Making Transition Work for Everyone

Poverty and Inequality in Europe and Central Asia

The World Bank
Washington, D.C.

Cover design by Tomoko Hirata

Library of Congress Cataloging-in-Publication Data has been applied for.

Contents

Foreword   v

The Report Team   vii

Acronyms and Abbreviations   ix

Overview   1

Part I   Dimensions of Poverty in Transition Economies   29

Chapter 1   The Nature and Evolution of Poverty   31

Chapter 2   A Profile of Income Poverty   65

Part II   Explaining the Increase in Poverty   107

Chapter 3   Understanding the Rise in Poverty:
             Initial Conditions, Institutional Legacies,
             and Policies   110

Chapter 4   A Look at Income Inequality   139

Part III   Public Action to Reduce Poverty   179

Chapter 5   Building Inclusive Institutions for
             Poverty Alleviation and Development   183

Chapter 6   Expanding Opportunities through Growth   206

Chapter 7   Improving Capabilities: Education   228

Chapter 8   Improving Capabilities: Health   257

Chapter 9   Providing Greater Security   287

Chapter 10   Reducing Income Inequality   331

Appendix A Measurement of Living Standards and Inequality   367

Appendix B Data Sources   378

Appendix C Variable Definitions for Poverty and
            Inequality Tables   382

Appendix D Poverty and Inequality Tables   421

Foreword

Poverty was not a central issue confronting policymakers a decade ago when Europe and Central Asian countries started embarking on the transition from plan to market. The general expectation was that poverty was limited, and that where it existed, it was very shallow. The presumption was that growth would come quickly as countries moved forward with the transition process, and that, with good labor mobility and high levels of education, it would reduce the incidence of poverty rapidly. Poverty was believed to be largely transitory in nature, and best addressed through the provision of adequate safety nets.

A decade or so later, it is clear that many of these suppositions have not materialized. The collapse in output was more severe than anticipated and the recovery in growth was much slower to come, especially in the CIS countries. The increase in inequality that occurred in many countries was also much larger than anticipated. Narrow sets of private interests, rather than the broader public good, have dominated the policy agenda in many countries and have derailed the reform process. Together these factors have given rise to a virtually unprecedented increase in poverty in the region. Moreover, there is a core group of very poor—notably the long-term unemployed and socially excluded—that is likely to be bypassed even by strong economic growth. And despite notable achievements in the education and health sectors in the past, both systems are under strain and are increasingly working to the detriment of poor families and the long-term economic mobility of their children.

Making Transition Work for Everyone: Poverty and Inequality in Europe and Central Asia offers a detailed look at the nature of poverty in transition countries, the factors that have contributed to the diverse outcomes across the region, and the institutional and policy issues involved in raising livings standards and reducing social exclusion. Drawing heavily on the framework of promoting opportunities, facilitating empowerment, and enhancing security on which the *World Development Report 2000/ 01: Attacking Poverty* is based, *Making Transition Work* focuses on the specific challenges facing the transition countries. It is an important contribution to our ongoing reflections about how we at the World Bank can work most productively with our clients and partners to reduce poverty. It is meant to stimulate debate. I hope it will be useful in forging a broad consensus on the actions needed to bring about better lives for the poor during a period of unparalleled economic, social, and political change.

Johannes F. Linn
Vice President
Europe and Central Asia Region

The Report Team

This book was prepared by a core team led by Christine Jones and Ana Revenga and comprising Asad Alam, Jeanine Braithwaite, Nora Dudwick, Maureen Lewis, Erzo Luttmer, James Lynch, Mansoora Rashid, Diane Steele, Nancy Vandycke and Ruslan Yemtsov. Marinette Guevara, Doreen Duff, and Ian Conachy provided additional assistance with the production of the report.

Additional material for the report was provided by Maria Amelina, Ritu Anand, Sue Berryman, Simon Blair, Mukesh Chawla, Csaba Csaki, Mark Davis, Henry Gordon, Lorraine Hawkins, Dorota Holzer, Tom Hoopengardner, Ede Jorge Ijjasz-Vasquez, Arvo Kuddo, Zvi Lerman, Montserrat Pallares-Miralles, Dena Ringold, Laura Rose, Maya Sandu, Brian Steven Smith, Verdon Staines, John Voss, Xiaoqing Yu.

In addition, many colleagues in ECA contributed invaluable comments and information.

Assistance with the analysis of the poverty and inequality data was provided by Robert Ackland, Richard Adams, Jane Falkingham, Franziska Grassman, Anna Ivanova, Ella Libanova, Michael Lokshin, Erzo Luttmer, Kalplana Mehra, Diane Steele, Jiri Vecernik, Xiao Ye, Ruslan Yemtsov, Erika Znidarsic.

Annette Dixon, Hafez Ghanem, Pradeep Mitra, and Michal Rutkowski, Marcelo Selowsky, and Michael Walton provided guidance to the report team at various stages. The work was carried out under the general direction of Johannes Linn, Vice President of the ECA region.

Alan Gelb, Louise Fox, Jeffrey Hammer, William Maloney, Branko Milanovic, Martin Ravallion, Carlos Silva-Jauregi, Kalanidhi Subbarao, Willem van Eeghen, and Ulrich Zachau were peer reviewers. The book also benefited substantially from comments received from participants in two consultations meetings held in Budapest in late March 2000 organized by Istvan Toth from TARKI, Budapest, Hungary, and the World Bank Institute SPRITE Program.

Book design, editing, and production were coordinated by the Production Services Unit of the World Bank's Office of the Publisher. Lucy Koons was the Production Editor and Barbara de Boinville edited the manuscript.

Acronyms and Abbreviations

AIDS	Acquired Immune Deficiency Syndrome
ALOS	Average Length of Hospital Stay
CDC	Centers for Disease Control
CEE	Central and Eastern European
CIS	Commonwealth of Independent States
CPI	Consumer Price Index
CSB	Central and South Eastern European and Baltic Countries
DALY	Disability-Adjusted Life Years
DHS	Demographic Health Survey
EBO	Employee Buyout
EBRD	European Bank for Reconstruction and Development
ECA	Europe and Central Asia
EU	European Union
FBS	Family Budget Survey
FSU	Former Soviet Union
GDP	Gross Domestic Product
GNP	Gross National Product
HIV	Human Immunodeficiency Virus
IALS	International Adult Literacy
IDD	Iodine Deficiency Disorder
IDP	Internal Displaced Persons
ILO	International Labor Organization
IMR	Infant Mortality Rate
LSMS	Living Standards Measurement Surveys
MBO	Management Buyout

MRI	Magnetic Resonance Imaging
NGO	Non-Government Organization
OECD	Organization of Economic Cooperation and Development
PAYGO	Pay-As-You-Go Pension System
PEM	Protein-Energy Malnutrition
PPP	Purchasing Power Parity
PSD	Private Sector Development
RLMS	Russian Longitudinal Monitoring Survey
SOE	State-Owned Enterprise
STD	Sexually Transmitted Diseases
TARKI	Social Research Informatics Center (in Hungary)
TB	Tuberculosis
UNDP	United Nations Development Program
UNICEF	United Nations Children's Fund
UNC	University of North Carolina
VAT	Value Added Tax
WDI	World Development Indicators
WDR	World Development Report
WHO	World Health Organization
WTO	World Trade Organization

Overview

In 1998 an estimated one out of every five people in the transition countries of Europe and Central Asia survived on less than $2.15 per day.[1] A decade ago fewer than one out of twenty-five lived in such absolute poverty. While these estimates are at best an approximation given serious data deficiencies, there is little doubt that poverty has increased dramatically in the region. Moreover, the increase in poverty is much larger and more persistent than many would have expected at the start of the process. Poland is a telling case: poverty has come down steadily from its peak in 1994 as the economy rebounded, yet poverty rates were still higher in 1998 than in 1991.

Absolute poverty in the aggregate is unlikely to diminish in the medium term unless the countries accounting for a large share of absolute poverty in the region, such as Russia, undertake substantial policy reforms that will lead to widespread improvements in living standards. Some countries in the region have moved more effectively than others to tackle poverty. But even the most successful reformers in the region can do more to foster the growth of productive employment, educate their children better to improve their labor productivity in the globalizing market economy, help people cope with the major risks of old age security, health, and unemployment in a fiscally sustainable manner, and address the needs of an emerging underclass of poor.

What is Unusual about Postsocialist Poverty?

The magnitude of the increase in poverty—and its persistence during the past decade—alone would probably suffice to distinguish the experience of the transition countries in the Europe and Central Asia region from other regions. The decline in economic output rivaled that of the Great Depression of the 1930s, and many countries have not yet recovered their pretransition level of GDP. Large as the collapse in living standards is, what truly sets it apart is that it has occurred in the context of profound and far-reaching systemic changes in political, economic, and social life.

On the political front, inhabitants of all but five of the postsocialist countries of Europe and Central Asia have found themselves suddenly living within new state borders, in nations that are fundamentally redefining their identities, and in political systems that in many cases have opened new avenues of political expression and expanded civil rights. On the economic front, transition to a market economy—in many countries not yet fully achieved—has brought new opportunities for many, while for others it has meant unaccustomed material hardship and loss of security. Successive economic shocks—loss of jobs or prolonged nonpayment of salaries, hyperinflation and loss of savings, and the drastic erosion of accustomed supports (such as low-cost or free social services, subsidies, and discounts on goods and services)—have made people feel unusually vulnerable, powerless, and unable to plan for the future.

For most of the new poor, transition has brought not only unaccustomed material hardship, but also the destruction of "normal" life and accustomed social patterns. In contrast to the majority of poor people in developing countries, most of the poor in transition countries are literate, many are well educated, and before the "transition" had secure employment and anticipated receiving regular pensions and allowances from the state after retirement. As jobs are lost and hidden unemployment grows, these sources of support—psychological and otherwise—are breaking down.

The poor expressed deep distress that their knowledge, skills, and formal and informal competencies have become irrelevant. They feel they have lost their sense of belonging to society and are no longer necessary to anyone. Their sense of personal failure, together with the loss of respected social roles and identities, has frequently given way to a paralyzing sense of shame and depression. Increased alcohol consumption, family tensions, and higher suicide rates are some of the manifestations of increased psychological and social stress that have surfaced in consultations with the poor. The psychological pain is as devastating as the material hardship:

"poverty is pain; it feels like a disease. It attacks a person not only materially but also morally. It eats away one's dignity and drives one into total despair" (a woman from Moldova, quoted in Narayan and others 2000, 2).

An important legacy of the past is the shame and stigma associated with being poor. In communist times poverty was largely regarded as a result of individual failings or deviancy, since the state provided guaranteed employment for the able-bodied and assistance to those who were otherwise unable to work. Moreover, the existence of widespread poverty would have been judged as a failing of the socialist state, and so the state tended to suppress any discussion of poverty. This, of course, is changing, but vestiges remain.

At the beginning of the twenty-first century, many of the politically fragile governments in Europe and Central Asia are reluctant to foster a public debate on poverty issues since poverty is on the rise, and nostalgia for the security of the former system is widespread. These factors tend to make societies reluctant to openly acknowledge the existence of poverty in its various manifestations. Experience elsewhere in the world suggests that more open dialogue at all levels of society about the causes and consequences of poverty and inequality helps improves outcomes for the poor. This book aims to contribute to that dialogue. It summarizes what is known about poverty and inequality in the region and explores the major challenges involved in reducing poverty and building more inclusive societies.

The Dimensions of Poverty in ECA

Levels of absolute income deprivation—measured by the $2.15 a day per person poverty line in 1996 PPP terms—vary considerably across the region, with the highest levels found in the Central Asia and the Caucasus region (figure 1). Based on the $2.15-a-day measure, there is virtually no absolute deprivation in many Central European countries. In contrast, the incidence of absolute poverty in Russia is close to 20 percent. The Russian poor accounted for about 60 percent of those living in absolute poverty in the region in the late 1990s. As a measure of absolute deprivation, the two-dollar-a day poverty line is preferred to the one-dollar-a-day line used in some other parts of the world because of the additional heating costs necessitated by the very cold winters prevailing in much of region. It also is at the bottom end of the range of national poverty lines, expressed in PPP terms, of the poorer countries in the region.

Although measures of absolute deprivation are useful in deriving regional estimates of poverty, they tell us little about the levels of resources individuals need to live with dignity and respect in a particular country. For this reason countries usually establish their own national poverty lines. These national poverty lines tend to increase with a country's income level. Therefore, even though the level of absolute deprivation based on the two-dollar-a-day line is very low in some Central European countries, poverty does exist in these countries, and it is a serious concern—just as it is in the United States or Western Europe. In the United States, for example, the poverty line for a family of four in 1998 was set at $11.41 per person per day. It was originally calculated in the mid-1960s as three times the minimum basket of food a family would need and since then adjusted for inflation. At this line, the official poverty rate in the United States in 1998 was 12.7 percent.

A Profile of Poverty in the Region

Despite some notable similarities, transition countries in ECA vary substantially in a number of ways, including their income levels, demographic profiles, degree of urbanization, pattern of labor market adjustment, and scope and targeting of public transfers. As a result, the pattern of poverty might be expected to vary across countries. But surprisingly, these patterns are quite similar across the region.

Figure 1   Percentage of Population Living in Absolute Poverty in ECA Transition Countries

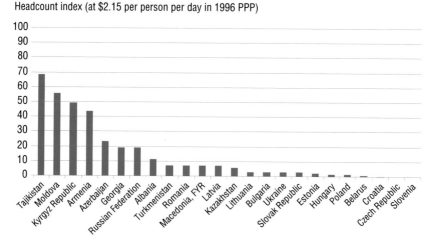

Headcount index (at $2.15 per person per day in 1996 PPP)

Source: Chapter 1, table 1.1.

Three major risk factors stand out: employment status, age, and location. First, employment status: not surprisingly, households with a head that is unemployed or inactive have a higher risk of poverty, relative to the rest of the population. Unemployment levels are correlated with education levels, and as a result people with only a primary school education have a higher risk of poverty than do people with a secondary education or higher. Second, age: in most countries, children are at a much higher risk of poverty than are the elderly, contrary to popular opinion. Likewise, the more children a household has, the higher its relative risk of poverty, even allowing for some economies of scale in consumption. Having more mouths to feed puts multichild households at higher risk of poverty, but lower levels of adult labor force participation also work to their disadvantage. Third, location: in most countries the rural population has a higher risk of poverty than the urban population, though there are a few exceptions, notably Ukraine.

Ethnicity is also a high risk factor in some cases. Although poverty data disaggregated by ethnic status are very limited, survey evidence for a few countries in Central and South Eastern Europe confirm that poverty rates for the Roma far exceed those of the overall population. In Hungary, for example, the Roma are about eight times more likely to be in long-term poverty than the general population (World Bank 2000a).

The unemployed, children, and rural populations have the highest relative risk of poverty, but in most countries they do not comprise a majority of the poor. The typical poor person is more likely to be between the ages of 15 and 64 and to live in an urban area in a household whose head is employed. Only in a few countries in Central Europe, where the relative risks of poverty are especially high for children or the rural population, is the typical poor person likely to be a child or live in a rural area. There are also a few countries in Central Asia where the majority of the poor are either children or rural residents, but this reflects these groups' large share of the population more than their high relative poverty risks.

Economic Insecurity

Another dimension of poverty is economic insecurity. If people are living on the margin of poverty, fluctuations in their incomes could easily push them into poverty, especially if they have few assets to rely on to smooth their consumption. As in other parts of the world, in Europe and Central Asia there is a high degree of volatility in incomes and consumption. One consequence is that there is a lot of movement in and out of poverty over time. Panel survey data from Russia, for example, show that the share of the population that has experienced at least one bout of poverty is more than double the fraction of the population in poverty in any one year; for Poland and Hungary the share is slightly less than double.

Although many households experience expenditure shocks—and some fall into poverty—many of those shocks are undone in subsequent periods. Over a long time horizon, economic positions are more stable. Stripping away the fluctuations and looking at the underlying pattern of expenditure reveal that poverty status is far more persistent. About 80 percent of those in the bottom quintile of the expenditure distribution in Poland, Hungary, and Russia remain stuck there. This more persistent picture of poverty is consistent with the long duration of unemployment, particularly in Central Europe. It appears that an underclass is forming, and with it the threat of long-term, structural poverty. Safety nets are needed to help people cope with temporary poverty in ways that do not dampen their incentives to earn income, but a potentially even more serious issue is how to improve the prospects of those with few opportunities to better their life chances.

Material deprivation and income insecurity are particularly important dimensions of poverty in Europe and Central Asia, given the fall in income and profound change in economic structures defining the transition process. The concept of poverty, however, goes beyond material deprivation. It encompasses poor health and lack of education as well as other nonmaterial dimensions of well-being, including powerlessness and social exclusion. Because of the positive achievements of the past, the poor in ECA fare much better than the poor in other parts of the world in terms of their education and access to health care. But there are signs that these past achievements are being undermined by cutbacks in the delivery of health and education services and, even more importantly, by the widespread rise in under-the-counter payments demanded by public service providers.

Deteriorating Health and Education Systems

School enrollment rates in ECA countries are significantly higher than those typically found in countries of similar income levels. Even in the poorest transition economies, primary school enrollments exceed 85 percent, and in many countries primary enrollment is effectively universal. Unfortunately, enrollment rates have started to fall in some of the poorest CIS countries: from more than 90 percent in 1989, primary school enrollment rates have fallen by about ten or more percentage points in Moldova, Armenia, Georgia, Turkmenistan, and Tajikistan during the past decade. In addition, there are signs of declining school attendance. The available evidence, sketchy as it is, suggests that poor children are the most likely to drop out of school or attend sporadically, and the least able to afford the costs (clothing, textbooks, transportation) of going to school.

The decline in funding for educational materials, unpaid teachers' wages, and lack of heat and maintenance for some schools contribute to a decline in the quality of schooling. Regional disparities also appear to be a problem in some countries, reducing the opportunities for children in poor rural areas to get a quality education. Moreover, as their salaries have fallen in a number of countries, some teachers have resorted to supplementing their incomes through tutoring—effectively requiring students to pay for tutoring to be awarded a passing grade. Parents also are being asked to pay bribes to obtain entrance to specialized schools for their children. These forms of corruption effectively result in unequal opportunities for children from poor families.

On the health side, indicators for the region are also far better in most cases than in countries of similar incomes, reflecting the universal provision of comprehensive health care services to consumers and high levels of education. Maternal mortality rates are low, ranging from less than 10 per 1,000 live births in Central Europe to less than 30 per 1,000 live births in Central Asia (with the exception of Turkmenistan), and they declined significantly between 1980 and 1987. Rises in under-five mortality rates have largely been contained. Even in the poorest countries in Central Asia, most children continue to be immunized, despite cuts in public expenditures on health.

Notwithstanding the relatively favorable indicators, disturbing health problems are surfacing. Most widely commented on has been the decrease in male life expectancy, particularly evident in many, though not all, of the countries in the former Soviet Union (FSU). Male life expectancy fell by around four years between 1989 and the mid-1990s in the Baltic countries and by more than five years in Russia, Ukraine, and Kazakhstan. By 1994 male life expectancy in Russia had fallen to 58 years—with a significant share of the decline attributable to the almost 100 percent increase since 1989 in the mortality rate of males between the ages of 40 and 59. Not all countries experienced a drop; life expectancy remained almost constant in Armenia and Turkmenistan. There has been a lively debate about reasons for the increase in deaths. The proximate cause is an increase in cardiovascular and circulatory diseases

and accidents and violence. Psychological stress in response to the difficulties of transition—which appears to have led to an upsurge in excessive alcohol consumption—may have contributed to excess deaths from
these causes. Mortality increases were lower in areas where social support systems were stronger.

Diseases such as tuberculosis that had been largely controlled are now
staging a resurgence, along with an explosion in sexually transmitted diseases and the related threat of an HIV/AIDS epidemic in parts of the region, most notably in Eastern Europe. Ukraine, Belarus, Moldova, and
Russia have the highest rates of HIV infections, with 1 percent of the adult
population of Ukraine estimated to be living with HIV/AIDS. In Russia
the number of reported HIV cases quadrupled between 1998 and 1999,
largely among injecting drug users. The skyrocketing increase in sexually
transmitted diseases suggests that in the future HIV is in danger of spread-
ing into the mainstream population through sexual transmission. Tuberculosis, including more drug resistant forms of the disease, also increased
during the 1990s. In Russia survey-based rates of drug resistant TB are
among the highest in the world. TB is neither diagnosed reliably nor treated
effectively, because of a lack of drugs and the use of nonstandard treatment protocols. If HIV becomes more widespread in the general population, it is likely to fuel a parallel increase in tuberculosis.

Less widely recognized—but with potentially serious implications for
child development—are signs of emerging nutritional deficiencies. Malnutrition is a concern: in several parts of the Caucasus and Central Asia,
wasting and stunting exceed WHO-determined threshold levels. The re-
emergence of iodine deficiencies, which leads to goiter, is another serious
concern, especially because of the risks it presents of severe mental retar-
dation. Salt iodization programs, the principal way of eliminating iodine
deficiencies, appear to have broken down in some countries, leading to a
rise in goiter rates. Goiter rates now approach 80 percent in parts of the
Caucasus and Central Asia.

While there is little hard evidence showing that health outcomes for the
poor are more negatively affected than the rest of the population, it is
clear that access to health care is becoming increasingly dependent on
whether a household can afford the "informal" payments to doctors and
others practicing in collapsed public institutions (figure 2)—and that the
poor have the least ability to pay. In some countries, notably the Caucasus,
informal payments account for more than 85 percent of all expenditures
in the sector. The poor sometimes go without medical care or drugs, or
they sell off their income-generating assets to scrape up the cash needed to
get treatment. The loss of access to free health care is of considerable

Figure 2   Share of Patients Making Informal Payments in Selected ECA Countries

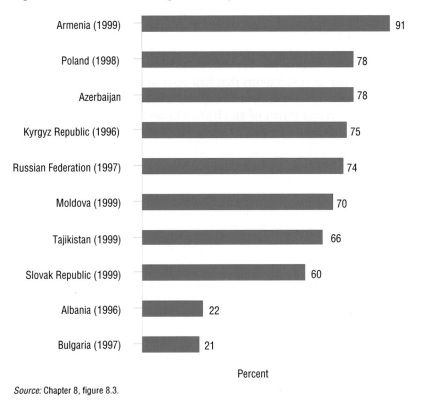

	Percent
Armenia (1999)	91
Poland (1998)	78
Azerbaijan	78
Kyrgyz Republic (1996)	75
Russian Federation (1997)	74
Moldova (1999)	70
Tajikistan (1999)	66
Slovak Republic (1999)	60
Albania (1996)	22
Bulgaria (1997)	21

Source: Chapter 8, figure 8.3.

concern to the poor and near poor and contributes deeply to their sense of growing vulnerability.

Growing Social Strains

The stresses of the transition are evident in many indicators. Families are no longer stable: divorce rates have increased in the Western CIS and Estonia, while marriage and birth rates have declined sharply throughout the region. Children and young adults are increasingly at risk. Poverty has led to an increase in the number of institutionalized infants ages 0 to 3, while a growing number of children are living on the street. In Russia alone the number of street children is estimated at one million. Youth unemployment is high in many countries, teen pregnancies have sharply increased, and the increase in unprotected sex has made young people vulnerable to sexually transmitted diseases including HIV/AIDS. Suicides of young males increased by more than 50 percent between 1989 and 1997 in Russia, Belarus, Lithuania, Slovenia, and the Czech Republic (UNICEF 1999); trafficking in young women is on the rise; and young men in the poor rural areas of Central Asia are increasingly being recruited into the drug trade. These trends presage the emergence of major social problems that threaten to complicate future efforts at poverty reduction.

Consultations with the poor reveal a decline in social cohesiveness. Poverty has reduced their ability to participate in informal networks of self-help. At the same time the consumption of the rich has become more conspicuous, fueling social tensions. The poor see the rich as people who have gotten where they are by exploiting their connections and by profiting dishonestly from their official positions. As one poor woman observed, the rich "have been plundering everything and eating so much that they cannot carry their own stomachs." Corruption, indifference, and ill treatment by those in power pervade virtually every aspect of the lives of the poor, whether it is dealing with social assistance and pension offices, obtaining health care, trying to run a small business, or seeking help from the police. Throughout the region the poor perceive the state as having effectively abandoned them. As one Georgian said: "Our leaders announced transition to new market relations and then left us to the mercy of fate, not asking whether we were prepared to accept the transition" (Dudwick 1999, 20).

Explanations for the Increase in Poverty

The main explanatory factor for the emergence of poverty in Europe and Central Asia is the social and economic dislocation of transition, and the resulting drop in output, government revenues, and household incomes. The impact of this economic collapse was accentuated by a large increase in income inequality. Coming as it did when incomes were falling, the increase in inequality meant that those at the bottom of the income distribution received an even smaller share of a shrinking pie.

Although they can account for much of the quantitative rise in poverty, these two factors—the collapse of output and increasing inequality—are in some sense just proximate causes, behind which lies a complex interaction of economic, social, and political processes. Both the extent of the output collapse and the rise in inequality were influenced by many interrelated factors: the degree of initial macroeconomic distortions, the familiarity of institutions and individuals with market mechanisms, the inherited economic structure, and the comprehensiveness and quality of the policy reform package. Most importantly, the path of output and incomes was conditioned by institutional legacies, which largely determined the behavior of policymakers during the transition and their interest and ability to deliver a consistent reform program, with adequate safeguards to protect the vulnerable.

The Fall in Output

The decline in output was pronounced throughout the region, but much more so in the CIS countries, where poverty has also risen the most. On average, the cumulative output decline in the CIS countries was almost 50 percent, while in the CSB (Central and South Eastern Europe and Baltic countries), output declined by about 15 percent before starting its recovery. The size of this output collapse is linked both to initial conditions and the choice of reform path. Less favorable initial conditions—larger economic distortions, less familiarity with market mechanisms and institutions, and less political reform—typically led to worse output performance. Yet while initial conditions are important, the choice of policies, and especially the comprehensiveness and quality of economic reforms, seem to have mattered even more. Some countries with highly unfavorable initial conditions have done well because they implemented strong reform packages, while others that started from a more favorable situation have done poorly. Overall, countries that implemented inconsistent or partial reforms experienced a larger drop in output than did those that reformed more quickly.

More importantly from a poverty perspective, these partial reformers experienced a sharper rise in poverty, for a given drop in output, than did countries that implemented more comprehensive reforms. This was mainly because inequality in these incomplete and partial reformers increased much more. People have mainly experienced the impact of the output collapse as a change in paid employment and in what wages can buy, and as a fall in government transfers and services.

Declining employment. All transition economies have experienced a sharp drop in the demand for labor. Falls in output across the region have entailed large declines in employment and wages. These effects have been amplified by the need to improve productivity and reduce the labor hoarding common to the old system. Most countries have also witnessed a decline in labor supply, as participation in the labor market has dropped because of early retirement, discouragement, or women choosing to stay at home. In all the transition countries of the region, the share of the population employed today is significantly smaller than it was at the start of the transition.

In most of the CSB countries, open unemployment rates are high and persistent. While the employed are benefiting from rapidly rising productivity and wages, the jobless—and especially the long-term unemployed—risk being left behind. Despite the strong resumption of GDP growth, job creation remains sluggish. The recovery of output has not resulted in much growth in net aggregate employment. Differences in standards of living between those with jobs and those without them are large and growing. Poverty is closely linked to unemployment.

In the CIS countries the decline in GDP was so abrupt and sizable that equivalent cuts in employment were politically and socially untenable. Enterprise restructuring has been limited, and the reduction in real wages or nonpayment of wages has been the dominant mode of labor market adjustment. Registered unemployment is low, but definitions based on household surveys suggest much higher rates of actual unemployment and inactivity. Hidden unemployment, with workers retaining formal ties to an enterprise but neither working nor receiving a wage, is also high. Yet income opportunities outside these attachments to nonviable and low-paying enterprises appear to be few. New private sector activities that could attract these workers have been slow to emerge, largely because of the incompleteness of reforms. Given the lack of alternatives, many families have turned to subsistence agriculture, or other forms of small-scale self-employment, to supplement their meager formal incomes. As a result, labor is channeled to these low-productivity activities rather than to new, higher-productivity jobs. GDP growth—where it has happened—has not brought about a recovery of employment levels. An extreme case of this is Armenia. Despite five years of continuous positive growth (averaging 5.2 percent per year) between 1994 and 1999, employment declined by 8.5 percent.

Shrinking fiscal revenues and transfers. The collapse in GDP also entailed a collapse in state revenues throughout the region. For many of the CIS countries, this was compounded by the loss of large fiscal transfers from Moscow as a result of independence. What happened to revenues dictated to a large extent whether countries were able to take action to cushion the social impact of the transition. Many of the CIS countries simply did not have the fiscal space to maintain basic social transfers—in some cases not even pensions. Many also had to slash spending in health and education, contributing to the spread of informal and under-the-table payments and hurting the poor more than the rich. Poor budget management and implementation in the face of shrinking revenues also led to the emergence of pervasive arrears in public sector payments, wages, and pensions in parts of the CIS (for example, Georgia, Moldova, Russia). These arrears have had a highly regressive aspect, since they fall disproportionately on the poor and are highest in poor regions.

Could fiscal adjustment have been carried out in a different, more pro-poor way? There is little doubt that, at least in the CIS, the quality of fiscal adjustment could have been much better. Across-the-board cuts in expenditures, with a bias toward cutting social and infrastructure spending, contributed to worsening inequality, and hence to increasing poverty. The absence of a safety net made it hard to restructure and lay off workers, and this contributed to slowing down growth and lengthening the recession. Moreover, by increasing inequality, these cuts may have contributed to slower growth. They certainly made it more difficult for necessary market-supporting institutions to develop: cash-starved governments that cannot pay their civil servants will find it impossible to develop an effective and accountable public administration and regulatory bodies.

In contrast to the CIS experience, expenditures in CSB countries were kept at very high levels. High levels of expenditures, especially in the social sectors, helped cushion the impact of the transition and made reforms more acceptable. In Poland, for example, pensions were critical to preventing the elderly from falling into poverty. In this manner high expenditures in the CSB may have been crucial to maintaining support for reforms and hence to the recovery of growth. The challenge for the CSB countries right now is how to reduce the fiscal burden imposed by these high levels of social spending without undermining their positive protective impact.

Rising Inequality

The collapse in output was critical in determining what happened to poverty. But what has happened to inequality has been equally important. The countries of Europe and Central Asia entered the transition process with some of the lowest levels of inequality in the world. But since then inequality has increased steadily in all transition countries—and dramatically in some of them (figure 3). Countries like Armenia, the Kyrgyz Republic, Moldova, and Russia are now among the most unequal in the world, with Gini coefficients nearly twice their pretransition levels.

The rise in inequality is in part attributable to positive developments: rising returns to education, a decompression of wages, and returns to risk taking and entrepreneurship. Despite the resulting increase in inequality,

Figure 3   Changes in Income Inequality in Selected ECA Countries during Transition

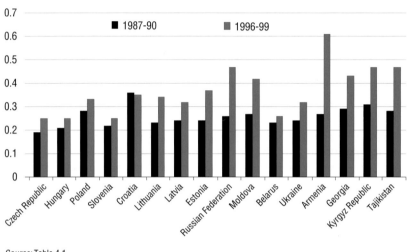

Source: Table 4.1.

these forces are welcome because they signal that the market is now working to reward skills and effort, as in more mature market economies. In the CSB countries, the rise in education premiums and wage dispersion has been dampened by strong social transfers and redistribution, in line with the demands that these societies have placed on their governments for such mechanisms. This has not been the case in the CIS, where social transfers have at best been negligible and in some instances even contributed to making inequality worse.

Rising educational premiums and wage dispersion are not sufficient to explain rising inequality in the CIS and, in fact, explain surprisingly little of it. Much of the rise in inequality in the CIS must be attributed instead to the apparent collapse of formal wages and income opportunities, the pervasiveness of wage arrears, and the resulting explosion of self-employment as the main source of household incomes. Unlike in the CSB, however, this emerging self-employment does not reflect new, private business activity but rather a large-scale move toward subsistence agriculture—a last-resort coping strategy to keep households afloat. New, formal job opportunities in the CIS are scarce, stifled by the lack of competitive markets and the pervasiveness of corruption and bribe-taking. People, except for a privileged few, are largely stuck in their low-paying (and sometimes nonpaying) jobs. Access to connections and informal networks, and an ability to pay, are key to finding a job and getting ahead. This has led to highly unequal outcomes.

Although these developments can explain the rise in inequality in the CIS, they are not the root of the problem. They are rather the manifestations of the failure to carry through with reforms aimed at the public good as a result of the state's capture by private interests. Those whose incomes depend on the continuation of opportunities for asset-stripping, monopoly rent-seeking, illegal enrichment, and tax evasion are a powerful force against policies that would foster widely shared prosperity. They have a strong interest in blocking further reforms that would allow for a true transition to a market economy and a more equal distribution of opportunities and incomes.

The Role of Institutions

Why were some countries so much more successful than others in managing the transition in a socially responsible way? And why were some countries more susceptible to capture by private interests from the start? The answer lies in the institutional structure these countries inherited, and the resulting incentives power holders faced to break with the past. Countries with stronger institutional checks and balances (resulting from stronger civil societies, more mature political democracies, and more developed market-supporting institutions) were better at establishing economic and political contestability from the start. As a result, these countries implemented more pro-poor policy choices: they carried out more comprehensive and decisive reforms, moved more quickly toward a market-based system for allocating resources (and away from the power- or access-based system that characterized late socialism), and carried out more socially focused adjustment. Because they were better at getting markets to work, these countries generated more new job and income-earning opportunities for their citizens. At the same time they also gave higher priority to keeping a strong social safety net and devoted a much larger share of their resources to this goal. Poverty and inequality increased, but much more moderately than in other parts of the region.

Other countries, most notably those of the CIS, failed to establish economic and political contestability. The partiality and incompleteness of economic and political reforms during the first stage of transition simply allowed some power groups—mainly traditional socialist elites in combination with some entrepreneurial newcomers—to cement and legalize the power relationships that existed at the end of socialism. In the absence of institutional checks and balances or other measures to restrain the arbitrary use of power, these groups were able to generate concentrated rents for themselves at a high cost in terms of increased inequality and poverty to the rest of society. These power groups are now the main obstacles to any further economic reform that would threaten their concentrated rents. With rent-seeking channels now firmly "institutionalized," politicians in much of the CIS are reluctant to let the process of democratization and market expansion move further, since this may jeopardize the status quo.

The partiality of the initial reforms—especially the lack of further efforts to deconcentrate economic power and create better-functioning markets—has stifled job creation and opportunities for all but these privileged parts of society. Formal wages and employment opportunities have collapsed, and with pervasive noncompetitive practices and corruption to contend with, there is little room for new small- and medium-scale private activity to emerge to create jobs. Resource-starved governments have revealed only limited interest (and ability) to protect the vulnerable: social spending has collapsed throughout much of the CIS, and along with it so has the social safety net. The result has been a virtually unprecedented increase in poverty and inequality.

Public Action to Reduce Poverty

Social and economic policies can go a long way to create opportunities, reduce poverty, and bring about a more egalitarian society—provided there is a political consensus for such policies. Such a consensus is unlikely to exist when institutions are not effective and do not act in the interests of the broad electorate. They are unlikely to work well when state capture or corruption are pronounced. Politicians captured by special interests have little incentive to advocate policies in the interest of all in society, including the poor. Public servants who earn their living through side payments for services rendered have little interest in forgoing corrupt practices. Captured and corrupt states are unlikely to "correct" themselves unless pressure comes from nonstate institutions and actors.

Building Institutions to Support Poverty Reduction Strategies

How can state capture and administrative corruption be tackled? The key is to address the underlying problems of institutional capacity and incentives faced by the state, civil society, and the private sector through a multipronged approach focused on increasing the cost of state capture to politicians and reducing the benefits from state capture to firms. There are five key building blocks: (a) increasing political accountability; (b) strengthening institutional restraints; (c) strengthening civil society participation and media oversight; (d) creating a competitive private sector; and (e) reforming public sector management. Increasing the transparency of the political process and political competition will make leaders more accountable to voters. Political participation by all segments of society can work to improve distributional equity, and it can improve social outcomes in health and education. Strengthening institutional restraints requires building and reinforcing the horizontal separation between the legislative, executive, and judicial branches, and turning them into legitimate and competent state institutions. The poor have much to gain from a well-functioning legal and judicial system and professional law enforcement, since police harassment, lawlessness, corruption, and violence deeply affect their daily lives. Building an effective public service is a key element in the strategy to reduce administrative corruption, and it can have a large impact on those most dependent on public service provision, the poor.

Once a state is captured, pressure must come from civil society and nonstate organizations, such as citizens groups, nongovernmental organizations, trade unions, religious organizations, and from the media. Long repressed during the socialist period, civil society will take some time to develop—especially where NGOs and other groups and the media are closely identified with government interests. Increasing economic competition will help dissolve the concentration of economic interests—though such a policy is likely to face strong resistance. Here, too, pressure from civil society will be key.

But even in states with governments that are not captured or corrupt, the poor are often voiceless, and their interests figure little in public policy. What can be done to increase their opportunities to make their concerns heard? One step is the creation of a concept of true public service, which when combined with mechanisms to monitor whether public servants are serving their clients effectively can help ensure that programs designed to serve the poor actually deliver their intended benefits. Another important advance is to ensure that the poor are made aware of their legal rights to receive benefits and public services, and have an effective means of redress if those rights are abrogated. Decentralization (a means of putting public officials in closer touch with the concerns of local populations) may give the poor greater opportunities for voice, provided issues of accountability and transparency are addressed.

Measures to build the social capital of the poor can play an important part in their empowerment. Reconstructing and empowering civil society, constructing new bases for community and social cohesion, and decentralizing government institutions are particularly important in ECA, given the devastating impact the strongly centralized, authoritarian socialist regimes had on "community" and "society." Where state capacity to deliver services is weak or absent, building accountable, inclusive local-level institutions can serve an important role. Yet such efforts are fraught with pitfalls: where local-level power structures are highly unequal, decentralization can increase exclusion and hurt the poor; widespread cynicism about public authority and politics and a tradition of alienation may slow down the development of civil society; the strong lack of community identity in many parts of the region—or identification with a social network that excludes other groups on ethnic or clan-related or other grounds—may work against the construction of an inclusive community able to act effectively on its own behalf. Building inclusive community-based institutions will not be fast or straightforward. But it may be the best hope for fostering the creation of national-level and state institutions that serve the broad interests of society—and are inclusive of, and accountable to, the poor.

Better-functioning and more inclusive institutions will facilitate the implementation of policies aimed at the broader public good, but even the best-intentioned governments will need a well-thought-out and coherent strategy to deliver improvements in living standards. Making transition work for everyone means first and foremost improving people's opportunities to earn a living through productive work. In turn, this means that everyone, including the poor, must have the capabilities needed to take advantage of those opportunities. Education and health systems must be reformed so that the poor as well as the rich can participate fully in the market. Making transition work for everyone also means providing for those who cannot participate in the market and helping citizens reduce the economic insecurity they face. In the past, socialist societies strongly emphasized security at the expense of individual achievement. Many citizens today want government to play an active role in providing for those who have no means of supporting themselves and in reducing the risks of inadequate income in old age and loss of income from employment. The challenge is how to do so in a way that is consistent with the fiscal resources available and does not dampen incentives to create new jobs. Governments can play an active role in reducing inequality and enhancing the mobility of those at the bottom—not only for reasons of social justice but also to foster social cohesion and long–run prospects for growth.

Creating Opportunities

Growth—and with it the generation of employment opportunities—is a sine qua non for poverty reduction. Living standards in very poor countries cannot be improved without growth. Provided it is equitably shared, growth can have a big impact on poverty reduction. In Poland, for example, the mean expenditures of the poor fall some 20 percent short of the relative poverty line—reflecting relatively shallow poverty. A 10 percent increase in mean income, equitably distributed, would reduce the incidence of poverty by 35 percent. But in Russia, by contrast, the incomes of the poor fall more than 30 percent short of the poverty line—hence deeper poverty. The same increase in mean incomes would reduce poverty by only 20 percent, far less than in Poland but still a respectable amount. In aggregate, absolute poverty could be reduced by more than 50 percent over a ten-year period if the region were to grow at 3.7 percent per year and that growth were to be shared evenly among the population. Were aggregate growth to be somewhat lower—2.7 percent per year— and inequality to worsen by 20 percent, however, poverty might actually increase in the region.[2] These simulations underscore the importance of robust, sustainable economic growth that is widely shared across the population. But this is far easier said than achieved.

While growth is essential to a continuing improvement in living standards, what matters ultimately is that growth generates jobs and that real wages rise over time as labor productivity increases. High unemployment rates and declines in labor participation rates in the CSB countries, and the considerable labor hoarding and low productivity prevalent in the CIS countries, suggest that job creation is likely to lag economic growth for some time to come. Even in the more successful reformers, such as Hungary and Poland, employment growth has lagged output growth by a considerable (and increasing) margin. In Hungary, for example, the number of jobs in 1997 was 30 percent lower than in 1989, even though output had recovered to its 1989 level. If the countries of the OECD are any guide for these economies, increasing the "job content" of output growth and tackling unemployment will require measures that go well beyond making the labor market more flexible. Increasing the flexibility of housing markets, deregulating product markets, and breaking up infrastructure monopolies are likely to be as important. Those measures are the key to the emergence of a competitive private sector that can be the engine of growth and rising labor demand.

Although some countries are on the road to growth, prospects are more uncertain in others. The challenges differ depending on where countries are in their reform efforts and on their income levels. Broad cross-cutting themes, however, are relevant to all countries First, fiscal adjustment remains central to the macroeconomic stabilization and growth prospects of all countries—and to poverty reduction efforts—since economic and financial crises are harmful to the poor. But the quality of that adjustment is paramount, if the state is to play its role in ensuring that all citizens have the capability to participate in the market and protect the vulnerable. Second, the enabling environment for private sector development—the key engine of job creation—remains deficient across the board. Third, virtually all countries face the problem of providing adequate social protection for those affected by economic restructuring. This, of course, is linked to the fiscal resources available, thereby closing the circle on the key set of needed reforms.

The more advanced market reformers have largely attained aggregate fiscal discipline, but they face quality issues in terms of managing off-budget fiscal risks generated by explicitly and implicitly guaranteed loans by government. Pension systems have threatened to undermine fiscal sustainability in many of the advanced market reformers as the ratio of contributors to dependents has fallen substantially over the transition period and will continue to fall. Pension reform is under way in many countries to reduce the burden on the budget and on contributors. This will help keep jobs in the formal economy, the number of covered workers high, and the future secure for senior citizens of today and tomorrow.

The less advanced market reformers have not yet achieved sustainable aggregate fiscal provision. This will require continuing efforts at revenue enhancement and expenditure retrenchment, with a particular focus on commitment control so that all expenditures are made on time and in cash. Key here will be inter- and intrasectoral budget tradeoffs, particularly with regard to the health and education sector, which accounts for a large share of budget spending. Soft budget constraints on the enterprise sector need to be eliminated in all their forms, because they not only compromise the tax and fiscal effort but also undermine restructuring and future growth prospects.

Although the advanced market reformers have made significant progress on the privatization and enterprise reform agenda, they still face challenges. They now confront the difficult challenge of privatizing infrastructure and utilities monopolies to bring in the new investment needed to modernize these sectors and maintain a competitive edge in the global economy. But for privatization to be successful, an appropriate legal and regulatory framework needs to be in place. Similarly, while the more advanced market reformers have in place the basic elements of frameworks for enterprise liquidation and insolvency, corporate governance, competition and antimonopoly policies, and regulation of the banking sector, these frameworks are sometimes deficient in key respects and inadequately enforced. The less advanced market reformers face the same challenges in improving the institutional structure that governs private sector activity. However, in addition, the enabling environment for small business remains sorely lacking, with excessive government micromanagement and corruption a major issue in many countries.

Moving ahead on the land reform agenda and promoting agricultural growth more broadly will contribute to overall growth and poverty eradication, especially in the low-income countries. Smallholder agriculture is more productive and labor intensive than is the newly privatized state and collective farm sector. While all countries have embarked upon agricultural reforms, considerably more progress must be made, especially in the areas of farm restructuring and liberalizing of marketing arrangements. Input markets are not functioning well in parts of the region. Governments may need to determine where this problem is attributable to excessive government interference and corruption and where there are more genuine market failures—for example, in the area of rural credit—in which they might usefully play a role.

Imposing hard budget constraints on enterprises and continuing the privatization process will increase the claims on the budget for severance payments, unemployment insurance, and other social assistance measures. Combined with measures to promote entry of new firms, this will generate a more productive economy over the medium term and over the long term more jobs. Considerable restructuring of the social sectors, including downsizing of personnel, will also be necessary to improve health and education services for the poor. But in the short term these measures may aggravate poverty. Freeing up fiscal resources to finance social assistance measures will be difficult, given the competing claims on the budget—hence the importance of improving revenue collections and prioritizing expenditures.

Improving Capabilities

To ensure that growth will be inclusive over the long term and to avoid the intergenerational transmission of poverty, ECA countries will need to pay particular attention to improving capabilities. While much has been achieved in this area under socialism, there are major deficiencies in health and education systems that affect much of the population, and especially the poor. Across the region people are increasingly being called on to make side payments to publicly financed health care providers. This is also a problem in the education system. Most governments have avoided making the tough decisions required to rationalize the intrasectoral allocation of expenditure within the two sectors as real social sector expenditures collapsed along with GDP. Personnel are underpaid or not paid at all, complementary expenditures (on materials, drugs, heat, and repairs, for example) are underfinanced, and the number of facilities and personnel significantly exceed OECD benchmarks. A major reallocation of expenditure—and greater accountability—is needed to ensure that governments can deliver on their commitments to provide universal primary education and basic health services to the population. Without a reallocation of funds, some of the poorest countries in the region risk not being able to provide universal primary education and essential health services. Rationalizing personnel and facilities, and allocating more funds where necessary, would help put both sectors on a sounder financial footing. In turn, this could eliminate the conditions that give rise to the "informal" payments that are rationing the poor out of the system at present, assuming there is government commitment to stamp out this form of corruption.

Beyond this lies the challenge of bringing the quality of the education and health systems up to OECD standards. Despite substantial achievements in these areas, neither system delivers high-quality health or education services. For the most part, education systems have not been adapted to prepare people for a modern market economy, which requires the ability to apply learning to new situations, rather than narrow specialization. Health systems have some ways to go in applying the most up-to-date treatment protocols and encouraging their population to change behaviors that lower adult life expectancy.

But these reforms are unlikely to fully address questions of differential access of the poor. The state, for example, may want to subsidize poor children's attendance at preschool programs. To keep their children in school, very poor parents may require additional assistance offsetting the loss in income children earn when kept out of school. And as cost-recovery measures are put in place for tertiary education, scholarship programs for the poor need to be instituted. Ensuring that the poor get access to health care entails deciding on the type of national health program to implement and how coverage for the poor will be financed. Of major importance to the poor is coverage for catastrophic illness—which they can least afford to pay for.

Reducing Destitution and Increasing Security

The key social protection challenge for most countries is to help the truly destitute and ensure that children do not suffer long-term developmental damage or fail to gain access to schooling and other opportunities for lack of funds. Once these objectives are met, societies can provide protection against adverse economic outcomes to a much broader range of the population. The challenge is to provide the right amount of social protection. Too much protection is fiscally costly and entails major disincentive effects, while too little protection may give rise to socially unacceptable levels of destitution and may irreparably harm children. Striking the right balance between protection and efficiency concerns is difficult for most countries, but it is especially tough in transition countries. First, as noted earlier, the choices between efficiency and protection are not clear-cut: higher expenditures on social protection programs to facilitate the reallocation of labor to more productive uses may serve long-term efficiency objectives. Second, the political challenges of reforming social protection systems are formidable. The socialist system provided a high degree of security that the public continues to want. For this reason, poor transition countries often have a more developed set of social protection programs than do other countries of similar income levels.

Despite the emphasis that has been placed on social protection measures, they have had only limited success in reaching the poor. Many countries spend about 1 percent of their income on social assistance programs, and even where they spend somewhat more, these programs for the most part have been poorly targeted, have covered only a limited number of poor, and have made little difference in their economic circumstances. Recent evaluations show that social assistance reaches only 2 percent of the poor in Latvia, for example. In some cases the bottom quintile gets only its share of total spending on social assistance, while in the best cases the bottom quintile receives roughly 40 percent of total spending. Thus, the bulk of spending is not going to the poorest.

In a number of countries, especially in the CIS, a great deal of money is spent subsidizing utility consumer prices—often by the utilities themselves from their capital budget—but most of this spending does not go to the poor, entails significant price distortions, and has deprived utilities of funds needed to maintain their infrastructure. The biggest chunk of social protection spending has gone to social insurance programs, especially pensions. Pensions have played a major role in helping countries (especially in

Central Europe) cope with transition shocks, reduce poverty in pensioner households, and dampen inequality.

A major challenge is to improve the targeting of social assistance programs and utility price subsidies. In all countries the priority should be the provision of adequate protection to the truly destitute and children at risk. But it is not easy to find cost-effective ways of doing this. In the poorer countries where poverty risks are not often well differentiated, categorical-based benefit systems are not likely to be well-targeted or to achieve high coverage—if they are affordable. Community-based benefit delivery might be used in conjunction with a transparent, interregional benefit allocation formula, especially in the poorer countries. Such programs might be supplemented by self-targeted programs, including work-fare schemes, which offer below market wages to avoid disincentive work effects. Middle- and high-income countries have the resources, financial and administrative, to adopt more universal, means-tested programs. Of particular concern for these richer countries are the high rates of poverty in multichild households, which ought to be a major focus of social protection programs. They also need to address the problems of socially excluded populations—in particular, the long-term unemployed and ethnic minorities such as the Roma.

Pension spending is high in transition countries, especially relative to income levels. The aging of the population—which will further reduce the number of contributors relative to the number of recipients—makes it all the more imperative to put pension systems on a more sustainable basis over the long term. The main public pension reform option in middle- and high-income countries is to tighten the benefit-contribution link, downsize public systems in order to reduce the burden on the budget, reduce contributors' tax rates, and create room for a funded program that would eventually supplement the publicly funded system. Low-income countries cannot afford the pension systems that they have—and hence they have let extensive pension arrears develop. In the short term it would be better to move to a flat distribution of payments that are paid on time. As economies grow and the contribution base widens, the benefits could be differentiated in line with contributions.

To deal with growing unemployment in the early years of transition, many countries initiated unemployment insurance programs similar to those in OECD countries. These programs proved to be expensive, not only because they had very generous benefits, but also because unemployment was high and persistent. Countries tightened provisions and often let benefits erode with inflation. While the programs may have helped cushion the shock of transition, they are not sustainable as they are. Unemployment insurance programs are more relevant for countries that can finance benefits at low tax rates, can administer benefits well, and can collect contributions attributed to individuals. Only some of the higher income transition countries are reaching this stage. Lower income countries may want to convert their unemployment insurance programs—which are not meeting their objectives—into unemployment assistance programs financed from general revenues and focused on flat-rate layoff packages, and coordinate them better with other social assistance schemes.

Reducing Inequality and Improving Mobility

Governments can also play an active role in reducing inequality and enhancing the mobility of those at the bottom. The main motivation for this may be social justice and a desire to maximize social welfare. But there are also other reasons for societies to be concerned about levels of inequality. For example, the existence of capital market imperfections combined with high levels of income inequality may effectively prevent equal educational opportunities. There is also evidence that high levels of inequality may threaten social cohesion, thereby deterring new investment and lowering long-run growth prospects.

While some increase in inequality as a result of transition was both anticipated and welcome—insofar as it provides incentives for risk-taking and hard work—the magnitude of this increase in some countries is worrisome: it raises doubts about the ability of some segments of society to participate fully in economic, social, and political life in the future. The agenda of policy actions described earlier that further the objective of transition are by and large consistent with a strategy to reduce inequality. Improving tax compliance—a major issue in most CIS and South Eastern European countries—would not only improve the fiscal situation and capacity for inequality-reducing transfers, but also could in itself help to reduce inequality. The aforementioned social assistance programs are a powerful tool for redistributing income to those at the bottom. Redistributive fiscal policy can also play a role in fostering the accumulation of public capital and promoting educational opportunities in poor rural regions in the higher income countries. In addition, many of the reforms described under the growth agenda—including further deregulation of the product market and financial sector development—will help reduce inequality. This is an important message because the popular perception is that market development and liberalization raise inequality. But the evidence for ECA suggests that this need not be the case.

Various other policy measures are often considered by societies that are committed to a more egalitarian distribution of income. Some can work, but others come at high cost. For example, policies to raise the wages of unskilled or low-skilled labor include those that establish a minimum wage or wage floor and those that facilitate investments in human capital and increase the productivity of the unskilled. The evidence from other regions suggests that minimum wages may lead to some decline in inequality (and somewhat larger positive effects on poverty), but they carry well-known risks, including a potentially negative effect on employment. Therefore, such policies are to be approached with caution. Training programs can also be used to provide workers with new skills better suited to the market economy. Evaluation of the effectiveness of training schemes for unemployed workers in three transition countries (the Czech Republic, Hungary, and Poland) found generally positive, though small, employment effects. Women and young workers benefited more than did male and older workers. While such programs may have a role to play in economies that are well advanced on structural reforms and are growing, they will do little to solve the problems in only partially reformed economies where the fundamental problem is collapsed labor demand. Policies that foster labor market participation of women may reduce poverty as well as having other beneficial effects, including reducing women's vulnerability to violence and increasing investments in children. The link between women's labor force participation, affordable childcare programs, and higher household incomes justifies a renewed focus on childcare—especially if it can be tied to early childhood education programs that improve the life chances of poor children.

Conclusions

Widespread poverty in transition countries in Europe and Central Asia need not be a permanent phenomenon. Economic and social policies have been effective in reducing poverty elsewhere in the world and could be effective in ECA—if governments choose to pursue them. Building public institutions that are accountable and responsive to a broad electorate is a prerequisite for more effective poverty reduction strategies. This, in turn, is linked to the development of a vibrant civil society in which information freely circulates and channels exist for making preferences known. Spurred in part by the prospects of accession to the European Union, some countries are moving quickly in that direction. But even in these countries, the poor may have little direct voice in shaping the interventions that affect them on a day-to-day basis. Effective poverty reduction strategies will entail removing the barriers to their equal participation in the market and in political life.

For countries where powerful private interests have captured the state, the challenge is particularly great. The cost of inaction is much higher as well, since these are the countries where the majority of the poor are found. It is essential to reduce state capture and make public institutions more broadly accountable. Societies can then confront the difficult challenges of expanding opportunities for productive work, improving the capabilities of the poor so that they can participate in the market, and providing the destitute with the basic essentials of life. Only then will transition work for everyone.

Notes

1. These estimates (World Bank 2000b) are based on 1993 PPP rates. Figure 1 reports the most recent available estimate of poverty by country, based on the newly available 1996 PPP rates, which are better for estimating poverty outcomes in the second half of the 1990s. Estimates based on the 1996 PPP rates are *not* comparable to estimates based on the 1993 PPP rates.

2. These projections are based on a $2.15 poverty line in 1993 purchasing power parity (World Bank 2000b).

References

Dudwick, Nora. "Georgia: A Qualitative Study of Impoverishment and Coping Strategies." In *Georgia: Poverty and Income Distribution*, vol. 2: *Technical Papers*. Report 1. 19348-GE. Washington, D.C.: World Bank. May.

Narayan, Deepa, and others. 2000. *Voices of the Poor: Can Anyone Hear Us?* New York: Oxford University Press.

UNICEF (United Nations Children's Fund). 1999. "Women in Transition." *Regional Monitoring Reports*, No. 6. Florence: UNICEF International Child Development Centre.

World Bank. 2000a. *Hungary: Long-Term Poverty, Social Protection, and the Labor Market.* Report 20645-HU. Washington, D.C. June.

————. 2000b. *Poverty Reduction and the World Bank: Progress in Fiscal 1999.* Report 2000-41. Washington, D.C.

PART I

DIMENSIONS OF POVERTY IN TRANSITION ECONOMIES

Poverty increased dramatically in the transition countries of Europe and Central Asia during the past decade—in part a result of the collapse in GDP rivaling that of the Great Depression of the 1930s. Not only is the increase in poverty unprecedented, but it has taken place in the context of profound changes in economic, social, and political life. These factors differentiate the experience of the poor in ECA from that of the poor in other parts of the world.

Chapter 1 explores the various dimensions of poverty within the broader context of the transition to a more market-oriented economy. For some the transition process has brought about a level of material deprivation unknown in the recent past, while many have experienced a decline in living standards. Achievements in education and health are being undermined as the poor are being rationed out of the system by their inability to pay. The security that was provided during the socialist period through guaranteed employment, old age pensions, and free health care and other services has given way to massive unemployment or underemployment, declining pensions, and services that are available to those who can pay. A strong sense of insecurity, vulnerability, and helplessness surfaces frequently in the voices of the poor, especially where prospects for economic recovery have been slow to materialize. While the transition has brought new economic and political opportunities to many, it also has widened the gulf between poor and rich. The poor often attribute much of this growing prosperity to corrupt and privileged access to resources and opportunities, which further entrenches the growing divide. As a result of these forces at play, social cohesion is no longer as strong, and social marginalization is increasing.

Chapter 2 takes a closer look at one important dimension of poverty—namely the characteristics of those whose incomes put them at the bottom of the income distribution. First, it examines the characteristics of the groups that have a higher than average risk of poverty, based on a relative poverty line for each country set at 50 percent of median income. Labor market status, location, and certain demographic characteristics show a strong correlation with poverty risks, more so in Central and South Eastern Europe and the Baltic states than in the Commonwealth of Independent States. Second, the chapter discusses the groups that make up the majority of the poor. For the most part they are the working poor with children. Third, the chapter explores the persistence of poverty over time. Survey data show that households tend to experience relatively large fluctuations in incomes over time that move many households in and out of poverty. From this, it would appear that poverty is largely a transitory phenomenon. However, a deeper look at panel survey data suggests that there is a greater degree of persistence in poverty. Indeed, an underclass may be forming.

CHAPTER 1

The Nature and Evolution of Poverty[1]

The poor in Europe and Central Asia have much in common with the poor elsewhere in the world—notably a lack of assets and access to resources and services, a low standard of living, poor health, limited social relationships, the sense of being stigmatized by the nonpoor, and feelings of powerlessness and insecurity (Narayan and others 1999). The region's socialist heritage, however, and the transition to a more market-oriented economy have made postsocialist poverty unusual in several respects.

The Unusual Features of Postsocialist Poverty

The magnitude of the increase in poverty would probably suffice to distinguish the experience of the ECA region from other regions in recent times. Between 1988 and 1998, absolute poverty rates in Europe and Central Asia increased from 2 to 21 percent.[2] While these estimates are an approximation given serious data deficiencies, there is little doubt that absolute poverty increased dramatically in the region.

In transition countries the decline in economic output and in the standard of living rivals that of the Great Depression of the 1930s, yet unlike the latter it has taken place in the context of far-reaching systemic changes in political, economic, and social life. Poverty has been accompanied by a feeling of profound disorientation: all the rules of the game changed overnight. As an employment services administrator in the Kyrgyz Republic explained, "Imagine traveling along in a car for seventy years and suddenly the road disappears and your car crashes. You don't know where to go" (Kuehnast 1993, 26).

In contrast to the majority of poor people in developing countries, most of the poor in transition countries are literate, many are well educated, and before the transition they had secure employment and anticipated regular pensions and allowances from the state after retirement. The poor in ECA tend to look to the past—with its guaranteed work, stable wages paid regularly, and predictable future—as a time of well-being. As a man from Bulgaria said, "In the past, with your salary you also got security—security that you would have free health care, access to a trade union sanitorium, that nobody would steal your money or that the bank would [not] go bankrupt" (World Bank 1999b, 23). Successive economic shocks—job loss or nonpayment of salaries, hyperinflation and loss of savings, and the increasing cost of education and health care—have made the poor in Europe and Central Asia unusually vulnerable and unable to plan for the future. As one Bulgarian acknowledged, "There's great insecurity now. You can't make any plans. For all I know, I might be told that we'll be laid off for a couple of months or that the factory is to be shut down. We work three days a week even now, and you're in for a surprise every day" (World Bank 1999b, 29).

For the new poor, poverty has brought not only unaccustomed material hardship, such as hunger (box 1.1), but also the destruction of "normal" life and accustomed social patterns. Under the socialist system, employment helped define an individual's social importance in formal networks (such as the work collective), and it provided the context for informal networks, an important source of support and information that helped people cope in a shortage economy. As jobs are lost and as hidden unem-

---

Box 1.1   Hunger as Experienced by the Very Poor

One important indicator of material deprivation is hunger. Relatively rare in the recent past, hunger is now more frequently experienced by the very poor (Narayan 2000b, 67).

Poverty is the fact that sometimes I go hungry to bed in the evening, because I do not have bread at home. *Macedonia, 1998*

That person is poor who for 20 days out of the month eats boiled potatoes without butter, drinks tea without sugar, and doesn't have enough money to buy subsidized bread. *Armenia, 1995*

Only God knows how we shall survive over the winter. At night you wake up because of a stomachache and because of hunger. *Moldova, 1997*

If I consider how other people live, then I feel poor because I cannot give my child what he needs. If an employed individual still has to worry about buying his or her child bread and has to scrape to make ends meet—this is not normal. *Latvia, 1997*

ployment grows, these sources of support—material, social, and psychological—are breaking down.

Poverty has further eroded the essential sources of support. Driven into isolation by poverty and shame, the poor lack the resources to maintain important social contacts. They find themselves increasingly cut off from informal supports at the very moment when unusually sharp competition over access to jobs, assets, and other resources have made "connections" more important than ever. Schoolchildren in Macedonia say, "School is no good if you don't have connections" (Narayan 2000b, 54). In a shrinking job market, there is a growing sense that qualifications matter less than do connections.

Although the poor in Europe and Central Asia hold governments and officials responsible for the widespread impoverishment, many also blame themselves. The poor expressed deep distress that their knowledge, skills, and formal and informal competencies have become irrelevant. They say they have lost their sense of belonging to society and are no longer necessary to anyone. In Bosnia and Herzegovina, for example, people explained that their inability to find a regular job made them feel worthless to themselves and their families (World Bank 1999a, 17).

Their sense of personal failure, together with the loss of respected social roles and identities, frequently have produced a paralyzing sense of shame. This has contributed to self-destructive responses such as alcoholism, depression, and even suicide. Poverty has greatly increased social stress. Respondents in Russia, for example, attributed the decrease in the birth rate, increases in mortality, growing alcoholism, rising divorce rates, and increasing crime to growing poverty (World Bank 1999e, 16). As one middle-aged Kyrgyz man said:

> As a result of poverty, people steal and rob, children run away from their parents, because of lack of clothes and shoes children can't attend school, the poor are humiliated by the rich, and people commit suicide. We've sold to China everything we had, even electric power lines. Everything built in the Soviet times was broken, stolen, taken apart (World Bank 1999d, 64).

The Extent of Material Deprivation

How many people are living in absolute deprivation in the transition countries of Europe and Central Asia? To answer this seemingly straightforward question, we use the so-called two-dollar-a-day poverty line (actually

$2.15 per person per day in 1996 purchasing power parity).[3] While in many parts of the world the one-dollar-a-day line is used to measure absolute deprivation, the two-dollar-a-day line is more appropriate for the ECA region because its very cold climate necessitates additional expenditures on heat, winter clothing, and food. The additional cost of heating expenditures for a modest apartment in Riga can easily run more than $0.50 cents per day per person for a family of four at current exchange rates. The lowest calorie-based national poverty line in the region, that of Moldova, is actually slightly above the two-dollar-a-day line, indicating that it is a reasonable threshold for absolute deprivation for the region.[4] Poverty levels are highest in Central Asia and the Caucasus; the incidence of poverty in Russia approaches 20 percent (table 1.1).

By and large, the poverty estimates appear plausible. Plotting the headcount indices based on the $4.30 poverty line (which does a better job of spreading out the high income countries) against 1998 GNP per capita in PPP, we find that poverty rates, as expected, decline as GNP increases. Some anomalies appear as well. Poverty rates seem low for Ukraine, Bulgaria, Turkmenistan, and Croatia, and somewhat high for Russia and possibly Romania (figure 1.1). However, the high level of inequality in Russia would lead to higher poverty levels for the same level of private consumption. It is also interesting to note that in Kazakhstan, Hungary, and Romania, mean expenditure per capita based on the survey results is substantially lower than private consumption per capita calculated from national account data. For Azerbaijan, Moldova, Ukraine, Belarus, and Croatia, on the other hand, ratios are high. It is not clear where the data shortcomings lie. Surveys may be systematically underreporting (overreporting) expenditures—in which case absolute poverty would be overestimated (underestimated).[5] Or they might be failing to adequately sample the better off in the society—if so, inequality would probably be underestimated but poverty measures might be fairly robust.[6] Or the national account data may be misestimating private consumption.

Another caution is in order regarding these estimates of absolute deprivation. They are based on PPP rates derived from the International Comparison Programme's price surveys carried out by the Organization for Economic Cooperation and Development (OECD) in 1996. According to these surveys, the prices of many services and some goods in ECA countries were extremely cheap relative to international prices. Measurement error may be a factor here, since it is very difficult to estimate prices when markets are developing and to take into account the value of ancillary benefits received by public sector employees. On average, market exchange

Table 1.1   Absolute Poverty Rates of Transition Economies in Europe and Central Asia,
Selected Years, 1995–99

Country	Survey year	Headcount index $2.15/ day	Headcount index $4.30/ day	Ratio of survey mean consumption to private consumption	1998 GNP in dollars per capita Atlas method	1998 GNP in dollars per capita 1996 PPP
Tajikistan	1999	68.3	95.8	1.02	370	1,040
Moldova	1999	55.4	84.6	0.67	380	1,995
Kyrgyz Republic	1998	49.1	84.1	0.83	380	2,247
Armenia	1999	43.5	86.2	0.62	460	2,074
Azerbaijan	1999	23.5	64.2	1.39	480	2,168
Georgia	1999	18.9	54.2	0.88	970	3,429
Russian Federation	1998	18.8	50.3	0.85	2,260	6,186
Albania[a]	1996	11.5	58.6	0.68	810	2,864
Turkmenistan	1998	7.0	34.4	0.89	502	2,875
Romania	1998	6.8	44.5	0.43	1,360	5,571
Macedonia, FYR	1996	6.7	43.9	0.69	1,290	4,224
Latvia	1998	6.6	34.8	0.68	2,420	5,777
Kazakhstan	1996	5.7	30.9	0.45	1,340	4,317
Bulgaria	1995	3.1	18.2	0.67	1,220	4,683
Lithuania	1999	3.1	22.5	0.69	2,540	6,283
Ukraine	1999	3.0	29.4	0.95	980	3,130
Slovak Republic	1997	2.6	8.6	0.75	3,700	9,624
Estonia	1998	2.1	19.3	0.80	3,360	7,563
Hungary	1997	1.3	15.4	0.47	4,510	9,832
Poland	1998	1.2	18.4	0.67	3,910	7,543
Belarus	1999	1.0	10.4	0.99	2,180	6,318
Croatia	1998	0.2	4.0	1.18	4,620	6,698
Czech Republic	1996	0.0	0.8	0.81	5,150	12,197
Slovenia	1997/98	0.0	0.7	0.94	9,780	14,399

Note: Recent household survey data are not available for Bosnia and Herzegovina and Uzbekistan. Private consumption data are not available for Tajikistan, Turkmenistan, Kazakhstan, Georgia, or Moldova. GDP per capita in current prices is used instead. GDP per capita (first half 1999) are used for Ukraine. The poverty headcount numbers are based on the international poverty lines of $2.15 and $4.30 per person per day.
a. The survey did not cover the capita city Tirana.
Source: Authors' estimates; see appendix for further details. GNP estimates from World Development Indicators database, World Bank.

rates are more than three times greater than the PPP rates in ECA countries—the largest divergence of any region in the world, including Africa. This is surprising since one would expect to find the greatest divergence between PPP rates and exchange rates in the poorest region of the world. If price estimates for transition countries are too low, the PPP rates would be biased downwards. A further source of distortion may occur from our use of PPP rates based on 1996 price surveys to estimate poverty based on household surveys carried out in later years. Although the PPP rates are

Figure 1.1   Incidence of Poverty vs. GNP in Selected ECA Countries

Headcount index at $4.30 per day

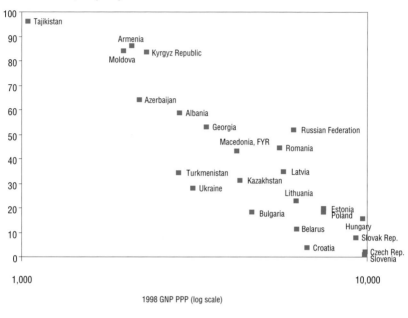

1998 GNP PPP (log scale)

Source: Table 1.1.

adjusted for inflation by the CPI index, they do not take into account changes in price structure that have occurred since 1996.[7] This may introduce another downwards bias. To the extent that the PPP rates are biased downwards, poverty rates would be biased downwards. For these reasons the poverty data presented in table 1.1—based on an international poverty line and PPP rates—should be used with caution, and only to gain an approximate picture of the extent and variation in absolute deprivation across the region.

More fundamentally, the international poverty lines intended to measure the extent of absolute deprivation tell us very little about the level of resources individuals in a particular country need to live with dignity and respect in that country.[8] For this reason countries establish their own national poverty lines—but even this is not without problems (box 1.2). National poverty lines tend to increase with a country's income level. Even though the level of absolute deprivation based on the two-dollar-a-day line is very low in some of the European Union (EU) accession countries, poverty does exist in these countries and is a serious concern—just as it is in the United States or Western Europe.[9] In the United States, for example, the poverty line for a family of four was $11.41 per person per day in 1998. It was originally calculated in the mid-1960s as three times the minimum basket of food a family would need, and since then it has been adjusted for inflation. At this line the official poverty rate in the United States was 12.7 percent.[10]

Income deprivation is the conventional objective measure of poverty. However, it does not necessarily accord well with people's own assessment of their economic welfare, as Ravallion and Lokshin (1999) demonstrate with data from Russia. They find that current household income is not closely correlated with people's self-reported assessments of their economic status. Adding other explanatory variables (such as educational attainment, health status, average income in the area of residence, and employment status) to household income and demographic measures substantially improves their ability to predict people's assessment of their economic welfare. Health and education are important aspects of well-being independent of their impact on income levels. Being unemployed or being afraid of losing one's job also lowers self-rated welfare, even controlling for household income.

Clearly, employment is valued for more than just the income it provides. Relative income also matters; if two people have the same income but live in different areas, the one living in the area of higher average income will perceive herself or himself to be worse off. The more income an individual earns, the better off the individual perceives her or his own economic welfare, even holding total household income constant. This suggests that earning income is important for more than the purchasing power it provides. These findings highlight the need to look beyond the conventional income-based measures of poverty to other factors that influence people's perception of their economic welfare.

Living Conditions

Living conditions for much of the population in Europe and Central Asia compare favorably with the conditions in countries of similar income levels. This is a positive legacy of the heavy investment in the past in infrastructure. Access to piped water, electricity, and central heating is high (table 1.3). However, the pattern of urban development is quite distorted. Many dwellings are located far from places of employment and the city center. Because of a lack of recent investment in housing infrastructure, housing conditions have seriously deteriorated, particu-

Box 1.2   Russia: How Many Poor?

Russia was the first country in the Commonwealth of Independent States to establish, in late 1992, an official methodology for measuring poverty. Since then Russia's statistical agency (Roskomstat) has produced monthly data on poverty incidence. Yet the question of how many people are poor in Russia is hotly debated because others have come up with alternative measures (table 1.2). Although estimates differ widely, all the data come from two basic surveys to

Table 1.2   Russia: Poverty Rates from Various Sources (percent)

Source	1991	1992	1993	1994	1995	1996	1997	1998
Based on official national poverty line								
Roskomstat official poverty incidence[a]	11.7	33.5	31.5	22.4	24.7	22.1	20.8	23.8
Roskomstat revised survey methodology[b]							32.2	37.8
RLMS (World Bank)[c]		26.8	36.9	30.9	41.1	43.2		49.1
RLMS (UNC)[d]		14.6	11.5	17.2	29.5	36.3		39.0
RLMS (World Bank) Panel[e]				37.6	39.6	43.1		
RLMS (C, T, Y) Panel[f]		48.3	40.7	33.7	35.6	36.2		
RLMS (Lokshin and Ravallion) Panel[g]						21.9		32.7
RLMS (Lokshin and Ravallion)						21.0		32.6
Based on $2.15 per day per capita in 1996 PPP								
Roskomstat official survey[h]		7.4		3.9			3.2	7.3
Roskomstat revised survey[i]								9.6
RLMS (World Bank)[j]		14.3	14.3	7.4	11.8	13.3		18.8
RLMS (C, T, Y) Panel[k]		13.5	14.0	6.7	11.0	9.3		
Based on $2.15 per day per capita in 1993 PPP								
RLMS (World Bank)[l]			19.6			24.4		25.1

RLMS = Russian Longitudinal Monitoring Survey.

a. Based on 49,175 households with 139,165 individuals, surveyed quarterly. Per capita total incomes (survey incomes with imputations to bring survey means to macroaggregates) compared to regional cost of official minimum subsistence basket. Source: Roskomstat: Russia in Figures, 1999. Official edition, p. 102. Moscow, 1999 (in Russian).

b. Consumption from Roskomstat's original household survey data, official poverty line. Source: *Roskomstat Statistical Bulletin* 11: 61 (November 1999).

c. Based on region-specific official poverty lines based on consumption per capita. Source: For 1992-96, Foley (1997, 78); for 1998, own estimate using raw data and official poverty line.

d. The UNC measure of poverty is based on incomes, not on consumption, and on region-specific poverty lines valued at survey-generated prices. Source: Mroz and others (1999).

e. Only panel households, two panels: rounds 1-4 (1992-93) and rounds 5-8 (1994-98). Source: World Bank (1999f, 6).

f. Based on local cost (estimated at survey unit values) of official poverty basket and per capita consumption; 1992 (average of rounds 1 and 2); 1993 (average of rounds 3 and 4); 1994 (round 5); 1995 (round 6); 1996 (round 7). Source: Commander, Tolstopiatenko, Yemtsov (1999).

g. Based on expenditures and region-specific poverty lines valued at survey-generated prices. Source: Lokshin and Ravallion (2000).

h. Bank estimates based on grouped data (official annual distribution of total income per capita, with macroimputations by deciles) and poverty line converted to local currency poverty line at average annual prices using national CPI. Sources: See note a.

i. Based on published consumption decile data. Source: See note b.

j. World Bank estimates based on raw data, full cross sections; national CPI data used to convert poverty line into local currency for survey months.

k. World Bank estimates based on raw data; see note e for panel definitions; regional price deflators used to calculate regional poverty lines corresponding to a national average of $2.15 at PPP in local prices.

l. Estimates by World Bank. See note j.

(Box continues on next page.)

Box 1.2 *(continued)*

measure living standards: the Family Budget Survey (FBS), carried out by Roskomstat, and the Russian Longitudinal Monitoring Survey (RLMS), carried out by the Institute of Sociology of the Russian Academy of Science with technical assistance from the University of North Carolina (UNC).

Why are there two different data sets? In part, it is a result of the inaccessibility of the Family Budget Survey, which for years has been off limits to outsiders and to a large degree to insiders as well. Until very recently all data collected at the regional level have been processed regionally, and no data set with national-level data existed. RLMS, on the other hand, is an open source, and it is the only microdata set on Russia available to everyone. The FBS sample as of 1998 is about 50,000 households, substantially larger than the RLMS survey, which has declined from approximately 5,500 households in 1992–93 to 3,619 households in 1990. It is widely debated which data set has more flaws, but most agree that neither is perfect.

Leaving aside issues of survey representativeness, we turn now to three methodological issues on which positions differ: (1) the definition of the welfare indicator; (2) the statistical methods applied to survey-generated numbers; and (3) the choice of poverty line. However abstract these issues may seem, all reflect important difficulties in measuring poverty in transition economies.

The definition of the welfare indicator. Very often welfare statistics rely on consumption or expenditure data rather than on income—often because income is underreported. The gap between household incomes reported in the Family Budget Survey and macro data from the national accounts is on the order of 30 percent and varies over time. Even when a consumption-based measure is used, there may be differences in the way the consumption aggregate is constructed. For example, the World Bank's Poverty Assessment for Russia uses a consumption indicator based on current expenditures, while the UNC data set computes one based on total spending, including consumer durables. Roskomstat, however, uses incomes as the main indicator of well-being but adjusts the income data.

The use of primary data and adjusted data. According to the poverty literature, raw primary data are generally better to use than adjusted data. Even if households tend to underreport their income, they do not have specific incentives to do so when asked about their spending. On the other hand, official estimates of Russian poverty are based on adjusted data: the information provided by the individual households is altered.

Roskomstat estimates for every region a measure called *total monetary income* based on household survey data, enterprise reports of wages, retail trade, and banking statistics. It is the amount of money spent by the population on purchases and payments on retail trade, net change in deposits and holdings of securities, net purchases by households of foreign currency and what is called "balance (*saldo*) of money holdings"—that is, the increase (decrease) of currency outside banks and enterprises. This aggregate regional figure is compared with what is reported by households for the same items in the Family Budget Surveys, and the latter is adjusted upwards to match the former. The difference is distributed across households based on log normal distribution.

These adjusted numbers result in lower poverty counts than the raw data from the Family Budget Surveys. Roskomstat claims that these adjustments are essential to overcome underreporting by respondents in household surveys. (The informal nature of many economic activities contributes to this underreporting.) Since total expenditures of households are checked against trade and monetary statistics, on an aggregate basis these corrections are probably justified. They may impose other errors on the data, however. In the final analysis it is not clear that adjusted data are preferable to estimates based more directly on the raw data.

(Box continues on next page.)

Box 1.2 *(continued)*

Recently, beginning in 1999, Roskomstat began making available estimates based on unadjusted data. It also published information on the magnitude of the adjustments. This resulted in in yet another estimate of poverty.

The choice of poverty line. All agree that absolute poverty is a real problem in Russia and that some absolute standard of basic needs should be used as a poverty threshold. One may argue that the poverty basket on which all measurements are based is out of date, since it was developed in 1992. Relative prices have changed enormously since then. But for the sake of comparisons over time, a poverty basket must be defined. Where researchers disagree is how to go from a basket of goods that is considered a subsistence minimum to the line expressed in currency units. There are two different approaches that yield dramatically different results. One approach, pursued by Roskomstat and the World Bank, is to use price data from price surveys to cost the minimum consumption basket. This produces regionally specific lines but, as many would argue, with a strong bias toward urban areas (where the price data are collected). The other approach, taken by UNC, is to use the unit values (prices reported by households) from the survey itself. Both approaches have merit. The different results reflect the geographic price differences in very imperfect transitional markets. Others have combined elements of both approaches (Lokshin and Ravallion 2000; Commander, Tolstopiatenko, and Yemtsov 1999).

Conclusion. Estimates of poverty in Russia, even estimates based on the same source of data, differ widely. Differences in methodologies are to be expected, given the serious problems of measurement presented by transition economies. Open access to data, more research, and a wide debate may help users converge on a more broadly accepted set of poverty estimates. The lack of a broadly agreed estimate of poverty makes it more difficult to have an informed dialogue about the extent of poverty and its causes.

Table 1.3   Households Connected to Utilities (percent)

Utility	Poverty Group	Armenia 1996[a]	Croatia 1998	Hungary 1997	Kyrgyz Republic 1999	Latvia 1997	Moldova 1998	Russian Fed. 1996	Ukraine 1996
Electricity	Nonpoor	99.0	99.8	n.a.	98.8	99.9	99.8	n.a.	99.9
	Poor	98.2	99.0	n.a.	99.2	98.7	97.7	n.a.	99.5
District heating	Nonpoor	9.0	33.4	26.6	30.0	69.9	35.9	72.7	31.2
	Poor	10.4	7.8	14.8	12.5	49.0	23.1	62.5	36.9
Network gas	Nonpoor	1.9	27.1	82.0	21.8	52.9	30.0	63.1	n.a.
	Poor	1.4	11.0	56.4	8.6	38.4	21.4	60.9	n.a.
Water	Nonpoor	88.4	96.6	93.4	76.2	83.9	35.0	79.2	57.8
	Poor	87.4	74.5	73.4	68.7	70.2	20.0	68.2	69.5
Hot water	Nonpoor	1.2	42.6	n.a.	0.7	59.0	32.9	61.4	24.3
	Poor	1.0	20.3	n.a.	0.1	39.3	19.3	45.3	24.8
Sewerage	Nonpoor	n.a.	79.6	92.8	n.a.	82.1	35.0	69.9	34.1
	Poor	n.a.	51.2	71.0	n.a.	66.4	20.0	57.4	39.8

n.a. = not available.
Note: The poverty line is set at two-thirds of median per capita consumption.
a. Households with connections to nonfunctioning utility services are not considered connected.
Source: Lovei (2000).

larly in high-rise dwellings built before the transition. Indeed, these dwellings may be uneconomic in the new structure of urban land prices. "Vertical" slums with their attendant social problems are likely to emerge in the future.[11]

In socialist times, utility services were highly subsidized. With the transition and the end of energy supply credits from Russia and Turkmenistan, energy supply became less reliable, and fuel shortages appeared in the Caucasus, Moldova, and parts of Central Asia. From 1992 to 1995 most of the population in Armenia received only 2 to 4 hours of electricity per day, and central heating and gas supply were virtually cut off (Lampietti and others 2000); since then conditions have improved substantially. The reliability of water supply also dropped. Access to safe water has become a significant problem in the poorest CIS countries (box 1.3). Despite government efforts to cushion the shocks through various subsidy mechanisms, poor consumers must pay higher prices even as their incomes fall. Even more distressing, poor consumers in some countries are paying more—but getting less—as service delivery becomes increasingly erratic.

Education and Health

The high level of education and health in Europe and Central Asia is one of the most important accomplishments of the socialist era. Today, school enrollment rates continue to be significantly higher than for countries of similar income levels. Even in the poorest countries in the region, primary school enrollment currently exceeds 85 percent, and in many countries it is effectively universal (see chapter 7). On the health side, indicators for the region are also generally better than in countries of similar incomes, reflecting high levels of education and the universal provision of comprehensive health care services to consumers in the past. Maternal mortality rates are low, ranging from less than 10 per 1,000 live births in Central Europe to less than 30 per thousand live births in Central Asia, with the exception of Turkmenistan, and they declined significantly between 1980 and 1987. Increases in the mortality rates of children under five have largely been contained. Even in the poorest countries in Central Asia, most children continue to be immunized, despite cuts in public health spending (Falkingham 2000).

The universal access to health and education that was publicly provided during the socialist era is being seriously undermined by families' inability to afford the charges that are now being levied by many public institutions. This problem includes the widespread under-the-counter pay-

Box 1.3   Water Supply: Low-Quality Services Hurt the Poor

Lack of access to some minimum quantity and quality of water supply services results in unhealthy living conditions and disproportionately affects the poor. Although official figures of water supply service coverage in Europe and Central Asia are very high, the quality of services has deteriorated rapidly. For example, in 1995 about 95 percent of all households in Baku were connected to the water supply system (World Bank 1995). However, based on results of a social assessment for a water rehabilitation project, water was available about 22 days per month, 4 hours per day. Eighty-seven percent of the population believed piped water was unsafe. The impact on the poor is higher (figure 1.2).

Figure 1.2   Water Availability in Baku, Azerbaijan, 1995

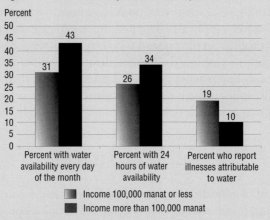

Percent

Legend:
- Income 100,000 manat or less
- Income more than 100,000 manat

Source: World Bank (1995).

Statistics on Armenians' access to drinking water can be misleading (Lampietti 2000). While most households have access to home water taps, water service is unreliable. Typically water is available for a few hours in the morning and in the evening, with urban consumers having fewer average hours of daily service. Fifty percent of Armenian households indicated that water was unavailable on average for 40 days. About 12 percent were without water for three months or more; breaks in service were particularly acute for the rural poor. Some villagers must travel far to fetch drinking water. In other villages water is for sale only from trucks, and lines for water can last all day, with family members replacing each other in line. When the need arises, about one-person-hour-per-day is spent finding, carrying, and storing water. In more than 60 percent of households, water collection is the responsibility of adult females. About a quarter of the households in Armenia treats the water before drinking it, the majority by boiling it.

Improved water services continues to be a priority for Armenia. In a 2000 survey, households were asked to rank Armenia's top three development priorities among 15 presented (unemployment, preventive health care, primary education, water supply, electricity, roads, public transportation, telephone, new housing, housing maintenance, solid waste collection, sewerage and wastewater, water level in Lake Sevan, social protection programs, and other). While unemployment and social protection are the top priority for three fourths of Armenians, water services is a leading "second tier" issue, selected as most important by 6 percent of the population (the same percentage, whether poor or nonpoor). Nearly a quarter of the population indicates water is one of Armenia's top three development priorities.

ments expected by doctors and teachers to supplement their income. As public spending on educational materials, teachers' wages, and maintenance of schools and heat becomes tighter, the burden shifts in many cases to parents. As household incomes decline, parents find it difficult to pay the rising costs associated with sending their children to school. Nearly universal school enrollment rates are being jeopardized in some of the poorest CIS countries. Primary school enrollment rates fell by ten or more percentage points in Moldova, Armenia, Georgia, Turkmenistan, and Tajikistan during the 1990s. The evidence, though sketchy, suggests that poor children are the most likely to drop out of school or to attend only sporadically. In 1997 a young Moldovan mother explained that she keeps her three school-age children out of school to help her scavenge cardboard: "We simply have to survive. If we had nothing to burn, we would die. My children can't go to school because, without them, I wouldn't be able to gather enough cardboard every day" (Narayan 2000b, 259).

Despite the relatively favorable indicators, disturbing health problems are surfacing. The decrease in male life expectancy, particularly in countries in the former Soviet Union, is noteworthy. Male life expectancy fell on average by four years between 1989 and the mid-1990s in the Baltic countries and by more than five years in Russia, Ukraine, and Kazakhstan. By 1994 male life expectancy in Russia had fallen to 58 years—with a significant share of the decline attributable to the almost 100 percent increase in the mortality rates of men between the ages of 40 and 59 since 1989. Not all countries experienced a drop; life expectancy remained almost constant in Armenia and Turkmenistan. There has been a lively debate about reasons for the increase in deaths. An increase in cardiovascular and circulatory diseases, accidents, and violence are the proximate causes, to which an upsurge in excessive alcohol consumption may have contributed (box 1.4). Mortality increases were lower in areas where social support systems were stronger (Shkolnikov and others 1999).

Diseases such as tuberculosis that had been largely controlled during the socialist period are staging a resurgence along with an explosion in sexually transmitted diseases and the related threat of an HIV/AIDS epidemic, notably in the Baltic and Slavic FSU countries. In Belarus and Ukraine, the incidence of syphilis and gonorrhea almost tripled between 1989 and 1997—presaging a likely HIV/AIDS epidemic in the next few years. The world's steepest increase in HIV/AIDS incidence in one year occurred in Russia in 1999, largely due to the rapid spread of HIV/AIDS among injecting drug users. Transmission among drug users has increased dramatically, resulting in the rapid rise in the number of HIV cases reported in 1999. At least 90 percent of newly registered HIV/AIDS cases

---

Box 1.4   Explaining the Decline in Male Mortality in Russian Federation

Between 1984 and 1987, life expectancy at birth increased from 61.7 years to 64.9 years for Russian males and from 73.0 years to 74.3 years for Russian females. The next few years, however, saw sharp declines, and between 1987 and 1994, life expectancy fell by 7.3 years for men and by 3.3 years for women.

Leon and others (1997) analyze age-specific and cause-specific patterns of mortality changes, and find that the largest increases in mortality rates are observed for alcohol-related deaths, accidents, and violence. Although other factors, such as nutrition and health services, may have been responsible, they find substantial evidence that significant changes in alcohol consumption over the period explain the main features of the observed mortality fluctuations.

In reviewing the evidence on historical patterns of alcohol consumption in Russia, McKee (1999) observes that the state at various times actually encouraged alcohol sales. By the early 1980s, the social cost of heavy drinking had become apparent. This led in 1985 to the imposition of then president Gorbachev's wide-ranging and initially highly effective anti-alcohol campaign, which included state restrictions on the sale and supply of alcohol as well as an increase in the price of alcoholic drinks. This trend continued into the 1990s, when sales of alcohol increased once more as the political will to restrict consumption evaporated and the price of alcohol fell relative to the costs of consumer goods, including basic foodstuffs. Annual consumption of pure alcohol per head, which had fallen from 14.2 liters in 1984 to a low of 10.7 liters in 1987, increased again to 14.5 liters by 1993. The experience of Russia demonstrates the important role that the state can play in containing alcohol consumption, and it highlights the importance of prevention measures designed to effect lifestyle changes.

---

have been attributed to intravenous drug use (Vinokur and others 1999). Preliminary studies suggest that drug use is becoming common among unemployed young people in many of the industrial cities of Russia and Ukraine (World Bank 2000c).

Poverty and Vulnerability

At the mercy of a corrupt bureaucracy, the poor are dependent on what little social assistance comes their way and humiliated by officials who treat them with little respect. While their standard of living worsens, they see officials enrich themselves through illegal actions. Institutions that should help them are, more often than not, part of the problem.

The Poor Feel Cheated Out of Assets

In many transition countries the state divested itself of assets, notably in the form of industrial enterprises, housing, and collective agricultural enterprises. The privatization of land and agricultural property was not always carried out transparently according to many poor. Abuses were reported more frequently by workers who chose to remain with newly privatized state and collective farms. The poor complained that collective and state farm managers often obtained the best and largest shares of land, agricultural equipment, and livestock. They accomplished this by exploiting legal ambiguities, taking advantage of the population's ignorance of the law, overtly intimidating collective farm employees, misrepresenting the facts, and sometimes refusing to accept documents or to abide by the law.

Armenia's far-reaching comprehensive land reform program distributed state and collective-owned land through a lottery system to villagers. The poor claimed that the nonpoor used their "connections" to undermine the fairness of the process, particularly as regards the distribution of livestock and machinery. "During privatization, those people who had a patron received five or six cows and the rest received nothing," complained one person. "The whole collective farm was plundered, and the chairman, together with the district leaders themselves, took the remaining 100 head of cattle to Turkey and sold them for $2 a kilo" (Dudwick 1995). When told of the strict state procurement regulations for milk, other farmers refused to take livestock. Not long after the privatization, the government lifted the procurement demands, which left these farmers feeling like they had been cheated (Holt 1995).

Officials and collective farm managers in Moldova frequently misinformed and intimidated collective farm workers who wanted to withdraw from the collectives. Dudwick (1997) reports that one mayor interviewed for the study openly acknowledged that he had tried to discourage pensioners and female collective farm workers from claiming their land shares by informing them that their land would be confiscated if they did not farm it. (The law does not make this provision.) On one farm the manager had effectively prevented pensioners from withdrawing from the collective by telling them (incorrectly) that they would lose their pensions if they withdrew. In other villages the collective farm managers kept people from leaving by threatening to prevent them from renting agricultural equipment; others refused to distribute the other assets (mainly agricultural machinery) to those who withdrew their land shares from the farm. As a stop-gap measure, one collective farm refused to allow people to withdraw until May, when it was too late to sow the crop.

A 1997 study carried out in two oblasts of Kazakhstan (Bilesim International 1997) found that farmland had become progressively more concentrated in the hands of a few. Fifteen percent of those interviewed had "voluntarily" given up their property shares as a result of intimidation, blackmail, and fraud. In some cases farm management intimidated farm workers by claiming that they could not take their shares because they had not paid their portion of the collective farm debts.

The Poor Feel Cheated Out of Entitlements

The poor often feel that they are being cheated out of their entitlements—although they do not always make the distinction between the state failing to make funds available to pay pensions and other social entitlements and misappropriation by social assistance officials. Informants in Kyrgyz Republic (World Bank 1999d, 99) believe that the payment of benefits in-kind is cheating them; they accuse officials from social assistance offices of distributing to them overpriced flour, oil, candies, and hosiery rather than cash. A pensioner in Kyrgyz Republic explained, "Corruption is one of the most important sources of poverty. The corrupt officials delay payment of our pensions and social benefits, because they use the money and profiteer on it" (World Bank 1999d, 49). In other countries people sometimes have to pay bribes to get pensions or disability assistance to which they are entitled. Informants in Javakhet, Georgia, for example, said that they had to pay twice the amount of their monthly pension in order to begin receiving their pension (Dudwick 1999). Adding insult to injury, the poor are ill-treated when they do seek help from public institutions, as these statements make clear:

> Poverty is humiliation, the sense of being dependent, and of being forced to accept rudeness, insults, and indifference when we seek help. *Latvia, 1998* (Narayan 2000b, 30)

> Why are they [post office employees] there? They don't even want to talk to us the way people do. We come to receive our own money, our pensions, and they treat us as though we come to take their own money away from them. *Kyrgyz Republic, 1999* (World Bank 1999d, 97)

Corruption in the Health and Education Sectors

Corruption in the health and education sectors is widespread but not new. During the socialist era, it was common to present teachers with small gifts and in some cases to pay bribes to improve grades or scores on university entrance examinations. As salaries have declined, teachers have compensated by stimulating demand for their tutoring services by threatening to fail students or by withholding knowledge required on university entrance exams. Bribes are often needed to enter prestigious departments and institutes. Similarly, during the Soviet era, patients presented doctors and nurses with gifts or small payments to ensure good care. But the costs were minimal compared with the fees today. If gifts once consisted of chocolates and cognac, or manageable cash amounts for surgery and child-birth, the same procedures now cost up to hundreds of dollars in under-the-table payments to doctors and hospitals. The following statements underscore the difference between then and now:

> Up to a few years ago I didn't even ask myself the question: What shall I cook? Today there are times I do not have anything to put on the stove and this is very difficult for a mother [crying]... Before we were not afraid of getting ill, everything was well regulated and there was health protection. Today we pray to God that nobody gets sick. What could we do? *Macedonia, 1998* (Narayan 2000b, 44)

> Before everyone could get healthcare, but now everyone just prays to God that they don't get sick because everywhere they just ask for money. *Bosnia and Herzegovina, 1999* (Narayan 2000a, 79)

Illness is dreaded by the poor who cannot afford the "informal" payments required to get medical care from doctors and others practicing in financially starved public institutions. In some countries, notably the Caucasus, informal payments account for more than 85 percent of all expenditures in the sector (Lewis 2000). The poor sometimes go without medical care or drugs, or sell off their income-generating assets, to scrape up the cash needed to get treatment. Illness can impoverish vulnerable families.

Crime

The poor express an extreme sense of isolation and defenselessness, especially in relation to crime and police corruption. During the Soviet period, police were fully prepared and equipped to preserve order and control the actions of ordinary citizens as well as those of criminals. Today the ability of the police to control crime appears to have weakened. Their interest in pursuing criminals is linked, in some instances, to whether they receive under-the-table payments.

Crime—petty street crimes as well as organized crime—has risen substantially throughout Europe and Central Asia during the transition. Crime, mostly in the form of theft, was the most frequently mentioned impact of poverty and ill-being by the poor in transition countries (Narayan and others 2000b). The crime wave derives from severe impoverishment of some sectors of the community, the enormous difficulties faced by poor unskilled youth in entering the labor market, and the weakening and corruption of state controls, particularly toward gang activity and organized crime. In the Kyrgyz Republic and Uzbekistan, livestock theft is a growing problem. In Ukraine storage bins in rural areas have been raided and livestock stolen. Theft from home gardens was viewed as a particular problem in Russia. "We watched over our potatoes with a gun. People from other towns pretend to come to pick mushrooms. They sprinkle a few mushrooms and some grass over the top of the basket, and underneath they have potatoes" (Narayan and others 2000a, 137).

Police corruption came up repeatedly during the consultations with the poor (Narayan 2000a, 144). "We feel absolutely insecure, they [the police] are corrupt," one Bulgarian respondent claimed. "If they catch a villain they let him walk; only those who can't give them anything are sent to prison" (World Bank 1999b, 74). In Georgia farmers say they live in a police state "in which police pay for their positions and freely harass citizens." Indeed, people prefer to contact "criminal authorities" rather than even come to the notice of the police who often extort payments from them" (Dudwick 1999, 67). In Moldova the poor also noted that the police lacked interest in helping the victims of crimes, and tended to blame the victim for theft or rape (De Soto and Dudwick 1997).

Organized crime has also become widespread, with "the network of criminals forming a state-within-a state and seizing certain sectors of the economy" (United Nations 1997). Mafia cartels operating throughout Europe—some organized along ethnic lines—do billions of dollars of business trafficking arms, drugs, and persons (as illegal migrants or prostitutes). The connection between the police and criminal organizations is a serious obstacle to small entrepreneurs, who find they have no recourse against rackets. This was a frequent complaint of small traders in ECA countries.

Drugs are becoming a major part of local informal economies, particularly in Central Asia and the Balkans. Geography and history make Kazakhstan, the Kyrgyz Republic, Tajikistan, Turkmenistan, and Uzbekistan attractive areas, because they are situated between the world's largest opium producers (Afghanistan, Pakistan, Iran, Burma, Laos, and Thailand) and the most lucrative markets in Western Europe. Poverty also makes for a fertile ground for recruiting young unemployed men to traffick drugs. The sale of drugs is more than an economic livelihood; it provides entire groups with means to advance political causes and finance military campaigns—undermining in some cases the ability of national governments to gain effective control over their boundaries. Drug-related crimes are becoming more frequent. The incidence of registered drug-related crimes in Kazakhstan in 1994 was 564; in the first three months of 1999, it rose to 5,247. In 1999, 185,000 drug-related crimes were registered in Russia, a 90 percent increase from 1996. Drugs contribute to the corruption of poorly paid police and other security forces (Olcott and Udalova 2000).

Another manifestation of the relationship between impoverishment, lack of economic opportunities at home, and criminality is the significant increase in the number of women and children (both boys and girls) involved in the sex industry in their own countries and in Western Europe, Israel, and the Persian Gulf. In Latvia authorities estimated that juveniles constituted 12 percent of those involved in prostitution in 1995 (Stukuls 1999). Many women are recruited through advertisements from ostensible modeling, tourist, or housekeeping agencies run by organized crime, or through offers to work abroad as waitresses. Traffickers often seize the women's passports, forcing women, without documents or means, to work their way out of servitude (Wedel 1999). According to the International Office of Migration, as many as 500,000 women are being trafficked to Western Europe alone, and Ukraine, Russia, and Belarus are becoming the center of the global trafficking of women. Although officials and law enforcement agencies acknowledge that a trafficking problem exists, many contend that the women are aware of the risks involved. Law enforcement agencies in countries of destination often treat trafficked women as illegal migrants and therefore as criminals—rather than as victims of crime.

Poverty and Helplessness

Many of the poor view the transition process as an event beyond their control, the reason for their downward mobility and loss of status. The transition is akin to a natural disaster with which they are powerless to cope. And while people may blame their downward slide on external causes, they nonetheless experience shame and humiliation in not being able to provide for their families and maintain connections with relatives and friends. Men have been particularly devastated by their inability to fulfill their expected role as the provider for the family. One man from Ozerny, Russia, admitted, "I cannot feed my children normally any more. [I] feel ashamed to come home (Narayan and others 2000a, 98).

Shame and helplessness have contributed to the increase in suicide, noted by many of the poor interviewed in various qualitative studies.

Speaking of four men that had recently committed suicide in the town of Kalofer, Bulgaria respondents noted, "They can't take the tension, have no job, must support three kids, so he takes the rope and that's it" (World Bank 1999b, 88). An elderly woman in Kyrgyz Republic observed that "the unemployed men are frustrated, because they no longer can play the part of family providers and protectors. They live on money made by their wives, and feel humiliated because of that. Suicides among young men have become more frequent" (World Bank 1999d, 110). Suicide rates skyrocketed the first half of the transition period, particularly in the former Soviet Union, and then came down some in the late 1990s (figure 1.3).

Marginalized Groups

If conditions have worsened considerably for the mainstream poor population, certain groups among them are in a particularly vulnerable situation, one that has worsened the effects of poverty or presented special obstacles to overcoming poverty. The vulnerability of some groups derives from external events, such as localized conflicts, war, or natural catastrophe. In other cases vulnerability is the outcome of long-term processes of marginalization related to minority ethnic or religious affiliation. Vul-

Figure 1.3   Suicide Rates in Selected ECA Countries, 1991–98

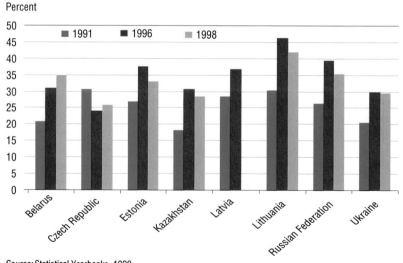

Percent

Source: Statistical Yearbooks, 1999.

nerability also relates to dependency. Given the current inability of states to provide care, the very young and very old, as well as people with severe disabilities or illnesses, have few alternative resources when their family support network breaks down. Because of the very nature of these marginalized groups, it is difficult to give precise descriptions of their size or the extent of absolute poverty among them. But there is little doubt that they are among the poorest and most socially excluded.

Displaced People

Although the countries of Europe and Central Asia contain only 7 percent of the world's population, they are home to an estimated 15 percent of the world's refugees and internally displaced persons, and some estimates go as high as 30 percent (Heleniak 1999). According to the U.S. Committee for Refugees (1999), conflicts in Southeastern Europe (Bosnia and Herzegovina, Croatia, and Kosovo), in the South Caucasus (Armenia, Azerbaijan, and Georgia), Russia (Chechnya, North Ossetia, and Dagestan), and Tajikistan have displaced almost 4.5 million people (including 1,270,000 refugees and 3,130,000 internally displaced persons). In some places, such as Kosovo, refugees have returned home within months. In most cases, however, displacement has lasted long enough to create pervasive effects on an entire generation. Displaced populations suffer multiple losses—of family members, homes, assets, livelihoods, and social networks—and they cope with high levels of physical, economic, and legal insecurity, particularly when the situations that caused their displacement remain unresolved. Postconflict transitions around the world have demonstrated that the social and economic impacts of long-term displacement linger far beyond the formal cessation of hostilities. In many countries so many are displaced that, despite international humanitarian assistance, public budgets are overwhelmed. During the late 1990s, Georgia allocated as much as 20 percent of its development budget to entitlements for internally displaced persons (IDPs). In such cases the displacement problem affects not only the vulnerable poor but the social fabric and economy of an entire country.

Unlike other poor people, many displaced persons have lost assets accumulated over a lifetime—including their homes. Years after the Dayton Accords of 1995, hundreds of thousands of refugees and IDPs in the Balkans are still displaced, unable to gain access to their properties. In Bosnia and Herzegovina some local authorities have transferred housing belonging to original owners to the new occupants, while contradictory laws in Croatia deliberately discourage return of displaced ethnic Serbs.

Displaced rural populations have lost access to land. Even when they return, they may be killed by landmines, as the mine-related casualties in the Gali region of Abkhazia or in Nagorno-Karabagh demonstrate. Some displaced persons have been physically disabled or psychologically traumatized by the conflict that caused their displacement, conditions that place even more obstacles in front of them.

Refugees and IDPs confront structural barriers that reduce their opportunities, often because they have few links to the structures of power in host communities. Bosnian IDPs, for example, complained that local employers routinely rejected them in favor of people native to the given municipality (World Bank 1999a). In the South Caucasus, where conflicts in Nagorno Karabakh, Abkhazia, and South Ossetia remain unresolved, IDPs in Azerbaijan and Georgia have been displaced for nearly a decade. The Azerbaijani and Georgian governments have not wished to facilitate integration of IDPs into host communities, which could weaken their claim on disputed territories. This has limited IDPs' legal access to land, permanent housing, and formal employment.

Refugees and IDPs face additional insecurities related to their uncertain legal status in the host country. In Moscow, which houses many refugees from conflicts in Tajikistan as well as other former Soviet countries, groups that lack a *propiska* (residence permit) are subject to harassment and extortion by police. Tajiks, many of whom work as loaders in local markets, reported that police beat them, confiscated their documents as a pretext for repeatedly fining them, and sometimes took their earnings (World Bank 1999e). In other cases the atrocities of war fueled continuing mistrust and hostility, which further reduce the ability of displaced persons to participate in local economies. For example, in South Eastern Europe (Bosnian Muslims, ethnic Serbs, and ethnic Croats returning to their former communities) or the Caucasus (South Ossetians returning to Georgia), local populations or nationalist groups have sometimes physically prevented displaced persons from returning, or pressured them to leave through hostile actions such as setting their houses on fire.

Many displaced persons live in conditions markedly worse than those of surrounding poor populations (box 1.5). In Azerbaijan, Georgia, and parts of the Balkans, displaced populations, dependent on humanitarian assistance and government-provided social services, continue to live in collective centers, camps, makeshift shelters, or public buildings. By the end of 1999, 75 percent of IDPs in Azerbaijan still lived in temporary and substandard accommodations. Many Crimean Tatars, some of whom left homes in Central Asia voluntarily but others under pressure of growing ethnic hostility in Uzbekistan, sold their assets to finance their move just before the hyper-

---

Box 1.5 Living Conditions for IDPs in Azerbaijan

Living conditions alone pose a huge burden for displaced families, many of whom live in accommodations never intended for habitation, remote from job opportunities, and apparently forgotten by authorities. IDPs in Azerbaijan asserted that improving their housing conditions was their first priority. A 30-year-old unemployed IDP in the basement of an unfinished apartment building in a remote district of Baku referred to his three children as "basement children." "We live here in this basement for five years now—all of us, my parent, my wife and three children, my brother and his family. This place is not for living, it is an underground utility area to keep water pipes. It is all made of cement, all the walls and the floor. That is why everyone is so sick here....we will all rot here soon." The entire extended family lives on the parents' pensions.

Source: Bank staff interviews.

---

inflation of the early 1990s. Since then, the majority of Tatars in Crimea have been living in temporary buildings without amenities, and lacking connections with municipal services (Wanner and Dudwick 1996; UNHCR 1997).

Ethnically-Based Exclusion

New state borders, the creation of new majority-minority relations, and sharp competition for reduced resources and employment opportunities can divide societies along ethnic lines. Some minorities live in considerable social and political isolation (such as Russians in the northern rust-belt communities of the Baltics). These Russians, however, are not necessarily at higher risk of poverty than the majority population. But for the Roma concentrated in Central and South Eastern Europe (box 1.6), social and political exclusion is linked to extreme poverty.

Marginalized socially and economically during the socialist era, the Roma during the transition have experienced an exclusion even more severe. As enterprises downsized, Roma were among the first to be laid off. Given their lack of skills and the discrimination against them, most are likely to remain unemployed. Roma who worked in collective agriculture but were not land owners lost access to land when restitution-based land reform was instituted. Many Roma reside in ghettoized neighborhoods on the peripheries of rural or urban settlements, and they have little access to municipal services. Few Roma children go beyond basic education in large part because of pervasive discrimination in the education system, where they are often labeled as "mentally disabled" and channeled into poorer quality special education. Attacks by skinheads, as well as mob violence,

---

Box 1.6   Who Are the Roma?

Approximately 5 million Roma—often called Gypsies—are thought to reside in Central and South Eastern Europe. The Roma are a unique minority because they have no historical homeland and live in nearly all countries in Europe and the former Soviet Union. Roma make up the largest share of the population in FYR Macedonia (11 percent); in Bulgaria, Slovakia, and Romania they represent about 9 percent of the population. Estimates of the size of the Roma population are very approximate because of undersampling (in censuses and household surveys) of areas in which Roma are likely to reside, difficulties in locating and identifying populations that may not be officially registered, and problems with self-reporting. Roma prefer not to self-identify for various reasons, including fear of discrimination. The "Roma community" is internally diverse. There are numerous subgroups differentiated by type of settlement and degree of assimilation, religion, and language. Some groups speak the Roma language, while others do not.

Source: Ringold (2000).

---

increased throughout Central and Eastern Europe in the 1990s. The Roma are not likely to be helped by the police; rather, many experience police violence on a daily basis (High Commissioner on National Minorities 2000). "The police are racists—when skinheads attack Gypsies and police turn up, they start beating the Gypsies too and let skinheads walk away scot-free. The skinheads are pampered rich kids. That's why they [the police] don't do anything" (World Bank 1999b, 38).

The levels of poverty among Roma are striking: according to a 1997 household survey in Bulgaria, more than 84 percent of Roma—compared with the national poverty rate of 36 percent—were living below the poverty line (World Bank 1999c). Comparisons with the 1995 data indicated that only 0.2 percent of Roma households had never been poor (in the bottom two quintiles) during both survey years (1995, 1997). The data for Hungary are also alarming: one-third of the long-term poor (households that were poor four or more times between 1992 and 1997) were Roma, although they comprise about only 5 percent of the population (World Bank 2000b, 14).

While some groups of Roma have organized to effectively represent their own interests, in most countries they remain politically fragmented. Recently, Roma communities have received a powerful boost from the European Union, as accession countries try to improve their human rights records. Governments and nongovernmental organizations have turned their attention to issues of improved health and education and promotion of employment opportunities. But the extent of political will on the part of governments varies. Success has also been limited because current programs addressed at Roma have insufficiently taken into account Roma cultural preferences for "independence, occupational flexibility, and the maintenance of a subsistence economy adapted to immediate needs"(Wheeler 1999, 6).

Dysfunctional Families and Children at Risk

The institution of the family has come under great stress during the transition, as evidenced by demographic indicators. Birth rates declined 26 percent on average between 1989 and 1998 in Central and South Eastern Europe and by 40 percent in the former Soviet Union (UNICEF, Transmonee database). Marriage rates fell by roughly the same percentage, with the largest declines in the Baltics and the Caucasus, and divorce rates increased significantly. Many of the poor report that poverty and unemployment have strained their marriages. Indeed, quarrels, drinking, and domestic violence have become more frequent. In discussions in Sarajevo and Mostar, for example, people explicitly attributed domestic violence to alcoholism, particularly on the part of demobilized soldiers who were frustrated at their inability to find regular employment. Alcoholics, whom many people regard as the "undeserving poor," are often excluded from networks of support. As a result, their families frequently live in extremely difficult conditions (box 1.7).

Dysfunctional family relations and parental inability to provide for children have increased dramatically the number of children at risk. The percentage of children 3 years of age and younger who are placed in infant homes has risen during the transition (figure 1.4), a telling indicator of greater family vulnerability and poor progress on child protection reforms. Poverty and other circumstances, including alcoholism, contribute to the incapacity of households to care for their children. In Estonia, Belarus, and Kazakhstan, for example, the number of children in infant homes increased by about 75 percent between 1990 and 1997. Bulgaria had the highest percentage of children in infant homes—about 1.2 percent of the population ages 0 to 3. Rates in Romania and Latvia are quite high as well (UNICEF 1999).

An extreme manifestation of child neglect and family breakdown in Europe and Central Asia is the appearance of "street children" (box 1.8). They regularly work on city streets and sometimes live there. Some are homeless, but many contribute their earnings to their families. Street children by and large are not orphans; most have at least one parent alive, and some spend their days on the street but return home to sleep.

Latvian authorities estimate as many as 4,000 street children in Latvia; for Romania, UNICEF reports between 2,500 and 3,500 street children (Schecter 1999). Concerned organizations estimate that the number of

---

Box 1.7   Three Perspectives on Alcoholic Families at Risk

Kyrgyz Republic. A woman from the Kenesh village in the Talas region of the Kyrgyz Republic expresses her view of local alcoholics in these words: "Some families in this village can't even afford food for their children. These people don't work on their land and offer it for lease to others. In many of such families children cannot attend school, because they don't have clothes and shoes. To some extent, these people are guilty . . . themselves. Many of the men are lazy and drink alcohol instead of working and providing for their families" (World Bank 1999d, 49).

Armenia. In Armenia the most striking examples of the "undeserving poor" were families with an adult alcoholic. Respondents identified these families as the poorest and most likely to be ignored by relatives. In such families the alcoholic husband was often unable to retain a job; if he did work occasionally, he often spent the cash or in-kind earnings on alcohol. Members of such families appeared hungry and dirty, living in horrifying conditions in dwellings that lacked the maintenance traditionally performed by the man of the house (Gomart 1998).

Ukraine. Olga V. is 31 years of age and has two sons, 11 and 9. They live in Ukraine. Her ex-husband is an alcoholic and provides no child support. When her older son was 6, she sent him to a state boarding school (*internat*) because she could not afford to raise him. The younger son told the interviewer, "Like my brother, I too want to go to the *internat.* There they eat four times a day. I want so much to eat. My mother has started to drink a lot lately. She washes or repairs things for people, gets some money, and drinks. There's not enough money for food." Indeed, Olga V. stated that since she lost her job as a milkmaid at the collective farm, she cannot even afford to feed her son twice a day. Often she has to decide who will eat, she or her son. "There's nothing to eat. We're constantly hungry. There's nothing to wear. There's no money to buy the child boots, or notebooks, pens or a bookbag. My life is just grief. That's all.... I don't even want to live. I gave birth to these kids and I have to raise them. But if I didn't, I would have put a rope around my neck and hung myself long ago" (Warner and Dudwick 1996, 15).

---

street children in Russia is 1 million. The children tend to be in poor health, incompletely vaccinated, and illiterate (or, at best, only occasionally attending school). Many earn money through hard physical work (such as loading at the market) and by begging, stealing, and engaging in prostitution.

Many street children have poorly educated parents or come from families with a history of criminal activity and serious personal problems. In some cases young families left their villages to engage in trade or business; others were unable to farm because they did not have enough able-bodied adults. Other street children were abandoned by young parents and taken in by elderly or disabled grandparents. Some of the street children have single mothers who lost work because of illness or when enterprises with a largely female work force closed. Other street children come from institutions that no longer have the resources to care for them and where viable community-based alternatives do not exist. In Central European countries, a disproportionate number of street children are Roma, many of whom are illiterate.

Figure 1.4 Children in Infant Homes

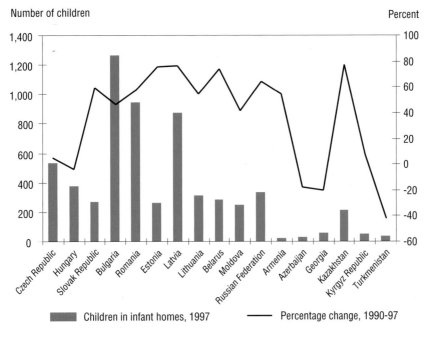

Note: Number of children in infant homes per 100,000 children ages 0 to 3.
Source: UNICEF (1999).

The Homeless

The most severely excluded persons in Europe and Central Asia are the
homeless, the beggars, and the scavengers. These groups are ranked at the
bottom of the economic ladder—worse even than those who live in poverty or even in extreme poverty. They are not considered members of normal society. In Bulgaria people referred to the most extreme form of poverty

---

Box 1.8 Street Children in Georgia

Interviews from Tbilisi, carried out by a volunteer from an NGO that works with them, reported that street children sleep in underground passes, elevators, and in abandoned kiosks.
A group of children, ages 6 to 14, sleep in the public toilet near Tbilisi's central market, near
the gathering spot of prostitutes and alcoholics. In winter these children sleep in the buildings that house communal boilers if apartment residents do not drive them away. According
to the interviewer, this group is the most difficult and troubled of the street children, and
many of them are well on their way to becoming fully criminalized (Dudwick 1999).

as *izpadnalite* ("those who have fallen out"). These people no longer have the respect of the community and often survive by rummaging in garbage cans (World Bank 1999b). In Russia and other parts of the former Soviet Union they are referred to as *bomzhi* (a Russian abbreviation signifying a person without a permanent place of residence) or *bichi* (Russian jargon for people who are homeless, or vagabond). Most people regard *bomzhi* with a mixture of pity and disgust. They are seen as drunkards, totally irresponsible, and blamed for their own condition. Most people avoid them because they consider them dirty, smelly and infested with fleas. They tend to be in ill health; a survey in Moscow revealed that 50 percent of those examined had TB. They survive by scavenging from garbage, begging, and stealing (World Bank 1999e; Vinoker and others 1999).

Little is known about the extent of homelessness across the region. Recent estimates from studies in Russia suggest that between 0.5 and 1 percent of the population in large Russian cities may be homeless, and the numbers are thought to be increasing. According to a survey carried out in 1995 of the homeless in St. Petersburg, 70 percent became homeless in the previous five years. Just over one-fifth became homeless in 1994, the year preceding the survey; 14 percent of those surveyed had been living on the street for more than 10 years. Almost 60 percent of the homeless lost their housing as result of previous criminal conviction and imprisonment, since imprisonment for more than six months deprives them of *propiska* and the right to occupy state-owned housing (Vinoker and others 1999, 19).

The Growing Divide between the Poor and the Rich

The poor see the rich as people who have gotten where they are, not by hard work and by taking advantage of new opportunities, but by exploiting their connections and through corrupt behavior. In Kyrgyz Republic, for example, informants explained that the very rich are "those that have made their fortune at the expense of the nation," selling metals, cotton, and other raw materials on conditions unfavorable for the country (World Bank 1999d, 39). The poor resent the conspicuous consumption of the rich, a change from the more discrete behavior of the rich in the past. The sense that the rich are those who have profited dishonestly from their official positions at the expense of the poor contributes strongly to social divisiveness, reduces credibility in the state, and leads to a sense of helplessness among the poor who have neither the connections nor the opportunities to enrich themselves. The very poor go hungry, while the rich "have been plundering everything and eating so much that they cannot carry their own stomachs" (Institute of Philosophy and Sociology 1998, 8).

Notes

1. This chapter draws heavily on World Bank (2000d), as well as the qualitative poverty assessments in Narayan (2000b) and the national synthesis papers for the "Voices of the Poor" consultation exercise summarized in Narayan and others (2000a).

2. These estimates are based on World Bank (2000d), which reports poverty estimates for the Europe and Central Asia Region, including Turkey. The estimates reported here do not include Turkey. The poverty line is set at $2.15 in 1993 purchasing power parity (PPP) terms. With the notable exception of Russia and a few other countries, the 1998 estimates are largely based on poverty rates projected from earlier surveys. Time series comparisons are problematic because of noncomparability of surveys before and after the transition (Milanovic 1998). An additional problem is the hyperinflation in many countries, especially in the former Soviet Union, which occurred during the first half of the 1990s. Hyperinflation introduces a potentially large margin of error in the calculation of the poverty lines in local currency for household surveys conducted in the post-hyperinflation period using the inflation-adjusted poverty lines based on the 1993 PPP rate.

Since the estimates reported in World Bank (2000d), new household survey data have become available as well as PPP rates based on 1996 price surveys. These estimates are reported in table 1.1. The 1996 PPP rates yield lower estimates of poverty than the 1993 rates, notably for Russia (box 1.2). Estimates of aggregate poverty for the region in 1998 based on 1996 rates are likely to be lower than estimates based on the 1993 rates. The trend, however, would remain unchanged.

3. The estimates based on the 1996 PPP rates are considered more reliable than the 1993 PPP rates because they take into account recent changes in the price structure following periods of hyperinflation in the early 1990s, trade liberalization, and real exchange rate realignment. The 1996 estimates are not comparable to estimates based on the 1993 rate.

4. The national poverty lines of Armenia, Georgia, and the Kyrgyz Republic fall between the $2.15 standard and $3.50 in 1996 PPP. The poverty line for Kazakhstan is roughly $4.70.

5. In principle, even if incomes are underreported, expenditures should be more reliable and take into account informal sources of income. So the size of the informal economy should not bias the survey results.

6. A study of household surveys in Latin America comes to this conclusion (Szekely and Hilgert 1999).

7. The CPI indices also have some deficiencies, including in a number of cases lack of good regional price deflators for many countries.

8. See World Bank (2000f) for a discussion of poverty lines.

9. Many Central European countries have not established official poverty lines, however.

10. Some important benefits, such as the earned income tax credit, and certain costs, such as the cost of child care, are excluded.

11. For a discussion of the spatial adjustment issues facing cities in the region, see World Bank (2000a).

References

Bilesim International, Kazakhstan. 1997. *Privatization in Agriculture in Akmola and Former Taldy-Korgan Oblasts.* Report prepared for World Bank, Environmentally and Socially Sustainable Development Sector Unit, Europe and Central Asia Region. Washington, D.C. Processed.

Commander, Simon, Andrei Tolstopiatenko, and Ruslan Yemtsov. 1999. "Channels of Redistribution: Inequality and Poverty in the Russian Transition." *Economics of Transition Journal* 7 (2): 411–47.

De Soto, Hermine G., and Nora Dudwick. 1999. "Poverty in Moldova: The Social Dimensions of Transition 1999." In *Moldova Poverty Assessment,* vol. 2: Technical Papers, Report 19846-MD. Washington, D.C.: World Bank. October.

Dudwick, Nora. 1995. "A Qualitative Assessment of the Living Standards of the Armenian Population, October 1994–March 1995." Working Paper 1. In *Armenia Poverty Assessment.* Washington, D.C.: World Bank.

———. 1997. *Land Reform in Moldova.* Report prepared for World Bank, Environmentally and Socially Sustainable Development Sector Unit, Europe and Central Asia Region. Washington, D.C. Processed.

———. 1999. "Georgia: A Qualitative Study of Impoverishment and Coping Strategies." In *Georgia Poverty and Income Distribution,* vol. 2: Technical Papers, Report 19348-G. Washington, D.C.: World Bank.

Falkingham, Jane. 2000. "From Security to Uncertainty: The Impact of Economic Change on Child Welfare in Central Asia." Innocenti Working Paper 76. Florence: UNICEF Innocenti Research Centre.

Foley, Mark. 1997. "Static and Dynamic Analyses of Poverty in Russia." In *Poverty in Russia: Public Policy and Private Responses,* ed. Jeni Klugman. Washington, D.C.: World Bank.

Gomart, Elizabeth. 1998. "Social Assessment of the Poorest of the Poor in Arme-nia, November-December 1997." World Bank, Environmentally and Socially Sustainable Development Sector Unit, Europe and Central Asia Region. Washington, D.C. Processed.

Holt, Sharon. 1995. "Using Land as a System of Social Protection: An Analysis of Rural Poverty in Armenia in the Aftermath of Land Privatization." Armenia Poverty Assessment Paper 3. Washington, D.C.: World Bank.

Institute of Philosophy and Sociology. 1998. *Listening to the Poor: A Social Assessment of Poverty in Latvia, 1998: Report on Research Findings (March–June 1998).* Prepared by the Institute of Philosophy and Sociology in Riga for World Bank, Environmentally and Socially Sustainable Development Sector Unit, Europe and Central Asia Region. Washington, D.C. Processed.

Kuehnast, Kathleen. 1993. "Women and Economic Changes in Kyrgyzstan: Coping Mechanisms and Attitudes Toward Social Policies: A Beneficiary Assessment." World Bank, Human Development Sector Unit, Europe and Central Asia Region, Washington, D.C. Processed.

Lampietti, Julian A., and others. 2000. *Utility Pricing and the Poor: Lessons from Armenia.* Washington, D.C.: World Bank.

Leon, David A., and others. 1997. "Huge Variation in Russian Mortality Rates, 1984–94: Artefact, Alcohol, or What?" *The Lancet* 350: 383-88.

Lewis, Maureen, 2000. "Who Is Paying for Health Care in Europe and Central Asia?" World Bank, Human Development Sector Unit, Europe and Central Asia Region, Washington, D.C.

Lokshin, Michael, and Martin Ravallion. 2000. "Welfare Impact of Russia's Financial Crisis and the Response of the Public Safety Net." Background Papers: Making Transition Work for Everyone: Poverty and Inequality in Europe and Central Asia. World Bank, Washington, D.C.

Lovei, Laslo. 2000. *Maintaining Utility Services for the Poor: Policies and Practices in Central and Eastern Europe and the Former Soviet Union.* World Bank Energy Sector Unit, Europe and Central Asia Region. Washington, D.C.

McKee, Martin. 1999. "Alcohol in Russia." *Alcohol and Alcoholism* 34(6): 824–29.

Milanovic, Branko. 1998. *Income, Inequality, and Poverty during the Transition to a Market Economy.* Washington, D.C.: World Bank.

Mroz, T., D. Mancini, and B. Popkin. 1999. "Monitoring Economic Conditions in the Russian Federation: The Russian Longitudinal Monitoring Survey 1992–98." Report submitted to the U.S. Agency for International Development. Carolina Population Center, University of North Carolina at Chapel Hill, North Carolina. March.

Narayan, Deepa, and others. 1999. *Global Synthesis: Consultations with the Poor.* Washington, D.C.: World Bank.

———. 2000a. *Crying out for Change: Voices of the Poor.* New York: Oxford University Press.

———. 2000b. *Voices of the Poor: Can Anyone Hear Us? New York:* Oxford University Press.

Olcott, Martha, and Natalia Udalova. 2000. "Drug Trafficking on the Great Silk Road: The Security Environment in Central Asia." World Papers 11, March. Carnegie Endowment for International Peace.

High Commissioner on National Minorities, Organization for Security and Co-operation in Europe (OSCE). 2000. *Report on the Situation of Roma and Sinti in the OSCE Area.* The Hague.

Ravallion, Martin, and Michael Lokshin. 1999. "Subjective Economic Welfare." Policy Research Working Paper 2106. Washington, D.C.: World Bank.

Ringold, Dena. 2000. "Roma and the Transition in Central and Eastern Europe: Trends and Challenges." World Bank, Human Development Sector Unit, Europe and Central Asia. Washington, D.C.

Schecter, Kate. 1999. "Social Development Strategy Note: Street Children in ECA." World Bank, Environmentally and Socially Sustainable Development Unit, Europe and Central Asia Region. Washington, D.C. Processed.

Shkolnikov, Vladimir, and others. 1999. "Causes of the Russian Mortality Crisis: Evidence and Interpretations." *World Development* 26 (11): 1995–2001.

Stukuls, Diana. 1999. "Body of the Nation: Mothering, Prostitution, and Women's Place in Postcommunist Latvia." *The Slavic Review* 58 (3).

Szekely, Miguel, and Marianne Hilgert. 1999. "What's Behind the Inequality We Measure? An Investigation Using Latin American Data for the 1990s." Washington, D.C.: Inter-American Development Bank. Processed.

UNDP (United Nations Development Programme). 1999. *Human Development Report for Central and Eastern Europe and the CIS, 1999.* New York.

UNHCR Regional Bureau for Europe. 1998. "Social Assessment of the Formerly Deported Population in the Autonomous Republic of Crimea: A Participatory Rapid Appraisal." European Series, vol. 4, no. 1.

UNICEF. 1999. *Women in Transition.* Regional Monitoring Report 6. Florence: UNICEF International Child Development Center.

United Nations. 1997. *National Human Development Report, Tajikistan.* New York.

Vinoker, Anatoly, Joana Godinho, Christopher Dye, and Nico Nagelkerke. 1999. "Russia: TB, HIV/AIDS and STIs: Portrait of a Crisis." World Bank, Human

Development Sector Unit, Europe and Central Asia Region. Washington, D.C. Processed.

Warner, Catherine, and Nora Dudwick. 1996. "An Ethnographic Study of Poverty in Ukraine." Prepared for Europe and Central Asia Region, World Bank.

Wedel, Janine R. 1999. "Trafficking in Women in Central and Eastern Europe and the Former Soviet Union: Highlights of the Problem." Prepared for the Environmentally and Socially Sustainable Development Sector Unit, Europe and Central Asia Region, World Bank. Processed.

Wheeler, Anthony. 1999. "Gypsies in Eastern Europe—Issues and Possible Actions." Washington, D.C.: World Bank, Human Development Unit, Europe and Central Asia Region.

World Bank. 1999a. *Bosnia: Consultations with the Poor* (a study to inform the *World Development Report 2000/1* prepared for the Global Synthesis Workshop, September 22-23, 1999). Poverty Group, Poverty Reduction and Economic Management Network. Washington, D.C.

———. 1999b. *Bulgaria: Consultations with the Poor* (a study to inform the *World Development Report 2000/1* prepared for the Global Synthesis Workshop, September 22-23, 1999). Poverty Group, Poverty Reduction and Economic Management Network. Washington, D.C.

———. 1999c. *Bulgaria: Poverty during the Transition.* Report 18411. Human Development Sector Unit. Europe and Central Asia Region. June 7.

———. 1999d. *Kyrgyz Republic: Consultations with the Poor* (a study to inform the *World Development Report 2000/1* prepared for the Global Synthesis Workshop, September 22-23, 1999). Poverty Group, Poverty Reduction and Economic Management Network. Washington, D.C.

———. 1999e. *Russia: Consultations with the Poor* (a study to inform the *World Development Report 2000/1* prepared for the Global Synthesis Workshop, September 22-23, 1999). Poverty Group, Poverty Reduction and Economic Management Network. Washington, D.C.

———. 1999f. *Russia: Targeting and the Longer-Term Poor.* Report 19377- RU. Washington, D.C. May.

———. 2000a. *From Commisssars to Mayors: Poverty and Cities in Transition Economies.* Washington, D.C.

———. 2000b. "Hungary: Long-Term Poverty, Social Protection, and the Labor Market." vol. 1, Main Report, Report 20645-HU. Washington, D.C. Draft.

———. 2000c. "Info Brief." Washington, D.C.: World Bank, Human Development Unit, Europe and Central Asia Region.

———. 2000d. *Poverty Reduction and the World Bank: Progress in Fiscal 1999.* Report R2000-41. Washington, D.C. March 30.

————. 2000e. *Toward a Social Development Strategy in ECA: Issues and Recommendations.* Environmentally and Socially Sustainable Development Sector Unit. Europe and Central Asia Region. Washington, D.C. June.

————. 2000f. *World Development Report 2000/1: Attacking Poverty.* New York: Oxford University Press.

CHAPTER 2

A Profile of Income Poverty

lthough the transition has led to widespread economic dislocation, its effect has not been uniform. This chapter begins with a
look at relative poverty risks, focusing on labor market, location,
and demographic factors. Certain subgroups of the population have a
higher incidence of poverty than others—particularly the unemployed,
the less well educated, the rural population, and children. But there are
important differences across the region as well, especially between the
countries of Central and South Eastern Europe and the Baltics (CSB) on
the one hand and the Commonwealth of Independent States (CIS) on the
other. Second, we look at the groups that predominate among the poor.
Although certain subgroups of the population may be at high risk of poverty, they make up a small share of the total population—and thus of the
poor. Many of the poor have a secondary school education, live in urban
areas, are of working age, and live in households with heads who are
employed—not the groups with the highest risk of poverty. Third, we
examine poverty outcomes over time. Although many people experience
fluctuations in their incomes and expenditures, the net effect over time is
one of far greater poverty persistence. There is relatively little mobility
out of poverty.

Factors Associated with an Increased Risk of Poverty

Comparing the pattern of poverty across countries immediately raises the
question of how to set the poverty line. The comparisons in this chapter
are based on the poverty profiles that result from setting the poverty line

in each county equal to 50 percent of median equivalent consumption.[1] Thus, the profiles give a picture of the characteristics of those who are at the bottom of the expenditure distribution in each country, that is, those who are poor relative to others in their own country. Using relative poverty lines allows us to explore the commonalities and the differences across countries in the characteristics of those who are at greatest risk of being left behind in the transition.[2]

To compare poverty risks across countries, however, we cannot use the poverty rates directly generated by the poverty profiles because the total poverty rates vary by country. A group whose incidence of poverty is 9 percent in Belarus has a very high risk of poverty relative to the 6 percent poverty rate of the Belarussian population as a whole. In contrast, a group in Ukraine having the same 9 percent poverty rate as our comparator in Belarus would have a much lower poverty risk than the Ukrainian population as a whole, which has a 22 percent incidence of poverty. To know whether a group is at high risk of poverty, we need to consider its poverty rate in relation to the national poverty rate. This ratio is sometimes called the relative poverty risk index (Foster and Toth 1999). An index value of one means a group faces the same risk as the population in total. The higher the value of the index, the greater the representation of that group among the poor population.

For groups at high risk of poverty (for households whose heads are unemployed, the rural population, and children), the relative poverty risk index is generally higher in CSB countries than in CIS countries. Thus, specific characteristics are more closely associated with poverty in CSB countries. In CIS countries more diverse factors combine to affect a household's poverty status so that distinctions based on one characteristic (for example, education) do not give rise to sharp differences in poverty risks. This is reflected in the fact that mean expenditures of groups at high risk of poverty relative to the population mean tend to be lower in CSB countries than in the CIS countries. Moreover, poverty is more shallow in CSB countries than in CIS countries: the shortfall between the average expenditures of the poor and the poverty line is about 20 percent in the CSB countries compared with 26 percent in the CIS countries—some 30 percent more. All other things being equal, poverty risks will tend to be higher for subgroups with the same mean expenditure (relative to the population) in countries where poverty is more shallow. Thus, the two factors—lower mean expenditures for subgroups at risk of poverty and more shallow poverty—combine to produce a more sharply differentiated poverty profile in the CSB countries than in the CIS countries.

The Labor Market and Poverty Risks

Across the region, the poor cite loss of stable income—that is, low pay, no pay, and unstable pay—as the overwhelming factor associated with poverty, with a decline in public transfers a close second. The poverty profiles show that poverty outcomes are indeed correlated with labor market outcomes—though differences in the relative poverty risk index between the CSB and the CIS countries are striking.

The unemployed are at higher risk of poverty, particularly in CSB countries. In most CSB countries, households whose head is unemployed or not in the labor market (grouped together under the term *nonworking heads*) are much more likely to be poor than the general population. (Retired heads are not included in the nonworking category.) In a number of CSB countries, the poverty risk for households with nonworking heads is more than double that of the population as a whole (figure 2.1). In the CIS countries, households with nonworking heads have a somewhat elevated relative risk of poverty compared with the population as a whole, but the indices are nevertheless close to one.[3]

The ratio of mean expenditures of households headed by nonworking heads to expenditures of households with employed heads is lower in CSB countries than in CIS countries. In CSB countries, mean expenditures in households with unemployed heads is only 68 percent of the mean of households with employed heads, compared with 85 percent in the CIS countries. Similarly, in CSB countries, mean expenditures of households with nonworking heads is 77 percent of the mean of households with employed heads, less than the 104 percent observed in the CIS countries. Households headed by the unemployed or the inactive are more likely to be poor in CSB countries than in CIS countries partly because their expenditures are lower relative to households headed by employed persons. Not being employed carries more of a penalty in the CSB countries—or, turning it around, being employed confers more of a benefit.

Households with fewer income earners have higher rates of poverty. In CSB countries, households with one income earner generally face an elevated relative risk of poverty, although households with two income earners have a relative poverty risk index of substantially less than one (figure 2.2). But in the CIS countries the differences in the relative poverty risk indices between one and two income earner households are not as striking as in the Central European countries. The risk of poverty in two income

Figure 2.1 Relative Poverty Risk of Households with Unemployed and Inactive Heads

Relative poverty risk index

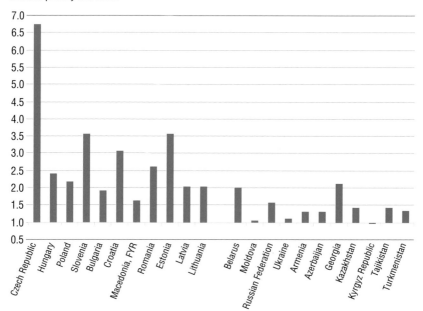

Note: For Armenia, Azerbaijan, and Slovenia, the poverty profile included information only on the unemployed. Inactive heads of households were not distinguished from pensioner heads of households, so the information presented in this figure pertains only to unemployed heads of households.
Source: Poverty profiles, appendix D.

earner households is reduced by 25 percent in the majority of CIS countries relative to the population as a whole, while in most CSB countries, the risk is reduced by over half. Single income earner households face only a slightly elevated risk of poverty compared with the population as a whole in the CIS countries. Having more income earners in CSB countries clearly helps keep households out of poverty, but it has less impact in the CIS countries.

Poorly educated households are at higher risk of poverty. Although pay scales in Soviet times were compressed and did not necessarily reward higher education, this is changing. Education and experience are rewarded much the same as in OECD countries, though there is some evidence that earnings peak at an earlier age in transition countries. Thus low levels of education would, all else being equal, result in less pay and thus correlate

Figure 2.2   Relative Poverty Risk by Number of Income Earners

Relative poverty risk index

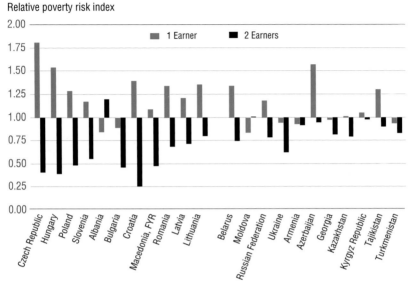

Source: Poverty profiles, appendix D.

with higher levels of poverty. This is indeed what the poverty profiles show: individuals with a secondary education have a lower relative risk of poverty (figure 2.3) than those with a primary education.

Again, there is a striking difference between the relative advantages conferred by primary and secondary education in the Eastern Europe and the CIS countries. Although individuals in the CIS countries with a secondary education generally have a lower relative poverty risk than individuals with a primary school education, the difference is far less pronounced in the CIS countries than in Central and South Eastern Europe. Education also carries a greater premium in CSB countries: mean expenditures of households headed by someone with a secondary school education are 28 percent higher than those of households whose head completed primary education, although in the CIS countries they are about 7 percent higher on average. In part, this may reflect the fact that the share of adults with a secondary or higher education is lower in the CSB countries than in the CIS countries. This would tend to result in a higher premium in CSB countries, all other things being equal. In Poland, the Czech Republic, and Romania, less than 10 percent of the adult population has a postsecondary education—better than 5 percent in Albania and

Figure 2.3 Relative Poverty Risk by Education Level

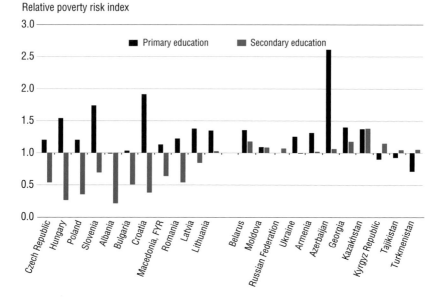

Note: For the Russian Federation, secondary education includes both primary and secondary.
Source: Poverty profiles, appendix D.

8 percent in FYR Macedonia, but still less than 13 percent in Kazakhstan, 14 percent in Latvia, 15 percent in Russia, or 19 percent in Armenia.

The smaller differential between the premium to secondary education and the premium to primary education in the CIS countries is consistent with the many reports that well-educated individuals cannot find employment at levels corresponding to their educational backgrounds. It is also consistent with results from the earnings functions for CIS countries. Although education is significantly and positively related to earnings, it (and other observable characteristics) explain only a very small part of the variation in earnings (chapter 4). Other factors—such as personal connections—are said by respondents to be the most important determinant of who gets a job and what kind of job.

Is poverty a result of having more dependents, lower labor market participation, or lower earnings of those who participate in the labor market? The answer is all of the above but to different degrees. The higher dependency ratio of poor households accounts for a small part of the difference in mean consumption levels between the top and bottom quintiles, the lower ratio of income earning adults to total adults accounts for slightly more, and the lower level of earnings per worker accounts for the largest part of the difference. In Poland, for example, the higher dependency ratios of the bottom quintile accounted for 12 percent of the difference in mean consumption between the top and bottom quintiles, the lower ratio of adults in the labor force accounted for 24 percent, and the lower level of resources contributed by each income earner accounted for the remaining 64 percent of the difference (figure 2.4). In contrast, in Russia, the lower level of resources contributed by each income earner accounted for 94 percent of the difference in consumption between the top and bottom quintiles.

Employment does not guarantee pay in CIS countries. An analysis of the Georgia household survey data (Yemtsov 1999) sheds some additional light on how labor participation and earning differences per worker are correlated with poverty outcomes. As noted above, the poor in Georgia have lower labor force participation rates than the nonpoor and higher rates of unemployment. Even when the poor work, they work in less well-paid and less secure positions than the nonpoor. Lower earnings are correlated with observable characteristics, such as education, age, or experience. The poor are also over-represented in the sectors that pay the lowest wages. Other factors, however, add to the earnings differentials between the poor and the nonpoor. The poor tend to work shorter hours— 36 hours per week on average compared with 40 hours per week for the nonpoor. Often this lower pay is the result of being forced to take involuntary leave or reduced hours. In addition, the earnings of the poor are more subject to delayed payments: the survey revealed than on average 22 percent of poor wage earners were owed back wages by their employers, compared with 8 percent of the nonpoor. The Tajikistan household survey showed a similar pattern. More than 35 percent of the employed suffered from wage arrears, but poorer households were hardest hit: arrears affected close to 41 percent of the households in the bottom two expenditure quintiles, compared with 31 percent in the top two quintiles. In Armenia, the situation was even more stark: in 1996, a quarter of all formally employed workers—80 percent of whom were not being paid— were on forced leave.

Wage arrears are endemic in many CIS countries: at end 1999, wage arrears in the public sector alone were equivalent to approximately 1 percent of GDP in Georgia, 1.6 percent in Moldova, and 2.7 percent in Armenia. More broadly, wage arrears in Russia in four sectors of the economy (industry, agriculture, transport, and construction) amounted to 2.9 percent of GDP in 1998 (Pinto, Drebentsov, and Morosov 2000).

Box 2.1   Differences in Consumption across Quintiles

Consumption per equivalent adult can be decomposed into five factors: measures of dependency ("mouths"), labor market participation ("labor participation"), labor earnings per income earner ("earnings"), share of other income in total income ("other income"), and ratio of consumption to income ("savings"), as the following equation shows:

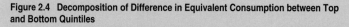

$$\frac{Consumption}{Eq.\ household\ size} = \frac{\#\ adults}{eq.\ household\ size} * \frac{income\ earners}{\#\ adults} * \frac{labor\ income}{\#\ income\ earners} * \frac{total\ income}{labor\ income} * \frac{consumption}{total\ income}$$

This equation can be transformed into logs to determine the share each factor contributes to consumption. The difference in mean equivalent consumption between the top and bottom quintiles is equal to the sum of the difference of the means of each factor between the top and bottom quintiles. We can then compute the share that the difference in each the five factors contributes to the overall difference in mean consumption between the top and bottom quintiles. A negative value for one of the factors means that the mean value of that factor was higher in the bottom quintile than in the top. Figure 2.4 shows how much of the difference is explained by each factor for seven countries across the region.

Figure 2.4   Decomposition of Difference in Equivalent Consumption between Top and Bottom Quintiles

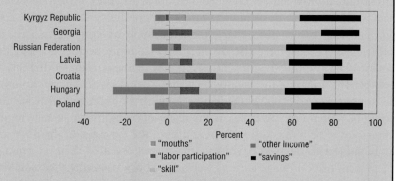

The factor "mouths," which captures the ratio of adults to total household size, is positive, indicating that households in the top quintile have a lower dependency ratio than households in the bottom quintile. Similarly, the top quintile has more income earners per adult (except Kyrgyz Republic), higher labor earnings per adult, and a much higher level of "savings" than the bottom quintile. Offsetting its smaller share of labor earnings per adult, the bottom quintile has a higher share of nonlabor income to total income in all countries.

Although labor participation is a relatively more important factor in Poland and Croatia than in the CIS countries, on average it accounts for roughly 20 percent of the difference in equivalent consumption. The higher share explained by the labor participation factor in the CSB countries may reflect the more sharply delineated nature of labor markets and the costs associated with unemployment in the CSB countries. "Savings"—which is more a measure of unreported income than true savings out of income—accounts for a low of 18 percent in Croatia to a high of 42 percent in Russia of the difference in mean log consumption between the top and bottom quintiles. The importance of the "savings" factor in Russia may be indicative of the highly informalized and nontransparent nature of markets in Russia. Lower dependency ratios account for only around 10 percent of the difference in mean consumption between the top and bottom quintiles across countries.

The analysis of Georgia provides some clues as to why the relative poverty risk index of households with unemployed heads is higher in CSB than in CIS countries, and the ratio of mean expenditures of unemployed-headed households to employed-headed households is lower. In contrast to the CSB countries, in many CIS countries workers have suffered a large collapse in real wages, many employees are on administrative leave and receive little or no pay, and their pay is subject to considerable arrears (box 2.2). Thus, in the CIS countries being unemployed likely does not entail a significant loss of income relative to what is earned by the nominally employed population. For example, the salaries of teachers—the most numerous group of public sector employees—are so low in some CIS countries that subsistence farming appears to be just as remunerative. A village official in Goris, Armenia, noted in 1995, "If a person keep one chicken [that] lays an egg every day, then he will have 800 drams a month—the salary of a teacher. If he has two chickens and gets two eggs a day, this gives him the salary of a professor" (Narayan 2000, 222).

To survive, many households in the CIS are forced to make do with various forms of informal activity, including cultivating household plots. In contrast, in CSB countries, real wages have not declined as significantly, there is far less unpaid administrative leave, and arrears are not as pronounced. Thus, in CSB countries, unemployment may constitute a real loss of income that is not entirely compensated for by social assistance payments, whereas in the CIS countries, many households, employed or not, must supplement their meager wages through other activities to make ends meet.

Despite late wages—or payment in kind in goods priced above actual market value—many people across the region have been slow to leave their jobs (box 2.3). This is especially true in the CIS. Workers frequently remain at their jobs in the hope that they will eventually receive their back wages. They fear that if they leave, they will never receive them. Others still believe that their enterprise may revive and become viable again. Workers over 45, who know their chances of finding new employment are very low and who understand the enormous transaction costs of relocating, have every reason to cling to enterprise jobs as long as possible (Zisk 1997). Workers of pre-pension age often prefer to keep poorly paid jobs in the state sector to achieve their 25-year seniority, which during the Soviet period guaranteed an additional 10 percent would be added to old-age pensions.

Even when employees receive salaries months late, they have access to job-linked benefits and services, which enterprises and managers often

---

Box 2.2   Work and Pay in Moldova

In its heyday the munitions plant in Balti, Moldova, employed 8,000 workers. Employment there was considered "prestigious" and attracted many workers. In 1997 the plant employed only 2,000 workers. They produce consumer items such as umbrellas, electric irons, toasters, and chandeliers, many of which remain in warehouses for lack of customers. Salaries have decreased from the once comfortable amount of 200 to 300 rubles a month to 100 to 150 lei, paid after a delay of two to three months. In many cases, employees are forced to receive goods in kind and must sell their supply of electric irons or toasters to local shops, or the market.

Source: De Soto and Dudwick (1999, 42).

---

continue to supply. These include housing, as well as health benefits, still considered to be of better quality than public health care (Zisk 1997). Despite late salaries, people also continue to work to preserve routine, to fulfill a sense of duty, and, through their work collectives, to maintain access to information, humanitarian assistance, bribes, public resources, and professional contacts. In their analysis of subjective measures of well-being, Ravallion and Lokshin (1999) find that the unemployed in Russia assess their economic well-being less favorably than employed workers, even after controlling for household income. The benefits of employment clearly transcend monetary remuneration.

Location and Poverty

Capital cities are better off—in many cases considerably better off. In every country where the capital city could be separated from other data, relative poverty rates were lower in the capital than in urban, rural, or other geographical areas (figure 2.5). Indeed, the director of a social assistance center in Latvia complained: "Don't let anyone tell me that prosperity in Latvia is developing; maybe a deputy or someone who makes large investments says that. We feel that there are two states in Latvia— Riga and the rest of the country" (Institute of Philosophy and Sociology 1998, 68). In Budapest, Warsaw, Moscow and St. Petersburg, and Dushanbe, the poverty rates are strikingly lower. A resident of Warsaw is six times less likely to be poor than the population at large. This represents a continuation from the past; the question is whether the disparities will grow between the capital and hinterland over time. This depends on many factors, including the scope for improving rural livelihoods.

Box 2.3   Job-linked Benefits in Moldova

In Moldova, although state-funded construction has stopped, people remain on job-linked waiting lists for housing. Many of them continue to live in crowded hostels for workers or hold onto jobs where they are not receiving salaries, sustained only by the hope that they will eventually receive an apartment. One worker at Moldova's Bucuria Candy Factory reported that when the factory fails to receive orders, she goes without a salary for several months. She is reluctant to look for another job, because the enterprise has promised her an apartment. "Now I live in a two-room apartment with my three children, my mother, and my husband, who is paralyzed. Where can I go?" Others take on a particular job simply in order to obtain a room in a hostel. Tatiana, a dressmaker, took on a job as a lab assistant so she and her husband could move into a 12-square-meter room in the Medical Institute's hostel, where they share the toilet, shower, and kitchen with five other families.

Source: De Soto and Dudwick (1999, 42).

Rural poverty rates are generally high. Given the strong bias in favor of capital cities, it is not surprising to find that in most countries the relative poverty risk index of rural areas is greater than one—implying that the incidence of poverty among rural households is greater than among urban ones (figure 2.6).[4] The difference is particularly pronounced in Central Europe and the Baltics, where (with the exception of the Czech Republic, Bulgaria, and Croatia) rural households are at least 50 percent more likely

Figure 2.5   Relative Poverty Risk by Capital City

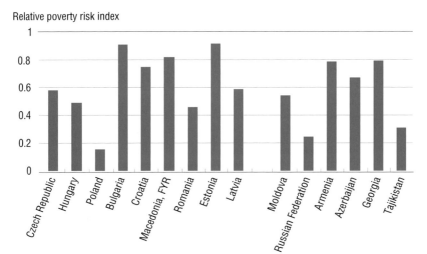

Relative poverty risk index

Note: For the Russian Federation, the data are for Moscow and St. Petersburg.
Source: Poverty profiles, appendix D.

Figure 2.6   Relative Poverty Risk by Rural Population

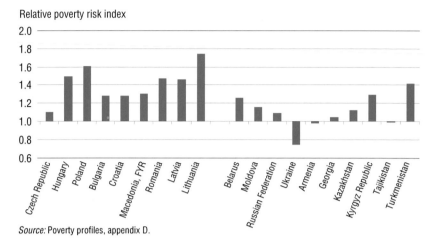

Relative poverty risk index

Source: Poverty profiles, appendix D.

to be poor than the population as a whole. In contrast, the relative poverty risk indices of rural residents are much closer to one in most of the CIS countries. In five of the ten CIS countries, mean expenditures of the rural population are close to one, and only in the Kyrgyz Republic and Turkmenistan are they substantially less than one.

The fact that relative poverty risks of rural areas are for the most part only slightly elevated (or, indeed, less than one) in most CIS countries reflects the dire situation of urbanized areas dependent on a collapsing industrial base more than it reflects prospering rural society. Urbanized areas may be doing better in CSB countries, where economic recovery is more advanced. The absence of high relative poverty risks for rural areas in most CIS countries also reflects the importance of household plots: often they enable a large share of the rural population to provide for some of their food needs. Kitchen gardens play a vital role in households' survival strategies in both urban and rural areas. In Georgia the share of home-produced food consumed in-kind constitutes 15 percent of total expenditures of the poorest decile; in Kazakhstan it constitutes 19 percent of total expenditures of the bottom quintile. What is somewhat surprising is that, in at least a few countries, it constitutes a larger share of total expenditures of richer households compared with poorer households: home-produced food accounts for 21 percent of total expenditures of the top decile in Georgia, and in Kazakhstan 27 percent of total expenditures of the top quintile.

Despite their capacity to produce some of their own food—which may keep many rural poor out of extreme poverty—conditions in rural areas remain difficult. Many rural households survive on subsistence. Households interested in farming lack the means to expand into more profitable farm activities. They tend to be cash-poor and therefore rely on barter. Cash-poor, with few opportunities to obtain credit, these households are unable to branch into more profitable crops because they cannot afford equipment, fertilizers, pesticides, seeds, or irrigation, and they often lack able-bodied adults. Wage labor for others, an option in some rural areas, is not the preferred option for populations with virtually no tradition of a rural labor market—especially when rural wages are very low (box 2.4).

In many places the disparities in employment opportunities and living standards have spurred the most skilled and entrepreneurial residents to migrate to urban areas for work. In FYR Macedonia and Albania, for example, they have virtually abandoned villages to the elderly. Elsewhere, young people who remain in the villages work only part-time in agriculture and remain idle for long winter months. Rural families in Latvia, the Kyrgyz Republic, Poland, and Moldova note a dramatic increase in alcoholism, even among youth, and growing youth involvement in both petty and violent crime. The obstacles facing rural youth have proved a boon to the expanding narcotics traffickers in Central Asia, who recruit heavily in impoverished mountainous villages.

Although conditions may be difficult in many rural areas, evidence from farm surveys in Russia, Moldova, and Ukraine suggests that land reform is having a positive impact on those who have decided to become private farmers. In the CIS countries, private farmers in most cases are former

---

Box 2.4   Views of Rural Wage Labor

Influenced by the ideological lessons that accompanied collectivization, rural workers have criticized the emergence of privatized agriculture as "slavery" (Georgia, the Kyrgyz Republic, Armenia) and "medieval work conditions" (Georgia). A wealthy Armenian farmer described how he had hired a married couple the previous year: "They looked after my cattle and their own. I worked their land, gave them the whole harvest, and paid them a salary. They never complained. But village people began to tease them; they called them wage laborers [a derogatory term] who worked for a 'lord.' When the couple worked for me, they had four cows. Now they only have two left, and they have not yet managed to plant their land. But they will not return to me, even though I still need workers." Expressing the predominant village perspective of this farmer, a young schoolteacher commented, "He may have become a big farmer, but we are not his serfs!"

Source: Dudwick (1996).

farm-enterprise employees who have decided to leave the collective for the new opportunity of becoming private farmers. The remaining farm-enterprise employees have basically the same training and experience as private farmers, but they have a different set of attitudes and priorities: they prefer the relative safety of the traditional collective framework to the risks and uncertainties associated with independent farming. Both groups give a fairly low evaluation of the general standard of living in their countries. Yet their responses show that farmers, on the whole, are better off and more optimistic than are employees of collective enterprises.

Farm surveys in Moldova, Russia, and Ukraine indicate that a much higher percentage of farm-enterprise employees than private farmers report that their earnings are only sufficient to sustain them at subsistence levels, if that. Correspondingly, a much higher percentage of farmers than employees report that they can afford more than just the bare subsistence needs, including the purchase of durables (figure 2.7a). Private farmers also evaluate the changes during the past few years more positively than do farm-enterprise employees: a significantly higher percentage of private farmers judge the situation to have improved, while most farm-enterprise employees at best regard the situation as unchanged (figure 2.7b). Finally, private farmers face the future with much greater optimism than do employees remaining in collective farm enterprises (figure 2.7c).

Employees of collective enterprises (now termed "shareholders") receive only meagre salaries paid partly in kind (now termed "dividends") often at below market value. They survive largely on what they produce in their household plots. Having remained as members of collective farms— and in some cases having ceded title to their land to the manager of the collective farm without full appreciation of what they were doing—farm employees have little recourse when they are not paid. Moldova collective farm workers complained that "farm managers use pretexts such as drought, bankruptcy, unforeseen expenditures, and farm indebtedness to cheat them of their actual earnings" (De Soto and Dudwick 1999, 27).

Land restitution was the primary process by which large-scale collective and state farm land was distributed in Central and South Eastern Europe. In 1991 in Romania land was restituted to former owners, while landless rural households that used to work for cooperatives or other landless rural inhabitants were granted ownership rights to up to one-half of a hectare (Chirca and Tesliuc 1999). As a result, most of the land was restituted to the elderly, who accounted for 41 percent of the rural population and owned 65 percent of the land. Young and middle-age farmers who depend on the land for a living lost out in the distribution of land. The

Figure 2.7a   Respondents in Moldova, the Russian Federation, and Ukraine Report What the Family Budget Buys

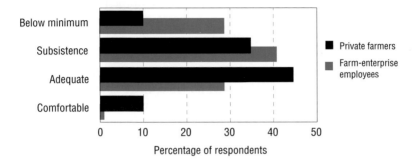

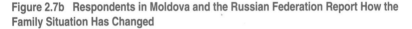

Percentage of respondents

Figure 2.7b   Respondents in Moldova and the Russian Federation Report How the Family Situation Has Changed

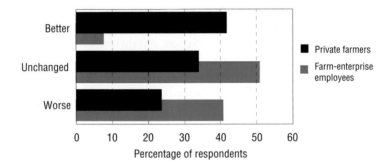

Percentage of respondents

Figure 2.7c   Respondents in Moldova, the Russian Federation, and Ukraine Report the Perception of Their Family's Prospects

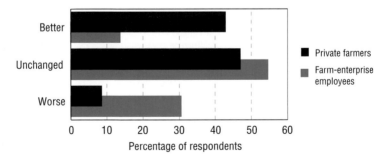

Percentage of respondents

Source: For the Russian Federation, Brooks and others (1996); for Ukraine, Csaki and Lerman (1997); for Moldova, Lerman, Csaki, and Moroz (1998).

pensioner households face a very low risk of poverty compared with young farmer households with little land or capital and have few alternatives to farming. A functioning land market, which is in the process of developing, will improve land-to-labor ratios, increase agricultural incomes, and help reduce poverty.

Regional differences are also pronounced. In most countries where a broad regional disaggregation was possible, there is at least one region with sharply higher poverty rates, reflecting country-specific regional factors. Table 2.1 shows the various areas that were identified in the poverty profiles as being at particularly high risk of poverty. For example, in North Hungary, an industrial region facing stagnant demand, the poverty rate was almost double that of the country. The Central Black Earth region in Russia has been especially hard-hit by a sharp contraction in light industry, as has East Ukraine. Particularly striking is the very high relative poverty index for parts of rural Kazakhstan, the Kyrgyz Republic, and Tajikistan. Belarus, Georgia, Moldova, and the Czech Republic had poverty rates with little regional variation, but this may reflect the broad level of disaggregation of the data.

Moreover, the broad level of regional disaggregation masks the fact that there are some very localized areas—particularly one-company

Table 2.1 Regions in Europe and Central Asia with a High Relative Poverty Risk Index

Country	Region	Relative poverty risk index
Hungary	Northern	1.92
	North Great Plain	1.54
Poland	East	1.42
Latvia	Latgale	1.45
	Kurzene	1.45
Albania	Kukes	3.63
Albania	Diber	2.59
Croatia	Central	1.51
Macedonia, FYR	Northeast	1.55
Romania	Northeast	1.50
Russian Federation	Central Black Earth	1.80
Ukraine	East	2.08
Kazakhstan	South	2.42
Kyrgyz Republic	Narunskaya	2.91
	Djala-Abadckaya	1.60
Tajikistan	Gorno-Badakhshan	2.09

Source: Poverty profiles, appendix D.

towns—that are at high risk of poverty. With very slack labor markets and constraints on labor mobility, workers in these towns often have limited alternatives (box 2.5).

The large disparities in regional poverty rates—echoed by disparities in regional unemployment rates and earnings—suggest that labor immobility may be an issue. Unemployed workers are often unwilling to move to regions that have better job prospects because of problems finding affordable housing, the cost of relocating, the risk of rupturing social support networks, and uncertainty about their own job prospects. In other cases they worry about abandoning elderly parents for whom they are responsible. Restrictions on relocation (such as the "propiska," or residence permit, still required by some large cities) continue to limit relocation opportunities or impose high costs.

Age and Household Type

During the transition the plight of various demographic groups has raised concern. Many fear for the elderly because of the erosion in the real value of pensions and inflation's severe toll on their savings. Children are also viewed as especially vulnerable to poverty in the transition (UNICEF 1999a,b; Falkingham 2000). Single mothers and elderly widows living alone are thought to be at high risk of poverty as well.

The Elderly. In fact, evidence on whether the elderly have a substantially increased risk of poverty is mixed. In most of the CSB countries, the

---

Box 2.5 The Plight of One-Company Towns

Entire communities sometimes grow up around a single industry, creating "company towns" or enterprises that function like mini-cities. In these communities enterprise closure or downsizing has contributed to high rates of poverty. This is the case in mining regions throughout Europe and Central Asia. One example is Tkibuli, Georgia, a coal mining town. In 1996, 80 percent of the population had been without work between one and five years, a third of the remaining 5,800 employees of the local coal mines were on indefinite leave without pay, and those still working had to wait six months to receive salaries and pensions.

Another example is Tekali, a mining town of around 27,000 people in Taldykorgan, Kazakhstan. It is one of the 57 towns in Kazakhstan that depended on one enterprise (or a few) during Soviet times and since the transition has shut down. In 1996 official unemployment in Tekali was 20 percent, with another 40 percent of the labor force subject to short hours or administrative leave.

Source: On Tkibuli, Dudwick (1999); on Tekali, World Bank (1998).

elderly (those 65 or older) are at lower risk than the population as a whole (figure 2.8). Bulgaria, Croatia, and Slovenia are clear exceptions. Another indication that the elderly in the CSB are generally better off than the population as a whole is the low relative rate of poverty of households with retired heads; again, Bulgaria and Croatia are exceptions (figure 2.9). Pensioner households have elevated relative risks of poverty in Estonia and Lithuania. In contrast, the elderly appear to have an elevated risk of poverty in a number of CIS countries—especially in Ukraine.[5] The relative poverty risk of households with retired heads tends to be somewhat elevated in the CIS countries, particularly Georgia. By and large, the CSB countries seem to have done a better job than the CIS countries in protecting their elderly during the transition process.

Pensioners in the CIS countries have long been accustomed to regular incomes. Even during the Soviet period, when they could count on receiving their pension, many had a very modest conception of what constituted a dignified old age. Today, considering it shameful to owe debts to the municipality, most elderly minimize their consumption of electricity, use of hot and cold water, and telephone. For example, pensioners in Moldova who could buy a loaf of bread and half a liter of milk a day before in-

Figure 2.8 Relative Poverty Risk of Children and Elderly

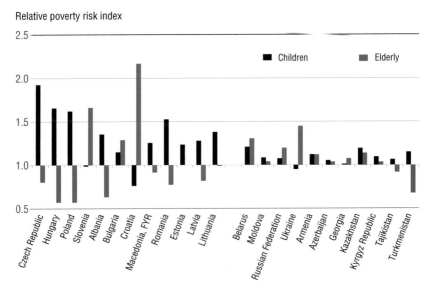

Source: Poverty profiles, appendix D.

Figure 2.9   Relative Poverty Risk of Households with Retired Heads

Relative poverty risk index

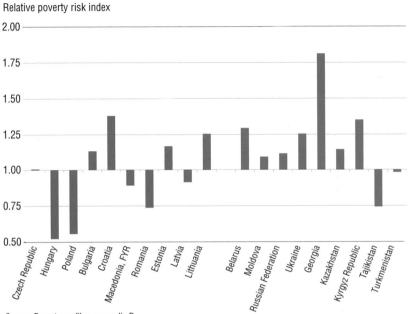

Source: Poverty profiles, appendix D.

dependence, can no longer afford basic staples, such as milk, on a daily basis (De Soto and Dudwick 1999). Pensioners also cut back on medical treatment, either substituting folk remedies or going without. Few are able to pay for the more complicated procedures that would make old age more bearable. In the past many people were able to save several thousand rubles of "funeral money." But the savings of numerous pensioners evaporated during hyperinflation. Now anxiety about who will pay for their funeral often matches day-to-day discomforts (Institute for Sociological and Political-Legal Research 1998; Wanner and Dudwick 1996).

To some extent, the condition of the elderly may be disguised by the average levels of consumption of the household, since the elderly often sacrifice their own well-being for their children or especially their grandchildren. Whether or not they bear sole responsibility for grandchildren, pensioners throughout ECA countries reported economizing to save money so they could help pay for their grandchildren's educational expenses. When the elderly live with children and grandchildren, they are even less likely to spend money on their own health care (Dudwick 1996, 1999). In Latvia the pension of an elderly parent often provided a major portion of a household's cash income, particularly when the adult child is an unemployed alcoholic (Institute of Sociology and Philosophy 1998).

Households that are headed by a single elderly female are perceived as being at high risk, because they are usually dependent on pensions and transfers from children and other relatives. They account for a very small share of the population—less than 4 percent in CSB countries and less than 2 percent in the CIS countries. In about half of the countries, they have a high relative risk of poverty, but again the small size of the population implies that the results may not be very robust. Only in two countries do they constitute more than 5 percent of the population—the Czech Republic and Latvia—and in both cases they have a relative risk less than one, as do the elderly in general in those countries.

The condition of the poorest elderly is dire indeed (box 2.6). Although Armenian respondents insisted that they would "never let anyone starve," elderly people with adult children or close relatives in other towns often received little help from neighbors, who felt that the pensioners were the moral responsibility of their own children (Dudwick 1997). Disabled or very poor elderly whose children are unable or unwilling to help them, either because they live far away or are also very poor, can find themselves in a particularly tragic situation.

Many elderly feel that they could survive if they received their pensions on time, but unfortunately even pensions have become vulnerable to economic uncertainties, political maneuvering, and petty corruption. In Moldova pensioners received their pensions up to nine months late (De Soto and Dudwick 1999). In Javakheti, Georgia, pensioners claimed they had to pay twice the amount of their monthly pension to start receiving pensions (Dudwick 1997). Sometimes local officials confiscated documents

---

Box 2.6 The Plight of the Elderly Poor

Jelena (72) is a childless single pensioner without close relatives. She lives alone in Riga with her dog. After paying 48 lats for communal services and rent, only 10 to 12 lats remain for the entire month. She believes that application to the municipality for social assistance was rejected because she is not a Latvian citizen, only a permanent resident. Her daily intake consists mainly of broth made from bones, cabbage and potatoes, but she often goes hungry. She tries to supplement her pension by collecting bottles from garbage containers. She can look for bottles only very early in the mornings, however, because later in the day, alcoholics and homeless people start collecting them. According to Jelena, they consider the garbage containers their personal property. Once one of them attacked her with a stick because she was about to take a bottle from his "personal" garbage container.

Source: Institute of Philosophy and Sociology (1998, 46).

for nonpayment of taxes, thereby preventing people from demonstrating eligibility for assistance. In Armenia a village chairman simply refused to distribute pensions until the pensioners had paid their land tax of $10 to $20; other local officials deducted the land tax from pensions (Dudwick 1996). Having looked forward to a secure old age, pensioners are embittered at finding themselves "standing at a broken trough" (Institute for Sociology and Philosophy 1998, 56).

Children. In contrast to the elderly, children have an elevated risk of poverty, particularly in CSB countries. Children have a strikingly high relative risk of poverty in many Central and Southern European countries (figure 2.8). In Hungary, Poland, and the Czech Republic, the risk was not elevated at the start of the transition. Yet, despite more progressive targeting of family assistance measures, it has been growing ever since (Foster and Toth 1999). In the CIS countries children also face an elevated relative risk of poverty, although it is not nearly as high in CSB countries. In about half of the CIS countries, children's relative risk of poverty is much higher than that of the elderly.

These findings, however, are sensitive to assumptions about economies of scale. If no economies of scale are assumed, children—who tend to live in large families—are at higher risk of poverty than the elderly—who tend to live in small families. But if substantial economies of scale are assumed (for example, an economies-of-scale parameter of 0.5), the elderly tend to be at higher relative risk of poverty.[6] In the absence of an unassailable methodology for determining the appropriate economies-of-scale parameter, there is no definitive answer to whether the children or the elderly are at greater risk. In a few countries, however, the results (at the relative poverty line of 50 percent of median equivalent expenditures) are robust to a range of values of the economies-of-scale parameter: children are consistently poorer than the elderly in the Czech Republic, Hungary, Poland, Albania, Croatia, and Slovenia.[7]

Single parent households, which are typically headed by women, have an elevated relative risk of poverty in many parts of the world.[8] Such households represent less than 3 percent of the population in Central European countries and slightly more than 4 percent of the population in the CIS countries. In a little more than half of the countries, single parent households have a relative poverty risk greater than one, but because they are such a small percentage of the population, these results are probably not very robust. Only in FYR Macedonia and Russia do they constitute more than 5 percent of the population. In Russia they have a poverty risk 50 percent higher than that of the general population.

In virtually all countries, the relative risk of poverty increases with the number of children in the family (figure 2.10). Why? On the one hand, it might be that households with more children have characteristics—such as low levels of education or low levels of labor market participation, particularly among women—that lead to lower earnings. Or it may be that they have relatively similar earnings as households with fewer children, but since they have more mouths to feed, consumption per equivalent adult is lower. To answer this question, we decomposed equivalent consumption into the five factors explained in box 2.1 and compared the differences between one-child and two-child households. The major reason that two-child households consume less per equivalent adult than one-child households is that two-child households have more mouths to feed (figure 2.11). However, the two-child households offset part of this disadvantage by participating more in the labor market. There is no clear pattern in the other factors across countries between one-child and two-child households.

A somewhat different pattern emerges when comparing households with three or more children and those with two children (figure 2.12). Mean consumption per equivalent adult is lower in households with three or more children than in households with two children, in part again because of the greater number of mouths to feed. But in this case households with three or more children have a lower ratio of income earners

Figure 2.10 Relative Poverty Risk by Number of Children

Relative poverty risk index

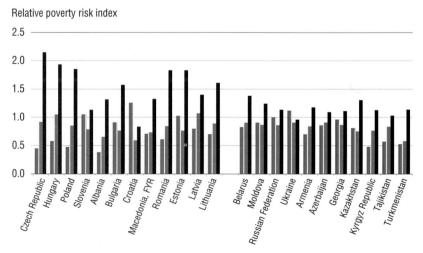

Source: Poverty profiles, appendix D.

Figure 2.11 Decomposition of the Difference in Equivalent Consumption between Households with Two Children and Households with One Child

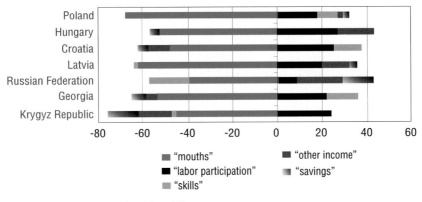

Note: See box 2.1 for an explanation of the variables.
Source: Household survey data, appendix B.

Figure 2.12 Decomposition of the Difference in Equivalent Consumption between Households with Three or More Children and Households with Two Children

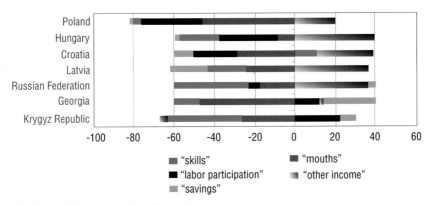

Note: See box 2.1 for an explanation of the variables.
Source: Household survey data, appendix B.

per adult ("labor participation") compared with households with two children, which contributes strongly to lowering their level of consumption in
all of the countries in the figure except Georgia and the Kyrgyz Republic.
Although labor earnings per income earner ("skills") is also lower in households with three or more children compared with those with two children
(except in Croatia), in four countries two-child households were able to
offset this loss through a higher ratio of nonlabor to other income. The key
to the sharp increase in poverty rates in multichildren households may lie
in the determinants of labor force participation. Across countries, the extent to which the poor are "bunched" around the poverty line plays a large
role in determining whether multichild households face a high relative risk
of poverty (box 2.7).

**Box 2.7   The Poverty Risk of Multichildren Households in Central Europe and in the
Commonwealth of Independent States**

Although having more children is associated with higher levels of poverty, the jump in the
relative risk of poverty with the number of children is much more pronounced in the Central
European countries than in the CIS countries. Take the comparison of Russia and Hungary. In
both countries the difference in log mean consumption per equivalent person of households
with one child and of households with three or more children is -0.29. So the percentage difference in the consumption levels of multichildren households in Hungary compared with one-
child households is the same as in Russia. But the relative risk of poverty of households with
three or more children compared with those with one child increases by only 56 percent in
Russia, compared with 186 percent in Hungary. Expenditures are much more closely bunched
around the poverty line in Hungary, so that the same percentage difference in mean expenditures translates into a higher relative poverty risk.

Figure 2.13   Differences in Mean Consumption and Poverty Risks of Households with One
Child and Three or More Children

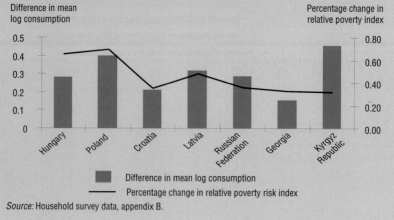

Difference in mean
log consumption

Percentage change in
relative poverty index

■ Difference in mean log consumption
── Percentage change in relative poverty risk index

Source: Household survey data, appendix B.

More children may mean less female labor force participation and higher rates of poverty. Analysis of the Georgia Labor Force Survey finds that if other personal and household characteristics are held constant, the number of children below the age of 7 and the number of elderly in a household are significant factors affecting the probability of urban females contributing to the labor force (Yemtsov 1999). This finding suggests that one of the causes of females dropping out of the labor force in urban areas might be the unavailability of childcare and household responsibilities assumed by women in extended households.[9] A study using Hungary Labor Force Survey data (UNICEF 1999b) found that the presence of children considerably reduced the probability of employment among women. For women ages 26 to 29, female employment went from 82 percent in households with no children, to 52 percent in households with one child, 35 percent in households with two children, and 11 percent in households with three or more children. For women ages 36 to 39, female employment dropped sharply—from 78 to 41 percent—as the number of children increased from two to three.

Women's responsibilities for care of the children and elderly may make it more difficult for them to find and keep jobs, even when they want to enter the labor force. Unemployment rates do not exhibit strong systematic bias against women across the region: female unemployment rates in 1997, based on standard criteria of the International Labour Organisation, were higher than male unemployment rates in some countries—the Czech Republic, Slovak Republic, Poland, and Romania, but not in others— Hungary, Slovenia, Bulgaria, Latvia, and Russia (UNICEF 1999b). Nevertheless, many qualitative poverty studies reported frequent complaints of discrimination against women in the labor market. Women complained that their appearance and age frequently worked against them, even for unskilled jobs. Many employers preferred young (under 30), attractive women. They explicitly refused to consider married women of child-bearing age, to avoid paying maternity benefits, or women with children, assuming these women would often have to take time off from work.

Poverty in childhood can permanently affect children's future by damaging the integrity and stability of their families, their health, their schooling, and, finally, their likelihood of either participating in the labor force or becoming economically and socially marginalized. Poverty affects children before birth when poor mothers are unable to pay for prenatal care or give birth in hospitals (Dudwick 1996, 1999). It continues at birth,

---

Box 2.8   Barriers to Female Employment

A comparative study of the impact of privatization carried out in Bulgaria, Poland, Russia, and Ukraine found pervasive discrimination against women, particularly in the private sector. In all countries, women faced discrimination in hiring. Prospective employers inquired about family status and childbearing plans, and then often explicitly rejected them if they had small children or planned to have children. Women over 40, even over 35, were less likely to be hired. As a Moscow woman declared, "I am a pregnancy threat and my mother an obsolescence threat. We both lost work—almost simultaneously within two days—in October 1998. I will agree to any secretarial position. But as soon as it becomes known that I am just married, it gives rise to suspicious looks at my waistline." In Bulgaria laws prohibiting employers from refusing to hire pregnant women, or mandating equal pay for equal work, have been removed.

State-owned companies were the least likely to ask women such personal questions; private companies, the most likely. Violations of employment contracts were most likely to occur in privatized firms in the food and services industries where women predominate. Women noted that employment in small privatized firms was often contingent on providing sexual favors to the boss. In Poland both male and female executives saw women as less devoted than men to their careers. The executives were convinced that women would eventually "have to withdraw from work to take care of family obligations."

Source: Women, Law, and Development International (2000).

---

with many ECA countries reporting an increased number of children placed in infant homes (chapter 1). Closure of childcare facilities has forced working parents to leave children as young as five home alone during working hours. Young children are increasingly responsible for household tasks, including cooking with dangerous, home-made cooking devices that poor households resort to when electricity and gas supplies are cut off (Dudwick 1997). Throughout Europe and Central Asia there are reports of children dropping out of school, in some cases to enter the labor force. In Moldova children as young as 10 may work as agricultural day laborers, not just for their own parents, but for farming associations or independent farmers (De Soto and Dudwick 1999).

Simple and Partial Poverty Risks

Univariate analysis looks at how poverty correlates with one other variable, such as employment, location, education, or demographic factors, broken by subcategory. Partial correlation analysis goes a step farther. It looks at the association between poverty status and the variable in question, controlling for the effects of other variables. For example, simple univariate analysis may show that poverty risks are not strongly differentiated by education level. This might occur if people living in rural areas are prone to poverty, in which case even people with high education in rural areas would have a higher risk of poverty. Were we to look at poverty risks in urban areas and rural areas separately, however, we might find that poverty risks are more clearly differentiated by education level. Or univariate analysis might show that poverty risks are strongly differentiated by education levels, while multivariate analysis might show that these risks are considerably weaker if other variables were taken into account. For example, if people with low education are heavily concentrated in rural areas, the strong correlation between education and poverty that would show up in a univariate poverty profile might be substantially diminished if we controlled for location.

The most common way to estimate partial relations is by ordinary least squares (OLS) regressions. Such regressions tell us whether variables are significantly related to the dependent variable (some measure of equivalent consumption). These regressions can then be used to calculate the poverty risks associated with various household characteristics, controlling for other household characteristics.[10] This is done by estimating what equivalent consumption a household would attain if its other characteristics were set equal to the population average. For example, suppose we are interested in poverty risks by education level, controlling for location. We run an OLS regression with education and location as independent variables. If the regression indicates that, holding education constant, living in urban areas is associated with a 20 percent increase in equivalent consumption (compared with the average), we estimate a new measure of equivalent consumption corrected for location by subtracting 20 percent from the equivalent consumption of individuals in urban areas. Then we calculate the risk of poverty by education category using the corrected measure of equivalent consumption. The resulting poverty rates show the partial relationship between education and poverty status, purged of the effects running through the location variable.

Many World Bank poverty assessments for transition countries estimate OLS regressions that show that most household characteristics—education, employment status, location, household demographics—are significantly associated with consumption levels in the expected directions. The Croatia poverty assessment (World Bank 2000) went a step farther to examine whether poverty risks change substantially when other variables are controlled for. The most dramatic change is that controlling for education substantially reduces poverty risks for the elderly, indicating that low levels of educational attainment are particularly pronounced among the elderly. This provides some insight into the channels that result in higher poverty among the elderly. Poverty risks also fall substantially in a number of regions once education is controlled for, indicating that low rates of education attainment are clustered in certain regions.

Figures 2.14a, 2.14b, and 2.14c show what happens to poverty risks by education levels in Croatia, the Kyrgyz Republic, and Russia respectively when we control for labor force participation (number of income earners per adult), dependency ratios (number of elderly per number of household members and number of children per number of household members), location (dummies for region multiplied by dummies for rural or urban location), and household size. The premium attached to higher education and vocational/technical education—which are associated with dramatically lower poverty risks—erodes, especially in the Kyrgyz Republic, and converges toward the poverty risk associated with secondary school. This suggests that higher education is correlated with other factors leading to a reduction in poverty, such as location and household size, reinforcing the often repeated observation that higher education is not much of a guarantee against poverty in parts of the CIS. The differences between the simple and the partial poverty risks are far less pronounced in Croatia and Russia, however.

As these examples show, in cases where characteristics associated with poverty are strongly correlated, multivariate analysis may provide a better understanding of the factors that put people most strongly at risk of poverty. Future work could usefully extend this analysis to determine whether poverty incidence by employment status, education, location, or household demographic characteristics (controlling for other variables) would yield a more sharply differentiated poverty profile—or a fuzzier one.

Targeting Groups for Poverty Assistance: The Challenges and Pitfalls

Identifying the groups that are at high risk of poverty as well as the groups that comprise the majority of the poor can help policymakers determine whether social assistance can be targeted at certain categories of poor. Targeting groups at high risk of poverty will minimize errors of inclusion, but if those groups comprise only a small share of the poor, there will be large errors of exclusion.[11] Similarly, targeting groups that comprise a large share of the poor will minimize errors of exclusion, but this risks large errors of inclusion if those groups have only a marginally elevated risk of poverty. Targeting households by employment status is not likely

Figure 2.14a   Croatia: Simple and Partial Relative Poverty Risks

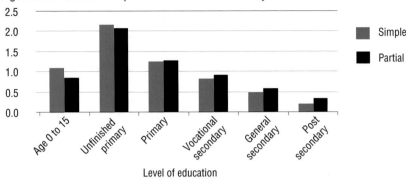

Level of education

Figure 2.14b   Kyrgyz Republic: Simple and Partial Relative Poverty Risks

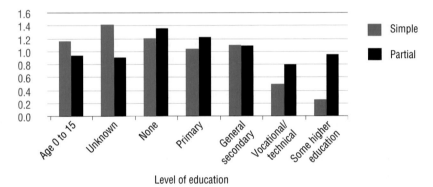

Level of education

Figure 2.14c   Russian Federation: Simple and Partial Relative Poverty Risks

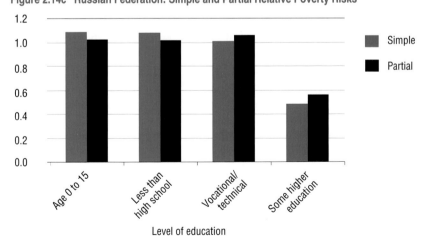

Level of education

Source: Household survey data, appendix B.

to be particularly effective in CSB or CIS countries; location and number of children hold out more promise for CSB countries.

Although households with unemployed or inactive heads are at high risk of poverty, they do not comprise the majority of the poor. Breaking down the poor by the employment status of the household head, we find that households with employed heads account for about 50 percent of the poor on average (figure 2.15), while pensioner households account for another 25 percent (figure 2.16). Thus, using unemployment of the household head as a targeting criterion would exclude most of the poor.

Children account for about one third of the poor (figure 2.17). But poor children live in poor households, and households with two or more children account for a sizable share of the poor, especially in a few Central European countries, where they also have a highly elevated risk of poverty (figure 2.18). They also account for a sizable share of the poor in the Caucasus and Central Europe. Households with two or more children account for more than three quarters of the population in all Central Asian countries except Kazakhstan. Thus, the number of children may be a useful targeting criterion in Central Europe, but not as useful in Central Asia, where errors of inclusion would be large.

The same is true for location. Although rural households tend to have a higher risk of poverty throughout the region, they are a minority of the population (except in Moldova, the Caucasus, and Central Asia). Because urban dwellers account for a large share of the population in many countries, they predominate among the poor in about half of the countries in the region—a noticeable difference from the rest of the world, in which the poor are overwhelmingly concentrated in rural areas (figure 2.19). Rural households constitute a majority of the poor in some CSB countries where they are not the majority of the population. Rural households also constitute the majority of the poor in Moldova, the Caucasus, and Central Asia, where they are the majority of the population. Hence, there would be fewer errors of inclusion in targeting rural households in CSB countries.

Changes in Economic Well-being over Time

At the start of the transition, it was thought that although households might fall into poverty as a result of the economic shocks, growth would quickly resume and living standards would rise. As it turned out, the output shocks were large and persistent, and poverty, rather than being short-lived, also proved persistent. Although in aggregate, poverty levels have remained high, individual outcomes are thought to be far more variable,

Figure 2.15   Share of Poor in Households with Employed Head

Percent

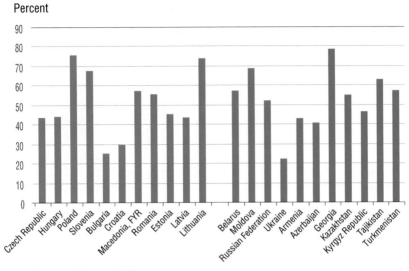

Source: Poverty profiles, appendix D.

Figure 2.16   Share of Poor in Households with Retired Head

Percent

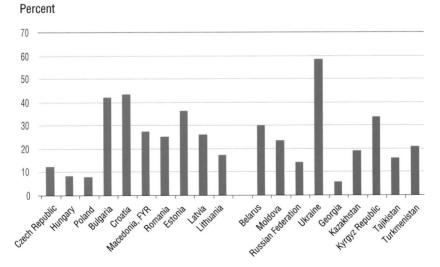

Source: Poverty profiles, appendix D.

Figure 2.17   Composition of Poor by Age Group

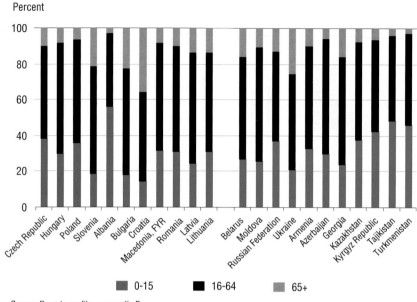

Source: Poverty profiles, appendix D.

Figure 2.18   Share of Poor Living in Households with Two or More Children

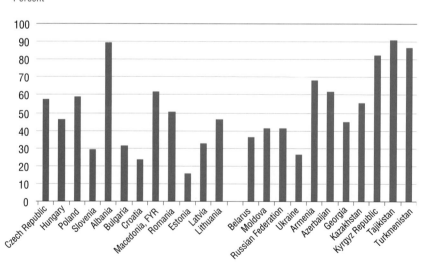

Source: Poverty profiles, appendix D.

Figure 2.19   Share of Poor in Rural Areas

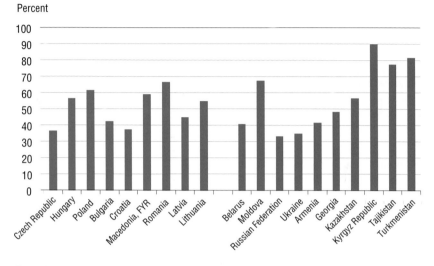

Percent

Source: Poverty profiles, appendix D.

depending on whether salaries are paid, transfers arrive, remittances come, or informal sector activities provide incomes. Following families over time through panel surveys allows us to examine the stability, or security, of their economic situations. Three countries—Poland, Hungary, and Russia—have long panels that can be used for this purpose.[12]

Panel surveys show that household incomes and expenditures are quite variable, but the shocks are largely transitory in nature. Between 1995 and 1996, the incomes of 43 percent of the population in Russia more than doubled or decreased by half. Between 1994 and 1995, the incomes of 4 percent of the population in Hungary and 14 percent of the population in Poland more than doubled or decreased by half, controlling for the mean income shock. Interestingly, fluctuations in expenditure are only slightly smaller than fluctuations in incomes, suggesting that families may find it difficult to smooth their consumption.

The large fluctuations in expenditure give rise to the phenomenon of *churning,* that is, households cycling in and out of poverty. Many households experience at least one bout of poverty. In Russia 45 percent of individuals are poor at least once over a four-year period—more than twice as many as the share in poverty (20 percent) in any one year (table 2.2).[13] In Poland a slightly smaller share of the population—37 percent—

Table 2.2 Transitory and Persistent Poverty in the Russian Federation, Poland, and Hungary
(percent)

Share of the population	Russian Federation (Expenditure)	Poland (Expenditure)	Hungary (Income)
A. Share of the population based on measured poverty			
Always poor (4 out of 4)	3.4	5.9	8.8
Sometimes poor (1, 2, or 3 times out of 4)	41.9	31.6	26.3
Never poor (0 times out of 4)	54.7	61.5	65.0
B. Share of the population based on simulations using "underlying" poverty transition probabilities			
Always poor (4 out of 4)	10.0	10.7	9.7
Sometimes poor (1, 2, or 3 times out of 4)	21.8	20.1	22.6
Never poor (0 times out of 4)	68.2	69.2	67.8

Note: Income and expenditure are adjusted for household size using an equivalence scale. The poverty line is set so that in each year 20 percent of the population is poor. Transition probabilities are shown in table 2.3, panel B.
Source: Luttmer (2000a).

experiences at least one bout of measured poverty. Movements in and out of poverty between two years are correspondingly high: 55 percent of the poor (11 percent of the total population) escaped poverty in Russia compared with 45 percent (8.8 percent of the population) in Poland and 40 percent (8 percent of the population) in Hungary (panel A of table 2.3).[14]

This churning, however, does not represent long-term movements into and out of poverty. Because a large part of the shock is undone in future years, long-term economic positions are considerably more stable than a simple look at year-to-year changes reveals. Purging the data of transitory shocks yields an estimate of the persistent component of expenditure (or income). This persistent component of expenditure we term "underlying" expenditure to distinguish it from the observed, or "traditionally" measured expenditure aggregate. Estimates of individuals' expenditures suggest that the shocks are largely transitory: about 86 percent of the expenditure shock in Russia, 76 percent of the expenditure shock in Poland, and 76 percent of the income shock was undone the following year. Panel B of table 2.3 reports the estimated flows in and out of poverty based on the expenditure (or income) data that is stripped of the transitory fluctuation. We call the latter movements in "underlying" poverty to

Table 2.3 Flows into and out of Poverty in the Russian Federation, Poland, and Hungary
(percent)

A. Movements in "traditionally measured" poverty			B. Movements in "underlying" poverty		
Russian Federation (1995-96)			**Russian Federation (1995-96)**		
Poverty status 12 months ago	This month's poverty status		Poverty status 12 months ago	This month's poverty status	
	Poor	Nonpoor		Poor	Nonpoor
Poor	44.7	55.3	Poor	79.4	20.6
Nonpoor	13.8	86.2	Nonpoor	5.2	94.8
Poland (1994-95)			**Poland (1994-95)**		
Poverty status 12 months ago	This month's poverty status		Poverty status 12 months ago	This month's poverty status	
	Poor	Nonpoor		Poor	Nonpoor
Poor	55.3	44.7	Poor	80.2	19.8
Nonpoor	11.2	88.8	Nonpoor	4.9	95.1
Hungary (1995-96)			**Hungary (1995-96)**		
Poverty status 12 months ago	This month's poverty status		Poverty status 12 months ago	This month's poverty status	
	Poor	Nonpoor		Poor	Nonpoor
Poor	60.5	39.5	Poor	78.5	21.6
Nonpoor	9.9	90.1	Nonpoor	5.4	94.6

Note: "Underlying" poverty measures assume log normality of expenditure distributions. See Luttmer (2000a) for a discussion of how "underlying" poverty flows are estimated. Poverty flows are based on expenditure data for Poland and Russia and on income data for Hungary from the TARKI panel. The poverty line is such that the poverty rate is 20 percent in all years. Standard errors are never larger than one fifth of the transition probabilities. Percentages in the table refer to share of poor (20 percent of the population) and nonpoor (80 percent of the population).
Source: Luttmer (2000a).

distinguish them from the "traditionally measured" flows in and out of poverty based on observed expenditure (or income) data.

The estimate of underlying expenditure is based on four years of panel data. The first and last years of the data (years 1 and 4) are used to estimate what part of the change in expenditure levels between year 2 and year 3 is from transitory fluctuations that are undone in the following year, and thus what part is from a permanent change in economic fortunes. To understand better the distinction, consider the example of someone who is not poor in year 2 but receives a negative income shock between year 2 and 3 that moves her into poverty in year 3. Suppose she then recovers in year 4 back to the level of expenditure she enjoyed in year 2. According to the observed measure, she would be classified as moving into poverty between years 2 and 3. But according to her estimated underlying expenditure path, she would be classified as persistently nonpoor between years 2 and 3 since the expenditure shock was short-lived and does not represent a permanent change in her economic fortunes. Table 2.3 reports both the traditionally measured and the underlying movements in and out of poverty between years 2 and 3.

By looking at movements in and out of poverty according to estimates of underlying expenditure levels, we can detect a much different picture of persistent poverty: in Poland, for example, only 20 percent of the poor escape poverty on a more permanent basis, less than half of what the movements based on traditionally measured poverty suggest, while 80 percent of the poor (16 percent of the population) in one year remain in poverty the following year according to their underlying status (column B of table 2.3). A much higher share of the poor remains in poverty in Hungary and Russia as well, according to the underlying estimate, than remains in poverty according to the traditionally measured share.

It is commonly thought that the transiently poor—those who escape poverty in some years—are most likely to benefit from an improvement in economic conditions. They are vulnerable to economic shocks but have characteristics that allow them to escape poverty at least some of the time. In contrast, the traditionally measured persistently poor—those who are observed to be poor in every period of observation—are thought to be an underclass that is unlikely to be able to take advantage of new economic opportunities. Given the large fluctuations in measured expenditures that move households in and out of poverty in this region, the number of individuals who are persistently poor according to their observed poverty status is quite small. Only 3.4 percent of Russians, 5.9 percent of Poles, and 8.8 percent of Hungarians were poor in all four years (table 2.2, panel A).

How useful is the measure of persistent poverty, which requires households to be poor in every period of observation, as a proxy for the size of the underclass? Because of the fluctuations in expenditure that are undone the following year and measurement error, an individual's economic fortunes may be considerably more stable than the year-to-year movements in observed poverty status suggest. A better estimate of persistent poverty might be based on the number of people whose underlying expenditures are below the poverty line in all four years. Such a measure can be derived by taking the probability that an individual will remain in poverty according to his or her underlying expenditures from one year to the next and using that probability to calculate the probability that the individual will remain in poverty for four consecutive years.[15] The share of the population remaining in poverty for a four-year period based on its underlying expenditures is shown in panel B of table 2.2. For all three countries, about 10 percent of the population is estimated to be always poor according to the underlying measure of expenditure—half the number of poor in any one given year. This is a lower bound. The number of persistently poor according to the underlying measure could reach 16 percent—the share of the population that remains in poverty between two consecutive years, if all of these people remain in poverty during the entire four-year period.

For Russia the lower bound measure for the share of the population in persistent poverty based on the underlying measure shown in panel B of table 2.2 is three times greater than the traditional estimate; for Poland it is 80 percent higher, while for Hungary it is only 10 percent higher. The reason the probability of remaining in persistent poverty based on the traditional measure of expenditure differs significantly among the three countries (despite the fact that the transition probabilities shown in panel B of table 2.3 for remaining in poverty are very similar) is the size of the transitory shock, which averages 45.3 percent in Russia, 19.2 percent in Poland, and only 11.4 percent in Hungary. When transitory shocks are large, traditional measures of persistent poverty will be low; underlying measures, which smooth out the transitory shocks, will be higher.

Traditional measures of poverty persistence, which require households to be poor in every period of observation, are likely to underestimate the share of the population stuck in poverty and thus understate the size of the incipient underclass forming, particularly when there are large, short-term fluctuations in income. Although some of these fluctuations may represent a real improvement in welfare, the fact that they are undone in subsequent periods suggests that these people are stuck in poverty. Therefore, estimations of persistent poverty based on the underlying measure of poverty may give a better sense of the size of the incipient underclass.

The long duration of unemployment rates supports the observation that an underclass may be forming. Data available for several Central and South Eastern European countries show that much of the unemployment is long term in nature. For example, as much as 80 percent of all the unemployed in FYR Macedonia are long-term unemployed, and this pattern is very similar across socioeconomic groups, in contrast to the more typical pattern found in Europe, where the incidence of unemployment increases with age. In Bulgaria 83 percent of unemployed people were unemployed the previous year, also indicating that unemployment is generally of long duration (World Bank 1999a). A study in Hungary found that the probability that an unemployed person will find a job within 12 months is on the order of 30 to 33 percent (Rutkowski 1999). The long duration of unemployment and its high correlation with poverty further support the notion that an underclass may be forming—especially in Central European countries.

Researchers have hypothesized that transient shocks may be a cause of long-term poverty. For example, people who suffer transient shocks, such as not being paid their salary over some period, might be forced to sell key income-generating assets, and this supposedly puts them on permanently lower income paths. However, Lokshin and Ravallion (2000) do not find evidence in the Hungarian panel data that transient shocks lead to long-term poverty. Persistent poverty is most likely the result of repeated transient shocks or characteristics that make it hard for households to escape poverty.

The Challenges Ahead

During the transition in Europe and Central Asia to a more market-oriented economy, some groups have fared relatively better and some relatively worse in terms of being at risk of poverty. An examination of underlying trends suggests that, despite the considerable fluctuations in incomes and expenditures, the overall picture is one of limited mobility: the same groups of people tend to remain at the bottom of the income distribution over time. Therefore, two challenges face policymakers and societies. One is to reduce downside fluctuations in incomes and, when they do occur, to protect the poor and near poor from the welfare losses associated with negative shocks. The second challenge is to enhance the opportunities of the persistently poor to improve their absolute level of living as well as their relative standing among the population.

Notes

1. In Czech Republic, the relative poverty line was set at two-thirds median equivalent consumption since only 2.8 percent of the population in Czech Republic fell under the 50 percent line. A moderate economies-of-scale parameter of 0.75 was used to calculate equivalent adult expenditure, based on the fact that housing and utility expenditures are typically a smaller share of household expenditures in most European and Central Asian countries than in OECD countries.

Children were weighted the same as adults. The broad conclusions in this chapter based on the profile results were not sensitive to the poverty line; profiles based on two-thirds of median household income were generally quite similar. See the appendixes for further discussion of the methodology, data sources, and poverty profile results.

2. Alternatively, comparisons could be made on the basis of absolute poverty lines. But since the levels of absolute poverty vary dramatically within the region (table 1.1), this would make intercountry comparisons of the characteristics of the poor in each country difficult.

3. Many poverty assessments confirmed that unemployed individuals were more likely to be poor than the overall population, although an individual's poverty status depends, of course, not only on his or her own income–generating capacity, but also on the income earned by other members of the household.

4. The distinction between rural and urban areas is an administrative one, and different countries may classify locations on the basis of very different criteria.

5. The elderly have a very low risk of poverty in Turkmenistan, but they are a very small share of the population so the results may not be robust.

6. See appendix A for further discussion of economies of scale.

7. Children also are poorer than the elderly in Turkmenistan, but the size of the elderly population there is quite small.

8. Such households comprise only a small share of female-headed households. The latter account for a little more than one-quarter of the population in the region, though the definition of a female-headed household is not uniform across poverty surveys. Female-headed households tend to be poorer than male-headed households, and many poverty assessments have found that this finding persists even after controlling for age, education, household size, and location.

9. The Latvia poverty assessment found that labor force participation of females between the ages of 25 and 35 was lower than for men. When predicted earnings were included in the regression analysis, participation rates of men were more highly correlated with the earnings they would be predicted to get in the labor market. But there was no significant correlation for women, indicating that other factors are associated with lower labor force participation rates by females.

10. See Luttmer (2000b) for a discussion of the methodology and results on Croatia.

11. Errors of inclusion occur when poverty benefits go to households that are not poor, while errors of exclusion occur when poverty benefits do not reach households that are poor.

12. This section is based heavily on Luttmer (2000a).

13. They either fall in the sometimes poor category (41.9 percent) or into the always poor category (3.4 percent).

14. The definition of poverty here is a relative one—the bottom quintile of the population. In a case such as Poland, where mean expenditures increased over time, these movements in and out of the bottom quintile would mostly likely

represent a significant change in the real standard of living. In Russia, which experienced overall a negative income shock, a movement out of the bottom quintile might not entail an absolute increase in expenditures.

15. The probability of remaining in poverty for four years based on the "underlying" poverty transition probability is obtained by raising the probability of remaining in poverty for two consecutive years to the third power multiplied by the share of the poor in the population, set at 20 percent.

References

Brooks, Karen, and others. 1996. "Agricultural Reform in Russia: A View from the Farm Level." World Bank Discussion Paper 327. Washington, D.C.

Chirca, Constantin, and Emil Daniel Tesliuc. 1999. "From Rural Poverty to Rural Development." National Commission for Statistics and World Bank. Processed.

Csaki, Csaba, and Zvi Lerman. 1997. "Land Reform in Ukraine: The First Five Years." World Bank Discussion Paper 371. Washington, D.C.

De Soto, Hermine, and Nora Dudwick. 1999. "Poverty in Moldova: The Social Dimensions of Transition 1999." In *Moldova Poverty Assessment*, vol. 2: Technical Papers, Report 19846-MD. Washington, D.C.: World Bank. October.

Dudwick Nora. 1996. "A Qualitative Assessment of the Living Standards of the Armenian Population, 1994-95." World Bank Working Paper 1. Washington, D.C.

———. 1997. "Land Reform in Moldova." World Bank, Environmentally and Socially Sustainable Development Sector Unit, Europe and Central Asia Region. Washington, D.C. Processed.

———. 1999. "Georgia: A Qualitative Study of Impoverishment and Coping Strategies." In *Georgia: Poverty and Income Distribution*, vol. 2: Technical Papers, Report 19348-GE. Washington, D.C.: World Bank. May 27.

Falkingham, Jane. 2000. "From Security to Uncertainty: The Impact of Economic Change on Child Welfare in Central Asia." Innocenti Working Paper 76. Florence: UNICEF Innocenti Research Centre.

Foley, Mark C. 1997. "Static and Dynamic Analyses of Poverty in Russia." In *Poverty in Russia: Public Policy and Private Responses*, edited by Jeni Klugman, 65-90. Washington, D.C.: World Bank.

Foster, Michael F., and Istvan Gyorgy Toth. 1999. "Trends in Child Poverty and Social Transfers in the Czech Republic, Hungary, and Poland: Experiences from the Years after Transition." Paper presented at the conference "Child Well-Being in Rich and Transition Countries: Are Children in Growing Danger of Social Exclusion?" September 30 - October 2, 1999, Luxemborg.

Institute of Philosophy and Sociology. 1998. "Listening to the Poor." Riga, Latvia. Processed.

Institute for Sociological and Political-Legal Research. 1998. "Qualitative Analysis of the Living Standards of the Population of the Republic of Macedonia." Skopje, Macedonia. Processed.

Lerman, Zvi, Csaba Csaki, and Victor Moroz. 1998. "Land Reform and Farm Restructuring in Moldova: Progress and Prospects." World Bank Discussion Paper 398. Washington, D.C.

Lokshin, Michael, and Martin Ravallion. 2000. "Short-Lived Shocks with Long-Lived Impacts? Household Income Dynamics in a Transition Economy." *Background Papers: Making Transition Work for Everyone: Poverty and Inequality in Europe and Central Asia*. World Bank. Washington, D.C.

Luttmer, Erzo. 2000a. "Inequality and Poverty Dynamics in Transition Economies: Disentangling Real Effects from Data." *Background Papers: Making Transition Work for Everyone: Poverty and Inequality in Europe and Central Asia*. World Bank. Washington, D.C.

———. 2000b. "Poverty and Inequality in Croatia." World Bank background paper for the Croatia: Economic Vulnerability and Welfare Study. Poverty Reduction and Economic Management Sector Unit, Europe and Central Asia Region. Washington, D.C. Processed.

Narayan, Deepa. 2000. *Voices of the Poor: Can Anyone Hear Us?* New York: Oxford University Press.

Pinto, Brian, Vladimir Drebentsov, and Alexander Morozov. 2000. "Dismantling Russia's Nonpayments System: Creating the Conditions for Growth." World Bank, Poverty Reduction and Economic Management Sector Unit, Europe and Central Asia Region. Washington, D.C. Processed.

Ravallion, Martin, and Michael Lokshin. 1999. "Subjective Economic Welfare." World Bank Policy Research Working Paper 2106. Washington, D.C.

Rutkowski, Jan. 1999. "Labor Market Disadvantage and Poverty: Evidence from Hungary Panel Data, 1992-97." World Bank, Europe and Central Asia Region. Washington D.C. Processed.

UNICEF (United Nations Children's Fund). 1999a. *After the Fall: The Human Impact of Ten Years of Transition*. Florence: International Child Development Centre.

———. 1999b. "Women in Transition." Regional Monitoring Report 6. Florence: International Child Development Centre.

Wanner, Catherine, and Nora Dudwick. 1996. "An Ethnographic Study of Poverty in Ukraine." World Bank, Europe and Central Asia Region. Washington, D.C. Processed.

Women, Law, and Development International. 2000. "Women's Rights under Privatization in Bulgaria, Poland, Russia and Ukraine." Washington, D.C. Processed.

World Bank.1998. *Kazakhstan: Living Standards during the Transition.* Report 17520-K2. Washington, D.C. March 23.

———. 1999a. *Bulgaria: Poverty during the Transition.* Report 18411. Washington, D.C. June 7.

———. 1999b. *Russia: Targeting and the Longer-Term Poor,* vol. 1: Main Report, Report 19377-RU. Washington, D.C. May.

———. 2000. *Croatia: Economic Vulnerability and Welfare Study.* Poverty Reduction and Economic Management Sector Unit, Europe and Central Asia Region. Washington, D.C. Processed.

Yemtsov, Ruslan. 1999. "Labor Markets, Inequality and Poverty." In *Georgia: Poverty and Income Distribution,* vol. 2: Technical Papers, Report 19348-GE. Washington, D.C.: World Bank. May 27.

Zisk, Kimberly Marten. 1997. *Weapons, Culture, and Self-interest: Soviet Defense Managers in the New Russia.* New York: Columbia University Press.

PART II

EXPLAINING THE INCREASE IN POVERTY

The emergence of widespread poverty in ECA is the outcome of a complex interaction of economic, social, and political processes. A proximate explanatory factor for the rise in poverty was the *economic collapse* of transition—the magnitude and duration of the drop in output and in household incomes. The extent of this collapse, however, was influenced by many interrelated factors: the degree of initial macroeconomic distortions; the familiarity of institutions and individuals with market mechanisms; the inherited economic structure; and the comprehensiveness and quality of the policy reform package. Most importantly, the path of output and incomes was conditioned by *institutional legacies*, which largely determined the behavior of policymakers during the transition process, and their interest and ability to deliver a consistent reform program, with adequate safeguards to protect the vulnerable.

Institutional legacies critically conditioned countries' ability (or inability) to break with their socialist past—and with old patterns of distribution of power and access to resources. Countries with stronger institutional checks and balances (resulting from stronger civil societies, more mature political democracies, and more developed market-supporting institutions) were better at establishing economic and political contestability from the start. As a result, these countries implemented better policy choices: they carried out more comprehensive and decisive reforms; moved more quickly toward a market-based system for allocating resources (and away from the power or access-based system that characterized late socialism); and carried out more socially focused adjustment. Because they were better at getting markets to work, these countries generated more new job and income-earning opportunities for their citizens. At the same time, they also gave higher priority to keeping a strong social safety net and devoted a much larger share of their resources to this goal. Poverty and deprivation increased in these countries—bearing witness to the social dislocation produced by the transition process—but the increase was much more moderate than in other parts of the region. This was, in general, the case of the more advanced reformers in Central Europe—the Czech Republic, Hungary, Poland, Slovenia—but also (albeit to varying degrees) of other Central and South Eastern European economies and of the Baltic states.

Other countries, most notably those of the Commonwealth of Independent States (CIS), failed to establish economic and political contestability. The partiality and incompleteness of economic and political reforms during the first stage of transition simply allowed some power groups—mainly traditional socialist elites in combination with some entrepreneurial newcomers—to cement and legalize the power relationships that existed at the end of socialism. In the absence of institutional checks and balances or other measures to restrain the arbitrary use of power, these groups were able to generate concentrated rents for themselves, at a high cost in terms of increased inequality and poverty to the rest of society. These power groups are now the main obstacles to any further economic reform that would threaten their concentrated rents. The partiality of the initial reforms—especially the lack of further efforts to deconcentrate economic power and create better-functioning markets—has stifled job creation and opportunities for all but these privileged parts of society. Formal wages and employment opportunities have collapsed, and with pervasive noncompetitive practices and corruption to contend with, there is little room for new small and medium-scale private activity to emerge and create jobs.

Resource-starved governments have revealed only limited interest (and ability) to protect the vulnerable: social spending has collapsed throughout much of the CIS, and along with it so has the social safety net. The result has been a spectacular increase in poverty and very high inequality. With rent-seeking channels now firmly "institutionalized," politicians in much of the CIS are reluctant to let the process of democratization and market expansion move further, since it may jeopardize the status quo. With a varying range of outcomes, this has been the case of most CIS Republics, starting with Russia but covering also many of the resource-rich Central Asian economies and the poorer countries of the Transcaucasus.

Part II explores this broad typology further by examining the interactions between institutional legacies, initial conditions, and policy choices, and by analyzing how these led to very different poverty and inequality outcomes across transition economies. Chapter 3 focuses mainly on understanding how institutions and history conditioned governments' ability to carry out economic reforms, and how these then jointly determined the path of output and incomes. Chapter 4 examines how policies and institutions have determined distributional outcomes and through this affected poverty.

Understanding the Rise in Poverty: Initial Conditions, Institutional Legacies, and Policies

The poor in Europe and Central Asia cite loss of stable income as the overwhelming factor associated with poverty. Poverty is largely the result of bad labor market outcomes, such as the loss of a paying job, the failure to be paid for work completed, or insufficient income because of a lack of the skills needed to compete in the new, more market-oriented economy. For those who are not able to work—children and the elderly—poverty is linked to a decline in public transfers and other forms of income support, and to being one of many dependents living on few and low incomes.

Similar causal forces underlie the rise in poverty in all ECA countries, namely the economic and social dislocation associated with transition, and the ensuing collapse in output and incomes. But poverty outcomes are vastly different across countries. Not only are the absolute levels of poverty different (chapter 1, table 1.1), but the characteristics of the poor vary also. In Central Europe, South Eastern Europe, and the Baltics (CSB), the risk of poverty is linked to well-identified household characteristics (education, number of income earners, employment status), which influence a household's ability to earn its income. Thus, the risk of poverty is especially high for households where the main income earner is unemployed, where there are many dependents living on a single income, or where workers' skills are no longer in demand. In contrast, relative poverty risks in the Commonwealth of Independent States (CIS) look remarkably similar across households that in theory would have widely differing income-earning opportunities. The bulk of the poor in the CIS are working poor, and they do not look all that different from the nonpoor.

Like poverty, the level of income inequality varies drastically across countries of the region—this being a critical contributing factor to the diversity of poverty outcomes. Some of the CSB countries remain very egalitarian by world standards, with Gini coefficients for consumption and income similar to those of the Scandinavian and Northern European countries. Much of the CIS, in contrast, compares to the highly unequal economies of Latin America and Africa (chapter 4, table 4.1). This divergence in inequality outcomes is particularly striking because the transition economies started the 1990s with fairly similar distributions of income. Although the CIS had, on average, somewhat higher initial levels of income inequality (with Ginis ranging from 0.23 to 0.3), the difference with respect to the CSB was at most 5 Gini points, not the wide gaps we see today.

These differences pose a puzzle. Why did apparently similar forces play out so differently in different countries? Was it the length and depth of the transitional recession that mattered? Was it initial conditions? Was it the choice and sequencing of policies? And what ultimately determined these choices? This chapter will attempt to untangle these issues. In particular, it will explore how institutions and history may have conditioned governments' ability to carry out economic reforms and how jointly these factors determined the path of output and incomes.

Transition and Poverty

In a narrow accounting sense the increase in poverty during the transition can be attributed to two distinct factors: the drop in output (and hence in consumption) and changes in its distribution. On average, the cumulative output decline in the CIS countries was almost 50 percent, while in the CSB countries output declined by about 15 percent before starting its recovery (figure 3.1). In and of itself, this massive decline in output led to a sharp rise in poverty. At the same time inequality was rising in all the transition countries—sometimes quite dramatically. While the increase in inequality was an expected, and to some degree necessary, development in the transition to market, in some countries the rise far exceeded what was anticipated and what had been seen before.

Although the collapse of output and increasing inequality can account for much of the quantitative rise in poverty, these two factors are in some sense just proximate causes, behind which lies a complex interaction of economic, social, and political processes. These underlying processes help explain why outcomes diverged as much as they did and are the key to

Figure 3.1   Evolution of Output in Transition Time

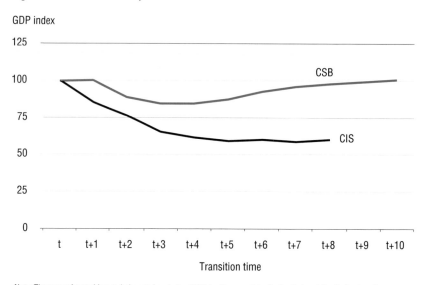

Note: The year of transition, t, is here taken to be 1989 for the countries in Central and South Eastern Europe and the Baltics (CSB) and 1991 for the countries in the Commonwealth of Independent States (CIS). The GDP index (t=100) is a population-weighted average for the countries in each group.
Source: World Bank, SIMA database.

how the worst outcomes may be improved. The question to answer is not so much whether poverty rose because output collapsed and inequality rose—the answer is an unambiguous yes—but why did output collapse so much more in some countries than in others? And why did inequality follow such different patterns?

One of the fundamental factors behind the path of output and incomes was the extent and quality of the economic reforms that countries chose to implement. There is a strong correlation between comprehensive reform and output performance (Aslund, Boone, and Johnson 1996; de Melo, Denizer, and Gelb 1996; Selowsky and Martin 1997; and EBRD 1999). Analysts, however, are beginning to realize that other factors may have mattered just as much: initial conditions (including location, initial economic distortions, and the resource endowment); the state of institutions at the start of the transition; and the political system. These factors had a direct and strong impact on output as well. Moreover, these nonpolicy factors fundamentally affected the choice of reforms and the extent to which countries were able to implement them (Bunce 1999; EBRD 1999). And these factors also had an independent impact on the distribution of income and consumption, and hence on the level of poverty.

In a recent paper de Melo and others (2000) show that initial conditions (including initial macroeconomic imbalances, unfamiliarity with the market process, and structural distortions) were indeed important in explaining both output performance and the speed of economic liberalization and reform across transition economies. They also show that political reform, in particular, was a critical determinant of the speed of economic liberalization. Their paper suggests, however, that while unfavorable initial conditions may have discouraged reforms, they did not make them less effective. On the contrary, the authors find that even in counties with highly unfavorable initial conditions, the effectiveness of reforms, once implemented, was not reduced. Moreover, they conclude that "countries cannot avoid the costs of non-reform, especially if deeply embedded in a disintegrating political and economic system" (de Melo and others 2000, 29). Although initial conditions are an important factor in explaining output performance, de Melo and others find that policy matters more (box 3.1, table 3.1).

As discussed in box 3.1, there is a strong link between policy reform and output performance. Countries that implemented inconsistent or partial reforms experienced larger drops in output than those that chose to move quickly. This relationship is reflected in the association between policies and poverty: good policies that allowed for a faster recovery of output appear to have led to lower poverty levels. Poverty is highest where reforms have stalled or been only partially implemented (figure 3.2). As shown in table 3.2, this relationship still holds if we control for initial income (as a proxy for the initial level of poverty) and other initial conditions (including the degree of political rights and civil liberties at the start of the transition and experience with market mechanisms as proxied by years under central planning). Moreover, the relationship between poverty rates and reform seems robust regardless of whether we measure poverty at the $2.15 per day line, or at the higher $4.30 per day line. This evidence suggests that countries that moved quickly and comprehensively to implement market reforms experienced a smaller increase in poverty than countries that delayed the start of reforms or stopped mid-way.

Some countries, such as Belarus, that have not started reforms appear to have maintained relatively low levels of poverty. Does this mean that it is better to not start reforms at all, rather than start and stop? The work by de Melo and others (2000) suggests that this is not necessarily the case, since delaying reforms is likely to increase future costs. Moreover, some of the peculiarities of the Belorussian economy suggest that measuring true

Box 3.1   The Role of Initial Conditions

Despite a common legacy and an apparent uniformity in their economic and political systems, transition economies differed widely in initial conditions, including their levels of development, macroeconomic distortions, memory of market-based institutions, and even in their histories as sovereign nations. de Melo and others (2000) explore the relative importance of initial distortions, institutional characteristics, and economic policies in explaining the highly divergent performance of transition economies. They use data on 28 transition economies (including China, Mongolia and Vietnam, Central and Eastern Europe, and the former Soviet Union) and span a period of five years.

de Melo and others find that while countries differ in many dimensions, empirically the variation in initial conditions can be summed up in two principal clusters: the first measures market imbalances and the degree of familiarity with market processes; the second presents the level of socialist development and associated structural distortions. They then explore the importance of these two clusters in determining the extent and speed of policy reform and economic performance. They find that initial conditions matter for both. Using cross-sectional averages and panel data, they find that adverse initial conditions were unambiguously associated with slower economic reform. However, adverse initial conditions do not diminish the effectiveness of reforms, and there are substantial costs to delaying or avoiding reforms. They also find that adverse initial conditions had an independent effect on economic performance. However, estimates of the relative importance of factors affecting performance reveal that policies still matter the most when it comes to explaining growth. According to their econometric model, policies account for 31 to 46 percent of the variation of growth across transition countries, while initial conditions account for 19 to 31 percent. For inflation, initial conditions dominate, with regional tensions coming in second. But when it comes to the determinants of policy reform proper, they find that the highest explanatory power comes from political reform (37 to 92 percent of the explained variance).

Table 3.1   Cross-country Variance in Outcomes: Policy versus Initial Conditions
(percentage of explained variance, maximum/minimum)

Indicator	Policy	Initial conditions	Regional tensions	Political freedom
Growth	46/31	31/19	28/28	7/0
Inflation	17/12	68/51	25/24	3/0
Policy	—	63/9	—	92/37

Source: de Melo and others (2000).

poverty in Belarus can be tricky (chapter 1). However, what is revealing about the Belarus case is the importance of what happens to *inequality* in determining poverty outcomes. Unlike in other CIS countries, the distribution of income in Belarus has remained relatively egalitarian: although the pie has been shrinking, it has not been redistributed to the rich as much as it has been in some neighboring countries. As we will see below, this has fundamental implications for poverty.

Figure 3.2   Overall Transition Indicators and Poverty

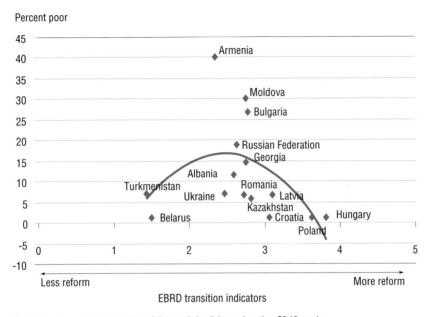

Note: Percent poor is the percentage of the population living on less than $2.15 per day.
Source: Team calculations based on latest representative household surveys.

Poverty outcomes depend not only on what happens to output, but more fundamentally on how these changes in output translate into changes in household consumption, and on what happens to the distribution of this consumption. The choice of policies can affect both the level and distribution of consumption. Thus, for a given change in output, poverty outcomes could differ markedly across countries. In other words, policy choices can significantly decrease or increase the poverty costs associated with a given output drop. Policies that shift much of the adjustment burden onto the poorest segments of society (for example, indiscriminate cuts in social spending and/or a reorientation of transfers to the better-off) can do much to worsen the poverty consequences of an output drop. Similarly, a policy and institutional environment that breeds corruption will lead to more unequal distributions of income, and hence to higher poverty rates at any given level of output. In extreme cases the distributional consequences of government policies and behaviors can even swamp the poverty-reducing impact of output growth.

Table 3.3 helps illustrate the importance of distributional outcomes for poverty. Column 1 shows that there is a negative relationship between the

Table 3.2 Poverty, Reforms, and Initial Conditions

Independent variables	At $2.15 per day				At $4.30 per day			
	(1)	(2)	(3)	(4)	(1)	(2)	(3)	(4)
Initial income (U.S. dollars)	—	-0.004 (-2.077)	-0.005 (-2.586)	-0.005 (-2.560)	—	-0.007 (-3.519)	-0.007 (-2.918)	-0.007 (-2.953)
Reform index[a]	2.571 (2.756)	2.102 (2.371)	2.170 (2.521)	1.673 (1.830)	4.181 (3.346)	3.298 (3.348)	3.302 (3.248)	2.651 (2.490)
Initial freedoms[b]	—	—	-5.078 (-1.449)	-4.459 (-1.294)	—	—	-0.335 (-0.081)	0.476 (0.119)
Planning[c]	—	—	—	0.381 (1.362)	—	—	—	0.499 (1.534)
Constant	4.309 (0.870)	26.534 (2.282)	91.305 (46.126)	63.164 (1.277)	23.332 (3.612)	65.150 (5.044)	69.428 (1.274)	32.525 (0.565)
R-squared	0.297	0.439	0.504	0.559	0.396	0.651	0.650	0.698
N	20	20	20	20	20	20	20	20

Note: The dependent variable is the percentage of the population below the poverty line. Regressions of percent poor were calculated on a set of independent variables for 20 countries. T-statistics are in parentheses.
a. The liberalization index computed by de Melo, Denizer, and Gelb (1996).
b. Index of political rights and civil liberties at start of transition, from Freedom House. We also experimented with other initial conditions variables such as location, initial trade distortions, etc., but none turned out to be significant.
c. Years under central planning.
Source: The percent poor is calculated using the latest representative household surveys (see chapter 1 and methodological appendix).

cumulative change in aggregate output and poverty outcomes across ECA countries, but also that there is a large *unexplained* residual. In fact, changes in output explain only a moderate fraction of the variance in poverty outcomes across the region. Putting in a variable to control for the distribution of consumption (or income) explains a big part of this residual (column 2). And while the output effect remains important, what happens to inequality (measured here by the end-period Gini coefficient) is even more fundamental in explaining cross-country differences in poverty outcomes.[1] It follows that policy choices that influence the distribution of income can have a large effect on poverty, independent of what happens to output.

Growth and distribution are not affected equally by macroeconomic developments and/or policy choices. This can present policymakers with difficult tradeoffs. Some developments, such as the liberalization of wages, can simultaneously lead to greater inequality (which would tend to increase poverty) and higher output (which would tend to reduce it). Similarly, cuts in fiscal expenditures that may be needed to reduce fiscal deficits

Table 3.3 Poverty, Output, and Inequality

Independent variables	At $2.15 per day		At $4.30 per day	
	(1)	(2)	(3)	(4)
Initial income per capita (US dollars)	-0.004 (-2.618)	-0.006 (-3.940)	-0.008 (-4.220)	-0.009 (-4.423)
Cumulative change in GDP[a] (percent)	-0.354 (-2.577)	-0.189 (-1.327)	-0.519 (-3.312)	-0.282 (-1.767)
Gini coefficient[b]	—	0.769 (2.261)	—	0.975 (2.158)
Expenditure dummy[c]	—	-20.399 (-2.788)	—	-15.530 (1.598)
Constant	26.351 (2.343)	17.947 (1.052)	66.277 (5.167)	46.692 (2.060)
R-squared	0.463	0.781	0.647	0.805
N	20	20	20	20

Note: The dependent variable is the percentage of the population below the poverty line.
a. From start of transition to year of poverty measurement.
b. The income or consumption Gini.
c. The dummy that equals 1 if Gini is based on consumption expenditures; 0 if for income.
Source: Regressions are based on PPP poverty rates (1996–99) and World Bank/EBRD data for 20 countries.

and sustain growth can, if not properly designed, have adverse distributional effects. In other cases, however, there are no obvious tradeoffs between pro-growth policies and pro-distribution policies. In fact, there may be large complementarities. Stabilization, for example, has been critical to restoring growth but also has had positive distributional outcomes. Similarly, efforts to reduce rent-seeking and corruption can be simultaneously beneficial for growth and for the distribution of income. Even when policy tradeoffs exist, policymakers can dampen their poverty impact by putting in place adequate safeguards and safety nets. Keane and Prasad (2000), for example, argue that Poland's social safety net has been relatively successful in achieving this purpose.

Countries have not always made the most pro-poor choices nor designed policies to dampen their adverse impact on the poor. Indeed, one of the most striking features of the transition is the divergence in the importance that governments have attached to maximizing social welfare and protecting the poor. To understand why this has been the case, we must look at the institutional and political context in which policy decisions are made.

Politics and Institutions as Determinants of Policy Choices

The importance that countries attribute to fighting poverty and the extent to which this importance is reflected in policy choices vary greatly across transition countries. At one extreme are countries, such as Poland, that spend a sizable fraction of their GDP redistributing resources toward the bottom of the distribution, with a demonstrated positive impact on poverty. At the other extreme are countries (such as Georgia and other members of the CIS) where, despite high levels of poverty and social distress, policymakers consistently fail to deliver on even the smallest commitment to the poor. How can these differences be explained? It is not just a question of assets and leadership. All politicians, if asked, will claim to be worried about poverty and social outcomes. But the incentives for politicians are radically different across ECA countries and consequently so are policy choices and actions. This is because policy choices do not occur in a vacuum but are embedded in political and institutional structures. Poverty and inequality outcomes are as much a product of *institutions*—or the lack of institutions—as of policies.

Institutions in Europe and Central Asia did not emerge overnight but were heavily conditioned by *historical legacies*. Countries with a longer experience of sovereignty began the transition with more developed public-sector institutions and better trained officials than did countries that gained independence more recently. They were also more likely to have adopted variants of socialism that provided for a smaller role of the state in the economy and allowed for a greater development of market-supporting institutions. As a consequence, transition in these countries required a lot less building and rebuilding of the state and private sectors (World Bank 2000a).

Countries with a longer experience of sovereignty also had—with some exceptions—more developed civil societies and a stronger tradition of collective action influencing the political process. Many of the Central European countries realized early on the strong interdependence between economic and political liberalization. Some initiated reforms as early as the 1960s. Although many of the reforms were later suppressed, these experiences provided a blueprint for the way in which social movements could bring about change. Much of the transition in Central Europe was initiated by civil society and fundamentally shaped by a process of social consultation and consensus. In contrast, in Russia and the CIS, the transition was initiated from the top by the Communist Party and managed by former Communist Party officials. A small group of well-placed elites made choices about the political system and economic reforms with little—if any—participation by broader segments of society. In many cases the same groups that controlled the allocation of state resources under socialism retained power after the transition; they simply legitimized their power through pseudo and partial reforms. Not surprisingly, given the low involvement of civil society, the CIS countries have demonstrated much less commitment to poverty alleviation and redistribution than have the countries of Central and Eastern Europe.

Country characteristics and history partly explain why attitudes toward reform and toward poverty have diverged so much. An equally important explanation lies in the *incentive structures* that enabled a postsocialist society and its power holders to abandon old socialist channels of distribution of power and resources and switch to the new market-based mechanisms. Where reform has stalled, the resistance to further reform has come not from those who have lost out—"the unemployed, the impoverished pensioners, or the superfluous state bureaucrats"—but from the winners of the initial stages—the enterprise insiders, commercial bankers, and local officials. The goal of these actors has been to "stall the reforms in a partial reform equilibrium that generates concentrated rents for themselves, while imposing high costs on the rest of the society" (Hellman 1998, 205).

The huge gains that can be made from the partiality of the reforms are the reason for the obstruction. Partial reforms have allowed the winners, usually the traditional socialist elites in combination with some entrepreneurial newcomers, to legalize the power relationships that existed at the end of socialism. Enterprise managers have been able to privatize the enterprises they manage and create banks to process the subsidies they extract from their former colleagues in power. This has given way to the phenomenon known as *state capture:* control of the policy-making and legislative processes by vested interests in collusion with those holding political power (box 3.2). Once these rent-seeking channels have been established, managers and politicians are reluctant to let democratization or market expansion move further as this could jeopardize the new status quo. The outcome is that the winners' consumption increases at a cost of deeper and more prolonged decline in the GDP. Data that relates the pace of reforms to the measurements of inequality support these observations: countries that have the highest variance of the reform score, used here as a proxy for "a more unbalanced progress across the different dimensions of economic reform," have the highest increase in the Gini coefficients and the highest increase in income of the top quintile of the population (Hellman 1998).

Box 3.2   State Capture and Administrative Corruption

State capture occurs when private interests use payments to public officials to influence the legal framework and policy-making process in an effort to secure rents and privileges. The degree of state capture is one of the variables that helps explain the divergence of outcomes among transition economies. This phenomenon is at the root of what may be broadly defined as pervasive corruption in parts of the ECA region, but it is distinct from *administrative corruption* per se and requires a different set of actions to confront it.

Figure 3.3 uses firm-level data to assess the extent of both state capture and administrative corruption across ECA countries. Administrative corruption measures bribes as a share of firms' annual revenues. State capture measures the average of the share of firms that report a significant impact on their business from several forms of state capture. These forms include "sale" of parliamentary votes and presidential decrees, sale of criminal court decisions to private interests, corrupt mishandling of Central Bank funds, and illegal contributions by private actors to political parties.

There is substantial variation in administrative corruption across ECA countries. Payments for administrative corruption range from a low of 1.1 percent of firm revenues in Croatia to a high of 5.7 percent in Azerbaijan. There is even more striking variation in the incidence of state capture: while only 6 percent of firms in Slovenia report a significant impact on their business from state capture, the share in Azerbaijan is 40 percent. If we group countries by quadrants of figure 3.3, we find that the first round of European Union accession economies, characterized by relatively low inequality and poverty, fall solidly into the bottom left quadrant. In comparison, most of the Commonwealth of Independent States, with its high inequality and high poverty rates, falls clearly into the top right quadrant (high state capture, high administrative corruption).

Figure 3.3   State Capture and Administrative Corruption

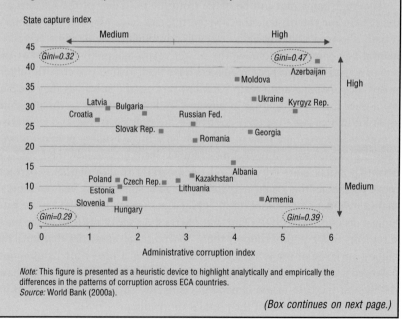

Note: This figure is presented as a heuristic device to highlight analytically and empirically the differences in the patterns of corruption across ECA countries.
Source: World Bank (2000a).

(Box continues on next page.)

Box 3.2 *(continued)*

Patterns of state capture are rooted in the type of political and institutional regime that evolved in the postsocialist period. Countries with a greater degree of political competition are less likely to suffer from state capture. In these more pluralistic regimes with developed channels of political contestability, competition between interest groups creates policing and accountability mechanisms that hold politicians and bureaucrats in check. At the other extreme are countries that have undergone partial political reforms but do not provide sufficient civil liberties and political competition to hold state officials accountable. In these countries the checks on abuses of power are insufficient to counterbalance the loss of control that resulted from the dismantling of the old system. Power tends to be concentrated at the top and distributed top down through the same types of patron-client structures that existed under the socialist system. There is one key difference, however: before, the Communist Party monopolized power; today the breakup of the party's monopoly and the proliferation of patron-client relationships contributes to disorder and institutional dysfunction. Rent-seeking arrangements are more pervasive and long term. Corruption in this context has become a systemic problem, complete with its own institutions.

Economic competition interacts strongly with political competition in determining susceptibility to capture. Lack of economic competition facilitates the concentration of productive assets and generates huge rents, increasing the incentives for old elites to retain control of the state and/or for new private interests to attempt to capture it. In countries where national wealth is heavily concentrated in a few key resource-based sectors (Azerbaijan, Russia, Kazakhstan, and Turkmenistan), incentives for private interests to try to secure control and ownership of these productive assets were (and remain) huge. The simultaneity of economic and political reform allowed these powerful private interests to influence the legislative and policy-making processes to gain control.

The scope of the countries that may be affected by these managerial strategies is large: of the 19 postsocialist countries, 10 have been listed as intermediary reformers, 4 as slow reformers, and only 5 have been qualified as advanced reformers. Among intermediary reformers, one finds many countries where the slowness of the reforms can be traced to the incentives faced by managers, bureaucrats, and politicians (Amelina 2000). In this context progress on reforms can be made only if the winners are restrained and their influence over the state reduced. This is a complicated challenge for two reasons: first, because of the path-dependent nature of postsocialist institutions, with each institution serving political and economic functions simultaneously; second, because the formal renaming of these functions does not necessarily mean their de facto transformation. For example, although local officials legally do not monitor the fulfillment of economic plans, they may have special relations with enterprise managers and assist them in obtaining preferential credits. A better understanding of postsocialist institutions and incentives is needed to be able to differentiate between actual and pro-forma reform.

Collusive socialist political and economic interactions in Europe and Central Asia can be carried over into the postsocialist structures, effectively slowing down the reform process, curbing economic growth, and increasing income inequality. Institutionally path-dependent structures aimed at supplying winners with rents rather than at promoting market-oriented production can perpetuate coordination failures between better- and worse-connected producers and politicians. Such coordination failures may leave a country in an undevelopment trap rather than propel it into the virtuous circle of more efficient production in a more democratic and more transparent environment.[2]

Channels of Transmission

As we have seen so far, poverty outcomes are the result of a complex interaction between policies and institutions in the economic and the political spheres. But how did these large-scale economic and political developments work themselves through to individual households and affect their living standards? The answer largely determines the type and characteristics of the poverty we see in transition economies. This makes it critical to the design of policies to help the poor.

Households have experienced the impact of macroeconomic developments and policy choices in three ways: through changes in the demand for labor, which fed through to changes in labor earnings—the main source of household incomes; through the collapse of fiscal transfers, which mediate between market-determined incomes and household consumption levels; and through changes in relative prices, which affect the consumption basket and purchasing power of households. Each of these three channels will be discussed in turn.

Shrinking Demand for Labor

People have mainly experienced the impact of economic reform as a change in paid employment and in what wages can buy. Falls in output across Europe and Central Asia have entailed large drops in real wages and employment (figures 3.4 and 3.5). These effects have been amplified by the need to improve productivity and reduce the labor hoarding common to the old system. The result has been high open unemployment in many countries—a relatively new phenomenon after decades of central planning—and high hidden unemployment in others.[3]

Figure 3.4   Changes in Employment in ECA Countries, 1991, 1994, 1998

Employment index (1989=100)

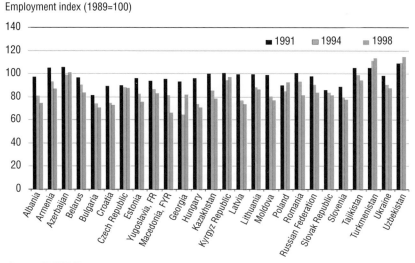

Source: UNICEF, Transmonee database.

All transition economies have experienced a sharp drop in the demand for labor and a decline in labor supply over time. But how these two underlying developments have manifested themselves in the labor market—in terms of open unemployment rates and tradeoffs between real wage and employment adjustment—has varied across countries.

Patterns of labor market adjustment. At the risk of oversimplifying, we can distinguish between two broad patterns of labor market adjustment. One is more typical of the countries of Central Europe, where the drop in output was more moderate and a steady recovery has been under way for some time. In these countries labor market adjustment occurred mainly through a sharp decline in employment, especially in the early stages of transition. During these early stages, job destruction rates in contracting enterprises far exceeded job creation rates in new or expanding firms, leading to high open unemployment. Between 1989 and 1992, rates of job destruction in the Central European economies averaged 12 to 16 percent annually, while job creation was a negligible 1 to 3 percent per year. The result was a sharp rise in unemployment from nearly zero to a range of 10 to 15 percent in Central Europe, 20 percent in Bulgaria, and 4 percent in the Czech Republic. Slow job destruction (and high inflows into self-employment and out of the labor force) in the Czech Republic

Figure 3.5 Changes in Real Wages

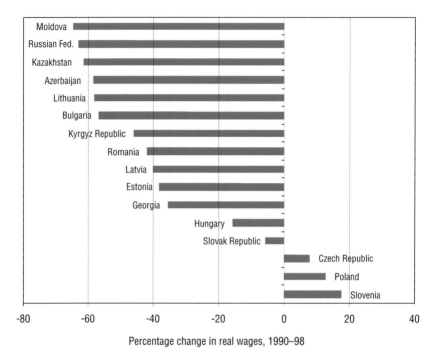

Percentage change in real wages, 1990–98

Source: UNICEF, Transmonee database.

underpinned the relatively low initial unemployment there, while rapid job destruction in Bulgaria was partly to blame for its high unemployment rate. But overall the forces at work were very similar across CSB countries, with job destruction concentrated in existing firms and job creation happening almost exclusively in new ones.

Since 1993, job destruction rates in the Central European countries have slowed dramatically to 2 to 3 percent per year, with the exception of Hungary, where it remained at 5.7 percent (Boeri, Burda, and Kollos 1998). And job creation rates have increased slightly to 3 to 4 percent per year (again with the exception of Hungary, where it remained at 1.3 percent). This has reduced the rate of joblessness. However, despite the strong resumption of GDP growth, job creation remains sluggish (table 3.4). The recovery of output has not resulted in much net aggregate employment growth. Differences in standards of living between those with jobs and those without them are large, and poverty is closely linked to unemployment.

The second pattern of labor market adjustment is more typical of the Commonwealth of Independent States (and of some slower reformers elsewhere, such as Romania). Here the declines in GDP were more abrupt and of longer duration, and proportional cuts in employment were politically and socially untenable. Enterprise restructuring has been limited (partly because of the slowness of the reforms proper). The reduction or nonpayment of wages (through the accumulation of wage arrears) has been the dominant mode of labor market adjustment. In many of these countries, people have turned to self-employment as a means of coping with low-paying (or even nonpaying) wage jobs. In the Central European countries self-employment first grew in the service sector and then rapidly expanded into manufacturing (Dabrowski, Gomulka, and Rostowski 2000). In contrast, self-employment in the CIS has been mainly limited to subsistence-type agriculture and small-scale trade. Registered unemployment is low,

Table 3.4   Growth, Employment, and Wages in Selected ECA Countries, 1990–98

Country and indicator	1990	1991	1992	1993	1994	1995	1996	1997	1998
Poland									
Real GDP (1989=100)	88.4	82.2	84.4	87.6	92.2	98.7	104.7	111.9	117.3
Real wages (1989=100)	75.6	75.4	73.3	71.2	71.6	73.7	77.9	82.4	85.2
Employment (1989=100)	95.8	90.1	86.3	84.3	85.1	86.7	88.3	93.3	93.4
Registered unemployment rate	3.4	9.2	12.9	14.9	16.5	15.2	14.3	11.5	10.0
Czech Republic									
Real GDP (1989=100)	98.8	84.7	79.3	79.8	82.0	87.2	90.5	90.8	88.7
Real wages (1989=100)	93.6	68.9	76.0	78.8	84.9	92.2	100.4	102.3	101.0
Employment (1989=100)	99.2	90.0	87.7	87.9	88.5	90.9	92.0	91.5	88.2
Registered unemployment rate	0.3	2.6	3.1	3.0	3.3	3.0	3.1	4.3	6.0
Bulgaria									
Real GDP (1989=100)	90.9	80.3	74.4	73.3	74.6	76.2	67.9	63.2	65.4
Real wages (1989=100)	111.5	68.0	76.7	77.6	63.7	60.2	49.6	40.1	48.1
Employment (1989=100)	93.9	81.6	75.0	73.8	74.3	75.2	75.3	73.3	71.2
Registered unemployment rate	—	—	13.2	15.8	14.0	11.4	11.1	14.0	12.2
Russian Federation									
Real GDP (1990=100)	100.0	95.0	81.2	74.2	64.8	62.2	60.0	60.6	57.8
Real wages (1990=100)	100.0	93.9	63.1	63.4	58.4	42.1	47.7	50.0	37.0
Employment (1990=100)	100.0	98.0	95.8	94.2	91.0	88.2	87.6	85.8	84.5
Registered unemployment rate	—	0.1	0.8	1.1	2.2	3.2	3.4	2.8	2.7
Georgia									
Real GDP (1990=100)	100.0	71.9	40.7	24.7	21.9	22.4	24.7	27.4	28.2
Real wages (1990=100)	100.0	68.8	45.4	21.7	30.1	25.4	37.9	51.3	64.5
Employment (1990=100)	100.0	91.1	71.8	64.8	63.3	69.9	73.7	80.8	80.8
Registered unemployment rate	—	0.2	2.3	6.6	3.6	2.6	2.4	5.0	5.0

— Not available
Source: World Bank SIMA database; UNICEF (1999).

but definitions based on household surveys suggest much higher rates of actual unemployment and inactivity. Hidden unemployment (workers retain formal ties to an enterprise but neither work nor receive a wage) is also high. Huge falls in output—with nominally less adjustment in employment—have meant that labor productivity has fallen. The result has been a steep fall in real wages and a big rise in the number of the working poor. In these countries the differences between employed and unemployed are small, and the working poor constitute the bulk of the poor. GDP growth—where it has happened—has not brought about a recovery of employment levels. Armenia is an extreme case: despite continuous positive growth between 1994 and 1999 (averaging 5.2 percent per year), employment declined by 8.5 percent. As a result of this continued drop in employment, the nonemployed proportion of the labor force increased by almost 55 percent.

Has one type of labor market adjustment been more socially costly? The answer depends greatly on the success of efforts to dampen and distribute the adjustment burden. Arguably, temporary unemployment, to the extent it is associated with a redeployment of factors to more productive endeavors, can lead to large economy-wide improvements in productivity and hence to better growth prospects. If some of this "growth payoff" can be redistributed to those bearing the burden—the unemployed—in the form of either transfers (unemployment insurance or early retirement) or investment (training), then the social costs of this mode of adjustment can be considerably dampened. Keane and Prasad (2000) argue that this has been the case in Poland. The success of this mode of adjustment, however, hinges on quick implementation of the reforms needed to allow a new, job-creating private sector to emerge. In the absence of such a dynamic new private sector, countries can get stuck in a spiral of fast job destruction with no new job creation. Bulgaria is an example.

Avoiding enterprise restructuring and job destruction, however, does not appear to be a recipe for lowering overall social costs. The CIS mode of adjustment—prolonged decline in output and productivity (linked to the lack of restructuring), stagnant employment flows, and large drops in real wages—leaves little hope for future growth and job creation. Although the adjustment burden may have been spread more widely than in CSB countries, its poverty consequences have been more severe. Moreover, in the absence of serious enterprise restructuring, prospects for increasing labor demand and productivity (the key to restoring incomes and lowering poverty) look fairly bleak.

There are useful examples from other countries of the tradeoffs faced in opting for one or the other mode of adjustment. Mexico in the early

1980s chose a path of large consensual declines in real wages to protect employment levels. This was hailed at the time as a sign of real wage flexibility, and unemployment levels remained below 5 percent during the whole decade. But despite widespread structural reforms, productivity growth remained stagnant and with it overall growth. With the benefit of hindsight, many analysts pointed to the failure of labor to reallocate between and within sectors as one of the reasons for Mexico's poor growth record in the 1980s (World Bank 1994). Poor productivity performance contributed to the structural imbalances that culminated in a crisis in the mid-1990s.

Spain had a different experience. During the 1980s and early 1990s, it drastically reduced its state sector and opened up the economy as part of its integration into the broader European economy. Spain protected real wage levels and underwent large labor shedding. As a consequence, it experienced double-digit unemployment for almost two decades. At its peak, unemployment reached 20 percent. Surprisingly, poverty and total income inequality declined (Revenga 1991; Jimeno and others 2000). This was because Spain put in place an extensive welfare system: in other words, it successfully redistributed some of its "growth payoff" (which was substantial) to those who had been hurt. Although unemployment remained a serious social problem, its costs in terms of poverty were significantly dampened.

Determinants of the labor market adjustment. Was the type of labor market adjustment in transition economies dictated entirely by the size of the output collapse? Or did the choice of policies and institutions play an important role? An important determinant of what happened to real wages was inflation. Large declines in real wages appear linked to the failure to stabilize quickly: those countries that experienced high average inflation rates during the period evidenced the largest declines in real wages. In some cases, such as Russia, this has been emphasized as a sign of real wage flexibility. A more pessimistic interpretation would suggest the failure of institutional mechanisms to protect the purchasing power of wages. Despite massive real wage declines, there was surprisingly little movement in employment—across sectors, between contracting and growing firms, or into and out of unemployment. This stagnation in employment flows most likely reflects the lack of alternative opportunities to low-wage employment in existing state and privatized enterprises.

In addition to stabilization, other factors influenced the type of labor market adjustment that countries followed. One was the extent to which hard budget constraints were imposed on existing enterprises, forcing them

Box 3.3   The Resurgence of Inflation Hurts the Poor

The 1998 financial crisis in Russia—although triggered by the East Asian crisis—was the result of structural weaknesses in the Russian economy. Inflation in Russia rose sharply in 1998–99. Other countries also saw a resurgence of inflation. By 1995 Albania, Bulgaria, and Romania had all succeeded in bringing inflation down. In Albania the 12-month inflation rate had fallen to 6 percent, while in Bulgaria and Romania it had declined to 35 percent. But by end-1997, inflation had shot back up to 40 percent, 580 percent, and 150 percent respectively. In Albania the emergence and rapid growth of pyramid schemes led to the financial crisis and public disorder of 1997, and to the resurgence of inflation. In Bulgaria widespread use of soft budget constraints in industry in the face of a weak financial sector led to hyperinflationary conditions. In Romania large financial support of farming and energy proved to be inflationary. These inflationary crises were unambiguously bad for poverty: absolute poverty in Russia (measured at the $2.15 PPP line) increased from 13.3 percent in 1996 to 18.8 percent in 1998, while in Romania poverty rose by 50 percent between 1996 and 1997.

Source: Chapter 1, box 1.1.

to restructure and improve productivity. In Central Europe hard budget constraints led state-owned enterprises (SOEs) to shed labor, restructure their product mix, and improve performance and productivity. Kollo (1996), for example, found that SOEs in Hungary shed labor even when experiencing growth in sales. Similarly, Pinto and van Winjbergen (1995) found that even in the early stages of transition Polish state firms underwent major employment restructuring. A second important factor was the extent to which new private sector entry was allowed through the creation of open and competitive markets. Here the difference between CSB and CIS is striking: the complete liberalization of entry in Poland, Hungary, and the Czech Republic made the new private sector the motor of growth and job creation. In Poland new private activity in manufacturing grew by as much as 40 percent in 1991 and then expanded at more than 25 percent per year for the next five years. In Russia new private activity remains modest. Much of this sluggishness is attributable to barriers to entry (including the bribe "tax"), as well as to the absence of truly competitive product markets (Boeri, Burda, and Kollos 1998). A third important influence over the mode of labor market adjustment has been the maintenance of a minimum credible safety net that allows workers to be laid off without falling into poverty. In Poland or Hungary workers could rely on a safety net, which functioned as a floor on real wage declines. In most of the CIS, safety nets have collapsed, and workers hang on to low-paying (or even nonpaying) jobs in order to keep their access to basic social services, and because the alternative—no income and no prospect of getting paid—looks worse.

Constraints on employment growth. The recovery of output growth is clearly a precondition for employment growth. Yet, as is evident from the CSB experience, output recovery and a recovery of employment have not always gone together. Even among the more successful reformers, employment growth has lagged behind output growth by a considerable (and increasing) margin (table 3.3). In Hungary—an extreme case of this—the number of jobs in 1997 was 30 percent lower than in 1989, even though output had recovered to its original level. There is one compelling reason to regard this "jobless" growth as a temporary phenomenon: transition was associated with a shift of labor from low-productivity activities to higher-productivity ones, and this will necessarily require that employment recover more slowly than output. However, these lags can be quite long: in Spain, for example, it took more than 15 years before employment growth caught up with output growth. The lag was partly attributable to policymakers' failure to tackle key structural labor market factors early on; they only did so after years of high unemployment. Once some of these critical structural issues were addressed, employment performance improved dramatically.[4] Indeed, the Spanish experience testifies to both the dangers of delay in confronting structural labor market problems and the benefits when action is finally taken.

There are a number of other factors that may help explain why employment growth has lagged behind output growth. First of all, despite years of downsizing, relative overstaffing remains a problem in many enterprises formerly run by the state. Even after the significant layoffs during the early 1990s, state-owned firms in Poland and the Czech Republic still have higher employment levels, other things being equal, than non-state-owned firms (Basu, Estrin, and Svejnar 1994). Second, existing idle capacity in most CSB economies is of poor quality, which may constrain the increase in employment associated with rising output (Boeri, Burda, and Kollos 1998). Since capital and labor are largely complementary in the production process, employment growth will be faster (for a given rise in output) if there is unused capital capacity that can quickly be brought on line. But if firms need to invest in new plant and equipment, the recovery of employment will be slowed down. Third, labor costs—especially nonwage components—are fairly high and may contribute to reducing overall labor demand. Skill mismatches also remain an important factor, since firms may have to factor into their labor costs a significant training component. Finally, rigidities outside the labor market (transport and housing problems, for example) can negatively affect employment outcomes.

Increasing the "job content" of output growth in the transition economies will require labor market reforms as well as reforms outside the labor market. Increasing the flexibility of housing markets and breaking up
infrastructure monopolies can be indispensable complements to labor
market reform.[5] Bulgaria, for example, has many of the features of
"Eurosclerotic" labor markets, but the reasons for its high unemployment
rates go well beyond narrow labor market issues (box 3.4).

Box 3.4   The Bulgarian Labor Market and Eurosclerosis

Many features of Bulgaria's labor market resemble those of the labor markets of France, Germany, and Italy. Bulgaria's unemployment is stubbornly stable at a double-digit level; long-term
unemployment, measured as the fraction of workers who have been unemployed for more than
a year, is about 50 percent; and the incidence of youth unemployment is high. Indeed, among
the Bulgarian workers unemployed for at least one year, as many as 25 percent are 24 years of
age or younger. Like some of the more poorly performing European countries, Bulgaria features
a dramatic level of "discouraged workers" (unemployed workers who appear to quit the labor
force). An unemployed person in Bulgaria is as likely to become employed as he or she is likely
to drop from the labor force. Finally, unemployment has a strong regional dimension, with a
dispersion in the unemployment rates across regions that is both increasing and persistent.

The term "Eurosclerosis" refers to an ailing labor market—one that displays the features
we have just described. Such a market is regulated by labor market policies and institutions that
are very rigid (for example, high payroll taxes, restrictive protection legislation, high minimum
wages, high unemployment benefits, and strong unions that do not coordinate their bargaining
activities). We will briefly review these characteristics in Bulgaria and compare them with
those observed in France, Germany, and Italy.

Payroll contributions. The level of payroll contributions in Bulgaria is by far the highest
among those observed in Central and Western European countries. By looking in further detail
at the composition and at the magnitude of payroll contributions in Bulgaria, we can see that the
sum of social security contributions, health care taxes, and contributions to the unemployment
fund reach 60 percent of gross income for many workers. The bulk of this burden is linked to
the social security contributions, which reached 54 percent of gross income in 1997 for primary workers, a set of workers that is entitled to early retirement benefits in light of their
particular jobs (for example, miners and teachers). The other contributions (for health care and
the unemployment fund) are sizable but still in line with those seen in Europe.

Employment protection legislation. Despite several revisions since the beginning of the
transition, there is an urgent need to revise the most restrictive provisions in Bulgaria's labor
code. The procedures for collective redundancies are quite rigid, they require difficult coordination with the trade unions, and they represent an obstacle to firm-level restructuring. While
employment termination for individual contracts is technically easy, there seems to be a
practical difficulty in implementing dismissal because of the jurisdictional bias in favor of
labor. In other dimensions, however, Bulgaria's labor code suits the needs of a market economy.
It avoids some of the restrictive provisions found in the codes of neighboring transition
economies (for example, the prohibition of fixed-term contracts and of part-time and additional work and unduly onerous standards governing firings and lay-offs).

(Box continues on next page.)

Box 3.4 *(continued)*

Minimum wage. One way to evaluate the minimum wage is to compare it with the average wage. While this ratio in Bulgaria was very high at the beginning of the transition, its level was cut throughout the 1990s and is now around 25 percent. In countries such as France and Germany, the ratio of the minimum wage to the average wage is much higher (about 50 percent).

Unemployment benefits. There are at least three ways to describe the generosity of the unemployment benefit level. The first one is the gross replacement rate, which represents the percentage of the unemployment benefit with respect to the average wage. The second measure is the coverage rate: the percentage of unemployed who receive unemployment benefits. A further measure is the duration of the unemployment period when workers can receive unemployment benefits. In each of these dimensions, Bulgaria's generosity is less than that observed in most other CEE economies. It also is lower than the indicators observed in France.

Union behavior. Unions in Bulgaria are fairly strong, at least when union membership is measured by union density (the share of employees who choose to join a union). However, industrial relations in Bulgaria are characterized by a high degree of cooperation between unions, and between unions and employer representatives, and wage pressures in Bulgaria do not appear to be too high. Some fine-tuning is needed (in particular, decentralized bargaining at the local level to address high regional unemployment persistence and differentials).

Conclusion. In sum, Bulgaria's payroll contributions are high, even when compared with the ailing European labor markets. However, its other labor market policies and institutions do not appear to be as rigid as those in France, Germany, and Italy. The poor performance of Bulgaria's labor market can be attributed only partly to its labor market institutions. The real culprit is Bulgaria's chronic inability to restructure its ailing industrial sector and to tackle fundamental structural problems.

Source: Garibaldi (2000).

Shrinking Budgets

We have discussed the first channel through which households and living standards are affected by macroeconomic developments—namely, changes in labor demand. A second channel is changes in fiscal taxation and spending.

The severe recession at the onset of the transition led to large declines in government revenues throughout Europe and Central Asia. For many of the CIS countries, independence from the Soviet Union also meant the loss of large fiscal transfers from Moscow, which compounded the declines in government revenues. Average tax collection rates for the CIS countries fell from 28 percent of GDP in 1992 to 22 percent of GDP in 1998. For the CSB countries, tax revenues fell from over 40 percent of GDP in 1989 to about 33 percent of GDP by 1992. These averages hide huge intercountry variations in the magnitude of the decline. In Georgia, for example, government revenues (excluding grants) dropped to single digits; in 1997 they represented only 7 percent of GDP. In the same year the Kyrgyz Republic and Tajikistan had collection rates of about 14 percent of GDP. In contrast, Hungary, the Czech Republic, Estonia, and Poland in 1997 had tax burdens exceeding 30 percent of GDP—comparable to tax collection rates in some advanced countries.

What happened to revenues dictated to a large extent whether countries could cushion the social impact of the transition. Many of the CIS countries simply did not have the fiscal space to maintain broad safety nets. Faced with a sharp drop in revenues and the need to stabilize their economies, governments had no choice but to cut expenditures. For the CIS countries, aggregate expenditures fell from about 50 percent of GDP in 1992 to 29 percent of GDP in 1998; for the CSB countries, expenditures fell from 53 percent in 1989 to 38 percent in 1998. In some cases the expenditure cuts were dramatic: in Georgia general government expenditures declined from around 36 percent of GDP in 1991–92 to just 11.6 percent in 1995. This was not enough to maintain basic social transfers—not even pensions, which fell to about US$6 per month, before recovering to US$12 per month in 1997. Many of the CIS countries had to slash spending in health and education. This increased informal and under-the-table payments and hurt the poor more than the rich. Poor budget management and implementation in the face of shrinking revenues led to pervasive arrears in public sector payments, wages, and pensions in parts of the CIS (for example, in Georgia, Moldova, and Russia). These arrears have had a highly regressive aspect since they fall disproportionately on the poor and are the highest in poor regions (Lehman, Wadsworth, and Acquisti 1999; Lehman, Wadsworth, and Yemtsov 2000).

The adverse impact on the poor came from two separate forces: first, the sheer size of the adjustment involved; second, the patterns of fiscal adjustment, which failed to protect pro-poor expenditures.

Could fiscal adjustment have been carried out in a way that hurt the poor less? There is little doubt that, at least in the CIS, the quality of fiscal adjustment could have been much better. Across-the-board cuts in expenditures, particularly for social services and infrastructure, worsened inequality and hence increased poverty. The absence of a safety net made it hard to restructure and lay off workers, slowing down growth and lengthening the recession. Broad cuts in expenditure also made it more difficult for market-supporting institutions to develop: cash-starved governments that cannot pay their civil servants face greater difficulty in building public administration and regulatory bodies that are effective and accountable.

In Central Europe, South East Europe, and the Baltics, unlike in the Commonwealth of Independent States, expenditures were kept at very high levels. Spending perhaps was too high since high labor taxation levels linked to generous social security systems may be stifling growth and employment creation. Yet on the positive side, high levels of expenditures, especially in the social sectors, helped cushion the impact of the transition and made reforms more acceptable. In Poland pensions were critical in preventing the elderly from falling into poverty (Keane and Prasad 2000). Indeed, high expenditures in the CSB may have buoyed support for reforms and been instrumental in the recovery of growth. The current challenge for the CSB countries is to reduce the fiscal burden imposed by these high levels of social spending without undermining their positive protective effects.

In many countries the transition brought about a needed overhaul of the tax system. In the pretransition economies, most tax revenue was generated from three sources: the turnover tax, the enterprise tax, and the payroll tax. The taxation system was grounded on the information provided in the plans, on the processing of payments through the state's monobank, and on the concentration of economic activities in a few large enterprises in the public sector. Moreover, considerations of equity or efficiency were not relevant to tax policy. The transition, however, fundamentally changed the old basis for taxation, and reform of tax policy and institutions became essential to the fiscal adjustment. Within the reduced overall burden of tax collection, transition saw a shift toward indirect taxes and introduced progressivity in income tax collections. The value added tax (VAT) has become a central part of the tax system in most ECA countries. While single rate VATs are regressive—and therefore trade off equity for efficiency considerations—reasonable tax thresholds and exemptions for essential food and medicine items have attempted to protect the poor. The equity considerations are also reflected in the progressivity of personal income taxes adopted in all transition economies. But weaknesses in tax administration, particularly in many CIS countries, have undermined the progressivity of the tax system. The collection of taxes from many of the largest taxpayers has been lax, and pernicious tax offsets have developed. Modernizing tax administration and expanding the taxpayer base would provide scope for generating additional revenues that could help finance pro-poor expenditures.

Changes in Relative Prices

A third transmission channel from macroeconomic developments to the household operates through changes in relative prices, which affect what household incomes can buy. Of particular importance to the poor are the prices of essential commodities.

In pretransition days the production and pricing patterns of key commodities consumed by the poor, such as utilities, were set administratively to facilitate the fulfillment of centrally prepared plans. Gas, electricity, and heating prices paid by residential consumers were particularly low. Households received a cross-subsidy from large (typically industrial) consumers who paid higher-than-average tariffs despite lower-than-average costs. Households also enjoyed an across-the-board subsidy provided to all consumers. These subsidies came in the form of budgetary transfers financing the capital costs of energy production, transport, and distribution.

Very early in the transition process, it became evident that the low household utility tariffs were unsustainable. The budget lacked the resources to cover the costs of the price subsidies, and the high industrial tariffs hurt the competitiveness of the industrial sector. Large price adjustments became necessary. In Ukraine household energy tariffs increased many times over in real terms between 1992 and 1995. (They increased fourfold for electricity and natural gas and more than twelvefold for district heating.) In other CIS countries large increases in tariffs also took place. In the CSB countries, the increases were less dramatic since the initial level of price distortions and subsidies was lower. Nonetheless, in Hungary, electricity, gas, and heating tariffs increased by about 50 percent between 1989 and 1999.

These large price increases directly hurt the poor, already suffering from declining incomes and increasing inequalities during this period. To mitigate the adverse effects of higher prices, governments introduced various subsidy schemes targeted at low-income households. Of particular importance were (1) life-line tariffs; (2) compensation to households for utility bills (which exceeded a given percentage of monthly household income); (3) tolerance of delinquent residential consumers (no disconnections for nonpayment); (4) price discounts for selected types of households; and (5) various types of earmarked cash and noncash transfers to poor households to help them meet their utility expenditures.

Different countries adopted different schemes. Many countries, including the Kyrgyz Republic, introduced lifeline rates for electricity. (Residential users were provided with an initial fixed amount of electricity that was priced below the cost of provision; higher blocks of usage were charged at progressively higher unit prices.) Many states in the former Soviet Union introduced subsidies to limit the burden placed by utility expenditures on household budgets. Cash transfer schemes earmarked for utility payments were started in Latvia, Hungary, Bulgaria, and several other countries.

These schemes differed in terms of their efficiency and equity impacts, but the share of expenditures spent on utilities remained within tolerable limits for most households, including poor households.[6] Despite the price increases, most countries retained energy prices at levels well below world prices. However, the effectiveness of such as strategy from a poverty-alleviation point of view remains questionable. A quicker move to world energy prices, with more focused targeting of assistance to the poor, might have done a better job of promoting growth and protecting the poor (box 3.5).

The hike in utility prices was perhaps the most significant from the perspective of the poor, but other price adjustments—for sugar, cooking oil, grains, and medicines—also affected the poor adversely by eroding their purchasing power. Most of these price increases took place in the early years of the transition. During 1992 the prices of bread, vegetable oil, and sugar in Russia rose three to four times faster than inflation.[7] Although the initial relative price changes were undoubtedly strong, particularly in the early years, they have stabilized with the progress of reforms.

Box 3.5   Energy Subsidies and Poverty: Why Slow Adjustment May Have Hurt the Poor

In Georgia the electricity sector provided power in 1999 at US$190 million below total cost (a subsidy roughly equivalent to 6.3 percent of GDP). The gap was mainly financed by arrears to energy sector suppliers. Georgia pursued this policy to protect its population from the impact of the steep price increases that would have been required had electricity been supplied at cost. But as documented in Chapter 8, these attempts to provide social protection via subsidized energy prices failed. Not only was this social protection very badly targeted, the resultant lack of cash in the system to buy fuel meant that there were persistent shortages of electricity. Like all FSU countries, network electricity access in Georgia is available to all, and depriving people of the actual service affects the poor disproportionately. They can least afford the more expensive alternatives to electricity. Arguably the implied subsidy of US$ 190 million could have done more to alleviate poverty had it been targeted directly, or devoted to alternative uses.

In Azerbaijan in 1999, US$250 million of the country's oil and gas was provided without payment for distribution to the economy and population through the electricity and gas system (an implied subsidy of 6.2 percent of GDP). All households—regardless of whether they were poor or not—received very cheap energy. (All households enjoy an electricity tariff of only 2US cents in a largely thermal system, and collections are only 12 percent of billings, even at that low tariff.) The US$250 million could have had a bigger impact on poverty had the money been better targeted. The winter of 1999 saw long electricity blackouts on a daily basis. In rural areas the blackouts were in peak hours (even though there is no piped gas available there as a substitute). In the capital, Baku, electricity blackouts were off-peak (even though piped gas is available). Since Baku is much richer than the rural areas, this rationing scheme was profoundly antipoor.

Source: Lovei (2000) and discussions with World Bank staff.

Notes

1. This is altogether a different exercise than trying to decompose changes in poverty rates within a country into growth versus distribution components. Here we are explaining the variance in poverty rates *across* countries as a function of the cumulative change in output and its distribution, as measured by the end-period Gini. Since countries started from roughly similar levels of inequality, the end-period Gini does indeed proxy for the change in distribution. But the coefficients cannot be interpreted as reflecting the contribution of growth versus distribution over time.

2. On coordination failures as a source of underdevelopment see Hoff (2000).

3. This is not necessarily reflected in high rates of *registered* unemployment, since in many countries the benefits of registering are low. Labor force surveys are better at capturing actual unemployment and uniformly yield higher rates.

4. Although it remains in double-digits, unemployment in Spain just reached its *lowest* level since the early 1980s.

5. See, for example, the discussion of recent Spanish economic reforms and the resulting creation of employment in Jimeno and others (2000).

6. For details on different types of schemes implemented in different countries and the analysis of their impacts on the poor, see World Bank (2000b).

7. Thus measures of poverty based on an overall CPI deflator may understate the true rise in poverty.

References

Amelina, Maria. 2000. "Why is the Russian Peasant Still a Kolkhoznik?" *Post-Soviet Geography and Economics*.

Aslund, Anders, Peter Boone, and Simon Johnson. 1996. "How to Stabilize: Lessons from Post-Communist Countries." *Brookings Papers on Economic Activity* 1: 217–313.

Basu, S., S. Estrin, and J. Svejnar. 1994. "Employment and Wage Behavior of Enterprises in Transition." Paper presented at the workshop on Enterprise Adjustment in Eastern Europe, Word Bank, September 1994.

Boeri, Tito, Michael C. Burda, and Janos Kollos. 1998. *Mediating the Transition: Labour Markets in Central and Eastern Europe*. New York: Institute for East-West Studies.

Bunce, Valerie. 1999. "The Political Economy of Post-Socialism." Cornell University. Processed.

Dabrowski, Marek, Stanislaw Gomulka, and Jacek Rostowski. 2000. "Whence Reform? A Critique of the Stiglitz Perspective." CASE, London School of Economics and Central European University. Processed.

De Melo, Martha, Cevet Denizer, and Alan Gelb. 1996. "From Plan to Market: Patterns of Transition." World Bank Policy Research Paper 1564. Washington, D.C.

De Melo, Martha, and others. 2000. "Circumstance and Choice: The Role of Initial Conditions and Policies in Transition." World Bank. Processed.

EBRD (European Bank for Reconstruction and Development). 1999. *Transition Report*. London.

Garibaldi, Pietro. 2000. "Bulgarian Labor Market: An Overview." World Bank. March. Processed.

Hellman, Joel S. 1998. "Winners Take All: The Politics of Partial Reforms in Post-Communist Transitions." *World Politics* 50: 203–34.

Hoff, Karla. 2000. *Beyond Rosenstein-Rodan: The Modern Theory of Underdevelopment Traps*. Paper prepared for the World Bank ABCDE Conference, Washington, D.C. April.

Jimeno, Juan F., Olga Cantó, Ana Rute Cardoso, Maria Izquierdo, and Carlos Farinha Rodrigues. 2000. "Integration and Inequality: Lessons from the Accessions of Portugal and Spain to the EU." *Background Papers: Making Transition Work for Everyone: Poverty and Inequality in Europe and Central Asia.* Washington, D.C.

Keane, Michael P., and Eswar S. Prasad. 2000. "Inequality, Transfers and Growth: New Evidence from the Economic Transition in Poland." IMF Working Paper. Washington, D.C. May.

Kollo, Janos. 1996. "Employment and Wage Setting in Three Stages of Hungary's Labour Market Transition." Paper presented at the workshop on "Unemployment, Restructuring and the Labour Market in Eastern Europe and Russia." World Bank/EDI, Washington, D.C. May.

Lehman, Hartmut, Jonathan Wadsworth, and Alessandro Acquisti. 1999. "Grime and Punishment: Job Insecurity and Wage Arrears in the Russian Federation." *Journal of Comparative Economics* 27 (December): 595–617.

Lehman, Hartmut, Jonathan Wadsworth, and Ruslan Yemtsov. 2000. "A Month for the Company: Wage Arrears and the Distribution of Earnings in Russia." Heriot-Watt University. Processed.

Lovei, Laszlo. 2000. *Maintaining Utility Services for the Poor: Policies and Practices in Central and Eastern Europe and the Former Soviet Union.* Energy Sector Unit, Europe and Central Asia Region. World Bank, Washington, D.C.

Pinto, Brian, and Sweder van Winjbergen. 1995. "Ownership and Corporate Control in Poland: Why State Firms Defied the Odds." CEPR Discussion Paper 1273. December.

Revenga, Ana. 1991. "La Liberalización Económica y la Distribución de la Renta: La Experiencia Española." *Moneda y Crédito*, no. 193, pp. 179-224.

Selowsky, Marcelo, and Ricardo Martin. 1997. "Policy Performance and Output Growth in the Transition Economies." *Proceedings of the American Economic Association*, vol. 87, no. 2.

UNICEF. 1999. "Women in Transition." *Regional Monitoring Reports*, No. 6, Florence: UNICEF International Child Development Center.

World Bank. 1994. *Mexico: Country Economic Memorandum*. Washington, D.C.

———. 2000a. *Anticorruption in Transition: A Contribution to the Policy Debate*. Washington, D.C.

———. 2000b. *Maintaining Utility Services for the Poor*. Washington, D.C.

CHAPTER 4

A Look at Income Inequality

The transition from a planned economy to a market economy was expected to lead to a rise in income disparities as wages and incomes moved to reflect individual productivity and effort. What was not expected was the range of distributional outcomes that we have seen. Although income disparities between the rich and the poor increased in all transition economies during the late 1980s and 1990s, the extent of the increase varied greatly from country to country.

In Hungary, for example, the increase was surprisingly modest: the Gini coefficient for per capita income rose only from 0.21 in 1987 to 0.25 ten years later. (The Gini is an often-used inequality index that is particularly sensitive to changes in the middle of the income distribution.) In the Czech Republic, Poland, and Latvia, inequality rose more substantially, but the distribution remained fairly egalitarian. And yet in another group of countries, most notably those of the Commonwealth of Independent States (CIS), the increase in inequality far exceeded anything ever seen before. In Russia, Armenia, Moldova, Tajikistan, and Turkmenistan, income Ginis almost doubled (table 4.1).

With Ginis around 0.5 or above, inequality in Russia, Armenia, Tajikistan, and the Kyrgyz Republic is now comparable to that observed in some of the most highly unequal economies in Latin America. Inequality in Estonia or Bulgaria rivals that of Peru or Venezuela (figure 4.1). However, unlike in Latin America where inequality has been high yet fairly stable, the deterioration of the income distribution in the CIS has occurred in only a decade—a change of unprecedented magnitude and speed. Not surprisingly, this has rendered the sense of relative deprivation of those at

Table 4.1   Income Inequality during the Transition, by Region, Selected Years 1987–99

Region and country	Gini coefficient for income per capita		
	1987–90 [a]	1993–94 [a]	1996–99 [b]
Central Europe			
Czech Republic	0.19	0.23	0.25
Hungary	0.21	0.23	0.25
Slovenia	0.22	0.29	0.25
Poland	0.28	0.28	0.33
South Eastern Europe			
Albania	—	—	0.27[c]
Bulgaria	0.23	0.38	0.41[d]
Croatia	0.36	—	0.35
Macedonia, FYR	—	—	0.37
Romania	0.23	0.29	0.30[c]
Baltics and Poland			
Lithuania	0.23	0.33	0.34
Latvia	0.24	0.31[e]	0.32
Estonia	0.24	0.35	0.37
Slavic countries			
Russian Federation	0.26	0.48	0.47
Ukraine	0.24	0.47[e]	0.33[c]
Moldova	0.27	—	0.42
Belarus	0.23	0.28[c]	0.28[c]
Caucasus and Central Asia			
Armenia	0.27	—	0.59
Georgia	0.29	—	0.43
Kyrgyz Republic	0.31	0.55	0.47
Kazakhstan	0.30	0.33	0.35[c]
Tajikistan	0.28	—	0.47
Turkmenistan	0.28	0.36	0.45[c]

— Not available.

Note: Income refers to **disposable income**—after-tax earned income. Identical calculations were performed for incomes per equivalent adult (theta=0.75) and using the OECD equivalence scale (theta=0.5).

a. The source was the Family Budget Surveys in Milanovic (1998) with these exceptions: the source for the Slavic republics in 1990 was Alexeev and Gaddy (1993); the source for the Czech Republic in 1994 was Flemming and Micklewright (1999); and the source for Poland for 1990 to 1994 was Keane and Prasad (2000).

b. The source was the authors' own computations from latest representative national household surveys. Incomes included in-kind consumption.

c. A consumption Gini was used because of a lack of data on incomes. See appendix A.

d. For 1995 because of problems with 1997 data.

e. For 1995.

Figure 4.1   Income Inequality: A Comparison of ECA, Latin American, and Southern European Countries

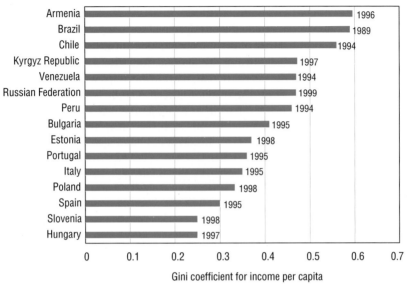

Gini coefficient for income per capita

Source: Table 4.1 and IADB (1998/99).

the bottom particularly acute. In contrast with the CIS experience, inequality in Central Europe remains low by world standards. Income Ginis in the Czech and Slovak Republics are roughly of the same magnitude as those of Sweden or Norway, while those in Hungary and Poland are on a par with Spain, France, and Germany.

This picture of rising disparities is even more extreme if we look at the social distance between the very rich and very poor. In 1998 in Russia the incomes of the top 10 percent of the population were 9 times those of the bottom decile. Decile ratios for per capita incomes in other CIS economies were equally high. In 1996-97 the top 10 percent of the distribution in Georgia earned nearly 7 times more than those at the bottom; in the Kyrgyz Republic and Tajikistan the comparable ratio was 10; in Armenia, an unbelievable 19. In Central Europe and the Baltics, on the other hand, the disparities between the very top and the very bottom remained relatively moderate: in 1996 incomes in the top decile in Hungary were only 3 times higher than those in the bottom decile—a smaller differential than in most countries belonging to the Organization for Economic Cooperation and Development (OECD).

Keane and Prasad (2000) and Garner and Terrell (1998) question whether the comparison of inequality indices before and after the transition is meaningful. They point out that pretransition figures on income distribution were often distorted and that comparisons are undermined by the use of surveys with differing methodologies, coverage, and objectives. Pretransition surveys were usually not designed to be representative of the entire population but rather of certain socioeconomic groups. As a result, they tended to be biased toward the average household and to exclude nonstandard households—in particular, marginal groups with a high probability of being poor. Thus, the distribution of income was usually truncated, leading to an underestimation of true income disparities.

The analysis of the individual country's survey methodologies, definitions, and coverage confirms that comparing income distributions before and after the transition is indeed difficult. For the countries of Central and South Eastern Europe and the Baltic states (CSB), however, the resulting biases appear to be small: most calculations may slightly overestimate the true change in inequality but not by much and not in all cases (Milanovic 1999). The problem is more severe for the CIS, where the increase in inequality may be much more seriously overestimated. Nevertheless, two findings appear to be fairly robust: first, the trend is one of rising inequality, even if the exact magnitude of the change is hard to measure (figure 4.2). Second, inequality in the CIS at the start of the transition was already significantly higher than in CSB countries, and at levels comparable to that of some of the more unequal OECD economies, such as the United States (Commander, Tolstopiatenko, and Yemtsov 1999).[1]

Even when surveys are comparable, measuring incomes accurately is problematic. Some economies have very large "gray" or "informal" sectors, and earnings generated there may not be adequately captured in the incomes reported by households. Such an omission could bias our measures of inequality, even if a priori we do not necessarily know whether it would tend to exacerbate or dampen true income disparities.[2] Indeed, when we compare reported household expenditures and incomes, we find that in some ECA countries the former systematically exceed the latter (for the CIS by as much as 20 to 40 percent). In these cases the observed underreporting of incomes may affect the reliability of our inequality estimates. It would be better, in these circumstances, to rely on measures of inequality that look at consumption or expenditures rather than incomes.

Consumption-based measures may also be preferable because consumption is less volatile than incomes and more likely to reflect permanent income. Incomes in Europe and Central Asia have become much more volatile than in the past and they fluctuate significantly from month to month. Recall periods are short in most of the surveys in the former Soviet Union (FSU): they vary between one and three months. Inequality mea-

Figure 4.2 Income Inequality in the Russian Federation, 1992–96

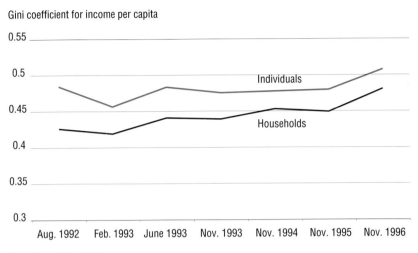

Gini coefficient for income per capita

Note: Constant June 1992 prices.
Source: Successive rounds of the Russian Longitudinal Monitoring Survey, which are comparable over time.
Commander, Tolstopiatenko, and Yemtsov (1999).

sures that rely on these "snapshots" will tend to overestimate the underlying inequality.[3]

How different are consumption-based measures of inequality from income-based ones? The short answer is that for most of the transition economies, with the exception of some CIS countries, measures of inequality
that are based on expenditures and those based on incomes are remarkably similar (table 4.2). However, for some CIS countries the differences
can be large. In fact, the existence of large differences between consumption inequality and income inequality correlates with our low/high inequality split. In other words, those countries that show the highest levels of
income inequality reveal the largest gap between consumption-based measures and income-based measures.

Several factors can explain this split between the economies of CSB
countries and those of the CIS. First, formal sources of labor incomes are
much more dominant among the former than among the latter. In CSB
economies, wages account for 60 to 80 percent of household incomes. In
contrast, among the economies of the CIS, wages represent less than 40
percent of total incomes and in some cases—Armenia and Georgia—less
than 15 percent. Second, state transfers are a much more important component of income among the CSB countries, where they comprise 25 to 30
percent of total incomes. In contrast, their importance among the econo-

Table 4.2   Consumption-Based and Income-Based Measures of Inequality

Country	Consumption-based measure			Income-based measure		
	Log deviation	Gini coefficient	90/10 ratio	Log deviation	Gini coefficient	90/10 ratio
Hungary	0.14	0.28	3.49	0.11	0.25	3.07
Latvia	0.19	0.34	4.54	0.19	0.32	4.13
Poland	0.19	0.34	4.29	0.17	0.32	4.25
Slovenia	0.14	0.28	3.67	0.11	0.25	3.04
Bulgaria	0.13	0.27	3.90	0.26	0.41	6.19
Croatia	0.17	0.32	4.29	0.22	0.35	3.76
Macedonia, FYR	0.16	0.34	3.83	0.24	0.37	5.77
Armenia	0.17	0.32	4.08	0.67	0.59	19.29
Georgia	0.24	0.37	5.69	0.33	0.43	6.65
Moldova	0.29	0.41	6.14	0.37	0.42	7.43
Kyrgyz Republic	0.30	0.42	6.35	0.42	0.47	10.40
Russian Federation	0.39	0.47	8.06	0.43	0.47	8.78
Tajikistan	0.17	0.32	4.04	0.41	0.47	10.60

Source: The authors' own calculations from latest representative household surveys.

mies of the CIS has shrunk drastically: state transfers still represent 16 percent of household incomes in Ukraine but less than 10 percent in Moldova and a miniscule 3 percent in Georgia.

Both wages and transfers can be measured quite accurately by household surveys, which may help explain why measured incomes in the CSB countries appear to be in line with measured expenditures. In contrast, other sources of income (more dominant in the CIS) are notoriously hard to measure. For self-employed individuals it is usually difficult to distinguish the part of their income that can be attributed to wages, the part that is the return to physical investment, and the part that is the value of their profit. Nonlabor earnings can be equally difficult to measure, particularly if they arise from a diversified portfolio of assets. Individuals may choose to underreport their incomes deliberately, and this is much easier to do the larger the fraction of nonwage earnings. To the extent that these other sources of income are measured with error, it is not surprising that the total distribution of income does not track the distribution of consumption all that well in the CIS.

For the economies of the CSB, income-based measures of inequality appear to be fairly accurate; or at least in line with what we observe on the consumption front as well. However, for the CIS, measurement is a much more difficult problem: "true" inequality in most CIS countries probably lies somewhere between observed consumption measures and observed income measures.

Box 4.1   Income Inequality and Income Mobility

Inequality measures that do not take into account income mobility may overestimate the underlying inequality. The measures presented in this chapter represent inequality in income (or expenditures) across individuals in a given recall period (one month, three months, or one year, depending on the survey). But measured incomes are often highly volatile from one period to the next. Part of this volatility may be attributed to "transitory" shocks, part may reflect seasonal patterns, and yet another part may reflect a permanent shift in incomes. When we rely on a one-time snapshot of inequality, we observe individuals subject to different types of income shocks. Some may have experienced a transitory shock to their incomes, some may truly have permanent higher incomes. Our measures treat all of these individuals in the same manner, mixing transitory and permanent, or long-term, inequality.

This can be a problem when comparing measures of inequality across countries. If surveys have different recall periods, and incomes are more volatile in some countries than in others, the different levels of inequality we measure could be spurious. Two countries could have similar levels of inequality on a yearly basis, for example, and yet a shorter recall period and higher month-to-month volatility in one of the countries would yield higher measured inequality.

For Russia and Poland, we have access to panel data that allow us to follow households over several years. We use this panel data to try to distinguish between "long-term" and "transitory" inequality. First, we average household income and expenditures successively over four periods (current month, current month plus 12 months ago, current month plus 24 months ago, and current month plus 36 months ago). The transitory components of income are averaged out as we average over more periods. As a result, the inequality of average income over four periods yields a better approximation of long-term inequality. Table 4.3 shows how inequality, as measured by the Gini coefficient, declines as we average over more periods. The absolute difference in inequality levels between the countries also declines.

Table 4.3a   Inequality Declines if Measured over Multiple Periods

| | Russian Federation, 1994–98 | | Poland, 1993–96 | |
Period	Income	Expenditure	Income	Expenditure
1-period Gini	0.437	0.446	0.305	0.285
2-period Gini	0.385	0.405	0.280	0.265
3-period Gini	0.360	0.384	0.269	0.255
4-period Gini	0.346	0.373	0.261	0.249

As a second approach we decompose household income into its transitory (expected to disappear within 12 months) and permanent (expected to last longer than 12 months) components. We then predict the inequality associated solely with the transitory components. The difference between this predicted value and measured levels of inequality gives us the underlying or long-term inequality.

(Box continues on next page.)

Box 4.1 (continued)

Table 4.3b   Monthly Inequality Compared with Long-Term Inequality

Component	Russian Federation (1995, 1996)		Poland (1994, 1995)	
	Income	Expenditure	Income	Expenditure
Total Gini	0.421	0.425	0.304	0.280
Long-term inequality	0.280	0.335	0.244	0.241
Total Gini	0.484	0.457	0.304	0.285
Long-term inequality	0.304	0.341	0.240	0.244

This second approach confirms that long-term inequality (in income or expenditures) is substantially less than inequality in any given month. In Russia, the difference is about 35 percent for income and 20 percent for expenditures. In Poland, the differences are somewhat smaller: 20 percent for income and 15 percent for expenditure.

Source: Luttmer (2000).

What, then, should we look at when carrying out our analysis? If our main interest is to understand how changes in distribution affect living standards and poverty, we should rely only on consumption-based measures of distribution. But if we want to understand what is driving changes in the distribution, and what underlying market forces are at work, we should rely on income-based measures since these can be linked more directly to household endowments and to market returns. If we want to compare the experience in the transition economies to that in other countries (especially in the OECD and Latin America), we must resort to income Ginis, which are more easily available on a comparable basis.

What Is Driving the Increase in Inequality?

The increase in income inequality across Europe and Central Asia has been driven by common forces acting with varying strength in different country settings and dampened or exacerbated by the actions of governments and other socioeconomic agents. The most important force driving inequality upward has been increased inequality of labor earnings. This increase derives from an increase in the dispersion of wages and from the growth of nonwage incomes associated with self-employment and entrepreneurial activities. The effect of increased inequality in labor earnings has been compounded in Bulgaria, Russia, and Ukraine by the impact of nonlabor earnings such as capital and property income. In many countries—such as the Czech and Slovak Republics, Estonia, Hungary, and Poland—government transfers and taxes have played an important equalizing role, dampening and undoing the effect of rising wage inequality. In other countries transfers have been mainly neutral. In still others, most notably in Russia, they have actually contributed to increasing inequality.

Increased Inequality of Labor Earnings

Most of the observable income inequality across households in transition economies is explained by inequality in labor earnings. Jointly, wage earnings and earnings from self-employment account for between 60 and 80 percent of all observed inequality of incomes (figure 4.3).[4] In this regard ECA is no different from, say, Latin America or the OECD, where earnings from labor explain most of the observable inequality.

Figure 4.3 Income Inequality in Selected ECA Countries, by Income Components, Selected Years, 1993–98

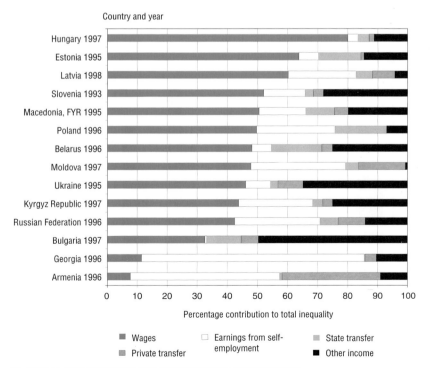

Source: The authors' computations from latest representative household surveys.

Inequality of labor earnings has increased markedly with the transition, independently of the speed of reforms. The dispersion of wages has increased everywhere: concentration coefficients for wages have risen from about 0.23 on average in CSB countries in the late1980s to about 0.32 in 1996; and from 0.25 in the CIS in 1989 to over 0.5 in 1996-97 (Milanovic 1999).[5] In addition, there has been a shift in the composition of income: a rising share of income is now derived from self-employment and entrepreneurial activities, and a declining share is derived from wages. Since incomes from these other sources tend to be more unequally distributed than wages, the shift in composition has also worked toward increasing overall inequality of labor earnings.

Rising wage inequality was the main factor behind the increase in inequality in many transition economies. According to Milanovic (1999), increasing dispersion of wages was responsible for the increase of between 3.5 and 8 Gini points in Central Europe.[6] Although the magnitudes differ

Figure 4.4 Earnings Disparities in Central and Eastern Europe, 1989 and 1997

Gini coefficient for monthly wage earnings

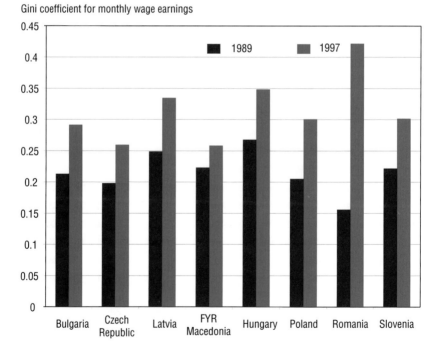

Source: Rutkowski (1999) and World Bank (1999). These sources used the UNICEF and TRANSMONEE database.

somewhat, these findings are consistent with those of Garner and Terrell (1998) for the Czech and Slovak Republics. Using comparable data from the Russian Longitudinal Monitoring Survey (RLMS), Commander, Tolstopiatenko, and Yemtsov (1999) find that the main factor driving changes in the distribution of income in Russia after 1992 was changes in income composition. According to their results, increasing wage dispersion alone would have been responsible for a nearly 9 point increase in the Gini, but its overall effect was dampened by the dramatic decline in wage shares. Rising entrepreneurial income was the single most important contributor to rising inequality in Russia, even though inequality of entrepreneurial income declined during the period.

Rising Returns to Education

Wage inequality has increased mainly because returns to education have risen rapidly. But we also see an increase in interindustry and occupational wage differentials, and a large increase in inequality within industry-occupation groups. In CSB countries, the increase in the education premiums happened very quickly. Rutkowski (1996, 1999) finds that the earnings differential between university-educated workers and workers with primary education in some of the advanced reformer countries more than doubled between 1989 and 1993. Poland is a good example: before the transition a university-educated worker earned about 35 percent more than a worker with a primary education. By 1993 this wage differential had increased to 75 percent. Interestingly, the increase in the education premium happened at the very beginning of transition; educational wage differentials in Poland in 1998 were roughly the same as in 1993.

As a result of this quick adjustment, returns to education in CSB countries are now in the range observed for established market economies (figure 4.5). The shares of total inequality determined by differences between education groups are also very similar to what we see in the OECD. Bailey (1997) finds that in 1992–94 differences between education groups alone explained between 12 and 16 percent of all income inequality in Poland, Hungary, and the Czech and Slovak Republics. Our own calculations with the latest available household surveys for those countries suggest that differences between education groups account for between 11 and 15 percent in Poland (1996), Hungary (1997), and FYR Macedonia (1996); nearly 20 percent in Slovenia (1993); and between 7 and 9 percent in Estonia (1995) and Latvia (1997–98). In contrast, differences between education groups explain only 2 to 3 percent of all observed inequality in the countries of the FSU and Bulgaria (figure 4.6).

Figure 4.5   Returns to a Year of Education during the Transition in CSB Countries, 1993–96

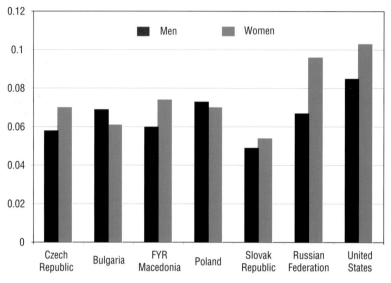

Returns to a year of education

Source: UNICEF and TRANSMONEE database.

Although rising educational premiums appear to have been the major factor driving the increase in inequality in Central and Eastern Europe and the Baltics, they have played only a minor role in the Commonwealth of Independent States. This is consistent with evidence from other studies: Lehman, Wadsworth and Yemtsov (2000) for Russia; Lindauer (1998) for Moldova; and Yemtsov (1999a and 1999b) for Armenia and Georgia. All find similar results. That education explains only a small share of observed wage inequality could be interpreted as reflecting the low market value of the stock of education inherited from the FSU. However, this explanation is at odds with the observed revaluation of education in the CSB countries, which had fairly similar education systems. It is more likely that the failure to find a strong link between education and wages in the FSU is symptomatic of other problems.

What factors—other than education—can explain rising wage inequality in Russia and other CIS republics? Simple decompositions of wage variance and/or human capital regressions reveal that individual characteristics play only a secondary role and that the share of wage inequality that remains "unexplained" is relatively large. Yemtsov (1999b) finds

Figure 4.6 Percentage of Total Inequality Explained by Differences between Education Groups, Selected ECA Countries, Selected Years, 1993–98

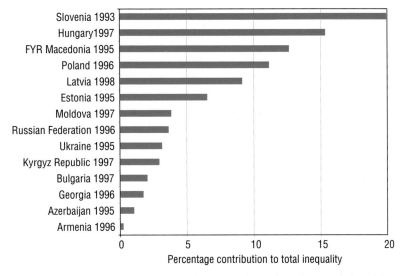

Source: The authors' computations from latest household surveys; income inequality per equivalent adult (theta = 0.75).

that some 45 percent of all wage variance in Georgia is unexplained or "residual." Similarly, Lehman, Wadsworth, and Yemtsov (2000) find that individual characteristics play a relatively minor role in explaining high wage inequality in Russia. They suggest that wage inequality in Russia is linked instead to "nonmarket" or distortionary factors—such as the existence of wage arrears.

Klugman (1998) attempts to quantify the impact of wage arrears on inequality for Uzbekistan. She finds that up to one half of the change in the Gini coefficient for wages between 1989 and 1995 can be attributed to the violation of wage contracts by employers. She also finds that these arrears are not randomly distributed. They are more likely to affect less educated and lower paid workers. Yemtsov (1999b) finds similar evidence for Georgia; Lehman, Wadsworth, and Acquisti (1999) find that in Russia arrears are regionally persistent, hence contributing to the large increase in intraregional wage disparities documented there. Using previously unavailable data from the Russian Labor Force Surveys, Lehman, Wadsworth and Yemtsov (2000) conclude that the main contributor to total inequality in Russia, among all explanatory variables, is regional location. However, they also find that most of the income inequality cannot be attributed to measurable factors. This stands in marked contrast to what is found in market economies, both developed and developing.

The Emergence of an Entrepreneurial Class

Transition has been associated with the elimination of legal restrictions on private ownership and activities, and with the removal of state subsidies. Both have radically altered the relative sizes of the public and private sectors. As noted earlier, one consequence of these shifts has been a re-evaluation of the value of education (at least in CSB countries) and a significant increase in wage disparities. Another consequence is the rise in self-employment and entrepreneurial income, which barely existed before, and the corresponding decline in the share of wages in total household incomes.

The share of income derived from self-employment or entrepreneurial activities has increased in all ECA countries: to about 5 to 10 percent in the CSB countries (with the exception of Poland, with its large agricultural sector, where income from self-employment reaches 18 percent); to 20 to 35 percent in Russia, Moldova, and Ukraine; and to more than 50 percent in the poorer republics of the Transcaucasus and Central Asia (reaching an incredible 72 percent in Georgia). Since self-employment and entrepreneurial income are more unequally distributed than wage incomes, this shift in income composition has contributed to increasing inequality. But its impact has been very different across countries: small in CSB countries and large in the FSU. For example, in Bulgaria, this shift in composition contributed only 2 to 3 percentage points to the change in the Gini; in Slovenia, about 1 to 2 percentage points. In Russia, however, it contributed toward increasing the Gini by nearly 12 percentage points (Milanovic 1999; Commander, Tolstopiatenko, and Yemtsov 1999).

Not only has the impact of self-employment differed in CSB and CIS countries, but the nature of this self-employment has also been very different. Self-employment in the CSB countries is associated mainly with the emergence of small, private entrepreneurs in industry and services. As discussed in Chapter 3, these new small-scale entrepreneurial activities have been an engine of growth and job creation. The scale on which this self-employment has appeared has been more or less in line with what exists in developed OECD economies. In fact, surveys of latent entrepreneurship suggest that there are no differences between Central European economies and Western economies in terms of the willingness of their populations to become self-employed. Nearly 80 percent of Poles, 58 percent of Slovenes, and 50 percent of Hungarians interviewed in a recent survey said they would prefer to be self-employed than an employee, if given the choice—compared with 70 percent of the Americans or 45 percent of the British who were interviewed (Dabrowski, Gomulka, and Rostowski 2000).

The rise in the share of self-employment income in the CIS, unlike in the CSB countries, has been largely concentrated in agricultural activities for self-consumption. The increase reflects the collapse of formal sector jobs and wages more than the emergence of new private opportunities. Less than 10 percent of Russian workers report that they are self-employed on a full-time basis; yet self-employment and entrepreneurial income account for more than 40 percent of total household incomes. With the exception of a few entrepreneurs concentrated at the top of the distribution, reported self-employment income in Russia and the CIS represents a complement to low (or unpaid) wages, and it is earned mainly through small-scale farming or petty trade (box 4.2). In marked contrast with attitudes in the CSB, only 33 percent of Russians responded that they would prefer to be self-employed. Thus, it seems that the emergence of self-employment on a large-scale in the CIS has been more a survival strategy in the face of collapsing formal incomes than a choice to take advantage of the entrepreneurial opportunities offered by liberalization. In line with this, most self-employment is not full time but reflects work done in parallel to a formal, low-paying (or even nonpaying) job.

There is a direct link between the emergence of this large-scale "survival" self-employment and high inequality in the CIS. There is a strong negative correlation between the level of total income inequality and the share of wages in total income; the correlation coefficient equals -0.80.[7] The highest inequality countries (Armenia, Georgia, Russia) are those in which the share of wages has fallen the most (and where as a consequence self-employment income accounts for a large part of household earnings). Lower wage shares are associated with higher inequality because well-functioning labor markets tend to play an equalizing role, linking the return to an individual's effort to his or her productivity and equalizing returns to comparable workers (to some degree) across sectors and occupations. In contrast, self-employment and entrepreneurial income, unlike wages, are critically tied to an individual's access to assets (including knowledge and information) and are thus often conditioned by initial assets or incomes. Even in a well-functioning market economy, self-employment incomes will be more unequal than wage employment. [8] In economies, such as those of the former Soviet Union, rife with distortions, regulations, barriers to entry, and opportunities for bribe taking, and where nontransparent connections can play a key role in securing contracts or

Box 4.2   Household Plots in the Commonwealth of Independent States

Household plots provide practically the entire rural population in the Commonwealth of Independent States (and part of the urban population) with a large proportion of their own food needs. The millions of small household plots, which average about 0.5 hectare and account for less than 10 percent of agricultural land, produce nearly 50 percent of gross agricultural output in the CIS. Most of the products from the household plot are consumed by the family, although some 10 to 20 percent of the output may be sold for cash in nearby markets. Altogether, these plots contribute some 40 to 70 percent of the family budget (including the value of home-grown products consumed by the family). They are thus a critical element of the survival strategies of many rural families in the CIS. Evidence from a 1998 World Bank farm survey in Moldova indicates that the share of income from the household plot increases from 28 percent of family income for households in the low income quartile to 34 percent for households in the high-income quartile. To earn the supplementary income from the household plots, rural residents work daily 5 hours on the family plot, in addition to 8 hours of work on the farm enterprise.

Table 4.4 Contribution of Household Plot to Rural Family Incomes in Selected CIS Countries
(percent)

Source of income	Ukraine	Moldova	Belarus	Russian Federation	Armenia
Salaries	42	55	51	45	8
Transfers and other income	15	12	6	15	15
Household plot (sales and own consumption)	43	33	43	40	76

Sources: For Ukraine, Moldova, Belarus, Armenia, World Bank (various years); for Russian Federation, Goskomstat (1994).

business opportunities, incomes from self-employment are bound to be critically tied to noneconomic factors and thus highly unequal. Moreover, they may be unequal in a way that may not be easily "explainable" by measured economic or individual variables.

Enterprise Privatization and Asset Transfers

The transition has meant the emergence of new private business; it also has been associated with the large-scale transfer of publicly owned assets into private hands. Nellis (1999) estimates that some 50,000 medium- and large-scale enterprises were privatized in the transition economies alone during the first half of the 1990s. In addition, hundreds of thousands of small-scale enterprises were privatized: more than 75,000 in Russia, 35,000 in Ukraine, and 22,000 in the Czech Republic. The European Bank for Reconstruction

Figure 4.7   Income Inequality and the Wage Share in Selected ECA Countries

Gini coefficient for income per capita

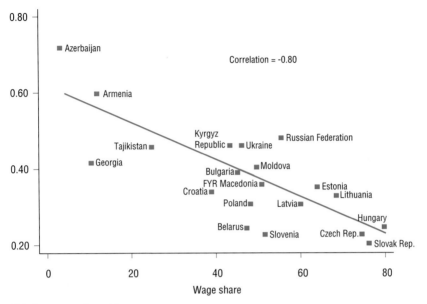

Wage share

Note: For years, see figure 4.6.
Source: The authors' calculations using latest representative household surveys.

and Development (EBRD) estimates that most of the countries of Central and Eastern Europe and the Baltics have privatized more than 50 percent of their medium- and large-scale enterprises and practically all of their small-scale ones. Among the Republics of the CIS, many (including Armenia, Georgia, the Kyrgyz Republic, Moldova, Russia, and Uzbekistan) have privatized at least one-third (and in some cases significantly more) of all medium- and large-scale enterprises and most of their small firms. Thus, at least on paper, the scale of the transfer has been truly massive.

Despite the likely quantitative importance of this asset transfer on the distribution of income and wealth, very little seems to be known about its actual impact. Indeed, the lack of surveys of household finances—a problem not limited to the transition economies—means that there is little reliable evidence. As a result, most analysis of the link between privatization and the distribution of wealth and income must be impressionistic and based mainly on qualitative and indirect evidence. In their attempt to go beyond anecdotal evidence and examine the distributional impact of privatization across the region, McHale and Pankov (1999) found that only limited value was transferred and that the largest gains went to the politically well connected and to insiders—especially managers—in more successful enterprises. Insider-driven privatization was the norm throughout much of the former Soviet Union and even in parts of Central and Eastern Europe. The resulting insider control slowed restructuring and had a negative impact on formal earnings. In those few countries (the Czech Republic, Estonia, Hungary, Poland) where a serious attempt was made to sell enterprises at fair market value (often to foreigners), more significant restructuring has taken place.

Countries that have privatized more and relied less on insider privatization have experienced smaller declines in the wage share (that is, a smaller collapse of formal incomes) and a smaller increase in the share of the unofficial economy—both of which have been associated with smaller increases in income inequality. Figure 4.8, a simple scatter plot of an index of privatization and the level of income inequality, appears to support this negative association between the scope of privatization and the level of inequality; the correlation coefficient equals -0.62.

The correlation between the privatization index and measures of inequality is even stronger if we weigh the index by the share of control given to insiders (correlation = -0.67). What seems to have mattered the most is the process through which privatization was achieved, and especially how privatization influenced the quality of resulting corporate governance. Programs that gave preferences to insiders or allowed vested interests to dominate the process were more likely to result in asset stripping and other predatory behaviors. Hence, these programs yielded more unequal outcomes and wider income disparities than did those that relied on fair market value and more transparent mechanisms (table 4.5). Similarly, processes that reduced administrative discretion or fostered the independent administration of the privatization program (as in Estonia or Hungary) may have resulted in more transparent transactions and thus in less unequal outcomes.

Housing Privatization

Like enterprise privatization, housing privatization has varied considerably across countries in Europe and Central Asia. In Albania the private share of housing rose from about 30 percent in 1989 to almost complete private ownership by 1995. In Lithuania the increase in the private sector share was from around 20 percent to around 80 percent. In 1997 private ownership of housing in Armenia was estimated at about 80 percent. Focusing on the share of state units privatized rather than the overall private

Figure 4.8 Income Inequality and Privatization Progress in Selected ECA Countries

Gini coefficient for income per capita

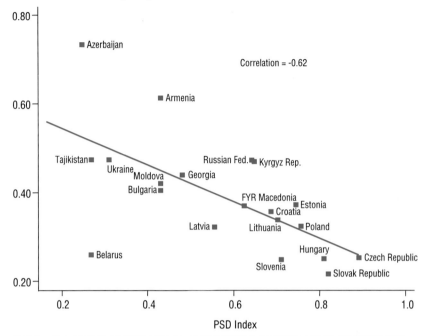

PSD Index

Note: For years, see figure 4.6. Dethier, Ghanem, and Zoli (1999) performed the same exercise with the EBRD index of privatization progress, and they obtained similar results. The correlation, if Belarus is excluded, equals –0.722. The PSD Index measures progress on privatization and other aspects of private sector development. For a detailed definition, see EBRD (1999).
Source: Dethier, Ghanem, and Zoli (1999); authors' own calculations based on the latest representative household surveys.

sector share, Struyk (1996) reports that over 90 percent of state-owned units in Bulgaria, and between 85 and 95 percent of units in Estonia, were in private hands as early as 1994. Elsewhere progress was slower. In Poland the private sector share was not much higher in 1995 than it was in 1989, at less than 30 percent. (Poland also has a large cooperatively owned housing sector.) In Russia the share of privately owned housing doubled over this period but remained below 40 percent (McHale and Pankov 1999).

Housing privatization appears to have had a progressive distributional impact even in the CIS. Buckley and Gurenko (1997) find that expanding the RLMS definition of income to include imputed housing income reduces both the level and the increase in Russian income inequality. Moreover, they argue that because housing wealth was more equally distributed

Table 4.5   Choice of Privatization Strategy and Inequality Outcome

Core privatization strategy	Inequality outcome	
	Low	High
Voucher-based privatization		
Equal access	Czech Rep. (P); Latvia (P); Lithuania (P); Slovak Rep. (S)	Armenia (P); Bulgaria (S); Kazakhstan (P); Kyrgyz Rep. (P)
Preferences to insiders		Armenia (S); Azerbaijan (P); Georgia (P); Moldova (P); Russian Fed. (P)
Sales to outsiders		
Large foreign participation	Estonia (P); Hungary (P)	
Little foreign participation	Slovenia (S)	Azerbaijan (S); Bulgaria (P); Czech Rep. (S); Kazakhstan (S); Latvia (S); FYR Macedonia (S); Moldova (S); Russian Fed. (S)
Insider buyouts		
EBOs	Croatia (P); Poland (P); Romania (P); Slovenia (P)	Kyrgyz Rep. (S)
MBO	Hungary (S); FYR Macedonia (P);Slovak Rep. (P)	Georgia (S); Estonia (S); Russian Fed. (T); Ukraine (P); Uzbekistan (P)
Other		
(includes restitution, liquidation)	Czech Rep. (T); Hungary (T)	Estonia (T)

Note: P is primary strategy; S, secondary strategy; T, tertiary strategy.
Source: EBRD (1999); McHale and Pankov (1999).

than nonresidential wealth, housing privatization had a strongly progressive effect on the wealth distribution in Russia, a conclusion shared by Alexeev (1999). McHale and Pankov (1999), on the other hand, suggest that privatization of housing has entrenched pre-existing differentials in the quality of housing. They conclude that privatization has resulted in a redistribution of housing wealth to those initially in possession of a "good-quality" state dwelling, while disadvantaging those without an initial attachment or with possession of an inferior quality unit.

Land Privatization and Land Reform

The land endowment in the individual sector, which includes traditional household plots as well as new private farms, increased dramatically during the 1990s. Indeed, the share of land cultivated by individuals (as opposed to collectives, cooperatives, and other corporate farms) soared from

20 percent to 70 percent in the CSB countries and from a mere 4 percent to 15 percent in the Commonwealth of Independent States.

The distributional impact of land privatization, like enterprise privatization, appears to have been fairly mixed. The outcome seems to depend highly on the quality and type of privatization process, although a strong correlation between the extent of privatization and more equitable outcomes can be discerned. The CSB countries (except Albania) largely relied on restitution programs that returned the land cultivated by large-scale collective farms and state farms to the former owners. The decision to restitute land according to precollectivization endowments was driven by the desire to treat the original owners fairly. The process, however, automatically created a different kind of injustice: many young workers on collective farms who did not own any land in the past remained land-less. In general, restitution procedures by their very design allocated much of the land to urban residents and to relatively old people in rural areas. In Romania, the elderly, who account for 41 percent of the rural population, got 65 percent of the land. Thus, there was a clear transfer of assets to certain groups of the population at the expense of others. However, in all these countries land can now be freely transferred and mortgaged. This has allowed inactive landowners, such as urban residents or elderly pensioners, to lease out their land to active and enterprising users in return for annual income in cash or in kind.

In the CIS the main mechanism of land reform involved the distribution of land above and beyond their household plot to active farm workers and farm pensioners. The implementation proceeded according to two different models. In the smaller countries (initially Armenia and Georgia; more recently Moldova and Azerbaijan), the former state and collective farms were dissolved and their land allocated in the form of equal physical plots among all farm members. As in the CSB, these plots in principle are freely transferable and even can be mortgaged. In practice, land transactions are very infrequent. This "small country" model has produced a highly equitable land ownership structure, but the average land plot is very small, ranging from 0.5 hectare to 1.5 hectares in most cases. This has created rural sectors with predominantly subsistence farming, since the small family farms lack the economies of scale for input acquisition, output marketing, and access to credit that the larger structures enjoy. Over the medium term land consolidation may improve productivity and thus the incomes of those remaining on the farms. Whether this worsens inequality will depend on whether those who are induced to sell off their land move on to other viable sources of income or become landless workers without assets.

In the larger CIS countries the collective farms have stayed intact, even if they have been nominally privatized and reorganized as joint-stock companies, limited-liability partnerships, or some other corporate shareholding form. According to this model—practiced in Russia, Ukraine, and Kazakhstan, among others—farm workers and pensioners are allocated paper certificates of entitlement (so-called land shares) instead of actual land plots. The new shareowners can keep their assets in the use of the corporation (in return for a promise of future dividends) or withdraw with a plot of land to establish an independent private farm outside the collectivist framework. Those who have left the collective with land report higher income and higher levels of satisfaction than those who have stayed. In practice, most rural residents prefer to keep their shares in the corporate farm. In such cases a formal contract is concluded with the new corporation and the shareholders typically have the right to specific dividends (usually output in kind at harvest). These dividends are intended to supplement the meager salaries of the farm workers, often the equivalent of a few hundred dollars a year including in-kind distributions, and the small state pensions of the rural retirees. In practice, however, most corporate farms in the CIS report losses and have no earnings for the distribution of dividends to their shareholders.

The system of land shares in the CIS has a potential for abuse by unscrupulous managers. They can take advantage of the naivete of the rural population and their traditional dependence on the collective farm to pressure the new shareowners into transferring or selling their shares without proper contractual arrangements. In exchange they may receive a vague promise that they can keep their job as long as the farm is operational. In Kazakhstan many recipients of land shares have been convinced to sign over their shares to the managers in exchange for rights to employment or dividends, but these rights are often unclear, undocumented, and unenforceable. These types of arrangements can create permanent and entrenched inequalities among the rural population.

Government Taxes and Transfers

Governments' tax and transfer policies have powerfully influenced the distribution of total disposable income in most ECA countries, but their effect has not been uniform. In the Czech and Slovak Republics, taxes and transfers almost entirely offset the sizable increase in overall income inequality from rising wage dispersion: the impact split roughly half and half between the two.[9] According to Garner and Terrell (1998), transfers' negative contribution to inequality in the Czech and Slovak Republics in 1989 was more than 20 percent. Moreover, this negative contribution increased markedly between 1989 and 1993, driven by an improvement in targeting and an increase in the share of transfers in total income. Similarly, Milanovic (1999) finds that better targeting of transfers in Latvia reduced inequality there by 1.5 Gini points following the introduction of flat pensions in 1992. For Hungary, Förster, Szivos, and Toth (1998) estimate that the impact of transfers was to reduce the overall income Gini in 1994 from about 0.5 pre-transfers to under 0.3 post-transfers. In Bulgaria and Slovenia, Milanovic (1999) estimates that the effect of transfers has been neutral, while the greater concentration of pensions in Poland may have contributed to increasing overall inequality. This last result has been challenged by Keane and Prasad (2000), who find that social transfers in Poland played an important role in dampening the increase in both poverty and inequality. Using unit record data from the Household Budget Surveys, they find that transfers were reasonably well targeted and mitigated the adverse distributional consequences of the transition process. They conclude that the pension system, in particular, served as an important safety net for older workers.

The story is quite different for the CIS, where government size and transfers have declined sharply. Institutional weaknesses, and in some circumstances lack of political will, have compounded punitive notional tax schedules. The result has been a sharp drop in revenues. This has curtailed governments' ability to provide essential public services and to finance redistributive programs. As discussed in chapter 3, the decline in government expenditures appears to have disproportionately hurt the poor and led to higher levels of income inequality

The most detailed studies of the impact of public policy on the distribution of income in the CIS have been carried out for Russia. Commander and Lee (1998) conclude that while transfers played a redistributive role at the start of the transition, their progressive impact on the distribution has dampened significantly, driven by both a decline in the share of the more progressive transfers (such as family allowances) and the increased concentration of the only growing component of transfers, namely pensions. They find that the share of transfers going to the upper quintiles of the distribution actually increased between 1992 and 1996. Although transfers contributed (weakly) to reducing inequality in 1992, they had increased inequality by 1994. This reversal was driven mainly by the changing concentration of pensions. Milanovic (1999) and Commander, Tolstopiatenko, and Yemtsov (1999) report similar results.

For taxation the story is somewhat different: Commander and Lee (1998) report a large negative effect of taxes on income inequality in Russia. This occurred primarily through the principal base for taxation, wages. As the share of wages in total income has fallen, the progressive effect of taxation has been reduced, even though taxes appear to have become slightly more progressive. By 1996 the overall effect was positive but relatively weak. Nevertheless, it speaks to the potential of taxation as a redistributive tool in the Russian economy.

To our knowledge, there are no CIS studies comparable to the Russian studies. We can, however, infer some conclusions concerning the role of transfers by examining simple decompositions of income inequality by income component (table 4.6). Results are fairly illustrative. In most CIS countries, state transfers contribute positively to increasing inequality (in absolute terms). Only in Armenia and Georgia is their overall impact neutral, reflecting both their miniscule share in total income and their essentially linear distribution (a direct result of having adopted flat pension rates early in the transition). Since transfers are still less regressively distributed than other sources of income, an increase in the share of transfers in household incomes with a corresponding decline in other sources (wages or self-employment) would *at the margin* reduce income inequality.

Table 4.6 Contribution of State Transfers to Total Income Inequality

Country	Share of total income (percent)	Concentration coefficient	Contribution to total inequality (percent)
CIS			
Armenia	4.9	0.104	0.8
Azerbaijan	12.9	0.235	4.2
Georgia	3.3	0.042	0.3
Kyrgyz Republic	7.4	0.202	3.4
Moldova	10.2	0.182	4.5
Russian Federation	17.5	0.184	7.4
Ukraine	4.7	0.241	1.2
Other ECA countries			
Bulgaria	20.2	0.004	0.2
Hungary	31.9	0.028	3.7
Estonia	14.2	-0.023	-0.9
Latvia	25.2	.070	5.5
Poland	29.6	0.182	17.3
Slovenia	20.1	0.042	2.9

Note: Incomes per equivalent adult.
Source: The authors' calculations based on latest representative household surveys.

In short, public policy as reflected in transfers and taxes has played a distinctly different role across ECA countries. In most of the CEE and the Baltics (in the "lower" inequality countries), taxes and transfers have significantly dampened the increase in inequality arising from growing dispersion of earnings. In contrast, in most of the high-inequality countries in the CIS, taxes and transfers have been at best neutral, and on occasion they have added to high levels of income inequality.

Why Is Inequality so Different across Transition Economies?

One of the most striking facts about transition and inequality is the wide diversity of outcomes. In many corners increasing income inequality has been portrayed as a socially costly *outcome* of transition, and more specifically of the big bang approach (UNDP 1999). Yet the comparison of country experiences in ECA poses a challenge to this conclusion since the most advanced and determined reformers have witnessed the smallest increases in overall inequality. In fact, the countries that have lagged in reforms, or undertaken reforms in a partial and inconsistent manner, have experienced the largest increases in inequality. How can this puzzle be explained?

As discussed above, both the changes and the levels of inequality in the CSB countries are relatively easy to explain since they reflect an (otherwise expected) increase in wage disparities. But neither education, nor access to assets, nor easily measurable variables appears to explain the rise of inequality (or its level) in the CIS. This suggests the need to look at less quantifiable and observable factors—such as access to connections, the impact of corruption, the role of institutions, and the effects of haphazard and often arbitrary reforms.

Income inequality is higher today in the "stalled transition" countries than in the more advanced reformers because of three interrelated institutional factors. First, we must note the failure to put in place the policies and institutions needed to allow product and factor markets to operate effectively as the main mechanism to allocate resources. A socially costly consequence of this failure has been the *disintegration of the formal labor market* (falling employment, collapsing wages, and growing wage arrears), which has pushed many people into self-employment and led directly to widening disparities in income. The second factor is the coopting of national governments by vested interests. These interests have blocked reforms that would erode their privileges and allow for a more equal distribution of opportunities and incomes. Finally, widespread rent-seeking

behaviors and corruption in public administration at the local and national levels have also contributed to high inequality. Such behaviors constrain the emergence of new private activity and nurture dysfunctional
governments. The toll on the poor is particularly high.

Each of these factors has played a role, and together they have powerfully reinforced the adverse distributional consequences. The pervasiveness of corruption explains why the markets in some CIS countries fail to
operate efficiently even when a notionally market-friendly environment
has been put in place. In these cases the liberalization of private activities
and entry clashes with the heavy "corruption tax" imposed on small entrepreneurs, which prevents them from effectively operating a small business and generating employment. This, in turn, leads to the failure of
reforms to "pay off" and to generate winners that can become advocates
for further reforms. The lack of such advocates reinforces the power of
vested interests and those who seek to block reform. The resulting vicious
cycle, dominated by rent-seeking behavior and disincentives to private
investment and employment generation, goes a long way toward explaining why inequality has increased as much as it has in parts of the CIS.

Liberalization, Deregulation, and Inequality

Inequality has increased significantly less in those countries that have been
able to build (and maintain) well-functioning product and factor markets.
The key market for the determination of household incomes is the labor
market, which determines the rewards to the one asset that households
typically possess: labor. As shown in figure 4.7, there is a strong negative
correlation between income inequality across ECA countries and one possible measure of labor market performance: the wage share as a measure
of the formalization of labor incomes. In those countries where wages
have remained the primary source of household incomes (countries with a
high wage share), inequality has increased much less than in those where
it has collapsed. Similarly, we find a strong correlation between other
measures of labor market performance and inequality. For instance, the
prevalence of wage contract violations (wage arrears) is positively correlated with income inequality (Klugman 1998; Lehman, Wadsworth, and
Acquisti 1999). Measures of labor turnover and mobility are negatively
associated with overall inequality.

Demand for labor is a derived demand and thus depends critically on
having competitive and well-functioning product markets. A quick comparison of reform experiences across ECA countries reveals a fairly strong

Figure 4.9 Income Inequality and Market Reforms

Gini coefficient for income per capita

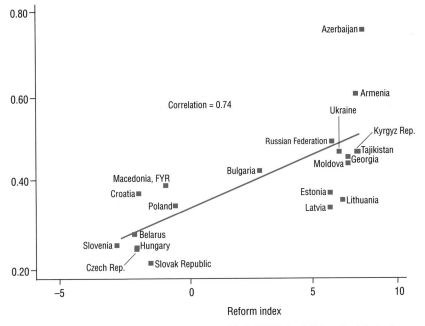

Reform index

Source: The market reform index is the De Melo, Denizer, and Gelb (1996) index. A higher value indicates *less* reform. Ginis are from the authors' own calculations using latest representative household surveys.

relationship between measures of product market development and over-all inequality. The simple cross-country correlation between the Gini for income and the De Melo, Denizer, and Gelb (1996) index of market re-forms is 0.74 (figure 4.9). Economies that have moved further in the direc-tion of letting the market allocate resources show less income inequality after the transition. As shown in table 4.7, this relationship still holds when we control for initial income and other initial conditions (such as measures of initial political freedoms or years under state planning). The relationship, moreover, appears to be unaffected by the choice of reform index (we also tried the liberalization index used by Dethier, Ghanem, and Zoli [1999] and the EBRD reform index) and by the use of alternative inequality measures. Of course, this evidence is far from conclusive. These types of indices are highly imperfect measures that attempt to aggregate progress on policy reform on many dimensions. Moreover, they largely measure *official* policy reforms, which may not always result in changes

Table 4.7   Market Reforms, Initial Conditions, and Income Inequality

Independent variable	(1)	(2)	(3)	(4)
Initial income per capita	-0.002 (-2.057)	-0.002 (-2.122)	-0.002 (-1.870)	-0.001 (-1.155)
Reform index[a]	1.987 (4.501)	1.416 (2.604)	2.399 (4.037)	1.780 (3.874)
Initial freedoms[b]	-0.666 (-0.482)	—	—	—
Planning[c]	—	0.264 (1.666)	—	—
Initial trade distortions[d]	—	—	-0.176 (-0.965)	—
Location[e]	—	—	—	-5.380 (-1.215)
R-square	0.638	0.659	0.651	0.663
N	24	24	24	24

Note: Regressions of Gini were performed on a set of independent variables for 24 countries. All regressions include a constant and a dummy for the use of a consumption Gini when the income Gini is not available. T-statistics are in parentheses.
a. A larger larger number means less reform.
b. The index of political rights and civil liberties at the start of the transition. Source: Freedom House (1999).
c. Years under central planning.
d. A measure of the importance of nonmarket trade at the start of the transition.
e. The dummy for proximity to Western Europe.
Sources: The Gini coefficients are from the authors' computations based on the latest representative household surveys. The reform index is from De Melo, Denizer, and Gelb (1996). All other variables are from Dethier, Ghanem, and Zoli (1999) database.

in the policy environment faced by economic agents on the ground. The official elimination of legal restrictions to private activity in a sector may not mean that there are no barriers to entry: corruptive practices and other forms of illegal taxation may constitute as large a barrier as the previous official restrictions. Evidence of this nature can only be suggestive, yet it is consistent with qualitative and case-study evidence from the region.

There are several channels through which liberalization and market development can have a *positive* impact on the distribution of income. A first, and obvious, channel is through their impact on labor demand. Liberalization is key to the emergence of new private sector activities that can absorb the outflow of workers from nonviable state enterprises. It is essential to the recovery of labor demand following the output collapse. Second, liberalization can foster the restructuring of state-owned enterprises (SOEs), allowing workers to break their ties with low-value enterprises where they get paid little or not at all. Where SOEs have not restructured, wage arrears and wage contract violations are more prevalent, increasing inequality. Finally, liberalization and deregulation dramatically reduce the opportunities for rent-seeking and corruption, which favors those with political power, connections, and the ability to pay bribes at the expense of those without political power.

Some evidence for these hypotheses is offered in table 4.8, which shows simple correlations between measures of liberalization, the wage share (a proxy for the state of the formal labor market and hence indirectly of labor demand), and measures of transparency. The correlation coefficient between the reform index and the wage share is 0.78. Countries that have moved farther in establishing markets have experienced a smaller collapse in wage shares. This can be interpreted as another manifestation of the strong negative relationship between progress on economic reforms and the collapse of formal labor demand (see chapter 3). Similarly, there is a strong correlation between measures of liberalization (or private sector development) and Transparency International's corruption perception index (TICP): competitive and well-functioning markets appear to be associated with better governance and less corruption (a higher TICP score). And there is a strong correlation between the TICP index and the wage share. The failure to establish competitive markets, the extent of corruption, and the collapse of formal labor demand appear to be closely interrelated.

The linkages between these three variables are too complex, and our observation points too few, to explore the causality in any depth. One reasonable line of argument would suggest that noncompetitive markets

Table 4.8   Market Reforms, Corruption, and the Wage Share

Index and wage share	Reform index	PSD index	TICP index	Wage share
Reform index	1.000			
PSD index	0.954	1.000		
TICP index	0.768	0.726	1.000	
Wage share	0.780	0.759	0.687	1.000

Source: The author's own computations using the latest household surveys; Dethier, Ghanem, and Zoli (1999) database, augmented with Transparency International's Corruption Perception Indices.

contribute to the emergence of widespread corruption. Both factors, in turn, are deterrents to private investment and private sector activity, and hence to the growth of labor demand. But the causality may run in the other direction: from weak governance and corruption, to state capture by powerful firms and lobbies, which can then distort the policy-making process in an effort to secure their concentrated rents at great cost to the rest of society.

Governance, Corruption, and Inequality

Corruption is an aspect of governance that directly affects the lives of the poor. Corruption hurts the poor through a variety of channels: lower economic growth, more regressive taxes, lower and more ineffective social spending, and disincentives to investment in the human capital of the poor. Corruption also increases income inequality and poverty by perpetuating unequal distribution of assets (box 4.3).

Corruption in Europe and Central Asia is among the worst worldwide. The EBRD and the World Bank recently conducted a Business Environment and Enterprise Performance Survey that covered 3,000 firms in 20 transition countries (EBRD 1999; World Bank 2000c). Almost 70 percent of firms in the Commonwealth of Independent States and about 50 percent in Central and Eastern Europe report corruption to be a problem

---

Box 4.3   Governance and Inequality

Governance can be understood as the norms, policies, and institutions through which power is exercised in the management of a country's economic and social resources. It includes the processes for selecting, monitoring, and replacing those in power; the capacity of government to manage its resources and to implement sound policies; and the respect that citizens and the state have for the institutions that govern economic and social interactions among them. Good governance is crucial for long-term economic growth (Knack and Keefer 1997; Mauro 1995). And there is increasing evidence that good governance can have strong *egalitarian* effects. Good governance can be measured in many different dimensions: the extent to which there are fair and transparent procedures for securing property rights and enforcing contracts; the incidence of government corruption; the quality and capacity of the public administration. Typically, these governance indicators are aggregated into single measures of "corruption" such as the Transparency International's Corruption Perception Index or the International Country Risk Guide Index. Empirically, these governance indicators have been associated with higher levels of social spending and more effective targeting of resources to the poor (Mauro 1998); better quality public services; and higher formalization of incomes (IADB 1998/99). Recent crosscountry studies find that good governance reduces poverty and improves the distribution of income (Gupta, Davoodi, and Alonso-Terme 1999; World Bank (2000c).

compared with 40 percent in Latin America and 15 percent in the OECD. Nearly three-quarters of firms surveyed by EBRD and the World Bank in the Kyrgyz Republic, Moldova, Russia, and Ukraine expressed little confidence in the security of their property rights. The same survey found that bribe payments for "administrative" corruption in the CIS averaged nearly 4 percent of annual firm revenues, while over 40 percent of firms in Russia, Moldova, Ukraine, and Azerbaijan reported that the sale of private interests of parliamentary votes or presidential decrees had an impact on their business. Although corruption is a problem in all ECA countries, there is considerable variation across the region in firms' perception of the severity of the problem. This variation makes it possible to analyze whether there is any apparent link, within ECA, between corruption and measures of income inequality.

At first glance, lower levels of corruption (measured as a higher TICP index) are statistically associated with lower levels of income inequality (figure 4.10). The simple correlation between the two is equal to –0.72. Similar negative associations are obtained if we use alternative measures of corruption (such as those drawn from the EBRD-World Bank survey)

Figure 4.10 Income Inequality and Corruption

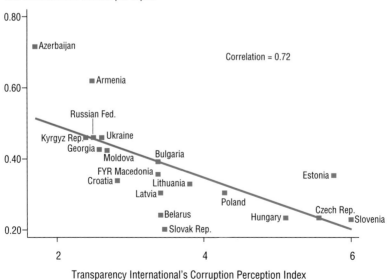

Source: Corruption Perception Index from Transparency International, 1999. Income Ginis are from table 4.1.

or an average of all available corruption measures (World Bank 2000a). More detailed analysis of the links between corruption and inequality suggests that the costs of corruption fall disproportionately on small firms and on the poor. Small firms pay bribes more frequently than do large firms, and these bribes represent a larger fraction of their incomes.[10] And while poor households are less likely to pay bribes, the bribes represent a much higher share of their incomes. The poor are also less likely to know where to go to get proper treatment when an official abuses his power (Anderson and others 2000). Corruption is thus a highly regressive phenomenon.

State Capture and Inequality

World Bank (2000a) documents the adverse impact of bureaucratic corruption on the transition economies and its negative distributional effects. But as it makes clear, the channel of influence from firms to the state may be even more damaging to the poor and to the distribution of income. There is increasing evidence that throughout the region firms often attempt to "capture" the state by using private payments to public officials as a way to influence the design of policy and the content of legislation, rules, and decrees. Through these efforts, firms can distort the legal framework and the policy-making process in an effort to gain large rents—to the detriment of the rest of society.

Transition economies are particularly vulnerable to state capture because of the socialist legacy of fused economic and political power and the lack of established markets and market-supporting institutions (see chapter 3). The lack of separation between economic and political power can blur the distinction between private and public interests and create perverse incentives for politicians and bureaucrats. At the same time the lack of markets can foster the emergence of huge rents to be fought over and appropriated by a privileged few. An increasing amount of the transition literature points to the problem of state capture as the root cause of the divergence in countries' performances and transition paths (EBRD 1999; Aslund 1999a and 1999b; Bunce 1999; and World Bank 2000b). Indeed, the speed and ability with which transition countries have implemented market reforms and developed supporting institutions seem to have been greatly conditioned by initial circumstances and the degree of political capture of governments.[11] The clearest example is Russia, where the early, chaotic stages of the transition allowed political power and wealth to be concentrated in the hands of well-placed business elites, who have since exerted a powerful influence over the pace of reform, blocking any progress that would erode their privileges. Much of the large increase in inequality in Russia happened during these early stages of transition (box 4.4).

State capture thrives when concentrated economic interests confront a weak state without sufficient accountability or control mechanisms. It has its origins in the choice of political institutions at the start of transition—a choice conditioned by both initial conditions and the nature of the exit from communism. Political institutions—and the extent of political competition in particular—influenced the susceptibility of different states to capture, and thus the path of economic reform. The social costs of state capture are huge: weakened investment and hence labor demand; informalization of labor market activities; taxes and expenditures biased

---

Box 4.4   The Legacy of the Early Years: Partial Reform, State Capture, and Inequality in Russia

Many economies in the former Soviet Union entered the transition with high levels of inequality. By 1992, for example, Russia already had an income Gini of 0.43—comparable to the United States in 1997—and only 4 Gini percentage points lower than the income Gini in Russia in 1999 (Commander, Tolstopiatenko, and Yemtsov 1999). Thus, much of the increase in inequality in Russia had occurred by the time the reformers took charge. This initial jump in inequality may be traced to partial and inconsistent reforms during the last years of the Soviet Union, which created a myriad of rent-seeking opportunities and behaviors (Aslund 1999a). The individuals best-placed to take advantage of these rent-seeking opportunities on a grand scale were state enterprise managers, in collaboration with well-placed government officials and politicians—the same groups that had "owned" political and economic power under the Soviet system. Firmly entrenched, these business elites were able to secure the ownership and control of the most valuable assets and resources in the country. Not surprisingly, this conditioned the pace and scope of further reform.

Aslund (1999a) identifies the following mechanisms for large-scale rent-seeking and private enrichment in the initial stages of the transition: the granting of exclusive licenses on the export of certain commodity goods; the privileged exploitation of arbitrage opportunities between controlled domestic commodity prices and world prices; and privileged access to subsidized credits from the Central Bank during hyperinflation. He estimates that jointly these activities may have reported private gains on the order of nearly 80 percent of Russia's GDP in 1992 alone. Easterly and Da Cunha (1994) estimate that credit emissions in Russia during 1992 totaled 33 percent of GDP, mostly in highly subsidized terms (nominal interest rates of 10 to 25 percent with average inflation exceeding 1000 percent). Like Aslund, they find that the credits went to selected enterprises and financial conglomerates. The cost of these directed credits was a huge inflation tax with significant distributional consequences: households and enterprises lacking the necessary political power suffered the most. The resulting hyperinflation led to the demonetization of the Russian economy, the collapse of formal incomes, and widespread informalization of labor market activities and labor earnings. This would set the stage for further increases in income inequality.

Table 4.9   State Capture and Inequality

Independent variable	(1)	(2)	(3)	(4)
State capture[a]	0.724	0.522	0.476	0.213
	(3.005)	(2.441)	(2.136)	(1.427)
Reform index[b]	—	—	—	1.428
				(1.998)
Initial freedoms[c]	-2.449	-0.539	-0.898	-0.752
	(-1.157)	(-0.285)	(-0.458)	(-0.422)
Planning[d]	—	0.485	0.378	0.170
		(2.811)	(1.748)	(0.769)
Location[e]	—	—	-4.742	-3.451
			(-0.829)	(-0.660)
R-squared	0.397	0.601	0.623	0.705
N	20	20	20	20

Note: The dependent variable is the Gini coefficient. Regressions of Gini were performed on a set of independent variables for 24 countries. All regressions include a constant and a dummy for the use of a consumption Gini when the income Gini is not available. T-statistics are in parentheses.
a. The percentage of firms responding that capture activities have a significant influence on their business.
b. A larger larger number means less reform.
c. The index of political rights and civil liberties at the start of the transition. Source: Freedom House (1999).
d. Years under central planning.
e. The dummy for proximity to Western Europe.
Sources: Same as table 4.7.

toward the rich and politically powerful; declining quality of social services; and underprovision of law and order. All of these costs affect the poor more than the rich and are therefore associated with more unequal outcomes.

The apparent association between state capture and high inequality is illustrated in table 4.9, which presents simple regressions of the Gini coefficient on measures of state capture and other initial condition variables. A higher degree of state capture is correlated with higher inequality, even when controlling for initial political freedoms, location, and years under state planning. The last column of the table shows, however, that the effect of state capture is dominated by the importance of economic reforms.

Notes

1. Standard household surveys in ECA, and especially in the FSU, are unable to capture the incomes of the richest segments of society, and hence our measures of inequality are most likely grossly underestimated.

2. A recent study of Georgia, for example, found that adjusting household incomes for "unreported cash incomes" (to match reported cash consumption) actually led to a *decrease* in the overall measures of inequality (World Bank 1999).

3. Some of the reported differences in income inequality measures in CSB countries and in the CIS could be attributable to differences in the recall period. Shorter recall periods in the CIS, combined with higher income volatility, could cause "measured" inequality to appear much higher than what you would obtain with a longer recall period.

4. In Central and Eastern Europe and in the Baltic states, most of the inequality in labor earnings is associated with wages; in the Commonwealth of Independent States, the bulk of inequality comes from self-employment earnings, reflecting the dramatic collapse of wage shares.

5. The concentration coefficient of wages measures how evenly or unevenly they are distributed. Negative values tell us it is progressive; a value of 0 means it is neutral; and positive values indicate that it is inequality increasing.

6. Milanovic (1999) also finds that the increase in wage inequality accounted for as much as a 15 to 24 point Gini increase in Latvia and Russia before and after the transition. However, the post-transition finding is not fully consistent with the results of Commander, Tolstopiatenko, and Yemtsov (1999).

7. McHale and Pankov (1999) also remark on this high apparent correlation. The simple correlation coefficient is -0.8, while the regression coefficient (shown in figure 4.7) equals –0.05 with a t-statistic of 5.481. The R-square for the regression is 0.64.

8. Inequality in Latin America is high in large part because of the prevalence of self-employment (World Bank 2000b). The same is likely to be true for the CIS.

9. Garner and Terrell (1998) find a larger impact for transfers than taxes in the Czech Republic, but conclude the reverse for Slovakia.

10. EBRD (1999) reveals that small firms are more than twice as likely to report paying bribes frequently than large firms (37 percent compared with 16 percent), and that on average these bribes represent a much larger tax on their revenues (5.4 percent compared with 2.8 percent).

11. Largely conditioned, in turn, by the extent to which countries were able to break with their socialist past, and by the nature of the political transition (see chapter 3).

References

Alexeev, Michael. 1999. "The Effect of Privatization on Wealth Distribution in Russia." *Economics of Transition.* 7, no. 2, pp. 449–65.

Alexeev, Michael, and Clifford G. Gaddy. 1993. "Income Distribution in the U.S.S.R. in the 1980s." *Review of Income and Wealth.* 39 (March): 23–36.

Anderson and others. 2000.

Aslund, Anders. 1999a. "Winner Takes All." Carnegie Endowment for International Peace. Processed.

Aslund, Anders. 1999b. "Problems with Economic Transformation in Ukraine." Paper prepared for the Fifth Dubrovnik Conference on Transition Economies, Dubrovnik, Croatia, June 23–25.

Bailey, Debra. 1997. "Separate but Equal? Comparing and Decomposing Income Inequality in Central and Eastern Europe." Center for Policy Research, Syracuse University.

Buckley, Robert M., and Eugene N. Gurenko. 1997. "Housing and Income Distribution in Russia: Zhivago's Legacy." *World Bank Research Observer,* 12:19-34.

Bunce, Valerie. 1999. "The Political Economy of Post-Socialism." Cornell University, New York. Processed.

Commander, Simon, and Une Lee. 1998. "How Does Public Policy Affect the Income Distribution? Evidence from Russia, 1992–96." London: European Bank for Reconstruction and Development.

Commander, Simon, Andrei Tolstopiatenko, and Ruslan Yemtsov. 1999. "Channels of Redistribution: Inequality and Poverty in the Russian Transition." *Economics of Transition* 7, No. 2, pp. 411–47.

Dabrowski, Marek, Stanislaw Gomulka, and Jacek Rostowski. 2000. "Whence Reform? A Critique of the Stiglitz Perspective." CASE, London School of Economics and Central European University. Processed.

De Melo, Martha, Cevet Denizer, and Alan Gelb. 1996. "From Plan to Market: Patterns of Transition." World Bank Policy Research Paper 1564. Washington, D.C.

De Melo, Martha, and others. 2000. "Circumstance and Choice: The Role of Initial Conditions and Policies in Transition." World Bank. Processed.

Deininger, Klaus, and Lyn Squire. 1996. "Measuring Income Inequality: A New Database." Development Discussion Paper No. 537. Harvard Institute for International Development, Cambridge, MA.

Dethier, Jean-Jacques, Hafez Ghanem, and Edda Zoli. 1999. "Does Democracy Facilitate the Economic Transition? An Empirical Study of Central and Eastern

Europe and the Former Soviet Union." Policy Research Working Paper 2194. World Bank, Europe and Central Asia Region, Poverty Reduction and Economic Management Sector Unit. October.

Easterly, William, and Paulo Vieria Da Cunha. 1994. "Financing the Storm: Macroeconomic Crisis in Russia." *Economics of Transition* 2 (December): 443–65.

EBRD (European Bank for Reconstruction and Development). 1999. *Transition Report.* London.

Flemming, John, and John Micklewright. 1999. "Income Distribution, Economic Systems and Transition." Innocenti Occasional Paper 70. Florence: UNICEF International Child Development Center. May.

Förster, Michael P., Peter Szivos, and Istvam György Toth. 1998. "Welfare Support and Poverty: The Experiences of Hungary and Other Visegrad Countries." In Kolosi, Tamas, Toth and Vukovich (eds.), *Social Report 1998*, Budapest: TARKI.

Freedom House. 1999. *Freedom in the World: The Annual Survey of Political Rights and Civil Liberties.*

Garner, Thesia I., and Katherine Terrell. 1998. "A Gini Decomposition Analysis of Inequality in the Czech and Slovak Republics during the Transition." Economics of Transition/European Bank for Reconstruction and Development (International); 6, 1:26-46, May 1998. European Bank for Reconstruction and Development, vol. 6, no. 1 (May): 23–46.

Goskomstat. 1994. *Russia Statistical Yearbook 1994.* Moscow.

Gupta, Sanjeev, Amid Davoodi, and Rosa Alonso-Terme. 1999. "Does Corruption Affect Income Inequality and Poverty?" Working Paper 76. International Monetary Fund, Washington, D.C.

IADB (Inter-American Development Bank). 1998/99. *Facing Up to Inequality in Latin America.* Economic and Social Progress in Latin America Annual Report. Washington, D.C.

Keane, Michael P., and Eswar S. Prasad. 2000. "Inequality, Transfers and Growth: New Evidence from the Economic Transition in Poland." May. Processed.

Klugman, Jeni. 1998. "Uzbekistan: Institutional Continuity Helps Performance." MOCT–MOST: Economic Policy in Transitional Economies, vol. 8, no. 1: 63–82.

Knack, Stephen and Philip Keefer. 1997. "Why Don't Poor Countries Catch Up? A Cross-National Test of An Institutional Explanation." *Economic Enquiry* 35 (July): 590–602.

Lehman, Hartmut, Jonathan Wadsworth, and Alessandro Acquisti. 1999. "Grime and Punishment: Job Insecurity and Wage Arrears in the Russian Federation." *Journal of Comparative Economics*, vol. 27, no. 4 (December): 595–617.

Lehman, Hartmut, Jonathan Wadsworth, and Ruslan Yemtsov. 2000. "A Month for the Company; Wage Arrears and the Distribution of Earnings in Russia." Heriot–Watt University. Edinburgh, Scotland. Processed.

Lindauer, David. 1998. "Labor and Poverty in the Republic of Moldova," *Moldova: Poverty Assessment Technical Papers 19846-MD*. Washington, D.C.: The World Bank.

Luttmer, Erzo. 2000. "Inequality and Poverty Dynamics in Transition Economies: Disentangling Real Effects from Data." *Background Papers: Making Transition Work for Everyone: Poverty and Inequality in Europe and Central Asia*. World Bank. Washington, D.C.

Mauro, Paolo. 1995. "Corruption and Growth." *Quarterly Journal of Economics* 110(3): 681–712.

———. 1998. "Corruption and the Composition of Government Expenditure." *Journal of Public Economics* 69: 263–79.

McHale, John, and Alexander Pankov. 1999. "Post-Communist Privatization and Wealth Distribution: What Do We Know?" Harvard University and World Bank. Draft.

Milanovic, Branko. 1998. *Income, Inequality, and Poverty during the Transition from Planned to Market Economy*. Washington, D.C.: The World Bank.

———. 1999. "Explaining the Increase in Inequality during the Transition." World Bank Policy Research Working Paper 1935. World Bank. Washington, D.C.

Nellis, John. 1999. "Time to Rethink Privatization in Transition Economies?" IFC Discussion Paper 38. World Bank. Washington, D.C.

Rutkowski, Jan. 1996. "High Skills Pay Off: The Changing Age Structure During Economic Transition in Poland." *Economics of Transition* 4 (1): 89–112.

———. 1999. "Wage Inequality in the Transition Economies of Central Europe: Trends and Patterns in the Late 1990s." World Bank, Human Development Sector Unit, Europe and Central Asia Region, Washington, D.C. Processed.

Shkratan, Maria. 1999. "The Impact of Corruption on the Poor in Transition Countries." World Bank. December. Processed.

Struyk, Raymond. 1996. *Economic Restructuring of the Former Soviet Bloc: The Case of Housing*. Washington, D.C.: Urban Institute Press.

Transparency International. Various Years. *Annual Report*. Berlin.

UNDP (United Nations Development Program). 1999. *Transition 1999: Human Development Report for Central and Eastern Europe and the CIS*. New York.

World Bank. Various Years. "Surveys of Small and Large Farmers (Armenia, Belarus, Moldova, Ukraine)."

———. 1999. *Georgia: Poverty and Income Distribution*. Report 19348-GE.

———. 2000a. *Anticorruption in Transition: A Contribution to the Policy Debate.* Poverty Reduction and Economic Management Sector Unit, Europe and Central Asia Region, World Bank.

———. 2000b. "Poverty and Policy in Latin America and the Caribbean." Draft. Washington, D.C.

———. 2000c. *World Development Report 2000/2001: Attacking Poverty.* Washington, D.C.

Yemtsov, Ruslan. 1999a. "Armenian Labor Market: Adjustments and Misalignments." *Improving Social Assistance in Armenia*, Annex 3, Report 19385-AM. Washington, D.C.: World Bank.

———. 1999b. "Inequality and Income Distribution," *Georgia: Poverty and Income Distribution.* Vol. 2: Technical Papers, Report 19348-GE. World Bank.

PART III

PUBLIC ACTION TO REDUCE POVERTY

Widespread poverty in Europe and Central Asia need not be a permanent phenomenon—even as it runs the risk of becoming one. As evidenced by the experience of many other countries, social and economic policies can go a long way to create opportunities, reduce poverty, and bring about a more egalitarian society. But in order for these policies to work, institutions must work well and must work in the interests of all parts of society, including the poor. Politicians captured by national elites or private interests have little incentive to act on behalf of the public good, and they are unlikely to implement the policies that will deliver better poverty outcomes. Indeed, it is hard to envision captured governments in much of the Commonwealth of Independent States (CIS) undertaking the actions needed to fight poverty and reduce inequality, when many of those actions (such as fostering the deconcentration of economic power through new entry and competition) may collide with their own private interests. If they are to attack poverty at all, governments throughout the region must first function effectively and be accountable and responsive to their broad electorates. Transition societies need to have mechanisms to ensure that different groups can express their preferences and demands in the political and social arena and that their voice is heard. With these fundamental elements in place, governments — and societies more broadly—will be better placed to design and implement a poverty strategy responsive to the needs of their citizenry.

Tackling state capture and building inclusive institutions are necessary elements of any effective antipoverty strategy in the transition economies. In all countries, even among the advanced reformers, there is scope to build more inclusive institutions and create better mechanisms for voice. But the problem is particularly acute in the CIS, where efforts to restart growth and make progress on the poverty agenda hinge on building accountable and responsible governments. Captured states, however, are unlikely to "correct" themselves. The pressure must come from nonstate institutions and actors—from the development of civil society and of inclusive institutions at the national and community levels. Chapter 5 addresses the issue of state capture and outlines a multiprong strategy to fight it. This strategy encompasses measures to increase the costs of state capture to bureaucrats and politicians (stronger checks and balances, more political competition, stronger oversight mechanisms and civil society); it also includes measures, such as more economic competition and further deregulation, to reduce the benefits to firms and individuals from engaging in capture activities. The chapter also emphasizes the importance of building civil society and inclusive community-based institutions—both as a means to pressure governments to change and as instruments to compensate for the limitations and failures of state institutions.

Institutional change alone, without progress on the economic policy front, will not be sufficient to reduce poverty and inequality. Better-functioning and more inclusive institutions will facilitate the implementation of policies aimed at the broader public good, but even the best-intentioned governments will need a well-thought-out and coherent strategy to deliver improvements in living standards.

Broad-based growth that translates into new jobs and higher incomes is a critical element of this strategy. Some countries are on the road to growth, but prospects are more uncertain in others. And all countries, even the advanced reformers, face the challenge of ensuring that growth translates into new jobs and employment. Chapter 6 lays out the main elements of a policy package that can underpin sustained growth and help translate growth into jobs. Some elements of this package (such as reforms to reduce widespread economic rents and foster competition) will be good for growth but will, in addition, facilitate institutional change and reduce inequality. Other reforms (such as efforts to fight discrimination) will help to ensure that the benefits of growth are widely distributed. Many of the transition countries still have highly distorted economies. Indeed, in many instances there are no explicit tradeoffs between growth and equity objectives; on the contrary, they tend to reinforce each other. In other instances there may be tradeoffs, and policy choices must be navigated with care. For example, in some of the countries in Central and South Eastern Europe and the Baltics (CSB), the need to carry out fiscal adjustment must be addressed without compromising the demonstrated effectiveness of the social safety net.

A second element in a strategy to fight poverty is building the capabilities of the poor, to allow them to take advantage of new employment and income-generating opportunities. The achievements of the education and health systems during the socialist era are undeniable. Countries are faced now with the challenge of reforming their systems to provide today's students with the skills they need to adapt to the changing demands of market-based economies. They are also faced with the challenge of providing their rapidly aging populations with high-quality health care that both households and the government can afford. The health and education systems have absorbed the large decline in financing that came with transition in ways that compromise quality and equity. Public sector salaries and expenditures on inputs (such as heat, textbooks, and drugs) have been downsized, but personnel and facilities have not. In this environment corruption has flourished as households have needed to make side payments to public sector employees to obtain services. Much of the burden of furnishing basic educational and health supplies has been *de facto* shifted to households. Serious illness is dreaded by poor households, since for many of them the costs of getting treatment are prohibitive. Chapter 7, on education, and Chapter 8, on health, suggest that poor communities and poor families are often the hardest hit by inadequate public spending and the rise in under-the-table payments. Chapters 7 and 8 review the important systemic reforms that are needed in each sector to ensure that the poor have the capabilities to participate as full members of society.

The transition has magnified the risks faced by households. Much of the security of the past was provided by guaranteed employment. This guarantee is gone. Largely because of the enormous fiscal contraction, programs that were intended to provide security and help people cope with economic shocks have had difficulty meeting their objectives. Free access to comprehensive health care has virtually disappeared in most countries. Under increasing stress, pension systems in some countries no longer provide a secure future for the elderly. Chapter 9 discusses how governments have tried to address the needs of the growing number of poor through expansion of social assistance programs, utility price compensation schemes, unemployment benefits, and pension reform. While many programs have provided some degree of support to families at risk, the sheer magnitude of the challenge has overwhelmed many countries' limited fiscal and administrative resources. Reform of pension programs is well under way across the region; still unresolved, however, are the inherent difficulties of identifying the poor and providing them with meaningful levels of social assistance while preserving work incentives.

Governments can play an active role in reducing inequality and enhancing the mobility of those at the bottom. While responding to societal preferences, better distributional outcomes have been shown to have an important positive impact on growth, on social cohesion, and on the functioning of democracy. Governments may want to influence inequality simply because they believe in social justice and in maximizing social welfare. Chapter 10 examines a set of policy options to affect the distribution of income. Some of these are policies that are needed to restore growth, but they also will have positive distributional effects. Others focus more directly on raising the income of those at the very bottom, essentially through two channels. The first is through measures to increase their earnings potential and remove barriers to their employment. The second is by rebuilding the capacity of governments to deliver basic services and carry out an effective fiscal policy, so that societies can achieve their distributional objectives.

CHAPTER 5

Building Inclusive Institutions for Poverty Alleviation and Development

I n countries making the transition to a more market-oriented economy, institutions have played a critical role in determining inequality and poverty outcomes—arguably as important a role as that played by economic factors. The weakness or strength of the institutional framework has, in the first instance, conditioned the ability (and desire) of governments throughout Europe and Central Asia to implement reforms for the public good. In this regard it has largely determined the path of output, incomes, and jobs. The institutional framework also has underpinned the quality of governance in these economies, with large spillover effects on growth, poverty, and distribution. Finally, the institutional framework has influenced the extent to which different parts of society have had a voice in the changes affecting them during the transition, and hence the degree of inclusiveness of policies and the policymaking process.[1]

Efforts to reduce poverty must address its economic, institutional, and political causes simultaneously. On the economic front, the key issue is access to assets and opportunities (chapters 6, 7, and 8). On the political and institutional front, the challenge is to ensure that state institutions and the political process do not discriminate against the poor. Policymakers must try to guarantee that the poor have recourse in the legal foundations and political processes of the country, that they have voice at the local and national levels, and that state institutions are responsive to all parts of society, the poor included. As important as economic growth is to poverty reduction, it cannot, by itself, alter the basic causes of persistent poverty (access to assets, opportunities, and political power) unless these institutional factors are also addressed.

Making institutions and policies more inclusive of the poor is complex, because the poor tend to have little political power, and their interests and needs may not be in line with those of more politically powerful groups. However, much can be done to create a social and political environment in which the advantages of pro-poor policies are widely accepted. A first step to building inclusive institutions is to ensure that they are representative of and accountable to of all parts of society, and most notably to the middle class. Indeed, the experience in the West suggests that a strong, informed middle class is at the core of effective, democratic, and transparent institutions and that any sustainable social contract must have the interests of the middle class at heart. To empower the middle class and to empower the poor require the same key elements: respect for political and civil liberties, respect for individual rights, and respect for all citizens' rights to participate in and influence social and economic decisions. This does not mean that a society with all these attributes will be strongly pro-poor and have institutions that are inclusive of all groups. But such a society will allow debate and expression of the society's preferences, and it will create the preconditions for pro-poor policies and empowerment to emerge.

In all countries of the region, there is scope to make institutions more inclusive. Even in the most advanced reformers, such as Poland or Hungary, the middle class has been shrinking as the polarization of incomes has grown (Birdsall and others 2000). The strongest risk factor for these economies is that high unemployment will lead to rising social exclusion among the long-term unemployed, much as it has in Western Europe. Programs and institutions that can bring the long-term unemployed and other disenfranchised groups back into social and economic life are thus urgently needed. The advanced reformers also face a problem with groups that are marginalized because of their ethnicity and consequently denied full and equal participation in social, economic, and political life.[2] The most notable example is the Roma population throughout Central Europe.

The challenge of inclusion is even larger in the Commonwealth of Independent States (CIS), because of the hijacking of the national agenda by powerful private interests at great social cost (chapter 3). The "capture" of the policymaking and legislative processes by special interests, and the ensuing weakness and arbitrariness of institutions, are fundamentally at odds with the emergence of a strong middle class. The system is, by definition, set up to create a polarization of society, a fundamental divide between the "haves"—with access to economic and political power—and the "have-nots." Such polarization provides a very unstable and weak foundation for the development of an open, democratic, market-based society. Tackling this "capture" of the state by private interests is of first priority if economic and political reforms are going to move forward and bring benefits to broader parts of society. It is also an essential aspect of rebuilding the credibility of the state and the trust of the broader population in the democratic process (box 5.1). This trust, in turn, is crucial to fostering civil and political participation, and to building a fully functioning democratic system.

Tackling state capture is just a first step in making institutions in the CIS more inclusive. It is a necessary but not sufficient condition for progress. Even in mature democracies with well-functioning institutions and accountable governments there are groups that are often voiceless and whose interests figure little in public policy. These groups, the poor among them, need a more direct voice in the interventions that affect them on a day-to-

---

Box 5.1   The Poor, Corruption, and Distrust

Corruption is one of the most visible manifestations of institutional weakness in transition economies. It is a problem in all countries of the region, although its extent and severity vary from country to country. The crippling nature of the problem is evident in the large amount of anecdotal and systematic evidence concerning the pervasiveness of corruption and bribery, the perceived risks of investing in the transition economies, and the emergence of huge disparities in wealth and incomes. Corruption has retarded growth, and it has affected the poor in many damaging ways: it has reduced the level of social spending, forced the poor to pay for even the most basic administrative and social public services, and constrained the emergence of small-scale enterprises and activities. Corruption of public institutions and authorities also has deepened the social exclusion of the poor, reinforcing their cynicism toward their leaders and the political system (World Bank 2000a, b).

World Bank poverty assessments in Europe and Central Asia are full of references to state corruption, government failure, and the poor's sense of abandonment by their leaders. Poor individuals have little reason to believe that the state represents their interests, and they feel hopeless, voiceless, and powerless. This feeds their alienation and disengagement from civil society and political life. "The state steals from us all the time," complained a person in the Ukraine, "so deceiving the state is not a sin" (Narayan 2000, 92). "They have been plundering everything and eating so much that they cannot carry their own stomachs," a Latvian reported (Narayan 2000, 82).

The poor often blame the government for their impoverishment and report widespread corruption and helplessness. "Our leaders announced transition to new market relations and then left us to the mercy of fate, not asking whether we were prepared to accept the transition," lamented one Georgian (Narayan 2000, 79). In Georgia, poor farmers equate privatization with theft and complain that the best land is distributed to those who work for the police, courts, school directors, and business people. In Moldova poor people equate independence, democracy, and the transition to market with lack of social justice. Workers on collective farms report being cheated out of their share of grains and denied access to equipment by those in control.

Source: World Bank (2000a, b).

day level, as well as the ability to organize and influence the political process. Actions are needed to bring down barriers—legal, political, and social—that work against their participation in the market and in political life. Institutions, however, are largely the outcome of the preferences and demands of civil society. For institutions to be inclusive of the poor, civil society itself must be inclusive. Customary practices, local and community networks, and discrimination can often work against inclusion. Removing this discrimination and managing ethnic and social divisions can be an important part of reducing poverty.

Building Effective National Institutions

Inclusive state institutions are a necessary precondition to fighting poverty in a sustainable way. But for state institutions to be inclusive, they first have to be effective, accountable, and representative. This cannot happen in a captured state. How can state capture be tackled? The key is to address the underlying problems of institutional capacity and incentives within the state, civil society, and the private sector.

State Capture and Administrative Corruption

World Bank (2000a) proposes a dual approach to the problem of corruption—namely, increasing the cost of state capture to politicians while simultaneously reducing the benefits from state capture to firms. This approach rests on five building blocks discussed in this section: (1) increasing political accountability; (2) strengthening institutional restraints within the state; (3) strengthening civil society participation and media oversight; (4) creating a competitive private sector; and (5) reforming public sector management.

Needless to say, efforts to challenge the control and rents secured by those who have captured the state will face stiff opposition. Those who benefit from the system have little incentive to change it. Those who are excluded may lack the political power and voice to demand change. The result is a vicious circle—a low status equilibrium that is hard to break. The pressure for change will have to come, in most cases, from nonstate institutions and actors—reinforced, if needed, by pressure from external sources. Therefore, it is important to build up civil society, empowering groups and communities to actively defend their interests on the national stage. This can strengthen the foundation for building trust and accountability from the bottom up. From the lessons of international experience in the fight against corruption and capture, we know that such progress is possible even if slow (box 5.2).

Increasing political accountability. To make politicians more accountable, governments must increase the transparency of the political process and increase political competition. Transparency provides the public with the information needed to monitor the state and make informed political choices. It can be fostered by protecting the right of the public to observe sessions in parliament, government, and the courts; by publishing the voting records of parliamentarians, the minutes of government meetings, and annual reports of government bodies; and by requiring public officials to disclose their income and assets and thus reveal conflicts of interest. Latvian law, for example, requires state officials to declare their assets, and it penalizes officials who cannot justify possession of assets in excess of their normal sources of income. Besides increasing overall accountability, increased transparency improves the likelihood that governments and officials will respond to the demands of the poor. Regular publication in the media of the transfer of social funds to specific districts, for example, can allow monitoring of the use of funds by public users, foster accountability, and improve the delivery of public services. The poor are likely to benefit the most from these reforms.

Box 5.2   Combatting Corruption and State Capture: Lessons from International Experience

Countries with very different governments have been successful in fighting corruption and reducing state capture. Hong Kong and Singapore implemented strong measures against corruption in public service. A key element of both programs was meritocratic pay schemes to create a professional civil service. These efforts were backed by fair and effective enforcement agencies, and they were supported by programs focused on education and prevention. As a result, both Hong Kong and Singapore have achieved dramatic reductions in public and private corruption since the early 1980s. Another successful example is the United States. During the late nineteenth and early twentieth centuries, gradual reform in the public sector reduced graft and corruption. Reform of the public system in the United States started slowly at the federal level, but it gained momentum as the beneficiaries of the reform process gained strength. Other countries have experimented with more partial reforms. Mexico, for example, recently implemented measures to improve its customs administration. It simplified procedures and improved pay and monitoring. In Argentina a scandal led to changes in accounting practices and management of the public reinsurance system. However, the sustainability of these partial reforms—as opposed to that of more comprehensive reforms—remains to be proven.

Source: Rose-Ackerman (1999, chap. 11); and World Bank (2000a).

Political competition limits the ability of any single powerful group to capture the state. It increases the likelihood that corruption will be checked by competing parties and punished by the electorate. In mature political systems, political parties constitute an important channel for broad constituencies to express their demands to political leaders. As an instrument of voice, political parties can be especially valuable for the disenfranchised and the poor, who have few other means of making their voices heard in national politics. Case studies from other countries suggest that political participation by all segments of society can increase distributional equity and improve social outcomes in education and health (Dreze and Sen 1996). Broad-based political parties are gaining credibility in Central and South Eastern Europe and the Baltics (CSB), but in many other transition economies they lack transparency and are only weakly representative of broad constituencies. This exacerbates politicians' dependence on powerful firms and financial interests.

Strengthening institutional restraints within the state. Under socialism economic, political, bureaucratic, and social power were fused. Transition involves the separation of the state from the economy and society, and the creation of independent legislative, executive, and judiciary functions. Yet the extent of separation of powers varies significantly by country. Legislatures and the judiciary in Central Europe and the Baltics have made great progress in establishing their independence from the executive branch of government and in strengthening their oversight function. Throughout the Commonwealth of Independent States, however, the legislative and judicial branches remain subject to the influences of powerful lobbies and the executive. Strengthening checks and balances in the system requires reinforcement of the horizontal separation between the legislative, executive, and judicial branches. This, in turn, will promote their transformation into legitimate and competent state institutions.

The first institutional priority is to build an independent and effective judiciary that can curb the arbitrary exercise of power by the state. Judicial independence, however, must not come at the expense of accountability. Monitoring mechanisms, such as the publication of trial records and judicial decisions, can help build this accountability and transparency. Objective selection criteria and high standards of qualification for judicial appointments, as in Georgia, will improve professionalism. Private lawyers can play an important role in curbing judicial corruption by acting as intermediaries between judges and litigants. The monitoring and enforcement of ethical and professional behavior in the legal arena also can be strengthened by the creation of associations that set and monitor standards of legal practice. In addition, the development of a system of consumer protection can advance the goal of an independent and effective judiciary.

A second priority is a strong legislature with well-defined oversight functions of other branches (as in much of central Europe). Mandatory disclosure of government documents, committees to audit public accounts, and mechanisms to sanction governments can strengthen this oversight function. Creating and strengthening independent watchdog institutions can also help build checks and balances. One good example of this is Poland's Supreme Audit Chamber, which investigates and publishes reports on abuses in procurement, management of public assets, and other diversions of public funds. Another key requirement is increasing the independence, effectiveness, and professionalism of law enforcement agencies.

Government decisions are less prone to corruption when they are based on clear and transparent administrative procedures rather than on the discretion of government bureaucrats. These procedures protect the rights of citizens by guaranteeing appropriate participation in government decisions by affected parties, as well as the right and availability of recourse. In an attempt to strengthen public administration and protect the rights of citizens, some transition countries (mainly in CSB) are developing their administrative procedures. Latvia, for example, is introducing legislation to set up a system of administrative courts dedicated to the adjudication of disputes between citizens and the state. Although these courts represent a large financial commitment, the Latvian government believes they are essential to the efficiency and credibility of government decisionmaking (World Bank 2000a).

Actions to lessen state capture and administrative corruption have a direct impact on the lives of the poor, who are often the most vulnerable to the arbitrary use of power. Police harassment, lawlessness, and violence deeply affect the daily lives of the poor. Hence, they have the most to gain from well-functioning legal and judicial systems and professional law enforcement (box 5.3).

Strengthening civil society participation and media oversight. Once a state is captured, the fusion of economic and political forces makes any reform difficult. It is hard for a captured and corrupt state to "correct" itself. Pressure must come from civil society and nonstate organizations—citizens groups, nongovernmental organizations, trade unions, religious organizations—and from the media. Under communism, however, civil society did not exist or was severely repressed. There were exceptions, such as a strong trade union movement in Poland and civic associations in other Central

> **Box 5.3   Lawlessness and the Poor**
>
> We feel absolutely insecure. The police are corrupt: if they catch a villain, they let him walk; only those who can't give them anything are sent to prison. (Kalaijdhzi, Bulgaria)
>
> It's the kind of police you have no hope of ever reaching. The police are for those at the top. (Yekaterinberg, Russia)
>
> In interviews Georgian entrepreneurs have stressed their need for a protector or *krysha*, which literally means "roof" in Russian. Such a person was said to be essential if an entrepreneur wanted to have good relations with important figures in the police force. The "protector" could publicize the fact of this relationships to protect the entrepreneur against unforeseen "accidents."
>
> *Source:* World Bank (2000b); on Georgian entrepreneurs, Dudwick (1999).

European countries, but these were not the norm. Even today, nongovernmental organizations (NGOs) in many transition economies remain closely tied to state institutions or to political and economic interests.

Recently, there has been a timid emergence of civil society activism in the transition countries, much of it focusing on corruption. To raise public awareness, many organizations have made use of country surveys on corruption as well as service delivery surveys. Public dissemination of this information has helped raise the electorate's awareness of the problem. One example of civil society activism is the People's Voice Program in Ukraine, which aims to build integrity at the municipal level by strengthening the voice of citizens' groups demanding better governance and service provision. This organization gathers information on problems associated with major public services. The information is then used to pressure local leaders to improve service delivery (World Bank 2000a).

The free functioning of nongovernmental organizations is necessary for a vibrant civil society, which can then influence the behavior of governments. The state must remove legal and other barriers to forming associations and provide an administrative and judicial framework that supports them. For example, Georgia's open and liberal policy toward NGOs makes it less cumbersome to obtain information on an NGO in Georgia than in neighboring countries. As a result, a number of civil society organizations have emerged since independence and are carrying out effective advocacy and monitoring work. These organizations are especially important in Georgia because of its weak institutional environment. They have played a crucial role in articulating and publicizing abuses of power and instances of corruption (World Bank 1999b). However, in some CIS countries—most notably those of Central Asia—nongovernmental organizations still face considerable restrictions as well as lingering state pressure.

Although civil society and the media can powerfully influence public officials, their roles are likely to be enhanced by a constructive state policy. For example, in 1998 an NGO in the Slovak Republic drafted the first version of the National Program for the Fight against Corruption, and it has regularly been invited by the government to monitor procurements and other state decisions. Governments that approach NGOs as partners rather than as enemies can spur productive results.

By uncovering abuses, a free media can be instrumental in checking the level of corruption and capture of the state by special interests. Since the fall of socialism, the media in many countries in Europe and Central Asia have become vocal critics of corruption. Although most countries in the region have a free and open press, its impact is weakened by lingering state controls, conflicts of interest generated by nontransparent ownership arrangements, and corruption in the press itself. In many transition countries, media organizations remain closely linked to (and often owned and funded by) the state, or they have been captured by powerful economic interests. Libel laws and intimidation can effectively constrain whistleblowers. In authoritarian parts of the region, state pressure and censorship often prevail.

A policy of openness, formalized in laws guaranteeing free access to information, is critical to strengthening the media's oversight function. Also important are efforts to professionalize journalism and to create a culture of "truth in reporting." Competition and policies to facilitate, rather than hinder, entry into the media market (including foreign entry) can reduce conflicts of interests and improve governance within the media.

Greater civil liberties, a freer press, and a stronger civil society are essential to building effective state institutions; they also have a direct positive impact on the fight against poverty. By bringing attention to the plight of the poor and fostering public debate, these measures can build social consensus on ways to combat poverty. They promote the formation of shared values, increase social solidarity, and pressure governments to respond to social needs.

Creating a competitive private sector. Reforms to improve the accountability of politicians and bureaucrats are critical to reducing corruption and state capture. However, it is also important to lessen the incentives that induce the private sector to engage in such capture activities. This requires dissolving the concentration of economic interests that has emerged during the transition. By lowering barriers to entry and requiring competitive restructuring, ECA governments can foster competition, reduce arbitrary rents, and nurture a private sector that alleviates poverty rather than worsens it. Parallel regulatory reform will reduce the ability of the state to extort bribes by decreasing the number and complexity of regulations and bureaucratic discretion. On positive example is Hungary, which has improved the quality of its regulations and eliminated many unnecessary ones. Although regulatory requirements are still substantial (nearly two-thirds of all firms must obtain licenses to operate), Hungary ranks first out of 20 transition countries in the Governance Index of the European Bank for Reconstruction and Development (World Bank 2000a).

Competition can also be facilitated by financial disclosure requirements, efficient registries, and supervision of monopolistic sectors by independent regulatory bodies. It is also important to redirect into legal channels the means by which firms seek to influence the state and the legislative process. Collective forms of interest representation—business associations, trade unions, and political parties—should be encouraged in this context.

In addition to reducing corruption, these measures can directly improve the income-generating opportunities of the poor. Barriers to entry and other regulatory hurdles are particularly harmful to the development of the small enterprise sector. Corruption itself represents a highly regressive tax on small businesses. Small enterprises in the region pay, on average, 5.4 percent of their revenues in bribes, compared with the 2.8 percent paid by large firms. They also face bribe demands more than twice as frequently as large firms do. Micro-enterprises—which represent an important source of employment and income for the poor—are particularly vulnerable to bribes in their interactions with the state. Thus, measures to reduce regulatory requirements, decrease barriers to entry, and stimulate competition in concentrated sectors can have useful spillover effects on the poor, and they can stimulate new small-scale activities in the private sector (EBRD 1999).

Reforming the public sector. A final key element in the strategy to reduce administrative corruption is an effective public administration—a true public service in which public officials can be relied upon to do their jobs well. What are the key elements of public sector reform? Meritocratic recruitment and promotion linked to performance are the most important structural features for improving bureaucratic performance. Where feasible, it can be useful to establish an independent body to oversee the civil service. This is currently happening in Poland, Latvia, and Kazakhstan. Low salary levels contribute to poor performance and encourage corruption. Therefore, ECA governments should endeavor to increase civil service salaries, link them to skill and performance, and monetize the extensive nonsalary benefits that now provide scope for corruption. Another important element is accountability in service delivery (especially in education and health). In Armenia, Latvia, and Albania, credible civil-society groups have initiated user surveys of service delivery, and they periodically publish their findings. This builds a culture of service delivery and accountability, with a large potential impact on those most dependent on public service provision—namely, the poor.

Also important are actions to improve fiscal management and administration, including measures to increase transparency in the budget process, provide transparent and comprehensive treasury operations, introduce competitive public procurement, and strengthen accounting and auditing. Tax and customs reform can be an important contributor to lowering corruption, while increasing much-needed state revenues. Reforms to simplify tax policy and eliminate discretionary exemptions can help lower corruption. Also important are the professionalization of staff, standardization of forms and procedures, and use of transparent systems such as computerized risk analysis at the borders. The key is to eliminate one-on-one contact between taxpayers and officials and ensure that operating and management systems are efficient and easily monitored, including through periodic taxpayer surveys.

Administrative corruption can be profoundly damaging to the level and quality of service delivery across sectors. It is often rooted in distorted policies, as evidenced in the energy and health sectors. Corruption is at the core of low collections and poor service delivery of electricity in many CIS countries, with negative spillover effects for growth, the emergence of a private sector, and ultimately poverty. Similarly, the absence of adequate governance, oversight, and monitoring has made the health sector fertile ground for corruption. The results are pervasive informal payments and a rationing of services to those who cannot pay. The effects of corruption in both energy and health appear to be very regressive, since the poor are the least able to make informal payments or to make formal payments for alternative services— for example, alternative sources of energy (Lovei 2000). Therefore, it is the poor who suffer the most from rationing of services.[3]

The voice of the poor: silent or heard? The quality of governance and democracy, the rule of law, and the efficacy of public administration influence the extent to which state institutions serve the poor. But their actual impact on poverty depends on how effectively they translate into empowerment of the poor at the micro level. Even in states with political and civil liberties and governments that are neither captured nor corrupt, the poor are often voiceless and their interests figure little in public policy.

Pluralistic and representative governments may not meet the needs of the poor for many reasons. The poor may not participate in the political process. They may lack information on the details and consequences of policy measures, and the time to follow up on issues. They are less able than the nonpoor to hold the elected officials accountable for their electoral promises. They also lack the necessary personal contacts, money, and time to pursue broad political goals. In addition, the poor may not have effective vehicles for organization. Sometimes the poor take little part in politics because participation seems futile or irrelevant to their primary concerns, or because they have little confidence about their ability to influence the government. In the words of one Armenian man, "People place their hopes in God, since the government is no longer involved in such matters" (Narayan and others 2000, 79). Other characteristics of the poor make collective action difficult. They are often geographically dispersed and socially heterogeneous, or feel isolated and ashamed. Or they may be excluded from political and economic processes by ethnicity and other identities.

What can be done to increase the voice of the poor in Europe and Central Asia? Empowerment—ensuring that the poor know their rights, have mechanisms to express them, and regain their trust in state institutions—is a good place to begin. Disseminating information on poverty, promoting public debate on poverty, fostering community participation, and building political support for pro-poor actions and coalitions are ways to increase the voice of the poor. Decentralization can put public officials in closer touch with the issues of greatest salience to local populations and give the poor more opportunities for expressing their concerns. Measures to build the social capital of the poor can play an important role, as well as efforts to foster the growth of pro-poor grassroots organizations. The state can facilitate interactions between local administrations and communities by reducing obstacles to community action and by encouraging greater collaboration between communities and local governments. These initiatives can have substantial political payoffs for governments by increasing legitimacy and popular support.

In creating political support for actions to help the poor, the state has a crucial part. From the state's point of view, bringing poor people into the mainstream is not only beneficial for overall social welfare; it also can improve political stability, make the investment climate more attractive, increase investment in education and human capital, build social cohesion, and induce growth. The well-being of poor people is of direct concern to the interests of the nonpoor. One distinct motivation for pro-poor action among the nonpoor worldwide is reduced crime and violence. A second, often-cited motivation is to prevent mass migration to urban centers and the ensuing problems of growing slums and heightened demands on already-stretched urban services. The nonpoor also have a strong interest in public health: in the context of communicable diseases, such as tuberculosis, it is impossible for any group to isolate itself completely from contagion. Poor people can be especially vulnerable to communicable diseases because they are undernourished and live in environments with greater exposure to infection (Moore and Putzel 1999).

Although the interests of the poor and the nonpoor are intertwined in these ways, the nonpoor do not always perceive the advantages of pro-poor action. Governments can do much to enhance the perceived common interests between the poor and nonpoor and to build political support for public action against poverty. Key to this is introducing into the public debate the notion that poverty reduction is a public good and will further the well-being of the nonpoor.

Building Inclusive Community-Based Institutions

Well-functioning states and accountable institutions are necessary for sustainable economic and social development. Yet one cannot assume that states will move in this direction without pressure from nonstate institutions and actors, or even from actors outside the given country. Countries in line for accession to the European Union hope accession will open to them many opportunities. Their desire to be part of the European Union has been a powerful catalyst for political leaders to push through broadranging institutional and policy reform. Of course, the Czech Republic, Estonia, Hungary, Poland, and Slovenia, because of country-specific advantages of history and location, have found it easier than other countries to meet the European Union half way. For many of the CIS countries, or the conflict-ridden countries of South Eastern Europe, state institutions are not coping well with the new demands.

Given how hard it is to change state-level institutions, building accountable and inclusive institutions at the local level can be a first step toward systemic change. Empowerment of the community takes on particular importance in Europe and Central Asia because the centralized and authoritarian socialist regimes had a devastating impact on "community" and "society." Depending on the length of time they maintained power, as well as the strength of pre-existing and countervailing institutions, socialist states significantly disempowered civil society by directly punishing autonomous initiatives. The destruction of civil society and traditional bases of community cohesion, together with the strong centralization of power, have, in a sense, provided the program for the rebuilding of more inclusive polities. In order to transform subjects back into citizens, governments may have to reconstruct and empower civil society, construct new bases for community and social cohesion, and decentralize government institutions.

Decentralization

Proponents of decentralization sing its praises. Particularly in the top-down, less-participatory ECA countries, decentralization, they say, will allow local governments to respond to local needs more effectively. It will place power and resources at a level closer to ordinary citizens, giving them new opportunities to participate in decisionmaking. Proponents differ, however, regarding the prerequisites essential to achieve these ends. Some argue that pre-existing traditions and channels for citizen participation are the key to successful decentralization, while others point to high levels of community cohesion and the ability to work together (often referred to as social capital). The presence of NGOs and other citizen groups may be an indicator of citizen participation, although such organizations can exclude segments of the citizenry. Proponents of decentralization believe it can stimulate demand for mechanisms through which people can voice their preferences. Where low levels of trust and cohesion limit interchange between citizens and their local governments, decentralization can be designed to build up participation around specific issues or projects.

Policymakers are now inclined to take a more careful look at decentralization. While decentralization can make the state more responsive to needs at the local level and stimulate participation, it also can do more harm than good if adequate support, structures, and accountability mechanisms are not in place. Where the accountability and the infrastructure of subnational governments are weak, decentralization can increase corruption and reduce access to basic social services as well as their quality. This has happened in parts of Central Asia, the South Caucasus, and the Baltics. When local-level power structures are themselves highly unequal, decentralization can increase exclusion and hurt the poor. Despite these cautions, the tendency in Europe and Central Asia has been to push for greater decentralization.

Civil Society: Model and Theory

Although one immediate aim of decentralization is to make government more accountable and responsible to citizens, this aim is often construed as part of the broader objective of strengthening civil society. Defined as a sphere of activity and discourse that mediates between individuals and families, civil society includes far more than NGOs and advocacy groups. It runs a broad gamut of formal and informal organizations and associations that exist outside the state—unions, professional and business associations, ethnic associations, religious organizations, student groups, cultural organizations, sports clubs, and informal community groups (box 5.4). Civil society and the state exist in a complicated, mutually dependent relationship, since actors need the protection of an institutionalized legal order to guard their autonomy and freedom of action.

Despite the current emphasis on rebuilding civil society in Europe and Central Asia, political theorists do not agree on the answer to this question: does civil society precede, follow, or accompany the development of political democracy? In any case, they warn that neither political democracy nor civil society ensures the existence of the other; rather, civil society requires institutional change in social and political systems, as well as a

---

Box 5.4 Civil Society Organizations

Civil society organizations, particularly the subset known as nongovernmental organizations, play a significant role in many domains of public life, including the provision of public services in partnership with government. Civil society in the Commonwealth of Independent States (particularly in Uzbekistan and Turkmenistan) has been subject to much greater pressure than in Central and South Eastern Europe and the Baltics. The legal and legislative framework, complex registration laws conditioned by state distrust of citizens' organizations, and pervasive poverty that allows little time for voluntarism have impeded the growth of this sector. Many trade unions and business organizations in CIS countries, unlike CSB countries, remain under state control and cannot be considered part of civil society.

Although some nongovernmental organizations were formed to promote certain issues or to advance the interests of members, many were created in response to the demands of donors for "grassroots" partners. As in CSB countries, these organizations tend to be loosely organized, not very accountable to their membership, and even less accountable to the donors with which they often work. Working with donors has improved NGOs in many respects, but some have become overextended because of donors' attempts to broaden their constituencies and beneficiaries to scales required by major projects. Generous funding and specific requirements have made some civil society organizations dependent on donors and less sustainable.

culture that legitimizes organized collective activity beyond family or ethnic bonds (Holm 1996). Even though in some countries (especially in Central Europe) the mobilization of civil society helped topple the socialist
system, that civil society has remained undeveloped in postsocialist states
with their weak and disorganized political institutions. Its development
has been hindered by widespread cynicism about public authority and
politics, and a tradition of alienation, which for many decades functioned
as a mode of resistance to oppressive state authorities (Diamond 1994;
Fish 1994).

Nevertheless, civil society programs and activities—religious, political,
business-oriented, and labor-oriented—mushroomed during the 1990s in
the ECA region, particularly in Central Europe and some CIS capitals.
What explains this activism? Some argue that the population sought to
create and use formal and informal organizations and groups as a viable
alternative to oppressive, inefficient, and narrowly defined state institutions and organizations. Thus far, however, many of these new organizations tend to be poorly funded, local, and "underinstitutionalized" because
of their creators' continuing aversion to formal procedures. Generous tax
incentives or lack of regulation have produced numerous foundations, many
of which have turned out to be tax shelters for businesses. In the more
authoritarian countries of the region, civil society organizations still operate under heavy pressure and are periodically closed down.

Civil Society and Social Cohesion

Another necessary ingredient for effective community-level institutions is
"social capital." The civic culture model of social capital stresses shared norms,
values, and generalized trust; the social structural model stresses social networks, which can be analyzed from the individual, group, community, or
even transnational perspective. These networks are a means of accessing
resources. The social network's position within a specific socioeconomic context limits or facilitates its access to resources (Foley and Edwards 1999).

Using the social structural definition of social capital, we can say that
while the socialist state crushed civil society, it did not destroy social capital, but rather provided different bases for it. Indeed, the need to cope
with the pervasive economy of shortages strengthened many social networks and forced people to rely heavily on social capital (particularly in
the absence of literal capital). The challenge for creating inclusive communities is to provide a "bridging mechanism" that can link individuals, households, groups, associations, and networks with each other, thereby reducing
the schisms and gaps that hinder the development of real communities.

Community-Level Institutions in the Absence of Communities

The strategy of rebuilding community-level institutions appears promising, but it rests on the premise that identifiable and viable communities already exist. In fact, the existence of communities in transition economies is questionable given the deliberate and often heavy-handed attempts by the state to crush local identities and solidarities. Numerous qualitative studies undertaken in ECA countries suggest that while people are members of many intersecting and locally based social networks (of work colleagues, neighbors, and kin), few identify with an abstract "community" or demonstrate much commitment to furthering the good of this community. In fact, many people view with deep suspicion appeals to support the "collective good." Moreover, the rapid socioeconomic stratification in the past ten years ruptured many of the social networks that linked people within geographic settlements. To the extent that such strong networks remain, they may or may not rely on identification with a neighborhood or village. Those trying to rebuild community institutions cannot take for granted that people living together perceive themselves as part of a community of common interests.

In a fascinating case study of Northern Albania, Douglas Saltmarshe (2000) explains how exclusivist, kin-based networks can provide social capital for their members but work against the construction of a community that can act effectively on its own behalf. His study compares two villages, which we will call Gura and Malaj. The residents of Gura were dominated by five *fis* (the extended families so important to Albanians' traditional social structure); only occasionally did the residents cooperate across kin lines to achieve immediate aims (such as pooling money to repair a burned out electrical transformer). The population in Malaj was more homogeneous than in Gura. Neighborhood alliances dominated in Malaj, and they laid the basis for a community-wide, corporate identity to emerge. The council successfully lobbied higher levels of government for resources. Malaj's ability to shed traditional norms allowed it to develop more responsive and effective local-level institutions.

Positive Examples of Local-Level Institutions

Because of the inadequacies of national-level institutions in Europe and Central Asia, local-level institutions have taken on more importance. Even in the most authoritarian and war-torn countries in the region, communities (whether defined in terms of shared interests or common locale) have assumed functions and services previously provided by the state. The greater ability of communities and groups to take initiative and collaborate is an aspect of the development of civil society in the postsocialist states. Case studies from a handful of countries suggest the variety of ways in which nonstate or local-level institutions have been able to act autonomously.

In Tajikistan, despite the absence of a stable or supportive state framework, people have managed to act together on their own behalf through long-standing institutions such as the mosque or through shared practical needs (supported by assistance from an international donor). The government's tolerance of greater religious freedom during the brief period between independence and civil war allowed Islamic institutions to grow. During the war, mosques suffered less damage than did other buildings, in part because of their more durable brick construction, in part because they were spared as symbols sacred to both warring parties. As a result, the mosques were able to serve as shelters in war-affected areas. In addition, Islamic institutions from abroad channeled assistance through local Islamic institutions, a much-needed conduit for assistance (Schoeberlein-Engel 1997).

Nonstate Rural Institutions

Another form of community development focuses on building communities of interest. In rural areas these have often taken the form of farmers' organizations or water users' associations. An apparently successful example is provided by the Leninsky District Farmers' Association (LDFA) in Tajikistan. Shortly after privatization, this association was formed with the assistance of the international relief organization CARE. The local *hakim* (mayor) supported its creation because he saw it as a means of better controlling taxation.

During the privatization process, the *hakim* and former collective farm chairman managed to acquire very large landholdings that they leased to farmers under extremely disadvantageous conditions. Because there were no minimum landholding requirements, the largest landholders dominated the LDFA board, and the *hakim* made most decisions. Farmers received $100 worth of seed and inputs, which they had to pay back 30 percent in cash or kind. Large landholders did not repay their credits, because the board of directors accepted all petitions for debt forgiveness from the landholders who constituted the *hakim's* network. Small farmers, on the other hand, repaid a far greater percentage of their debt than did the elite. Because of the provision of quality seeds and fertilizer, yields of most crops dramatically increased. During the second year of operation, the LDFA enlisted more households that were poor and headed by a female, and it set a 15-hectare maximum landholding for members. It then required 70 percent repayment in cash, not kind, stopped accepting petitions for nonrepayment, and disqualified many large farms from receiving further credit due to their failure to repay previous credits. CARE targeted further credits at small landholders (1.5 to 5 hectares). By the third year the LDFA had grown from 650 to 1,500 members. CARE then introduced mini-associations, redrafting the bylaws to favor more participation by members. Despite the *hakim's* heavy-handed attempt to subvert the secret balloting, farmers resisted and managed to elect the leaders whom they desired. The LDFA has since taken over control of local-level irrigation networks. Because of striking increases in productivity, farmers in adjacent districts have expressed interest in establishing a similar farmers' association.[4]

Water-user associations (WUAs) in Albania exemplify how donors' intensive involvement and farmers' strong self-interest can enable farmers to solve their own problems despite a weak state and extreme distrust of the public sector by the general public. A Bank-led project originally set a modest target of developing small, village-based water-user associations to manage tertiary canals. Within a year the farmers overcame their initial resistance to working across villages and decided to consolidate for greater efficiency into larger, hydraulic-based associations. The farmers demanded financial autonomy and more responsibility because they did not want to depend on the unreliable services of the state's water enterprises. In 1996, 150 Albanian representatives of WUAs went on study tours to Turkey and Italy. When they returned they transformed their water-user associations into larger, hydraulic-based groups and started taking over responsibility for secondary canals. After the 1997 turmoil that followed collapse of the pyramid schemes, it became apparent that the state's water enterprises could not manage the primary irrigation facilities. It is now not only the farmers' preference but also the government's policy to transfer all irrigation management to local water-user associations and to the recently formed Federation of Water-User Associations. In addition to contributing to higher rural incomes, WUAs have fostered more community-based cooperation.

As in any new community organization, subversion is a danger. Water-user associations tend to be dominated by large farmers, thereby excluding the poorest farmers. Conflicts have arisen regarding equity, since upstream villages are able to receive more water than downstream villages get. The project has begun to address these issues. Presidents of the Federation of Water-User Associations are now elected from the less advantaged villages or through a rotation system. The challenges facing these associations in Albania include improving responsiveness to members' common needs, building trust between members, and increasing the water users' sense of ownership.[5]

Examples of Municipal Reform

Obninsk, a city of 110,000 people a few hours drive from Moscow, has declared itself an experimental city. With help from Eurasia Foundation grants, Obninsk has sought to improve and develop links between authorities and citizens to increase participation in municipal decisionmaking and to fight corruption. The city administration now puts the draft budget on its internet web site (www.obninsk.ru), along with the previous year's budget (including taxes, revenues, and expenses), to encourage comments from the community. It is procuring public goods over the internet on a pilot basis, and community members can use the computer terminals at city hall to check up on such information. A former mayor of Obninsk and a champion of governance reform at the city level is now a provincial legislator working with other legislators to reform province administration. Other civic leaders from Obninsk are beginning to work with counterparts elsewhere in Russia to provide assistance in governance reform.

Another example of municipal reform comes from Romania. Romanians have long viewed their local governments as unresponsive. This image was reinforced by guard cages at building entrances, where uniformed guards regulated who could enter. In 1995 the elected leadership of Ialomita County (population 380,000) made the decision to establish a citizens' information center to provide information about country services and to encourage citizens' participation in community services. The center is the first handicapped-accessible facility in a local government office in Romania. It provides printed brochures about the areas of responsibility and functions of local councils and governments, as well as material from local NGOs and other local governments. The center averages about 25 requests a day for information. Impressed by Ialomita County's center, the mayor of Bucharest has begun to develop a similar one.

Community-Building Interventions: Do They Work?

As we have seen, nonstate institutions can be efficient. They also can be highly exclusive and dysfunctional when local elites capture the benefits or powerful local networks subvert broad participation.

Many donor-aided efforts to rebuild communities have attempted to build on indigenous neighborhood institutions, such as the Central Asian *mahalla* (neighborhood). This traditional institution has become the basic organ of local self-governance. Usually, a respected member of the mahalla is elected the chairman. In urban areas a mahalla committee governs 350 to 400 households, although in rural areas the mahalla may be the entire settlement. The mahalla committee usually includes two paid positions (one is an elected chairman). This election usually follows the recommendation of the *hokimiyat* (mayor's office) and his secretary (and therefore may be subject to political capture).

Among its other responsibilities, the committee allocates and distributes subsidies and social assistance to poor families, and it decides, in conjunction with village council and collective farm leaders, the allocation of household plots. The committee gives legal advice, settles family disputes, and occasionally provides material aid in addition to government assistance. Donor organizations have found the mahalla committees to be a useful intermediary close to the community. However, the more state and donor money that is channeled through the mahallas, the greater the danger of coopting them. The mahalla leadership has been accused of corruption and rent-seeking, which highlights the dangers of promoting apparently indigenous but no less exclusionary forms of "community." To prevent local-level or nonstate institutions from reinforcing exclusionary norms and behaviors, policymakers must provide incentives for these community-based institutions to become inclusive.

Reconstructing and empowering civil society, and constructing new bases for community and social cohesion, will not be fast or straightforward. But these are essential foundations for the creation of inclusive and accountable institutions at the local, national, and state levels— institutions that serve the broad interests of society, including those of the poor.

Notes

1. This chapter draws heavily on World Bank (2000a,b).

2. This is very much the same problem that exists in richer and more established market economies, such as the United States, where groups of the population also suffer from social exclusion.

3. The discussion of the LDFA is based on an interview in November 1999 by Mike Thurman.

4. The discussion of the water-user associations in Albania is based on an interview with the task manager, Toru Konishi, World Bank, Europe and Central Asia Region, carried out by Evelin Lehis.

References

Birdsall, Nancy, and others. 2000. "Building a Market-Friendly Middle Class." Remarks made at the World Bank Annual Conference on Development Economics, April 18, Washington, D.C. Comments revised May 8.

Diamond, Larry. 1994. "Rethinking Civil Society." *Journal of Democracy,* vol. 5, no. 3.

Dreze, Jean, and Amartya Sen. 1996. *India: Economic Development and Social Opportunity.* New Dehli: Oxford University Press.

Dudwick, Nora. 1999. "Georgia: A Qualitative Study of Impoverishment and Coping Strategies." World Bank Technical Paper 4. Washington, D.C.

EBRD (European Bank for Reconstruction and Development). 1999. *Transition Report.* London.

Fish, Steven. 1994. "Russia's Fourth Transition." *Journal of Democracy,* vol. 5, no. 3.

Foley, Michael, and Bob Edwards. 1999. "Is It Time to Disinvest in Social Capital?" *Journal of Public Policy,* vol. 19, no. 2, 141-73.

Holm, John. 1996. "The Development of Civil Society in a Democratic State: The Botswana Model." *African Studies Review* 39 (September): 43–69.

Lovei, Laszlo. 2000. *Maintaining Utility Services for the Poor: Policies and Practices in Central and Eastern Europe and the Former Soviet Union.* Energy Sector Unit, Europe and Central Asia Region. Washington, D.C.: World Bank.

Moore, Mick, and James Putzel. 1999. "Politics and Poverty." World Bank paper commissioned by the *World Development Report 2000/2001: Attacking Poverty.* New York: Oxford University Press.

Narayan, Deepa, and others. 2000. *Can Anyone Hear Us? Voices of the Poor.* New York: Oxford University Press.

Rose-Ackerman, Susan. 1999. *Corruption and Government: Causes, Consequences, and Reform.* Cambridge, U.K.: Cambridge University Press.

Ruzica, Miroslav. 2000. "Central and Eastern European Third Sector after 1989." Paper prepared for the World Bank. Washington, D.C.

Saltmarshe, Douglas. 2000. "Local Government in Practice: Evidence from Two Villages in North Albania." In *Public Administration and Development.*

Schoeberlein-Engel, John. 1997. "Overcoming the Ravages of Tajikistan's Civil War." In Michael Cernea and Ayse Kudat, eds., *Social Assessments for Better Development: Case Studies in Russia and Central Asia*. Washington, D.C.: World Bank.

World Bank. 1995. *A Qualitative Assessment of the Living Standards of the Armenian Population*. Washington, D.C.

———. 1996. *Ethonographic Study of Poverty in Ukraine*. Washington, D.C.

———. 1997a. *Poverty in Georgia: The Social Dimensions of Transition*. Washington, D.C.

———. 1997b. *Report on the Qualitative Analysis Research into the Living Standards of Inhabitants in Aluksne District*. Washington, D.C.

———. 1999a. "Consultations with the Poor." Paper prepared for the World Bank Global Synthesis Workshop, September.

———. 1999b. *Georgia: Poverty and Income Distribution*. Report 19348-GE. Washington, D.C.

———. 2000a. *Anticorruption in Transition: A Contribution to the Policy Debate*. Washington, D.C.

———. 2000b. *Consultations with the Poor: Global Synthesis Workshop, 2000*. Washington, D.C.

———. Forthcoming. *ECA Social Development Strategy*.

CHAPTER 6

Expanding Opportunities
through Growth

Given the exceptional collapse in output and household incomes in transition economies, prospects for reducing poverty depend critically on the resurgence of robust, stable, and equitable growth. Growth is a necessary condition in order to provide income-earning opportunities for households, thereby enabling them to improve their incomes and living standards. This is as true for the transition economies as it is for other countries.[1] Moreover, without the increase in the size of the national income and of the fiscal resources available, governments will find it difficult to finance the required investments in social, human, and physical capital, or the redistributive policies needed to protect the poorest.

What Can Governments of Transition Countries Do to Promote Growth?

The size and role of government in transition economies have diminished, but government continues to play a critical role in fostering the development of policies and institutions that would do the most to spur growth. The resurgence of growth in many of the countries in Central and South Eastern Europe and the Baltics (CSB) has already shown that this is possible. At the same time experience from some of the countries in the Commonwealth of Independent States (CIS) has demonstrated that bad government policies and inadequate institutional arrangements can also make things worse. Partial reforms that permit a greater capture of the state by oligarchs, loose fiscal policies, excessive licensing and regulation, poor incentives for new enterprise development, and lawlessness all compromise growth and deny the poor the opportunities they need to improve their welfare.

In developing these policies and institutions, governments need to bear in mind two sets of issues. First, transition remains a holistic process that requires movement along many fronts and that necessarily stretches the limited implementation capacity of most of the countries. Mistakes may occur, but it is important to stay the course on the general direction of policy change. In this vein the costs of "partial reform" are high and highlight the interdependencies between policy and institutional reforms, and between macroeconomic and microeconomic reforms. These have been highlighted in recent years by the global financial crises. The prolonged period of rapid growth in the East Asian "tigers" was broken off by a financial crisis because the structural and institutional weaknesses of these economies led to a build-up of external vulnerability (Stiglitz 1998). Similarly, the short period of macroeconomic stability in Russia and many other transition countries was abruptly interrupted in 1998, not only from the reverberations of the East Asian crisis, but also from their own structural and institutional weaknesses.[2]

Second, the growth of economic opportunities will have higher payoffs for the poor if that growth generates employment and real wages rise over time with increases in labor productivity. This requires that the poor gain more than proportionally from the emergent growth—an enormous challenge in view of the experience that job creation typically lags behind economic growth. But countries can adopt measures to enhance the job content of growth. For example, reducing labor market frictions and developing housing markets will help match workers with jobs and reduce barriers to job creation. Similarly, deregulating product markets, reducing barriers to entry for small businesses, and upgrading vital infrastructure will foster the development of a more competitive private sector and maximize the potential for job creation.

Whatever the specific package of growth policies adopted in transition economies, these policies must take into account the large variation in policy, performance, and vulnerabilities among the countries or groups of countries. Most of the CSB countries are more advanced along the reform path than are the CIS countries. For example, Estonia, Hungary, Poland, and the Slovak Republic have progressed substantially along the transition path and have in place a good set of policies. The objective of European Union membership for these countries, as well as for other countries of the CSB, provides a strong driving force for comprehensive reforms. By contrast, countries of the CIS are lagging along the reform path.

Turkmenistan and Belarus, for example, have a long way to go. In terms of economic performance, growth in the CSB countries has been driven by rising exports to Western markets and by buoyant capital inflows into restructured and new private enterprises. For many of the countries in the CIS, growth is still elusive. Even in Armenia, where the economy has grown steadily in per capita terms since 1995, the original collapse in output was so large that current output is still only half of its pretransition level.

Economic vulnerabilities are also quite different across the transition countries. In Poland, Hungary, and Slovenia, growth prospects are likely to be relatively resilient to external shocks. In Bulgaria, the Czech Republic, and the Slovak Republic, insufficient financial discipline and soft budget constraints have generated excessive borrowing abroad, quasi-fiscal contingent liabilities, and a very high share of bad loans in banks' portfolios—all of which render these economies more vulnerable to external shocks. Then there are other countries in both the CSB and the CIS that have strong economic links with Russia and that are therefore vulnerable to economic fluctuations in that country. Some of the CIS countries are resource rich, which makes them vulnerable to "Dutch Disease" effects—the negative effects of an inadequately managed natural resource boom. This may amplify the problems of transition (Sachs and Warner 1995; Rosenberg and Saavalainen 1998). Some other countries in the region are simply poor and heavily burdened with external debt. Others have only recently emerged from ethnic conflict and civil war or have been adversely affected by the consequent influx of refugees from these countries and the disruption in trade and thus are prone to social and ethnic tensions.

The forward-looking policy agenda must recognize these differences among countries and groups of countries. However, commonalities in the growth agenda exist in terms of broad themes that cut across all countries (table 6.1). First, the restructuring of existing state enterprises and the creation of new private businesses through new entry and privatization are priorities in all transition countries and the future engine of growth. Second, this restructuring has to be supported by a sound fiscal policy that can provide the basis for macroeconomic stability while allowing for adequate social protection for displaced workers and other vulnerable groups. This fiscal policy also has to permit critical investments in health, education, and social infrastructure, so as to enable the population to take advantage of the benefits offered by the emerging market economy. Third, the challenge of social protection in the face of enterprise restructuring and tightening budgets implies that social policy must be reconfigured in a way that makes the provision of social services more cost-effective. The rest of this chapter discusses these crosscutting themes; chapters 7, 8, and

Table 6.1   Key Policy Measures to Promote Poverty-Reducing Growth

Type of country	Policies to improve the competitive environment	Policies to strengthen fiscal reforms	Policies to enhance social development
Advanced market reformers	• Develop adequate legal and regulatory frameworks for infrastructure and utility privatization • Promote entry and exit • Improve competition policies • Support financial sector development • Promote export competition • Improve labor market policies	• Reduce contingent fiscal liabilities • Improve the system of intergovernmental finance • Strengthen public administration • Reduce pension expenditures	• Reform pensions • Reduce entitlements • Introduce social programs to upgrade workers' skills • Improve delivery of education services
Less advanced market reformers	• Introduce hard budget constraints • Remove barriers to entry and exit and enhance competition policies • Reduce transaction costs for small businesses • Improve labor market policies • Strengthen the financial sector • Promote incentives for export growth • Undertake agriculture land reforms • Liberalize agriculture marketing and pricing • Introduce greater efficiency in the use of irrigation	• Reduce deficits through appropriate expenditure cuts and revenue increases • Re-orient public expenditures towards human and physical capital investments • Manage external borrowings carefully • Improve systems for budget and public expenditure management	• Consolidate social assistance • Improve poverty targeting and cost-effectiveness of social assistance services • Improve quality and cost-effectiveness of education services

9 then address in more detail the issues in social policy given their importance to the future challenge of transition.

Improving the Business Environment

The fundamental sources of growth for the transition economies will come from productivity gains from industrial as well as agricultural enterprises. Enterprise productivity will rise with improved incentives for better performance in restructured state and privatized enterprises. In addition, the growth of new businesses will lead to employment, higher incomes, and growth. The business environment must encourage the movement of resources to economic activities where they are the most productive. Progress has already been made in most transition economies in terms of establishing many of the necessary changes in the policy environment, although a wide dispersion among the countries remains in terms of these policies. But there is a wider dispersion in terms of the institutional framework needed for the policies to be effective. The rules and regulations governing economic activity differ markedly from country to country. This section describes five significant actions transition economies can take to improve their business environment: strengthen the competitive environment; reduce obstacles for private business; privatize large enterprises, infrastructure monopolies, and utilities; strengthen the financial sector; and promote agricultural growth. Each country will define these actions in the context of its own development.

Strengthen the Competitive Environment

Much has been written regarding the perceived failures of the privatization programs in some countries, the stripping of assets, insider-control, the lack of restructuring, and the capture of assets by oligarchs. Some observers believe that such outcomes, particularly in Russia, were the result of imbalances between market and institutional reforms (Stiglitz 1999). But the extent to which market institutions can be promoted ahead of effective demand for them remains unclear (Dabrowski and others 2000). These market institutions include the following: rules for fair and open competition (hard budget constraints, removal of barriers to entry and exit, and enforcement of bankruptcy), transparent laws that protect property rights and are effectively enforced, a framework for sound corporate governance of firms (including protection of the minority rights of shareholders and creditors), and fair, open, and transparent rules for foreign trade and investment.

To foster the restructuring of nonviable enterprises, governments need to establish hard budget constraints. Managers of state enterprises will then know that the budgets set for them by the government are fixed and that losses will not be financed out of general revenues or by the central bank. They will thus bear the responsibility for both their losses and their profits. Poland provides one of the most robust empirical results from the transition experience—namely, the crucial link between the resumption of growth and enterprise-level hard budget constraints (Pinto, Belka, and Krajewski 1993). Such constraints enable the efficient use of existing assets in an enterprise and the efficient allocation of resources in the economy through exit and entry of enterprises, affording countries opportunities to resume growth even before the productivity gains from privatization are realized.

The lack of hard budget constraints is a significant weakness in the incentive environment in the CIS countries. No country has witnessed the problems associated with this shortcoming as much as Russia has (box 6.1). Russia's failure to impose hard budget constraints on enterprises led to the development of a serious payments problems. What started off as a microeconomic problem developed into a macroeconomic problem, undermined the fiscal stabilization effort, and led ultimately to the financial meltdown in 1998.

In many countries the performance and restructuring prospects of the newly privatized enterprises have been compromised by the predominance of insider ownership. Experience from transition and other countries has shown that this leads to less restructuring, since such firms tend to underinvest, prefer high wages instead of long-term growth, depend too much on credit, and do not attract foreign investments. Given the better performance of foreign-owned enterprises compared with domestic-owned ones (for example in Slovenia), governments need to give priority to attracting more foreign ownership and investments into the privatization programs. Even the advanced market reformers need to ensure an appropriate set of conditions that would support adequate entry and exit and encourage the restructuring of privatized firms. This, in turn, would re-

---

Box 6.1 Hard Budget Constraints, Nonpayments, and Growth in the Russian Federation

The problem of nonpayments is perhaps most stark in Russia. The problem was fueled by an inconsistent policy mix of rapid disinflation, inadequate fiscal adjustment, and soft budget constraints for enterprises. From 1995 to 1998, the government, at the macro level, sought to achieve rapid stabilization by fixing the exchange rate and tightening credit even as fiscal reforms and the consolidation of the government budget lagged behind. This led to expenditure arrears and a sharp increase in public borrowings. At the micro level, the government sought to maintain the social safety net by continuing the subsidization of enterprises, maintaining employment, and avoiding enterprise exit. These (mostly implicit) subsidies—equivalent to between 7 and 10 percent of GDP over the 1995-97 period—were in the form of payments arrears and noncash settlements for energy payments. The costs were passed on by the energy monopolies to the budget in the form of tax arrears. This contributed to the large chronic shortfalls in tax revenues. Given the fiscal shortfalls, public borrowings rose (averaging 7 percent of GDP over the 1995-97 period), and real interest rates increased sharply, causing liquidity problems for enterprises. This pushed enterprises farther toward noncash settlements while increasing the need for more implicit subsidies, tax arrears, cash shortfalls, and government borrowing. A financial meltdown occurred in 1998 as public debt service reached unsupportable levels.

Source: Pinto (2000).

quire good frameworks for enterprise liquidation and insolvency, strong mechanisms for corporate governance, adequate enforcement of competition and antimonopoly policies, and equality of treatment of foreign and national investors.

A key mechanism for strengthening the competitive environment is the maintenance of open trade regimes with flexible exchange rates. This is essential to maintain competitive pressures on the import-substituting sectors and enhance the competitiveness of the export sector. Flexibility of exchange rates will help to contain real appreciation. For those countries with restricted current accounts—such as Uzbekistan, Turkmenistan, and Belarus—trade and exchange rate liberalization may carry the risk, over the short run, of current account deterioration because imports may rise in response to repressed demand. But such a deterioration can be managed with appropriately tight fiscal and monetary policies, and an external financing plan supported by international financial institutions. Over the medium term, the current account, as well as prospects for financing it, will improve with an acceleration in exports and capital inflows.

But trade liberalization by itself is not enough to permit countries to maximize the gains from trade if market access is not broadened. Many of the CIS countries are small, landlocked countries for whom trade is essential to provide opportunities for growth. Market access needs to be improved with advanced economies as well as with traditional regional trading partners. Strong trade linkages with growing markets of the OECD countries can be an important channel for growth in the transition economies.[3] Given the regional proximity of the European Union, access to EU markets needs to be enhanced. This is planned to occur for the CSB countries that are negotiating EU accession, but the countries of the CIS also need access to EU markets. An institutional arrangement that may promote this is World Trade Organization (WTO) membership. China's expected membership in the WTO will enable WTO members of the CIS—such as the Kyrgyz Republic—to extend trade links with its eastern neighbor. In the more specific regional context of Central Asia, the lack of openness to trade in Uzbekistan is a serious limitation to the growth of neighboring countries as well as its own.

Reduce Obstacles for Private Businesses

The environment for private businesses—particularly small firms, which are generally recognized as an engine of growth in the advanced market reformers—remains lacking (box 6.2). A variety of these microeconomic impediments—both policy and institutional—is still prevalent in all transition countries, but perhaps more so in the CIS countries. Of particular importance are the institutional arrangements for good governance (World Bank 2000). This requires a major transformation of the public sector to encompass reforms in public expenditure management, auditing, administration, and legal and judicial services. In addition, transparency needs to be promoted vigorously, especially in the context of the privatization programs. High levels of corruption and rent-seeking have bred pessimism about the chances of new entrepreneurs to start a business.

Box 6.2   Obstacles to Private Businesses in Transition Countries

In 1999 the World Bank and the European Bank for Reconstruction and Development (EBRD) conducted a survey of the business environment of more than 3,000 enterprises in 20 transition countries. This survey is very revealing. The vast majority of firms were small and medium-size enterprises. The survey asked the manager of each enterprise to assess the extent to which different aspects of the business environment in the country were an obstacle to the operation and growth of the firm (figure 6.1). A score of 4 indicates a major obstacle, while a score of 1 represents no obstacle. An unweighted average of the scores for advanced and less advanced market reformers shows that these obstacles—mostly microeconomic and institutional—are serious in both groups of countries, but they are more acute in the less advanced market reformers.

Figure 6.1   Advanced Market Reformers and Less Advanced Market Reformers Rank the Importance of Ten Aspects of the Business Environment

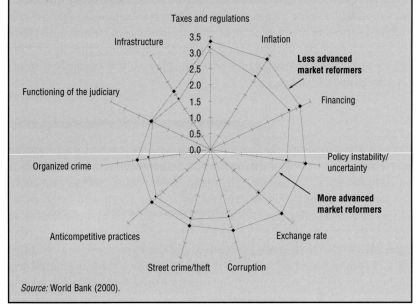

Source: World Bank (2000).

For small businesses, excessive government micromanagement of enterprises is particularly onerous. In Ukraine, for instance, more than 100 separate governmental agencies are empowered to inspect enterprises. Even small enterprises must submit to an average of 78 inspections per year, requiring 68 separate written responses. Dealing with these inspections and audits consumes two days per week of the average manager's time and requires a cash outlay of $2,000. Similarly, surveys have shown that shops in Moscow are visited by a much larger number of inspectors than shops in Warsaw (Frye and Schleifer 1997). To reduce such burdens on small enterprises, governments must (1) strengthen the institutional environment through a reduction in rules, permits, inspections, audits, and red tape; simplification of taxation; provision of information; and legal and accounting training; (2) strengthen financial intermediaries targeted to reach these small businesses; and (3) develop support networks through fostering business associations, chambers of commerce, and partnerships with external agencies (EBRD 1999).

In addition, countries emerging from conflict face the specific challenge of consolidating the rule of law. While this is a political challenge as well, much can be achieved by a prosecution and judicial system in which all citizens have confidence. Its establishment requires the creation of an independent, impartial, and multiethnic judiciary, vigorous prosecution of organized crime, corruption, and other violence; better public information about citizens' rights; and an equitable mechanism for enforcing legal rulings. Insurance also is needed to mitigate the noncommercial risk involved in private investment. In Bosnia the Investment Guarantee Agency has been an important instrument for providing such insurance. It is evolving into an export credit agency that can play an increasing role in attracting private financing.

Privatize Large Enterprises, Infrastructure Monopolies, and Utilities

Even as the advanced market reformers have embarked on sweeping privatization programs, the privatization and enterprise reform agenda is far from complete. For instance, in Poland, despite significant privatization, the state still owns 3,000 enterprises (including about 120 large enterprises) employing 40 percent of the industrial workers and continuing to impose a costly burden on the budget (through loss-making enterprises especially in the coal, steel, railroad, and defense sectors). Across all of the CIS progress has been made in the privatization of housing, small and medium enterprises, and banks, but large enterprise privatization is largely unfinished. In addition, there remains the very difficult privatization of infrastructure monopolies and utilities.

The privatization of infrastructure monopolies and utilities is an important area, especially for the CSB countries and the larger countries of the CIS. It has been obvious since the start of transition that the existing infrastructure networks needed extensive restructuring to meet the demands and standards of a market economy (Broadman and Recanatini 1999). Yet reforms are very nascent, and there is still inadequate recognition that the socially optimal industrial structure is increasingly competitive—given changes in markets and technology—with unbundling of service offerings and open entry and exit. While the commercialization and privatization of these monopolies should carefully follow the development of appropriate legal and regulatory frameworks that provide for transparency, simplicity, and accountability—including the establishment of independent regulatory agencies—movement toward the reform of infrastructure monopoly sectors is needed to address current inefficiencies and the future needs of the economy. The state will continue to be the main source for infrastructure investments—particularly in poor countries such as Tajikistan and Albania—but these investments need to be complemented by private sector participation wherever possible.

Strengthen the Financial Sector

A growing private sector requires a healthy financial sector. Banking and capital market reforms, under way in all transition countries, need to be continued; of course, different countries are at different points in these reforms. Some countries, such as Bulgaria, should strengthen the liquidation procedures for insolvent banks. This is needed not only to facilitate the exit of the least viable banks but also to enable the consolidation or merger of banks as the accession process to the EU intensifies competitive pressures. In other countries, such as Estonia, the environment for foreign portfolio investments needs to be strengthened by revising securities law to spell out clear reporting requirements and specific rules for transparency, disclosure, and the restraint of insider trading.

Banking reforms will also promote financial deepening. The depth of the financial system is a strong predictor of long-term economic growth. But financial depth remains low, particularly in the CIS. One of the factors that may have led to low financial depth in some countries (Armenia, for example) is excessively tight monetary policy. The combination of large budget deficits with low inflation targets and a stable exchange rate has meant that credit has been very tight and real interest rates high. This, in

turn, may have excessively restricted enterprise borrowing and the overall level of financial intermediation, dampening growth prospects.

Promote Agricultural Growth

Big gains in growth and improvement in living standards will come from
a resurgence in agriculture. Given the structure of many of the transition
economies, agriculture will remain a significant portion of the national
economy. In many countries, particularly in the CIS, agricultural reforms
have been partial and uneven, and political support for them, despite
obvious gains for the rural poor, has been lacking. The most difficult
reforms have been those going against the long tradition of public ownership of land and the high-cost policy of securing sufficient supplies of
basic agricultural goods for the domestic market through export limitations. For the CIS, the agenda for agricultural reforms remains vast and
includes the following long-term objectives: advancing land reform and
restructuring the traditional collective and state farms, creating a conducive policy and institutional environment for rural finance, liberalizing
the market environment on both the input and output side, privatizing
agro-processing and trade, reducing payments arrears among agricultural
enterprises, scaling down agricultural trade controls, and creating a new
institutional framework for the sector (box 6.3). Particularly essential is
phasing out state monopolies on inputs and state monopsonies on grain
and other cash crops. The relative importance of each long-term objective
differs from country to country, and the sequencing of actions must be
adjusted to different conditions.

In the CSB countries, privatization of agricultural land ownership has
largely been achieved, but the excessive fragmentation of land ownership
risks making efficient farming operations difficult. Land market development needs to be actively supported by the government. Challenges still
to be met include the development of a modern and efficient land titling
system with adequate land and cadastre legislation, the speedy settlement
of land ownership issues, the provision of proper proof of ownership to
facilitate growth of the land mortgage market, and an improved system
for collecting and disseminating information on land market prices.

In addition, the irrigation networks need to be strengthened in most
countries. Cost recovery in irrigation is a desirable objective, not only for
fiscal reasons but also to support efficient water use. This is particularly
important in countries such as Uzbekistan where excessive irrigation, poor
drainage, and inefficient water management have raised soil salinity and
aggravated environmental problems. However, cost recovery for water use

---

Box 6.3   Agriculture Reforms for CIS Countries

Agricultural growth is central to the growth strategies of the low-income countries, given the large size of the agricultural sector in most of the Commonwealth of Independent States. Measures to promote agricultural growth need to include land reform, farm restructuring, marketing liberalization, promotion of value-added linkages, and support for rural credit and irrigation.

The process of land reform and farm restructuring must be intensified. Private ownership of land will improve the incentive to invest and the efficiency in resource use and—given the price liberalization that has already taken place—it is likely to unleash a virtuous cycle of investment, growth, and higher incomes. The CIS countries have followed divergent reform strategies. Russia and Ukraine, which control the bulk of the farmland resources in the region, legally recognize private ownership, but they restrict the buying and selling of land in practice; therefore, land transactions are mainly limited to leasing. Moreover, individuals usually receive paper shares certifying their entitlements to land without specifying a concrete physical plot. The remaining countries (with the exception of Azerbaijan, Armenia, Georgia, and Moldova) generally do not recognize private land ownership, but they differ in their attitude toward land transactions. Land use rights are secure and transferable in Kazakhstan, Kyrgyz Republic, and now in Tajikistan, but Turkmenistan, Uzbekistan, and Belarus prohibit any transactions in land.

Farm restructuring still has a long way to go. Even where the share of the old collective and state farms has come down substantially, and new forms of ownership have taken root, evidence suggests that not much may have changed on the ground. For instance, qualitative surveys in Moldova reveal that members of the new "joint stock companies"—the erstwhile collective farms—are often treated essentially like wage workers and have little say in decisionmaking. Farm managers largely retained the role that they played in the collectives, and members felt inhibited in exercising their choice with respect to the appropriate use of land and nonland assets.

Marketing arrangements need to be liberalized, particularly where monopolistic marketing boards control the sale of key cash crops. While this is not unique to these CIS countries, they can afford the cost from inefficiencies in the marketing chain less than other countries can. Tajikistan is already in the process of opening up its cotton export business. The liberalization of marketing arrangements will facilitate the development of forward linkages in order to provide for greater domestic value added for export crops. In Moldova, for instance, much of its agricultural produce is exported unprocessed, and its perishability therefore limits the geographical reach of the country's exports. Existing agro-processing facilities are either outmoded or produce goods that are not competitive in the international marketplace. A capital injection, especially from foreign investors, could provide the technological upgrade to revive this sector. The gains will not only come from the additional value-added but also from seasonal credit to farmers these enterprises can provide, growth in knowledge about other markets, the establishment of new production chains, and the possibility of larger investible surpluses to farmers, which if reinvested, can rev the engine of growth for these countries. All of this, of course, will require adequate provision of agricultural inputs—irrigation, rural credit—which need to be strengthened.

---

can only take place with better prices for farmers' products. If charges are unaffordable, as in Bulgaria, they may become a significant disincentive to irrigation. Moreover, investments in irrigation should carefully target viable schemes, and responsibility for the maintenance of the infrastructure schemes should be passed on to local associations of water users.

Broadening access of agricultural exports and the development of agriculture will remain critical to the growth prospects of many countries. More than trade and price liberalization and subsidy reduction are needed, although these reforms are important. Growth will also require the completion of structural reforms in the sector. Even in advanced market reformers, such as Poland, government intervention in the form of price supports, import tariffs, social transfers, and other measures is widespread. While some measures may be justified on social grounds, long-term measures need to be adopted for enhancing productivity and competitiveness in the sector.

Finally, institutions required by a market-based agriculture must be strengthened or developed. State institutions in the sector should only be concerned with the provision of public goods and services. With institutions still lacking in areas such as rural credit, agricultural and rural policy, veterinary and phyto-sanitary measures, food safety, research and advisory services, public-private partnerships should be developed that will help to overcome financing problems. Further institution building in the nongovernmental sector, such as producer and trader associations, is also needed to create an informed constituency that supports market-based agricultural growth and development.

Strengthening Fiscal Reforms

Thus far the chapter has examined how transition countries can promote poverty-reducing growth by improving the business environment. Ways to strengthen fiscal reforms will now be discussed.

The objectives of fiscal reforms are numerous: a sustainable fiscal deficit that is compatible with low and moderate levels of inflation and public debt, the resumption and sustenance of growth through low and stable levels of taxation and necessary investments in human and physical capital, and improved equity by creating the necessary fiscal space to finance key social services and targeted interventions for the poor and the vulnerable. These objectives are central to the growth prospects of transition economies. While the importance of continuing fiscal reforms is common to most countries, they take on different emphases depending on country-specific situations.

Establish and Maintain Aggregate Fiscal Discipline

Aggregate fiscal discipline needs to be established and maintained in many of the CIS countries. The reduction of the fiscal deficit, consistent with noninflationary financing, calls for sustained efforts at revenue enhancement and expenditure retrenchment.

Revenue collection is highly variable across the CIS countries, with a low of 9 percent of GDP in Georgia and a high of 45 percent in Belarus.[4] Shortcomings in tax policy and enforcement persist that undermine tax collection and distort incentives for growth. In the Kyrgyz Republic tax exemptions are estimated to cost between 5 and 7 percent of GDP, even as revenue collection remains low at 16 percent of GDP. In Russia nonpayments of taxes compromised macroeconomic stability (as noted earlier in box 6.1). A potentially large tax base is distorted as a result of arbitrary tax exemptions granted by federal and subnational authorities. Moreover, the multiplicity of taxes—and cumbersome and often contradictory tax regulations—erode further the potential for tax collections. In some other countries such as Uzbekistan, where revenue collections are relatively successful at more than 31 percent of GDP, the instruments for enforcing tax legislation have negative implications for growth. Tax enforcement has been partly accomplished through the use of the banking system. While this arrangement may have helped prevent the collapse in tax revenues that has afflicted many CIS countries, it erodes the confidentiality and trust in the banking system, leading to low levels of intermediation and hence low growth.

Many CIS countries also need to reduce expenditures. In Russia expenditure cuts will facilitate macroeconomic stabilization and provide for some fiscal space in the face of the high debt service burden. In the Kyrgyz Republic subsidies—particularly in the form of losses in energy utilities—are estimated at about 6 percent of GDP. In Armenia expenditures need to be reduced by ensuring more cost recovery in irrigation. In Kazakhstan expenditure cuts are needed to reduce public sector borrowing and lower real interest rates. In Moldova reduced spending is necessary to lessen the dependence on external financing, which is currently between 25 and 30 percent of the budget. In some countries, especially the CSB countries, the fiscal burden of social expenditures is very high and needs to be reduced. In Slovenia public pension expenditures have climbed to more than 13 percent of GDP—a doubling of pretransition levels—and they are not sustainable. The fiscal burden of pension systems increased not only with steady declines in tax compliance and the contribution base, but also with an increased use of benefits to ease the social costs of transition (Tanzi and Tsibouris 1999). For instance, the promotion of early retirements in the early years of transition—while beneficial for employment growth by providing space for new jobs—added to the fiscal burden.

For four low-income countries—Georgia, the Kyrgyz Republic, Moldova, and Tajikistan—the fiscal envelope is severely constrained by the external debt service burden. These countries face very tight liquidity constraints and, in the face of slow growth, a long-term solvency constraint. For fiscal sustainability, these countries need not only generous debt relief but also new concessional financing from external sources to enable them to rally from their encumbering debt. Some countries need new concessional financing, but others, especially those emerging from conflict (such as Bosnia), need to be weaned off dependence on donor resources. As the resources decline over time both in terms of magnitude and the element of concessionality, these countries will have to find their own resources for the ongoing physical and social reconstruction work. To that end, they need to start developing a medium-term strategy for fiscal adjustment. Essential elements of such a strategy should include measures for reducing the level of public expenditures and for mobilizing additional revenues from improved tax policies and administration.

Improve Allocative Efficiency of Expenditures

For countries of the CIS, governments need to reallocate their expenditures toward growth-enhancing activities. At the heart of this challenge is defining the strategic priorities for state involvement. Far-reaching developments in the global economy have redefined the role of the state—what it can and cannot do, and how it can do it best—yet most of these countries still struggle to unshackle themselves from a history of pervasive state interventions. Of primary importance is ensuring that the overall budget reflects the expenditure priorities of the policy framework. These priorities need to be established with due consideration of the inter- and intrasectoral policy tradeoffs as well as the tradeoffs between expenditures on investments and expenditures on operations and maintenance, between new and continuing programs and projects, and between social sector expenditures and those on physical investments. Such consideration and discussion need to be broadened not only with government but also with civil society, including parliamentary representatives of the people.

The prioritization of expenditures takes more urgency in view of the loss of revenues from the decline in the state-owned enterprises, the need to provide social assistance to those adversely affected by enterprise restructuring, and the imperative to maintain low taxes on the emerging private sector so as to induce more rapid growth. Social expenditures are the overriding concern over the short term in many countries, but these needs should be balanced against the need for public investments in infrastructure, something that has been neglected during the past ten years. The underinvestments in physical infrastructure now risk undermining growth prospects. In both Kazakhstan and Azerbaijan, public investments had fallen to 2 percent of GDP by 1998-99. While the infrastructure needs are large, and some of them can be met through privatization (for instance, of utilities, telecommunications, and transport), other sectors (principally roads, bridges, irrigation and drainage, and urban infrastructure) are likely to remain in the public domain.

Strengthening the allocative efficiency of budgets also requires the development of effective tools for monitoring and executing the budget. While treasury systems are being developed in all of the transition countries, their scope is still much too limited, and no where are they fully functional (Tanzi and Tsibouris 1999). These systems are necessary to provide comprehensive budgeting, payment, and accounting information for effective financial management. Treasury systems take a long time to develop, and it is therefore imperative that governments persevere in implementing them throughout government.

Improve Public Administration

As the transition economies prepare for a robust market economy, they need to improve public administration by establishing a merit-based civil service and rationalizing administrative entities. In Estonia economies of scale in the delivery of public services can be derived from the consolidation of the numerous administrative entities—16 regional administrations and 254 local governments (two-thirds of which have populations less than 3,000). The rationalization of government units would allow the decentralization of public administration to be matched with stronger administrative capacity and accountability systems at the decentralized level. The overemployment in health and education at local levels in Estonia could then be reduced. In Armenia, by reducing the high ratio of teachers to students of 1:9, the government can find the fiscal space for remunerating teachers better or reallocating funds for higher priority expenditures.

Public administration reforms can open the way for improvements in the system of intergovernmental finance that are particularly important in the large transition countries. In Russia and Ukraine reforms are crucial in order to eliminate arbitrary political bargaining in determining budgetary transfers and discretionary tax exemptions, and to lay down a stronger basis for fiscal stability.

There are several ways in which governments can make a useful contribution here. The first relates to a clear assignment of expenditure obligations and revenue responsibilities. This will help to strengthen the foundations of fiscal management. In this connection local governments need to develop their own sources of revenue (for example, through fees for local services, and property taxes), and have greater autonomy over revenues. Remaining transfers to them should be made as transparent (formula-based) and stable as possible, so as to create the correct incentives for local revenue collection. Second, governments need to improve the efficiency of delivery of public services. This requires exploring economies of scale in the provision of services at subnational levels, organizing effective regional associations, and enhancing discipline in local government finance (including adequate systems of financial management). Third, where local government borrowings take place, adequate safeguards are needed—such as rules requiring borrowings only to finance investments—at least during the early years of fiscal decentralization. With time, and as markets for subnational debt develop in some of the countries that are able to adequately price risk, these formal constraints can be relaxed. In either case the legal and regulatory framework for subnational borrowing should be strengthened.

Reduce Contingent Fiscal Liabilities

The CIS countries wrestle with basic problems of fiscal control, but more advanced market reformers have largely attained aggregate fiscal discipline. New types of fiscal risks now have become important in the CSB, and they need to be contained and reduced (box 6.4). Still invisible in fiscal records, and often not officially recognized by the government, is the stock of hidden public debt that has emerged outside the budget as a result of borrowings by various agencies to finance off-budget expenditures. Off-budget fiscal risks have become more visible in some countries, such as the Czech Republic, where explicitly and implicitly guaranteed loans by the government have generated significant claims on the budget. The growth in these contingent fiscal liabilities risks generating sudden and not entirely expected claims on the budget, thus endangering future fiscal stability.

To minimize these risks, governments need to consolidate fiscal accounts to cover off-budget programs, which do not reflect the strategic choices

---

Box 6.4   Contingent Fiscal Liabilities

Contingent fiscal liabilities, financial obligations triggered by a discrete but uncertain event, are a major hidden fiscal risk. These liabilities may be explicit or implicit. Explicit liabilities are specific government obligations defined by law or contract. The government is then legally mandated to settle the obligation when it becomes due. Implicit liabilities represent a moral obligation or expected burden for the government—not in the legal sense but based on public expectations and political pressures.

   Although all transition economies face particularly large fiscal risks from contingent fiscal liabilities, the advanced market reformers have contingent fiscal liabilities at the fore of their fiscal agenda now that aggregate fiscal discipline has largely been achieved. These contingent liabilities arise from various sources. For instance, public expenditure policies over the long term have imparted a presumed liability for pensions. Current and projected economic and demographic developments impose sizable liabilities on governments. Often governments are also compelled to cover the uncovered losses and obligations of state-owned enterprises, the banking system, or budgetary and extrabudgetary agencies. Contingent liabilities grow with weaknesses in the financial sector, macroeconomic policies, regulatory and supervisory systems, and information disclosure.

   Governments can undertake various measures to contain and reduce these fiscal risks. First, policymakers need to identify, classify, and understand the full range of fiscal risks. Understanding them will encourage policymakers to avoid those that are bound to surface in a politically meaningful timeframe. Second, fiscal analysis must factor in the cost of implicit subsidies provided by contingent support programs. Such analysis should include the ordering of these risks by their significance. Third, governments should undertake steps to limit their risk exposure. One way to do this would be to treat noncash programs involving contingent fiscal risks like any other pending item and to make the potential fiscal cost of off-budget programs visible in advance. Also helpful are rules on full disclosure of fiscal risks, on dealing with state guarantees and insurance programs, and on the behavior of public agencies and subnational governments.

Source: World Bank (1998).

---

made in the budget process. Also needed are effective regulations with respect to the amounts of government-guaranteed loans and government risk exposure to them when agencies design programs with contingent budget support. Reporting requirements should include bank and nonbank financial institutions or funds that may generate any such risk in the future.

Strengthening Social Policies

Government policies in the social sphere need to have a dual focus: providing social assistance to those adversely affected by enterprise restructuring and other macroeconomic and structural reforms and strengthening the education and skill development required for future growth.

Improve Targeting and Cost-Effectiveness of Social Protection

To accommodate the social fallout from tightened budgetary constraints on enterprises, transition economies need to strengthen the formal social protection system. This need not result in a net increase in the fiscal burden—which may not be feasible for many countries given the fiscal constraint—if accompanied by a reduction in explicit and implicit subsidies and in untargeted benefits. The social role of the state should be reoriented away from paternalistic, poorly targeted benefits conveyed largely through extensive cross-subsidies and toward policies that address poverty and vulnerability directly. How to improve the targeting of benefits to the poor—whether through income-tested assistance, community-based schemes, targeting based on indicators of poverty, or self-targeting—is a complex matter that depends on the administrative capacity of the government (see chapter 9 for a fuller discussion). Whatever the mechanism, such a system should try to provide an adequate minimum poverty benefit to the poor, an adequate minimum pension, and special provisions for vulnerable groups.

Improvements need to be made in unemployment benefits and severance pay arrangements to make benefits affordable while preserving incentives for labor reallocation. Options for such measures include a flat benefit at a reasonable level above subsistence with tight eligibility and for limited duration, special budget-financed severance pay schemes whereby workers would be eligible for one-off payments conditional on enterprise restructuring or closure, and special interventions to address the economically devastated or backward areas and single company towns.

At the same time changes in the demographics, retirement ages, and macroeconomic outcomes have put the pension systems in all countries under strain. In the absence of reforms, these systems will experience chronic and growing deficits and become a fiscal liability. Pension reforms should include increasing the minimum retirement age, restricting the scope of benefits, linking contributions and benefits, ensuring a reasonable minimum pension, and ultimately introducing a multipillar system. These measures will not only make the provision of pensions more efficient but also reduce their high fiscal burden. While ongoing pension reforms (for example, in Latvia and Poland) have focused on an array of measures to make pensions fiscally more affordable, more countries need to undertake such reforms in order to secure the future for their senior citizens.

Transition countries should also consolidate their multiple social assistance programs into a single, targeted poverty benefit. The targeting of benefits is currently inadequate. In Russia, for instance, only 8 percent of social assistance is distributed to the poorest decile, and some 20 percent of poor households receive no benefits at all. By better targeting of benefits, governments can manage more wisely the social fallout from enterprise restructuring.

Invest in Education and Skills and Improve Service Delivery

The slow demographic growth in most of these countries implies that growth will come primarily from an increase in labor productivity rather than from an expansion of the labor force. While workers' productivity is closely related to the level of capital investment, it can also be enhanced by human capital investments through education and training activities, and by improvement in education service delivery. In many countries, on-the-job training opportunities are limited, and there is excessive emphasis on high-cost vocational training with unclear job market advantages due to the rapid change in technical requirements and market developments. The educational system inherited from the pretransition days does not meet the demands of the rapidly changing marketplace. Some transition countries face a particular challenge. High unemployment and poverty rates in rural areas force many children to complete only basic education and bow to economic pressures by going to work at an early age. This risks causing inequities in educational opportunities between rural and urban children. The following chapters shed light on specific measures that can help to address the education and training needs in transition economies.

Conclusions

Ten years into the transition, a wide variety of policies and performance marks the transition countries. This diversity defines the new set of initial conditions for the future and requires a differentiated set of policy measures to promote broad-based employment-generating growth, a *sine qua non* for poverty reduction. As the competitive environment is strengthened, prospects for enterprise restructuring and output gains will improve. But so will the demand for adequate social protection for those workers affected adversely by the restructuring. At the same time, the budget will need to provide for the maintenance of low and stable levels of inflation and for the necessary investments in human and physical capital. This will require continued fiscal adjustment. However, even with additional fiscal savings, social policy will need to become more effective through better targeting and cost-effectiveness in service delivery so as to reduce the fiscal cost of these services. Movement along these three fronts requires a concerted, integrated approach by the governments. Such an approach will provide the transition economies with the best hope for unlocking the sources of growth, while ensuring that the poor can take advantage of the emerging economic opportunities and are protected from any adverse economic effects.

Notes

1. Recent empirical work strongly suggests that incomes of the poor rise in the same proportion as overall growth. In particular, the evidence suggests that what is good for the economy as a whole—openness to foreign trade, low inflation, fiscal discipline, low government consumption, and good rule of law—is also good for the poor (Dollar and Kray 2000).

2. For a succinct analysis of some of the structural and institutional weaknesses that contributed to the Russian financial meltdown in 1998, see Pinto (2000).

3. See Easterly (1999) for an empirical analysis that suggests that OECD growth rates are important for developing countries' own growth performance.

4. The revenue figures are for 1998.

References

Broadman, H., and F. Recanatini. 1999. "Corruption and Market Institutions in Transition Economies." Washington, D.C.: World Bank.

Dabrowski, Marek, Stanislaw Gomulka, and Jacek Rostowski. 2000. "Whence Reform? A Critique of the Stiglitz Perspective." CASE, London School of Economics and Central European University. Processed.

Dollar, D., and A. Kray. 2000. "Growth is Good for the Poor." World Bank paper. Washington, D.C. Processed.

Easterly, W. 1999. "The Lost Decades: Explaining Developing Countries' Stagnation: 1980-98." World Bank paper. Washington, D.C. Processed.

EBRD (European Bank for Reconstruction and Development). 1999. *Transition Report*. London.

Frye, A., and A. Schleifer. 1997. "The Invisible Hand and the Grabbing Hand." *American Economic Review* 87 (2): 354-58.

Pinto, B. 2000. "Give Growth and Macroeconomic Stability in Russia a Chance: Harden Budgets by Eliminating Nonpayments." *The Economics of Transition*, forthcoming.

Pinto, B., P. Belka, and R. Krajewski. 1993. "Transforming State Enterprises in Poland: Evidence on Adjustment by Manufacturing Firms." *Brookings Papers on Economic Activity* 1: 213-70.

Rosenberg, C., and Tapio Saavalainen. 1998. "How to Deal with Azerbaijan's Oil Boom? Policy Strategies in a Resource-Rich Transition Economy." IMF Working Paper WP/98/6. Washington, D.C: International Monetary Fund.

Sachs, J., and A. Warner. 1995. "Natural Resource Abundance and Economic Growth." NBER Working Paper 5398. Cambridge, Mass.: National Bureau of Economic Research.

Stiglitz, J. 1998. "The Role of International Financial Institutions in the Current Global Economy." Speech to the Council on Foreign Relations, Chicago, February 17.

———. 1999. "Whither Reforms?" Paper presented at the World Bank Annual Conference on Development Economics. April.

Tanzi, V., and G. Tsibouris. 1999. "Fiscal Reform over Ten Years of Transition." Paper presented to the Fifth Dubrovnik Conference on Transition Economies, July 23-25. International Monetary Fund.

World Bank. 1998. "Contingent Government Liabilities: A Hidden Risk for Fiscal Stability." World Bank Working Paper 1989. Washington, D.C. October.

———. 2000. *Anticorruption in Transition: A Contribution to the Policy Debate.* Poverty Reduction and Economic Management Sector Unit, Europe and Central Asia Region, World Bank.

CHAPTER 7

Improving Capabilities: Education

Accomplishments in education were one of the triumphs of socialism. Levels of education attainment were high compared with other countries at similar levels of economic development. At the start of transition, adult literacy was generally universal; participation and completion rates for children and youth of both genders were high at all levels of education; teachers came to work; students had textbooks; and repetition and drop out rates were low (World Bank 2000c).

Now, however, poor children are increasingly at risk of not getting the education they need to participate productively in the market economy. In Bosnia, Georgia, Azerbaijan, and Tajikistan, the education of thousands of children was severely disrupted by ethnic strife, war, and civil unrest. In nonwar countries, differences in learning opportunities have emerged, one of the indicators being a decline in enrollment rates, particularly at the preschool and upper secondary levels.[1]

Declines in enrollment and attendance are related to poverty in complex ways. As poverty increases many poor parents find it harder to finance the costs associated with sending their children to school (clothing costs, for example). In addition, educational systems in many countries have responded to the decline in real public education expenditures and rising input costs by shifting part of the costs formerly paid by the public sector to households. Parents are increasingly called upon to buy textbooks and other materials not provided by schools, and in some cases they are even asked to contribute to school maintenance, heat, and teachers' salaries. Under-the-table payments to school personnel are on the rise, making it harder for children of poor families to muster the resources needed to attend upper secondary schools and universities. Substantial differences in educational opportunities between rural and urban areas are also beginning to be documented. Since relative rural poverty risks are already high in a number of countries, educational policies may be enhancing disparities and increasing the intergenerational transmission of poverty, rather than improving socioeconomic mobility.

Finally, the education provided in the public school system emphasizes factual learning and does not adequately prepare students to compete in an increasingly knowledge-based environment. Thus, for ECA transition countries, the challenge is to maintain the almost universal access to education achieved through decades of heavy investment while improving the quality of education to ensure that the poor have opportunities to advance in a market economy.

Who Is—and Isn't—Attending School

Enrollment rates are the best available measure of learning opportunities in the transition countries. The picture of enrollment rates varies substantially across the region, but in some countries there have been significant declines in enrollment—a major concern because of the strong correlation throughout the world between educational attainment and poverty status. A number of Central European countries show little change at the various levels of schooling. In contrast, some of the CIS countries show significant declines in enrollment rates.[2]

In the first half of the 1990s, enrollment rates in preschools dropped in many countries, with falls of 15 to 17 percentage points in South Eastern Europe, the Western CIS, and Central Asia, and by 25 percentage points in the Caucasus. In FSU countries, 32,000 preschools were closed during 1991-95, and the total number of places fell by a fifth (UNICEF 1998). In Ukraine, for example, the number of preschools has dropped by 43 percent since 1992. Only part of the dramatic decline in preschool enrollments can be explained by falling birth rates (box 7.1). It should be recognized that daycare for children under the age of four was combined with preschool so that the declines in enrollment rates reflect reductions in both types of programs.

The fall in preschool enrollment is now widening the gap between rich and poor children in terms of their readiness to learn. In pretransition days, enterprises provided preschool services to their employees. Following the collapse of communism, enterprises began facing hard budget constraints that compelled them to cut spending that did not contribute directly to profitability. Preschools were early casualties. In most cases, attempts have been made to transfer the financial responsibility for preschools from enterprises to municipalities. However, municipalities have often lacked the means to finance them. They have had to close them or introduce user charges to finance them. As a result, only children from families that can afford to pay are able to attend preschools.

In terms of enrollment rates in (compulsory) basic education, Central and South Eastern European countries have maintained the previous achievement of virtually universal education (figure 7.1). In contrast, in Western CIS, the Caucasus, and Central Asia, there is some evidence of deterioration. At one extreme, enrollment rates in Georgia fell by 15 percentage points between 1989 and 1996.

Declining overall enrollment rates at the upper secondary (general, vocational/technical) level signal emerging and important educational inequalities (figure 7.2). By 1997 enrollment rates in general secondary education—the academic stream—had declined, except in Central Europe, South Eastern Europe, and the Baltics, Belarus, Russia, Ukraine, and Kazakhstan. In a number of CIS countries, enrollment rates fell precipitously: between 1989 and 1997, enrollment rates fell by 15, 40, and 45 percent in Armenia, Georgia, and Tajikistan, respectively. These statistics are of concern because a solid upper secondary education seems to produce the skill levels required in a market economy. Failing to complete secondary school will, on average, increasingly place individuals at a disadvantage in the labor market and at risk of poverty (chapter 2).

Figure 7.1   Gross Enrollment Rates in Basic Education, 1989–97

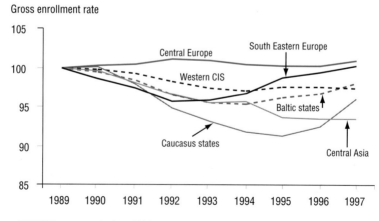

Source: UNICEF, Transmonee database, 2000.

Box 7.1   Preschools in Ukraine

In Ukraine more than half of the children ages 1 to 6 do not attend preschools (including daycare centers). In rural areas only 20 percent of the children attend. In recent years the attendance at preschools has fallen dramatically. In rural areas, the attendance fell by more than 50 percent between 1990 and 1998. Despite the closure of a large number of preschools, there is still a large unused capacity. The dramatic decline in preschool enrollments can be explained in part by the collapse in the birth rate since the start of the transition. The rest appears to be linked to Ukraine's economic collapse. A large share of preschool education was provided by factories. Factory failures, together with the withdrawal of women from the labor force, appear to account for a major share of the decline in preschool enrollments.

Table 7.1   Preschool Enrollment in Ukraine

Indicator	1990	1995	1998	Percentage change, 1998-90
Number of schools (thousands)	24.5	21.4	17.6	-28.2
Urban areas	11.9	10.5	8.2	-31.1
Rural areas	12.6	10.9	9.4	-25.4
Number of children enrolled (thousands)	2,428	1,536	1,103	-54.6
Urban areas	1,877	1,222	896	-52.3
Rural areas	551	314	207	-62.4
Enrollment rates of children ages 1 to 7 (in percent)	57	44	38	-33.3
Urban areas	64	53	40	-37.5
Rural areas	43	28	20	-53.5
Number of children per 100 places	107	76	67	-37.4
Urban areas	113	84	77	-31.9
Rural areas	90	57	43	-52.2

Source: Ukraine, Committee on National Statistics.

Enrollment rates in the vocational/technical stream of secondary education fell in most of the region. In some cases the declines reflect a shift toward general secondary education—a positive shift since general secondary education teaches more fungible skills that equip graduates to adapt to evolving market demands. In Hungary and Slovakia, for example, the changes in vocational/technical enrollment exactly balance the rise in general secondary education, so the overall enrollment rate at the upper secondary level remained unchanged. In contrast, in the CIS countries, there has been a remarkable decline in both general and vocational/technical secondary education.

Enrollment rates in tertiary education display a variety of patterns. There have been some noted increases in Central and South Eastern Europe—from 14 percent in Hungary in 1989 to 24 percent in 1997 and

Figure 7.2 Gross Enrollment Rates in General Secondary Education, 1989–97

Gross enrollment rate

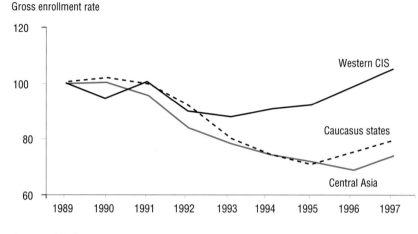

Source: UNICEF, Transmonee database.

from 16.8 percent in Bulgaria in 1989 to 27.1 percent in 1997—and (relatively small increases) in most of the CIS countries. Enrollment rates increased from 17 percent in 1989 to 19 percent in 1997 in Russia, and from 15 percent in 1989 to 20 percent in 1997 in Ukraine.

Particularly disturbing is scattered evidence suggesting that the decline in enrollment rates and school attendance is concentrated among the poor. In Bulgaria, for example, the drop in basic education enrollment rates was the sharpest among children in the lowest quintile (World Bank 1999a). In Russia, the proportion of teenagers (ages 17 to 19) from low-income households in school is more than one-third below that of children of high-income groups; the share in tertiary education is half that of young people of high-income groups (UNICEF 1998).

While there is little systematic evidence on actual attendance in school, absenteeism appears more prevalent among the poor. The 1995 Azerbaijan Survey of Living Conditions estimated an extended absence rate for children 6 to 16 years of age of 10 percent compared with the official estimate of 0.6 percent. The rate for nonpoor families was lower than the rates for very poor and poor families (World Bank 1997). In Armenia, only 52 percent of poor rural households said that their children attended school very regularly, compared with 68 percent of nonpoor households. The poor physical condition of the schools and lack of heat, water, and electricity was the reason most commonly given for irregular attendance (World Bank 1996). In Tajikistan, nonattendance rates in basic education were particularly high among the lowest income group—41 percent for the first quintile as opposed to 31.7 percent for the fifth quintile. More than 70 percent of students coming from the very poor families reported "no clothing" and "bad weather" as the two main reasons for nonattendance of basic education (World Bank 2000b). A woman from the Tash Bulak village in the Kyrgyz Republic thus expresses the hardship felt by many poor families:

> When our children were small it was easier to take care of them. Now they need to go to school, which means–they need clothes, and shoes, and school supplies. We don't have enough money, so only two of our children, two sons, attend school and our daughters stay at home, because they have no shoes and the school is located very far from here, 6 kilometers. The boys walk this distance. Occasionally some driver would pity them and give them a free ride. (World Bank 2000a, 76)

And finally, when poor parents send their children to school, they forgo the income that their children might otherwise be contributing to the household's survival. This may be a factor contributing to declining attendance and enrollment in the poorest countries of the region. In Central Asia and the Caucasus, young children, instead of going to school, are increasingly required to work to supplement family income (World Bank 1999c). In Moldova parents take children out of school to help with farm work (World Bank 1999f).

There is some evidence of reduced educational access for minorities—in particular Roma children—who are among the poorest children in Europe.[3] The education status of Roma has historically been low across Europe. While significant gains were made in enrolling Roma children during the socialist era, education attainment of Roma lags significantly behind the non-Roma population, with Roma much less likely to continue on to secondary and postsecondary education than the rest of the population. In Romania in 1994, 41 percent of Roma children ages 7 to 14 were not attending school compared with 7 percent of the rest of the population. In Bulgaria enrollment rates for Roma children ages 6 to 14 whose household incomes placed them in the bottom quintile (where most of the Roma are concentrated) were 33 percentage points lower than for the total population of children in the bottom quintile. In Hungary, where preschool is compulsory for all children at age 5, 11 percent of Roma did not attend school in 1997. Roma children are also less likely to continue from primary to secondary school. While 62 percent of all students in Hungary in 1995 continued from primary to secondary school, only 9 percent of Roma did so.

In addition, during the socialist era Roma children were channeled into "special schools" for the mentally and physically handicapped (box 7.2). This parallel system of education persists today. Compared with mainstream schools, these special schools provide Roma children with lower quality education and fewer opportunities to progress within the educational system and the labor market. In the Czech Republic, for example, students leaving special schools are only allowed to enter technical secondary schools, which puts them at a disadvantage in the labor market.[4] The practice of channeling Roma into special schools is most widespread in the Czech and Slovak Republics and in Hungary. In 1997 in the Czech Republic 64 percent of Roma children in primary school were in special schools compared with 4.2 percent of the total popula-

---

Box 7.2   Entrance to Remedial Special Schools in the Czech Republic

Roma children end up in special schools for many reasons. A study of this process in the Czech Republic found that because of discrimination and the highly discretionary nature of the placement, many more Roma children end up in special schools than should be the case.

Children can be enrolled or transferred from a regular basic school into special schools. By law, placement is based on the recommendation of the school director in consultation with the parent and an educational psychologist. In some cases parental consent is not obtained, or it is abused. Parents may not realize that they are authorizing their children to be shifted into a special school:

> My daughter is in the second year of basic school. She is doing alright. One day in November 1997 her teacher came to see me saying, "We want to move her to another class which will be better for her." He gave me a piece of paper to sign. I should have read it but it was long and I didn't think a teacher would try to cheat us, so I just signed it.... The next day I got a letter saying that my daughter had been moved to a remedial special school. Roma parent, Prague

Educational psychologists play a pivotal role in determining whether children will be sent to special schools, since they recommend students for examination and administer the exams. These procedures were found to be highly discretionary. In some cases children were even recommended for transfer without undergoing the required psychological exam. The tests themselves are problematic. Many are culturally biased. In addition, Roma children often start school with little or no knowledge of Czech. Not surprisingly, many children fail the tests and are subsequently evaluated as handicapped.

Because of the widespread abuses that have been documented, parents of 18 Roma children from the Czech town of Ostrava initiated legal proceedings against the government last year. In the district of Ostrava, Roma children outnumber non-Roma in special schools by more than 27 to one. Although they represent less than 5 percent of all primary-school-age students in the district, they constitute 50 percent of the special school population. The Czech Constitutional Court ruled in favor of the government. An appeals process opened in April 2000 in front of the European Court of Human Rights in Strasbourg.

Source: European Roma Rights Center (1999).

tion. Similarly, in Hungary about half the number of students enrolled in special schools were Roma.

Public Spending Decisions Do Not Favor the Poor

In a number of ECA countries, essential educational inputs (such as textbooks, school supplies, and school maintenance) are being squeezed between the falling education budget and a sizeable wage bill. This has compromised the quality of education of many countries, particularly in poor regions that have been forced to bear a disproportionate share of the adjustment. In Albania, for example, where 50 percent of the population live in rural areas, villages often depend on ad hoc strategies to get textbooks from urban centers to the village. Rural schools have fewer teaching materials and less equipment than urban schools have (World Bank 2000c). Students in rural schools, which are often in worse physical condition than urban schools, sit under umbrellas on rainy days because of leaks in roofs. In the worst cases the schools have broken walls and roofs and are open to the weather (World Bank 2000c). In Georgia, there is a similar urban bias: in 1996, for example, 43 percent of primary and secondary school directors in urban areas reported that textbooks were available for all children, compared with 27 percent of directors in rural areas (World Bank 1999c). And in many countries this bias extends to teacher qualifications as well (box 7.3).

In Russia, a few regions have been able to capitalize on their resource endowments, location, and other factors to increase their income. These regions have been able to spend more on education and other social areas.

Box 7.3   The Inequality of Learning in Rural and Urban Regions of Albania

In Albania, rural areas have a much smaller percentage of teachers with higher education qualifications than urban areas have, especially at the basic education level (44 percent compared with 70 percent). Villages with no access to a road attract qualified teachers only with great difficulty—teachers may have to walk as far as 2 miles in hard terrain to reach the school. School inspectors confirm that many teachers in rural and remote village schools lack subject matter knowledge *and* pedagogic skills. Urban settings offer more tutoring opportunities because the families tend to be wealthier. These opportunities make teachers reluctant to take teaching posts in rural areas. If they do commute from urban to rural areas to teach, they may leave their schools sometimes before the end of the school day in order to return to the city to tutor (World Bank 2000c).

In contrast, the poorest regions, with low per capita incomes and little fiscal capacity, have been struggling to maintain the basic requirements for high learning achievements in schools (World Bank 1999g). In Hungary, the decentralization resulted in a highly unequal distribution of resources across municipalities. Such effects had serious implications for the quality of education across regions, especially between poor rural communities and wealthier urban communities.

In many ECA countries the state does not allocate enough funds to meet the basic needs of the school system. This shifts educational costs to families. Many preschools and some institutions of higher education are now charging fees, effectively discouraging participation by the poor. When schools stop providing textbooks, parents are required to buy them. When the quality of teaching suffers, parents must pay for extracurricular tutorials for their children to learn. When buildings are not maintained, parents are asked to help pay for heat or repairs so that their children's school surroundings are conducive to learning. And when teachers are not paid or underpaid, parents are sometimes required to make informal payments to supplement teachers' salaries.

Informal payments are particularly an issue in entrance to secondary or university facilities. These payments may by outright "gifts," or they may take the form of tutorials to prepare students for examinations that the tutor is writing. Although the payment of bribes to achieve entrance is a practice that predates the transition, it has worsened in recent years. It excludes gifted students from poor families from university education, as well as undermines the value of university degrees and the fairness of the educational system. In Russia, for example, parents can gain access for their children to some elite secondary schools only by donating expensive items of equipment. Unfortunately, little is known about the magnitude of informal payments and their equity effects. But it is likely that the additional demands from supplementary charges and informal payments are highly regressive, since poor parents tend to have more children and less capacity to make such payments than parents who are wealthier.[5]

Particularly in countries where the formal labor market has collapsed and returns to higher education are not promising, poor parents may be unwilling to pay these costs. As one Armenian father explained in 1996: "Because I have no money, I cannot support my son's studies at the institute. There would be food, transport, and lodging expenses—without mentioning the bribes of which even a first-grader is aware. Now my son is keeping cows for 10,000 drams a day. Education is not the future" (Narayan 2000, 209).

Education Expenditures by the Poor and Nonpoor

Poor parents spend a large share of their incomes on schooling, but they cannot afford to spend as much in absolute terms as nonpoor households. In Tajikistan, households from the poorest quintile spend about 17 percent of their per capita expenditures on education; the share for households from the top quintile, however, was only about 5 percent (World Bank 2000a). In the Kyrgyz Republic, the extremely poor spent 17 percent of their per capita expenditures on education in 1997, compared with 13 percent for the nonpoor (table 7.2). In absolute terms the level of private expenditures on education (including fees) was two and a half times lower for the poor than for the nonpoor (Dorabawila, Lewis, and Staines 1999). In the former Yugoslav Republic of Macedonia in 1996, the poor spent two times more on education (as a percentage of per capita expenditures) than did the nonpoor, across all levels of education, but in total they spent less than half of what the nonpoor spent (table 7.3). In every case the differentiated ability to pay the cost of getting an education is likely to result in differentiated access to education.

Public spending on basic education is mildly progressive, but spending on secondary and higher education is not. Expenditure incidence analysis matches information from household surveys on school attendance by income quintile with information on the fiscal cost of providing different levels of education. Table 7.4 shows the distribution of public spending on education, by level of education, for the poorest (bottom 20 percent) and the richest (top 20 percent) quintiles of the population. The spending is progressive if the share received by the poor is greater than 20 percent (their share in the population). As shown, spending on primary education

Table 7.2 Annual Education Expenditures by Poverty Group, Kyrgyz Republic, 1997
(in som and percent)

Expenditure item	Extremely poor	Poor	Nonpoor
Tuition	21	53	375
Books, uniforms, fees, tutors	193	228	356
School repairs, classroom supplies, teachers, outings	36	43	64
Meals, transport, other	43	82	350
Total annual education expenditures	*293*	*406*	*1145*
Total as a percentage of per capita consumption	16.9	14.1	13.1

Source: World Bank (1999e).

Table 7.3   Private Expenditures on Education for the Poor by Level of Education,
FYR Macedonia, 1996

(in denar and percent)

	Primary education		Secondary education		Tertiary education	
Expenditure item	Poor	Nonpoor	Poor	Nonpoor	Poor	Nonpoor
Admission fee	0	0	0	96	0	4,916
Coaching	0	1,435	0	1,082	0	672
Transport	22	248	1,870	3,176	3,446	4,347
Books/supplies	1,871	2,923	1,760	3,186	2,676	3,714
Other expenditures	60	668	53	428	249	133
Total expenditures on education	1,953	5,274	3,683	7,968	6,371	13,782
Total as a percentage of per capita consumption	6.6	4.2	12.5	6.4	21.6	11.1

Source: World Bank (1999b).

is mildly pro-poor. (There is little difference in enrollment rates between rich and poor children, and poor families tend to have more children.)

Spending on secondary and tertiary education, however, benefits the poor the least. In Bulgaria, the poorest quintile benefits from 21 percent of the public spending on primary education, but only 11 percent on tertiary education, largely because of the very low enrollments of poor young adults in tertiary education. Some countries have scholarship programs that, in principle, favor poor families. However, benefit-incidence analysis

Table 7.4   Incidence of Public Expenditures on Education in Selected ECA Countries

Country	Preschool	Primary	Secondary	Tertiary
Romania (1997)				
Bottom 20%	—	21.0	26.0	**10.0**
Top 20%	—	10.0	12.0	**24.0**
Bulgaria (1997)				
Bottom 20%	23.0	21.0	**16.0**	11.0
Top 20%	—	—	—	—
FYR Macedonia (1996)				
Bottom 20%	24.9	25.4	**12.6**	7.1
Top 20%	17.5	14.0	**22.3**	46.0
Albania (1996)				
Bottom 20%	—	27.0	**7.2**	7.5
Top 20%	—	11.8	**32.3**	31.6

Note: Expenditures for tertiary education are marked in bold when not pro-poor.
Source: Tesliuc and Pop (2000); Rashid, Dorabawila, and Adams (1999); and World Bank (1999a, 1999b).

of scholarship programs in Romania shows that these programs have a regressive distributive impact in favor of children from the middle and upper classes. In the design phase most of the scholarships are justified on social grounds; only a few of them are awarded for "merit." Ex post, however, most of the scholarships went to the nonpoor (Tesliuc and Pop 2000). In sum, public financing of secondary and tertiary education benefits those who are better off and the most able to pay to send their children to school.

Inadequacy of the Knowledge and Skills Acquired in the Education System

Public education in Europe and Central Asia does not provide the poor—or the nonpoor—with the capabilities they need to participate in a market economy. Despite remarkable achievements, the education system does not adequately prepare its students to meet the growing challenge of global competition. This affects both poor and nonpoor alike, but the poor cannot afford to take advantage of costly opportunities that might improve their capabilities.

The education system in ECA countries has stressed memorized factual and procedural knowledge—not learning skills that provide the basis for a flexible labor force able to adapt to changing markets and employer needs. In theory, education performs three functions: the transmission of knowledge; the transmission of skills; and the acquisition of "behavioral traits" (that is, values and attitudes shaping behavior). What "formal education does...is not so much to train workers, as to make them trainable" (Blaug 1993, 28). Evidence from the OECD International Adult Literacy Survey (IALS) suggests that formal education in ECA countries provides students with knowledge but not the skills to prosper in a modern market economy (World Bank 2000c).

The IALS defines functional literacy as the information-processing skills that adults need to perform school tasks encountered at work, at home, or in the community—considerably more than the ability to read and write. Literacy measures how well a person can apply knowledge to solve problems he or she may not have encountered before. Even in economically advanced countries with strong education systems, many adults have difficulties coping with the reading and numeracy activities that are common in modern life (OECD 2000). Although adults with serious literacy problems can be found in any country, the patterns differ greatly from one country to another. Using three different scales of literacy (prose, document, and quantitative), figure 7.3 shows that there is a high percentage of adults in Poland, Hungary, and Slovenia with low literacy levels compared with adults in other OECD countries.[6] Literacy levels in the Czech Republic, however, compare favorably.

Another problem with education in Europe and Central Asia is that it is excessively specialized. In planned economies, the education system prepares specialists who know what job they will have in the future and what their professional responsibilities will be. Thus, education is narrowly tailored to niches in the economy. The narrow specialization is not desirable in a market-oriented environment where professional needs are less predictable. Students with a vocational/technical secondary education are not well equipped to respond to market signals and adapt to the rapidly changing market conditions in transition Europe.

Policy Challenges Faced by Governments

Inequities in learning opportunities have been growing during the transition process. Perhaps the most important lever for addressing these emerging inequities is education finance reform. There are five basic challenges. The first is to ensure an adequate level of financing for the sector so that all students have the opportunity to get a basic education. The second challenge is to allocate the education budget across levels of education and the

Figure 7.3 Percentage of 16–65 Year-Olds Who Test at Low Literacy Level, 1994–98

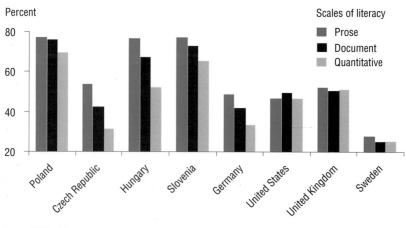

Source: OECD (2000).

third challenge across education inputs, so that resources are used in the most cost-effective manner possible. This will help to eliminate the conditions that give rise to informal payments and reduce the burden of education being shifted onto parents. The fourth challenge is to distribute the financing equitably across jurisdictions to ensure that all children have access to educational opportunities. The fifth challenge is make sure that a move toward greater reliance on private financing does not disadvantage the poor. Each of these challenges will be discussed in turn.

Ensuring Adequate Financing for Public Education

One of the most important decisions countries must make is the level and allocation of government financing to education. International experience provides some guidelines for setting the priorities. OECD countries spend on average 6 percent of their national income on education (with 1 to 2 percent of private spending), while middle-income countries spend, on average, 4 percent of their national income on education (OECD 1998).

If countries are not spending enough on education, the poor are likely to suffer. Indeed, real spending on education has declined substantially during the transition in many countries, as real GDP fell. But most countries have shown a strong public commitment to education during the transition by maintaining a reasonable level of spending on education relative to their GDP. Public spending on education as a share of GDP remained high: on average ECA countries spent 4.4 percent of GDP in 1998 (figure 7.4). This compares favorably with the 4.9 percent of GDP that OECD countries—with ten times transition countries' GDP per capita—spent on average on education (OECD 1998). But in a few countries, notably the Caucasus, basic education for all is threatened. In Armenia and Georgia and Tajikistan, education expenditures are two percentage points or more lower than the OECD average.

Improving the Allocation of Expenditures across Levels of Education

Basic (compulsory) education (grades 1 to 9). Basic education should have first claim on public education resources for at least two reasons: first, a sound basic education lays the "base" for subsequent learning; second, deficiencies at this level of schooling strongly affect the incidence of poverty. Publicly supported mandatory education is an attainable goal in the short term in almost all ECA countries, except possibly in Armenia, Azerbaijan, Georgia, and Tajikistan. In these four countries, the overall

Figure 7.4 Public Expenditures on Education in Transition Economies, 1998

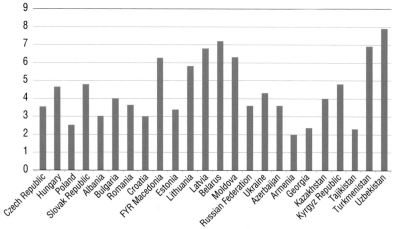

Education expenditures as a percentage of GDP

Note: For Croatia, Czech Republic, Estonia, and Poland, expenditure is spending by central government only. For FYR Macedonia, the year is 1996. For Estonia and Lithuania, the year is 1997.
Source: International Monetary Fund data.

budgetary environment is so tight that it may not be possible to offer universal basic education. Obviously, this is a highly undesirable outcome. In these countries, the overall budget for education may need to be increased to achieve universal basic education. And in those countries in which basic education is secured, governments can expand educational services in other directions.

Preschool education. Public resources should be devoted to preschools for children ages 4 to 6 for the following reasons. First, children who have developmentally appropriate stimulation before they are 6 years old can be educated at lower cost and to higher levels than can children who do not. Neurological evidence shows that children are primed to learn during the first years of life. Since preschools organized to develop the child cognitively can improve children's educational achievements at all levels, preschool should be thought of as part of the general education system.

Second, preschooling is a powerful antipoverty device. In the absence of preschools, early childhood opportunities are defined by the socioeconomic status of each child's family. This means that children from poor families are likely to arrive at school at ages six or seven already at a learning disadvantage that can never be entirely mitigated. Affordable preschools can help level the playing field for children from poor families.

Preschool services do not have to be compulsory, but they should be universally accessible. Through parent-teacher associations, local communities could help schools and teachers compensate for the limited resources of regional and central governments. Communities could be involved in the organization of early childhood development programs. Governments can, in turn, play a facilitative role in mobilizing local communities to create these programs (UNICEF 1998). Childhood development programs have the side benefit of freeing poor mothers (who cannot afford the tuition of regular preschools) to go to work. Access to preschools for the poor could be eased by granting them exemptions for school fees.

Vocational/technical secondary education. In most ECA countries, students must choose early on between a general education or a vocational/ technical education. Although the share of the relevant age group enrolled in vocational/technical upper secondary education varied in 1997 from a low of 15 percent (Albania) to a high of 85 percent (Czech Republic), in most ECA countries more than half of the students continue to be enrolled in the vocational/technical track (World Bank 2000c). This is very unfortunate. Early specialization, especially in narrowly defined vocational tracks, is inconsistent with the market needs for flexibility in learning. It does not make sense to teach a large number of students highly specific vocational skills that are rapidly rendered obsolete by the technological change characteristic of a dynamic modern economy. Moreover, it is very costly to run highly specialized schools. They cost more than general academic/vocational training, which does a better job of preparing students for the market. Thus, expensive specialized education should be replaced by a broadly based vocational/technical education that is better integrated with academic training. Highly specialized vocational training is best left to on-site training by employers.

Higher education. ECA countries have expanded higher education enrollments rapidly—a goal consistent with the human capital demands of the mixed market economies that are emerging in the region. However, with rapidly expanding enrollments and no change in spending per pupil, the higher education budget is likely to absorb an increasing share of the public education budget. Higher education in Moldova and Ukraine represents 15 percent and 19 percent, respectively, of the education budget— a fairly high percentage. This could endanger public spending on levels of education that should have a higher priority. In order to expand the quality and quantity of higher education—which is a highly desirable outcome—without crowding out public spending on other education levels, countries must lower the costs per student and increase the share of the costs borne by students. How to deal with the equity implications of the latter is an important issue taken up below.

Optimizing the Input Mix to Improve Education Conditions for All

Virtually all countries face significant cost pressure from several sources. First on the demand side, there is increasing pressure to increase upper secondary and tertiary education in response to the skill demands of market economies. While falling birth rates in many countries will moderate fiscal pressure on the system, these upper levels of education are more expensive, and are likely to lead to higher education costs in the future. In addition, the costs of many inputs have risen, and there is likely to be more cost pressures on the system in the future. The energy bill has increased substantially, as countries have whittled down energy subsidies and let energy prices reflect world energy scarcities. Maintenance on infrastructure, often deferred during the transition, has deteriorated greatly in some areas. Substantial allocations will be needed to bring maintenance up to par. Publication of educational materials, once subsidized, is more expensive today. Indeed, many countries are trying to replace their entire stock of textbooks to reflect the new realities of the transition. Teachers' salaries, which often fell relative to the average wage, may be bid up over time as labor markets begin to function better. These additional cost pressures make it imperative that governments adjust their spending to get the most out of what they do spend on education. The major challenges ECA countries face are to reduce their energy costs, rationalize their infrastructure, and bring down the wage bill.

Reduce energy costs. Some ECA countries spend between 30 and 50 percent of their total education budget on energy—although the energy bills are often unpaid. Freeing up funding for other uses by conserving energy will take sustained cooperation among all the sectors of government—and will take time. Energy-conserving school designs can gradually reduce energy use as new schools replace old ones. However, this process will take years. In the short term other measures—insulating school walls, double-glazing windows, and installing meters so that schools are billed only for energy used—will help reduce the energy bill.

Consolidate schools and increase spending on infrastructure. Falling enrollment rates in preschool and basic education have resulted in underuse of schools, yet the fixed cost of operating school buildings remains high.

Moreover, underfunding—often nonfunding—of school maintenance over the years of transition has created an education infrastructure crisis in Europe and Central Asia, especially in the FSU countries. It is impossible to estimate the total value of the repairs required in the region, although estimates for Albania ($270 million) and Latvia ($850 million) suggest the magnitude of the problem (World Bank 2000c). In some countries, such as Albania, some schools are in such a decrepit condition that school safety is a major concern. Data from Albania and a few other countries suggest that correcting the infrastructure problems resulting from deferred maintenance could absorb at least double the annual education budget.

A cost-effectiveness analysis could help determine the schools to be consolidated and those requiring rehabilitation and re-engineering investments. Consolidation is politically difficult to achieve, since it usually entails downsizing of personnel. It must be done with care not to increase urban-rural disparities that would make it more difficult for poor rural children to attend school (box 7.4).

The option of consolidation may not be desirable in areas with low population density or where there are issues of maintaining schooling in

---

Box 7.4   Constraints on Rationalization of Small Rural Schools in Novgorod

The special problems encountered in many rural schools throughout Russia are exemplified in Novgorod, where approximately 70 percent of the schools and 50 percent of the teachers are located in rural areas, whereas only 25 percent of the students live in rural areas. As a result, teachers and facilities are relatively underutilized in rural areas of the region. Average expenditure per student across regions varies from 2,100 to 3,000 new rubles (about $350 to $570).

Whether teachers are teaching full loads or not, student-teacher ratios in most rural schools are much lower than in cities. Rural classes rarely approach 25 students (the maximum allowed by federal regulations), and in some locations they dip as low as 2 students in a class. In 1995, the average student-teacher ratio was 8:1. Teachers in rural areas receive 25 percent higher salaries than those teaching in urban areas. In theory, they receive free housing. Teachers must pay for housing first and then claim reimbursement from the region. Given current budgetary constraints, many rural teachers do not receive their housing allowances—or not, at least, in a timely fashion. There have also been delays of varying duration in the payment of teachers' salaries in Novgorod.

Although multigrade teaching is common in OECD countries and is used in some parts of the Novgorod region, it is seen as undesirable and, at best, a stop-gap solution. Because most teachers do not have the training for multigrade teaching, this approach may compromise student learning. Regional Administration staff suspect that teachers in rural schools who are teaching more than one subject are not acceptably proficient in the second subject. Most teachers with a university education and/or good teaching qualifications do not want to live in rural areas. This raises the issue of retraining for rural school teachers (World Bank 1999g).

minority areas. In most cases these schools should be maintained in order
to ensure equitable access for poor rural families and minorities, even if
this results in small class size. A multigrade system of instruction can offer
a cost-effective way to provide education in such circumstances, if done
correctly. The practice of multigrade teaching has been found effective
when teachers have been properly trained to teach classes comprising students of different grade levels, when teachers have been provided with
proper teaching materials, and when students have appropriate, specially
designed textbooks. Maintaining small schools in villages may be needed
only in the earliest years of education (through grades 3 or 4). From about
the age of 10, however, children are old enough to attend schools farther
from home. Savings from school consolidation might be used to fund student transport in such circumstances.

Rationalize the wage bill. At the same time that governments have
curtailed expenditures on materials and maintenance, they have increased
the number of teachers—even though the number of students has been
falling (figure 7.5). And many of the systems are thought to have been
overstaffed at the outset, like the rest of the economy. In Bulgaria, the
total number of teachers increased by 3.5 percent, despite attempts to
scale back civil service employment (World Bank 1999a). In Central Asia,
the increases range up to 25 percent (Klugman 1999). In Russia, *every*
region increased its number of teachers in public employment—an overall
increase of 25 percent—between 1989 and 1996 (World Bank 1999g): the

Figure 7.5   Student-Teacher Ratio, 1989–97 (1989=100)

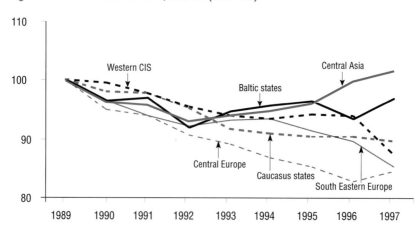

Source: UNICEF, TransMonee database, 2000.

national number of teachers grew three times as fast as the number of students: the student-teacher ratio declined from 15.8 in 1989 to 11.9 in 1997.[7]

In Ukraine, spending on items vital for the provision of quality education (textbooks and capital repair) has fallen, while spending on staff has increased. Allocations for textbooks fell by 70 percent between 1995 and 1998. Spending on capital maintenance was reduced to 2.2 percent of the education budget. Table 7.5 shows the discrepancy between the growth in the number of teachers (and schools) on the one hand and the number of students on the other hand. For example, in tertiary education, Ukraine expanded the number of teachers by 9.4 percent and the number of schools by 5.5 percent between 1990 and 1997, while the average number of students remained almost constant.

Using OECD standards as a benchmark, we estimate that up to a third of the teaching labor force (and even more of the nonteaching force) should be reduced.[8] The reduction in excessive staffing should be done while preserving the quality of education and adequately compensating those who must leave the education sector. Experience in some ECA countries suggests that a step-by-step approach is politically and socially desirable. An up-front reduction in staffing would lead to an undesirable outcome:

Table 7.5   Changes in Education Supply and Enrollment in Ukraine, Selected Periods, 1985–97

Indicator	1990/1985 (in percent)	1997/1990 (in percent)	1997 (in thousands)
Preschool			
Urban areas			
Number of schools	1.7	-26.9	8.7
Number of children	-8.4	-49.3	952
Rural areas			
Number of schools	12.5	-23.0	9.7
Number of children	-0.2	-60.3	219
Basic education			
Average number of students per class	-12.1	-3.5	22.4[a]
Number of teachers	13.5	6.3	571
Tertiary education			
Number of schools	1.6	5.5	940
Number of teachers	5.4	9.4	119
Number of students	-1.4	-0.1	1,636

a. Not in thousands.
Source: Ukraine, Committee on National Statistics.

good teachers would leave the profession and lower quality teachers or highly specialized teachers would stay. Therefore, an attestation mechanism could be designed to select high-quality teachers. Once the attestation is implemented on a national scale, teachers' wages would be brought up to nationally competitive levels, and severance pay (as well as training and opportunities for self-employment) would be granted to those who leave the education sector (Vandycke 2000).

It does not make sense to search for additional cost savings by allowing teachers' wages to fall relative to other wages and running up wage arrears. Instead, rationalizing the labor force might permit a net reduction in the wage bill and at the same time permit an increase in salaries in countries where teachers are poorly paid.

Distributing Financing Equitably across Government Jurisdictions

Ensuring equality of educational opportunity, measured at a minimum by equality in educational spending, is a strong argument for a high degree of centralized financing in countries in which income inequality is high. Almost all ECA countries—except Bosnia and Herzegovina, Russia, and Georgia—rely on centrally generated revenues to finance basic education.[9] While most education financing is generated nationally, it is often channeled through local governments. In Armenia and Bulgaria, the grants are earmarked exclusively for education. In most other countries (such as Albania, Azerbaijan, Georgia, Hungary, Poland, Moldova, Romania, Russia, Tajikistan, and Ukraine), local governments rely on block grants that are not earmarked exclusively for education. In these countries education spending has not always been protected, though typically social assistance expenditures have been the first to be cut.

Although most ECA countries now raise revenues for the sector centrally, many countries are considering devolving responsibility for revenue generation to local governments. However, centralized financing of education in ECA countries has a number of important advantages (Hoopengardner 1999), especially that of improving the equity of educational outcomes. The tax bases (personal and business income tax, turnover tax, and property tax) of ECA countries differ widely among localities. In other words, there is a "horizontal fiscal imbalance." The ratio of high to low per capita income across localities is typically five to one or greater. If subnational governments pay for the education of children only in their jurisdictions, geographic differences in income would translate into unequal educational opportunities. Poor regions would be likely to have poor education systems that produce poor educational outcomes that result in low incomes that reinforce regional poverty. The experience of Georgia (box 7.5) reveals some of these problems.

In principle, locally generated resources could be redistributed through some sort of equalization fund, which essentially confiscates resources in one jurisdiction and applies them to another. However, it is politically and administratively easier to distribute national revenues to localities in ways that help equalize education opportunities among jurisdictions. Centralized financing, combined with a system in which "money follows stu-

---

Box 7.5   Decentralization of Education Spending in Georgia

Since Georgia's independence, government spending on education has declined dramatically. Not only did GDP fall dramatically—more than 75 percent reduction between 1991 and 1994—but the share of GDP allocated to education—from more than 7 percent in 1991 to 1 percent in 1994—fell as well. Since 1995 a modest recovery has taken place. In 1998 education spending as a share of GDP amounted to 2.4 percent. Compared with OECD standards, the education sector is severely underfinanced.

The responsibility for education spending is shared between the central government (higher, vocational, and specialized education) and the district (rayon) authorities (preschool, primary, and general secondary education). In 1998 about two-thirds of education spending was made by the rayons. Education spending by rayons is financed from various sources, including earmarked grants for education from the central government, general purpose grants from the central government, and own local fiscal revenues.

In its implementation, this system raised a number of problems:

- In 1998, 48 rayons, out of Georgia's 61 rayons, received budget transfers with funds earmarked for education. For the remaining ones, no funds were earmarked for education, presumably because the central government thought that the fiscal capacity of these rayons was adequate to finance the needs of the education sector and did not necessitate central government transfers.

- The majority of public spending on education is financed from revenue generated and collected at the rayon level. The fiscal capacity of rayons appears, however, to be highly variable. For instance, in 1998 the expenditure per student varied between a low of Laris 70 to a high of Laris 279. This extreme variation in expenditure per student could be warranted by conditions of population density, income, or other factors. While geographical remoteness and low student/teacher ratios explain some of the differences, the discrepancy in per student expenditure raises questions about the equity of education spending across the country.

- Criteria for calculating the transfers and their earmarked portions for education are nontransparent.

Most rayons allocate the bulk of their education budget to the payment of salaries, at the expense of spending on other necessary items, such as textbooks, utilities, and maintenance of schools. Yet teachers' salaries have not been paid on time. In 1998 about 70 percent of teachers had salary payment in arrears. Arrears accumulation is partly linked to shortfalls in central government financing. It is also related to the low capacity of rayons to mobilize revenues.

dents," can give poor children in poor areas fair life chances if resources are distributed equitably among jurisdictions. In the past, funding in ECA countries was usually allocated on the basis of norms for inputs. Jurisdictions with the most school buildings and teachers generally received the most money. Now, however, it is almost universally accepted that money should follow students. This has become the preferred mechanism for determining how spending is distributed among spending units. The funding formula per student can be adjusted for factors that result in differences in costs, such as population density or in the education challenges that different student bodies present.

Decisions about who raises the money and who controls it are separate decisions. Centralized revenue generation need not imply centralized control over the use of resources. Local jurisdictions or institutions can be given the flexibility to allocate resources as they see fit to improve the quality and cost-effectiveness of the services they offer.

Supplementing Public Financing with Private Funds without Disadvantaging the Poor

To supplement tax revenues for the education sector, all ECA countries use cost-recovery mechanisms such as user charges and fund-raising efforts at the school level. These mechanisms have merit to the extent that they increase the total resources available to the sector and promote greater ownership and participation by the contributors, who are often the beneficiaries (students and their parents). The risks of excluding the poor, however, are high.

Increase user charges on a limited basis. User charges (payments by recipients for identifiable services) are direct financial supports for education. Tuition for preschool students, charges for textbooks or laboratory materials, and tuition and dormitory fees for university students are examples of user charges. The rationale for user charges is that since individual students receive a large part of the benefit from education, they (their families) should bear part of the cost directly. Although user charges can improve the quality of education beyond that which would be possible with government financing alone, they entail significant risks of excluding the poor, especially for basic education. In addition, they may increase regional disparities since the schools best positioned to raise money through user charges may be in relatively rich jurisdictions where educational opportunities are already good.

The case for user charges is strongest for higher education. Most of the benefits of higher education are private: higher lifetime earnings for the individual receiving the education. Several ECA countries have already introduced tuition and fees to shift a share of costs from the taxpayer to students and their parents—often through creative means to circumvent legal provisions that prevent the countries from charging tuition. In Poland, for example, in the past, "extramural students" attended one weekend and evening program. Now these students are allowed to attend regular day classes along with day students who do not pay tuition charges. The poor are already underrepresented in higher education, and care must be taken not to further aggravate the inequity through the imposition of user charges.

Means tested scholarships and student loan schemes are important vehicles for ensuring that the talented poor can attend university. Unfortunately, they are difficult to implement successfully. First, applying a means test to identify students who are eligible for state subsidies is difficult and costly. Countries that operate subsidized student-loan schemes and scholarship programs rely on reports of income and wealth to the tax authorities in order to estimate ability to pay for schooling and capacity to repay loans. However, tax compliance in ECA countries tends to be low, and self-reporting tends to be inaccurate. Second, double-digit inflation rates that persist in a number of ECA countries make nominal interest rates on fixed rate loans very high. These rates impose large risks on borrowers if inflationary expectations are not realized. Innovative lending products that index the unpaid principal amount of the loan to a price index or that adjust interest rates frequently might be considered. Third, implementing a student loan scheme requires solving the problems inherent in lending large sums of money on a long-term basis without collateral. Students generally do not have an established credit history that might be used to assess their character. Moreover, the enforcement of loan repayment is usually facilitated by the borrower's sense that the lender has a legitimate claim on the borrower. This sense of obligation derives from a recognition that the loan has supported the purchase of something of value and that the terms of the purchase were fair. The history of highly subsidized higher education in the region undermines this sense of obligation. Since consumer credit is underdeveloped in most ECA countries, there is little tradition of voluntary repayment of credit and little onus attached to default.

Adopting an income-contingent repayment scheme might be an option for financing higher education, but it is largely untested. In this scheme low-earnings students are protected in both the short and long run. Repayment of a student's loan is based on a percentage of his or her subsequent earnings, collected alongside income tax or a social insurance contribution, until the loan and interest have been repaid. However, implementing such a scheme requires a large tax administrative capacity to effectively administer income tax—an institution often lacking in ECA countries. In theory, the scheme should improve the access of the poor to higher education. Actual evidence is needed, however, on the extent to which the scheme is *de facto* fair, equitable, and reaches the poor. The Hungarian government is in the process of adopting such a scheme (Barr 1999). This will provide valuable evidence on how well the scheme works in practice.

Stamp out or legitimize informal user charges. Informal user charges are payments that are not explicit or publicly mandated. In some cases they result from corrupt practices, as when teachers threaten to fail students unless students pay teachers for extra tutoring outside school. In other cases they cover legitimate costs of education, such as the cost of heating school buildings, which are shifted to parents or to the community. In the latter case, there is often inadequate financial control over the informal parental contributions.

As noted earlier, informal payments are widespread in connection with entrance to university education. In the absence of reliable assessment for school-leavers, higher education institutions are obliged to organize their own entrance examinations, which consume scarce financial resources and give rise to opportunities to extract bribes from parents. Objective university entrance examinations would reduce this pernicious practice. Objective standards at all levels of education would provide students, their parents, and the community at large a means for assessing how well schools are performing—and thus how well tax revenues are being spent.

Informal payments—even those that actually go to legitimate school expenses—contribute to the exclusion of the poor from education. Ensuring that schools are accountable for how the money is spent on legitimate expenses will reduce opportunities for corruption, but it will not necessarily address equity concerns. Prohibiting the informal payments that are effectively bribes would improve equity concerns, but this is unlikely to succeed unless the conditions that give rise to the informal payments are addressed. A more efficient and equitable deployment of resources will reduce the conditions that lead to the proliferation of legitimate and illegitimate informal payments—and reduce disparities in educational opportunities between the poor and nonpoor.

Conclusion

The reforms described in this chapter will contribute to promoting equitable education opportunities for all and to keeping the poor from being excluded from the education they need in today's world. Yet even with the broad agenda outlined above, the educational needs of the poor may not be entirely met. Additional measures may be needed to improve educational access and quality in particular locations, such as rural areas, or for certain population groups that present particular challenges.

In some cases the causes of unequal opportunities can be fixed with money—for example, subsidizing poor parents so that they can buy required textbooks or clothing for their children. Linking attendance in school to receipt of the benefit may be worth considering if the objective of the assistance is to enable poor children to attend school—as long as the benefit is sufficient to cover the incremental costs of school attendance. In other cases the reasons for poor children's lack of attendance are more complicated. If they are too isolated, rural areas may not be able to retain good teachers. In this case improving roads and transport options may have an impact on the quality of rural schools and also on the school attendance of children in rural areas.

Issues of ethnicity also present particular challenges. Although poverty keeps many Roma children out of school, there are other reasons: lack of proficiency in the national language, fear of assimilation among some traditional Roma families that decreases demand for education, and discrimination by non-Roma parents, children, and teachers. A number of programs are under way to address these issues. One example is targeted preschool programs, which prepare children for the classroom environment and overcome language and cultural differences. In Hungary, Bulgaria, and Romania, the Open Society Foundation is supporting programs at the primary-school level based on the Headstart initiative of the United States in both Roma and non-Roma communities. Secondary schools targeted to Roma children have recently been opened in Hungary and the Czech Republic. These schools incorporate Romani studies into the curriculum and aim to provide a supportive environment through teacher training and parental involvement. Systematic evaluation of the programs is needed to determine whether they are breaking down the barriers that prevent the Roma (and other groups suffering ethnic discrimination) from closing the education gap.

Notes

1. *Preschool education* refers to schooling for children 0 to 6–7 years of age. It includes daycare centers. *Basic education* refers to primary grades 1 to 4 and lower secondary grades 5 to 9. *Upper secondary education* is split into general ("academic") and vocational/technical tracks. *Tertiary* (or higher or university) *education* refers to postcompulsory education.

2. Gross enrollment rates for the ECA region must be treated cautiously: the age-specific population numbers are somewhat suspect since the last credible censuses were conducted at the end of the 1980s. During the transition, the civil registration of births and deaths declined sharply, while mobility across borders increased. The enrollment numbers are questionable for those countries or regions within countries engaged in conflict.

3. The section on the Roma is based on material summarized in Ringold (2000).

4. As of spring 2000, the Czech Parliament was considering legislation that would allow graduates of special schools to continue in the mainstream school system.

5. More investigation is needed on the price elasticity of the demand for education in ECA countries.

6. Low literacy is defined as the sum of literacy scores for Level 1 and Level 2. Individuals need to attain a level of 3 or greater to function in a modern workplace.

7. The student-teacher ratios are likely to fall farther in the years ahead as the smaller cohorts from lower birth rates pass through the education system.

8. On average, the student-teacher ratio in OECD countries is 10:1. The ratio in Georgia and Armenia is 9.2:1 and 8.7:1, respectively.

9. Russia's oblasts are as big as most ECA countries. In Russia, decentralization from national to subnational levels of government should be thought of in terms of decentralization from oblast to suboblast levels of government.

References

Barr, Nicholas. 1999. "Higher Education Finance: Lessons from International Experience." *Republic of Hungary: Higher Education Reform Project: Consulting Services for Student Loan Program.* London: Department of Economics, London School of Economics.

Blaug, Mark. 1993. "Education and the Employment Contract." *Education Economics* 1(1): 21–33.

Dorabawila, Vajeera, Maureen Lewis, and Verdon Staines. 1999. "Trend and Status of Education and Private Expenditure, Kyrgyz 1993–97." Human Development Sector Unit, Europe and Central Asia Region, World Bank. Processed.

European Roma Rights Center. 1999. "A Special Remedy: Roma and Schools for the Mentally Handicapped in the Czech Republic." Country Report 8.

Hoopengardner, Tom. 1999. "Patterns of Education Finance in ECA Countries." Human Development Sector Unit, Europe and Central Asia Region, World Bank. Processed.

Klugman, Jeni. 1999. "Financing and Governance of Education in Central Asia." *MOST Special Issue* (unpublished).

OECD (Organisation for Economic Co-operation and Development). 1997. *Literacy Skills for the Knowledge Society.* Paris: OECD; Canada: Human Resources Development Canada, and Statistics.

———. 1998. *Human Capital Investment: An International Comparison.* Paris: Centre for Educational Research and Innovation.

———. 2000. *Literacy in the Information Age.* Final Report of the International Adult Literacy Survey. Paris: OECD; Canada: Human Resources Development Canada, and Statistics.

Rashid, Mansoora, Vajeera Dorabawila, and Richard Adams. 1999. "Household Welfare, Labor Market, and Public Programs in Albania." Human Development Sector Unit, Europe and Central Asia Region, World Bank. Processed.

Ringold, Dena. 2000. "Education and the Roma in Central and Eastern Europe: Trends and Challenges." World Bank.

Tesliuc, Cornelia, and Lucian Pop. 2000. "Poverty, Inequality, and Social Protection." In *Economic Transition in Romania: Past, Present, and Future,* edited by Christof Rühl and Daniel Daianu. Bucharest: World Bank and Romanian Center for Economic Policies. (Proceedings of the Conference: Romania 2000: Ten Years of Transition: Past, Present, and Future, October 21–22, 1999, Bucharest, Romania.)

UNICEF. 1998. "Education for All?" *Regional Monitoring Report* No. 5. Florence: UNICEF Child Development Centre.

UNICEF-IDC, TransMONEE Database 3.0. http://www.unicef-icdc.org/information/databases. Florence: UNICEF International Development Center.

Vandycke, Nancy. 2000. "Programmatic Adjustment Loan in Ukraine: Education Component." Human Development Sector Unit, Europe and Central Asia Region, World Bank. Processed.

World Bank. 1996. "Armenia: Confronting Poverty Issues." Report 15693–AM. Washington, D.C.

———. 1997. "Azerbaijan Poverty Assessment." Report 15601–AZ. Washington, D.C.

———. 1999a. "Bulgaria: Poverty during the Transition." Report 18411. Washington, D.C.

————. 1999b. "Former Yugoslav Republic of Macedonia: Focusing on the Poor." Report 19348-GE. Washington, D.C. June 11.

————. 1999c. "Georgia: Poverty and Income Distribution." Report 19348-GE. Washington, D.C. May 27.

————. 1999d. *Global Synthesis. Consultations with the Poor.* Reports on Bulgaria, Bosnia and Herzegovina, Russia, and Uzbekistan. Prepared for *Global Synthesis Workshop*, September 22–23, 1999. Poverty Group, Poverty Reduction and Economic Management Sector Unit, World Bank.

————. 1999e. "Kyrgyz Republic: Update on Poverty in the Kyrgyz Republic." Report 19425-KG. Washington, D.C. June.

————. 1999f. "Moldova: Poverty Assessment." A World Bank Country Study. Washington, D.C. May.

————. 1999g. "Russia: Regional Education Study." Report 18666-RU. Washington, D.C.

————. 2000a. *Kyrgyz Republic: Consultations with the Poor* (a study to inform the *World Development Report 2000/1* prepared for the Global Synthesis Workshop, September 22–23, 1999). Poverty Group, Poverty Reduction and Economic Management Sector Unit. Washington, D.C.

————. 2000b. "Republic of Tajikistan. Poverty Assessment." Report 20285. Washington, D.C. June 29.

————. 2000c. "The Hidden Challenges to ECA's Education Systems: ECA Education Sector Strategy Paper." Washington, D.C.

CHAPTER 8

Improving Capabilities: Health

During the socialist era transition countries in Europe and Central Asia made major strides in the health arena. They increased life expectancy, lowered child mortality, immunized virtually all children, improved access to safe water and better sanitation, alleviated acute malnutrition and micronutrient deficiencies, and sought to control communicable diseases. The broad-based nature of these interventions, together with the strong emphasis on education, considerably improved the health outcomes of the population—including the least advantaged. By the mid-1950s health indicators in ECA countries reached levels comparable to most Western countries. By the mid-1960s, average life expectancy at birth in these countries was only 1 to 2 years shorter than in the West.

As a result of sound investments to promote good health, the major disease burden in Europe and Central Asia is similar to that in higher income countries. Lung cancer, liver cirrhosis, cardiovascular disease, and injuries are the major causes of mortality and morbidity in the region. Cardiovascular disease was responsible for 26.2 percent of premature deaths, as measured by disability adjusted life years (DALYs),[1] substantially exceeding the industrialized country average of 19.4 percent (Murray and Lopez 1997). While there are no data on the incidence of these diseases across income groups, they clearly affect the poor as well as the nonpoor. The high rates of tobacco and alcohol consumption in the region contribute strongly to premature deaths from cardiovascular and pulmonary diseases.[2] Lifestyle changes could substantially reduce these risks. In general, governments have placed little emphasis on prevention, although a reduction in alcohol availability in Russia in the mid-1980s resulted in a noticeable decline in premature deaths.

Emerging Threats to Good Health for the Poor

In addition to achievements in reducing life expectancy, ECA countries realized another major achievement in the creation of a health system that offered universal entitlement to comprehensive, free health care. Health systems have remained remarkably resilient despite the fiscal shock they have endured. The most troubling reversal of improving health outcomes—the decline in adult life expectancy in some countries, most notably Russia during the transition—has not been attributed to a serious worsening of the health system. But there are signs that the achievements of the past are being undermined to the detriment of the poor. First, although not widespread, slippages in basic public health investments are beginning to appear and are likely to differentially affect the poor. Second, countries are not doing enough to address the re-emergence or emergence of new public health threats, notably tuberculosis and HIV/AIDS—which, especially in the case of TB, may disproportionately affect the poor and most marginalized populations. Third, the access that the population has historically enjoyed to universal, free health care is giving way to a system in which access to health care is conditional on making under-the-table, illegal payments to public health care providers. The poor, who can least afford to pay, are the most negatively affected.

Stalled Progress on Basic Health Outcomes

Slippage in basic health outcomes interventions is emerging in some parts of the region, particularly in immunization coverage and treatment of undernutrition and micronutrient deficiencies.

Immunizable diseases, such as measles and tetanus, are being controlled by vaccination programs, although there have been notable lapses in the region. In Georgia only 63 percent of children under a year old had been immunized against measles in 1998, and no child was immunized in 1994-95 because of a lack of vaccines (World Bank 1999); in Azerbaijan immunizations were handled by Doctors without Borders (World Bank 1997). Physicians in Eastern Europe have reported numerous measles outbreaks among Roma (gypsy) communities, suggesting uneven vaccination coverage (ECOHOST 2000). Data from a few Demographic and Health Surveys indicate that coverage is lower than desirable in some countries. In Uzbekistan in 1996, only 80 percent of children ages 12 to 23 months had received the Bacille Calmette Guerin (BCG) vaccine, 3 doses each of the diphtheria, pertussis, and tetanus (DPT) vaccine and oral polio vaccine (OPV), and a measles vaccine, while in Kyrgyz Republic only 70 percent of children had. More worrisome is Kazakhstan: not only is the rate of fully immunized children low, but the rates vary substantially by household wealth. Data from the Demographic and Health Survey in 1995, though now somewhat dated, showed that only 41 percent of children in the poorest quintile had received these vaccinations compared with 82 percent in the upper quintile (figure 8.1). Thus, some problems have emerged with the traditional and vitally important child immunization programs, but these are largely in some of the countries in the Commonwealth of Independent States (CIS).

Environmental health and adequate potable water and sanitation remain policy and resource challenges for the region, particularly in the former Soviet Union (FSU). The legacy of environmental degradation and contamination of land and water, growing air pollution in cities, and eroding water and sanitation systems will only worsen without adequate attention

Figure 8.1   Childhood Immunization Rates in Kazakhstan by Wealth Quintile, 1995

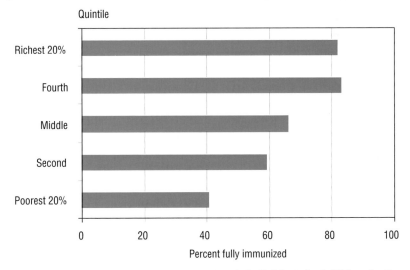

Note: Percentage of living children 12 to 23 months who received the Bacille Calmette Guerin (BCG) vaccine; three doses each of the diphtheria, pertussis, and tetanus (DPT) vaccine and the oral polio vaccine (OPV); and measles vaccination at the time of the Demographic and Health Survey.
Source: Bank staff estimates based on a 1995 Demographic and Health Survey.

Table 8.1 Wasting and Stunting Prevalence in Europe and Central Asia, Selected
Countries, Selected Years
(percent)

Country	Year	Public health concern	
		Wasting prevalence above 5 percent	Stunting revalence above 20 percent
Kazakhstan[a]	1995		
Urban		(3.3)	(15.8)
Rural		(3.0)	21.8
Kyrgyz Republic[a]	1997	(3.4)	24.8
Tajikistan[c]	1998	7.0	55.0
Uzbekistan[a]	1996	11.6	31.3
Azerbaijan[b]	1996	(2.9)	22.2
Albania[b]	1997	7.4	22.7

Note: Stunting is low height-for-age because of chronic malnutrition. Wasting is low-weight-for height as a result of acute malnutrition. They are defined as the proportion of children falling below minus two Z-scores of the standard established by the World Health Organization and the U.S. National Center for Health Statistics. Comparable data are not available for Georgia. Armenia does not quite meet the triggers: wasting rates in 1998 were 4.1 percent and stunting rates were 12.6 percent. Figures in parentheses are below the threshold levels.
a. Rates are for children ages 0 to 35 months.
b. Rates are for children ages 0 to 59 months.
c. Rates are for children ages 6 to 59 months.
Sources: Galloway, Rokx, and Brown (2000).

from governments in the short to medium term. Access to clean water is particularly a problem in the rural parts of Central Asia.

Undernutrition may be a more serious problem as poverty levels rise. As table 8-1 shows, undernutrition in children under five years of age is a problem in parts of Central Asia, the Caucasus, and Albania. By the standards of the World Health Organization (WHO), national prevalence rates greater than 5 percent for wasting and 20 percent for stunting indicate a serious public health problem. Tajikistan saw sharp increases in stunting and some rise in wasting between 1994 and 1998 probably due to war and the dramatic declines in incomes and sharp increases in prices as subsidies were withdrawn. Between 1994 and 1998 wasting more than doubled, increasing from 3 to 7 percent of children ages 6 to 59 months, and stunting increased from 41 to 55 percent. Kyrgyz Republic also exhibits wasting levels of about 10 percent between ages 1 and 2. In both countries the early introduction of tea, and inappropriate weaning foods such as cow's milk, have had negative effects on child nutrition (Galloway, Rokx, and Brown 2000).

Micronutrient malnutrition is the result of poor intakes of vitamins and minerals, which cause a number of poor health outcomes, such as

compromised growth and immune functions, reduced mental development and educational achievement, decreased productivity, and lessened
reproductive capacity. Three micronutrients—iron, iodine, and vitamin
A—are the most important in preventing the aforementioned afflictions.
They are easily tracked and addressed. Despite this, there is limited information in the ECA region on the prevalence of iron and iodine deficiency
and virtually none on the status of Vitamin A, but what evidence does
exist is cause for concern. There appear to be areas in Central Asia and
the Caucasus where Vitamin A deficiency and anemia from iron deficiencies are quite prevalent. Anemia rates among women of reproductive age
are extremely high in the Aral Sea region of Kazakhstan and Uzbekistan,
reaching over 60 percent in Uzbekistan (Galloway, Rokx, and Brown
2000).

Goiter prevalence stemming from iodine deficiency disorder (IDD) is
emerging as a serious public health concern in many parts of the region
outside Central Europe. Goiter rates of 25 percent have recently been reported in Bosnia and Herzegovina; 15 to 25 percent of children and women
are affected in Central Russia and up to 40 percent in other parts of Russia. Among certain groups, such as internally displaced persons, levels are
higher, with prevalence (23 percent) more than double that of the general
population (10 percent) in Azerbaijan. Studies in selected districts of Kyrgyz
Republic suggest IDD rates as high as 87 percent of preschoolers in Osh
and 52 percent prevalence of iodine deficiency among preschoolers in Issy
Kul. In one region of Tajikistan, goiter prevalence is as high as 80 percent.
In Georgia IDD rates of 54 to 78 percent have been reported. IDD is
highest in the mountainous regions, where poverty is most widespread. If
confirmed, these findings have serious implications for the next generation and for longer term economic prospects given the severe negative
effects of iodine deficiency on learning. Sadly, these prevalence figures
reflect a breakdown in salt fortification, an inexpensive and simple preventive method to control IDD (box 8.1).

Communicable Diseases: A Looming Threat

Tuberculosis, the major communicable disease in the region and one that
disproportionately affects the poor, was largely brought under control
during the pre-transition era. But this trend is being reversed. Between
1991 and 1998, TB incidence in Russia climbed from 50,400 to 110,900
cases a year, more than a 100 percent increase. In 1997 alone, Russia
represented 35 percent of all cases reported to the WHO European Region. Despite this, experts indicate that as of 1998 more than one-fifth of

---

Box 8.1   Iodine Deficiency Disorders in the Former Soviet Union

The former Soviet Union began iodizing salt in the 1950s, and by 1970 much of the iodine deficiency disorders (IDD) in the CIS had been eliminated. Poor monitoring led to a rise in un-iodized salt, causing a resurgence in IDD prevalence beginning in the 1980s. Declines in iodized salt were linked to a lack of sodium thiosulphate needed to iodate salt. Cases of goiter in certain Oblasts in the Ukraine increased by 100 percent between 1980 and 1990, and in Belarus a 300 percent increase in goiter prevalence occurred in some oblasts after 1986.

Exacerbating this was a decline in the consumption of fish, a rich source of iodine, throughout the region. The cost of fish rose and supplies declined with the demise of the Soviet fishing fleet. Some progress is being made in reviving iodization programs: Armenia, and Ukraine revived their programs in 1997, Turkmenistan in 1998, and Georgia more recently. Central Europe has fared somewhat better: the Slovak and Czech Republics continued their iodization programs during the transition period; Bulgaria reintroduced its program in 1995 and Poland in 1997.

Source: Galloway, Rokx, and Brown (2000).

---

new cases go undiagnosed. Epidemiological data suggest that TB is disproportionately prevalent among alcohol and drug addicts, the homeless, criminals, and economically marginalized populations. In 1997 a Russian was 7 times more likely to die of tuberculosis than was a European Union (EU) resident and 28 times more likely to die of TB than was an American. Most troublesome is recent analysis showing that the exponential increase in HIV infection could make TB almost uncontrollable in Russia since the two diseases reinforce the negative effects of the other (Vinokur and others 1999).

Of grave concern is the unprecedented increase in HIV/AIDS. The number of persons living with HIV/AIDS increased more than tenfold between 1995 and 1999 in Eastern Europe and Central Asia; indeed, the number of reported cases reached 420,000 in 1999 (UNAIDS 2000). The number of new cases in Russia quadrupled between 1998 and 1999, the steepest one-year increase reported across the world in 1999 (figure 8.2). Ukraine, Belarus, Moldova, Poland, and Russia have the most reported cases. An estimated 1 percent of Ukraine's adult population (those 15 to 49 years of age) is now living with HIV/AIDS (UNAIDS 2000). Prevalence among intravenous drug users in Belarus, Russia, and Ukraine has reached 60 to 70 percent (World Bank 2000c), and the disease is likely to move soon into the mainstream of the population. Efforts to address the problem to date have been limited.

Deteriorating Access to Care for the Poor

Figure 8.2   New Reported HIV Infection Cases in the Russian Federation, 1991–99

Number of cases

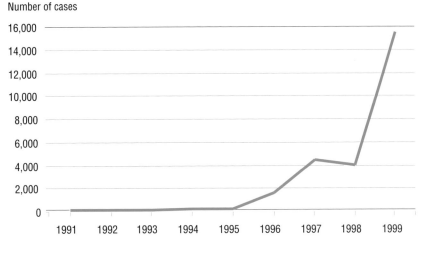

Source: Russian Federal AIDS Center, Moscow, 1999.

The issue of greatest concern to the poor is the deterioration in their access to good-quality and affordable health care. The most significant achievement of the pre-transition period—delivery of comprehensive, free health care services to all—has come under severe strain because of increasingly scarce financial resources. Many ECA countries are finding it harder and harder to fund the vast state machinery of health care production inherited from the socialist period. Unpaid or underpaid public workers frequently tap patients—illegally for the most part—for funding to make up for inadequate public spending on salaries and supplies. The poor have been least able to pay. Moreover, health care workers do not pay taxes on the money they earn under the table—further reducing the public resources available to fund health care.

Out-of-pocket, informal payments for health services, whether as gratuities or as bribes, are becoming increasingly commonplace in many countries of the region. Historically, informal or "envelope" payments were used throughout the region to expedite services, obtain popular providers, or otherwise facilitate better access. This undermined the free service policy of the government, but at least it made providers somewhat accountable to their customers. But the use of informal payments exploded in the 1990s. Figure 8.3 summarizes the frequency with which patients made informal payments in selected ECA countries during the 1990s. In a number of countries more than two-thirds of patients made informal payments. This

Figure 8.3   Share of Patients Who Made Informal Payments in Selected ECA Countries
(percent)

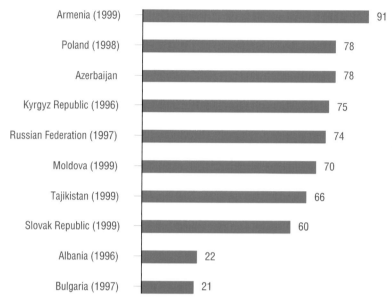

Armenia (1999)	91
Poland (1998)	78
Azerbaijan	78
Kyrgyz Republic (1996)	75
Russian Federation (1997)	74
Moldova (1999)	70
Tajikistan (1999)	66
Slovak Republic (1999)	60
Albania (1996)	22
Bulgaria (1997)	21

Source: Lewis (2000).

reflects a collapsed public system that is now financed on a fee-for-service basis. In addition to making payments to health professionals, patients in parts of the CIS must purchase or furnish their own food, sheets, and medical materials. Public facilities no longer have the means to provide them.

The effect on the poor within countries is noteworthy in two respects. First, for the poor, paying for inpatient care is particularly onerous and often requires families to sell assets to finance health care. In the Kyrgyz Republic almost one-third of all patients seeking inpatient care borrowed money, while in rural areas almost half of such patients sold produce or livestock (Abel-Smith and Falkingham 1996). Similar figures are reported for Georgia, Tajikistan, and Ukraine (World Bank 1999; KIIS 1999; Falkingham forthcoming). Second, the poor are more likely to forgo care because they cannot afford it. In 1997, 41 percent of all Russian patients could not afford to purchase drugs, and 11 percent could not afford any kind of medical treatment (Boikov and Feeley 1999). Similarly, 32 percent of those reporting an illness in Tajikistan in 1999 could not seek professional treatment because it was unaffordable, and 37 percent of pregnant women reported that they did not have prenatal care, with more than half citing inability to pay as the main reason. Thirty-five percent of women in the bottom quintile delivered their last child at home, compared with 20 percent of the women in the top quintile. In contrast, during the Soviet period, 90 percent of all births were delivered in maternity wards. Trend data for informal payments are limited, however; box 8.2 traces the evolution of informal payments for health care in the Kyrgyz Republic.

The equity implications of informal payments are highly problematic. Informal payments introduce perverse incentives into the system that undermine prospects for health reform. Introduction of a series of innovative reforms in Hungary, for example, had little impact on performance, contrary to the experiences of the industrialized countries. Financial incentives proved less attractive than potential earnings from charging patients, regardless of the fact that such charges are illegal. By tolerating informal payments to make up for low or nonexistent wages paid to health care providers, governments can continue to dodge the need for reform while preserving the fiction of universal, free heath care.

In addition to being forced to pay—often illegally—to get care through the public health system—the care the poor receive may not be of high quality. Treatment protocols are not based on up-to-date evidence of what works and what is most cost-effective. Physicians and hospital staff have incentives to continue with treatments that are not necessarily the most appropriate, because hospitalizations increase their opportunities for supplementing their wages through informal payments. As a result, treat-

---

Box 8.2 Out-of-Pocket Payments for Health Care in the Kyrgyz Republic

In the early years of independence, the government of the Kyrgyz Republic suffered a large decline in GDP, and its spending on health declined by more than 60 percent in real terms between 1990 and 1995. At the same time patients' out-of-pocket expenditures (official and informal) increased. Although only 11 percent of those seeking consultations with a physician reported making a payment in 1993, this number rose to 25 percent in 1994 and to 51 percent in 1996. Paying for inpatient care was extremely uncommon in 1993, but by 1996, 74 percent of all patients reported making a payment for an inpatient visit. As expected, the poor have been much more adversely affected than the rich. In 1994, among those who were ill, only 41 percent of the patients of the lowest quintile sought professional care compared with 62 percent in the highest quintile. Among those prescribed medicines, 41 percent of patients in the bottom quintile did not obtain the prescribed medicines compared with 21 percent in the highest quintile.

Source: Abel-Smith and Falkingham (1996) and Dorabawila (2000).

ment protocols are often biased toward hospitalization and long hospital stays, even when they are not medically indicated (box 8.3). Not only are the poor paying to get treatment, they are often paying for treatment that is not the most cost-effective for their condition. In sum, the poor are being increasingly rationed out of access to decent quality, affordable care.

The Way Forward

Most countries in the region are not delivering on their stated goal of providing universal, free health care for all—and especially for the poor, who can least afford private alternatives. Nor are they adequately addressing the public health challenges they face. What can be done?

There are many ways to organize a health system, and no country has found the ideal health system in terms of financing, organization, and

---

Box 8.3 Inappropriate Treatment Protocols

Hospitalization remains common in Europe and Central Asia for conditions (such as minor osteoarthritis, varicose veins, mild hypertension, and mild asthma) that are not criteria for admission in most countries. The over-reliance on injectable (intramuscular) medications is a major reason for hospitalization for conditions that elsewhere would be treated with oral medications (Klugman and Scheiber 1996).

Protocols for diagnosing and treating tuberculosis are also deficient. TB patients are hospitalized for an excessive period of time (9 to 12 months) through most of the region. Furthermore, patients are not treated with the standard regimens recommended by the World Health Organization. Instead, drug combinations tend to be individualized, and this, combined with a serious lack of essential drugs, results in low cure rates and cases of chronic infections, often with drug-resistant strains. Increasing treatment default rates also favor continued production of the bacilli and drug resistance.

Another example of inappropriate medical protocols is treatment for sexually transmitted diseases. Throughout most of the region, all confirmed syphilis cases are hospitalized for a one-month course of injections (given several times a day). This practice is contrary to international evidence and practice with respect to both the type of drug given and the hospitalization. Hospitalization also is encouraged for gonorrhea cases, and the therapies used are not proven in the internationally accepted literature. Although officials have argued that hospitalization is warranted by fears of an epidemic, it does very little to prevent the spread of STDs.

In many countries, and especially in the CIS, abortion is the most commonly used method of fertility control. Because of a lack of alternative forms of contraception, women have relied heavily on abortion to terminate unwanted pregnancy, despite the high incidence of side effects (infection and sterility). Abortions are typically carried out as in-patient procedures in hospitals. In 1996 in Romania and in 1995 in Russia, 63 percent of pregnancies ended in abortion.

delivery of health care. Tradeoffs across objectives are inevitable, and thus policymakers must weigh the tradeoffs according to national preferences. One of the key organizing principles is the nature and extent of government's role in health care. While there is clearly a role for government in the financing, provision, monitoring, and regulation of the health system (box 8.4), that role varies greatly across countries, even within the Organisation for Economic Co-operation and Development (OECD). With regard to the effectiveness of health care delivery, sound arguments can be made for both public provision and private provision. The objectives of the health system in each society should drive the policies on who should pay, who should deliver, and who should regulate.

Whatever role is adopted for government, four things are clear. First, the poor will not be well served by publicly financed health care systems if those systems are not financed on a sustainable basis and if they are poorly managed. OECD countries have found that the key to sustainable financing is to contain the volume of care, with particular focus on (1) preventing open-ended fee-for-service systems where doctors and patients are reimbursed for any and all cared desired, (2) controlling technology acquisitions, and (3) containing the number of doctors.

Second, in virtually all health systems there is a role for the private sector, both in delivering and financing health care. This can take the form

---

Box 8.4   Rationale for Government's Role in Health Care

- Poor health is often a random event. Risk pooling is essential for equity and access since, in any given year, 70 percent of all health expenditures are for only about 10 percent of the population. In the absence of appropriate risk-pooling measures, efficient and effective resource allocation and utilization become skewed and biased toward those who can pay for health care.
- Providers, not consumers, usually decide what care is consumed because patients typically delegate medical decisions to physicians as their "agents." Once demand is not contained by prices, the incentives facing providers drive up health care utilization and therefore cost. How providers are paid and managed then becomes critical to controlling the volume and cost of health care services.
- With third party payment of medical bills under insurance, both the insured and the providers become insensitive to the cost of health care services. This leads to situations of demand-side and supply-side moral hazard: consumers overconsume and providers overproduce because they have no responsibility for the resulting costs.
- Private insurance options require rigorous public regulatory systems if they are to remain financially solvent and protect consumers.
- Public health threats must be addressed by government. The private sector does not have incentives to pay for investments or treatments that benefit the population at large (the free-rider problem).

of services offered by private providers and private financing that supplements, complements, or replaces publicly provided coverage. To replace regressive illegal payments, ECA countries need to develop a more equitable, transparent, and legal basis for charging for health services in the public sector as well as the private sector. Whatever the mix of private and public services, there is an absolutely critical role for the government to play in regulating the sector. Health service quality must be regulated to protect consumers, and financing bodies (for example, insurers) must be regulated to protect the financial market as well as consumers and providers. Both forms of regulation underpin a fair and credible private health sector.

Third, governments have a vital public health role to play in promoting healthier lifestyles and lessening the transmission of communicable diseases. And finally, while a well-functioning health system will address the needs of most of the population, including most of the poor, it will take special efforts on the part of government to address the needs of the most socially marginalized populations. These issues are dealt with in turn.

Spend Better, Not Necessarily More

ECA countries are likely to continue to use public systems to deliver health care to much of the population. The major issue facing the system is not that countries spend too little of the public budget on health care but that the spending is inefficient. By and large, ECA governments are spending a significant share of their gross domestic product on health care (figure 8.4)—even though real expenditures have fallen during the transition along with the collapse in government revenues and real GDP (figure 8.5).

However, a few countries—Georgia, Azerbaijan, and Tajikistan—are spending too little. In 1998 public expenditure on health in Georgia was only 0.6 percent of GDP. The challenge for these countries is to increase and maintain a minimum level of spending while improving the efficiency of that spending. At the other extreme, governments in Croatia, Lithuania, Slovenia, and the Czech Republic are spending a higher percentage of their GDP on health care than some of the richest OECD countries, despite the fact that their GDPs are only a half to a third as much. These countries may need to consider whether at the margin their programs are affordable given competing uses for public spending. In any event, they should ensure that they are getting value for the large sums they spend on health care and that the public financing requirements of their health care systems are fiscally sustainable over time.

Figure 8.4   Public Health Expenditures as a Share of GDP, Selected ECA and OECD Countries

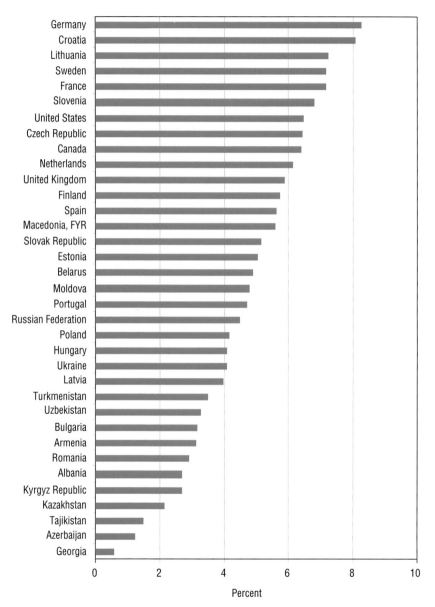

Note: Data are for 1998 or the most recent year available: 1996 for Romania; 1997 for Albania, Azerbaijan, Croatia, France, Moldova, Turkmenistan, United States, and Uzbekistan; and 1999 for Tajikistan.
Source: The World Bank's World Development Indicators database.

Figure 8.5   Average Annual Percentage Change in Real Expenditures on Public Health
and GDP

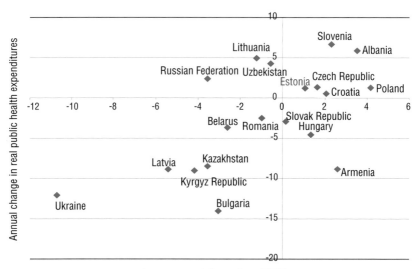

Average annual change in real GDP

Note: Health expenditures are deflated by CPI; GDP is deflated by the GDP deflator. The starting and the ending years for the above countries are as follows: Ukraine (1992/1997); Latvia (1991/1998); Kyrgyz Republic (1992/1998); Russian Federation (1990/1997); Kazakhstan (1993/1998); Bulgaria (1990/1998); Belarus (1990/1998); Lithuania (1992/1998); Romania (1990/1996); Uzbekistan (1990/1997); Slovak Republic (1990/1998); Estonia (1992/1998); Hungary (1992/1998); Czech Republic (1993/1998); Croatia (1990/1997); Slovenia (1991/1998); Armenia (1992/1997); Albania (1990/1998); and Poland (1991/1998).
Source: World Bank World Development Indicators database.

Downsize the Health Sector

There is substantial room in ECA countries for governments to get more value out of the money they spend on health care while at the same time putting health systems on a more sustainable financial basis. The root of the problem is that there are more facilities and more personnel than are needed to deliver quality care. Excess capacity has become a bigger problem during the transition, as real spending on health fell in response to the collapse in GDP. Resources are being spread too thinly, leading among other things to the surge in informal payments particularly detrimental to the poor. Resources wasted on half-empty facilities, poorly insulated buildings, or medical technologies that do not function rob the system of resources that could be put to effective use in the diagnosis and treatment of patients and providing care for the poor. In Moldova 60 percent of the health budget is spent on utilities, often for underutilized or unused health facilities. The health sector must downsize, and this can facilitate the reforms needed to improve the quality and efficiency of care.

ECA countries have more hospital beds and more physicians than do other middle- and high-income countries. Partly as a result of the emphasis on universal access in the pre-transition era, huge networks of medical facilities were set up, staffed generously, and supplied with a large number of hospital beds. Countries in the CIS averaged 10.22 hospital beds per 1,000 population compared with 7.39 beds in Western Europe and 6.9 beds in other middle- and high-income countries like Australia, Canada, Japan, and the United States, where ongoing reforms are continuing to reduce these levels. Moreover, they averaged 3.73 physicians per 1,000 population compared with 2.71 physicians in Western Europe and 1.63 physicians in the other countries just mentioned (World Bank 1998).

Infrastructure. Thus, a key challenge is rationalizing physical infrastructure. Downsizing physical infrastructure will improve efficiency and can provide the resources to maintain and upgrade a core set of services. Optimal downsizing requires sizable up-front investments in smaller, better configured, better equipped facilities. The investment needs far exceed what donors have spent—which points to the need for private financing as well as asset sales and retention of proceeds to finance new investment. Georgia's plan to sell unused buildings establishes the resources to consolidate and improve the rest of its health care delivery system and makes available resources to deal with the energy needs that plague facilities in the northern and mountainous regions (box 8.5).

Personnel. Rationalizing the number of personnel is also crucial. Public sector health employees' wages account for a large share of total health expenditures throughout the region, especially in the Commonwealth of Independent States. In Central and Eastern Europe salaries generally account for a smaller share of expenditures than in OECD countries. In many countries only wages are paid; where finances have dried up, wages are in chronic arrears as well. Indeed, focus groups in Moldova, Armenia, and the Ukraine specifically note the need to compensate physicians because the state fails to pay them (Ruzica and others 1999; Kurkchiyan 1999; KIIS 1999). The issue is not that health sector workers are paid too much, but rather that there are too many workers, especially physicians. Containing the number of physicians trained is an important cost containment mechanism. International evidence shows that the number of physicians correlates with the volume and cost of care.

> **Box 8.5   Georgia's Strategy to Downsize Hospitals**
>
> Between 1991 and 1998 the Georgian government decreased the number of hospital beds by almost 60 percent and physicians by 32 percent. In 1998 there were nearly 11,000 beds in 51 hospitals serving a population of 1.38 million.
>
> The three-phase rationalization program initiated in 1998 will reduce hospital beds in Tbilisi by 6,500. This program has twin objectives: to increase operational efficiency and to improve quality of infrastructure and services.
>
> The plan identified 12 hospitals that were to remain publicly owned and operated. Other facilities were targeted for privatization via direct sale to staff, for private sale as a health facility, or for unrestricted private sale. The total value of the real estate to be vacated was estimated at US$35 million with $11.9 million realizable in phase one. The total proceeds of sale will be retained for utilization by the recently established Hospital Restructuring Fund. Initial proceeds from completed sales are currently being utilized to upgrade two of the major facilities; services from the closed hospitals will be relocated to them.
>
> Seven hospitals are slated for sale, and the government is committed to overall capacity reduction as indicated by the sale of facilities "for closure" rather than for conversion to a private inpatient facility.

Where the state cannot pay public servants, separation with severance for excess personnel offers an important alternative. Assistance in obtaining loans for new businesses, retraining (to address shortages of nurses and therapists), and other interventions may be needed to assist the process. The magnitude of the downsizing needed is considerable, and major political obstacles will arise. But if the problem of excess personnel is not confronted, underpaid workers will continue to augment their salaries with illegal payments from patients.

Controlling Costs and Improving Care: Other Measures

Clinical effectiveness will save resources and improve the quality of care. Evidence-based medicine has replaced tradition as the basis for clinical care in the industrialized countries. It allows the most effective treatments to substitute for those that were less effective or had no clinical impact. Modern specialist care relies on research on the impacts of interventions on patients to guide protocol selection. In many OECD countries, pharmaceuticals are not only screened to ensure their safety and therapeutic effects. They also are reviewed for cost-effectiveness as a basis for determining whether and to what extent the health system should reimburse the costs of each drug. Medical protocols in the region should be tested against evidence of their impact on patients. This will save resource use—because ineffective methods and inputs are removed—and it will improve the effectiveness and quality of care.

Reduce hospitalizations and lengths of stay. Reducing hospitalizations and lengths of stay will have a beneficial effect on efficacy and quality as well. During the past few decades, much hospital care in the industrialized world was moved to outpatient settings, reducing morbidity and mortality in patients and significantly reducing costs per case. Better outcomes occurred, since long hospital stays tend to delay recovery. Lengths of hospital stays have been declining dramatically in acute care hospitals, reaching 5 days in the mid-1990s in Sweden and the United Kingdom. In transition countries, hospitalizations are too frequent and too long compared with OECD averages (figure 8.6). Some progress, however, has been made. For example, Georgia reduced patients' length of hospital stays from 16.2 days in 1993 to 11.7 days in 1998. Estonia reduced the length of stay from 17.4 days in 1990 to 10.3 days in 1998. Clearly, there is scope for further progress.

Figure 8.6   Average Lengths of Stay in Acute Care Hospitals, Selected ECA and OECD Countries, 1996–97

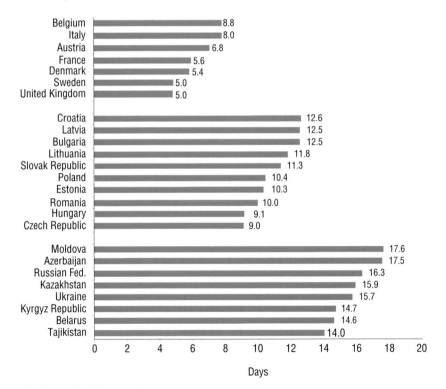

Source: OECD health data; WHO (2000).

A major reason for long hospital stays in many ECA countries is that hospital budgets are based on the number of hospital beds and the length of the stay. Hospital administrators and physicians have little incentive to minimize stays. Altering this system of financing has proved to be very difficult. Indeed, the introduction of certain payment methods for care (for example, the German "points system") in a number of Central and Eastern European countries during the transition has entrenched these patterns. These payment models cover costs based on the number of days spent in the hospital, contrary to the trend in many OECD countries of paying hospitals based on a predetermined number of days for a given condition—a scheme that discourages long hospital stays.

Improve provider incentives to control costs. To produce efficient care of a high quality, policymakers in transition countries must change the way in which health care providers are compensated. In designing an optimum compensation mechanism, policymakers should target multiple objectives: efficient use of resources, better quality of care, greater freedom of choice for patients, and freedom of operation for the provider. The compensation system should clearly specify what procedures and services are covered as well as how patients will be protected from any potential adverse consequences that may result from these arrangements.

In outpatient settings capitation mechanisms encourage physicians to provide only the amount of care needed, since providers are paid on a per patient basis. Capitation payments in Poland—when combined with family physician training—have promoted cost effectiveness and reduced the role of informal payments (box 8.6). But capitation mechanisms can also engender problems. Unless accompanied by additional incentives to see patients, provide a range of services, and achieve targets for improving care (for example, immunization coverage), this payment model can give doctors an incentive to provide minimal services and refer costly complex cases elsewhere.

The shift from specialists to family medicine practitioners in much of the region has also been prompted by a desire to improve contact with patients and lower costs. Family practitioners can be less costly than specialists, and they can more effectively coordinate care for patients. But to make family practice work, governments must provide complementary incentives that encourage treatment at the lowest possible level of care. They also must reward providers for efficiency, compensate for real costs incurred, and target high-risk behaviors and diseases. The overall system should be one that imposes discipline on primary care providers as part of broader reforms. This package of incentives has been lacking in the ECA

Box 8.6   Experimenting with Family Practice in Krakow, Poland

In a significant departure from the traditional model of primary care provision, where health care was provided by salaried physicians trained in internal medicine, pediatrics, and gynecology, the provincial and city governments of Krakow, Poland, introduced a new model of primary health care delivery in 1996 based on the concept of family medicine. The physicians' practice provides a comprehensive set of services—including consultations, diagnostic and laboratory services, and minor surgeries—for all members of the family.

The family physicians are paid out of the state budget but on the basis of a capitation fee per enrollee instead of the traditional salary-based compensation. To maintain patient enrollment, the physicians have an incentive to maintain a high-quality services. At the same time they must keep treatment costs low. These family practices are still small in number (a little over 1.5 percent of all outpatient services in Krakow). Patients' level of satisfaction, however, is significantly than for public ambulatory services. And out-of-pocket patient expenditures, including spending on drugs, is 40 percent less than in public ambulatory services. Most importantly, patients' informal payments (commonly known in Poland as "envelope payments"), reported to be commonplace in the public sector, are conspicuously absent in the practices of family physicians.

Source: Chawla, Berman, and Kawiorska (1998).

---

countries where a shift to family practice has been tried. Therefore, the benefits of reform have not been fully realized.

In addition to initial high investments in strengthening primary care, the Czech Republic has invested in upgrading hospitals. There has been real growth in physicians' salaries and an expansion of private sector alternatives. High-risk populations, such as infants and cardiovascular patients, have been targeted. Together these reforms have led to lower mortality and broad access to subsidized care (World Bank 1999a, 2000b).

Open-ended fee-for-service systems (doctors and patients are reimbursed for any and all care desired) should be avoided. Estonia and the Czech Republic have introduced mixed-remuneration systems incorporating controllable elements of fee-for-service and incentives to control costs, including capitation for outpatient care (SWECO International 2000; World Bank 1999; World Bank 2000b). The results have been encouraging, but a better understanding of the dynamics is needed before firm conclusions can be drawn.

Many ECA countries have set up health insurance funds, often in the form of an independent health insurance agency, to provide a consistent source of financing for the health system and to spur rationalization of the health delivery system. Georgia, Hungary, Kazakhstan, and Romania exemplify this approach, and none has benefited in ways that industrialized countries have experienced. The fundamental problem is that the funds were not a force for containing costs. The system continued to provide "free" care to all through public facilities, and it failed to reduce the number of facilities or medical staffers. Therefore, the conditions that gave rise to informal payments were not remedied. Instead, public insurance systems became alternative means for raising and managing health sector revenues. There were few incentives to push for greater effectiveness and efficiency.

Limit technology, drugs, benefits. Limiting technology, drugs, and benefits is essential to controlling costs. Essentially, the breadth of historical coverage is not affordable, and adding costly new technologies and drugs will make systems even less affordable, even though they have the potential to enhance quality. Limiting the purchase of technology that has high capital and recurrent costs (for example, CAT scans and MRIs) is necessary to keep overall medical expenditures under control. By deciding on what technologies will be available and issuing licenses to determine the number purchased by the public and private sectors, governments can avoid excessive technology acquisitions that often spiral costs through intensive use in an effort to amortize expensive medical equipment. Health insurance systems in Europe and Central Asia frequently promise coverage for services (such as spa treatment, free eye glasses, free dental care) that are not available under many social insurance or public health systems in more affluent countries. Unfortunately, ECA countries do not have the resources to provide extensive health coverage for all.

Make health care providers more accountable. It is a common practice in OECD countries to make health care providers, from physicians to hospitals, account for their outputs and their use of inputs. Providers must report specific achievements (such as number of patients) and indicators of outcomes (such as disease incidence). But health care managers in many ECA countries, particularly in the CIS, are not free to make management decisions or allocate resources. Penalizing poor performance or rewarding good performance is difficult because the rules are vague, and managers do not have the authority to make decisions and answer for them. This lack of accountability is true across the region, although there are notable exceptions within some countries (some hospitals in the Czech Republic, for example).

Increasing autonomy—that is, giving managers full control, or at least greater control, over resources and production—is a means of overcoming the lethargy in decisionmaking in bureaucratic organizations. Autonomy is often accompanied by increasing the scope for raising hospital or clinic revenue and retaining that revenue. More autonomy also may lead to changes in the compensation mechanisms for health providers working in these facilities, which can alter the structure of incentives in the organization. In OECD countries, increasing autonomy, through transferring the responsibility of management and production to the facility-level staff, is usually accompanied by systems that ensure high levels of accountability. Delegation of responsibility without accountability permits unrestrained freedom, which may have undesirable consequences.

Expand Private Sector Financing While Protecting the Access of the Poor

Few governments can afford to deliver comprehensive, free health services to all their citizens, and ECA countries, operating under tight budgetary constraints, are no exception. Although downsizing will free up some resources, comprehensive free coverage will remain unaffordable. Moving to a system in which some individuals finance some of their own health care—in addition to government financing health care—is inevitable. Typically, the establishment and growth of private sector financing takes place on an individual basis or through private insurance schemes.

Most industrialized countries have a private insurance system in which citizens can enroll. In Germany roughly 9 percent of the population has private insurance. In Australia 45 percent has supplementary insurance. Even in the United Kingdom about 10 percent of the population has supplementary health insurance that complements the National Health Service expenditures (Chollet and Lewis 1997). In addition to private insurance schemes, most countries require patients to make some copayment for the publicly financed care they receive. This discourages inappropriate or unnecessary use and contributes to the cost of care. In France patients cover 25 percent of outpatient services, and in Australia patients cover 20 percent of costs. Austria, Finland, and Portugal charge a flat fee for inpatient care (OECD 1994). Publicly provided care may be nominally free in ECA countries, but in practice individuals are paying—and paying a good deal—under the table.

Rationalize informal payments. The problem with the current system of informal payments is that it is not transparent and illegal in most countries. Rationalizing private participation through transparent and legal copayment mechanisms would take advantage of the existing ability and willingness to pay for medical care. Rationalization also could reverse the regressive nature of private contributions. Consumer information and consumer complaint mechanisms are needed as well. They can play an important role in publicizing official payment policies and in providing avenues for redress for illegal demands. But any campaign against informal payments is prone to failure unless accompanied by (1) measures to improve the incomes of health professionals and (2) a national policy that makes it clear that side payments and other "off-budget" exchanges between public employees and citizens are unacceptable. Health sector managers who permit such activities need to be held accountable.

Public systems could move to formal copayments with waivers for the indigent. Because government cannot finance all the services populations want, and users tend to overuse when services are free (the moral hazard problem in health), some form of copayment can contribute toward the cost of care and discourage overuse. Official fees are common in many countries (including Armenia, Georgia, and Russia), but unofficial fees are dramatically higher, indicating a willingness to pay among some segments of the population. Using these paid charges as a starting point, governments could raise copayments for services and offer waivers for those who cannot pay based on income. Such approaches are common in industrialized countries (OECD 1992, 1994) and elsewhere in the developing world (Gertler and Hammer 1997).

The "basic package" approach to rationing, where only a set of high-priority services is financed, could be subsumed within a broader approach of specifying a schedule of available services that have differentiated requirements for copayments. Setting the fees is less problematic than establishing and implementing a fair waiver system. Piggybacking on the social assistance or unemployment systems in ECA countries where the poor are identified may be a cost-effective way to determine patients' income levels.

Rationalize drug financing policy. Pharmaceutical policy is another area where private payments have a role to play in reducing public expenditures. Indeed, many governments in Europe and Central Asia are already charging for drugs. The problem is that budgets have exploded as supply options have expanded. To control drug expenditures, Western European countries have taken a variety of measures: requiring copayments, controlling the range of drugs prescribed, favoring generics, and intervening in the pharmaceutical market (table 8.2). Pharmaceutical policy is one of the most complex areas for intervention, but the current pattern of public expenditures on drugs—in some countries too low, while in others too high—is untenable. Where public expenditures on drugs are low, serious

Table 8.2 Alternative Cost-Containment Strategies in the Pharmaceutical Sector in EU Countries

Strategy	Country experience
Provider incentives	
Fixed budgets for doctors	Fundholding GPs in the United Kingdom
Indicative budgets for doctors	Germany; nonfundholding GPs in the United Kingdom
Fixed budgets for pharmaceutical expenditures	Germany, Italy
Practice guidelines	France
Cost-effectiveness guidelines	United Kingdom
Prescription auditing	Several countries (not in a systematic way, except in the United Kingdom)
Positive and/or negative lists of drugs	All countries
Controlling the number of products	Denmark, Netherlands, Norway
Development of a market for generics	Mainly Denmark; also Germany, Netherlands, United Kingdom
Capitation or salary payment for first-contact doctor	Several countries including Ireland, Italy, Netherlands, Spain, Sweden, United Kingdom
Ceilings on advertising spending	United Kingdom
Flat rate payment to pharmacists on a percentage basis	Netherlands, United Kingdom
Patients' incentives	
Cost sharing	All countries except Netherlands
Health education programs	Netherlands, United Kingdom
Market interventions	
Price controls	All countries except Denmark, Germany, United Kingdom
Profit ceilings	United Kingdom
Reference prices	Denmark, Germany, Netherlands, Sweden
Industry contributions when budgets are exceeded	Germany in 1993, France from 1995
Fixed or revenue budgets for the industry	France, Spain
Taxes on promotional spending	France, Spain, Sweden
Promoting generics	Mainly Denmark; also Germany, Netherlands, United Kingdom

Source: Mossialos, Kanavos, and Abel-Smith (1997).

equity concerns arise. In much of Central Asia, governments are no longer subsidizing drugs for all patients. Where public expenditures on drugs are high (for example, in the Slovak Republic), the pharmaceutical policy is likely to be fiscally unsustainable.

Develop private mechanisms for pooling risk. Alternatives to publicly financed health services should be fostered. This, however, requires a regulatory structure that ensures consumer rights, quality products, and the financial responsibility of insurers. We do not suggest that a private system should replace public health insurance. On the contrary, it should complement or supplement it. Public systems cover the poor, and fully private systems will not, unless financed by or forced to do so by government. This is clearly reflected in the health care systems in the Netherlands, the United Kingdom, Switzerland, and the United States. Private risk management arrangements encompass traditional indemnity insurance, supplementary insurance that can be private or quasi-public, managed care where enrollees pre-pay, and medical savings accounts that are overseen by government but are individuals' savings for health care (Scheiber 1997). In countries where the obstacles to development of private insurance are great (because of weakness in the rule of law or the absence of reputable financial institutions, for example), there may be a place for smaller community-based or provider-based initiatives for pooling and redistributing out-of-pocket payments for some health services.

Government regulation is an absolute necessity regardless of the strategy adopted for increasing private sector participation in financing and delivery. The Czech Republic's failure to regulate the 27 private health insurers early on in its comprehensive health reform led to bankruptcies that shifted debt to the central government and reduced trust in the system. Subsequently, the population manifested an overwhelming preference for enrolling in the government health insurance company instead of private alternatives. The debt overhang remains on the public books, and suppliers have still not been paid (World Bank 1999). Regulation can prevent some of this dislocation and the eroding trust in government that accompanies such failure.

Increase private investment. Capital investments are underfunded, and creative means are required to improve health care quality. In many OECD countries, the private sector is the predominant source of finance for health investments. Private ownership can be an effective, efficient, and consumer-responsive option for health care facilities that are relatively small, non-specialized, and competitive (for example, primary health care, pharmacy, dentistry, diagnostic services, and nursing homes). In the better-performing transition economies, private owners of these services are able to access capital markets to finance investment. In some ECA countries (Bosnia is one example), health care providers are accessing micro-credit. Other countries (such as Romania and Bulgaria) are considering development of special lending schemes for private primary care providers.

Acute hospital care exhibits some natural monopoly characteristics, except in very large metropolitan areas. Hospital services are complex and difficult to contract. However, private financing options for public sector investment in hospitals (such as build-operate-transfer contracts) have been used successfully in some OECD countries (notably the United Kingdom). In ECA countries with a reasonable degree of economic and political stability, they also may be a feasible alternative.

Pay More Attention to Public Health Priorities

Government must be responsible for public health, and certain initiatives deserve priority. The first priority should be micro-nutrient fortification of salt (iodine) and wheat (iron). This is simple and low-cost, and it demonstrates high benefits, especially for the poor.

Second, ECA governments should address communicable disease threats through information (especially for rising and fatal threats such as AIDS), immunization where vaccines exist, diagnosis (TB and AIDS are the most important in this region), and treatment (TB and other diseases that present). Those with mild or negligible symptoms may have limited interest in diagnosis, but the public interest is extensive. Hence, the government needs to intervene.

The types of common screening mechanisms in use are inefficient. Tuberculosis screening in much of the region relies on mass miniature radiography of a large share of the population. This is expensive and inefficient. In parts of the region, employees are screened biannually for STDs and skin infections. This is not cost effective: few cases are detected per thousands screened. In addition to being cost ineffective, such screening raises privacy and ethical considerations.

Third, governments in Europe and Central Asia must establish policies on prevention and disincentives for behaviors that lead to health problems. Information about life styles (smoking and excessive drinking), diet, and sedentary habits is crucial to bringing down high cardiovascular disease and early death. Consumers need to learn about the importance of positive and negative (even dangerous) behaviors that affect both well-being and mortality. Commercial advertising, information brochures in public facilities, broad information campaigns, and outreach to high-risk groups can be effective. "Sin taxes" on tobacco and alcohol have reduced overconsumption of these products in industrialized countries, and they hold promise in the ECA region. Aggressive information campaigns to mitigate the spread of AIDS and TB should be a high priority and could overlap with the other public information campaigns discussed earlier.

Improve the Health of Hard-to-Reach Populations

A well-functioning health care system is the single most important element in reaching the poor with prevention and treatment. The reforms discussed earlier can shape a health system that will better both the population at large and the poor. But additional effort may be required to address the needs of the hard-to-reach poor. Without special efforts, public health systems in ECA countries are not likely to reach these vulnerable groups: internally displaced persons who are victims of regional conflicts, the homeless, the disabled, and substance abusers. In many cases their health problems are different from those of the population at large, and they require special attention.

A particularly thorny issue in Central and South Eastern Europe is the significant and growing population of Roma. They are sicker than the population at large (box 8.7) and have less access to care because of isolation, limited incomes, and discrimination. Experience from Western Europe suggests that programs should be tailored to the Roma because their customs and practices differ from much of the rest of the population. More general initiatives have not fared well (Ringold 2000).

The overall availability of funding for health will influence the effort and resources that can and should be targeted at hard-to-reach groups. Improving the educational opportunities for these groups may have beneficial spillover effects on their health. It may not be feasible for countries that spend relatively little on health care to develop special programs that provide comprehensive care to special groups. However, much of Europe and Central Asia spends a rather large amount of resources on health care. Ensuring that marginalized groups have access to basic health services may be an important part of a wider effort to integrate these groups into society, especially where poor health limits their productivity and well-being.

Conclusion

Policy reforms in the health sector can make an important contribution to promoting economic growth and reducing poverty. The inefficiencies and inequities that have emerged during the transition in the health systems of much of the region are significant. Policymakers face a major challenge in determining how best to raise the quality of health care, improve the allocation of scarce public resources, and meet the needs of the

---

Box 8.7 Health and the Roma Minority

Roma comprise a significant minority population in many of the countries of Central and Eastern Europe and the former Yugoslavia. They represent 6 to 10 percent of the population in Hungary, Romania, Slovakia, the former Yugoslav Republic of Macedonia, and the Czech Republic. Roma have long been a marginalized group in Europe, and they entered the transition period with lower levels of welfare and access to social services, including health care, than non-Roma. However, a growing body of evidence suggests that these gaps have widened during the transition.

Although comprehensive and reliable information on the health status of Roma is lacking, the available evidence suggests that mortality and morbidity are notably higher among Roma than non-Roma communities. A review of studies in Hungary estimated that life expectancy of Roma was 10 to 15 years lower than for the non-Roma population, and infant mortality was significantly higher as well (Puporka and Zadori 1999). A similar gap was identified in the Czech and Slovak Republics, where infant mortality rates were estimated to be double for Roma than non-Roma (ECOHOST 2000). In all three countries, high infant and child mortality has been linked to a significant prevalence of low-birth-weight babies associated with poor nutrition and maternal health.

In addition, health status is severely affected by poor living conditions. Roma housing is frequently overcrowded, and the public services, inadequate. Access to clean water, sanitary facilities, and waste removal is lacking. Low educational levels and lack of awareness about public health issues exacerbate the health problems of the Roma population. Communicable diseases associated with poor living conditions and life styles are prevalent among Roma. Epidemics of tuberculosis, hepatitis, and infectious skin diseases among Roma communities have been frequently reported in the Czech and Slovak Republics and in Hungary. Although little evidence is available, there are early indications that Roma are increasingly at risk of life-style-related diseases including sexually transmitted diseases (including HIV) and drug abuse (ECOHOST 2000).

Source: Ringold (2000).

---

most vulnerable. Without attention to the functioning of the health system and how it is financed, health outcomes will be compromised, and public resources will be wasted. It is the poor who will suffer disproportionately.

Notes

1. DALYs are time-based health outcome measures that adjust for time spent in less-than-perfect health and permit global comparisons of premature mortality (Murray and Lopez 1997).

2. Tobacco accounted for 12.5 percent and alcohol for 8.3 percent of all premature deaths (DALYs) in Europe and Central Asia (Murray and Lopez 1997). These rates of premature deaths from tobacco and alcohol consumption are some of the highest recorded by any region in the world.

References

Abel-Smith, Brian, and Jane Falkingham. 1996. *Financing Health Services in Krygyzstan: The Extent of Private Payments.* Report for the British Government Know How Fund. London: London School of Economics.

Belli, Paolo. 2000. "Reforming Health Systems in ECA: A Review of Experience." World Bank, Human Development Sector Unit, Europe and Central Asia Region. Washington, D.C. Processed.

Boikov, V. E., and F. G. Feeley. 1999. "Russian Household Expenditures on Drugs and Medical Care." Boston: Boston University. Processed.

Chawla, Mukesh, Peter Berman, and Dorota Kawiorska. 1998. "Financing Health Services in Poland: New Evidence on Private Expenditures." *Health Economics*, vol. 7, no. 4, 337–46.

Chollet, Deborah, and Maureen Lewis, 1997. "Private Insurance: Principles and Practice." *Innovations in Health Care Financing: Proceedings of a World Bank Conference, March 10-11, 1997.* World Bank Discussion Paper 365. Washington, D.C.

Dorabawila, Vajeera. 2000. "Health Status and Private Health Expenditures in the Kyrgyz Republic, 1993-97." World Bank, Human Development Sector Unit, Europe and Central Asia Region. Washington, D.C. Processed.

ECHOHOST (European Centre on Health of Societies in Transition). 2000. "Health Needs of the Roma Population in the Czech and the Slovak Republics: Literature Review." Prepared for the World Bank, Human Development Sector Unit, Europe and Central Asia Region. Washington, D.C. Processed.

Falkingham, Jane. 1998-99. "Barriers to Access." *EuroHealth*, vol. 4, no. 6.

———. forthcoming. "Poverty, Out-of-Pocket Payments and Inequality in Access to Health Care: Evidence from Tajikistan." *Social Science and Medicine.*

Galloway, Rae., Claudia Rokx, and Lynn Brown. 2000. "Nutrition Status and Issues in ECA." Washington, D.C. Processed.

Gertler, Paul J., and Jeffrey S. Hammer. 1997. "Strategies for Pricing Publicly Provided Health Services." *Innovations in Health Care Financing: Proceedings of a World Bank Conference, March 10-11, 1997.* World Bank Discussion Paper 365. Washington D.C.

Godinho, Joana. 2000. "Health Promotion in World Bank–Financed Projects in Europe and Central Asia." World Bank, Human Development Sector Unit, Europe and Central Asia Region. Washington, D.C.

KIIS (Kiev International Institute of Sociology). 1999. *Level of Availability and Quality of Medical Care in Ukraine.* Study by KIIS and the World Bank. Kiev, Ukraine. Processed.

Klugman, Jeni, and George Scheiber. 1996. "A Survey of Health Reform in Central Asia." World Bank Technical Paper 344. Washington, D.C.

Kurkchiyan, Marian. 1999. "The Change in the Health Care in Post-Soviet Countries: A Case Study of Armenia." World Bank, Human Development Sector Unit, Europe and Central Asia Region. Washington, D.C. Processed.

Lewis, Maureen. 2000. "Who Is Paying for Health Care in Eastern Europe and Central Asia?" World Bank, Human Development Sector Unit, Europe and Central Asia Region. Washington, D.C.

Mossialos, Elias, Panos Kanavos, and Brian Abel-Smith. 1997. "Will Managed Care Work in Europe?" *PharmacoEconomics* 11 (April): 297-305.

Murray, C. J. L., and A. D. Lopez. 1997. "Global Mortality, Disability, and the Contribution of Risk Factors: Global Burden of Disease Study." *The Lancet*, vol. 359 (May 17).

OECD (Organisation for Economic Co-operation and Development). 1992. "The Reform of Health Care: A Comparative Analysis of Seven OECD Countries." Health Policy Studies No. 2. Paris.

———. 1994. "The Reform of Health Care Systems: A Review of Seventeen OECD Countries." Health Policy Studies No. 5. Paris.

Puporka, Lajos, and Zsolt Zadori. 1999. "The Health Status of Romas in Hungary." Hungary NGO Studies No. 2. Budapest: World Bank Regional Office.

Ringold, Dena. 2000. *Roma and the Transition in Central and Eastern Europe: Trends and Challenges.* World Bank, Human Development Sector Unit, Europe and Central Asia Region. Washington, D.C.

Ruzica, Miroslav. 1999. "Moldova Health Reform: Social and Institutional Analysis." World Bank, Environmentally and Socially Sustainable Development Unit, Europe and Central Asia Region. Washington, D.C. Processed.

Saltman, Richard, and Joseph Figueres. 1997. "European Health Care Reform: Analysis of Current Strategies." Copenhagen: Regional WHO Office for Europe.

Scheiber, George. 1997. "Innovations in Health Care Financing." World Bank Discussion Paper 365. Washington, D.C.

SWECO International. 2000. "Estonia Hospital Master Plan 2015." Scandinavian Care Consultants AB.

UNAIDS. 2000. *Report on the Global HIV/AIDS Epidemic.* Geneva. June.

Vinokur, Anatoly, and others. 1999. "Russia: TB, HIV/AIDS, and STIs: Portrait of a Crisis." World Bank, Human Development Sector Unit, Europe and Central Asia Region. Washington, D.C. Processed.

WHO (World Health Organization). 2000. Regional Office for Europe, Health for All Database.

World Bank. 1999. "Czech Republic: Toward EU Accession." Washington, D.C.

———. 2000a. *Armenia Institutional and Governance Review*. Report 20269. Washington, D.C.: World Bank.

———. 2000b. "Czech Republic Public Expenditure Review: Health." World Bank, Human Development Sector Unit, Europe and Central Asia Region. Washington, D.C. Processed.

———. 2000c. "Info Brief." World Bank, Human Development Sector Unit, Europe and Central Asia Region. Washington, D.C. Processed.

———. 2000d. *Tajikistan Poverty Assessment*. Report 20285-TJ. Washington, D.C. June 29.

CHAPTER 9

Providing Greater Security[1]

E quity and income security were the cornerstones of the socialist system. These objectives were achieved through an equitable wage structure, guaranteed employment, and wide-ranging subsidies on basic consumer goods and enterprise-provided services. Explicit social protection programs were essentially limited to public pension systems that provided generous benefits to the retired and social assistance programs that helped those with special needs, such as the disabled and orphans. Extensive privileges were also available to particular groups as a reward for their contribution to society (for example, veterans and teachers) or because of the hardship or danger imposed by their occupation (for example, miners).

With the transition to market, the guaranteed employment, retirement security, and consumer subsidies promised by the socialist system diminished substantially at the same time that the real incomes of households fell. By and large, Central and Eastern European countries used cash assistance programs to provide income support to the growing number of poor, and they relied on early retirement and unemployment insurance programs to facilitate the layoff of a large number of workers (Garibaldi and Brixiova 1997). In the Commonwealth of Independent States (CIS), however, the state continued to protect employment by not imposing hard budget constraints on enterprises, and it adjusted subsidies for housing and utilities in response to rising prices. Cash assistance programs and unemployment insurance programs have been less important.

Despite expansion, existing social programs have only had varied success in reaching the poor. Central and Eastern European countries have spent a larger share of their gross domestic product on social programs, but many of these programs—with the exception of pensions—have had a limited impact on poverty. In the CIS, and in some countries in Central and South Eastern Europe and the Baltics (CSB), high rates of inflation have eroded the value of benefits provided by most programs, and the few benefits that exist on paper are often provided in arrears or sometimes not at all. Across the region utility and housing subsidies have primarily gone to the nonpoor. They impose a heavy burden on the budget but are politically difficult to remove. In virtually all countries, groups dependent on institutionalized care live in miserable conditions made worse by dwindling levels of public support.

What are the key objectives for social protection programs in the future? Most societies would like to help the most destitute and ensure that children's mental and physical development is not impaired. This ought to be the overriding objective of social protection programs. Indeed, for very poor countries this may be all that they can afford. Substantial reforms of social protection systems will be required to achieve this objective. As the level of income increases, countries may be able to afford to do more. The state can play an important role in insuring individuals against the loss of income from unemployment through unemployment insurance programs and in helping individuals smooth income over the life cycle through pension schemes.

An Overview of the Most Important Social Protection Programs

The main types of cash assistance provided by transition countries are child allowances and (means-tested) social assistance.[2] *Family and child benefits* were the most common form of cash benefits before the transition. As poverty worsened in transition countries, child allowances became a key instrument used by the government to reduce the impoverishment of the population. Some countries (Romania and Estonia) have introduced universal child allowances. Others have targeted previously universal benefits (Poland, Belarus, Russia) or introduced new targeted benefits (Czech Republic, Lithuania). Still others, under fiscal pressure, have sharply reduced real benefits (the former Yugoslav Republic of Macedonia) or eliminated child allowances altogether (Armenia, Georgia). In Romania child benefits are now conditional on participation in school. The design of benefits has varied as well. Often benefits are differentiated according to the number and age of children (Romania), the presence of a single mother, and location.

In the early 1990s many countries began to introduce or broaden *poverty cash benefit programs* to supplement child allowance programs. Poverty cash benefit programs were intended to address the needs of the newly emerging groups of poor who did not qualify for help under the existing pension and child allowance programs or under newly created unemployment insurance programs—namely, the long-term unemployed and those who had exhausted other benefits, the elderly poor with very low pensions or none at all, and families without children. Poland, Hungary, and the Czech and Slovak Republics passed new legislation on social assistance in the early 1990s that built upon existing programs. FYR Macedonia, Estonia, and Latvia introduced new means-tested social assistance programs in the early 1990s, and in 1995 the Kyrgyz Republic was the first country in the former Soviet Union (FSU) to adopt a national poverty benefit.[3] Recently, Armenia and Georgia replaced child allowances with a single cash poverty benefit.

Many countries also introduced a variety of *utility price subsidization mechanisms* to help consumers cope with rising utility prices during the 1990s. Gas, electricity, and heat prices were set particularly low during the socialist era. But by the mid-1990s these low household utility tariffs became unsustainable: the budgets of many countries in Europe and Central Asia lacked the resources to cover the costs of price subsidies, and the utilities found it increasingly difficult to shoulder the losses associated with low residential tariffs. Most countries have adjusted prices slowly, often at the expense of making needed investments in infrastructure to keep the utility services running smoothly and efficiently. To protect the poor, governments used other policies as well. "No disconnection" policies are quite usual in South Eastern Europe and in the former Soviet Union, although they are less common in Central and Eastern European countries. Most countries in Central and Eastern Europe have abandoned across-the-board utility and housing subsidies, but these remain popular in the CIS countries. The CIS countries also retain energy-related subsidies— "privileges"—for particular groups, such as the police, judges, and individuals with birth defects. These privileges have proved difficult to reorient toward the poor (box 9.1).

Spurred on by the ever-increasing number of unemployed and the need to facilitate layoffs and promote restructuring, many countries created *unemployment insurance programs* similar to those in member countries of the Organisation for Economic Co-operation and Development (OECD). Unlike such programs in most OECD countries, these programs did not require individuals to "contribute" for a minimum time in order to qualify for insurance payments. In the first few years of the transition, unemploy-

---

Box 9.1   Rationalizing Privileges in the Kyrgyz Republic and Moldova

Privileges represent special benefits (cash, in-kind payments, and/or price subsidies) for categories of individuals. They are a mix between entitlements for status (for example, for World War II participants), remuneration for public sector employment (for example, police, judges), and category-based targeting of social assistance (for example, fourth children). Some privileges exist only on paper, since they have never been financed by government budgets. Some are funded by utility and service providers that are obliged to provide free or reduced-price services to privileged individuals. In many cases these service providers receive indirect subsidies or support from the state (for example, assumption by the state of energy arrears of utilities to foreign suppliers). Other privileges are funded (at least partially) through government budgets.

Many privileges were introduced in the Soviet era. They were aimed at providing benefits to those deserving special merit because of their service to the state. Since then various new privileges have been introduced. These tend to be more category-based assistance. Privileges range from discounts on utility prices (energy, telephone, water, sewage), public transportation, housing rental, and medicine to free cars and sanatorium treatments to actual cash grants.

In the Kyrgyz Republic privileges are granted to about 10 percent of the population and are targeted to 26 categories of people. In 2000 the total cost of the privileges that were functioning is estimated at 452 million som (US$9.5 million) or less than 1 percent of GDP, of which 340 million som (US$7 million) were actually budgeted and the remainder were "implicit." About half the total cost of privileges is on energy tariff discounts. The government has gradually been extending privileges—mainly for energy tariff discounts—as a form of social protection. In 1998–99 energy privileges were extended to some categories of poor families: single nonworking pensioners with pensions under 400 soms, families receiving pensions because of the loss of the income-earning head of the household, Unified Monthly Benefit recipients, and families with invalid children. In 2000 a new income-tested category—families with a per capita monthly cash income of 200 soms ($4.20) or less—was added.

---

ment insurance programs were quite generous; privileges were equivalent to OECD norms—especially in CSB countries.[4] For example, new entrants to the labor force were eligible for benefits (Romania); duration of benefits was long (24 months in FYR Macedonia), or it was open ended (Poland). But as growth in unemployment and layoffs reduced the ratio of contributors to beneficiaries, the financial costs of financing generous schemes rose sharply and countries reduced benefits.

During the socialist period, countries developed comprehensive defined-benefit PAYG (pay-as-you-go) schemes providing *old-age, disability, and survivor pensions*, as well as other insurance-based benefits and short-term benefits for sickness and maternity leave. As in Western countries, pension systems in Eastern Europe evolved out of growing concerns about old-age poverty in the wake of industrialization, and later they were used to help the prewar generation share in the fruits of the postwar economic boom.[5] The pension systems covered a large share of the labor force because of the formalized nature of employment under the socialist system.

Box 9.1 *(continued)*

Using categorical and income-testing approaches, the government of the Kyrgyz Republic is taking steps to reduce the overall budgetary cost of privileges and to reorient social protection benefits toward those families in greatest need. In 2000 it submitted a draft law to Parliament that would reduce the number of broad categories from eleven to seven categories better targeted to needy sectors of the population. The proposed legislation also would reduce benefit levels significantly in many of the remaining categories. If enacted, the changes would reduce the total cost of the functioning entitlements by 40 percent, to 276 million som (US$5.8 million or 0.5 percent of GDP), and reorient the privileges to the neediest, increasing their share from less than 40 percent to 70 percent of the total cost.

In Moldova privileges were granted to 447,540 recipients (or about 12 percent of the population) in 37 categories, as of January 2000. The total cost of privileges functioning in 2000 is estimated at 367.5 million lei (US$30 million or about 3 percent of GDP), of which only 207 million lei (US$17 million) are budgeted. Recognizing that the system was unsustainable, the government and Parliament attempted to rationalize it. After several failed efforts, the Parliament in April 2000 approved a targeted compensation scheme that abolishes energy-related privileges issued in the past by law or government decree. In its place is a category-based energy subsidy scheme intended to cover poor and vulnerable sectors of the population via direct payments to consumers for partial energy discounts. Because of difficulties in applying means-testing, the new program covers nine categories of the population that are presumed to be the poorest and most vulnerable segment of the population. The new program became effective on June 22, 2000. The total cost of privileges is estimated to fall from $30 million to $25.5 million in 2000. Although the cost savings are not large, the new system is much better targeted to the poor than the old one was. In addition, significant savings have been achieved by completely eliminating energy compensations. Almost 1 million Moldovans were entitled to these subsidies, and the cost of the system was estimated at 270 million lei (or US$21 million) in 1999.

Eligibility criteria for old-age, disability (box 9.2 on Poland), and survivor pensions were generous. High dependency ratios—the ratio of workers to pensioners—in the region, like in Western Europe, led to a demographic profile in the postwar era that supported low retirement ages, commonly 60 for men and 55 for women.[6] In addition, various occupational groups, such as miners and teachers, were eligible to retire even earlier. Benefit levels were quite generous, with system replacement rates as high as 80 percent in Poland, Yugoslavia, and for some groups of pensioners in Russia. The weak link between contributions and benefits led to considerable internal redistribution between classes of workers.

Growing unemployment, layoffs, poor tax compliance from the informal economy, and early retirement policies increased the ratio of pensioners to contributors and created financial problems for most pension systems in transition economies (figure 9.1). Although many systems began the transition with three contributors financing each pensioner, now there are fewer than two contributors for each pensioner. The inherited gener-

Figure 9.1 The Dependency Ratio of Pension Systems in Selected Countries in Europe and Central Asia, Various Years

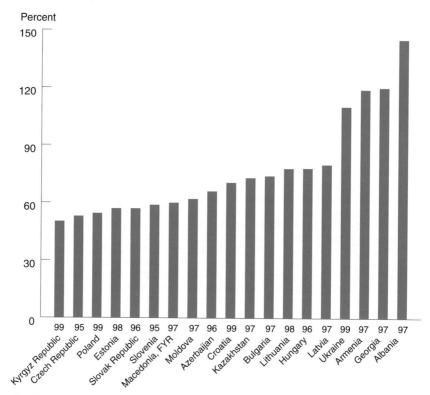

Note: The dependency ratio is the number of pensioners to the number of contributors to the pension system.
Source: World Bank (2000b).

osity of public pension systems further reduced the fiscal viability of pension systems. As a result, some pension systems—particularly those in the CIS—found it increasingly difficult to pay beneficiaries.

The tendency of transition countries to spend most of their social protection budget on pension programs reflects their historical legacy of well-developed pension schemes. Spending on social insurance programs averages more than 10 percent of GDP in CSB countries compared with about half that in CIS countries. Budgets for cash social assistance and child allowance programs typically range between 0.5 and 2 percent of GDP across the region, with CSB countries spending more than CIS countries. A few countries spend 13 percent or more of GDP on pensions—notably Croatia, Poland, Slovenia, and Slovakia. CIS countries in the

Caucasus and in Tajikistan spend less than 4 percent of GDP on pensions and very little on social assistance, with the exception of Armenia, which spent more than 2 percent of GDP on its targeted means-tested poverty benefit in 1999. In 1998 Georgia spent less than 3 percent of GDP on pensions—and less than 0.1 percent of GDP on family benefits. In 1999 Tajikistan—the poorest country in the region—spent 1.8 percent of GDP

Box 9.2   Poland's Disability Pension System

Disability is a costly problem in Poland. Disability pensions total more than 3.3 percent of GDP, and they require a payroll tax of more than 7 percent of the wage bill.

The high cost of Poland's disability pension system can be attributed to its large number of beneficiaries relative to other ECA countries and to its relatively generous benefits. More than 15 percent of the working-age population in Poland is disabled, compared with 10 percent in Hungary and Latvia (countries with disability systems similar to Poland's prior to the transition), less than 7 percent in Germany, and only 4 percent in Switzerland. Health problems and injuries do not account for Poland's high share of disabled. Program design and implementation seem to have encouraged an extraordinary number of people to apply for, and qualify for, disability pensions. In a household survey conducted in 1996, one-third of the people who said that they had qualified for benefits answered questions about their well-being in a way that revealed that they did not meet International Classification of Impairments, Disabilities and Handicaps (ICIDH) criteria for disability. They were legally but not physiologically disabled.

Persons with the least serious kinds of disabilities have been generously treated. Until 1997 individuals suffering from a long-term medical problem could qualify for the weakest category even if work capacity was unimpaired. In 1997 a law mapped the old three categories into three new degrees of disability, and the critical element became loss of work capacity rather than just health problems. Even so, people with a "slight" degree of disability remain eligible for disability insurance benefits, and they continue to count in the quota and Sheltered Work Establishment systems (see box 10.2 in chapter 10).

Eligibility criteria have not been strictly enforced. This was especially true in the early 1990s when applications for certificates of disability jumped. It appears that people substitute disability benefits for unemployment benefits because they are easier to qualify for and they do not expire automatically. This helps to explain why the number of beneficiaries grew so rapidly in the early 1990s. There is even evidence that moral hazard has led to corruption involving workers, certifying physicians, and sometimes employers. A qualitative study on informal payments in the health sector found that some people reported "purchasing" sick leave, a disability certificate, or exemption from military service (Shahriari, Belli, and Lewis 2000). People reported that a disability certificate could cost as much as 3000 zlotys (about US$750).

In response to the rapid growth of disability beneficiaries and the high cost of benefits, the government modified Poland's disability pension system significantly in terms of administrative procedures and eligibility criteria. In 1998 the number of new disability beneficiaries declined by 10 percent compared with the number of new disability beneficiaries in 1997, the first decline ever. Unfortunately, the numbers are likely to resume growing because of continued economic restructuring and the aging of the population.

Source: Andrews and Hoopengardner (1999).

on pensions and only 0.2 percent on poverty benefits; the monthly poverty benefit was sufficient to cover only the cost of two loaves of bread (World Bank 2000f).

Sizable amounts, especially in CIS countries, are spent subsidizing the consumption of utilities. In many cases the subsidy is borne by the utility, rather than the budget, so the amount is difficult to ascertain. The spending gap between CIS countries and CSB countries would narrow if compensation for utility prices were factored in. CIS countries have been much slower than CSB countries to price energy and other utilities at world prices.

Thus, the challenge facing transition countries is not so much to increase the overall envelope allocated to social protection as it is to ensure that the money is used effectively to address the most acute manifestations of poverty. In what follows, we look at the impact of social protection programs on poverty and explore how they might be reformed to be more effective.

Social Assistance Programs and the Poor

The poverty impact of social assistance programs is often evaluated using three common measures—coverage, targeting, and effectiveness. *Coverage* is the share of the poor who receive the benefit; *targeting* is the share of expenditures from the benefit that is received by the poor; and *effectiveness* is the share of the benefit relative to average household expenditure. There are tradeoffs between these various objectives. To include as many poor households as possible, policymakers may make the eligibility criteria very broad. In such circumstances, targeting efficiency is likely to be low since some of the benefits will go to nonpoor households. Tradeoffs also are made between coverage and effectiveness: the more broadly social assistance expenditures are distributed across households, the smaller the amount going to any one household is likely to be. In a world of imperfect information, limited funds, and electoral demands, policymakers face difficult choices in trying to reach as many poor households as possible with a meaningful level of assistance. The evidence discussed below suggests that the coverage of the poor provided by social assistance programs is quite low. Child allowances are somewhat better targeted than means-tested cash benefits, but both programs end up benefiting many nonpoor. Program effectiveness is generally not very high.

The Performace of Cash Benefit Schemes

Despite growing poverty in Europe and Central Asia, cash benefit schemes in the first half of the 1990s performed poorly. In some countries the coverage of the population measured as the proportion of all households receiving the poverty benefit was quite low, to the point many schemes were termed "irrelevant" (Milanovic 1998). More than 20 percent of households in Hungary received social assistance, but the receipt rate was only 13 percent for Russia, and a negligible 4 percent for Bulgaria, Estonia, and Poland. The coverage of poor households receiving social assistance also was low across the region; only Hungary reported high coverage of the poorest households (table 9.1).

Evaluations of the performance of programs in the second half of the decade show that many programs continue to have limited coverage of the poor (tables 9.2 and 9.3). In Romania and Latvia, coverage is particularly low. Croatia is an exception: half of the poor are covered by the social assistance program. The poverty line in Croatia, however, is very low, so that only 2 percent of households fall below it.

Why do social assistance programs do an inadequate job of reaching the poor? There are many reasons. Poor people often lack information regarding poverty programs. Even those who are eligible for benefits may not apply for the programs because they have difficulty obtaining and understanding the numerous documents required. Some may feel there is a stigma attached to claiming resources. For pregnant women and women with small children, and for others, the long wait in line to receive benefits can be discouraging. Some poor people cannot afford transport fees or under-the-counter fees to obtain documents. In addition, the means-testing formulas applied in many programs may inaccurately assess the household's income status.

The *targeting efficiency* of social assistance to the poor varies considerably. For programs evaluated in the first half of the 1990s, poverty benefits are not particularly well targeted. In every country except Russia, the bottom decile received some 20 to 35 percent of total expenditure on the benefit. In Russia the bottom decile received less than its share in the total population (table 9.1). A number of programs also performed poorly in the second half of the decade. In Kazakhstan, as in Russia, where the payment of social assistance out of block grants is left to the discretion of regional authorities, social assistance programs fared particularly poorly. But there are some good examples of targeting, such as Romania and to a lesser extent Hungary. Interestingly, some of the lower income countries—

Table 9.1   Coverage, Targeting Efficiency, and Effectiveness of Benefits in Selected ECA
Countries, 1993–95

Indicator	Poland	Hungary	Bulgaria	Russian Federation	Estonia
Percentage of households below national poverty line	38	8	2	36	3
Coverage					
Percentage of households	4	24	3	13	3
Percentage of poor	6	43	10	13	10
Inclusion errors[a]	36	86	92	84	65
Exclusion errors[b]	94	57	90	87	90
Targeting efficiency[c]	21	27	22	8	35
Effectiveness[d]	22	5	4	4	15
Type of benefit	MT	NMT	NMT	NMT	MT

MT = means tested; NMT = not means tested.
Note: Poverty line is the national poverty line for each country.
a. Share of the nonpoor who receive social assistance.
b. Share of the poor who do not receive social assistance.
c. Share of total transfer expenditures to bottom decile.
d. Social assistance as a share of expenditures of recipients.
Source: Braithwaite, Grootaert, and Milanovic (1998).

Table 9.2   Coverage, Targeting Efficiency, and Effectiveness of Benefits in Croatia
and Latvia, Various Years

Indicator	Croatia, 1998	Latvia, 1997–98
Percentage of households below national poverty line	2	15
Coverage		
Percentage of poor	50	2
Inclusion errors[a]	77	77
Exclusion errors[b]	50	98
Targeting efficiency[c]	30	15
Effectiveness[d]	12	20

Note: Poverty line is the national poverty line for each country.
a. Share of the nonpoor who receive social assistance.
b. Share of the poor who do not receive social assistance.
c. Share of total transfer expenditures to bottom decile.
d. Social assistance as a share of expenditures of recipients.
Source: World Bank (2000a, 2000e).

Table 9.3 Share of Poor Households Receiving Transfers in Bulgaria, Romania,
and Kazakhstan, Various Years
(percent)

Cash benefit	Bulgaria (1997)`	Romania (1997)	Kazakhstan (1996)
Social assistance	17	8	—
Child allowances	30 and above	60 and above	6

— Not available.
Note: The poor are defined as follows: Bulgaria, 36 percent; 31 percent; Romania, 31 percent; and
Kazakhstan, 35 percent. Bulgaria has diverse programs of social assistance with no means test.
The child allowances in Bulgaria and Romania are universal; in Kazakhstan they are means tested.
Source: World Bank (1998, 1999a); Tesliuc and Pop (2000).

FYR Macedonia and Albania, for example—do as well or better than
higher income countries in targeting their social assistance (table 9.4).

Targeting can be assessed by an evaluation of inclusion and exclusion
errors in the social assistance system. *Exclusion errors*—the share of poor
households excluded from assistance—are very high in the region. Evidence from the first half of the 1990s (table 9.1) showed that (with the
exception of Hungary) close to 90 percent of the eligible poor were excluded from receiving benefits in most countries! Inclusion errors, or the
share of nonpoor receiving assistance, were also quite high, with the exception of Poland. In more recent years comparable evidence from Latvia
and Croatia shows that exclusion and inclusion errors remained high: inclusion errors were 77 percent in both countries, while exclusion errors
were 50 percent in Croatia and an astonishing 98 percent in Latvia (based
on national poverty lines). Programs need not have both high inclusion
and high exclusion errors. In the FYR Macedonia, for example, exclusion
errors were low, but there was considerable leakage of social assistance
benefits to the nonpoor.

How *effective* are cash transfers in alleviating poverty? Programs evaluated in the first half of the 1990s show that social assistance represented a
relatively small share of recipients' household expenditures, although in
Poland they amounted to 22 percent. Latvia performed almost as well as
Poland in the second half of the decade. Additional evidence is available
from recent poverty assessments on transfer effectiveness for the bottom
quintile or, in the case of Bulgaria, of the poor as defined by the country-
specific poverty line (table 9.5). Social assistance comprises about 10 to
20 percent of household expenditures of poor households in Bulgaria,
Romania, and FYR Macedonia, but it covers only 1 percent of total expenditures of the poor in Kazakhstan. Are programs adequate in alleviat-

Table 9.4 The Share of Total Cash Transfer Expenditures Received by the
Bottom Quintile in Selected ECA Countries, Various Years

| Country and year | Cash benefit | |
	Social assistance	Child/family allowances
Latvia 1998	20	29
Croatia 1998	25	28
Romania 1997	79	51
Macedonia, FYR 1997	47	5
Albania 1996	47	—
Kazakhstan 1996	6	24
Uzbekistan 1999	23	—
Hungary 1997	46	20
Estonia 1995	44	40
Armenia 1996	—	25

— Not available.
Note: For all countries the "poor" are defined as the bottom quintile except Romania (bottom 31 percent) and Estonia (bottom 30 percent). The type of poverty cash benefit for Croatia, Romania, FYR Macedonia, Uzbekistan, Albania, Hungary, and Estonia is means-tested social assistance. Bulgaria and Kazakhstan have diverse social assistance programs; no means test. Latvia has a poverty benefit based on minimum subsistence. Child allowances in Armenia, Bulgaria, Romania, and Estonia are universal but targeted by age; in Kazakhstan, FYR Macedonia, Uzbekistan, and Croatia, they are means tested. Latvia has diverse family-benefit programs.
Source: World Bank (1998, 1999b, 1999d, 2000a, 2000c, 2000e); Tesliuc and Pop (2000); Rashid, Dorabawila, and Adams (1999); Coudouel and Marnie (1999).

ing poverty? Evidence from FYR Macedonia and Bulgaria indicates that social assistance and child allowance programs do have some impact on poverty reduction, but the impact is very small (in relation to pensions, for example) and not sufficient to move most households out of poverty.

Table 9.5 Cash Transfers as a Percentage of Household Expenditures of Poor
in Selected ECA Countries, Various Years

| Country and year | Cash benefit | |
	Social assistance	Child/family allowances
Bulgaria 1997	15	5
Romania 1997	22	11
Macedonia, FYR 1997	12	0.3
Kazakhstan 1996	2.3	2.2

Note: The "poor" are defined as follows: Macedonia and Kazakhstan, bottom 20 percent; Romania, bottom 31 percent; Bulgaria, bottom 36 percent. The type of poverty cash benefit is as follows: Croatia, Romania, and FYR Macedonia, means-tested social assistance; Bulgaria and Kazakhstan, diverse social assistance programs with no means test. Child allowances: Bulgaria, Romania (universal); Kazakhstan, FYR Macedonia (means tested).
Source: World Bank (1998, 1999a, 1999b); Tesliuc and Pop (2000).

The evidence presented above highlights the tension between coverage, targeting, and adequacy. For example, in Romania the social assistance system is better targeted and more adequate than in Croatia, but limited resources mean that the coverage is lower. Coverage is also very low in Latvia, but the benefit adequacy is better. In contrast, in Croatia the coverage is relatively much higher (for a much more restricted number of poor). In most countries, social assistance programs do not do a particularly good job of reaching the poor, concentrating their expenditures on the poor, and lifting the poor out of poverty.

The Performance of Child Allowance Programs

Evidence on the *coverage* of child allowance programs is more limited than on the coverage of cash benefit programs, but it appears to vary considerably as well. In the few countries where data on both types of coverage are available, the coverage of child allowances is much higher than for social assistance. This may be because child allowances, by targeting children rather than income or other characteristics, reach a large share of the poor.

There is considerable variation in the *targeting efficiency* of child allowances. The efficiency of targeting does not appear to be related to the nature of the benefit—means tested or universal. In Croatia means-tested child allowances are relatively well targeted, but means-tested child allowances perform much worse in FYR Macedonia. Universal child allowances are reasonably well targeted to the poor in Romania, reflecting the strong correlation between family size and poverty status.

Therefore, using child allowance programs to target the poor, at least from this sample, does not appear to be superior to using social assistance. In Croatia and Kazakhstan means-tested child allowances are relatively better targeted than means-tested social assistance. However, the opposite is true in FYR Macedonia. In Estonia universal child allowances do no better than means-tested social assistance, while in Romania they do much worse than means-tested social assistance programs. In other cases, despite disparate methods of targeting (Estonia, Croatia), both programs do about the same.

The *effectiveness* of child allowances is minimal, and (except for Romania) these allowances cover less than 5 percent of household expenditures for the poor. This is largely because these programs receive a minimal amount of funding. Although the coverage of child allowance programs is better than social assistance coverage, even where child allowance programs are well targeted, limited funding makes them a very weak tool for poverty alleviation.

Options for Reform

Social assistance and child allowance schemes are reaching the poor with limited success, although some do better than others. The key reason for social assistance reform in most countries is the need to channel scarce resources in the most efficient way to provide basic needs—food, shelter, clothing—for the most destitute, while avoiding the creation of "poverty traps" or a culture of benefit dependency.

To achieve this objective, transition countries must address these fundamental questions: What type of protection (cash or in kind, broad-based or categorical) will be provided? Is there a need for a variety of programs to cater to different groups of poor? How can programs be administered effectively? Who will finance and deliver the social assistance? A country's income level often influences program design.

High-income and upper-middle-income transition countries. These countries have lower absolute poverty rates, more fiscal resources, and in general greater administrative capacity than lower-middle- and low-income countries have. As a result, they should be able to help not only the truly destitute but also a broader group of poor. The high-income and upper-middle-income countries—especially in Central Europe—tend to have a high concentration of child poverty as well as rural poverty; long-term unemployment also is a problem. Meeting the needs of these disparate groups of poor is not easy.

In principle, a broad poverty benefit based on means and asset testing would be the choice social assistance mechanism. This would ensure that "holes" in targeting that are prevalent in category-based benefits can be plugged. In higher income countries where the informal economy is limited, and where administrative capacity and record keeping and registration of assets are fairly advanced, means testing of income and assets to target the cash benefit to the poor is more feasible. While means testing does not always work, some means-tested systems do perform well (box 9.3). Further analysis is needed to identify which, if any, aspects of the means-testing criteria leads to better targeting efficiency.

Given that means testing is never perfect, child allowances may ensure that families with children, who appear to have the highest risk of poverty in many transition countries, obtain some cash assistance if means tests fail. In countries where child poverty is a particular concern and means-

---

Box 9.3   The Social Assistance Program in the Former Yugoslav Republic of Macedonia

The social assistance program in FYR Macedonia guarantees households a certain minimum income level that varies by household size. Households claiming the benefit are subject to a combined income and asset test, implemented and monitored by the local welfare offices. The social assistance program provides a cash transfer if the household income falls below the minimum.

Social assistance benefits appear to be relatively well targeted from several perspectives. Data from 1997 show that the bottom two deciles receive almost half of all public spending on social assistance. Without this income support, the severity of poverty would double in rural areas (World Bank 1999b). Social assistance benefits are largely received by the unemployed and by households headed by uneducated or less educated individuals. According to the review of the government in 1999, benefits also reached certain ethnic groups where poverty incidence is high (the Albanian population and Roma). For example, 12.7 percent of the social assistance beneficiaries were Roma, although, as an ethnic group, Roma account for only about 2.2 percent of the total population.

Whether social assistance programs can reach and provide effective assistance to the needy depends on the policy and institutional capacity. In terms of policy, the Macedonian government has been able to define income- and asset-testing criteria that allow the system to capture the most vulnerable groups. In terms of administration of the program, Macedonia has inherited from the former Yugoslav system a relatively developed local-welfare-office structure that collects a significant amount of information on households. A set of stringent reporting and screening requirements is enforced. Macedonia's relatively strong legal infrastructure has largely held the administration accountable for program delivery. A grievance mechanism is used by households that do not agree with the judgment of the social assistance office.

The number of beneficiaries and nominal expenditure on social assistance increased steadily in recent years, and the average benefit duration is long. This is partly attributable to continuing difficulty in monitoring and verifying claims. There is significant inclusion error, and the welfare offices are short of staff to adequately monitor the change-of-asset status of households. Coordination with other social programs and government agencies has not been very efficient in terms of information access and benefit payment. The government is committed to improving program efficiency by developing tighter eligibility criteria and improving the quality of service.

---

tested poverty benefits cover a limited number of the poor, the benefits could be supplemented (or replaced if they were performing particularly poorly) by universal or indictor-targeted child allowances. In cases where countries provide both cash assistance and child allowances, child allowances (universal or categorically targeted), should be added to the income of recipient households to avoid double counting. Another vulnerable group, elderly nonpensioners, might also be targeted in this way. Where the social assistance system is performing well in reaching the poor, including those with children, child allowances could be merged with the social assistance system. In such cases, the social assistance benefit scale is set so as to increase the threshold level of benefit per child.[7]

Work incentives will be an important issue if cash benefit programs provide a reasonable level of benefit, and income thresholds (means tests) are used for determining program eligibility. Keeping the level of benefit low (relative to the average or minimum wage) will create fewer work disincentives, but will be less effective in pushing households out of poverty. Incorporating work incentives into cash benefit programs entails fiscal and administrative costs that must be carefully considered. More sophisticated incentives should be developed if there are large stagnant pools of beneficiaries in the system—probably the case of the long-term unemployed in many CSB countries. A key question is whether benefits should be of unlimited duration, particularly for working-age adults.

To address this problem, social assistance programs in transition countries have incorporated labor market incentives in different ways. In Bulgaria 30 percent of wage income is disregarded in the calculation of eligibility for benefits. Some countries require beneficiaries to be registered with labor offices, limit the duration of social assistance benefits, or keep benefit levels low. In Estonia nonworking household members of working age are not included in benefit calculations. In FYR Macedonia income thresholds were reduced, and benefit duration was limited to reduce the adverse effects of incentives. Before this reform, the maximum benefit for a four-member family was equivalent to the average wage. (The average wage for unskilled labor in the country was about 30 percent of the average wage.) Now the maximum threshold for a similar family is 40 percent of the average wage.

In many other Central and Eastern European countries, work incentives are weak or nonexistent. Where benefit levels are high and close to the reservation wage, there are no incentives for individuals to seek work or report their true unemployment status instead of claiming benefits. There has been little systematic evaluation of the experience on implementation, efficiency, and effectiveness of work incentives in transition countries. This information would be useful in ascertaining which incentive effects are best at reducing welfare dependency.

Lower-middle-income countries. In lower-middle-income countries a meaningful level of means-tested poverty benefit for all poor may not be possible to finance or administer. Social assistance may be able to protect only some groups of poor. This is an extremely difficult choice for policymakers. The poverty profiles may provide useful guidance in such cases. For example, groups in deepest poverty or those that cannot work might be targeted. If resources are severely limited, children may be targeted in preference to the elderly to avoid irreversible impacts on the human capital development of children.

If it is difficult to verify incomes—the case when there is a high degree of informality in the economy, means testing will probably not work very well. Under such circumstances it is usually preferable to have categorically targeted benefits. Child allowances or demogrants (cash transfers based on age) for nonpensioned elderly might be easily targeted benefits to alleviate poverty. Child allowances would protect the most vulnerable households with unemployed members, but they would do little to protect young unemployed workers without families. Where budget constraints are particularly severe, child allowances may do the best job of protecting those at greatest risk.

Targeting of categorical or in-kind benefits can be universal or based on indicators that are correlated with the characteristics of the poor. *Universal targeting* has greater acceptability and political appeal.[8] But it runs the risk of transferring small amounts of benefit to many recipients, doing little to help the truly destitute. In lieu of universal targeting, countries can deliver child allowances by *indicator targeting*. For example, child allowances can be targeted to families with two or more children and limited by age of child. In countries where the poor with many children are an ethnic minority, indicator targeting may not be politically acceptable. If the nominal value of child allowances is capped, economic growth will reduce the percentage of families receiving allowances automatically in the future, even if initially the allowances were received by the majority of the population. In that way the allocation of social assistance expenditures can gradually be targeted to the residual poverty population once economic growth resumes.

Where categorical targeting is too expensive or has high errors of inclusion or exclusion, governments may want to use a *proxy means test* to target the poor. This type of means test uses several indicators (with appropriate weights) rather than simply income to target the poor. Armenia and Russia are experimenting with these mechanisms for targeting a broad-based poverty benefit. It is not yet clear, however, that this mechanism performs better than indicator targeting or a means test.

Low-income countries. Countries (mainly in the former Soviet Union) with very low incomes have few resources for social assistance benefits and limited administrative capacity. Their key challenge is to identify a few cash and in-kind benefits or services that are administratively easy to target and deliver to the very poorest groups or regions in the country. Social assistance might be limited to addressing the most serious manifestations of malnutrition or hunger, or lack of school attendance linked to poverty among particular population groups. Where possible, benefits or services might be designed to serve two purposes. In addition to alleviating household cash constraints, they might keep children in school or reduce malnutrition.

Several targeting mechanisms may be particularly appropriate for very poor countries. For example, poor countries may want to use *geographical targeting*, especially if resources are limited, and the poor are concentrated in certain areas of the country. In many countries there are pockets with extremely high poverty rates (chapter 2). Like categorical targeting, geographic targeting is, by definition, inequitable, since there may be pockets of poor in nontargeted regions. But if there are identifiable pockets of severe poverty, geographical targeting may be a reasonably efficient way of addressing problems of acute malnutrition or low school attendance.

Self-targeting is perhaps the most simple way of targeting the poor in low-income countries. It means that a subsidized good or service is available to all, but designed in such a way that only the poor will choose to use it. Work fare programs, where the wage is set very low, are self-targeting.[9] Two successful workfare programs are the Maharashtra Employment Guarantee Scheme in India and the Trabajar program in Argentina. Both concentrate on infrastructure projects that are labor intensive, benefit the local community, and target poor areas. The Trabajar program was expanded in the mid-1990s to cope with rising unemployment, which reached 18 percent in 1996–97 and was concentrated among the poor (World Bank 2000g). Public works programs are best viewed as a means of targeting income support to the poor rather than as a way of getting the unemployed back into the labor market (World Bank 2000b).

Self-targeting provides a gradual exit criteria: once individuals or families are back on their feet after a crisis, they will opt out of self-targeted programs. However, program design is key. In Albania and FYR Macedonia, where workfare programs were used, wages were not set low enough to attract only the poorest workers. Perhaps because there is considerable income from the informal sector, people in FYR Macedonia did not wish to join public works programs even though the benefit was set at the average wage. A few other countries in the region have experimented with public works programs, but to date there has been no systematic evaluation of their effectiveness.

Given the limited role of the state in delivering benefits, some countries, namely Albania and Uzbekistan, have used *community targeting* to deliver benefits (box 9.4). As noted earlier, communities may know more about the poor in their area than central or regional officials do, and they will have more information about how to reach the poor and ensure that they receive benefits. In community targeting, some local authority or committee is empowered to make decisions about who should receive program benefits.

Given the success of intracommunity targeting evidenced in these programs, a generalized poverty benefit administered by local communities for low-income countries based on some means-testing criteria cannot be dismissed out of hand and may work in particular institutional settings (Coudouel, Marnie, and Micklewright 1998; Alderman 1999). But community-targeted systems have several drawbacks. Benefits may be captured by local elites, allowing a few individuals to determine who receives assistance. Another problem, emerging from evidence on Albania, is that community targeting does not necessarily facilitate equitable targeting across regions.

Issues that Cut across Country Income Groups

Institutional and financing arrangements for social assistance differ across countries. Although in some countries assistance is centrally funded and administered, in others (such as Bulgaria, Romania, Latvia, and Kazakhstan) responsibility for financing social assistance has been transferred to local governments, with some support through central budget transfers.

Decentralization. A lack of earmarking of budget transfers for social assistance means that funds are often not used for this purpose. Local governments frequently have few resources to finance social assistance. In Hungary, however, the administration and financing of social assistance programs are completely decentralized. Decentralization can give rise to inequities across jurisdictions or to low levels of financing. In Kazakhstan, for example, Almaty city spends roughly 8 times more per poor person on social assistance than do some of the poorest oblasts (World Bank 2000d).[10]

Poor regions with the highest rate of poverty have the fewest resources to address their poverty needs. A key role for central governments is to ensure that regional disparities are not accentuated, but are mitigated, by the distribution of benefits. The central government should determine the level or threshold of social assistance or types of services for which individuals across the country will be eligible and ensure that social assistance programs are adequately financed. However, in some cases the state

---

Box 9.4 Community Targeting of Cash Benefits in Uzbekistan

An alternative approach to federally determined targeting rules is to allow local communities to determine eligibility for social assistance benefits, while the financing of the benefit remains a federal responsibility. Several countries follow this approach including Uzbekistan.

Faced in 1994 with the dissolution of guaranteed employment and consumer subsidies—the main safety net in the socialist era—the government of Uzbekistan created a targeted lump-sum cash benefit program. The unique feature of this program is that Uzbekistan uses a traditional community group, the Mahalla committee, to target and administer the benefit. The Mahalla committee is a community-based entity, the chairman of which is elected by the local community from candidates nominated by the local political authority. Salaries of the chairman and secretary of the Mahalla committee are paid by the state.

The choice of the appropriate level of benefit (between one and three times the minimum wage) and the definition of who is poor (within broad federal guidelines) are decentralized to the Mahalla committee level. This program assumes that Mahallas are better informed than the federal government about who is poor and the appropriate level of benefit they should receive. Eligibility for the benefit is based on many factors in addition to income. These include assets, number of working household members, and assessment of whether household members are shirking (for example, whether they could obtain more revenue from better use of their agricultural plot). If the Mahalla committee votes to give assistance, the recipient is entitled to receive a monthly benefit of between one and three times the minimum wage for a period of three months.

In 1997 the universal child benefit was replaced with a child allowance benefit targeted to the poorest households using the Mahalla committee system. The procedure for obtaining assistance is quite similar to that for the poverty benefit. The main difference is that the family must provide detailed information on its income for the past 12 months, as well as documentation on its children. Mahallas have some discretion in setting the size of the minimum monthly per capita income threshold for determining eligibility as well as discretion in determining who should be awarded assistance even if the family meets the income test. The size of the benefit depends on the number of children in the family. Coudouel and Marnie (1999)

---

may delegate the exact type of service, or identification of the poor (according to some guidelines), to the community. The community has an advantage over the state, because it knows the needs and conditions of its population better. Yet the state needs to monitor local governments to ensure that they are allocating resources and delivering services according to the agreed upon rules.

Groups with special needs. An issue that cuts across all transition countries is how to provide for populations with special needs. Institutional care, which includes the provision of shelter and food, is generally available in the region to orphans, children with special needs, the severely disabled, and the elderly in need of assistance. Transition countries have tended to rely too heavily on institutions to care for disadvantaged groups, at the same time that resources for institutions have been squeezed. Institutionalized groups, given the lack of voice in society, are most often the

---

Box 9.4 *(continued)*

conducted an evaluation of the system based on household surveys in 1995 and 1999 in the Fergana Valley oblast.

How well have Mahalla performed the task of allocating the low-income benefit? In 1999 the low-income benefit was distributed progressively: the poor in the Fergana oblast received a larger share of benefits than the well off. In 1999 the bottom two quintiles received almost half of all expenditure. Despite this relatively favorable result, targeting efficiency has declined slightly over time, down from 59 percent in 1995. In 1995, 27 percent of all expenditures on the low-income benefits were targeted to the lowest quintile, but in 1999 the lowest quintile received 23 percent of total program expenditures.

The program appears to be well administered in the Fergana oblast. Most households know about the program, and program knowledge has increased over time. Few households report "waiting for an answer" on their applications. More than two-thirds of those who did not apply said that they would do so if they were ever in need. The most common reason stated for not wanting to turn to the Mahalla for help was a complicated application procedure and discomfort at having their situation discussed in public. Few—about 5 percent of those refused assistance—cited corruption at the Mahalla level as a reason for not receiving the benefit.

Nevertheless, there appears to be room for improvement. In 1999, nearly 22 percent of top-quintile households applied for the program (as in 1995), and about 8 percent received assistance. Of the bottom quintile, only 42 percent applied and 27 percent were granted help. Apparently, many of those who would be most likely to receive the benefit are choosing not to apply.

How much has coverage of full allowances improved? In 1999 nearly 40 percent of poor households received child allowances compared with 12 percent of poor households in 1995. This shows that a greater number of poor are receiving child allowances through the Mahalla system.

Source: Coudouel and Marnie (1999).

---

first to be penalized when resources are scarce. Providing protection for these groups must be an integral part of a social assistance strategy for all countries, no matter what their level of income, but reforms are needed to improve opportunities for these groups while reducing the overall cost of the program. A few countries are experimenting with innovative reforms in this area (box 9.5).

Diversification. The state can also move away from relying solely on the public sector to deliver social services and work with nongovernmental organizations to deliver services. However, NGOs require an effective legislative environment that allows them to raise revenues and enter into contractual arrangements—an environment lacking in some transition countries. High-income transition economies may be in a better position than low-income countries to diversify provision of social assistance and

---

Box 9.5   The Shift Away from Institutionalized Care in Transition Economies

One of the most deleterious legacies of socialist social assistance programs was their over-reliance on residential institutions for social care. Institutionalization was often the only option for the elderly who were unable to live on their own, adults with physical and mental disabilities, and children in difficult circumstances because of poverty, ethnicity, disability, or other risk factors. In many cases the most vulnerable and marginalized members of society were placed in institutions.

Recent data suggest that nearly 1.3 million people—820,000 of them children—live in about 7,400 highly structured institutions in Central and Eastern Europe and Central Asia. As the effects of economic decline weakened families, the lack of community alternatives forced families to rely on these large institutions. As a result, the number of individuals in custodial care has increased (chapter 1) at the same time that living conditions in these institutions have deteriorated significantly because of shrinking budgets and higher operating costs.

Many transition economies have begun exploring alternatives to institutions. Experience in Western Europe and the United States suggests that community-based services, such as home care and day care services, and special education programs for children with learning disabilities can be more effective, efficient, and humane. Transition economies are well positioned to begin developing such services. Decentralization and increased NGO activity and community participation in civil society have laid the groundwork for greater consumer involvement in social services.

Making the move to community-based care involves significant changes in social policy. Six elements form a comprehensive and integrated strategy:
- Changing public opinion and mobilizing community support.
- Strengthening the community-oriented social welfare infrastructure, such as schools of social work, training programs for staff in residential institutions, and staff in local social assistance offices.
- Piloting community-based social service programs to provide the flexibility for testing a wide range of approaches.
- Designing pilot projects to reduce the flow of individuals entering residential institutions and to reintegrate individuals into the community.
- Redesigning, converting, or closing individual institutions.
- Developing a national system of community-based social services.

A few transition economies are leading the way in this transformation. For example, in 1996 Lithuania introduced day schools for handicapped children and multiservice community centers—serving battered women, socially vulnerable children, and former prisoners. These pilot projects have already demonstrated noteworthy achievements, including deinstitutionalization of severely disabled children in Moletai and Utena, sharply reduced demand for an elderly home in Svencionys, and provision of safe and stable care for battered women and their children in Vilnius. In Constanza, Romania, apartments with house parents are used to care for HIV-positive children who attend a regular school. And in Shkodra, Albania, a center for at-risk families provides counseling, home visiting, parent training, and referral services.

Source: Tobis (1999).

---

social services to NGOs. However, low-income transition economies can begin to develop the necessary legislative framework for future involvement. In high-income countries some social services and institutionalized care could be provided mainly through community organizations and

NGOs. Partnership with nonstate actors can help increase the range of social services that is available, improve quality through competition, and foster greater public participation and ownership of social assistance programs in civil society.

Utility Subsidization Programs and the Poor

Unlike other parts of the world, in Europe and Central Asia many of the poor are connected to a variety of utility services. In most parts of the region, close to 100 percent of the poor are connected to electricity, and two-thirds are connected to water (except in Moldova). Significantly fewer benefit from centralized provision of gas, sewerage, hot water, and heat. The relatively high connection rates reflect the heavy investment in infrastructure during the socialist period, the high degree of urbanization and urban poverty, as well as the exigencies of the cold climate prevailing in much of the region. Because of these factors, affordability of these services is a major poverty issue in the ECA region.

Approaches to Energy Subsidization for the Poor

Utility subsidies for households can be grouped into three broad categories: no disconnection of delinquent households; price subsidies of various types (across-the-board price subsidies, life-line tariffs, and price discounts to "privileged" households), and compensatory household income support (burden limits and other earmarked cash transfers). This section looks at the merits of each of these approaches in terms of coverage of the poor, the efficiency with which resources are targeted to the poor, the impact on prices, and administrative ease.

No disconnection of delinquent households. In a few countries—notably in the Commonwealth of Independent States and in South and Eastern Europe—utilities are pressured by governments not to disconnect households that do not pay their bills. Although one might expect that poor households would be over-represented among households with payment arrears, evidence shows that there is considerable leakage of this benefit to the nonpoor. Some poor households do not benefit from this policy—in part because its application tends to be erratic and not formalized: governments are reluctant to make "no disconnection of delinquent households" an official public policy. Moreover, benefits may accrue disproportionately to nonpoor households to the extent that their monthly utility bills are larger than those of the poor. Targeting efficiency is low. This policy has little to recommend it except administrative simplicity.

Across-the-board price subsidies. Across-the-board subsidies cover all households that are connected to the utility—so while coverage of connected poor households is universal, there is considerable leakage to the nonpoor. Targeting efficiency is further undermined to the extent that utility consumption increases with income. While across-the-board price subsidies are simple to administer, they distort energy prices for all consumers.

Life-line tariffs. Many governments in Europe and Central Asia introduced life-line tariffs for utility services with metered or relatively easily estimated consumption, especially electricity and gas. Under this system the price subsidy is restricted to the initial block of consumption called the basic need level. This offers a less costly alternative to across-the board-price subsidies since only part of consumption is subsidized; coverage is provided to all consumers connected to the utility. Targeting efficiency is increased by restricting the size of the first block so that it does not exceed the consumption levels of the poor—assuming that consumption increases with income. Targeting can be further improved by a three-block tariff structure, assuming that the third block is set above cost, so it includes a negative subsidy. Under this system nonpoor households effectively subsidize poor households. Thus, for the same total cost a bigger subsidy can be granted on the price of the first block.

Price distortions can be kept relatively low in a two-block tariff as long as the first block is kept sufficiently small so most consumers, including the poor, consume more than the first block. This ensures that the last unit of consumption is priced correctly. A three-block tariff structure distorts the marginal price signal more, however. Life-line tariffs are more complex to administer than across-the-board price subsidies, since they require reliable, tamper-proof metering or a reasonable consumption proxy. They are not suitable for water and sewerage in countries where residential water use is not metered.

Price discount for privileged consumers. Some countries provide price discounts to certain households selected on the basis of such factors as occupation, medical history, age, and merit. The FSU countries operated a system of merit-based utility price discounts—not only to reduce poverty but to reward service in certain occupations and to compensate for human suffering (war, hard labor, catastrophe). Price discounts ranged from 25 to 100 percent. While the Baltic states have made inroads on eliminating the system of privileges, many CIS countries have made less progress. Since the primary goal of the system of privileges is not poverty alleviation, it is not surprising that the system only covered some of the poor. For example, in Moldova in 1997 only about 35 percent of the people benefiting from electricity price privileges were poor. Moreover, the privileges tended to be inadequately targeted to the extent that the poor consume less utility services than do the nonpoor. Like across-the-board price subsidies, privileges can be highly distortionary, although they create distortions only for a selected group of consumers. Privileges are also administratively more demanding than the no-disconnection, across-the-board price subsidy or life-line tariff mechanisms, since they require the government to issue a list of privileged consumers that the utility then must take note of when calculating the monthly bill.

Burden limits (housing allowances). Starting in 1995, a number of FSU countries introduced subsidies to limit the burden placed by utility expenditures on household incomes. Housing allowance offices in government receive their funding from the budget and make payments to utilities on behalf of households whose combined utility expenditures exceed a certain share of their income. This share—the burden limit—typically varies from 15 to 30 percent, and its calculation may include fuel costs (in rural areas) or rental payments on apartments in cities.

Coverage of the poor depends on whether the poor apply for the benefit, and if they meet the eligibility criteria. Evidence suggests that many poor do not receive the benefit. Burden limits do an inadequate job of targeting resources to the poor because of the weak connection between per capita household income and the share of the utility bill in household consumption. A solution for the problem of low targeting efficiency is to replace actual utility expenditures with normative utility expenditures in the formula that is used to calculate the allowance. The norms can be set on the basis of per capita norms for apartment space (and associated heating requirements) and water and electricity consumption. Since the norms are independent of income, the allowance that a household receives under this modified burden limit mechanism is inversely related to income.[11] It is crucial, however, to set the norms sufficiently low (below the old "sanitary" norms applied in the former Soviet Union) in order to keep the number of beneficiaries limited and the amount of support affordable for the budget.

For example, the Kyrgyz Republic operates a system of housing allowances based on normative utility expenditures in Bishkek, the capital city.

To be eligible for the allowance, a household must live in an apartment building, and its normative utility expenditures (electricity excluded) should exceed 23 percent of its income (the burden limit). Normative utility expenditures depend on the number of people in the household and on the level of utility tariffs. In 1999 about 2,600 households received the support—a coverage ratio of 11 percent of poor households, assuming that there are about 23,000 poor households in Bishkek falling below the relative poverty line.[12] Burden limit schemes are highly distortionary insofar as the price of an additional unit of utility service covered under the scheme is effectively zero. Using normative consumption to fix the level of utility expenditures for the purpose of subsidy calculation can significantly reduce the distortionary effect. Like other income-tested schemes, burden limit schemes are fairly complex to administer.

Other earmarked cash transfers. Some countries provide other forms of earmarked energy benefits for low-income households. In Riga, Latvia, the energy benefit is calculated as the amount needed to cover utility costs so that the household is left with a minimum specified amount of income after paying its energy bill. In Bulgaria the guaranteed minimum income benefit includes an energy benefit component provided monthly to eligible households during the heating season. This supplement is intended to defray part of the energy costs. Schemes like the one in Riga can be highly distortionary to the extent that they make the cost of an additional unit of utility consumption zero for eligible households. On the other hand, the Bulgarian energy benefit in 1998–99 was paid in cash, so energy consumption patterns were not distorted. Earmarked cash transfers are administratively complex because eligibility is based on means testing. Although means testing reduces coverage of poor households with utility connections (to the extent that means testing is imperfect), it probably improves targeting.

Reform Options

Many countries in the region have extensive utility coverage that poor consumers are finding unaffordable as their incomes fall and utility prices are brought in line with the cost of supply. For political and other reasons—including the need to ensure adequate levels of heat for the poor—the way forward is not to abandon provision of these services but to improve the cost efficiency of the utility services, increase bill collections from those who can pay, while helping the poor cope with the higher prices. Some form of subsidy for the very poor may be necessary for a period of time until their incomes rise. The challenge is subsidize the cost of utility provision to the poor in the least costly and distortionary way possible.

In determining how to reform utility and housing benefits, governments must decide whether an energy-specific benefit, in addition to or instead of a generalized cash-transfer poverty benefit, is needed. A couple of considerations come into play. From a political economy angle, nonearmarked social assistance transfers lack the appeal of a benefit that is directly tied to the cost of consuming the commodity or service in question. Since energy costs are such a large share of household expenditure—unlike other commodities—a tied benefit certainly has considerable appeal.

Countries that do have a well-functioning cash benefit system may want to rely solely on it to cushion utility price shocks for the poor. The administratively less demanding attributes of life-line tariffs are presumably not a major advantage when countries can deliver means-tested benefits adequately. However, life-line tariffs may still be preferred because they provide universal coverage of the connected poor—which even well-functioning income-tested benefits are unlikely to do. The disadvantage is that life-line tariffs tend to introduce more price distortions than do nonearmarked cash benefits, something that countries with the ability to implement nonearmarked cash benefit schemes should consider. Burden limit schemes based on actual utility expenditures are not efficiently targeted and introduce price distortions. Burden limit schemes based on normative prices do a better job on targeting, but they are not clearly preferable to a cash benefit or a life-line tariff.

Life-line tariffs are the best option for countries that do not have the ability to operate an effective means-tested cash benefit program—likely the case for low-income countries. Life-line tariffs tend to be better targeted than across-the-boards price subsidies. Price distortions are usually less in two-block systems than in three-block systems, but the latter score better on targeting criteria. In the case of nonmetered water supply where no good proxy exists for actual consumption and where life-line tariffs are not feasible, an across-the-board price subsidy is the best option.

Price discounts for privileged consumers fare poorly on a number of counts. They generally do a poor job of reaching the poor, they introduce price distortions, and they require special agencies to certify eligibility, which in turn must be taken into account by the utility in calculating consumers' bills. Although it may not be possible for political reasons to eliminate all privileges, they can be phased out slowly by grand-fathering those currently on the rolls and/or keeping the amount of the benefit fixed. Assuming some inflation, such benefit caps will erode in real terms over time, freeing up resources that can be used for more effective social assistance programs or other urgent fiscal needs.

The Performance of Social Insurance Programs

In transition countries there are two main social insurance programs: pensions (including old-age, disability, and survivors' insurance) and unemployment. Social insurance programs enable individuals to smooth consumption against particular adverse events (such as unemployment or disability) or over their lifetime. They also have (explicit or implicit) redistributive objectives in reaching the poor. In most countries the ability of programs to insure individuals has been constrained, but pension programs have had an important poverty alleviation impact.

The Performance of Unemployment Benefit Programs

The ability of unemployment insurance programs to insure individuals against unemployment has been limited in most countries because of continual changes in contractual terms over time, delay, and nonpayment of benefits. During the transition, the first cohort of the unemployed was relatively more advantaged because it received more generous net benefits than did later cohorts.

In response to tighter financial conditions, many Central and Eastern European (CEE) countries reduced the level of benefits, cut generous eligibility conditions, and limited the duration of benefits in the second half of the 1990s. The long-term unemployed were the hardest hit. Poland limited benefit duration to one year, and FYR Macedonia, to 18 months. In Hungary, the Czech Republic, and Slovenia, maximum duration was halved. In many FSU countries, benefit duration was set even lower, at about six months. Benefit replacement rates were reduced, and maximums were established to cap growth in the level of the benefit. These changes were applied to all recipients in some countries (the Czech and Slovak Republics), while in Poland and Hungary changes were grand fathered.

In many countries real benefits fell because of high and persistent inflation. As a result, they became flat and close to the minimum wage, with almost no link to contribution history (of limited application during the transition). This was particularly the case in Russia and other FSU countries, where the real level of benefits has declined so much that most eligible unemployed do not claim benefits (World Bank 2000b). Moreover, in many FSU countries, benefits are often unpaid. In Russia, for example, benefit arrears have sometimes reached three to four months.

Even countries that have had trouble meeting their obligations in these programs have found it difficult to reduce benefits. In Romania and Bulgaria new entrants to the labor market (such as graduates of secondary school) remain eligible for assistance. This is not the case in most OECD programs.[13] In Romania it was politically impossible to reduce eligibility because of the participation of youth in the revolution. In FYR Macedonia a reduction in benefit for some insured was made politically palatable by increasing benefits for other recipients. Although the maximum benefit was reduced from 24 to 18 months for most workers, the maximum duration of benefit for those with a long contribution history (35 years) was increased until retirement, despite continuous deficits in the employment fund. In FSU countries, despite nonpayment of benefit or payment in kind, programs are still politically difficult to remove. Understandably, citizens want their government to fulfill its promises rather than make its obligations more consistent with financial realities. As a result, benefits in many countries are not paid or are paid sporadically.

Do unemployment insurance programs help the poor? It is difficult to say much about the *coverage* of the poor given very sparse evidence. Evidence on the *targeting efficiency* of programs suggests that, with the exception of FYR Macedonia and Latvia, program spending received by the poor is greater than their share in the population. In Estonia and Romania 60 to 70 percent of benefits are received by the bottom third of the population. Perhaps this is not surprising given the high correlation of unemployment and poverty in some countries. The targeting efficiency of unemployment benefit programs, where comparable data exist, is higher than for child allowances and social assistance in all countries (except for social assistance in FYR Macedonia, Romania, and Albania). However, the *effectiveness* of benefits tends to be low—more comparable to child allowances than social assistance, given the low share of total public spending on unemployment benefits. The lack of resources in CIS countries likely makes the effectiveness of programs particularly low in those countries (table 9.6).

Options for Reform of Unemployment Insurance Programs

Unemployment insurance programs are appropriate for a number of transition countries. They are useful risk-pooling programs when the number of unemployed is small relative to the pool of people employed in the

Table 9.6 Coverage, Targeting Efficiency, and Effectiveness of Unemployment Benefits in Selected ECA Countries, Various Years

Country and year	Cash benefit		
	Coverage[a]	Targeting efficiency[b]	Effectiveness[c]
Bulgaria 1997	6	—	17
Macedonia, FYR 1997	—	17	2
Albania 1996	—	25	—
Armenia 1996	—	26	—
Estonia 1995	—	60	—
Romania 1997	13	68	21
Croatia 1998	—	39	—
Latvia 1998	—	26	—
Kazakhstan 1996	2	33	1

— Not available.

Note: The "poor" are defined in Bulgaria as the bottom 36 percent; Romania, bottom 31 percent; Estonia, bottom 30 percent; and in Albania, FYR Macedonia, Armenia, Croatia, and Latvia, bottom 20 percent. For Kazakhstan, for targeting efficiency and effectiveness the "poor" are defined as the bottom quintile and for coverage as the bottom 35 percent.

a. Percentage of poor receiving benefits.

b. Percentage of total benefit expenditures received by poor.

c. Benefit as percentage of household expenditures.

Source: World Bank (1996a, 1998, 1999a, 1999b, 1999d, 2000a, 2000e); Rashid, Dorabawila, and Adams (1999); Tesliuc and Pop (2000).

formal sector. But they are a very costly way to deal with massive unemployment as a result of restructuring. Insurance-based programs are more appropriate for countries that can administer benefits well, can finance benefits at low tax rates, and can collect contributions attributed to individuals than they are for low-income countries. The transition economies in Central Europe and the Baltics are reaching this stage.

High-income countries. Where unemployment insurance is provided, the overall program should be affordable and financed without the imposition of high tax rates on contributors. One way to cap program benefits might be to set the tax rate for the program to a low and less distortionary level (say 1 to 2 percent), which is roughly at the lower end of the range of tax rates in transition countries. Imposing the tax on employer and employee, as in most OECD countries, would make the insurance link more clear to employees. Otherwise, when tax rates are quite high and the benefit provided is negligible, providing unemployment insurance results in a greater informalization of the economy.

Benefit duration should be limited to six to nine months to reduce work disincentives. This is based on a key finding in the literature for developed economies. The generosity of the unemployment insurance system, particularly the duration of benefit, has strong work disincentives. Most studies find that benefit duration is strongly and positively associated with the duration (not incidence) of unemployment.

In transition countries, however, the reduction in the generosity of benefit has not increased incentives to work. Outflows from unemployment to work have not increased. The exit from unemployment status does appear to be related to benefit duration—for example, in Romania—unemployment duration peaked at nine months, the maximum level of benefit. Once the benefit was exhausted, however, most of the unemployed withdrew from the labor force altogether (Boeri, Burda, and Köllo 1998), instead of returning to work.[14] One reason for limited incentive effects is the creation of social assistance benefits for which many unemployed qualify. In many transition countries these social assistance benefits continue to be of indefinite duration. Many unemployed shift to social assistance after their unemployment benefits expire. Reducing the unemployment benefit by supplanting it with another generous benefit counters any positive incentive effect from stricter benefit conditions.

Eligibility conditions should exclude, when politically possible, students and new entrants to the labor force. To preclude the moral hazard problems common in any form of insurance, unemployment insurance programs typically include co-payment as well as restrictions on eligibility.[15] As in OECD countries, incentives in Europe and Central Asia should include waiting periods for receiving benefits and eligibility restrictions on workers who have left the labor force voluntarily and because of misconduct or a labor dispute. There are penalties for false claims, and benefits can be suspended if two or more reasonable job offers are refused. In low-income countries—such as the Kyrgyz Republic and FYR Macedonia—and even in some lower-middle-income countries—such as Russia—moral hazard provisions are less relevant given the low level of benefit, but in upper-middle-income countries, such as Poland and Hungary, these provisions may reduce false claims.

Unemployment insurance programs might provide more generous benefits if it is found that in doing so, at least for a short period of time, enterprise restructuring is facilitated. But generous unemployment benefits are difficult to reduce or phase out, as many Central European countries have discovered. A more attractive option is the use of one-off generous severance payments paid by the central government (without increasing statutory severance payments) to spur layoffs and restructuring in state enterprises.

The administration of unemployment programs remains a challenge even for many of the higher-income transition economies. First, in countries where employment offices are not computerized or linked by automation to other programs, cross-checking across programs or regions for fraud is extremely difficult if not impossible. Another problem is that registration for unemployment is not limited to those who are genuinely seeking work or who have been in the formal labor market. Registration for unemployment, as an indicator that the person is seeking work, is a means to get poverty or health benefits. As a result, many people who have no intention of entering the labor market appear on registered unemployment rolls. Finally, in higher-income countries, employment services offices sometimes intervene too heavily in the job search process by forcing individuals and firms to legitimize employment offers through the employment bureau, driving up hiring costs, or creating incentives for firms and individuals to enter into contracts illegally.

Lower-middle income and low-income countries. Low-income transition economies are in a very different situation with respect to unemployment insurance programs for a number of reasons. First, contributory schemes have little relevance, given the large informal economy and the limited administrative capacity to implement contributory schemes. Second, since enterprise restructuring is still at a relatively early stage in a number of countries, more layoffs are likely once restructuring takes place. The cost of instituting or maintaining traditional unemployment insurance schemes with reasonably generous benefits of long duration would be very high under these circumstances. The risk is that resources spent on unemployment insurance programs would take benefits away from these countries' overriding poverty-reduction objective—namely, making sure that the basic needs of the poorest households and children at risk are met.

Can any case be made for unemployment assistance? This answer is probably yes, especially in countries where workers in restructured enterprises have actually been working and being paid by the enterprise. While enterprises may have statutory severance obligations, many are probably not in a position to pay them. The loss of income in such cases may make such households vulnerable to poverty. There also may be a strong political rationale for providing some assistance if it significantly facilitates enterprise restructuring. Under these circumstances, low-income countries should convert unemployment insurance programs into unemployment assistance programs financed from general revenues. In these cases the flat unemployment assistance can be offered (in lieu or in combination, depending on fiscal resources) as a severance package for laid-off workers. This assistance should be simple, affordable, flat-rate, and highly limited in duration. It also should take into account severance pay and other layoff arrangements provided directly by the enterprise. The political costs of converting schemes from a contributory to a flat rate basis are not insurmountable, as the examples of Poland and Albania, both of which have flat schemes, demonstrate.

The unemployment assistance benefit structure must be coordinated with social assistance benefits and with community works programs, for which the unemployed may become eligible after exhausting unemployment benefits. Rather than having a separate unemployment assistance benefit, many countries may find it simpler to have one noncontributory poverty benefit with eligibility based on weights for unemployment and poverty-related (number of children) characteristics. Combining unemployment with cash benefits may also be more administratively efficient, since unemployment offices do little more than pay benefits.

The Performance of Pension Systems

During the early part of the transition period, pension systems were often used to facilitate enterprise restructuring. They became unaffordable as pension costs rapidly increased. The deterioration of pension-fund financing led countries, in the short run, to meet pension obligations through a combination of lower wage replacement rates, higher payroll taxes, and higher deficits. High-income transition economies that maintained a large share of formal employment, and strong revenue collection performance, experienced modest declines in the covered wage bill. Through a combination of budget transfers and high contribution rates, these transition economies were able to maintain reasonably high benefit levels relative to wage levels.

But in countries that realized much greater declines in their GDP, such as Armenia and Georgia, the general inability to collect contributions or other taxes meant pensions often were unpaid, or they were allowed to erode in real terms. In many countries (Albania and Ukraine are two examples), the ratio of maximum to minimum pensions is already close to one; while in some other countries the distinction between social assistance and pension programs has vanished and a flat pension has been paid since 1996. As the link between contributions and benefits has weakened and pension systems have come under increasing stress, they have been less able to deliver on their insurance objective.

However, pension systems have played an important role in protecting beneficiaries against poverty. Indeed, as chapter 2 showed, in most countries the incidence of poverty for households headed by pensioners is much lower than for other socioeconomic groups, such as the unemployed or working poor. In addition, the elderly have a lower relative risk of poverty than other demographic groups have. But single elderly women with low survivor pensions are particularly vulnerable. In Croatia and Slovenia, pension spending as a share of GDP is very high, but poverty among the elderly or households headed by pensioners is high relative to other demographic groups. This indicates that pension spending is very unevenly distributed. In Croatia in 1998, 47 percent of pensioners received pension benefits of less than 1,000 kunas per month–slightly more than half of the mean monthly per capita household expenditure. Moreover, more than one fourth of persons in Croatia who are 60 years or older do not receive any pension benefit.

Pension benefits represent a large share of total public expenditures in CSB countries. This means that pension systems (for countries where comparable data are available) provide more generous benefits than social assistance and are therefore more effective. In some countries pension systems have the single largest impact of any cash transfer on reducing the incidence and depth of poverty and reducing inequality. In FYR Macedonia the incidence of poverty would have doubled (all else constant) had the pension system not existed. By contrast (and all else equal), the incidence of poverty would fall at most one or two points if social assistance or unemployment benefits were discontinued. Similarly, in Bulgaria, pensions contribute the most to raising households out of poverty. Almost 40 percent of households that were poor prior to the receipt of social transfers relied on pensions as the primary means of moving out of poverty. Social assistance, unemployment benefits, and child allowances contributed much less to reducing poverty in the country.

The targeting of pension expenditures is not as efficient as unemployment or social assistance benefits (table 9.7). This is to be expected since pension spending is more generally linked to prior wage earnings.

Pension System Reform Options

The most important immediate reason to reform pension systems is that the obligations of the public system are unaffordable and are becoming more so over time as populations age. Countries have taken a number of important steps to improve the long-term sustainability of their pension

Table 9.7 Coverage, Targeting Efficiency, and Effectiveness of Pensions in Selected ECA Countries, Various Years

Country and year	Cash benefit		
	Coverage[a]	Targeting efficiency[b]	Effectiveness[c]
Bulgaria 1997	68	—	48
Macedonia, FYR 1997	—	7	17
Albania 1996	—	18	—
Armenia 1996	—	19	—
Estonia 1995	—	17	—
Latvia 1998	—	12	—
Croatia 1998	—	12	—
Kazakhstan 1996	23	11	15

— Not available.
Note: The "poor" are defined in Bulgaria as the bottom 36 percent; Romania, bottom 31 percent; Estonia, bottom 30 percent; and in Albania, FYR Macedonia, Armenia, Croatia, and Latvia, bottom 20 percent. For Kazakhstan, for targeting efficiency and effectiveness the "poor" are defined as the bottom quintile and for coverage as the bottom 35 percent.
a. Percentage of poor receiving benefits.
b. Percentage of total benefit expenditures received by poor.
c. Benefit as percentage of household expenditures.
Source: World Bank (1996a, 1998, 1999a, 1999b, 1999d, 2000a, 2000e); World Bank 1999c, Rashid, Dorabawila, and Adams (1999).

schemes (Palacios and Rocha 1998; Gora and Rutkowski 1998; Government of Slovenia 1997; and Jelinek and Schneider 1997). They have raised actual or effective retirement ages, and they have changed indication rules from a link to wages to a combination of wage and price indexes (Hungary, Poland, Czech Republic) or price index (Croatia). While the high-income countries are doing a better job of meeting their obligations, the size of the required payroll taxes offers a substantial incentive for workers to opt out of the formal sector. Additional reforms are needed to enable pensions to meet their objectives of reducing old-age poverty and helping individuals smooth consumption over their life cycle.

Middle-income and high-income countries. The main public pension reform challenges for middle-income and high-income transition countries is to tighten the benefit-contribution link to maintain workers' incentives to contribute to the system, downsize public systems in order to reduce the burden on public finances, lower tax rates on employees (and employers), and create room for the eventual introduction of a defined contribution plan. The way to pursue this objective is to convert the PAYG pillar into the one based on the notional defined contributions principle, or to modify and downsize the earning-related defined benefit schemes.[16] In both cases the public system would continue to provide either a minimum pension or social assistance to the elderly to address poverty objectives. It is particularly important to reduce the demands of the public pension system on the budget if there are major unmet poverty needs in the country. Often, however, there is significant political opposition to pension reforms.

Upper-middle and high-income countries may wish to consider introducing a multipillar system, assuming that financial market administrative capacities are adequately developed, the government can effectively regulate and supervise funds, and the transition costs can be financed—conditions few transition countries currently meet.[17] These reforms allow individuals to obtain pensions from two sources: a benefit obtained from the downsized public-defined benefit pension system (or the first pillar) and the benefit obtained from a portion of mandatory individual contributions that accumulate in individual accounts and are invested (eventually) in a diverse portfolio of assets (second pillar). The accounts are managed by the private sector, which typically has a better performance record than the state in managing funds. The state, however, regulates and supervises the accounts.

Investing a portion of mandatory individual contributions in individual accounts is considered to have several advantages. First, in essence, this reform entails the conversion of the implicit debt of pension systems to an explicit pension fund deficit. Second, it allows individuals to obtain savings that reflect market returns on contributions. Third, by allowing individual contributions to be invested in the public system and in portfolios managed by private companies, and by allowing eventual international diversification of portfolios, individuals can diversify risk across countries/regions or assets.

To date, only two of the CSB countries, Hungary and Poland, have adopted a multipillar system. In Hungary 1.2 million workers—mostly under age 40—have diverted part of their pension contributions to private pension providers. All new labor market entrants are required to join. In Poland the new private pension funds are being licensed. In 1999 workers in Poland between the ages of 30 and 50 were given the choice to divert one-fifth of their overall pension contribution to these new funds. Workers under 30 will automatically join the new scheme. In Romania, Croatia, Latvia, Slovenia, and FYR Macedonia, the introduction of the second pillar is being planned. So far only one FSU country, Kazakhstan, has introduced a multipillar system. Kazakhstan is distinct in that it has fully privatized the pension scheme, leaving the public sector's role as one of coping with the risks of poverty in old age or disability.[18]

Countries adopting a multipillar system face a host of challenges (World Bank 2000b; Palacios and Rocha 1998). They must manage the financial costs of the transition, redefine the government's role as supervisor, design the institutions in the second pillar, and implement parallel reforms to ensure the success of the multipillar scheme.

Low-income countries. Low-income countries must ensure that the pension system does not let elderly pensioners fall into destitution, and they must free up resources to address the needs of others living in destitution. To accomplish these overriding objectives, poor countries may have to substantially flatten the distribution of the pension or adopt a flat pension. Special privileges accorded to particular groups of workers should be reduced. In the meantime these countries should focus on developing the institutional capacity for the eventual introduction of funded pension systems. When the wages start growing, these countries should consider a step-by-step movement toward a multipillar system.

Political opposition to pension reforms is considerable. Georgia recently introduced a flat pension, and now there is a huge debate about reintroducing differentiation in the benefit. In FYR Macedonia, despite the major financial problems with the pension fund, successive governments have promised increases in benefits prior to elections.

Administrative issues also plague many transition countries, especially the poorest ones. Actuarial capacity to forecast pension expenditures and revenues is still limited in many low-income countries. Collection of contributions remains a major problem, particularly given the emergence of the private (and informal) sector. Pension funds are often not audited. Because of borrowing and lending across insurance funds, the financial conditions of many funds are opaque. Particularly in CIS countries, record-keeping of individual work history and pensioner information remains deficient. As countries move to a multipillar system, selection of management of private pension systems, development of legislation, proper management of accounts, collection of contributions, and ways to build institutional capacity to regulate and supervise private funds become critically important.

Conclusions

Table 9.8 summarizes the programs that are likely to be the most appropriate for countries, given their income level.

Table 9.8 Typology of Reform Options by Country and Program

Income level	Social assistance	Social insurance unemployment	Pensions
High and upper-middle	Means-tested cash benefit assistance program, possibly supplemented by indicator targeting De-institutionalization	Insurance	Multipillar with minimum poverty-based benefit
Lower-middle	Categorical cash benefit (universal or targeted by indicator; means test possibly only where local institutions are strong) Life-line tariffs De-institutionalization	Flat benefit or severance	Reformed PAYG linking contributions with benefits, with minimum poverty-based benefit
Low	Limited cash benefit probably based on geographic targeting or indicator targeting Life-line utilities tariff Self-targeting (for example, workfare) De-institutionalization	Flat benefit or severance	Flat benefit

Transition countries face tough political choices. Governments are under great pressure to provide a high level of security to their populations, a number of whom find the uncertainty and reliance on self required by the market system difficult to bear. For this reason, poor transition countries often have a more developed set of social protection programs than do other countries with a similar level of income. In some countries the levels of protection are not fiscally sustainable. They undermine the development of formal labor markets and sometimes undermine recipients' incentives to work. In Europe and Central Asia, like elsewhere in the world, political considerations often dictate that programs be expanded beyond the truly needy in order to ensure a more secure resource stream. Indeed, many countries in Western Europe spend substantial amounts on programs that provide support to all or most families with children. The United States is an exception in that it concentrates its social assistance expenditures on the poor (Bradbury and Janti 1999).

Democratization has allowed some groups to form powerful lobbies that can direct subsidies in their direction. Political pressure groups may explain why some countries (for example, Latvia) continue to subsidize utilities for urban groups when rural areas have almost no access to hot water and heating. Political pressure appears to have privileged pensioners while leaving many rural and urban populations and multichild households at high risk of poverty. Similarly, continued privileges to particular groups, and even an increase in groups with privileged benefits, attest to the importance of political influence in the design of social assistance systems in many CIS countries.

Social protection reforms may have to compromise program design for greater acceptance of overall program objectives. Flat benefits targeted to the most needy may not enjoy broad-based support. Programs for the poor often need broader participation in order to ensure that schemes are continued and adequately funded. What is unfortunate is when broad participation undermines the provision of adequate benefits to the truly destitute or to parents who cannot afford to feed their children, provide them with adequate health care, or send them to school.

Notes

1. This chapter draws heavily on World Bank (2000b), and the work of Andrews and Ringold (1999), Palacios, Rutkowski, and Yu (1999), and Rashid and Rutkowski (1999), as well as on the work on the paper of Lovei (2000).

2. Other family benefits—including birth grants, parental leave benefits, and maternity leave introduced early on in the transition—still exist, but they are negligible in value compared with these two types.

3. Most countries have a regular monthly-benefit social assistance program as well as occasional benefits for households in temporary need of assistance. In countries where social assistance means-tested programs were added to already existing programs (such as in Romania, FYR Macedonia, and the Slovak Republic); other benefits were included in the calculation of household income, so that double counting of cash benefits was avoided.

4. In OECD countries, eligibility for unemployment benefits requires minimum coverage (six months on average); benefits are capped, and duration varies between 8 and 36 weeks. Benefit replacement rates range from 40 percent to 75 percent of past earnings, and they are based on an average of recent wages. To reduce false claims, OECD countries impose waiting periods and require applicants to be capable and willing to work, and registered at the Employment Bureau. Laid-off workers and those who have not left work voluntarily, or due to strike, or as a result of misconduct are generally eligible for benefits. Refusing a reasonable job offer without good reason is cause for suspension of benefit (Tzannatos and Roddis 1998).

5. The Union of Soviet Socialist Republics (USSR) introduced a range of social insurance programs, including contribution-based old-age pensions, in the 1920s after the Russian Revolution.

6. In OECD countries, public systems are financed as pay-as-you-go, and they are composed of a flat rate pension and an earnings-related tier. Tax rates vary considerably, ranging from 38 percent in Germany to 6 percent in the United States. Program expenditures vary between 6 and 10 percent of GDP. The retirement age is about 65 years (at least for men); many countries have lower retirement ages for women. System replacement rates are far in excess of 40 percent per couple as stated in a convention of the International Labour Office. Eligibility restrictions include minimum years of contribution. Many countries have reformed their pension systems because of financial problems.

7. Cash benefits are not always allocated appropriately within a household. To address this problem, some countries provide benefits directly to the mother. In the United Kingdom this policy is followed because mothers are assumed to be less likely to use the cash for the consumption of goods that may not reduce—or (in the case of alcohol) aggravate—poverty. This approach could be considered for means-tested cash assistance in transition countries where differences in intrahousehold spending preferences are strong. This is an area that has not been well researched in transition countries.

8. The concept of "affluence testing" to exclude the rich as opposed to including the poor is gaining attention in OECD countries.

9. In higher-income countries, self-targeting is often achieved by imposing a cost to receiving social assistance—formally through a work requirement and informally by having long queues to receive benefits. The shame associated with receiving social assistance benefits may deter some individuals from applying. These costs will lower the net benefit to the poor from the program and must be considered in evaluating how cost-effective the program is.

10. This is calculated by dividing social assistance spending by the number of poor as estimated using the household survey. Not all of the spending actually goes to the poor.

11. The allowance (A) is equal to $pcN - bY$ (or zero, whichever is larger), where p is the price of a unit of utility, b is the burden limit, Y is household income, c is the norm for per capita utility consumption, and N is the number of persons in the household. Since pcN does not change with income, the allowance decreases as household income grows.

12. For the purposes of the analysis, the relative poverty line is set at two-thirds median consumption. See Lovei (2000).

13. In some OECD countries, school leavers are eligible for benefits during recessions (Tzannatos and Roddis 1998).

14. Most hiring in transition economies has been from the ranks of the employed, not from the pool of unemployed. One reason cited for this phenomenon is the large surplus labor still existing in enterprises, and the low skill base of the

unemployed or those who have been laid off. There is very little unemployment among college or university graduates in Central European countries.

15. Moral hazard exists, for example, when program administrators do not have perfect information about beneficiaries. In this case individuals may try to keep benefits to which they are not entitled by claiming they are unemployed when they are not, or they may shirk on the job in order to get fired so that they can receive benefits.

16. The prototype of notional defined contribution (NDC) scheme reforms in transition economies was developed by Latvia. (Latvia followed the reform designed in Sweden.) The NDC system is based on individual accounts. Pension contributions are notionally accumulated (indexed), and the pension depends on the accumulated amount divided by the average life expectancy at the retirement age. Therefore, the system has automatic stabilizers enabling the pension level to be adjusted to changes in life expectancy. The system encourages recipients to work longer since the increases in the pension amounts are actuarial, not linear. This means that at the age of 62 or 63, one working year longer yields an 8 to 9 percent increase in the amount of the pension, not a 2 to 3 percent increase.

Despite certain advantages, the NDC system is an unfunded pay-as-you-go system, subject to some of the risks associated with these schemes. Countries may choose to modify their Defined Benefit Scheme by making benefits more tightly linked to contributions. This can be achieved by increasing the retirement age, reducing excessive target replacement rates, and introducing a lifetime assessment period. This particular first-pillar option has been adopted by Hungary in its multipillar system, and it is being considered by FYR Macedonia and Romania as an integral part of their pension reform programs. To reduce costs, many countries have raised retirement ages (Hungary, Poland, the Czech Republic, and FYR Macedonia) or effective retirement ages (Latvia); changed indexation rules from wage to a combination of wage and price (Hungary, Poland, Czech Republic); price (Croatia), or public sector wage; and changed the benefit formula (FYR Macedonia, which reduced replacement rates, and Slovenia).

17. The transition costs are not real costs since the implicit debt to future generations is paid. See Rutkowski (1998) for an overview of the movement toward multipillar systems in both transition economies.

18. In this regard the Kazakhstan reform resembles the Chilean, El Salvadoran, and Peruvian reforms in which no residual, unfunded public contributory scheme remained after the reform.

References

Alderman, Harold. 1999. *Decentralization and Targeted Transfers: Social Assistance in Albania*. Washington, D.C.: World Bank.

Andrews, Emily, and Dena Ringold. 1999. "Social Safety Nets in Transition Economies: Toward a Reform Strategy." World Bank Social Protection Discussion
Paper 9914. Washington, D.C.

Andrews, Emily, and Mansoora Rashid. 1996. "The Financing of Pension Systems in Central and Eastern Europe: An Overview of Major Trends and Their
Determinants, 1990-93." World Bank Technical Paper 339, Social Challenges
of Transition Series. Washington, D.C.

Andrews, Emily S., and Tom Hoopengardner. 1999. "Disability and Work in Poland." World Bank Discussion Note. Human Development Sector Unit, Europe
and Central Asia Region. December. Processed.

Boeri, Tito, Michael C. Burda, and Janos Köllo. 1998. "Mediating the Transition:
Labour Markets in Central and Eastern Europe." In *Forum Report of the Eco-
nomic Policy Initiative*, no. 4, edited by Lorand Ambrus-Lakatos and Mark R.
Schaeffer. New York: Institute for EastWest Studies.

Bradbury, Bruce, and Markus Janti. 1999. "Child Poverty across Industrialized
Nations." Innocent Occasional Paper 71, Economic and Social Policy Series.
Florence: UNICEF International Child Development Centre.

Braithwaite, Jeanine, Christiaan Grootaert, and Branko Milanovic. 1998. *Determinants of Poverty and Targeting of Social Assistance in Eastern Europe and
the Former Soviet Union*. Washington, D.C.: World Bank.

Coudouel, Aline, and Sheila Marnie. 1998. "The Mahalla System of Allocating
Social Assistance in Uzbekistan." New York: United Nations Development
Programme.

———. 1999. "From Universal to Targeted Social Assistance: An Assessment of
the Uzbek Experience." Draft.

Coudouel, Aline, Sheila Marnie, and John Micklewright. 1998. "Targeting Social
Assistance in a Transition Economy: The Mahallas in Uzbekistan." Innocenti
Occasional Paper 63, Economic and Social Policy Series. Florence: UNICEF
International Child Development Centre.

Garibaldi, Pietro, and Zuzana Brixiova. 1997. "Labor Market Institutions and
Unemployment Dynamics in Transition Economies." International Monetary
Fund Working Paper Wp/97/137. Washington, D.C.

Gora, Marek, and Michal Rutkowski. 1998. "The Quest for Pension Reform:
Poland's Security through Diversity." World Bank Social Protection Discussion
Paper 9815. Washington, D.C.

Government of Slovenia. 1997. "White Paper on Pension Reform." Ljubljana.

Jelinek, Tomas, and Ondrey Schneider. 1997. "Time for Pension Reform in the
Czech Republic." *Transitions*, vol. 4, no. 1 (June).

Lovei, Laszlo. 2000. *Maintaining Utility Services for the Poor: Policies and Practices in Central and Eastern Europe and the Former Soviet Union.* World Bank, Energy Sector Unit, Europe and Central Asia Region. Washington, D.C.

Milanovic, Branko. 1998. *Income, Inequality, and Poverty during the Transition from Planned to Market Economy.* Washington, D.C.: World Bank.

Palacios, Robert, and Roberto Rocha. 1998. "The Hungarian Pension System in Transition." World Bank Social Protection Discussion Paper 9805. Washington, D.C.

Palacios, Robert, Michal Rutkowski, and Xiaoqing Yu. 1999. "Pension Reform Strategy in ECA Countries." Washington, D.C.: World Bank. Processed.

Rashid, Mansoora, and Jan Rutkowski. 1999. "Labor Markets in Transition Economies: Legacy, Recent Developments, and Strategic Options." Washington, D.C.: World Bank.

Rashid, Mansoora, Vajeera Dorabawila, and Richard Adams. 1999. "Household Welfare, the Labor Market, and Public Programs in Albania." World Bank paper. Washington, D.C. Processed.

Shahriari, Helen, Paolo Belli, and Maureen Lewis. 2000. "Institutional Issues in Informal Health Payments in Poland." World Bank, Human Development Sector Unit, Europe and Central Asia Region, Washington, D.C. Processed.

Tesliuc, Cornelia M., and Lucian Pop. 2000. "Poverty, Inequality, and Social Protection." In *Economic Transition in Romania*, ed. Christop Rühl and Daniel Daianu, 173-243. Bucharest: Arta Grafica.

Tobis, David. 1999. "Moving from Residential Institutions to Community-Based Services in Eastern Europe and the Former Soviet Union." Washington, D.C.: World Bank.

Tzannatos, Zafiros, and Susan Roddis. 1998. "Unemployment Benefits." World Bank paper. Washington, D.C. Processed.

World Bank. 1996a. *Estonia: Living Standards during the Transition: A Poverty Assessment.* Report 15647-EE. Washington, D.C. June 17.

———. 1996b. *Poverty in Ukraine.* Report 15602-UA. Washington, D.C. June 27.

———. 1998. *Kazakhstan: Living Standards during the Transition.* Report 17520-KZ. Washington, D.C. March 23.

———. 1999a. *Bulgaria: Poverty during the Transition.* Report. 18411. Washington, D.C. June.

———. 1999b. *Former Yugoslav Republic of Macedonia: Focusing on the Poor,* vol. 1. Report 19411-MK. Washington, D.C. June 11.

———. 1999c. *Georgia: Poverty and Income Distribution,* vol. 1. Report 19348-GE. Washington, D.C. May 27.

———. 1999d. *Improving Social Assistance in Armenia.* Report 19385-AM. Washington, D.C. June 8.

———. 1999e. *Moldova Poverty Assessment.* Report 19926-MD. Washington, D.C. November.

———. 1999f. *Russia: Targeting and the Longer-Term Poor*, vol. 1. Report 19377-RU. Washington, D.C. May 1999

———. 2000a. *Croatia, Economic Vulnerability and Welfare Study.* World Bank, Poverty Reduction and Economic Management Sector Unit, Europe and Central Asia Region. Washington, D.C. Processed.

———. 2000b. "ECA Social Protection Strategy: Balancing Protection and Opportunity." World Bank, Human Development Sector Unit, Europe and Central Asia Region. Washington, D.C. Processed.

———. 2000c. "Hungary: Long-Term Poverty, Social Protection, and the Labor Market." Report 20645-HU. Washington, D.C. Draft.

———. 2000d. *Kazakhstan: Public Expenditure Review.* Report 20489-KZ. Washington, D.C. June 27.

———. 2000e. *The Republic of Latvia Poverty Assessment*, vol. 1. Report 20707-LV. Washington, D.C. June 14.

———. 2000f. *Tajikistan: Poverty Assessment.* Report 20285-TJ. Washington, D.C. June 29.

———. 2000g. *World Development Report 2000/1: Attacking Poverty.* New York: Oxford University Press.

CHAPTER 10

Reducing Income Inequality

Much of the increase in income inequality in Europe and Central Asia (ECA) reflects a welcome adjustment to an incentive and remuneration structure that rewards individual productivity. It is the natural and positive outcome of unleashing market forces and allowing individual returns to reflect individual effort. However, the polarization of incomes, severe in parts of the region, is not easily explained by productivity differentials or individual characteristics. In other countries of the world high inequality has impeded growth, undermined poverty alleviation, and fueled social tensions. Should policymakers in ECA then be concerned about the observed rise in inequality?

Should ECA Policymakers Worry about Inequality?

There is mounting evidence that high inequality is bad for growth (Benabou 1997; Aghion, Caroli, and Garcia-Penalosa 1999). Recent empirical studies have documented an unambiguous negative correlation between the average rate of growth and measures of inequality across countries and periods. And recent theoretical work has shown that these empirical findings are consistent with modern microeconomic theories of incentives.[1] There are also links between economic inequality and other social goals. Medical researchers have found that high and increasing inequality, within countries, is highly correlated with worsening health outcomes and increasing mortality (Smeeding 1997). High inequality is also correlated with greater social exclusion, declining confidence in the government, and impaired functioning of democracy.

For all these *instrumental* reasons, policymakers in Europe and Central Asia should worry about inequality. But they also should worry about inequality in its *own right*: because they believe in social justice and in maximizing social welfare. The new theoretical insights in economics show that, contrary to the traditional view, there need not be a tradeoff between social justice and productive efficiency (and/or growth). Redistribution can be good for growth.

Whether there are tradeoffs to reducing inequality or not depends greatly on the underlying forces that give rise to unequal outcomes. If disparities in outcomes arise purely from differences in effort and other decision variables of individuals, interventions to equalize outcomes may affect incentives and motivation, with negative consequences for overall social welfare. However, if unequal outcomes or achievements are related not exclusively to differences in effort but reflect also the impact of different human characteristics, which, in turn, affect individual capabilities (Sen 1992), the disincentive problem is fundamentally altered. If inequality of capabilities is related to gender or ethnicity (factors that cannot be easily changed), special treatment for the disadvantaged group may not generate the usual incentive problem. Thus, the ability of government action to influence inequality without major tradeoffs will depend critically on the specific policies, institutions, and social arrangements that underpin the distribution of income.

What Can Governments Do to Reduce Inequality?

Some of the forces that have given rise to high inequality in parts of Europe and Central Asia may prove temporary, especially if the transition process deepens and appropriate institutions to support the market and a pluralistic society develop. An important part of the jump in inequality (especially in the Commonwealth of Independent States) reflects the widespread quasi-rents resulting from incomplete or noncompetitive markets, from distortionary policies, or from corrupt government practices. If markets start to function better and governance improves, we would expect inequality in much of the CIS to come down.

However, the move toward less inequality is not automatic. Current inequities can become entrenched and affect the development of institutions and policies in ways that are not easily reversible. More accountable and less corrupt governments, better-functioning markets, and appropriate institutions can emerge only if society at large demands it. Yet inequality of the magnitude seen in some of the CIS republics is already eroding the ability of those at the bottom (and possibly those in the middle) to influence political outcomes and government action. This can only lead to a greater polarization of society, increased economic insecurity, impaired democracy, and rising violence and social dislocation.

Governments can do much to mitigate the unequal outcomes that the transition may generate (table 10.1). They can also make things worse.

Table 10.1   Policy Measures to Reduce Inequality, by Subregion

Policy	Central and Eastern Europe and the Baltics	Southern Europe and the Balkans	Commonwealth of Independent States	Caucasus and Central Asia
Building transparent and efficient product markets[a]	Fairly advanced but taxes and regulation burdensome for new firms.	More progress needed. Licensing, regulations, and anticompetitive practices hamper expansion of private firms.	High priority. Anticompetitive practices, licensing, regulations, and corruption hamper entry and expansion of new private firms.	High priority. Anticompetitive practices, licensing, regulations, and corruption hamper entry and expansion of new private firms.
Expanding financial markets[a]	Shallow by OECD and East Asia standards, but comparable to Latin America and the Caribbean. New firms and especially small enterprises still face difficulties accessing long-term finance.	Very shallow credit markets; private/small firms and SOEs have differential access.	Very shallow credit markets; unequal access for private/small firms and SOEs; connections are important.	Very shallow credit markets; unequal access; small firms face problems financing even working capital.
Raising the incomes of those at the bottom through labor market reforms[b]	Focus on raising incomes of low-skilled workers while maintaining wage flexibility. Antidiscrimination policies.	Focus on raising incomes of low-skilled workers while maintaining wage flexibility. Antidiscrimination policies.	Wage inequality high. Product markets and governance are key. Skill upgrading for poorest important in medium term.	Wage inequality high. Product markets and governance are key. Skill upgrading for poorest important in medium term.
Using distributive fiscal policy	Large scope for using fiscal policy. Focus on improving targeting of transfers. Policies to foster accumulation of public capital and education in poorest regions (within countries).	Scope to improve taxation and tax compliance, as well as targeting of transfers. Restoring fiscal balance is key. Possible scope for regional policies.	Scope to improve tax compliance and budget execution (arrears). Improve targeting of transfers. Possible scope for regional policies.	Priority is improving tax compliance, expenditure prioritization, and budget execution. Limited role for transfers in short to medium term (too poor).

a. A policy that is needed to sustain growth; it also will have positive distributional effects.
b. The focus of this policy is to change the distribution of income.
Source: Chapter 10.

As chapter 4 explained, governments' bad policies—excessive regulation and licensing, subsidized directed credit, protection of vested interests at the expense of the broader population—contributed significantly to the large income disparities in the CIS. History is rife with other examples: many Latin American governments tried for decades to mitigate entrenched inequality with populist policies (massive subsidy schemes, unmanageable progressive taxation, restrictive labor legislation), and they achieved mostly the opposite effect (IADB 1998).

To be effective, government policy must reflect an understanding of the nature and causes of inequality. Policies to reduce inequality in Europe and Central Asia must also recognize the diversity of causes and the large variance in institutional capacity across the region. In the countries of Central and South Eastern Europe and the Baltics (CSB), strong governments are in place, markets are functioning quite well, and the development of market-supporting institutions is well advanced; therefore, much can be accomplished through properly designed redistributive fiscal policy. There is also scope to improve the distribution of income through measures aimed at building the skills (and hence the income-earning opportunities) of less-educated workers and of marginalized groups. Moreover, the process of accession to the European Union can provide an invaluable mechanism for reducing regional disparities (structural funds) and for continuing economic and social reform.

Reducing inequality in the Commonwealth of Independent States will be much more complicated. Inequality in the CIS appears linked to failed government policy and especially to the failure to carry out reforms that go against the powerful vested interests that have grown out of the early stages of transition. Thus, there is much less political support for redistribution and for the measures that may be required than in the more advanced reformer countries. The problem of state capture in some of these countries is severe, and a captured state is unlikely to be responsive to distributional concerns. Policies to address poverty and reduce inequality in these countries must be linked to political reform and to efforts to build institutions that will deliver accountable and responsive governments with adequate checks and balances. The discussion in this chapter focuses on what can be accomplished through *economic* policy to reduce inequality and improve distributional outcomes. The need for accompanying *political* reform and an appropriate institutional context was discussed in chapter 5.

Given these constraints, what can governments do to reduce inequality in the CIS? The choice of policy measures relates to the factors that caused the collapse of formal employment and incomes. A first priority would be to eliminate excessive regulation, licensing, and other product market distortions; correct misdirected credit and financial sector policies; and build a functioning labor market (that is, governments need to continue on a determined path of economic reform, paying particular attention to building more open and efficient product and factor markets). These policies are necessary to restore and sustain growth, but they will also have positive distributional implications.

Second, CIS governments can focus more directly on affecting the distribution of income. They can try and raise the incomes of those at the very bottom through measures, such as antidiscrimination policies and legislation, that will enhance their earnings potential and remove barriers to their employment. In addition, these governments should rebuild their capacity to deliver basic services and carry out an effective fiscal policy (by collecting taxes in a fair and effective way, setting expenditure priorities in a transparent and accountable manner, and monitoring the delivery and quality of public services). Superimposed on these two priorities, and of special importance in Europe and Central Asia, is the need to prevent governments from being coopted by special interests and to ensure that governments are representative and accountable to their populations (chapter 5).

Building Transparent and Efficient Product Markets

Without well-functioning product markets, new formal sector employment opportunities, the key to reducing income disparities, will not emerge (EBRD 1999).[2] Competitive product markets are also essential to stimulating the restructuring of nonviable enterprises. Such restructuring would reduce the prevalence of wage arrears (or forced borrowing from workers), which is contributing to high wage inequality in the CIS.[3] Increased competition, liberalization, and deregulation would reduce monopoly rents. This, in turn, would diminish the gains to firms from lobbying and corrupting the state. State capture would be reduced and overall governance improved. All of these developments can promote growth, and they can improve distributional outcomes.

How much of an impact could continued market liberalization have on reducing inequality among the high-inequality ECA countries? To answer this question we compare high- and low-inequality countries and then simulate a simple counterfactual. Table 10.2 shows the regression of the Gini coefficient on measures of overall reform and on initial conditions for (1) a cross-section of ECA countries at one point in time and (2) for a pooled sample of countries over several years. For the cross-section regressions,

Table 10.2 Regressions of Income Ginis on Liberalization Index and Initial Conditions

Index	Cross-section of ECA countries 1996–97		Pooled sample, multiple years[c]	
	All available Gini statistics (24 countries)	Only income Ginis (24 countries)	All available Gini statistics (24 countries)	Only income Ginis (24 countries)
De Melo, Denizer, and Gelb reform index[a]	1.480	1.528 (2.860)	— (2.821)	—
Liberalization index[b]	—	—	27.027 (2.635)	28.294 (2.390)
Initial Gini (1989–90)	113.41 (1.981)	136.85 (2.052)	152.84 (3.350)	155.11 (3.275)
Initial income per capita	-0.0008 (-0.607)	-.0002 (-0.138)	-0.001 (-0.960)	-0.001 (-1.028)
Dummy for consumption Gini	-10.48 (-2.040)	—	-10.668 (-2.474)	—
R^2	0.699	0.703	0.413	0.419

Note: dummy =1 if Gini is consumption Gini.
a. A higher value means less reform (not available for pooled data).
b. From Dethier, Ghanem, and Zoli (1999). A higher value means less reform (used in pooled regressions).
c. Standard errors corrected for nonindependence across observations on same country.
Source: Dethier, Ghanem, and Zoli (1999) data combined with Ginis from latest household surveys.

we use the De Melo, Denizer, and Gelb (1996) reform index, which is a comprehensive index of progress on diverse reform fronts. A higher value indicates less reform: thus, a positive coefficient indicates that countries that have made less progress on reforms are also the ones with higher inequality outcomes. For the pooled regressions we do not have the De Melo, Denizer, and Gelb index; therefore, we use an alternative liberalization index provided by Dethier, Ghanem, and Zoli (1999). Unlike in the cross-section regressions, in the pooled regressions the estimated coefficients are influenced by variation in the data across countries as well as by changes over time within countries. However, the relationship between reforms and inequality appears to be the same.

Table 10.3 presents predicted inequality from the cross-section regressions shown in table 10.2 under two scenarios. The first scenario maintains the explanatory variables at their actual levels; the second assumes that the CIS countries achieved the same level of progress toward com-

Table 10.3 Predicted Gini Coefficients for the Commonwealth of Independent States under Alternative Scenarios

Explanatory variables	At actual levels	CIS progress resembles CSB progress
Reform progress	0.46	0.38
Initial conditions	—	0.40

Note: The predicted inequality for Central and Eastern Europe is 0.31. This is for a cross-section sample. Members of the CIS are Armenia, Azerbaijan, Belarus, Georgia, the Kyrgyz Republic, Moldova, Russian Federation, Ukraine, Tajikistan. The countries in Central and South Eastern Europe and the Baltics are Bulgaria, Croatia, the Czech Republic, Estonia, Hungary, Latvia, Lithuania, FYR Macedonia, Poland, Slovak Republic, and Slovenia.
Source: Simulations based on table 10.2.

petitive markets as the group of CSB countries (but keeping the initial conditions distinct). We also predict what the level of inequality would be for the CIS sample if the initial conditions had been the same as in the CSB, but progress on liberalization had followed its actual path. The results suggest that if the CIS countries were to achieve the same level of market development as the average CSB country, the predicted income Gini would drop by 8 Gini points. Changing the initial conditions for the CIS without altering its liberalization path would reduce the predicted income Gini but not by as much.

Continued progress in building competitive markets appears to be good for distribution and good for growth. But what aspects of market development should countries focus on? Is domestic price liberalization more or less important to inequality than the liberalization of external transactions? And how do these factors compare with other aspects of macroeconomic stability? While we are limited by the availability of comparable data across countries, some suggestive evidence can be inferred from regressions of the income Gini on alternative measures of reform progress. Because the cross-section sample is too limited to carry these out, we present the results only for the pooled sample (table 10.4).

This exercise is hampered by the difficulties of measuring progress on any of these fronts accurately. Because the measures are highly correlated among themselves, attempts to isolate their individual effects may be futile. However, some interesting findings do emerge. If we limit our analysis to the liberalization variables, we find that price liberalization is more correlated with inequality than with the liberalization of external transactions or other measures of private sector development (columns 1 and 2). However, this result largely disappears when measures of macroeconomic stability and the governments' fiscal stance are added to the regression.

Table 10.4 Liberalization and Inequality, Alternative Specifications

	(1)	(2)	(3)	(4)	(5)	(6)
Trade and foreign exchange	-7.129	-12.271	-0.191	-5.348	-8.944	-4.579
	(-0.372)	(-0.623)	(-0.011)	(-0.337)	(-0.406)	(-0.165)
Price liberalization	-39.262	-38.088	-24.303	-10.203	-3.416	-44.066
	(-1.761)	(-1.686)	(-1.142)	(-0.489)	(-0.108)	(-1.502)
Private sector development	—	5.396	—	—	—	—
		(0.634)				
Government expenditures (% of GDP)	—	—	-5.447	-6.309	—	—
			(-2.493)	(-2.939)		
Government deficit (% of GDP)	—	—	—	8.563	—	—
				(2.241)		
Volatility 1 (standard deviation of inflation)	—	—	—	—	0.0144	—
					(3.041)	
Volatility 2 (standard deviation of GDP growth)	—	—	—	—	—	0.650
						(1.958)
Initial Gini	135.27	135.53	143.59	105.53	72.485	91.069
	(2.883)	(2.866)	(2.832)	(2.303)	(1.364)	(2.247)
Initial income per capita	-0.0001	-0.0001	-0.0001	0.0001	-0.001	-0.001
	(-1.403)	(-1.363)	(-0.786)	(0.288)	(-1.011)	(-0.890)
R^2	0.485	0.488	0.498	0.601	0.581	0.534

Note: Regressions on pooled data for 20 ECA countries (multiple observations by country). Standard errors were corrected for heteroskedasticity and autocorrelation.
Source: Same as table 10.2.

The inclusion of the macroeconomic variables swamps the liberalization effect and renders it insignificant, suggesting that stabilization is a prerequisite for the development of markets and further reform. Both of our measures of macroeconomic instability—the standard deviation of inflation over the period and the standard deviation of real GDP growth—are positively, and significantly, related to inequality. The effect of inflation is particularly strong, highlighting its important distributional costs. The fiscal variables are also significantly correlated to inequality. The size of government spending (expenditures as a percentage of GDP) has an inequality-reducing effect, but this effect is not independent of the size of the government deficit. Government deficits, in fact, have a regressive impact on the distribution of income, and this impact is of a magnitude largely similar to the positive effect of government spending.

Expanding Financial Markets and Building Sound Credit Policies

This book has highlighted the role of low wages, particularly for the less educated, as an important determinant of income inequality and poverty. But wages are markedly influenced by the amount of capital with which workers can operate. When formal labor markets become relatively unimportant and households resort to self-employment and small-scale entrepreneurial activity for their main source of income, the availability of credit to finance capital investments becomes critical. Indeed, it can become the key determinant of the returns to labor and hence of a family's well-being. This is especially true for rural families who may depend solely on the income generated from their farming activities. World Bank (1999c) found that in Georgia rural families with access to credit and/or to capital inputs complementary to land were much less likely to be poor than those without such complementary inputs.

Well-functioning credit markets are needed to sustain formal employment. In Latin America, for example, shallow financial markets have been directly associated with high informalization of employment (IADB 1998). As the Latin America experience illustrates, formalization is usually a hallmark of the development of a market economy, but this process can be short-circuited if the domestic financial system is not up to the task. When financial markets are shallow, entrepreneurs and the self-employed often remain involved in small-scale, informal activities because they cannot obtain the credit to finance the expansion and formalization of their enterprise.

Credit markets are likely to be especially distorted in Europe and Central Asia because of the legacy of central planning, under which credit was allocated on a noneconomic basis to different activities and frequently used as a political tool. Moreover, many ECA countries started the transition with bouts of hyperinflation, which wiped out financial savings and destroyed much of the incipient financial system. The resulting scarcity of capital has negatively affected not only economic growth but also the distribution of income: poor households were more affected by the disappearance of prior savings and less able to gain access to credit, even informal credit, following hyperinflation (World Bank 1999a, 1999c; Gomart 1999).

In many ECA countries the shortage of credit has not been alleviated with the return to stable (and low) inflation rates: large fiscal deficits financed through high-yield government emissions have, in some countries, siphoned away scarce domestic (and foreign) savings from productive investments, which do not yield the same return in the short-term. World Bank (1999f) showed that more than three-quarters of the portfolios of the largest banks in Armenia were invested in government bonds, leaving only a miniscule fraction of resources available for loans to productive private sector endeavors. Even in an advanced reformer country like Slovenia, the public sector is crowding out a substantial share of the resources that could be available to the private sector (World Bank 1999e). The resulting scarcity of credit is particularly severe for small businesses and potential entrepreneurs, whose financial needs are typically greater and whose creditworthiness is more difficult to assess. This shortage of credit restricts the ability of small businesses to obtain access to the working capital and physical capital necessary to raise their productivity and expand their enterprises.

Shallow Financial Markets Contribute to High Inequality

In Europe and Central Asia financial depth—measured either as the ratio of broad money supply to GDP or as financial system credit to the private sector as a percentage of GDP— is much lower than in East Asia or even in Latin America (figure 10.1). The exceptions are the more advanced EU accession countries, where financial markets appear fairly comparable to those in Latin America in terms of depth although they are still much shallower than those in the OECD. At the other extreme we find the economies of the Caucasus and Central Asia. These countries have financial markets that are underdeveloped even by the standards of low-income countries. With ratios of broad money to GDP in the range of 7 to 12 percent, and banking sector credit to the private sector in the range of 2 to 6 percent, the financial markets of those countries are shallower than those in much of South Asia and parts of Africa. Other measures of financial market development, such as stock market capitalization, yield a similar picture.

Squire and Zou (1998) found that shallow financial markets are strongly associated with higher income inequality. In fact, they find that financial depth has one of the largest quantitative impacts on the Gini coefficient among all the variables considered. A similar, albeit weaker, correlation between financial depth and inequality was found with regard to Latin

Figure 10.1   Banking Sector Credit to Private Sector in Selected ECA and Latin American Countries

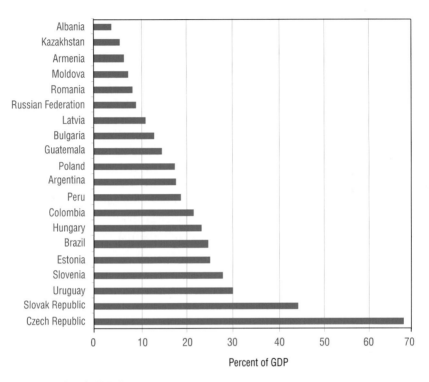

Source: World Bank SIMA database.

America (IADB 1998). Shallow and inefficient financial markets in Europe and Central Asia, and especially in the CIS, may be one of the reasons for the emergence of such high disparities in income.

Financial markets affect income inequality in a number of ways. Deep financial markets facilitate savings and the accumulation of capital, raising labor productivity and wages and driving down the returns to capital. This tends to improve the distribution of income because most households depend on wage incomes, while capital income accrues mainly to a more concentrated group of individuals. Higher capital accumulation promotes growth, which tends to feed back to wages. In contrast, if financial markets are not functioning effectively, domestic investment will be lowered, and the ensuing scarcity of capital will affect both growth and the distribution of income. If financial markets are weak, credit becomes particularly inaccessible to low-income individuals and small businesses. This has implications for the earnings of those who rely on small-scale activities to make their living. Therefore, there is a direct impact on inequality. But shortage of credit to small businesses can also have a negative impact on overall employment creation and thus on average wages and incomes.

There is evidence that the banking system provides limited credit to small enterprises even in the more successful reformer countries. EBRD (1999) finds that inadequate access to financing ranks second among the main barriers to entry and expansion of new private firms in Central and South Eastern Europe (after taxes and regulations). Access to long-term financing is a particular problem, even in advanced reformer countries such as Hungary or Poland. Small entrepreneurs' access to credit is even more restricted in the CIS, where access to working capital can be difficult. Throughout the region access to finance is significantly more difficult for start-ups and new firms than for state-owned enterprises (SOEs), and it is shown to depend greatly on special connections to banks and on other noncompetitive practices (EBRD 1999).

Financial Policies to Reduce Inequality

Chapter 6 discussed the major obstacles to the development of well-functioning financial systems in many ECA countries and proposed policy instruments to foster this development. However, even relatively well-functioning financial systems can fail to serve small and low-income borrowers. This is because small borrowers face particular obstacles in securing credit. From the point of view of the lender, monitoring small loans is much more expensive (as a fraction of loan size) than monitoring larger loans; moreover, the cost of enforcing repayment, if forced to go through the legal system, is proportionately much higher. Hence, if credit is to be made available to the poor, even greater care needs to be taken to ensure an appropriate regulatory and legal framework.

Beyond the standard measures to liberalize and create competitive financial markets and to establish appropriate supervisory institutions, what other reforms are needed to ensure that credit in ECA countries is available to the poor? Reforms to promote broader availability of credit may include, first of all, appropriate regulation and supervision of banking institutions that lend to small and microenterprises. Standard prudential banking regulations and supervisory practices (designed with traditional commercial-bank-lending technology and large loan sizes in mind) may unintentionally impede lending to small and microenterprises. Lending technology for micro loans can differ in important ways from that which is appropriate for larger customers. Applying supervisory norms appropriate for larger loans may make micro loans too expensive and reduce supply. To allow for micro lending, the regulatory and supervisory framework may have to be adapted with regard to operational restrictions, documentation requirements, capital requirements, and the treatment of collateral.

To promote expanded access to credit by small enterprises, ECA governments must establish an adequate legal and institutional framework for secured transactions. In much of the region, inadequate or nonexistent legal registries impede the use of movable goods or real property as collateral to secure loans. While this problem affects all firms, its greatest impact is on small firms. Sometimes the problem is the law itself. In Armenia, for example, the law restricts the kinds of goods that can be used as collateral (allowing only nonmovable property). This effectively limits access to credit for many small entrepreneurs. Even when the law allows for the use of different types of collateral, access to credit can be impeded by the lack of supporting institutions and implementation mechanisms. For example, a pervasive problem in the region is the lack of appropriate collateral registration procedures and of legal registries that allow a lender to ensure that there are no prior superior claims on an asset that a borrower pledges as collateral. The lack of legal registries is bound to be a more serious problem for small borrowers with no established reputation than for larger borrowers with well-established assets, reputations, and connections.

The most egregious failure in this regard is the lack of adequate land registries in many of the CIS countries, which impedes the use of the most important potential source of collateral for many households. Some countries have attempted to lessen this problem through extensive land titling programs to regularize the property rights of small farmers and tenants. Even in the absence of well-functioning legal registries, such titling can provide beneficiaries with an acceptable form of collateral and thus greater access to credit. However, progress with land titling in parts of the region has been fairly slow. In some cases progress has been hindered by land titling fees and property taxes, which some cash-strapped farmers have not been able to pay (Gomart 1999).

Other measures to improve the availability of credit to small borrowers could include establishing or strengthening credit bureaus, improving the legal framework for leasing and factoring, facilitating the development of small capitalization rural banks, and fostering the development of credit unions. Experiences to date with the promotion of rural credit unions in Armenia, Georgia, and Moldova have been very successful (chapter 5).

Labor Market Policies to Improve Distribution

Much of the inequality in Europe and Central Asia is associated with the collapse of formal wages and incomes for unskilled workers. Unskilled workers in Central and Eastern Europe and in the Baltics have seen their wages fall relative to those of more educated workers; and in some cases (Bulgaria and Estonia, for example), they have seen their real wages collapse in absolute terms as well. The formal incomes of unskilled workers in the CIS have plummeted in an even more striking manner. As a result, many of these workers have had to resort to secondary employment in either agriculture or trade as the sole means to maintain household incomes. Throughout the region, wage structures have shifted, devaluing the work of production workers relative to nonproduction activities (thus reversing the relative overvaluation of physical labor imposed by central planning).

At the core of these developments is reduced demand for low-skilled workers in response to (1) the restructuring of the formerly planned economies and (2) the removal of institutional constraints on wage setting. The pattern of this demand shift has differed markedly within the region. In the CSB countries there have been shifts in relative labor demands: low-skilled and poorly educated workers have lost out. In the CIS the real problem is the collapse of labor demand altogether; demand for both low-skilled and high-skilled workers has crashed.

In this context what can government policies do to reduce wage inequality? Given the differences in the underlying forces at work, will policies differ between CSB and CIS countries? The issue of regenerating formal labor demand in the CIS is intrinsically linked to establishing well-functioning factor and product markets that will allow private enterprise and demand for labor to spring up. Measures to support this were discussed in chapter 6. Here we will focus instead on policies to raise the wages of the unskilled.[4]

Policies to raise the wages of unskilled or low-skilled labor fall into two categories: policies to establish a minimum wage or wage floor; and policies to facilitate investments in human capital and to increase the productivity of the less skilled. Also important in the ECA context are policies to protect the income of workers who become temporarily unemployed, since these workers are likely to be low-educated or unskilled. These policies, discussed at length in chapter 8, will not be addressed here, except to note their impact on the distribution of wage incomes. Finally, policies to foster the labor force participation of women (and remove constraints such as discrimination or lack of childcare) can also have an important distributional impact.

Minimum Wages

The minimum wage has been used worldwide as a redistributive mechanism and an income protection mechanism for the poorest workers. Under central planning, the minimum wage directly and indirectly played this role in Europe and Central Asia as well. The intention was to provide a minimum acceptable threshold of wages (reflecting minimum living standards) for less-skilled workers. With the transition, however, the old standards for the minimum wage in many countries (especially in the former Soviet Union) have become meaningless or are not enforced. Given the observed large increase in inequality in much of the region, is there a renewed role for minimum wages?

The minimum wage plays a very different role in the CSB countries than it does in the CIS (figure 10.2). Minimum wages in the Eastern European countries are set at around 30 to 40 percent of the average wage—a level that is not high by OECD standards but high enough to provide a floor for low-skilled wages. In the case of Poland, the earnings distribution shows a big spike at the level of the minimum wage, which appears to be binding for blue-collar workers in some low-paying sectors (Rashid and Rutkowski 2000). In contrast, minimum wages in most of the CIS have fallen well-below subsistence levels, and they represent a negligible share of the average wage. In these countries minimum wages—when observed—are irrelevant as a policy for protecting workers.

There is an intense debate in both industrial and developing countries over the effectiveness of minimum wages as a redistributive tool. The overall evidence suggests that minimum wages may lead to small declines in inequality and somewhat larger positive effects on poverty. One study for the United States found that the decline of the real value of the minimum wage explained about one-third of the increase in wage inequality during the 1980s (Dinardo, Fortin, and Lemieux 1995). A different study, however, found only modest effects on earnings inequality and virtually no effect on family income inequality (Horrigan and Mincy 1993). In developing countries, most of the evidence points to very small effects. Bell (1997), for example, found that in Columbia the impact of the minimum

Figure 10.2   Minimum Wages in Europe and Central Asia, Selected Countries, 1997

Percentage or average wages

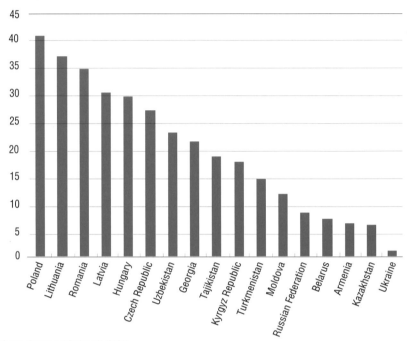

Source: Rashid and Rutkowski (2000).

wage on inequality was small, and it persisted during the period of economic recession. Ramos and Reis (1995) found a similarly small impact of minimum wages on inequality in Brazil. And the IADB (1998) found that reductions in minimum-wage purchasing power were associated with increases in the concentration of incomes (and vice versa) in 11 Latin American countries.

However, the use of minimum wages also has well-known risks. Some studies, mainly on OECD countries, have documented a negative effect of minimum wages (when set too high) on growth and employment, with long-term adverse effects for the poor. When labor markets are dualistic, as in many developing countries, minimum wages can work to lower the wages of workers in the informal sector, who are typically more needy (World Bank 1995). Once a minimum wage is set, pressures for it to be raised in real terms can be considerable. The risks of setting a too high minimum wage in Europe and Central Asia are of particular concern for the EU accession countries, where pressures to raise minimum wages to

European levels ahead of labor productivity could increase unemployment. Consider the experiences of Spain and Portugal following their accession to the European Union. Although both countries suffered similar economic shocks and had similar labor market institutions, Portugal has weathered the postaccession process with significantly less unemployment than has Spain. One possible reason for this is that Portugal has a much lower statutory minimum wage and less binding wage floors arising from collective bargaining. As a result, it has had more real wage flexibility at the bottom of the distribution than has Spain (box 10.1).

For the minimum wage to raise the real incomes of the poorest workers, it must meet three conditions. First, it must not reduce aggregate employment demand. Typically, this will require that the minimum wage be set low (below 40 percent of the average wage). When the minimum wage is low, it does not noticeably affect aggregate employment levels. When it is high, the employment destruction effects can be severe; the experience

---

Box 10.1   EU Accession and Income Inequality: The Cases of Spain and Portugal

Economic integration can exert a powerful influence over the distribution of income. In much of Latin America, economic integration has been associated with increasing inequality. Both Mexico and Chile, for example, experienced sharp increases in wage dispersion and growing inequality of incomes. However, the experience of those countries that recently acceded to the European Union was quite different. In both Spain and Portugal, income disparities declined during the 1980s following their accession into the EU. During the 1990s, household income inequality increased in Portugal but remained fairly flat in Spain. In both countries, market forces may have worked toward increasing disparities, but in Spain this was countered by the impact of taxes and transfers. In Portugal, on the contrary, national redistributive policies have been less relevant in terms of shaping the distribution of income.

EU regional policies and transfers have reduced regional differences in labor productivity in both countries. But given the low fraction of total income inequality explained by differences between regions, and the divergence of regional employment rates (especially in Spain), the overall impact of EU regional policy instruments has been relatively small.

Wage inequality has increased in both Spain and Portugal, reflecting a shift in the demand for labor toward higher skilled workers. The reduction of employment and wage shares of manual, semi-skilled, and low-skilled workers has been strong in manufacturing as well as in nontradable sectors such as transport. However, in Portugal, trade patterns favoring labor-intensive products, such as textiles, have sustained the wages of low-skilled workers and led to relatively low unemployment. In Spain, the sharp decline in demand for low-skilled workers combined with a rigid labor market; the result was very high levels of unemployment. Institutional arrangements, such as collective bargaining and the minimum wage, protected the wages of low-skilled workers in Spain more than in Portugal. Wages at the bottom of the distribution actually increased in Spain. This was another factor adding to high unemployment.

Source: Jimeno and others (2000).

of Puerto Rico during the 1970s, when it (briefly) adopted the U.S. minimum wage, is an example. Puerto Rico's experience, along with that of other countries, suggest that with high minimum wages, the elasticity of employment with respect to changes in the minimum wage can be over 1 (Castillo-Freeman and Freeman 1990).

Minimum wages in Europe and Central Asia are not especially high (figure 10.2), and they are unlikely to have significant aggregate employment effects. In the Czech Republic, for example, less than 10 percent of all employees earn the minimum wage (World Bank 1999b). However, in some CSB countries with higher minimum wages, most notably Poland, the minimum wage may be binding for certain groups (low-skilled, manual workers in low-paying sectors), and it may be hurting youth employment (Rashid and Rutkowski 2000). This suggests the need for caution in raising the real level of the minimum wage, particularly as these countries face EU accession.

Second, for the minimum wage to be effective as a redistributive mechanism, compliance must be high. This again will require that the minimum wage be set low: if the minimum is set so high that it affects employment, displaced workers and employers will collude to evade it. Evasion is likely to be as much of a problem in large enterprises as in small ones. In Venezuela and El Salvador, six out of every ten workers paid significantly less than the minimum wage are employed by large enterprises (IADB 1998). Unfortunately, reliable evidence on compliance with minimum wages in Europe and Central Asia is scarce. In Central Europe compliance is estimated to be quite high. However, in the CIS, getting enterprises to comply with payroll and other tax regulations is difficult. This signals that compliance would likely be a serious problem there as well.

Third, the minimum wage, to be effective, must be set at a level that covers a substantial group of low-income workers. Even when the minimum wage is set low, it can be badly targeted. In Argentina, where the minimum wage is set very low, only 30 percent of workers earning that level of wages come from the poorest quintile of the population. Just above 20 percent belong to the second quintile, and the rest come from middle-class and upper-class families. More than half of those who earn the minimum wage are young people who may or may not come from low earner households (IADB 1998). No comparable information is available for ECA countries, but evidence from Poland suggests that the minimum wage there may disproportionately affect young workers, independent of their household income. In this case, and even in the best of circumstances (no employment effect and high compliance), increases in the minimum wage will affect the overall distribution of income only slightly. In other words, as a tool to influence the distribution of income, the minimum wage will be largely ineffective.

One possibility for improving the targeting of the minimum wage is to distinguish between the wage paid to young workers and that paid to potential heads of household. Governments can establish a lower minimum wage for young workers, as is done in many European countries. An additional advantage of this approach is that it can reduce employers' disincentive to hire young workers with little or no experience, which is likely to exist when the adult minimum wage is binding for them as well.

An alternative to the minimum wage is to use wage supplements for low-income workers. In the United States the earned income tax credit is an example of this type of tool. It works as a negative tax for low-income workers and is administered by the tax collection office. These programs, however, can introduce perverse incentive effects. Indeed, there is the danger of creating a "poverty trap." Moreover, wage supplement programs are administratively very burdensome—and hence unsuited to many ECA countries with weak institutional capacity. Another alternative is to subsidize enterprises that contract workers below a certain income level. The hope would be that the subsidy would reduce unemployment of low-skilled workers and thus affect the distribution of earnings. However, as the experience in industrial countries has shown, enterprises often simply "churn" low-wage workers, with few real gains in terms of overall employment and incomes. Programs in the Czech Republic, Poland, and Hungary have yielded mixed results. Positive and lasting employment effects have been identified in Poland, but the benefits in the other two countries are less clear (Fretwell, Benus, and O'Leary 1999).

Training and Investments in Worker Productivity

Formal education affects income inequality through its long-term effects on the earnings potential of children from low-income families and through its effect on labor supply decisions of women. But formal education holds little hope for raising the income or employment possibilities of low-educated adults who have long since left school. For these individuals, training programs and other forms of assistance to increase their skills could, however, make a difference. Such training would aim at providing them with new skills better suited to the market economy.

The effectiveness of training schemes has been debated for a long time. There is a wealth of evaluation studies, with different methodologies and settings and with widely different results. This makes it hard to arrive at any firm conclusions. However, the general evidence suggests that some types of training programs, especially those directly linked to potential employers, can be effective. Program size and design are critical to their performance. Standardized training programs do not fit all workers; the programs must be targeted and tailored carefully. A recent study evaluated training schemes for unemployed workers in three transition countries (the Czech Republic, Hungary, and Poland) and found generally positive, although very small, employment effects. The employment effect was larger for women than for men (a finding common to most evaluations of OECD training schemes), and for young and middle-age workers than for older workers. Training was also found to be more effective for workers with low levels of education (primary and secondary as opposed to postsecondary education)—a finding consistent with the large skill-mismatches within these economies resulting from the low level and low quality of the educational stock (Fretwell, Benus, and O'Leary 1999).

The Fretwell, Benus, and O'Leary study, unfortunately, was limited to evaluating programs in those three higher-income Central European transition countries. We know little about the actual or potential effectiveness of programs in other countries of the region. The potential for training or other types of active labor market policies in countries with large informal markets, a collapsed formal labor demand, limited administrative capacity, and a limited information base may, in fact, be very small.

Training programs can help individuals with or without experience upgrade their skills, but the training must be offered on a selective basis and only after a careful examination of labor market conditions. All programs should have an impact evaluation component built in from the start. Preferably, training should be carried out in association with the potential employer and involve an on-the-job component. General training in skills widely in demand (languages, computers) can be considered as well as other alternatives, such as assistance with re-entry to institutes of higher learning. Private sector provision of training should be given priority, and constraints to individuals engaging on their own in such activities must be assessed to minimize the extent to which the intervention may have displacement effects.

Policies to Foster the Participation of Women in the Labor Force

Whether or not women participate in the labor force makes a significant difference in the distribution of family income. Throughout Europe and Central Asia families with low dependency ratios have higher household incomes and a much lower probability of being poor (chapter 2). Women's labor force participation also has beneficial effects on the intrahousehold distribution of consumption, reduces women's vulnerability to violence, and improves investments in children.

Prior to the transition, more women in ECA countries participated in the labor force than in almost any other industrialized country. In the Soviet Union in the 1980s, about 90 percent of prime-age women were either employed or went to school (UNICEF 1999). Participation rates for women in Central and Eastern Europe averaged between 65 and 75 percent. These high rates of labor force participation were built, to a large extent, on the availability of government-subsidized child care programs (nurseries, preschool, kindergartens, and after-school programs) in all ECA countries before the transition.

Women's labor force participation rates were expected to decline with the transition to levels more in line with OECD countries. Indeed, between 1989 and 1996 the rates fell by about 12 percentage points in the Czech Republic (for the female population 15 and older); by 8 percentage points in the Slovak Republic; by 12 percentage points in Slovenia; and by nearly 20 percentage points in Hungary (World Bank 1999b, 1999e; Loshkin 1999; Paukert 1998). The drops in labor force participation were not equally distributed across income classes, however, and they disproportionately affected women with little education and skills and from poor households (Loshkin 1999; Yemtsov 1999).

In Russia the decline in female labor force participation rates has been linked to an increase in the cost of child care, especially among low-income families (Loshkin 1999). Loshkin finds that labor force participation decisions of Russian women are strongly influenced by the cost of child care, which has increased sharply with the transition.[5] He concludes that lowering the cost of child care would have a strong positive effect on the labor activity of women and hence indirectly on household incomes. The positive effect of lowering child care costs on household incomes, and hence indirectly on poverty, would be larger than what is obtained via the existing system of family transfers (child allowances).

The link between women's labor force participation, family incomes, and child care (as well as the existing evidence on the positive impact of child care on child development) could justify a renewed role for ECA governments in ensuring that quality care is available for children. Governments need not provide or finance all child care, but they have an important role to play in regulating and providing the right environment for these services to develop. Governments can leverage scarce public resources by supporting existing private and/or informal arrangements and by building partnerships with community groups, nongovernmental and religious organizations, existing social services, and the private sector.

Government also has an important role to play in providing financial support to the poorest families to guarantee them access to affordable child care.

Policies to Reduce Discrimination against Women in the Labor Market

In most transition economies the wage gap between men and women has either fallen or remained relatively stable since the start of the transition. Only in Bulgaria has the gender wage gap increased sharply (by about 5 percentage points since 1989). Controlling for human capital and other job-related factors, we find that the gender wage gap ranges from a low of 11 to 16 percent in the Federal Republic of Yugoslavia, Hungary, and Poland, to a high of 39.5 percent in Azerbaijan (UNICEF 1999).

A number of factors have reduced the pay gap between men and women since the start of the transition. First, since women on average have higher educational attainment than men throughout the region, the increase in labor market returns to education has worked in their favor. Second, there has been a slight trend toward a reduction of occupational segregation, which was high under socialism, again with beneficial effects for women. Countering these positive developments, however, is evidence suggesting that in high-unemployment settings, women may face greater difficulties than men in finding jobs.

A survey of unemployed people in Poland revealed that 40 percent of men but only 25 percent of women found work within a year of becoming unemployed. The main explanation for this gender difference was marital status. Married men were twice as likely to find work as were married women. This reflects women's greater responsibility for child care, which hampers job hunting and may limit employment options, as well as some discrimination by employers (UNICEF 1999).

In part, these discriminatory attitudes may be linked to the high level of mandated maternity benefits in most ECA countries, a policy that may indirectly hurt the employment prospects of married women. Contributing to this discrimination are cultural factors and pervasive gender stereotypes. By shortening the length of mandated maternity benefits and allowing small and medium firms greater flexibility in the level of benefits they offer, governments may reduce employers' reluctance to hire married women. Labor laws in many countries prohibit women from performing certain types of heavy work and from dangerous occupations, which also constricts women's employment opportunities. Modernizing this legal framework to allow for greater *de jure* equality could help reduce occupational segregation and discrimination against women.

Women seem to suffer more from wage arrears than do men, although this finding appears linked to their higher participation in industries where arrears are common, especially health care, education, and finance. Gender does not seem to be a factor in determining the risk of wage arrears at an individual level, indicating that the decisions of employers and managers related to arrears were not determined by gender bias per se.

Overall, there is no clear trend on whether the labor market situation of women has improved relative to that of men, or worsened, during the transition. However, in many countries in the region, and despite constitutional affirmations that women and men are legally equal, women do face some forms of structural discrimination, which spill over into the labor market and into differing opportunities for men and women. One area in which discrimination is particularly strong is family law. The rules of joint property in the Czech Republic and Azerbaijan, for example, do not adequately support women in divorce situations or in nonmarital unions. Laws in Bulgaria, Ukraine, and Armenia actively discriminate against women and fail to protect girls by allowing a lower legal marriage age for girls than for boys.

While the broad legal framework for equality seems to be in place in most countries, there is much to do in terms of making it a reality in the workplace, family, and community. Progress on this front is crucial to ensuring that women and children get a fair share of opportunities and to reducing inequalities between the sexes over the medium term.

Policies to Foster Labor Force Participation of People with Disabilities

Labor force participation rates for people with disabilities are low everywhere in the world. Drawing people with disabilities into the labor force is a stated objective in most countries. Two approaches predominate: economic incentives designed to encourage people with disabilities to work and to encourage employers to hire people with disabilities; and legislation empowering people with disabilities to combat discrimination with the force of law—that is, a "civil rights" approach. The economic incentive approach is based on the notion that disability is a medical condition that reduces productivity. Economic incentives are needed to compensate for lower productivity. The civil rights approach is based on the notion that prejudice and misunderstanding are the greatest obstacles to the employment of people with disabilities. Legislation is needed to reduce physical and social obstacles that unnecessarily exclude people with impairments. Poland has chosen to rely very heavily on economic incentives, almost to the exclusion of the civil rights approach—without, however, great success. Poland was the first country in the world to implement a "quota-levy" system (box 10.2). The system began in 1920, following the return home of soldiers injured in the Great War.

Quota levy systems still exist in over half of the EU countries, but other countries are moving away from them. The United Kingdom abandoned its quota system and Netherlands gave up on a planned system. Portugal considered but decided against a quota system, and Ireland and Belgium have limited their systems to the public sector. Germany and France reformed existing systems.[6]

Instead, countries in Europe and elsewhere are relying more on antidiscrimination legislation. The flagship for this approach is the U.S. Americans with Disabilities Act of 1990 (together with earlier legislation on civil rights and disability). Australia's Disability Discrimination Act of 1993 outlaws all discrimination on the grounds of disability. England's Disability Discrimination Act of 1995 makes it illegal to discriminate against people with disabilities in employment and commerce. Austria, Germany,

---

Box 10.2 Poland's Experience with the Quota-Levy System

The quota-levy system currently in place in Poland requires enterprises to reach an employment quota of 6 percent persons with disabilities or to pay a levy. The levy is about 40 percent of the average wage for each person short of the quota. Most enterprises choose to pay the levy rather than hire any workers with disabilities at all. As a revenue-generator, the quota-levy system is a success—it is like a 2.4 percent wage tax. As a mechanism to increase the employment of persons with disabilities, though, it must be considered a failure.

The revenue generated by the quota-levy system, together with generous tax privileges, finances Sheltered Work Establishments (SWEs). At least 40 percent of the people they employ must have disabilities and 10 percent of them must have moderate or severe disabilities. In fact, most people with disabilities employed by SWEs have only slight disabilities—in many countries, they would not be considered disabled. At the end of 1998, 3,100 SWEs employed about 230,000 people with disabilities out of about 700,000 people with disabilities who were employed. SWEs are obligated to spend the subsidies they receive to improve working conditions for employees with disabilities. However, Polish critics of the SWE system argue that it does not encourage inclusion of workers with disabilities into the mainstream labor force and that the money serves mainly to enrich entrepreneurs clever enough to exploit the subsidies. Critics also charge that the SWE system is politically self-perpetuating, because the subsidies to SWEs create the means for disability entrepreneurs to make contributions to politicians who then champion their cause.

and Finland have all amended their constitutions to prohibit discrimination on the grounds of disability.[5]

The economic incentives and civil rights approaches are based on different philosophies, but at least in principle they should complement each other. With proper coordination, each has the potential to make the other more effective.

Using the Redistributive Power of Fiscal Policy

A key role of governments in most societies is to combat market failure—which includes the inability of purely private endeavor to provide adequate sustenance for everyone in the population. Governments throughout the world have traditionally played an important role in improving the distribution of income and directing resources to the poor. In the centrally planned economies, the state's redistributive role was of central importance. Today, as those economies turn toward the market, the state still has a role to play, albeit an altered one. Indeed, a broad majority of the population of the transition economies believes that the state ought to play such a redistributive role, even in a market-oriented economy. A recent survey of Russian households showed that three out of every four Russians believe that the government should "tax the incomes of the very rich and help the poor" (Ravallion and Lokshin 1999). Similarly, interviews with poor individuals through the region reveal that they believe the state has a responsibility to help them (World Bank 1999a). Many of these individuals, however, have little hope that the state will be able to fulfill that responsibility (box 10.3).

Before the transition the role of the state in all centrally planned economies was similar. Today, however, the size of the state, as measured by the share of public spending in GDP, varies greatly across ECA countries. In much of Central and Eastern Europe, public spending remains large, and in line with that observed in most OECD economies. These large public expenditures, particularly those spent on social programs and transfers, have lessened the inequality arising from pure market-determined outcomes. In contrast, much of the CIS has seen the size of the state shrink dramatically—in some cases to levels incompatible with the delivery of the most basic government functions. This collapse of state spending, along with deteriorating targeting of transfers, has accentuated the increase in inequality.

The apparent correlation between the size of the state and the extent of inequality in the transition economies does not mean that a bigger government is necessarily better for the poor. The impact of public spending

> ## Box 10.3   Citizens' View of Government in Europe and Central Asia
>
> Many in the the former Soviet Union believe that the state has abandoned its citizens. The prevalent view of state government in the wake of the Soviet collapse is of a dishonest, uncaring institution. Even in some Eastern European countries, there is nostalgia for the relative egalitarian system of the past.
>
> > *Politicians don't care about the suffering population.* (Moldova, 1997)
> >
> > *People place their hope in God, since the government is no longer involved in such matters.* (Armenia, 1995)
> >
> > [The state is] *a parent which should take care of its children.* (Georgia, 1997)
> >
> > [In the socialist era] *there were no such great differences between people, there was no poverty. There was a middle class that lived well.* (Macedonia, 1998)
>
> *Source:* World Bank (1999a).

on the distribution of income is not driven by the total amount of resources spent. Instead it depends on the efficiency with which those resources are spent and on how well they are targeted. An extreme example of this can be found in Brazil, which has the largest government in all of Latin America (in line with that of a developed country) and yet the highest inequality in the world. What is different between the CSB countries and those of the CIS is not just that public spending has collapsed more in the latter, driven by the dramatic fall in revenues. The significant difference is that in the CSB the state has been able to use its resources more effectively and deliver its services more efficiently, including that of improving the distribution of income.

Figure 10.3 plots the size of the state, as measured by the ratio of public spending to GDP, against post-transition levels of income inequality. The countries where public spending has shrunk the most are those with the worst distributions of income. This is consistent with the regression estimates in table 10.4, which indicated that the size of government spending had a progressive impact on overall inequality, even when controlling for initial conditions and for progress on liberalization. Interestingly, the effect of government spending was not found to be independent of the government deficit. In fact, the negative impact of government deficits on the distribution of income could swamp the positive expenditure effect.

Figure 10.3 also shows where other regions would fall in the inequality-government spending relationship. This highlights the huge variance in ECA countries with regard to the size of government. Most of the countries of the CSB have spending levels that are well above even OECD standards. The Slavic republics tend to fall between OECD levels of spend-

Figure 10.3   Government Spending and Inequality in Europe and Central Asia and Elsewhere

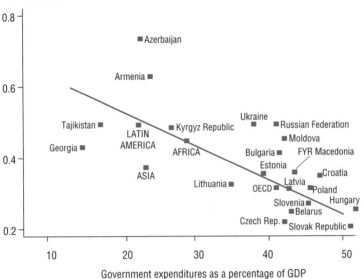

Note: The correlation equals -0.71. The observations of the inequality-government spending relationship for non-ECA regions were not used to calculate the correlation and implicit line. They were simply added to this figure for comparative purposes.
Source: For Europe and Central Asia, authors' calculations from Dethier, Ghanem, and Zoli (1999) dataset and representative household surveys. For other regions, IADB (1999).

ing and those of other regions but are notably above the latter. The Caucasus and the poorer countries of Central Asia, on the other hand, stand out for their very low public spending levels, which are below the average for Latin America, Asia, or Africa.

Figure 10.3 suggests that the potential to use fiscal policy as a redistributive tool varies greatly across ECA countries. Tax and expenditure priorities also may be different across countries. Based on this diversity, we can distinguish between three broad groups of countries:

- The countries of Central and South Eastern Europe, where governments are relatively strong and where a broader revenue base suggests that there is significant scope for using fiscal policy to affect the distribution of income;

- The middle-income Slavic republics, the Baltics, and middle-income Central Asian republics, where government is modest in size but where, given improvements in tax collections and better targeting of expenditures, there is potential for fiscal policy to have some redistributive effect; and

- The low-income countries of the Caucasus and Central Asia, where public spending is currently insufficient for governments to fulfill even their most essential tasks and deliver basic social services. In these countries the focus must be on raising revenues enough to finance a minimum level of government services, including appropriate spending on health and education. The potential for fiscal policy to play a short-term redistributive role is limited, but its importance in preventing the entrenchment of long-term inequality is large.

Fiscal Policy in CSB Countries

Taxes and transfers have had a significant redistributive impact in most of the Central and South Eastern European countries, and especially in the first round of EU accession candidates (Garner and Terrell 1999; Keane and Prasad 1999; Milanovic 1999). These redistributive policies have played an important role in dampening the increase in poverty and preventing the emergence of large social and income disparities. However, this achievement has not been without costs. Social insurance systems (pensions and unemployment insurance)—used extensively to cushion the impact of large-scale redundancies and protect the elderly from poverty—are running increasing deficits and posing a growing fiscal burden that could threaten macro stability in the medium term. In some countries overly generous systems may be distorting consumption and labor choices and fostering an incipient culture of dependency (chapter 8). Most importantly, by relying on high payroll taxes to support these generous systems, CSB countries run the risk of following in the European Union's footsteps and building a labor market environment that is biased against low-wage and low-skill workers. In much of the European Union, high nonwage labor costs have contributed to high rates of unemployment among low-skilled workers (Dolado and others 1986; Bean and Blanchard 1997; and Bentolila and Revenga 1995). This is a trap that CSB needs to avoid. High tax burdens also pose a disincentive to investment and can ultimately slow down growth.

A fiscal priority in this subregion is to reform social assistance and social insurance systems. The goal is to improve their efficiency and reduce their fiscal costs while maintaining their demonstrated effectiveness at protecting the unemployed, the elderly, the poor, and other vulnerable groups. Pension reform is at the top of the agenda because of the accumulation of large contingent liabilities in this area. Some of these countries have already introduced multipillar systems quite successfully (Hungary, Poland, and Slovenia); others are in the process of doing so (Romania, Croatia, Latvia, and FYR Macedonia). Another priority on the expenditure side is to streamline social assistance programs, improve their targeting, and introduce work incentives to avoid welfare dependency. There also is scope for improving schemes of help the unemployed, mainly by tightening eligibility criteria, lowering payroll taxes, and distributing the burden more equally between employees and employers. An alternative for countries with less administrative capacity is to opt for one-time severance pay schemes, which are easier to administer and may have less perverse incentive effects.

Fiscal Policy in Middle-Income Transition Economies: The Baltics, the Slavic Republics, and Central Asia

The redistributive impact of taxation in this group of countries seems to be small. In both Estonia and Lithuania, despite fairly high tax compliance, the total redistributive impact of direct taxation amounts to only 1 and 2 Gini points respectively (Cornelius and Weder 1999). Computations for Russia similarly indicate that the total redistributive impact of taxation is modest (Commander and Lee 1998). Although the Russian tax system is progressive on paper and became more progressive during the 1990s, the principal base for taxation is wages, and since its share in total incomes has dropped, so has the distributional impact of taxes. More importantly, the overall effect of taxation is directly conditioned by significant tax arrears, whose incidence is not random but somewhat regressive (Alexeev and Grady 1993).

There is room for making taxation more progressive in most of these republics, particularly through the elimination of tax exemptions, the reduction of tax arrears, and through measures that eventually will increase the share of formal wages in total incomes. But the scope for influencing the distribution of income via progressive taxation of labor earnings may be limited—certainly more limited than in Central Europe. Recent theoretical and empirical research on Chile, for example, suggests that the more unequal the pre-tax distribution, the less the scope for directly improving income distribution via progressive taxes (Engel, Galetovic, and Raddatz 1998). In Russia and large parts of the CIS, tax evasion is a major problem, rendering progressive taxation less effective. Labor incomes—which represent the part of household incomes most easily taxed and least subject to evasion—are relatively low in all but the top decile. This results in a relatively low average tax rate and relatively little redistribution. It may be more promising for governments to focus on the average tax rate and then target expenditures: high-yield, indirect taxes (such as the broad-based value added tax) may be much more effective at raising revenues and ultimately prove to be more progressive if spending is adequately targeted. The analysis on Chile suggests that distributional considerations should affect only the decision on the size of the overall tax burden. Once this is decided, revenues should be raised with the most efficient tax, and income inequality addressed through the expenditure side.

There is more potential for affecting the distribution of income through expenditure policy. The priority in this regard is to improve the targeting of transfers and make them more progressive. Commander and Lee (1998) and Commander and others (1999) show that the incidence of transfers in Russia (especially pensions) has become more regressive during the transition (with 50 percent of total transfers accruing to the top 20 percent of the distribution). Those transfers that are better targeted, such as child allowances, have become nearly insignificant. The overall effect is to make total transfers regressive: that is, they contribute to increasing total income inequality rather than reducing it. In contrast, in all three Baltic countries, pensions and social assistance are progressively distributed and contribute significantly to increasing welfare and to reducing inequality (Cornelius and Weder 1999; Milanovic 1999).

Improvements in targeting will not be easy to achieve. And efforts to increase the coverage and effectiveness of social transfers must be weighed against existing resource constraints to ensure that programs provide protection without compromising efficiency and growth. There is, however, much scope for improving the efficiency with which resources are used by simplifying schemes and adapting them to countries' levels of income, by improving their administration, and by tailoring programs to groups truly in need (chapter 8).

Fiscal Policy in the Low-Income Transition Economies

The top fiscal priority in these countries is to increase tax revenues to a level that will allow governments to perform at least their most basic functions. The complete collapse of state revenues in some of the poorer countries of the region has endangered the delivery of basic education and health services as well as the maintenance of public infrastructure and law and order. Countries cannot provide income-earning opportunities to their citizens without a functioning state. And such a state needs a minimum level of revenues. With revenues on the order of 9 percent of GDP, Georgia provides less than $6 per capita per year to the public education system. Families with means can make up for the ensuing collapse in quality through private lessons and other informal mechanisms. The poor cannot. This handicaps the earnings potential of their children. In the absence of a minimally functioning state, income and social disparities can become deeply entrenched, passed on from one generation to the next.

The key to raising revenues—more important even than improving administration or lessening corruption—is political will. Weak or captured states may have little ability to enforce tax compliance by politically powerful groups. Therefore, reforms to strengthen the state and reduce state capture are critical (chapter 5). Also promising may be efforts to separate the management and administration of revenues from the political sphere. Georgia's recent subcontracting of customs management to a private company will provide an interesting case study for the region in this regard (World Bank 1999p).

Tax instruments in these countries must be adapted to the level of income. Because of the large informal sectors and low-income levels in these countries, direct taxation is unlikely to yield significant revenues in the foreseeable future. Reliance on high-yield, indirect taxes such as the VAT makes more sense, even if such a consumption tax can appear regressive. As the experience of Chile and other developing countries illustrates, a well-administered VAT can yield high revenues that can be spent progressively, with an overall positive effect on the distribution of income. Like other low-income countries, the poor countries in Europe and Central Asia will need to depend extensively on excise and international trade taxes as a source of revenue. Improvement of customs administration and enforcement is thus critical.

On the expenditure side, the priority in these countries is not to engage in redistributive policies per se but to ensure a minimum level of equal opportunity for all. The highest priority spending must be in education and health to ensure adequate access to and quality of services to the poor. Spending on law and order as well as on basic infrastructure is also of crucial importance to the poor. Given the resource constraints, the scope for using transfers is limited. But small, well-targeted transfers can have an impact. Simulations for Georgia, for example, show that even a modest transfer envelope of 1 percent of GDP, if accurately targeted, can have a large impact on poverty (World Bank 1999a). Unfortunately, for these programs to work there needs to be a firm commitment from the government to deliver this benefit. Georgia's experience with a very limited poverty benefit has been disappointing. In 1999, only 37 percent of the budget allocated for the poverty benefit was actually paid out to its intended beneficiaries—even though the total planned budget for the program was only 14 million laris, or 1.2 percent of consolidated government spending (0.3 percent of GDP). Actual paid expenditures on the poverty benefit were a miniscule 0.4 percent of consolidated budget spending, or less than 0.1 percent of GDP. Armenia and the Kyrgyz Republic have been far more successful at introducing and operating limited benefit schemes targeted to the poor.

Notes

1. There are many reasons why inequality can have a direct negative impact on growth. If capital markets are imperfect, inequality can reduce investment opportunities and worsen borrowers' incentives, with negative consequences for growth. High inequality can also increase macroeconomic volatility and hence indirectly affect growth. And greater inequality can create large divergences in interests, which can prevent the adoption of socially efficient policies.

2. Nonfinancial micro-constraints constitute the main barrier to the emergence and expansion of new private enterprises throughout the region. Inflation comes next, followed by lack of financing, corruption, and anticompetitive practices.

3. Arrears fall disproportionately on workers with low wages and little education (chapter 4).

4. Once demand for labor recovers in the CIS, patterns are likely to follow the trend we have seen in Central and Eastern Europe: low skilled and poorly educated workers lose out. As this happens, these policies will gain in importance for the CIS as well as for CSB.

5. According to GosKomStat, Russia's statistical agency, the proportion of Russian children in preschool facilities dropped by more than 50 percent between the mid-1980s and the mid-1990s. This sharp decline in the number of kindergartens and nurseries was accompanied throughout the region by an increase in the cost of government-provided care. Before the transition, childcare costs were typically covered (partially or totally) by subsidies from the federal and local governments or by employers. By 2000, most company-provided daycare services in the CIS had been transferred to local and municipal governments, which usually lack the resources to operate them at all.

6. The material in these paragraphs draws heavily on Metts (2000).

References

Aghion, Philippe, Eva Caroli, and Cecilia Garcia-Peñalosa. 1999. "Inequality and Growth: The Perspective of the New Growth Theories." *Journal of Economic Literature*, vol. 37.

Alexeev, Michal, and Clifford G. Gaddy. 1993. "Income Distribution in the U.S.S.R. in the 1980s." *Review of Income and Wealth* 39 (March): 23–36.

Bell, Linda. 1997. "The Impact of Minimum Wages in Mexico and Colombia." *Journal of Labor Economics* (U.S.) 15 (July): S102–S135.

Benabou, Roland. 1997. "Inequality and Growth." *NBER Macroeconomic Annual*. National Bureau of Economic Research.

Bentolila, Samuel, and Ana Revenga. 1995. "The Employment Content of Output Growth: A Cross-Country Analysis." Paper prepared for the CEPR Conference on Unemployment Policy, Vigo, September 1994. Also available as Documento de Trabajo N. 9517, Banco de España (April 1995).

Blanchard, Olivier. 1998. "Revisiting European Unemployment: Unemployment, Capital Accumulation and Factor Prices." National Bureau of Economic Research (NBER) Working Paper Series (U.S.), No. 6566:1–39. May.

Castillo-Freeman, Alida, and Richard Freeman. 1990. "Minimum Wages in Puerto Rico: Textbook Case of a Wage Floor?" National Bureau of Economic Research Working Paper Series (U.S.), No. 3759:1–23. June.

Commander, Simon, and Une Lee. 1998. "How Does Public Policy Affect the Income Distribution? Evidence from Russia, 1992–96." London: European Bank for Reconstruction and Development. Processed.

Commander, Simon, Andrei Tolstopiatenko, and Ruslan Yemtsov. 1999. "Channels of Redistribution: Inequality and Poverty in the Russian Transition." *Economics of Transition* 7(2): 411–47.

Cornelius, Peter K., and Beatrice Weder. 1996. "Economic Transformation and Income Distribution: Some Evidence from the Baltic Countries." Staff Papers, International Monetary Fund (International); 43:587–604. September.

De Melo, Martha, Cevdet Denizer, and Alan Gelb. 1996. "From Plan to Market: Patterns of Transition." World Bank Policy Research Paper 1564. Washington, D.C.

Dethier, Jean-Jacques, Hafez Ghanem, and Edda Zoli. 1999. "Does Democracy Facilitate the Economic Transition? An Empirical Study of Central and Eastern Europe and the Former Soviet Union." Policy Research Working Paper 2194, World Bank, Poverty Reduction and Economic Management Sector Unit, Europe and Central Asia Region. Washington, D.C. October.

Dinardo, John, Nicole Fortin, and Thomas Lemieux. 1995. "Labor Market Institutions and the Distribution of Wages, 1973–1992: A Semiparametric Approach." National Bureau of Economic Research Working Paper Series (U.S.), No. 5093:1–62. April.

Dolado, Juan J., and Jose Luis Malo de Molina. 1986. "Spanish Industrial Unemployment: Some Explanatory Factors." *Economica* (UK) 53 (Supplement): S313–S334.

EBRD (European Bank for Reconstruction and Development). 1999. *Transition Report*. London.

Engel, Eduardo, Alexander Galetovic, and Claudio Raddatz. 1998. "Taxes and Income Distribution in Chile: Some Unpleasant Redistributive Arithmetic." Centro de Economia Aplicada (Chile), Documentos de Trabajo No. 41. September.

Fretwell, Benus, and O'Leary. 1999. "Evaluating the Impact of Active Labor Market Programs." World Bank Social Protection Discussion Paper 9915. June.

Garner, Thesia I., and Katherine Terrell. 1998. "A Gini Decomposition Analysis of Inequality in the Czech and Slovak Republics during the Transition." *Economics of Transition* 6(1):23–46.

Gomart, Elizabeth. 1999. "Armenia: Social Assessment of the Poorest of the Poor." In *Improving Social Assistance in Armenia*, Report 19385-AM. Washington, D.C.: World Bank.

Harrigan, Michael W., and Ronald B. Mincy. 1993. *The Minimum Wage and Earnings and Income Inequality*. New York: Russell Sage Foundation.

IADB (Inter-American Development Bank). 1998/99. *Facing Up to Inequality in Latin America*. Economic and Social Progress in Latin America Annual Report. Washington D.C.

Jimeno, Juan F. and others. 2000. "Integration and Inequality: Lessons from the Accessions of Portugal and Spain to the EU." *Background Papers: Making the Transition Work for Everyone: Poverty and Inequality in Europe and Central Asia*, Washington, D.C.

Keane, Michael P., and Eswar S. Prasad. 2000. "Inequality, Transfers and Growth: New Evidence from the Economic Transition in Poland." IMF Working Paper. May.

Lokshin, Michael. 1999. "Household Child Care Choices and Women's Work Behavior in Russia." Working Paper 2206. World Bank, Development Research Group, Poverty and Human Resources.

Metts, Robert. 2000. "Disability Issues, Trends, and Recommendations for the World Bank." Social Protection Discussion Paper 0007. Washington, D.C.: World Bank.

Milanovic, Branko. 1999. "Explaining the Increase in Inequality during the Transition." Policy Research Working Paper 1935. World Bank, Washington, D.C.

Paukert, L. 1998. "Economic Transformation and Women's Employment in Four Central European Countries: 1989–1994." Labor Market Paper 7. International Labor Office.

Ramos, Lauro, and Jose G. A. Reis. 1995. "Salario minimo, distribuicao de renda, e pobreze no Brasil." *Pesquisae Planejamento Economico* 25 (April):99–114.

Rashid, Mansoora, and Jan Rutkowski. 2000. *Labor Markets in Transition Economies.* World Bank Strategy Paper. March.

Ravallion, Maartin, and Michael Lokshin. 1999. "Subjective Economic Welfare." World Bank, Development Research Group, Poverty and Human Resources. Washington, D.C. Processed.

Sen, Amartya. 1992. *Inequality Reexamined.* Oxford: Clarendon Press, and Cambridge, Mass.: Harvard University Press.

Smeeding, Tim. 1997. "American Income Inequality in a Cross-National Perspective." Luxembourg Income Study Working Paper 157.

Squire, Lyn, and Heng-Fu Zou. 1998. "Explaining International and Intertemporal Variations in Income Inequality." *Economic Journal: The Journal of the Royal Economic Society* (U.K.) 108 (January):26–43.

UNICEF. 1999. "Women in Transition." *Regional Monitoring Reports,* No. 6. Florence: UNICEF International Child Development Center.

World Bank. 1995. *Workers in an Integrating World.* New York: Oxford University Press.

———. 1999a. "Consultations with the Poor: A Review of World Bank Participatory Poverty Assessments." (Includes Armenia, 1995; Georgia, 1997; FYR Macedonia, 1998; and Moldova, 1997.)

———. 1999b. *Czech Republic: Towards EU Accession, 1999.*

———. 1999c. *Georgia: Poverty and Income Distribution.* Report 19348-GE, 1999, vols. 1 and 2.

———. 1999d. *Georgia: Structural Reforms Support Project.*

———. 1999e. *Slovenia: Economic Transformation and EU Accession.*

———. 1999f. "An Informal Note on the Banking Sector in Armenia." Processed.

Yemtsov, Ruslan. 1999. "Inequality and Income Distribution." *Georgia: Poverty and Income Distribution,* 1999. vol. 2: Technical Papers, Report 19348-GE.

Measurement of Living Standards and Inequality

Measurement of Living Standards

To examine poverty and inequality, we need a measure of well-being. Ideally, this measure should correspond as closely as possible to the way individuals experience their standards of living, including the effects of access to social services; social stigma; stress; insecurity; vulnerability; and social exclusion. Here we focus only on material well-being, which we measure using information on household expenditure or income.

The construction of the measure of material well-being involves two steps. First, we need to decide whether to base it on income or consumption, and which components of income or consumption to include. Second, we need to decide how to adjust the income or consumption measure for economies of scale at the household level.

To estimate a poverty rate based on the measure of well-being, we need to establish a poverty line. The poverty line is discussed below. More detailed information on the measurement of living standards and the calculation of poverty and inequality statistics can be found in World Bank (1993), Ravallion (1994), and Deaton (1997). This measure of well-being can also be used to calculate inequality statistics.

Material Well-Being as a Consumption or Income Aggregate

There are several reasons why household consumption (money expenditures plus the value of food produced on a household plot) is believed to be more accurate than income for measuring well-being in transition economies. In many CIS countries people are paid very irregularly, with several months of wage arrears common. In this context, consumption is smoothed while income is very erratic. Furthermore, income underreporting is marked, because survey respondents are not willing to fully disclose illegal or semilegal income sources. Finally, produce from the household plot has become a mainstay of food consumption and this is not a standard component of money income.

Hence, in this book, we rely mainly on consumption-based measures of poverty, although we use income-based ones for a few countries where a measure of consumption information is available.[1] Consumption is generally defined as the sum of expenditures on current purchases plus the value of food produced and consumed by the household. Ideally, the use-value rather than the purchase expenditures of consumer durables and real estate should be included. In practice, the imputation of these use-values is not always possible and the monetary value of home-production is not always known. Hence, the consumption definitions used for the countries in this study vary somewhat in their treatment of consumer durables and the value of food produced by the household (see table C.2 for details).

This book uses both the income and consumption aggregates to calculate measures of inequality. While consumption may be a more accurate measure of material well-being, examining income inequality offers two benefits. First, it is easier to make international comparisons using income inequality since income inequality statistics are available for more countries. Second, we can obtain insights into the drivers of inequality by decomposing income inequality into the contributions of the various income sources.

Adjustment for Economies of Scale

Household income or expenditure needs to be adjusted for household composition to be a useful measure of material well-being. Clearly, a one-person household living on $250 per month is materially better off than a five-person household living on $250 per month. A simple solution is to divide by the number of household members, but most people would agree that a five-person household with $250 per month is better off than a single person having to live on $50 per month because of economies of scale in consumption. Economies of scale arise in many ways—for example, by sharing certain expenditures such as expenditures on housing, utilities, cars, or newspapers. Apart from household size, the age or gender of household members may also influence the amount of income or consumption needed to attain a certain level of well-being. It is commonly thought, for example, that the consumption needs of very young children are less than working-age adults.

Economies of scale can be approximated by adjusting the household size variable to derive a variable called equivalent household size. For example, a household with an equivalent size of 3.5 needs to spend 3.5 times as much as a single adult in order to be equally well off as the single adult. The equivalence scale usually takes both the age structure and the number of individuals in a household into account. A large class of two-parameter equivalence scales can be described by the formula

$$\text{Equivalent size} = (adults + \alpha * children)^\theta$$

where *adults* stands for the number of adults in the household, *children* stands for the number of children ages 15 and below, and α and θ are parameters between 0 and 1. A higher θ implies fewer economies of scale. A lower value of α gives less weight to children's consumption. A simplified one-parameter version of this scale allows only household size to vary:

$$\text{Equivalent size} = (\text{household size})^\theta.$$

The special case of both α and $\theta = 1$ yields the familiar per capita measure.

Some commonly used scales do not fall in the category of equivalence scales described by the above formula. The OECD, for example, has used the following equivalence scale:

$$\text{Equivalent size} = 0.3 + 0.7 * adults + 0.5 * children.$$

The OECD currently uses a revised scale with stronger scale economies:

$$\text{Equivalent size} = 0.5 + 0.5 * adults + 0.3 * children.$$

Unfortunately, there is no accepted way to estimate equivalence scales (Deaton and Paxon 1996, Deaton 1997). A number of methods are used, but each has major drawbacks. As a result, a wide variety of equivalence scales is used in various countries. This makes intercountry comparisons of poverty and inequality difficult, because measures of poverty and inequality are sensitive to the equivalence scale used. The literature suggests that a one-parameter scale (based on household size) give fairly similar results to two-parameter equivalence scales; results based on the OECD scales show similar results to one-parameter equivalence scales with a value of θ around 0.5–0.6 (Figini 1998). Varying the economy of scale parameter may change the relative poverty risks of different demographic subgroups of the population, notably the elderly and children, as Lanjouw and others (2000) show.

Because there is no generally accepted way to estimate equivalence scales, in this book we calculate poverty and inequality measures using three different values of θ = 0.5, 0.75, and 1.00 for the poverty line set at 50 percent of median expenditure (or income). In the main text we report results based on θ = 0.75, which seems a reasonable estimate for transition countries, in light of the fact that energy prices are subsidized and housing costs are not included in expenditure estimates—two major sources of economies of scale in OECD economies.

Poverty Lines

The third task is to set a poverty line. There are two types of poverty lines: absolute and relative. Absolute lines set an absolute minimum standard of living and are typically based on a fixed basket of food products (deemed to represent minimum nutritional intake necessary for good health) plus an allowance for other expenditures (such as housing and clothing). Hence absolute lines can vary across countries, depending on the composition of the consumption basket.

To facilitate comparisons across countries, a poverty line is fixed in U.S. dollars and then converted into national currency units using purchasing power parity (PPP) exchange rates. PPP rates measure the relative purchasing power of different currencies over equivalent goods and services. Market exchange rates are not appropriate for welfare comparisons because they do not account for the sometimes substantial differences in relative prices between economies. PPP rates also take into account differences in the structure of consumption between countries. However, they are not without problems (see World Bank 2000).

This book uses an absolute poverty line of $2.15 per person per day to derive cross-country estimates of absolute deprivation. This poverty line is roughly equal to the lowest absolute poverty lines that are used by transition countries in the Europe and Central Asia region and that are based on a nationally determined minimum food basket plus an allowance for nonfood expenditures. Because most transition countries have national absolute poverty lines that exceed $2.15 per day per person, we also provide poverty estimates based on an absolute poverty line of $4.30 per day per person. The absolute poverty lines are converted into national currency using 1996 PPP exchange rates (the most recent ones available). Next, the absolute poverty line, expressed in 1996 national currency, is adjusted for inflation using the national consumer price index to yield an absolute poverty line for the year in which the consumption or income data were collected.

Irrespective of absolute needs, people may consider themselves poor when their living standards are substantially below those of others in their country. This type of poverty is captured by relative poverty lines, which define poverty relative to national living standards. Relative poverty lines are useful for international comparisons of the *characteristics* of the worst off individuals in each country. Relative poverty lines are usually set as a fixed percentage of median or mean equivalent household income. We calculate poverty profiles using three common relative poverty lines. For clarity of exposition, we use 50 percent of median income as our base relative poverty line in the main text. However, Appendix D also reports poverty estimates for one-third and two-thirds of median consumption.

Poverty and Inequality Statistics

Poverty Statistics

The simplest and most commonly used measure of poverty is the headcount index, which is given by the fraction of individuals with equivalent consumption below the poverty line.[2] This measure, however, does not tell us whether the poor are only slightly below the poverty line or whether their consumption falls substantially short of the poverty line. Moreover, the headcount measure also does not reveal whether all the poor are about equally poor or whether some are very poor and others just below the poverty line.

To examine these three dimensions of poverty—headcount, shortfall, and inequality among the poor—we use the Foster, Greer, and Thorbecke (1984) class of poverty measures. This class is described by

$$P(\alpha) = \frac{1}{n} \sum_{i=1}^{n} \left[\max \left(\frac{z - c_i}{z}, 0 \right) \right]^{\alpha}$$

where α is the parameter (explained below), z is the poverty line, c_i is equivalent consumption of individual i, and n is the total number of individuals. If we set α equal to 0, we obtain P(0), or the *poverty headcount index*. P(0) simply measures the fraction of individuals below the poverty line. If we set α equal to 1, we obtain P(1), or the *poverty deficit*. The poverty deficit is a poverty measure that takes into account how far the poor, on average, are below the poverty line. One can show

$$P(1) = P(0) * (Average\ Deficit)$$

where the average deficit is the amount, measured as a percentage of the poverty line, by which the mean consumption of the poor on average falls short of the poverty line. An average deficit of 20 percent means that mean consumption of the poor falls 20 percent short of the poverty line. A poverty deficit of 5 percent means that if a country could mobilize resources equal to 5 percent of the poverty line for every individual and distribute these resources to the poor in the amount needed to bring each individual up to the poverty line, then, in theory, poverty could be eliminated.

Finally, if we set α equal to 2, we obtain $P(2)$, sometimes also called the *severity of poverty* or *FGT(2)*. This poverty measure captures difference in the severity of poverty, since it effectively gives more weight to those consumption of the poorest.

In our presentation of the poverty results, we rely mainly on the head-count index.

Inequality Statistics

There are many ways to measure inequality because inequality is a multi-dimensional concept. This book relies mostly on three types of inequality measures: (1) quantile ratios; (2) Gini coefficients; and (3) Theil inequality measures.

Quantile ratios are straightforward indicators of inequality that are easy to interpret. The most common quantile ratio is the 90/10 ratio, which is the equivalent consumption at the 90th percentile of the equivalent consumption distribution divided by the equivalent income at the 10th percentile. This measure is easy to interpret. For example, if the 90/10 ratio is equal to 4, then the poorest person of the richest 10 percent of the population consumes 4 times as much as the richest person of the poorest 10 percent. The 90/10 ratio can be decomposed; it is equal to the product of the 90/50 ratio and the 50/10 ratio. This decomposition tells us to what extent the 90/10 ratio is driven by inequality in the top of the distribution versus inequality at the bottom end. Quantile ratios are insensitive to outliers either in the very top or very bottom tail of the consumption distribution. However, quantile ratios do not reflect what happens in other parts of the distribution. For example, no change in inequality anywhere between the 11th and the 89th percentile would ever be reflected in a 90/10 ratio. To address this shortcoming, we also use Gini and Theil coefficients.

The Gini coefficient is given by:

$$G = \frac{2}{\mu n^2} \sum_{i=1}^{n} \left(r_i - \frac{n+1}{2} \right) c_i$$

where there are n individuals indexed by i, their equivalent consumption is given by c_i, mean equivalent consumption is denoted by μ, and where r_i is household's i rank in the equivalent consumption ranking (that is, for the household with the lowest equivalent consumption r_i equals 1, while for the household with the highest equivalent consumption r_i equals n). The Gini coefficient is bounded between 0 and 1, with 0 indicating absolute equality and 1 indicating absolute inequality. The Gini coefficient is especially sensitive to changes in inequality in the middle of the equivalent consumption distribution.

Another widely used class of inequality indicators is the generalized entropy class developed by Theil. Within that class, we use the *Theil mean log deviation index*,

$$E(0) = \frac{1}{n} \sum_{i=1}^{n} \ln \left(\frac{\mu}{c_i} \right) = \ln \left(\frac{1}{n} \sum_{i=1}^{n} c_i \right) - \frac{1}{n} \sum_{i=1}^{n} \ln(c_i).$$

and the *Theil entropy index*,

$$E(1) = \frac{1}{n} \sum_{i=1}^{n} \frac{c_i}{\mu} \ln \left(\frac{c_i}{\mu} \right).$$

Both measures are zero for perfect equality. For complete inequality (one person consumes everything), $E(0)$ goes to infinity while $E(1)$ reaches $n\ln(n)$. The two Theil inequality measures differ in their sensitivity to inequality in different parts of the distribution. The entropy measure, $E(1)$, is most sensitive to inequality in the top range in the distribution, while the mean log deviation measure, $E(0)$, is most sensitive to inequality in the bottom range of the distribution.

Inequality can be decomposed along two dimensions. One can decompose total inequality in equivalent consumption into the contribution of each component of equivalent consumption. Because equivalent consumption has relatively uninteresting components, this decomposition is usually performed for income inequality by the sources of income (labor income, self-employment income, state transfers, and so on). This decomposition can be performed using the Gini coefficient. The second way of decomposing inequality is to decompose it into inequality within population subgroups and between subgroups. This decomposition can be performed using the Theil indices.

Inequality Decomposition by Income Source Using Gini Coefficient

Since the source decomposition is typically performed using income, we present it for income rather than equivalent consumption. Following Shorrocks (1982), we decompose the Gini coefficient into the contribution of income sources. The contribution of each income source is the product of a concentration coefficient for that income source and the fraction of that income source in total income.

More formally, G_k^*, the concentration coefficient for income component k, is given by

$$G_k^* = \frac{2}{\mu n^2} \sum_{i=1}^n \left(r_i - \frac{n+1}{2} \right) y_{k,i}$$

where $y_{k,i}$ is component k of the income of individual i, mean **total** income is denoted by μ, and r_i is household's i rank in the ranking of **total** income. The Gini coefficient is a weighted sum of the concentration coefficients

$$G = \sum_{k=1}^K \frac{\mu_k}{\mu} G_k^* = \sum_{k=1}^K S_k G_k^*$$

where $S_k = \mu_k/\mu$ is the share of the component k in total income. The percentage contribution of income source k to total income equality is found to be

$$P_k = S_k \frac{G_k^*}{G} \times 100 \%.$$

The expression above gives the *overall* contribution of income source k to inequality. However, we may also wish to know the *marginal* contribution of each source to inequality. In other words, by what percentage would inequality increase if income source k increased by x percent? Lerman and Yitzhaki (1994) show that the elasticity of the Gini coefficient with respect to S_k is given by:

$$\in_{G,S_k} = \frac{S_k \left(G_k^* - G \right)}{G}.$$

Hence, whenever the concentration coefficient of income source k is greater than the overall Gini coefficient, an increase in the income source k (holding everything else constant) will increase inequality. In particular, if the share of income source k increases by 1 percent, overall inequality will increase by $\in_{G,S_k}$ percent.

Inequality Decomposition by Population Subgroup Using Theil Indices

The Gini coefficient does not lend itself well to a decomposition by population groups. For that purpose, the Theil generalized entropy class of inequality measures is used.

Decomposition by population groups allows us to look more closely at the causes of inequality. Following Bourguignon (1979) and Shorrocks (1980), we decompose total inequality into a component that is due to inequality across population subgroups, and into a component that is due to inequality within these subgroups. This decomposition can be performed for various population groupings.

Let the population be divided into m mutually exclusive and exhaustive subgroups. Let the population share of the jth group in the population be given by w_j, and the consumption share by v_j.

We can now rewrite the *Theil mean log deviation index* as

$$E(0) = \sum_{j=1}^{m} w_j E(0)_j + \sum_{j=1}^{m} w_j \ln\left(\frac{w_j}{v_j}\right)$$

where $E(0)_j$ is the mean log deviation measure calculated for all individuals in subgroup j. The first summation is a weighted average (using population shares as weights) of the mean log deviation measures calculated for the subgroups. Hence, this first term gives the component of overall inequality that is due to inequality *within* subgroups. The second summation is the mean log deviation measure calculated on mean consumption of each subgroup (and weighting each subgroup by its population share). Hence, this second term gives the component of inequality that is due to *between*-group differences.

The decomposition for the *Theil entropy measure* is similar and given by

$$E(1) = \sum_{j=1}^{m} v_j E(1)_j + \sum_{j=1}^{m} w_j \left[\frac{v_j}{w_j} \ln\left(\frac{v_j}{w_j}\right)\right]$$

where $E(1)_j$ is the Theil entropy measure calculated for all individuals in subgroup j. The first summation is a weighted average (using consumption shares as weights) of the entropy measures calculated for the subgroups. Hence, this first term gives the component of overall inequality that is due to inequality *within* subgroups. The second summation is the entropy measure calculated on mean consumption of each subgroup (and weighting each subgroup by its population share). Hence, this second term gives the component of inequality that is due to *between*-group differences.

Notes

1. Countries where we used income-based measures include Hungary and the Slovak Republic.

2. The exposition of the poverty and inequality measures is phrased in terms of equivalent consumption, but the same measures could be applied to equivalent income.

References

Bourguignon, François. 1979. "Decomposable Income Inequality Measures," *Econometrica* 47(4): 901–20.

Deaton, Angus. 1997. *The Analysis of Household Surveys: A Microeconomic Approach to Development Policy.* Washington, D.C.: World Bank.

Deaton, Angus, and Christina Paxon. 1996. "Economies of Scale, Household Size, and the Demand for Food." Research Program in Development Studies, Princeton University, Princeton, N.J. Processed.

Figini, Paolo. 1998. "Inequality Measures, Equivalence Scales and Adjustment for Household Size and Composition." LIS Working Paper No. 185 (available on LIS web site).

Foster, James, Joel Greer, and Eric Thorbecke. 1984. "A Class of Decomposable Poverty Measures." *Econometrica* 52(3): 761–65.

Lanjouw, Peter, Branko Milanovic, and Stefano Paternostro. 1998. "Poverty and the Economic Transition: How Do Changes in Economies of Scale Affect Poverty Rates for Different Households?" Policy Research Working Paper 2009. World Bank: Washington, D.C.

Lerman, Robert I., and Shlomo Yitzhaki. 1994. "Effect of Marginal Changes in Income Sources on U.S. Income Inequality." *Public Finance Quarterly* 22(4): 403–17.

Ravallion, Martin. 1994. *Poverty Comparisons*. Chur, Switzerland: Harwood Academic Publishers.

Shorrocks, Anthony. 1980. "The Class of Additively Decomposable Inequality Measures." *Econometrica* 48(1): 613–25.

———. 1982. "Inequality Decomposition by Factor Components." *Econometrica* 50(1): 193–211.

World Bank. 1993. *Poverty Reduction Handbook*. Washington, D.C.: World Bank.

———. 2000. *World Development Indicators*. Washington, D.C.

Appendix B

Data Sources

These technical notes discuss the sources and methods used to compile the poverty and inequality indicators presented in appendix D. The notes are organized by table and within table, and by indicator in order of appearance.

Sources

The poverty and inequality data presented in appendix D and used throughout this book are taken from household-level surveys implemented in the countries. The tables were created directly from the source data with the exception of Estonia 1995. The data used to prepare the tables for Estonia 1995 were taken from the household expenditures and income data for transitional economies (HEIDE) dataset.[1] The data included in all of the surveys included in the analyses are nationally representative, with the exception of the "Albania 1996 Employment and Welfare Survey." The data from this survey do not include the capital city of Tirana.

Data Consistency and Reliability

The definitions for the indicators included in the tables have been standardized to the extent possible, but differences remain. The definitions of the individual indicators change depending on the information available in the surveys used to provide the tables. Individual definitions of the variables used in the poverty and inequality tables are included in appendix C (tables C1.1 through C1.5). Definitions of the components included in the consumption and income aggregates are included in appendix C.

Poverty Profiles and Inequality Measures

Poverty profiles and inequality measures for the most recent survey, with exceptions as noted below, are presented in appendix D.

Country	Survey	Year(s)	Sample size	Sampling weights used
Albania	Employment and Welfare Survey	1996	1,506 households 7,619 individuals (does not include Tirana)	Yes
Armenia	Living Standards Survey	1998–99	3,600 households 15,632 individuals	No
	Household Expenditure Survey	1996	4,920 households 19,407 individuals	No
Azerbaijan	Azerbaijan's Study of People's Priorities	1999	1,011 households 5,161 individuals	Yes
	Living Standards Measurement Study	1995	2,016 households 10,012 individuals	Yes
Belarus	Household Sample Survey	1999	5,152 households 14,964 individuals	Yes
	Household Sample Survey	1996	5,069 households 14,893 individuals	Yes
Bulgaria	Integrated Household Survey	1997	2,322 households 6,497 individuals	No
	Integrated Household Survey	1995	2,468 households 7,199 individuals	No
Croatia	Household Budget Survey	1998	3,123 households 9,433 individuals	Yes
Czech Republic	Microcensus	1996	28,148 households 71,836 individuals	Yes
	Microcensus	1992	15,676 households 41,896 individuals	Yes

(Table continues on next page.)

Country	Survey	Year(s)	Sample size	Sampling weights used
Estonia	Household Income and Expenditures Survey	1998, 4th quarter	2,397 households 6,588 individuals	Yes
	Household Income and Expenditures Survey	1995	2,818 households 8,758 individuals	Yes
Georgia	Survey of Georgian Households[1]	1999, 4th quarter	2,842 households 9,817 individuals	Yes
	Survey of Georgian households	1996–97	2,520–2,699 households 9,319–9,962 individuals	Yes
Hungary	Household Budget Survey	1997	7,559 households 20,073 individuals	No
Kazakhstan	Living Standards Measurement Survey	1996	1,996 households 7,224 individuals	No
Kyrgyz Republic	Living Standards Measurement Survey[1]	1998	2,962 households 15,301 individuals	Yes
	Living Standards Measurement Survey	1997	2,693 households 13,630 individuals	Yes
Latvia	Household Budget Survey	1997–98	7,690 households 21,693 individuals	Yes
Lithuania	Household Budget Survey	1999	4,029 households 11,994 individuals	Yes
Macedonia, FYR	Household Budget Survey	1996	1,514 households 6,242 individuals	Yes
Moldova[2]	Household Budget Survey	1999, 4th quarter	1,539 households 4,315 individuals	Yes
	Household Budget Survey	1997, 3rd quarter	1,962 households 5,857 individuals	Yes
Poland	Household Budget Survey	1998	31,708 households 100,613 individuals	Yes
Romania	Living Standards Measurement Survey	1998	32,054 households 98,876 individuals	Yes
Russian Federation	Russian Longitudinal Measurement Survey	1998	3,619 households 10,222 individuals	Yes

(Table continues on next page.)

Country	Survey	Year(s)	Sample size	Sampling weights used
Slovak Republic[1,3]	Microcensus	1997	16,336 households 48,740 individuals	Yes
Slovenia	Household Income and Expenditures Survey	1997–98	2,577 households 7,792 individuals	No
	Household Income and Expenditures Survey	1993	3,270 households 11,078 individuals	Yes
Tajikistan	Living Standards Measurement Survey	1999	2,000 households 14,142 individuals	No
Turkmenistan	Living Standards Measurement Survey	1998	2,096 households 12,138 individuals	No
Ukraine	Household Income and Expenditures Survey[1]	1999	9,320 households 26,156 individuals	Yes
	Household Income and Expenditures Survey	1996	2,322 households 5,403 individuals	No
	Household Income and Expenditures Survey	1995	2,024 households 4,567 individuals	No

Notes:
1. Poverty profile tables are not available for this survey.
2. The poverty profile is based on data drawn from the June 1996 through December 1997 quarterly data. The absolute poverty rates are based on the 1999 fourth quarter data.
3. Household level data only included in the survey. Number of individuals calculated by summing the value found in the variable in which the number of household members is detailed across the entire data set. The survey reports on income received in 1996.

Note

1. See Jeanine Braithwaithe, Christiaan Grootaert, and Branko Milanovic (1999), *Poverty and Social Assistance in Transition Countries,* New York: St. Martin's Press, for a description of the HEIDE data set.

Variable Definitions for Poverty and Inequality Tables

Table C.1   Education

Country	Year	Primary	General secondary	Specialized secondary	Tertiary
Albania	1996	Highest level of education completed includes creche, pre-school, elementary, or middle school.	Highest level of education completed is general secondary.	Highest level of education completed is technical/vocational secondary.	Highest level of education completed is post-secondary, vocational, or university.
Armenia	1996	Highest level of education completed is 7 years.	Adult with highest grade completed: general secondary school, 8 to 12 years.	Highest level of education completed is vocational/professional/technical.	Highest level of education completed is any year of college, institute, university, academy, or post-graduate courses, or internships.
Armenia	1998–99	Highest level of education completed is 7 years.	Adult with highest grade completed: general secondary school, 8 to 12 years.	Highest level of education is vocational/professional/technical.	Highest level of education completed is any year of college, institute, university, academy, or post-graduate courses, or internships.
Azerbaijan	1995	Highest level of education completed is 8 years.	Highest level of education completed is secondary.	Highest level of education completed is professional/technical, secondary technical, or specialized secondary.	Highest level of education completed is higher education, Candidate of Science, Doctor of Science, or Professor.

(Table continues on next page.)

Table C.1 *(continued)*

Country	Year	Primary	General secondary	Specialized secondary	Tertiary
Azerbaijan	1999	Highest level of education completed is 8 years.	Highest level of education completed is secondary.	Highest level of education completed is professional/technical, secondary technical, or specialized secondary.	Highest level of education completed is higher education, Candidate of Science, Doctor of Science, or Professor.
Belarus	1996	Highest level of education completed is 7 years.	Highest level of education completed is secondary education (8–12 years).	Highest level of education completed is vocational/professional/technical.	Highest level of education completed is any year of college, institute, university, academy, or post-graduate courses, or internships.
Belarus	1999	Highest level of education completed is primary (3 years) or incomplete secondary (fewer than 8 years).	Highest level of education completed is general secondary education (8 years).	Highest level of education completed is vocational/professional/technical.	Highest level of education completed is any year of college, institute, university, academy, or post-graduate courses, or internships.
Bulgaria	1995	Highest level of education completed is from 1st year of elementary school to 3rd year of middle school.	Highest level of education completed is 4th year of middle school to 3rd year of general secondary school.	Highest level of education completed is any year of technical secondary or any year of vocational secondary.	Highest level of education is at least 1st year of university or occupation-specific higher education.
Bulgaria	1997	Highest level of education completed is from 1st year of elementary school to 3rd year of middle school.	Highest level of education completed is 4th year of middle school to 3rd year of general secondary.	Highest level of education completed is any year of technical secondary or any year of vocational secondary.	Highest level of education is at least 1st year of university or occupation-specific higher education.

(Table continues on next page.)

383

Table C.1 (continued)

Country	Year	Primary	General secondary	Specialized secondary	Tertiary
Croatia	1998	Primary or less.	"Secondary": 4-year vocational secondary and grammar school.	"Basic vocational"; Basic vocational school (1–3 years).	Post-secondary and higher education.
Czech Republic	1992	8 or 9 years of elementary school, including negligible percentage of not completed primary education.	General: General high school with matura (gymnasium); vocational: vocational school or lower secondary (2–3 years), education without matura.	Specialized high school with matura (commercial school, etc.) or post-high school, including the lowest college degree (2 years of university).	Completed university education.
Czech Republic	1996	8 or 9 years of elementary school, including negligible percentage of not completed primary education.	General: General high school with matura (gymnasium); vocational: vocational school or lower secondary (2–3 years) education without matura.	Specialized high school with matura (commercial school, etc.) or post-high school, including the lowest college degree (2 years of university).	Completed university education.
Estonia	1995	No formal education; primary.	Secondary; specialized secondary.	Secondary plus other courses; apprenticeship degree.	Higher education.
Estonia	1998	No individual-level data are available, only household-level data.			
Georgia	1996–97	Highest level of education completed is 7 years.	Adult with highest grade completed: general secondary school (8 to 12 years).	Highest level of education completed is vocational/professional/technical.	Highest level of education completed is any year of college, institute, university, academy, or post-graduate courses or internships.

(Table continues on next page.)

384

Table C.1 (continued)

Country	Year	Primary	General secondary	Specialized secondary	Tertiary
Hungary	1997	Completed 8 or fewer years in elementary school.	Completed secondary grammar school.	Completed vocational training school, vocational school, or vocational secondary school.	Completed college or university.
Kazakhstan	1996	Highest level of education completed is 1 to 7 years.	Highest level of education completed is 8 to 12 years.	Highest level of education completed is additional technical training after completing general secondary school.	Highest level of education completed is any year of college, institute, university, academy, or post-graduate courses or internships.
Kyrgyz Republic	1993	Highest level of education completed is 8 or fewer years.	Highest level of education completed is any year of high school (8–10 years).	Highest level of education completed is high school and other.	Highest level of education completed is 10 or more years of primary and secondary schooling, and one or more additional levels.
Kyrgyz Republic	1997	Highest grade completed is 7 or fewer years.	Adult with highest grade completed: secondary school is 8 to 12 or highest diploma or certificate received is incomplete secondary or complete secondary.	Highest diploma or certificate received is professional, technical school, or technikum.	Highest diploma or certificate received is higher education, diploma, candidate of science, or doctor of science.
Latvia	1997–98	Primary, lower than primary, or did not study.	Secondary, secondary technical, or special secondary.	Vocational.	Higher education.
Lithuania	1999	Variable provided in data set, no definition given.	Variable provided in data set, no definition given.	Variable provided in data set, no definition given.	Variable provided in data set, no definition given.

(Table continues on next page.)

385

Table C.1 *(continued)*

Country	Year	Primary	General secondary	Specialized secondary	Tertiary
Macedonia, FYR	1996	Completed primary.	Completed secondary.		High and higher education.
Moldova	1997	Primary, incomplete primary, or no school.	General secondary, incomplete secondary.	Specialized secondary (vocational or technical).	Higher and incomplete higher.
Poland	1998	Primary or less.	"Secondary": Vocational secondary and general secondary	"Basic vocational": Basic vocational school.	Post-secondary and higher education.
Romania	1998	Adults with 8 years of education or less. Separate categories were computed for those younger than 15, and for adults without school.	Vocational: completed vocational school or 10 years of education.	High school or post-high school. Completed 12 years of education (high school), or vocation post-high school.	College (14 years of education) or university (including post-graduate studies) completed.
Russian Federation	1998	Highest level of education completed is 8 years or less.	Highest level of education completed is any year of high school (8–11 years).	Highest diploma or certificate received is professional, technical school, or technikum.	Highest diploma or certificate received is higher education, diploma, candidate of science, or doctor of science.
Slovenia	1993	Completed 8 or fewer years of schooling.	Completed occupational school or high school.		Completed 3- or 4-year courses in university or completed post-graduate degrees or higher.
Slovenia	1997–98	Primary school and first phase of secondary education.	Second phase of secondary education.		Higher education.

(Table continues on next page.)

Table C.1 (continued)

Country	Year	Primary	General secondary	Specialized secondary	Tertiary
Tajikistan	1999	Highest level of education completed is 8 years.	Highest level of education completed is secondary education.	Highest level of education completed is professional or technical, secondary technical, or specialized secondary.	Highest level of education completed is higher education, candidate of science, doctor of science, or professor.
Turkmenistan	1998	Completed 6 or fewer years of schooling.	Completed between the 7th to 9th or 10th grades.		Any education after 9th or 10th grades, including vocational training and colleges.
Ukraine	1995	7 years of education or less.	Incomplete secondary (fewer than 10 years), complete secondary (10–11 years), or specialized secondary (college and so on).	Vocational training school after 7–8 years or vocational training school after 10–11 years.	Incomplete higher (3 years or more), or higher.
Ukraine	1996	7 years of education or less.	Incomplete secondary (less than 10 years), complete secondary (10–11 years), or specialized secondary (college and so on).	Vocational training school after 7–8 years or vocational training school after 10–11 years.	Incomplete higher (3 years or more), or higher.

Table C.2 Location/Access to Land and Automobile

Country	Year	Urban	Rural	Region	Access to land	Access to automobile
Albania	1996	Definition based on administrative units used to select the sample.	Definition based on administrative units used to select the sample.	Not used because variable in the data set was apparently badly defined.	Do you have access to any agricultural land that could be used to produce crops or raise livestock?	Do you have a car, not used for business?
Armenia	1996	Urban settlements or "Gorodskoi" (administrative definition based on 1991 Census).	Rural settlements and "poselki" (administrative definition based on 1991 Census).	New administrative regions (marzes) collapsed.	Access to private plot, does not imply ownership.	Estimated based on car fuel spending or payments for parking lot.
Armenia	1998–99	Urban settlements or "Gorodskoi" (administrative definition based on 1991 Census).	Rural settlements and "poselki" (administrative definition based on 1991 Census).	New administrative regions (marzes) collapsed.	Access to private plot, does not imply ownership.	Do you have a car?
Azerbaijan	1995	Variable provided in data set, no definition given.	Variable provided in data set, no definition given.	Variable provided in data set, no definition given.	Either now or at any time during the last 12 months, has your family had any land at its disposal?	Families who own a car or displaced persons who brought their cars with them.
Azerbaijan	1999	Baku only.	Non-Baku.	Variable provided in data set, no definition given.	Not used in the analyses.	Not used in the analyses.

(Table continues on next page.)

Table C.2 *(continued)*

Country	Year	Urban	Rural	Region	Access to land	Access to automobile
Belarus	1996	Large cities (population more than 100,000).	Variable provided in data set, no definition given.	South (Brest and Gomel regions (oblast)). Central (Minsk and Minsk regions (oblast)). West (Grodno region (oblast)). East (Mogilev and Vitebsk regions (oblast)).	Does your family have any land in use?	How many cars does your family have? - None. - One. - Two. - Three or more. - Does not know, refuses to answer.
Belarus	1999	Large cities (population more than 100,000).	Variable provided in data set, no definition given.	South (Brest and Gomel regions (oblast)). Central (Minsk and Minsk regions (oblast)). West (Grodno region (oblast)). East (Mogilev and Vitebsk regions (oblast)).	Does your family have any land in use?	How many cars does your family have? - None. - One. - Two. - Three or more. - Does not know, refuses to answer.
Bulgaria	1995	Variable provided in data set, no definition given.	Variable provided in data set, no definition given.	Variable provided in data set, no definition given.	Do you have access to any agricultural land that you use to produce crops or raise livestock?	Do you have a car?
Bulgaria	1997	Variable provided in data set, no definition given.	Variable provided in data set, no definition given.	Variable provided in data set, no definition given.	Do you have access to any agricultural land that you use to produce crops or raise livestock?	Do you have a car?

(Table continues on next page.)

389

Table C.2 *(continued)*

Country	Year	Urban	Rural	Region	Access to land	Access to automobile
Croatia	1998	Variable provided in data set, no definition given.	Variable provided in data set, no definition given.	Counties are grouped by regions: "Zagreb": Grad Zagreb and Zagrebacka. "Central": Krapinsko-zagorska, Sisacko-moslavacka, Karlovacka, Varazdinska, Koprivnicko-krizevacka, Bjelovarsko-bilogorska and Medjimurska. "Istra (N. Coast)": Primorsko-goranska, Licko-senjska and Istarska. "Dalmacija (S. Coast)": Zadarska, Sibensko-kninska, Splitsko-dalmatinska and Dubrovacko-neretvanska. "Slavonija": Viroviticko-podravska, Pozesko-slavonska, Brodsko-posavska, Osjecko-baranjska and Vukovarsko-srijemska.	Does household use agricultural land?	Possession by the household of a car.
Czech Republic	1992	Urban 1: settlements of urban character (statistical definition); Urban 2: capi-	Urban 1: settlements of rural character (statistical definition); Urban 2: all	Former administrative regions collapsed: Middle (Prague and Central	In-kind income (food consumption) estimated 500 Czech Koruna and over	Household or a private firm of any household member owns car.

(Table continues on next page.)

Table C.2 *(continued)*

Country	Year	Urban	Rural	Region	Access to land	Access to automobile
		tal—only Prague; cities—settlements with 100,000 inhabitants and more; towns—other settlements of urban character.	settlements of rural character.	Bohemia), West (West and North Bohemia), South (South Bohemia and South Moravia), North (North Bohemia and North Moravia).	monthly (about 10 percent of monetary per capita income).	
Czech Republic	1996	Urban 1: settlements of urban character (statistical definition); Urban 2: capital—only Prague; cities—settlements with 100,000 inhabitants and more; towns—other settlements of urban character.	Urban 1: settlements of rural character (statistical definition); Urban 2: all settlements of rural character.	Former administrative regions collapsed: Middle (Prague and Central Bohemia), West (West and North Bohemia), South (South Bohemia and South Moravia), North (North Bohemia and North Moravia).	In kind income (food consumption) estimated 500 Czech Koruna and over monthly (about 10 percent of monetary per capita income).	Household or a private firm of any household member owns car.
Estonia	1995	Variable provided in data set, no definition given.	Variable provided in data set, no definition given.	Variable provided in data set, no definition given.	Access to private plot, does not imply ownership.	Do you own a car?
Estonia	1998	Variable provided in data set, no definition given.	Variable provided in data set, no definition given.	Not included in data set.	Not included in data set.	Not included in data set.
Georgia	1996–97	Urban settlements or "Gorodskoi" (administrative definition based on 1991 Census).	Rural settlements or "poselki" (administrative definition based on 1991 Census).	New administrative regions collapsed.	Access to private plot, does not imply ownership.	Do you have a car?

(Table continues on next page.)

Table C.2 (continued)

Country	Year	Urban'	Rural	Region	Access to land	Access to automobile
Hungary	1997	Variable provided in data set, no definition given.	Variable provided in data set, no definition given.	Variable provided in data set, no definition given.	Used information on total area of cultivated land available to household.	Number of cars owned by household.
Kazakhstan	1996	Variable provided in data set, no definition given.	Variable provided in data set, no definition given.	Variable provided in data set, no definition given.	Did your family have a private plot (a back yard, an orchard, a plot for vegetables, family farm, rented plot) during the past 12 months?	Do you have in your household a passenger car?
Kyrgyz Republic	1993	Urban settlements or "Gorodskoi."	Rural settlements, often equivalent to villages.	Variable provided in data set, no definition given.	Either now or at any time during the last 12 months, has your family had any land at its disposal?	Do you have an auto or truck?
Kyrgyz Republic	1997	Variable provided in data set, no definition given.	Variable provided in data set, no definition given.	Variable provided in data set, no definition given.	Households who reported positively to having any land available in the agricultural module.	Do members of your household own a car?
Latvia	1997–98	Variable provided in data set, no definition given.	Variable provided in data set, no definition given.	Variable provided in data set, no definition given.	Used information on total area of land for farming, plot beside summer house, or small garden.	Information on whether household owns car and number owned.

(Table continues on next page.)

392

Table C.2 *(continued)*

Country	Year	Urban	Rural	Region	Access to land	Access to automobile
Lithuania	1999	Large towns are formed by the 5 biggest towns in Lithuania (Vilnius, Kaunas, Klaipeda, Siauliai, Panevezys).			Does your household use a plot of land?	Household owns car (possession of durable goods).
Macedonia, FYR	1996	Variable provided in data set, no definition given.	Variable provided in data set, no definition given.	Capital and rest of the republic.	Area of cultivable land greater than zero.	Number of cars greater than zero.
Moldova	1997	Variable provided in data set, no definition given.	Variable provided in data set, no definition given.	Variable provided in data set, no definition given.	Household has access to land for growing food.	Information on whether household owns car and number owned.
Poland	1998	Variable provided in data set, no definition given.	Variable provided in data set, no definition given.	Voivodships (counties) are grouped by regions. "North": Bydgoszcz, Elblag, Gdansk, Koszalin, Pila, Plock, Slupsk, and Szczecin. "Center": Ciechanow, Kalisz, Leszno, Lodz, Piotrkow, Radom, Siedlce, Sieradz, Skierniewice, Torun, Warsaw, and Wloclawek. "East": Bialystok, Bielsk Podlaski, Chelmno, Lomza, Lublin, Olsztyn, Ostroleka, Prze-	Does household use land?	Possession by the household of a motorcar.

(Table continues on next page.)

Table C.2 *(continued)*

Country	Year	Urban`	Rural	Region	Access to land	Access to automobile
				mysl, Rzeszow, Suwalki, Tarnobrzeg, and Zamosc. "West": Gorzow, Jelenia Gora, Konin, Legnica, Poznan, Walbrzych, Wroclaw, and Zielona Gora. "South": Bielsko-Biala, Cracow, Czestochowa, Katowice, Kielce, and Krosno.		
Romania	1998	Administrative definition: urban areas are defined by law.	Administrative definition: what is not classified as urban: villages and communes.	Administrative definition: From an administrative point of view, Romania is organized in 41 judets. Recently (1998) 8 development regions have been defined (by merging neighboring judets), with responsibilities for regional development policy design and implementation. These development regions do not have administrative functions.	The household owns or rents agricultural land.	At least one household member owns a car.

(Table continues on next page.)

Table C.2 *(continued)*

Country	Year	Urban`	Rural	Region	Access to land	Access to automobile
Russian Federation	1998	Variable definition provided in data set, no definition given.	Variable definition provided in data set, no definition given.	Variable definition provided in data set, no definition given.	Households who reported positively to having any land available in the agricultural module.	Do members of your household own a car?
Slovenia	1993	Variable definition provided in data set, no definition given.	Variable definition provided in data set, no definition given.			Number of automobiles was greater than zero.
Slovenia	1997-98	Information not included in data set.	Information not included in data set.	Information not included in data set.	Households with cultivated land.	Number of automobiles was greater than zero.
Tajikistan	1999	Definition based on administrative units used to select the sample.	Definition based on administrative units used to select the sample.	Administrative definition: From an administrative point of view, Tajikistan is divided into four regions: Gorno-Badakhshan Autonomous Oblast in the east, Khatlon Oblast in the south, Leninabad Oblast in the north, and RRS in the central part. The capital, Dushanbe, is also counted as a 5th seat of regional government.	How many sotkas are available to you and members of your household? (includes 8 types of land: individual garden plot, cotton production, wheat production, other production, raising animals (pasture), orchard/vineyard, fallow, other uses).	Do any members of your household own a passenger automobile?

(Table continues on next page.)

Table C.2 *(continued)*

Country	Year	Urban*	Rural	Region	Access to land	Access to automobile
Turkmenistan	1998	Variable provided in data set, no definition given.	Variable provided in data set, no definition given.	Not available in the data.	How many sotkas are available to your household? If the total is greater than zero, the household had access to land.	Number of automobiles was greater than zero, including motor boat, motorcycle, car, truck, or tractors.
Ukraine	1995	Urban: Settlement size of 100,001 people or more. Semi-urban: settlement size of 10,001 to 100,000 people.	Settlement size smaller than 10,000 people.	Used regional breakdown as found in poverty analysis.	Work on a land lot, cattle/poultry breeding, and so on, which belongs to you or to your household; fishing, hunting, berries, and mushroom gathering.	In your household, do you have a motor vehicle?
Ukraine	1996	Urban: Settlement size of 100,001 people or more. Semi-urban: settlement size of 10,001 to 100,000 people.	Settlement size smaller than 10,000 people.	Used regional breakdown as found in poverty analysis.	Has your household been using any land (a land lot, kitchen garden, summer cottage, subsidiary farm, and so on) during the last 12 months?	Does any member of your household own a car?

396

Table C.3 Demographics

Country	Year	Elderly	Adults	Household head
Albania	1996	65 years of age or older	15 years of age or older	Head of household identified by the household when filling in the roster of the questionnaire.
Armenia	1996	65 years of age or older	15 years of age or older	Oldest male aged 18–59 with earnings; if no males with earnings 18–59 then oldest female with earnings aged 18–54; if no one with earnings, oldest person.
Armenia	1998–99	65 years of age or older	15 years of age or older	Head of household identified by the household when filling in the roster of the questionnaire.
Azerbaijan	1995	65 years of age or older	15 years of age or older	Head of household identified by the household when filling in the roster of the questionnaire.
Azerbaijan	1999	65 years of age or older	15 years of age or older	Head of household identified by the household when filling in the roster of the questionnaire.
Belarus	1996	65 years of age or older	15 years of age or older	Head of household identified by the household when filling in the roster of the questionnaire.
Belarus	1999	65 years of age or older	15 years of age or older	Head of household identified by the household when filling in the roster of the questionnaire.
Bulgaria	1995	65 years of age or older	15 years of age or older	Head of household identified by the household when filling in the roster of the questionnaire.
Bulgaria	1997	65 years of age or older	15 years of age or older	Head of household identified by the household when filling in the roster of the questionnaire.

(Table continues on next page.)

397

Table C.3 *(continued)*

Country	Year	Elderly	Adults	Household head
Croatia	1998	65 years of age or older	15 years of age or older	Head of household identified by the household when filling in the roster of the questionnaire.
Czech Republic	1992	65 years of age or older	15 years of age or older	Man in the couple, if one couple; economically active man if two couples (man with higher income if two active men), economically active woman if more women (woman with higher income if two active women).
Czech Republic	1996	65 years of age or older	15 years of age or older	Man in the couple, if one couple; economically active man if two couples (man with higher income if two active men), economically active woman if more women (woman with higher income if two active women).
Estonia	1995	65 years of age or older	15 years of age or older	Oldest male aged 18–59; if no males 18–59 then oldest female aged 18–54; if no females 18–54 then youngest male aged 60 or older; if no males 18 or older then youngest female aged 55 or older; if no females 18 or older then oldest person.
Estonia	1998	No individual level data are available, only household level data	No individual level data are available, only household level data	Variable provided in the data set, no definition given.
Georgia	1996–97	65 years of age or older	15 years of age or older	Head of household identified by the household when filling in the roster of the questionnaire.

(Table continues on next page.)

Table C.3 *(continued)*

Country	Year	Elderly	Adults	Household head
Hungary	1997	65 years of age or older	15 years of age or older	Oldest male 18–59; if no male aged 18–59, oldest female 18–54; if no female aged 18–54, youngest male 60⁺; if no male 60⁺, youngest female 55⁺; if no female 55⁺, oldest person.
Kazakhstan	1996	65 years of age or older	15 years of age or older	Variable provided in data set, no definition given.
Kyrgyz Republic	1993	65 years of age or older	15 years of age or older	Oldest male aged 18–59; if no males 18–59 then oldest female aged 18–54; if no females 18–54 then youngest male aged 60 or older; if no males 18 or older then youngest female aged 55 or older; if no females 18 or older then oldest person.
Kyrgyz Republic	1997	65 years of age or older	15 years of age or older	Head of household identified by the household when filling in the roster of the questionnaire.
Latvia	1997–98	65 years of age or older	15 years of age or older	Head of household identified by the household when filling in the roster of the questionnaire.
Lithuania	1999	65 years of age or older	15 years of age or older	Individual with the highest yearly income in the household.
FYR Macedonia	1996	65 years of age or older	15 years of age or older	Identified by household in the roster.
Moldova	1997	65 years of age or older	15 years of age or older	Head of household identified by the household when filling in the roster of the questionnaire.
Poland	1998	65 years of age or older	15 years of age or older	Head of household identified by the household when filling in the roster of the questionnaire.

(Table continues on next page.)

399

Table C.3 *(continued)*

Country	Year	Elderly	Adults	Household head
Romania	1998	65 years of age or older	15 years of age or older	Reported by a household member. The interviewer collects information from as many members of the household as possible, and asks who is the head.
Russian Federation	1998	65 years of age or older	16 years of age or older	Oldest male aged 18–59; if no males 18–59 then oldest female aged 18–54; if no females 18–54 then youngest male aged 60 or older; if no males 18 or older then youngest female aged 55 or older; if no females 18 or older then oldest person.
Slovenia	1993	65 years of age or older	15 years of age or older	Variable provided in data set, no definition given.
Slovenia	1997-98	65 years of age or older	15 years of age or older	Variable provided in data set, no definition given.
Tajikistan	1999	65 years of age or older	15 years of age or older	Head of household identified by the household when filling in the roster of the questionnaire.
Turkmenistan	1998	65 years of age or older	15 years of age or older	Head of household identified by the household when filling in the roster.
Ukraine	1995	65 years of age or older	15 years of age or older	Identified by age, gender, and member bringing in the largest share of household income to have 4 values: male under 59, male over 59, female under 54, or female over 54. (Indicator was missing for 10% of the households.)
Ukraine	1996	65 years of age or older	15 years of age or older	Head of household identified by the household when filling in the roster.

Table C.4 Employment

Country	Year	Employed	Self-employed/ employer	Unemployed	Not employed/ not in workforce	Retired
Albania	1996	If working during the past 7 days in a permanent wage job, a temporary job with no contract or a temporary job with a contract.	If working during the past 7 days in own business or farm.		Not working in the past 7 days and not looking for a job because of illness, child care, education, or housekeeping.	Not working in the past 7 days and not looking because retired.
Armenia	1996	Self-identification reference: one month, criterion—at least one day employed.	If working during the past month in own business or farm.	Self-identification—no work, no earnings, and active search for work.	Others, except retired.	Not working and receiving a pension.
Armenia	1998–99	i) During the last week, respondent performed any activity aimed at obtaining means for life (for at least one hour). Or, (ii) even if respondent did not work last week, the respondent had a job to return to. Or, (iii) even if respondent is unpaid family worker, pensioner, housewife, jobless, or in school, the respondent did during the last week at least one hour of work for money, benefits in-kind, or family gain.	If working during the past 7 days in own business or farm.	If working during the past 7 days actively seeking work, without work and available for work.	Others, except retired.	Not working and receiving a pension.

(Table continues on next page.)

Table C.4 (continued)

Country	Year	Employed	Self-employed/ employer	Unemployed	Not employed/ not in workforce	Retired
Azerbaijan	1995	Work for wages.	Work for wages and identify self as self-employed, owner, or employer.	Does not work for wages, but looked for a job during the last week.	Does not work for wages, did not look for a job during the last week, and not retired.	Does not work for wages, did not look for a job during the last week, and identifies self as retired.
Azerbaijan	1999	Variable provided in data set, no definition given.	Variable provided in data set, no definition given.	Variable provided in data set, no definition given.	Variable provided in data set, no definition given.	Variable provided in data set, no definition given.
Belarus	1996	Blue-collar worker, white-collar worker, collective farmer, military service person, and other employed.	Farmers and self-employed as reported by the respondent.	Unemployed (as reported by the respondent).	Students, disabled, housewives, and others not in the labor force.	Pensioners.
Belarus	1999	Blue-collar worker, white-collar worker, collective farmer, military service person, and other employed.	Farmers and self-employed as reported by the respondent.	Unemployed (as reported by the respondent).	Students, disabled, housewives, and others not in the labor force.	Pensioners.
Bulgaria	1995	Working for a wage or revenue during past 7 days at a permanent or temporary job.	Working for a wage or revenue during the past 7 days at own business or own farm.	Not working for wage or revenue during the past 7 days and is currently looking for work.	Not working for a wage or revenue during past 7 days due to sick leave, maternity leave, vacation, seasonal or company closed.	Not working for a wage or revenue during the past 7 days, and not currently looking for work because is pensioner.

(Table continues on next page.)

Table C.4 (continued)

Country	Year	Employed	Self-employed/ employer	Unemployed	Not employed/ not in workforce	Retired
Bulgaria	1997	Working for a wage or revenue during past 7 days at a permanent or temporary job.	Working for a wage or revenue during the past 7 days at own business or own farm.	Not working for wage or revenue during the past 7 days and is currently looking for work.	Not working for a wage or revenue during past 7 days due to sick leave, maternity leave, vacation, seasonal or company closed.	Not working for a wage or revenue during the past 7 days, and not currently looking for work because is pensioner.
Croatia	1998	(i) During the last week, respondent performed any activity aimed at obtaining means for life (for at least one hour). Or, (ii) even if respondent did not work last week, the respondent had a job to which to return. Or, (iii) even if respondent is unpaid family worker, pensioner, housewife, jobless, or in school, the respondent did during the last week at least one hour of work for money, benefits in-kind, or family gain.		(i) Respondent is not "employed" (see previous definition), has looked for a job or tried to set up own firm or business over the last four weeks and is able to start working within the next two weeks. Or, (ii) respondent has found a job which starts soon and is able to start working within the next two weeks.	Not "employed" (see previous definition), not "unemployed" (see previous definition) and not "retired" (see next definition).	Not "employed" (see previous definition) and receives pension income.

(Table continues on next page.)

Table C.4 *(continued)*

Country	Year	Employed	Self-employed/ employer	Unemployed	Not employed/ not in workforce	Retired
Czech Republic	1992	According to self-declaration, employed or self-employed the last day of the referring period (31 December 1996).	According to self-declaration, relates to the last day of the referring period (31 December 1996).	Not employed and registered in the local labor office, not regarding if receiving unemployment benefits, the last day of the referring period (31 December 1996).		Not employed in a permanent job and receiving old-age or disability pension benefits the last day of the referring period (31 December 1996).
Czech Republic	1996	According to self-declaration, employed or self-employed the last day of the referring period (31 December 1996).	According to self-declaration, relates to the last day of the referring period (31 December 1996).	Not employed and registered in the local labor office, not regarding if receiving unemployment benefits, the last day of the referring period (31 December 1996).		Not employed in a permanent job and receiving old-age or disability pension benefits the last day of the referring period (31 December 1996).
Estonia	1995	Variable provided in data set, no definition given.		Variable provided in data set, no definition given.	Variable provided in data set, no definition given.	
Estonia	1998	Variable provided in data set, no definition given.	Variable provided in data set, no definition given.	Variable provided in data set, no definition given.	Variable provided in data set, no definition given.	Variable provided in data set, no definition given.
Georgia	1996–97	i) During the last week, respondent performed any activity aimed at obtaining means for life (for at least	If working during the past 7 days, in own business or farm.	If working during the past 7 days actively seeking work, without work and available for work.	Others, except retired.	Not working and receiving a pension.

(Table continues on next page.)

Table C.4 *(continued)*

Country	Year	Employed	Self-employed/ employer	Unemployed	Not employed/ not in workforce	Retired
		one hour). Or, (ii) even if respondent did not work last week, the respondent had a job to return to. Or, (iii) even if respondent is unpaid family worker, pensioner, housewife, jobless, or in school, the respondent did during the last week at least one hour of work for money, benefits in-kind, or family gain.				
Hungary	1997	Because of lack of documentation, this had to be ascertained indirectly. Deemed to be employed if of working age (>=16 years and <=55 if female or <=60 if male), earned income, wage share of personal income exceeded share from unemployment benefits, self-employment income not largest share of total household income.	Deemed to be self-employed if of working age (>=16 years and <=55 if female or <=60 if male), earned income, wage share of personal income exceeded share from unemployment benefits, self-employment income personal income zero and largest share of total household income.	Deemed to be unemployed if of working age (>=16 years and <=55 if female or <=60 if male), earned income, wage share of personal income less than share from un-employment benefits or personal income zero and seeking employment.	Deemed to be not in labor force if not employed, self-employed, or unemployed and <=55 if female or <=60 if male.	Deemed to be retired if does not fall into any of previous categories.

(Table continues on next page.)

Table C.4 (continued)

Country	Year	Employed	Self-employed/ employer	Unemployed	Not employed/ not in workforce	Retired
Kazakhstan	1996	Currently employed by an enterprise, organization, collective farm, state farm, cooperative with no further specifications.	Owner: Employed and answered yes to, "Are you the owner of the enterprise where you mainly work?"	Not "employed" (see previous definition) and answered yes to, "Did you look for a job or try to start your own business during the last 7 days?"	Not "employed" (see previous definition), did not look for work, not a pensioner.	Not "employed" (see previous definition), did not look for work because is a pensioner.
Kyrgyz Republic	1993	Employed full-time or part-time as hired labor in an enterprise, organization, collective or state farm or cooperative.		Not employed by an enterprise and so on, not self-employed, not full-time student, and has attempted to find work during the last 30 days.	Not currently in employment and not looking for employment.	
Kyrgyz Republic	1997	During the last 7 days worked or had a business and did not classify self as employer.	Employer: Employed (see previous) and classified self as employer.	Not employed (see previous definition) and looked for a job in the last 7 days.	Not employed (see previous definition) and did not look for a job in the last 7 days.	Not employed (see previous definition), did not look for a job in the last 7 days because is pensioner or old.
Latvia	1997–98	Major source of income from working and self-employment income not largest share of total household income.	Major source of income from working and self-employment income largest share of total household income.	Did not work in last week and has looked for work in past month or major source of income from unemployment benefit.	Deemed to be not in labor force if not employed, self-employed, or unemployed and <=55 if female or <=60 if male.	Deemed to be retired if does not fall into any of previous categories.

(Table continues on next page.)

Table C.4 *(continued)*

Country	Year	Employed	Self-employed/ employer	Unemployed	Not employed/ not in workforce	Retired
Lithuania	1999	Has been working in any activity for earning income (in cash or in-kind) more than one hour during the past 7 days; or has a job or business, but has not been working due to weekend, vacation, illness, childcare, and so on.			Has been looking for a job during the past 4 weeks.	Has not been looking for a job because individual is pensioner.
FYR Macedonia	1996	Variable provided in the data set, no definition given.	Variable provided in the data set, no definition given.	Variable provided in the data set, no definition given.		Identified self as pensioner only.
Moldova	1997	Farmer or worked in agriculture or nonagriculture sector.	Worked as entrepreneur.	Not employed or self-employed, looked for work in last 7 days, would be able to work next week.	Major source of income was not from working and <=55 if female or <=60 if male.	Deemed to be retired if does not fall into any of above categories.
Poland	1998	(i) Over the last 7 days, respondent performed any gainful or income-earning work or helped free of charge in family business. Or, (ii) over the last 7 days,		Respondent is not "employed" (see previous definition), has been looking for work over the last four weeks and is	Not "employed" (see previous definition), not "unemployed" (see previous definition), and not "retired" (see next definition).	Not "employed" (see previous definition) and age 65 years or older.

(Table continues on next page.)

Table C.4 (continued)

Country	Year	Employed	Self-employed/ employer	Unemployed	Not employed/ not in workforce	Retired
		respondent had a job as hired laborer, self-employed or helping free of charge in family business, or was temporarily absent from the previously mentioned activities.		ready to undertake work this or next week.		
Romania	1998	Labeled: employee, wage-earner.	This category was split into: a) employer (owner of a registered business that hires employees); b) self-employed in non-agricultural activities; c) farmers—self-employed in agricultural activities. This split was operated because we noted differences in poverty risks among these groups.	Not employed and looked for a job in the last 7 days (ILO definition).	Residual category: without a job, but not looking. Here we included registered unemployed who reported that they are not looking for a job.	Pensioners (recipient of pension income).
Russian Fed.	1998	Currently employed by an enterprise organization, collective farm, state farm, or cooperative with no further specifications.		Not "employed" and answered yes to, "Did you look for a job or try to start your own business during the last 30 days?"	Not employed and did not look for a job in the last 30 days.	Not employed, and did not look for work because is a pensioner.

(Table continues on next page.)

Table C.4 (continued)

Country	Year	Employed	Self-employed/ employer	Unemployed	Not employed/ not in workforce	Retired
Slovenia	1993	Variable provided in data set, no definition given.	Variable provided in data set, no definition given.	Variable provided in data set, no definition given.		Variable provided in data set, no definition given.
Slovenia	1997-98	Individual is currently working, or is temporarily not working (illness, vacation).		Individual defined as unemployed in data set.	Individual defined as retired, pupil, or student, involved in non-economic activity, unable to work, in military service, or less than 15 years old.	
Tajikistan	1999	ILO definitions	ILO definitions	ILO definitions	ILO definitions	ILO definitions
Turkmenistan	1998	If working in past 7 days and claimed not to be self-employed nor an independent entrepreneur.	If working past 7 days and claimed to be self employed or an entrepreneur.	If not working in past 7 days and looking for a job, or not looking because the respondent thought there were no jobs or no good jobs to look for.	Not working in the past 7 days and not looking because of being a student, taking care of children, no time, retraining, or maternity leave.	Not working in the past 7 days and not looking because is pensioner or old.
Ukraine	1995	Main occupation is "work," during the last 7 days employed by someone outside of the family or worked on a land lot,	Main occupation is "work," during the last 7 days employed by someone outside the family or worked on a	Main occupation is "work," during the past 7 days was not employed by someone outside the family or worked on a	Main occupation is householder, pupil of secondary school, college student, full-time student of higher institute.	Main occupation is pensioner. Identifies self as pensioner.

(Table continues on next page.)

409

Table C.4 *(continued)*

Country	Year	Employed	Self-employed/ employer	Unemployed	Not employed/ not in workforce	Retired
		and was a hired worker with a private person, company, agency or was individual lessee.	land lot, and owner of a company having employees, or co-owner of a company having employees or was self-employed.	land lot, and did not work in the last 7 days because waiting for a reply from a company, organization, employment agency, or waiting for a new company to open.		
Ukraine	1996	Main occupation is "work," major income comes from job at an enterprise, organization, company, collective farm, or work at a farmstead economy, land lot, or summer cottage, and does not identify self as owner.	Employer: Main occupation is "work," major income comes from job at an enterprise, organization, company, collective farm, or work at a farmstead economy, land lot, or summer cottage, and identifies self as owner. Self: Main occupation is "work," major income comes from work/occupation made by self or together with other people out of organization, company, or enterprise.	Reason for not having a job which brought income in the last 7 days is being registered for a job and waiting for an answer or waiting for an answer from an enterprise, organization, private person.	Identifies self as housekeeper, pupil in secondary school, college student, or full-time student of higher education institute.	

410

Table C.5 Income Earners/State Transfers/Private Transfers

Country	Year	Income earner	State transfers	Private transfers
Albania	1996	Number of people who worked during the past 7 days.		
Armenia	1996	In the last month respondent had income from wages, self-employment, or from agriculture or forestry (including benefits from private plot).	Money income from social assistance benefits and other social transfers; all in-kind transfers (food and non-food given for free or discount coupons for fuel/electricity).	Gifts, alimony, and income from remittances received in cash and in-kind.
Armenia	1998–99	In the last month respondent had income from wages, self-employment, or from agriculture or forestry (including benefits from private plot).	Money income from social assistance benefits and other social transfers; all in-kind transfers (food and non-food given for free or discount coupons for electricity).	Gifts, alimony, and income from remittances received in cash and in-kind.
Azerbaijan	1995	Number of people listed as "employed."	Income from pensions, pension allowances, bread allowances, child allowances, and other state allowances, in money.	Gifts from people who are not members of the household.
Azerbaijan	1999	Not used in the analyses.	Not used in the analyses.	Not used in the analyses.
Belarus	1996	Number of people who report that they "work at present."	Income from pensions, subsidies for fuel (heating), Chernobyl benefits, child allowances, household student grants, unemployment benefits, and other state subsidies and benefits.	Financial assistance received from relatives or friends not living with family or from charitable organizations, as well as alimony received by the household.
Belarus	1999	Number of people who report that they "work at present."		

(Table continues on next page.)

Table C.5 *(continued)*

Country	Year	Income earner	State transfers	Private transfers
Bulgaria	1995	Working for a wage or revenue during past 7 days or performed activity for cash or in-kind remuneration.	Child allowances, disability, household, maternal, medical, public pension, private pension, stipend, survival pension, transport, and unemployment allowances.	Income from remittances received.
Bulgaria	1997	Working for a wage or revenue during past 7 days or performed activity for cash or in-kind remuneration.	Child allowances, disability, household, maternal, medical, public pension, private pension, stipend, survival pension, transport, and unemployment allowances.	Income from remittances received.
Croatia	1998	In the past 12 months respondent had income from wages, self-employment, or from agriculture or forestry (including benefits from private plot).	Receipts from disability, old-age or survivor's pension (including from abroad), child allowance, layette assistance, allowance for nursing other persons or allowance for physical disablement, social welfare support, compensation for rehabilitation or employment of disabled persons.	Scholarship or schooling allowance, gifts in cash and in-kind (including transfers from abroad).
Czech Republic	1992	Number of people employed and self-employed.	Pension benefits, sickness benefits, family allowances, unemployment benefits and all benefits from the state social support scheme	Income from private insurance companies and other private institutions, and from gifts and inheritance.

(Table continues on next page.)

Table C.5 *(continued)*

Country	Year	Income earner	State transfers	Private transfers
Czech Republic	1996	Number of people employed and self-employed.	Pension benefits, sickness benefits, family allowances, unemployment benefits, and all benefits from the state social support scheme.	Income from private insurance companies and other private institutions, and from gifts and inheritance.
Estonia	1995	Number of people listed as employed.	Old-age pension, disability pension, and loss-of-provider pension.	Cash private transfers.
Estonia	1998	Information not included in data set.	Information not included in data set.	Information not included in data set.
Georgia	1996–97	In the last 3 months respondent had income from wages, self-employment, or from agriculture or forestry (including benefits from private plot).	Money income from social assistance benefits and other social transfers; estimated value of food in-kind transfers, averaged over the last 3 months.	Gifts, alimony, and income from remittances received in cash and in kind averaged over the last 3 months.
Hungary	1997	Number of people listed as employed (see previous definition).	Pension, family-related benefits, social assistance, unemployment benefits, other social transfers and stipends.	Cash gifts from family and friends.
Kazakhstan	1996	Worked for money or had profitable business during the last 7 days.	Income from maternity grants, maintenance grants for children, single mother subsistence allowance, allowance for children of men serving their military term, allowance for unemployed mothers that have 4 or more children under 7, and allowance for individuals with AIDS.	

(Table continues on next page.)

Table C.5 (continued)

Country	Year	Income earner	State transfers	Private transfers
Kyrgyz Republic	1993	Number of people listed as employed (see previous definition).	Income from social assistance benefits and other social transfers.	Private gifts received.
Kyrgyz Republic	1997	Number of people listed as employed (see previous definition).	Income from social benefits: pensions and other allowances.	Gross transfers received.
Latvia	1997–98	Number of people listed as employed (see previous definition).	Old-age and other (such as disability) pensions, family-related benefits, social assistance, unemployment benefits, other social transfers and stipends.	Cash and in-kind gifts from family and friends.
Lithuania	1999	Income earner is defined as having a main source of income, such as an individual who is not dependent according to questionnaire.	Income from retirement pension plus unemployment benefits plus other pensions and benefits.	
FYR Macedonia	1996	Number of employed persons.	Child benefits, retirement pensions, social assistance, invalid and other subventions, scholarships.	Remittances from abroad and foreign pensions.
Moldova	1997	Number of people listed as employed (see previous definition).	Old-age and other (such as disability) pensions, family-related benefits, social assistance, unemployment benefits, other social transfers, and stipends.	Gifts received.

(Table continues on next page.)

Table C.5 *(continued)*

Country	Year	Income earner	State transfers	Private transfers
Poland	1998	During the past month respondent had income from wages or self-employment.	Income from: old-age pensions, disability pensions, unemployment benefits, other benefits from the labor fund, family pensions, maternity allowances, upbringing allowances, childbirth, funeral, sickness allowances (after cessation of employment relationship), rehabilitation allowance, family allowances, nursing allowances, housing supplementary allowances, regular benefits from social welfare, temporary benefits from social welfare, benefits for pregnant women and persons raising children, other benefits from social welfare, child-support payments from child-support fund, assistance from non-commercial institutions, and other social-welfare type income.	
Romania	1998	All recipients of primary market incomes (employers, self-employed, employees, farmers) or pensioners.	Pensions, unemployment benefits, family benefits, social aid (MIG) program, other allowances from state or local budget.	Gifts from other households, in cash or in-kind.
Russian Federation	1998		Income from social benefits: pensions and other allowances.	Gross transfers received.

(Table continues on next page.)

Table C.5 *(continued)*

Country	Year	Income earner	State transfers	Private transfers
Slovenia	1993	Number of people listed as employed.	Income from pensions and other social insurance disbursements.	Income from abroad.
Slovenia	1997–98	Number of people listed as employed.		
Tajikistan	1999	Number of people listed as employed (see previous definition).	Income from social assistance benefits and other social transfers.	Gifts and remittances from persons outside the household, including aid from international relief organizations.
Turkmenistan	1998	Number of people who worked last 7 days.	Income from old age pension, disability pension, pension in case of loss of provider, allowances for temporary disability, maternity leave, disaster, social pensions, family benefits, and other allowances not mentioned above.	Remittance from family members, relatives, and nonrelatives.
Ukraine	1995	Number of people who during the last 7 days were employed with someone not a member of their household, worked on a land lot, cattle or poultry breeding which belonged to the household, or was self-employed or in a joint profitable activity with other people.	Income from old-age pension, service pension on privileged terms, disability or sickness pension, loss of breadwinner pension, merit pension, other pension, child allowance, unemployment allowance, low-income allowance, allowance for those who suffered from Chernobyl, and other allowances from the state or local authorities.	Income from anyone outside the household (whether in Ukraine or abroad), trade union or company management, charity foundations of Ukraine, religious organizations of Ukraine, charity foundations and religious organizations of other countries, including humanitarian aid, and other organizations.

(Table continues on next page.)

416

Table C.5 *(continued)*

Country	Year	Income earner	State transfers	Private transfers
Ukraine	1996	Number of people listed as employed or employer.	Money received as old-age pension, service pension, old-age pension on privileged terms, disability or sickness pension, loss of breadwinner pension, merit pension, and unemployment benefits.	Money received as gifts from family members who live apart or from nonrelatives.

Table C.6 Components of the Consumption Aggregate

Country	Year	Food — Bought	Food — Gift	Food — Home produced consumption	Food — Meals outside	Food	Education	Medical	Other	Rent	Utilities	Durables
Albania	1996	✓	✓	✓	✓	✓	✓	✓	✓	✓	✓	✓[2]
Armenia	1996	✓	✓	✓	✓	✓	✓	✓	✓	✓	✓	
Armenia	1998–99	✓[3]	✓[3]	✓[3]	✓	✓	✓	✓	✓	✓	✓	
Azerbaijan	1995	✓	✓	✓	✓	✓			✓	✓	✓	
Azerbaijan	1999	✓	✓	✓	✓	✓	✓	✓	✓			✓[1]
Belarus	1996	✓	✓	✓	✓	✓	✓	✓	✓	✓	✓	
Belarus	1999	✓	✓	✓	✓	✓	✓	✓	✓	✓	✓	
Bulgaria	1995	✓	✓	✓		✓	✓	✓	✓	✓	✓	✓[2]
Bulgaria	1997	✓	✓	✓		✓	✓	✓	✓	✓	✓	✓[2]
Croatia	1998	✓	✓	✓	✓	✓	✓	✓	✓		✓	✓[1]
Estonia (HEIDE)	1995	✓		✓		✓	✓	✓	✓	✓		
Estonia	1998	✓		✓		✓	✓	✓	✓			
Georgia	1996	✓	✓	✓[4]	✓	✓	✓	✓	✓	✓	✓	
Hungary	1997	✓	✓	✓	✓	✓	✓	✓	✓	✓	✓	✓[1]
Kazakhstan	1996	✓	✓		✓	✓	✓	✓	✓		✓	✓[2]
Kyrgyz Republic	1993	✓		✓	✓	✓	✓	✓	✓	✓	✓	✓[1]
Kyrgyz Republic	1997	✓	✓	✓	✓	✓	✓	✓	✓	✓	✓	✓[2]
Kyrgyz Republic	1998	✓	✓	✓	✓	✓	✓	✓	✓	✓	✓	✓[2]
Latvia	1997–98	✓	✓	✓	✓	✓	✓	✓	✓	✓	✓	✓[1]
Lithuania	1999	✓	✓			✓	✓	✓	✓	✓	✓	✓[1]
FYR Macedonia	1996	✓	✓[5]	✓[5]	✓	✓	✓	✓	✓	✓	✓	✓[1]
Moldova	1997	✓	✓	✓	✓	✓	✓	✓	✓	✓	✓	✓[1]
Poland	1998	✓	✓	✓	✓	✓	✓[6]	✓[6]	✓	✓	✓	✓[1]
Romania	1998	✓	✓	✓	✓	✓	✓	✓	✓	✓	✓	

(Table continues on next page.)

418

Table C.6 (continued)

Country	Year	Food			Meals outside	Food	Education	Medical	Other	Rent	Utilities	Durables
		Bought	Gift	Home produced consumption								
Russian Federation	1998	✓	✓		✓	✓	✓	✓	✓	✓	✓	✓²
Slovenia	1997–98	✓		✓	✓	✓	✓	✓	✓	✓	✓	✓¹
Tajikistan	1999	✓	✓	✓	✓		✓	✓	✓	✓	✓	✓¹
Turkmenistan	1998	✓		✓	✓	✓	✓	✓	✓	✓		✓¹
Ukraine	1995	✓⁷	✓⁸	✓⁸	✓	✓	✓	✓	✓	✓	✓	
Ukraine	1996	✓⁷	✓⁸	✓⁸	✓	✓	✓		✓	✓	✓	

Notes: If the survey is not listed, consumption data were not analyzed.
1. Indicates purchase price is included.
2. Indicates use value has been calculated.
3. Value based on question on total consumption of food by household, which did not distinguish consumption by source (bought, gift, home-produced).
4. Value based on longer recall (three months) than other food items.
5. In-kind food consumption is recorded, but not separated out by gift or consumption of home production.
6. Education and health expenditures are only included if the household paid for them.
7. Consumed food rather than purchased food.
8. Food as gifts and consumption of home production were considered as both income and expenditures.

419

Table C.7 Components of the Income Aggregate

Country	Year	Cash	In-kind	Agri-cultural	Nonagri-cultural	Home con-sumption	Social transfers	Rent	Private transfers	Other income	Taxes
		Wages		*Self-employment*							
Albania	1996	✓			✓		✓	✓	✓	✓	
Armenia	1996	✓		✓	✓	✓	✓		✓	✓	
Armenia	1998–99	✓			✓		✓		✓	✓	
Azerbaijan	1995	✓			✓		✓	✓	✓	✓	
Bulgaria	1995	✓		✓	✓		✓		✓	✓	
Bulgaria	1997	✓		✓	✓		✓		✓	✓	
Croatia	1998	✓	✓	✓	✓		✓		✓	✓	
Czech Republic	1992	✓		✓	✓		✓			✓	
Czech Republic	1996	✓		✓	✓		✓			✓	
Estonia (HEIDE)	1995	✓	✓	✓	✓	✓[1]	✓	✓	✓	✓	✓
Estonia	1998	✓		✓	✓		✓	✓		✓	
Georgia	1996	✓		✓	✓		✓		✓	✓	
Hungary	1997	✓		✓	✓	✓	✓	✓	✓	✓	✓
Kazakhstan	1996	✓		✓	✓	✓	✓	✓	✓	✓	
Kyrgyz Republic	1993	✓		✓	✓	✓	✓		✓	✓	✓
Latvia	1997–98	✓	✓	✓	✓	✓[1]	✓	✓	✓	✓	
Lithuania	1999	✓	✓	✓	✓	✓	✓	✓	✓	✓	
FYR Macedonia	1996	✓	✓	✓	✓		✓	✓	✓	✓	
Moldova	1997	✓		✓	✓		✓	✓	✓	✓	
Poland	1998	✓		✓	✓		✓	✓	✓	✓	
Russian Federation	1998	✓	✓	✓	✓		✓		✓	✓	
Slovak Republic[3]	1997	✓	✓	✓	✓		✓		✓	✓	
Slovenia	1993	✓		✓[2]	✓[2]		✓				
Tajikistan	1999	✓	✓	✓[2]	✓	✓[1]	✓		✓	✓	
Ukraine	1995	✓	✓	✓		✓[1]	✓		✓		
Ukraine	1996	✓	✓	✓		✓[1]	✓		✓	✓	

Notes: If the survey is not listed, income data were not analyzed.
1. Home consumption included as both income and expenditure.
2. Net income from self-employment (not specified as agricultural or non-agricultural).
3. Survey was administered in 1997 and collected information on income in 1996.

APPENDIX D

Poverty and Inequality Tables

Distribution of Consumption and Expenditures

ALBANIA: Distribution of Consumption: Summary Statistics, 1996

Indicator	OECD equivalence scale (theta=0.5)	Equivalent adults (theta=0.75)	Individuals, per capita (theta=1)
A. Consumption			
Decile ratio: (90/10)	2.93	3.16	3.56
of which: (50/10)	1.81	1.80	1.89
(90/50)	1.62	1.76	1.89
Gini coefficient	0.23	0.25	0.27
Theil entropy measure	0.09	0.10	0.12
Mean log deviation measure	0.09	0.10	0.12

Note: The data do not include Tirana.

ARMENIA: Distribution of Consumption and Incomes: Summary Statistics, 1998/99

Indicator	OECD equivalence scale (theta=0.5)	Equivalent adults (theta=0.75)	Individuals, per capita (theta=1)
A. Consumption			
Decile ratio: (90/10)	3.83	3.88	4.08
of which: (50/10)	1.95	1.95	2.03
(90/50)	1.96	1.99	2.01
Gini coefficient	0.31	0.31	0.32
Theil entropy measure	0.17	0.17	0.18
Mean log deviation measure	0.16	0.16	0.17
B. Incomes			
Decile ratio: (90/10)	18.97	19.40	19.29
of which: (50/10)	5.10	5.19	5.19
(90/50)	3.72	3.74	3.72
Gini coefficient	0.58	0.58	0.59
Theil entropy measure	0.69	0.69	0.71
Mean log deviation measure	0.65	0.65	0.67

AZERBAIJAN: Distribution of Consumption: Summary Statistics, 1995

Indicator	OECD equivalence scale (theta=0.5)	Equivalent adults (theta=0.75)	Individuals, per capita (theta=1)
A. Consumption			
Decile ratio: (90/10)	7.07	7.09	7.14
of which: (50/10)	2.89	2.93	2.83
(90/50)	2.44	2.42	2.52
Gini coefficient	0.42	0.43	0.44
Theil entropy measure	0.33	0.34	0.37
Mean log deviation measure	0.32	0.33	0.34

AZERBAIJAN: Distribution of Consumption: Summary Statistics, 1999

Indicator	OECD equivalence scale (theta=0.5)	Equivalent adults (theta=0.75)	Individuals, per capita (theta=1)
A. Consumption			
Decile ratio: (90/10)	4.87	5.03	5.26
of which: (50/10)	2.16	2.15	2.18
(90/50)	2.26	2.34	2.41
Gini coefficient	0.42	0.42	0.43
Theil entropy measure	0.45	0.46	0.48
Mean log deviation measure	0.31	0.32	0.33

BELARUS: Distribution of Consumption and Incomes: Summary Statistics, 1999

Indicator	OECD equivalence scale (theta=0.5)	Equivalent adults (theta=0.75)	Individuals, per capita (theta=1)
A. Consumption			
Decile ratio: (90/10)	3.90	3.85	4.06
of which: (50/10)	2.02	1.98	1.99
(90/50)	1.93	1.95	2.04
Gini coefficient	0.29	0.30	0.31
Theil entropy measure	0.15	0.15	0.17
Mean log deviation measure	0.15	0.15	0.16
B. Incomes			
Decile ratio: (90/10)	3.14	3.01	3.14
of which: (50/10)	1.83	1.77	1.79
(90/50)	1.71	1.71	1.76
Gini coefficient	0.26	0.25	0.26
Theil entropy measure	0.12	0.12	0.13
Mean log deviation measure	0.11	0.11	0.11

Note: Due to the structure of the questionnaire, it is likely that income from self-employment may be underreported and hence income inequality underestimated.

BELARUS: Distribution of Consumption and Incomes: Summary Statistics, 1996

Indicator	OECD equivalence scale (theta=0.5)	Equivalent adults (theta=0.75)	Individuals, per capita (theta=1)
A. Consumption			
Decile ratio: (90/10)	2.99	3.10	3.38
of which: (50/10)	1.74	1.72	1.80
(90/50)	1.72	1.80	1.88
Gini coefficient	0.26	0.26	0.28
Theil entropy measure	0.12	0.12	0.14
Mean log deviation measure	0.11	0.11	0.13
B. Incomes			
Decile ratio: (90/10)	2.93	2.84	2.98
of which: (50/10)	1.73	1.66	1.70
(90/50)	1.69	1.71	1.76
Gini coefficient	0.25	0.25	0.26
Theil entropy measure	0.12	0.11	0.12
Mean log deviation measure	0.11	0.10	0.11

BULGARIA: Distribution of Consumption and Incomes: Summary Statistics, 1995

Indicator	OECD equivalence scale (theta=0.5)	Equivalent adults (theta=0.75)	Individuals, per capita (theta=1)
A. Consumption			
Decile ratio: (90/10)	3.54	3.30	3.40
of which: (50/10)	1.93	1.83	1.89
(90/50)	1.83	1.80	1.80
Gini coefficient	0.27	0.27	0.27
Theil entropy measure	0.13	0.12	0.13
Mean log deviation measure	0.13	0.12	0.13
B. Incomes			
Decile ratio: (90/10)	6.08	5.88	6.19
of which: (50/10)	2.89	2.87	2.95
(90/50)	2.11	2.06	2.09
Gini coefficient	0.41	0.40	0.41
Theil entropy measure	0.40	0.41	0.43
Mean log deviation measure	0.25	0.25	0.26

CROATIA: Distribution of Consumption and Incomes: Summary Statistics, 1998

Indicator	OECD equivalence scale (theta=0.5)	Equivalent adults (theta=0.75)	Individuals, per capita (theta=1)
A. Consumption			
Decile ratio: (90/10)	4.03	3.83	3.91
of which: (50/10)	2.05	1.91	1.90
(90/50)	1.97	2.00	2.06
Gini coefficient	0.30	0.30	0.30
Theil entropy measure	0.16	0.15	0.16
Mean log deviation measure	0.16	0.15	0.15
B. Incomes			
Decile ratio: (90/10)	4.16	3.78	3.76
of which: (50/10)	2.12	1.93	1.86
(90/50)	1.97	1.96	2.02
Gini coefficient	0.36	0.35	0.35
Theil entropy measure	0.34	0.33	0.33
Mean log deviation measure	0.24	0.22	0.22

CZECH REPUBLIC: Distribution of Consumption and Incomes: Summary Statistics, 1996

Indicator	OECD equivalence scale (theta=0.5)	Equivalent adults (theta=0.75)	Individuals, per capita (theta=1)
A. Consumption			
Decile ratio: (90/10)	2.87	2.74	2.96
of which: (50/10)	1.64	1.59	1.66
(90/50)	1.76	1.73	1.77
Gini coefficient	0.25	0.24	0.25
Theil entropy measure	0.11	0.10	0.11
Mean log deviation measure	0.10	0.10	0.10
B. Incomes			
Decile ratio: (90/10)	2.87	2.74	2.97
of which: (50/10)	1.64	1.59	1.66
(90/50)	1.76	1.73	1.79
Gini coefficient	0.25	0.24	0.25
Theil entropy measure	0.11	0.10	0.11
Mean log deviation measure	0.10	0.10	0.10

ESTONIA: Distribution of Consumption and Incomes: Summary Statistics, 1998

Indicator	OECD equivalence scale (theta=0.5)	Equivalent adults (theta=0.75)	Individuals, per capita (theta=1)
A. Consumption			
Decile ratio: (90/10)	5.36	5.07	5.38
of which: (50/10)	2.09	2.03	2.07
(90/50)	2.56	2.50	2.61
Gini coefficient	0.37	0.37	0.38
Theil entropy measure	0.24	0.24	0.26
Mean log deviation measure	0.23	0.22	0.23
B. Incomes			
Decile ratio: (90/10)	4.74	4.42	4.70
of which: (50/10)	2.09	1.96	2.03
(90/50)	2.27	2.26	2.32
Gini coefficient	0.37	0.36	0.37
Theil entropy measure	0.25	0.24	0.26
Mean log deviation measure	0.23	0.22	0.23

GEORGIA: Distribution of Consumption and Incomes: Summary Statistics, 1996/97

Indicator	OECD equivalence scale (theta=0.5)	Equivalent adults (theta=0.75)	Individuals, per capita (theta=1)
A. Consumption			
Decile ratio: (90/10)	5.16	5.29	5.69
of which: (50/10)	2.45	2.47	2.51
(90/50)	2.11	2.14	2.27
Gini coefficient	0.35	0.35	0.37
Theil entropy measure	0.21	0.22	0.24
Mean log deviation measure	0.21	0.22	0.24
A. Incomes			
Decile ratio: (90/10)	5.96	6.16	6.65
of which: (50/10)	2.56	2.56	2.60
(90/50)	2.33	2.41	2.55
Gini coefficient	0.41	0.41	0.43
Theil entropy measure	0.34	0.36	0.40
Mean log deviation measure	0.29	0.30	0.33

HUNGARY: Distribution of Consumption and Incomes: Summary Statistics, 1997

Indicator	OECD equivalence scale (theta=0.5)	Equivalent adults (theta=0.75)	Individuals, per capita (theta=1)
A. Consumption			
Decile ratio: (90/10)	3.13	3.18	3.49
of which: (50/10)	1.74	1.76	1.87
(90/50)	1.79	1.81	1.87
Gini coefficient	0.26	0.27	0.28
Theil entropy measure	0.12	0.13	0.15
Mean log deviation measure	0.11	0.12	0.14
B. Incomes			
Decile ratio: (90/10)	2.80	2.81	3.07
of which: (50/10)	1.68	1.68	1.79
(90/50)	1.67	1.67	1.71
Gini coefficient	0.24	0.24	0.25
Theil entropy measure	0.10	0.10	0.11
Mean log deviation measure	0.09	0.10	0.11

KAZAKHSTAN: Distribution of Consumption: Summary Statistics, 1996

Indicator	OECD equivalence scale (theta=0.5)	Equivalent adults (theta=0.75)	Individuals, per capita (theta=1)
A. Consumption			
Decile ratio: (90/10)	4.73	4.83	5.23
of which: (50/10)	2.19	2.21	2.28
(90/50)	2.16	2.18	2.29
Gini coefficient	0.33	0.34	0.35
Theil entropy measure	0.18	0.19	0.21
Mean log deviation measure	0.19	0.19	0.21

KYRGYZ REPUBLIC: Distribution of Consumption and Incomes: Summary Statistics, 1997

Indicator	OECD equivalence scale (theta=0.5)	Equivalent adults (theta=0.75)	Individuals, per capita (theta=1)
A. Consumption			
Decile ratio: (90/10)	5.05	5.52	6.35
of which: (50/10)	2.08	2.14	2.19
(90/50)	2.43	2.58	2.90
Gini coefficient	0.36	0.39	0.42
Theil entropy measure	0.22	0.26	0.33
Mean log deviation measure	0.22	0.25	0.30
B. Incomes			
Decile ratio: (90/10)	8.39	9.27	10.38
of which: (50/10)	3.09	3.15	3.27
(90/50)	2.72	2.94	3.18
Gini coefficient	0.42	0.44	0.47
Theil entropy measure	0.33	0.36	0.42
Mean log deviation measure	0.34	0.37	0.42

LATVIA: Distribution of Consumption and Incomes: Summary Statistics, 1997/98

Indicator	OECD equivalence scale (theta=0.5)	Equivalent adults (theta=0.75)	Individuals, per capita (theta=1)
A. Consumption			
Decile ratio: (90/10)	4.25	4.23	4.54
of which: (50/10)	2.06	2.07	2.18
(90/50)	2.06	2.04	2.08
Gini coefficient	0.32	0.32	0.34
Theil entropy measure	0.18	0.18	0.20
Mean log deviation measure	0.17	0.17	0.19
B. Incomes			
Decile ratio: (90/10)	3.94	3.82	4.13
of which: (50/10)	1.92	1.92	2.10
(90/50)	2.05	1.99	1.97
Gini coefficient	0.32	0.32	0.32
Theil entropy measure	0.23	0.21	0.21
Mean log deviation measure	0.19	0.18	0.19

LITHUANIA: Distribution of Consumption and Incomes: Summary Statistics, 1999

Indicator	OECD equivalence scale (theta=0.5)	Equivalent adults (theta=0.75)	Individuals, per capita (theta=1)
A. Consumption			
Decile ratio: (90/10)	3.89	4.01	4.25
of which: (50/10)	1.93	1.95	2.02
(90/50)	2.02	2.05	2.10
Gini coefficient	0.32	0.32	0.34
Theil entropy measure	0.19	0.20	0.22
Mean log deviation measure	0.17	0.17	0.19
B. Incomes			
Decile ratio: (90/10)	4.45	4.52	4.89
of which: (50/10)	2.21	2.20	2.33
(90/50)	2.02	2.05	2.10
Gini coefficient	0.34	0.33	0.34
Theil entropy measure	0.20	0.20	0.21
Mean log deviation measure	0.18	0.17	0.19

FYR MACEDONIA: Distribution of Consumption and Incomes: Summary Statistics, 1996

Indicator	OECD equivalence scale (theta=0.5)	Equivalent adults (theta=0.75)	Individuals, per capita (theta=1)
A. Consumption			
Decile ratio: (90/10)	4.38	4.44	4.80
of which: (50/10)	2.20	2.26	2.41
(90/50)	1.99	1.96	1.99
Gini coefficient	0.31	0.32	0.34
Theil entropy measure	0.17	0.18	0.20
Mean log deviation measure	0.16	0.17	0.19
B. Incomes			
Decile ratio: (90/10)	5.20	5.42	5.79
of which: (50/10)	2.40	2.46	2.58
(90/50)	2.17	2.20	2.24
Gini coefficient	0.35	0.36	0.37
Theil entropy measure	0.23	0.23	0.25
Mean log deviation measure	0.22	0.23	0.25

MOLDOVA: Distribution of Consumption and Incomes: Summary Statistics, 1997

Indicator	OECD equivalence scale (theta=0.5)	Equivalent adults (theta=0.75)	Individuals, per capita (theta=1)
A. Consumption			
Decile ratio: (90/10)	5.79	5.77	6.14
of which: (50/10)	2.32	2.32	2.39
(90/50)	2.49	2.49	2.57
Gini coefficient	0.39	0.40	0.41
Theil entropy measure	0.28	0.29	0.30
Mean log deviation measure	0.27	0.27	0.29
B. Incomes			
Decile ratio: (90/10)	7.17	7.23	7.43
of which: (50/10)	2.81	2.81	2.78
(90/50)	2.55	2.58	2.67
Gini coefficient	0.41	0.41	0.42
Theil entropy measure	0.30	0.30	0.32
Mean log deviation measure	0.35	0.35	0.37

POLAND: Distribution of Consumption and Incomes: Summary Statistics, 1998

Indicator	OECD equivalence scale (theta=0.5)	Equivalent adults (theta=0.75)	Individuals, per capita (theta=1)
A. Consumption			
Decile ratio: (90/10)	3.44	3.72	4.29
of which: (50/10)	1.80	1.87	2.00
(90/50)	1.91	1.99	2.14
Gini coefficient	0.29	0.31	0.34
Theil entropy measure	0.16	0.18	0.21
Mean log deviation measure	0.14	0.16	0.19
B. Incomes			
Decile ratio: (90/10)	3.48	3.71	4.25
of which: (50/10)	1.90	1.98	2.14
(90/50)	1.83	1.87	1.98
Gini coefficient	0.29	0.30	0.32
Theil entropy measure	0.16	0.17	0.19
Mean log deviation measure	0.13	0.14	0.17

ROMANIA: Distribution of Consumption: Summary Statistics, 1998

Indicator	OECD equivalence scale (theta=0.5)	Equivalent adults (theta=0.75)	Individuals, per capita (theta=1)
A. Consumption			
Decile ratio: (90/10)	3.17	3.24	3.62
of which: (50/10)	1.78	1.80	1.92
(90/50)	1.78	1.80	1.88
Gini coefficient	0.27	0.27	0.30
Theil entropy measure	0.14	0.15	0.17
Mean log deviation measure	0.12	0.13	0.15

**RUSSIAN FEDERATION: Distribution of Consumption and Incomes:
Summary Statistics, 1998**

Indicator	OECD equivalence scale (theta=0.5)	Equivalent adults (theta=0.75)	Individuals, per capita (theta=1)
A. Consumption			
Decile ratio: (90/10)	7.79	7.68	8.06
of which: (50/10)	2.95	2.82	2.83
(90/50)	2.64	2.72	2.85
Gini coefficient	0.46	0.46	0.47
Theil entropy measure	0.42	0.41	0.43
Mean log deviation measure	0.38	0.38	0.39
B. Incomes			
Decile ratio: (90/10)	8.29	8.39	8.78
of which: (50/10)	3.30	3.37	3.51
(90/50)	2.51	2.49	2.51
Gini coefficient	0.46	0.46	0.47
Theil entropy measure	0.59	0.60	0.61
Mean log deviation measure	0.41	0.41	0.43

SLOVENIA: Distribution of Consumption and Incomes: Summary Statistics, 1997/98

Indicator	OECD equivalence scale (theta=0.5)	Equivalent adults (theta=0.75)	Individuals, per capita (theta=1)
A. Consumption			
Decile ratio: (90/10)	3.31	3.35	3.67
of which: (50/10)	1.79	1.73	1.82
(90/50)	1.84	1.94	2.02
Gini coefficient	0.26	0.27	0.28
Theil entropy measure	0.11	0.12	0.14
Mean log deviation measure	0.11	0.12	0.13
B. Incomes			
Decile ratio: (90/10)	2.94	2.84	3.03
of which: (50/10)	1.82	1.72	1.74
(90/50)	1.61	1.65	1.74
Gini coefficient	0.24	0.24	0.25
Theil entropy measure	0.09	0.09	0.11
Mean log deviation measure	0.10	0.10	0.11

TAJIKISTAN: Distribution of Consumption and Incomes: Summary Statistics, 1999

Indicator	OECD equivalence scale (theta=0.5)	Equivalent adults (theta=0.75)	Individuals, per capita (theta=1)
A. Consumption			
Decile ratio: (90/10)	4.04	3.97	4.07
of which: (50/10)	2.03	2.07	2.04
(90/50)	1.99	1.92	2.00
Gini coefficient	0.31	0.31	0.32
Theil entropy measure	0.17	0.17	0.18
Mean log deviation measure	0.16	0.16	0.17
B. Incomes			
Decile ratio: (90/10)	10.42	10.37	10.60
of which: (50/10)	3.66	3.72	3.67
(90/50)	2.85	2.79	2.89
Gini coefficient	0.47	0.47	0.47
Theil entropy measure	0.41	0.40	0.41
Mean log deviation measure	0.41	0.40	0.41

TURKMENISTAN: Distribution of Consumption: Summary Statistics, 1998

Indicator	OECD equivalence scale (theta=0.5)	Equivalent adults (theta=0.75)	Individuals, per capita (theta=1)
A. Consumption			
Decile ratio: (90/10)	5.35	5.59	6.13
of which: (50/10)	2.21	2.22	2.29
(90/50)	2.42	2.52	2.68
Gini coefficient	0.37	0.39	0.41
Theil entropy measure	0.26	0.27	0.31
Mean log deviation measure	0.23	0.25	0.28

UKRAINE: Distribution of Consumption: Summary Statistics, 1995

Indicator	OECD equivalence scale (theta=0.5)	Equivalent adults (theta=0.75)	Individuals, per capita (theta=1)
A. Consumption			
Decile ratio: (90/10)	5.71	5.41	5.48
of which: (50/10)	2.40	2.31	2.34
(90/50)	2.38	2.34	2.34
Gini coefficient	0.39	0.38	0.39
Theil entropy measure	0.28	0.28	0.30
Mean log deviation measure	0.26	0.26	0.27
B. Incomes			
Decile ratio: (90/10)	8.63	8.71	9.10
of which: (50/10)	3.18	3.18	3.21
(90/50)	2.71	2.74	2.83
Gini coefficient	0.47	0.60	0.47
Theil entropy measure	0.42	0.42	0.44
Mean log deviation measure	0.38	0.38	0.39

UKRAINE: Distribution of Consumption and Incomes: Summary Statistics, 1999

Indicator	OECD equivalence scale (theta=0.5)	Equivalent adults (theta=0.75)	Individuals, per capita (theta=1)
A. Consumption			
Decile ratio: (90/10)	3.87	3.94	4.29
of which: (50/10)	1.95	1.96	2.06
(90/50)	1.99	2.01	2.08
Gini coefficient	0.31	0.32	0.33
Theil entropy measure	0.17	0.18	0.20
Mean log deviation measure	0.15	0.16	0.18
B. Incomes			
Decile ratio: (90/10)	4.04	3.92	4.19
of which: (50/10)	2.07	2.00	2.06
(90/50)	1.95	1.96	2.03
Gini coefficient	0.31	0.31	0.32
Theil entropy measure	0.17	0.18	0.19
Mean log deviation measure	0.17	0.16	0.18

Composition of Poverty

ALBANIA: Composition of Poverty, 1996

Poverty line	33% of median	67% of median	50% of median	50% of median	50% of median	
Economies of scale	Theta=.75	Theta=.75	Theta=1	Theta=.75	Theta=.50	
	Share of poor	Share of poor	Share of poor	Share of poor	Share of poor	Share of population
Age in years						
0–15	63.1	48.8	57.0	56.2	49.9	35.1
16–64	32.0	47.2	40.2	41.0	44.5	58.8
65⁺	4.9	4.0	2.8	2.8	5.5	6.1
Total	100.0	100.0	100.0	100.0	100.0	100.0
Education						
Age less than 15	63.1	48.8	57.0	56.2	49.9	35.1
None	7.2	5.4	4.2	5.1	8.3	4.6
Primary (less than 7 years)	29.7	36.5	33.4	32.7	34.9	35.6
General secondary (8–12 years)	0.0	1.7	1.4	2.1	1.8	7.8
Vocational/specialized secondary	0.0	7.2	3.8	3.5	4.5	13.6
Some higher	0.0	0.4	0.2	0.5	0.6	3.3
Total	100.0	100.0	100.0	100.0	100.0	100.0
Location						
Rural	100.0	91.4	92.6	88.5	85.7	65.2
Urban	0.0	8.6	7.4	11.5	14.3	34.8
Total	100.0	100.0	100.0	100.0	100.0	100.0
Access to land						
No	0.0	12.5	12.5	20.3	25.5	37.7
Yes	100.0	87.5	87.5	79.7	74.5	62.3
Total	100.0	100.0	100.0	100.0	100.0	100.0
Own automobile						
No	100.0	100.0	100.0	100.0	100.0	97.8
Yes	0.0	0.0	0.0	0.0	0.0	2.2
Total	100.0	100.0	100.0	100.0	100.0	100.0
Household typology						
Single parent with child(ren)	0.0	0.5	1.0	1.5	1.8	0.5
Other households with child(ren)	96.6	92.2	97.2	94.2	85.1	80.2
Single elderly male	0.0	0.0	0.0	0.0	0.3	0.0
Single elderly female	0.0	0.4	0.0	0.5	1.5	0.3

(Table continues on next page)

ALBANIA (continued)

Poverty line	33% of median	67% of median	50% of median	50% of median	50% of median	
Economies of scale	Theta=.75	Theta=.75	Theta=1	Theta=.75	Theta=.50	
	Share of poor	Share of poor	Share of poor	Share of poor	Share of poor	Share of population
Multiple elderly only	0.0	0.2	0.0	0.0	1.0	0.4
Other households without child(ren)	3.4	6.7	1.8	3.8	10.4	18.5
Total	100.0	100.0	100.0	100.0	100.0	100.0
No. of children under 15						
Zero	3.4	7.3	1.8	4.3	13.2	19.3
One	0.0	13.4	6.4	6.6	7.0	20.5
Two	10.5	17.1	12.2	15.6	16.1	30.1
Three or more	86.2	62.2	79.6	73.5	63.7	30.1
Total	100.0	100.0	100.0	100.0	100.0	100.0
No. of elderly						
Zero	71.5	80.0	83.0	85.0	82.8	74.7
One	14.5	16.3	12.3	13.3	14.1	19.4
Two or more	13.9	3.7	4.7	1.7	3.1	6.0
Total	100.0	100.0	100.0	100.0	100.0	100.0
Household head, gender						
Male	68.0	91.3	88.6	83.8	80.2	90.8
Female	32.0	8.7	11.4	16.2	19.8	9.1
Total	100.0	100.0	100.0	100.0	100.0	100.0
Household head, labor market status						
Unknown	0.0	11.6	12.2	18.5	20.3	13.0
Employed	0.0	8.2	4.1	5.6	5.6	18.3
Self-employed or employer	46.6	61.3	65.7	54.7	46.5	42.2
Not in workforce	39.5	11.0	10.6	12.5	17.7	8.7
Retired	13.9	7.8	7.4	8.8	9.9	17.7
Total	100.0	100.0	100.0	100.0	100.0	100.0
No. of income earners						
Zero	17.5	15.0	15.0	22.4	29.8	17.9
One	47.9	24.2	29.8	38.6	34.3	28.7
Two	34.5	40.1	36.3	27.4	30.3	33.5
Three or more	0.0	20.7	18.9	11.6	5.5	19.9
Total	100.0	100.0	100.0	100.0	100.0	100.0

Source: Albania 1996 Employment and Welfare Survey.

ARMENIA: Composition of Poverty, 1998/99

Poverty line	33% of median	67% of median	50% of median	50% of median	50% of median	
Economies of scale	Theta=.75	Theta=.75	Theta=1	Theta=.75	Theta=.50	
	Share of poor	Share of poor	Share of poor	Share of poor	Share of poor	Share of population
Age in years						
0–15	32.1	31.9	34.6	33.0	30.2	29.4
16–64	57.2	58.3	57.2	56.7	56.4	61.5
65+	10.7	9.8	8.2	10.3	13.4	9.1
Total	100.0	100.0	100.0	100.0	100.0	100.0
Education						
Age less than 15	32.1	31.9	34.6	33.0	30.2	29.4
None	1.7	1.6	1.9	1.6	1.6	1.6
Primary	5.2	4.8	4.9	5.3	5.6	4.1
Secondary or specialized secondary	55.2	53.0	52.1	52.9	53.7	51.7
Higher	5.8	8.8	6.5	7.2	9.0	13.3
Total	100.0	100.0	100.0	100.0	100.0	100.0
Location						
Urban	48.7	58.4	56.4	58.0	62.2	57.1
Rural	51.3	41.7	43.6	42.0	37.9	42.9
Total	100.0	100.0	100.0	100.0	100.0	100.0
Region						
Aragotsotn	20.2	8.0	9.8	9.7	8.2	6.2
Ararat	0.3	9.4	7.6	8.6	7.6	9.5
Armavir	2.9	5.8	6.3	5.0	6.1	11.5
Gegarkunik	10.3	8.8	10.0	10.9	8.7	8.3
Lori	19.1	12.9	14.2	15.6	17.0	8.5
Kotaik	10.3	10.0	11.3	8.4	8.9	9.3
Shirak	12.6	13.2	10.7	13.3	15.1	9.4
Sunik	2.6	3.9	4.1	5.0	4.2	4.8
Vaits Dzor	2.4	1.7	1.6	1.8	1.3	1.9
Tavush	0.0	0.5	0.3	0.1	0.2	2.9
Capital	19.4	25.8	24.2	21.6	22.7	27.7
Total	100.0	100.0	100.0	100.0	100.0	100.0
Access to land						
No	42.8	54.4	51.5	51.8	57.8	48.3
Yes	57.2	45.6	48.5	48.2	42.2	51.7
Total	100.0	100.0	100.0	100.0	100.0	100.0
Own automobile						
No	93.0	89.9	90.4	92.4	94.0	77.3
Yes	7.0	10.1	9.6	7.6	6.0	22.7
Total	100.0	100.0	100.0	100.0	100.0	100.0

(Table continues on next page)

ARMENIA (continued)

Poverty line	33% of median	67% of median	50% of median	50% of median	50% of median	
Economies of scale	Theta=.75	Theta=.75	Theta=1	Theta=.75	Theta=.50	
	Share of poor	Share of poor	Share of poor	Share of poor	Share of poor	Share of population
Household typology						
Single parent with child(ren)	2.4	3.4	3.1	4.1	5.5	2.2
Other household with child(ren)	79.8	77.6	85.6	79.4	68.8	74.1
Single elderly male	0.0	0.1	0.0	0.1	0.2	0.2
Single elderly female	1.5	1.0	0.3	1.2	3.3	0.8
Multiple elderly only	0.6	1.3	0.2	0.8	1.9	1.4
Other households without child(ren)	15.8	16.7	10.8	14.4	20.3	21.4
Total	100.0	100.0	100.0	100.0	100.0	100.0
No. of children under 15						
Zero	17.9	19.0	11.3	16.5	25.7	23.7
One	15.3	15.1	13.9	15.4	16.7	18.4
Two	40.8	33.2	34.2	34.1	31.9	32.0
Three or more	26.1	32.6	40.6	34.0	25.7	25.9
Total	100.0	100.0	100.0	100.0	100.0	100.0
No. of elderly						
Zero	61.6	63.7	61.0	61.1	62.8	68.5
One	25.2	25.6	27.2	28.0	27.8	22.5
Two	13.2	10.8	11.8	11.0	9.4	8.9
Three or more	0.0	0.0	0.0	0.0	0.0	0.1
Total	100.0	100.0	100.0	100.0	100.0	100.0
Household head, gender						
Male	73.6	75.4	76.2	72.9	66.9	78.4
Female	26.4	24.6	23.8	27.1	33.1	21.6
Total	100.0	100.0	100.0	100.0	100.0	100.0
Household head, labor market status						
Inactive	46.6	35.8	37.2	38.7	41.3	29.7
Unemployed	15.0	20.6	19.0	18.2	18.7	15.5
Employed	38.4	43.6	43.9	43.1	40.0	54.9
Total	100.0	100.0	100.0	100.0	100.0	100.0
No. of income earners						
Zero	31.7	32.3	29.4	32.2	39.2	22.0
One	23.5	26.0	24.8	26.2	27.8	28.2
Two	24.3	24.9	24.0	26.5	22.2	29.0
Three or more	20.5	16.8	21.8	15.1	10.8	20.8
Total	100.0	100.0	100.0	100.0	100.0	100.0

Source: Armenia 1998/99 Integrated Survey of Living Standards.

AZERBAIJAN: Composition of Poverty, 1999

Poverty line	33% of median	67% of median	50% of median	50% of median	50% of median	
Economies of scale	Theta=.75	Theta=.75	Theta=1	Theta=.75	Theta=.50	
	Share of poor	Share of poor	Share of poor	Share of poor	Share of poor	Share of population
Age in years						
0–15	27.9	30.8	31.5	29.8	29.8	28.4
16–64	68.6	62.8	62.5	64.1	64.1	65.8
65+	3.5	6.5	6.0	6.1	6.2	5.8
Total	100.0	100.0	100.0	100.0	100.0	100.0
Education						
Age less than 15	27.9	30.8	31.5	29.8	29.8	28.3
Unknown	0.0	0.1	0.0	0.2	0.2	0.2
None	2.7	3.3	3.8	3.9	3.9	2.5
Primary	5.8	3.6	4.9	5.2	5.5	2.0
Incomplete secondary	10.5	11.9	9.6	9.4	8.7	9.7
General secondary	36.8	30.8	31.1	30.7	31.3	27.8
Technical secondary	3.9	2.8	2.6	2.7	2.8	4.3
Professional	9.0	11.0	11.8	13.9	13.3	12.0
Higher	3.5	5.8	4.7	4.4	4.6	13.3
Total	100.0	100.0	100.0	100.0	100.0	100.0
Location						
Baku	6.4	16.3	13.3	16.3	14.7	26.6
Non-Baku	93.6	83.7	86.7	83.7	85.3	73.4
Total	100	100	100	100	100	100
Household typology						
Single parent with child(ren)	1.6	2.1	2.0	2.2	3.3	1.9
Other households with child(ren)	70.9	71.1	73.5	70.8	69.5	68.3
Single elderly female	0.0	0.0	0.0	0.0	0.0	0.0
Multiple elderly only	2.3	8.9	8.9	7.0	5.8	6.1
Other households without child(ren)	25.2	18.0	15.7	20.1	21.5	23.6
Total	100.0	100.0	100.0	100.0	100.0	100.0
No. of children under 15						
Zero	25.2	19.5	16.3	21.5	23.0	25.2
One	17.0	14.9	14.3	16.6	18.5	18.2
Two	35.0	36.9	36.5	33.3	32.1	30.5
Three or more	22.8	28.8	32.9	28.6	26.5	26.0
Total	100.0	100.0	100.0	100.0	100.0	100.0
No. of elderly						
Zero	84.9	70.3	71.7	74.3	74.2	74.0
One	12.8	20.8	19.4	18.8	19.9	19.9
Two or more	2.3	8.9	8.9	7.0	5.8	6.1
Total	100.0	100.0	100.0	100.0	100.0	100.0

(Table continues on next page)

AZERBAIJAN (continued)

Poverty line	33% of median	67% of median	50% of median	50% of median	50% of median	
Economies of scale	Theta=.75	Theta=.75	Theta=1	Theta=.75	Theta=.50	
	Share of poor	Share of poor	Share of poor	Share of poor	Share of poor	Share of population
Household head, gender						
Male	78.0	74.7	73.4	72.4	70.7	80.7
Female	22.0	25.3	26.6	27.6	29.3	19.3
Total	100.0	100.0	100.0	100.0	100.0	100.0
Household head, labor market status						
Unknown	0.0	0.8	0.9	0.0	0.0	0.3
Government	12.5	11.6	10.0	10.7	10.6	17.4
Education	11.2	4.0	3.7	4.3	4.5	5.4
Health	0.0	0.6	1.2	1.3	1.4	2.4
Agriculture	4.4	8.4	5.3	5.1	5.8	6.9
Private industry	4.3	1.6	1.4	1.6	1.7	3.2
Trade	11.2	5.1	6.6	6.4	5.3	6.3
Housekeeping	30.6	38.3	38.1	38.1	39.9	31.9
Unemployed	23.6	26.2	28.1	27.3	25.5	20.7
Other	2.3	3.3	4.6	5.3	5.5	5.6
Total	100.0	100.0	100.0	100.0	100.0	100.0
No. of income earners						
Zero	4.3	3.3	2.7	3.1	3.2	1.8
One	5.4	9.1	8.9	9.9	10.4	6.3
Two	22.8	17.0	13.2	15.2	14.3	16.1
Three	16.3	14.1	15.3	16.7	19.0	17.1
Four	21.0	17.5	15.7	15.7	16.4	22.7
Five or more	30.3	39.0	44.2	39.4	36.7	36.1
Total	100.0	100.0	100.0	100.0	100.0	100.0

Source: Azerbaijan 1999 Household Survey Data.

BELARUS: Composition of Poverty, 1999

Poverty line	33% of median	67% of median	50% of median	50% of median	50% of median	
Economies of scale	Theta=.75	Theta=.75	Theta=1	Theta=.75	Theta=.50	
	Share of poor	Share of poor	Share of poor	Share of poor	Share of poor	Share of population
Age in years						
0–15	25.9	27.5	32.7	26.8	20.2	22.2
16–64	58.3	57.1	58.5	57.1	51.9	65.6
65+	15.7	15.3	8.9	16.1	27.9	12.2
Total	100.0	100.0	100.0	100.0	100.0	100.0
Education						
Age less than 15	29.6	29.4	35.3	29.4	22.0	24.0
Unknown	1.9	2.4	2.3	2.6	1.5	2.3
None	6.5	4.7	3.0	5.3	9.6	2.6
Primary	25.0	20.4	16.5	20.2	29.1	14.9
General secondary	16.7	18.4	20.1	20.8	18.0	17.7
Vocational or specialized secondary	20.4	21.5	20.5	19.6	17.8	27.0
Some Higher		3.3	2.4	2.2	2.0	11.6
Total	100.0	100.0	100.0	100.0	100.0	100.0
Location						
Urban	33.6	29.6	27.2	29.8	30.8	43.3
Semi-urban	41.5	23.4	26.2	29.6	27.3	24.5
Rural	24.9	47.0	46.7	40.6	41.9	32.2
Total	100.0	100.0	100.0	100.0	100.0	100.0
Region						
South (Brest and Gomel oblasts)	38.9	35.7	38.2	37.5	35.9	31.7
Central (Minsk and Minsk oblasts)	32.3	22.4	22.1	22.8	22.3	30.6
West (Grodno oblast)	10.6	11.1	9.1	6.0	7.7	12.5
East (Mogilev, Vitebsk)	18.3	30.8	30.6	33.7	34.1	25.2
Total	100.0	100.0	100.0	100.0	100.0	100.0
Access to land						
No	49.1	30.5	30.0	31.8	34.1	34.1
Yes	50.9	69.5	70.0	68.2	65.9	65.9
Total	100.0	100.0	100.0	100.0	100.0	100.0
Own automobile						
No	92.0	91.9	90.9	93.1	95.0	75.0
Yes	8.0	8.1	9.1	6.9	5.0	25.0
Total	100.0	100.0	100.0	100.0	100.0	100.0
Household typology						
Single parent with child(ren)	5.5	4.5	4.1	5.4	7.1	2.9
Other households with child(ren)	57.6	60.2	72.3	59.4	39.1	54.6

(Table continues on next page)

BELARUS *(continued)*

Poverty line	33% of median	67% of median	50% of median	50% of median	50% of median	
Economies of scale	Theta=.75	Theta=.75	Theta=1	Theta=.75	Theta=.50	
	Share of poor	Share of poor	Share of poor	Share of poor	Share of poor	Share of population
Single elderly male	0.0	0.3	0.0	0.5	0.9	0.4
Single elderly female	9.4	5.8	1.9	7.1	16.7	3.5
Multiple elderly only	1.7	4.6	2.5	4.1	6.1	4.1
Other households without child(ren)	25.8	24.7	19.2	23.5	30.1	34.4
Total	100.0	100.0	100.0	100.0	100.0	100.0
No. of children under 15						
Zero	37.0	35.4	23.6	35.1	53.8	42.5
One	20.6	27.5	28.6	28.7	21.9	31.5
Two	42.4	24.7	27.7	25.8	19.3	20.9
Three or more	0.0	12.4	20.1	10.4	5.0	5.1
Total	100.0	100.0	100.0	100.0	100.0	100.0
No. of elderly						
Zero	70.3	75.1	81.7	73.2	62.8	78.6
One	28.1	16.7	11.4	19.6	29.6	14.9
Two	1.7	8.1	6.9	7.3	7.6	6.4
Three or more	0.0	0.1	0.0	0.0	0.0	0.1
Total	100.0	100.0	100.0	100.0	100.0	100.0
Household head, gender						
Male	29.9	47.3	50.6	41.9	31.4	48.7
Female	70.1	52.7	49.4	58.1	68.6	51.3
Total	100.0	100.0	100.0	100.0	100.0	100.0
Household head, labor market status						
Unknown	2.6	0.2	0.3	0.5	0.7	0.2
Employed	65.7	60.1	66.3	56.1	42.8	68.6
Self-employed or employer	0.0	0.9	0.9	1.0		1.6
Unemployed, but looking for work	4.1	5.4	6.1	6.7	6.4	3.2
Not in workforce	4.3	3.6	5.1	5.8	5.5	3.0
Retired	23.3	29.9	21.3	30.0	44.7	23.3
Total	100.0	100.0	100.0	100.0	100.0	100.0
No. of income earners						
Zero	26.9	20.5	11.7	22.9	40.3	14.7
One	40.2	29.2	28.1	31.3	33.2	23.4
Two	32.8	41.7	48.0	37.2	24.0	49.6
Three or more	0.0	8.6	12.3	8.5	2.6	12.2
Total	100	100	100	100	100	100

Source: Belarus 1999 Household Sample Survey.

BULGARIA: Composition of Poverty, 1997

Poverty line	33% of median	67% of median	50% of median	50% of median	50% of median	
Economies of scale	Theta=.75	Theta=.75	Theta=1	Theta=.75	Theta=.50	
	Share of poor	Share of poor	Share of poor	Share of poor	Share of poor	Share of population
Age in years						
0-15	25.4	17.7	21.3	18.1	15.0	15.7
16-64	56.6	59.4	62.4	59.0	54.4	66.5
65+	18.0	22.9	16.3	22.9	30.6	17.8
Total	100.0	100.0	100.0	100.0	100.0	100.0
Education						
Age less than 15	25.4	17.7	21.2	18.0	15.0	15.7
Unknown	5.3	3.0	4.0	4.6	4.1	1.4
None	33.8	29.5	27.4	31.7	35.5	19.4
Primary (less than 7 years)	21.1	25.2	25.5	26.6	25.9	25.6
General secondary (8-12 years)	8.8	13.5	11.9	10.4	10.5	21.3
Vocational or specialized secondary	2.6	8.9	6.8	5.5	6.0	14.0
Some higher	3.1	2.3	3.3	3.3	3.0	2.5
Total	100.0	100.0	100.0	100.0	100.0	100.0
Location						
Urban	49.1	59.7	57.0	57.4	59.9	67.1
Rural	50.9	40.3	43.0	42.6	40.1	32.9
Total	100.0	100.0	100.0	100.0	100.0	100.0
Region						
Sofia	14.8	13.1	12.2	12.0	13.1	13.0
Other urban	34.3	46.7	44.8	45.3	46.8	54.1
Other rural	50.9	40.3	43.0	42.6	40.1	32.9
Total	100.0	100.0	100.0	100.0	100.0	100.0
Access to land						
No	87.8	68.2	69.7	70.7	72.3	57.8
Yes	12.2	31.8	30.3	29.3	27.7	42.2
Total	100.0	100.0	100.0	100.0	100.0	100.0
Own automobile						
No	95.0	79.7	80.7	84.6	88.1	56.3
Yes	5.0	20.3	19.3	15.4	12.0	43.7
Total	100.0	100.0	100.0	100.0	100.0	100.0
Household typology						
Single parent with child(ren)	0.0	1.1	0.3	0.9	1.0	0.9
Other households with child(ren)	57.4	41.8	52.2	43.1	35.6	41.0
Single elderly male	0.9	1.3	0.3	1.4	2.5	1.0

(Table continues on next page)

BULGARIA *(continued)*

Poverty line	33% of median	67% of median	50% of median	50% of median	50% of median	
Economies of scale	Theta=.75	Theta=.75	Theta=1	Theta=.75	Theta=.50	
	Share of poor	Share of poor	Share of poor	Share of poor	Share of poor	Share of population
Single elderly female	4.8	4.9	2.5	5.4	9.7	2.9
Multiple elderly only	13.9	16.6	14.6	16.0	17.4	11.8
Other households without child(ren)	23.0	34.3	30.0	33.2	33.8	42.4
Total	100.0	100.0	100.0	100.0	100.0	100.0
No. of children under 15						
Zero	33.9	52.8	41.4	50.4	59.5	56.2
One	16.5	19.1	20.9	18.1	13.0	23.7
Two	21.3	17.1	20.0	15.9	13.0	16.3
Three or more	28.3	11.1	17.7	15.6	14.6	3.9
Total	100.0	100.0	100.0	100.0	100.0	100.0
No. of elderly						
Zero	60.9	60.4	62.7	56.7	53.6	66.6
One	25.2	23.0	22.6	27.3	29.2	21.5
Two	13.9	16.2	14.3	15.6	17.0	11.8
Three or more	0.0	0.5	0.3	0.4	0.5	0.1
Total	100.0	100.0	100.0	100.0	100.2	100.0
Household head, gender						
Male	77.4	79.6	82.9	80.0	74.4	85.6
Female	22.6	20.4	17.1	20.0	25.6	14.4
Total	100.0	100.0	100.0	100.0	100.0	100.0
Household head, labor market status						
Unknown	22.6	8.1	10.3	11.5	11.5	6.1
Employed	20.9	29.2	30.2	24.3	18.8	41.8
Self-employed or employer	1.3	1.4	0.3	0.8	0.9	3.7
Unemployed, but looking for work	25.7	14.6	20.0	19.3	21.0	8.7
Not in workforce	0.0	2.9	3.0	2.3	1.0	2.6
Retired	29.6	43.8	36.1	42.0	46.9	37.3
Total	100.0	100.0	100.0	100.0	100.0	100.0
No. of income earners						
Zero	67.4	47.1	47.1	56.7	65.2	30.2
One	17.0	25.9	25.2	23.4	20.7	26.5
Two	9.6	23.3	22.0	15.6	10.6	34.6
Three or more	6.1	3.6	5.6	4.3	3.6	8.8
Total	100.0	100.0	100.0	100.0	100.0	100.0

Source: Bulgaria 1997 Integrated Household Survey.

CROATIA: Composition of Poverty, 1998

Poverty line	33% of median	67% of median	50% of median	50% of median	50% of median	
Economies of scale	Theta=.75	Theta=.75	Theta=1	Theta=.75	Theta=.50	
	Share of poor	Share of poor	Share of poor	Share of poor	Share of poor	Share of population
Age in years						
0-15	9.8	17.1	22.6	14.1	8.4	18.4
16-64	53.1	50.9	54.8	50.2	43.8	65.3
65+	37.1	32.1	22.6	35.7	47.7	16.3
Total	100.0	100.0	100.0	100.0	100.0	100.0
Education						
Age less than 15	9.8	17.1	22.6	14.1	8.4	18.4
Primary	74.5	56.1	51.0	63.3	70.8	32.9
Basic vocational	7.9	13.6	14.0	12.3	11.2	15.0
Secondary	7.2	11.3	11.4	9.1	7.9	24.0
Higher	0.5	1.9	1.0	1.3	1.7	9.6
Total	100.0	100.0	100.0	100.0	100.0	100.0
Location						
Zagreb	10.4	14.2	15.2	13.3	15.9	17.6
City	48.0	49.6	47.9	49.3	50.7	53.4
Rural	41.6	36.2	36.9	37.4	33.4	29.0
Total	100.0	100.0	100.0	100.0	100.0	100.0
Region						
Zagreb	15.5	23.2	23.8	20.6	22.4	26.6
Central	35.1	28.5	33.1	35.7	31.1	23.5
Istra (N. Coast)	2.1	11.7	10.2	10.7	12.7	12.9
Dalmacija (S. Coast)	16.1	12.6	10.1	10.8	12.0	18.5
Slavonia	31.3	24.1	22.8	22.2	21.8	18.5
Total	100.0	100.0	100.0	100.0	100.0	100.0
Access to land						
No	52.8	45.5	41.3	48.5	53.4	48.8
Yes	47.2	54.5	58.7	51.5	46.6	51.2
Total	100.0	100.0	100.0	100.0	100.0	100.0
Own automobile						
No	94.6	72.8	69.2	83.2	89.7	37.0
Yes	5.4	27.2	30.8	16.8	10.3	63.0
Total	100.0	100.0	100.0	100.0	100.0	100.0
Household typology						
Single parent with child(ren)	0.8	2.6	1.4	1.3	1.7	2.1
Other households with child(ren)	25.8	41.0	56.6	34.3	18.5	46.7
Single elderly male	3.5	1.3	0.9	1.3	3.1	0.8

(Table continues on next page)

CROATIA (continued)

Poverty line	33% of median	67% of median	50% of median	50% of median	50% of median	
Economies of scale	Theta=.75	Theta=.75	Theta=1	Theta=.75	Theta=.50	
	Share of poor	Share of poor	Share of poor	Share of poor	Share of poor	Share of population
Single elderly female	9.6	8.9	3.1	10.2	20.0	3.4
Multiple elderly only	13.8	11.8	7.2	13.4	15.6	5.0
Other households						
without child(ren)	46.5	34.5	30.8	39.5	41.1	42.0
Total	100.0	100.0	100.0	100.0	100.0	100.0
No. of children under 15						
Zero	73.4	56.5	42.0	64.4	79.8	51.2
One	11.4	15.0	16.7	12.4	7.8	21.0
Two	7.5	19.3	24.3	16.1	9.0	20.0
Three or more	7.7	9.2	17.1	7.1	3.5	7.7
Total	100.0	100.0	100.0	100.0	100.0	100.0
No. of elderly						
Zero	52.6	49.6	53.6	47.7	41.3	68.2
One	23.5	30.0	25.0	30.9	38.9	21.6
Two	24.0	19.3	19.9	20.9	19.4	9.7
Three or more	0.0	1.1	1.6	0.5	0.4	0.5
Total	100.0	100.0	100.0	100.0	100.0	100.0
Household head, gender						
Female	29.7	27.9	20.1	30.1	39.7	22.0
Male	70.3	72.1	79.9	69.9	60.4	78.0
Total	100	100	100	100	100	100
Household head, labor market status						
Employed	20.0	39.3	41.9	30.0	22.8	59.9
Unemployed	12.7	6.9	9.5	8.5	6.5	2.9
Retired	40.3	42.6	35.8	43.6	56.1	31.5
Other	27.1	11.3	12.9	17.9	14.7	5.6
Total	100.0	100.0	100.0	100.0	100.0	100.0
No. of income earners						
Zero	41.3	24.5	19.9	34.8	40.6	12.5
One	53.6	50.7	49.5	51.8	51.5	37.0
Two	1.5	17.7	18.3	9.0	5.8	35.8
Three or more	3.6	7.2	12.3	4.5	2.1	14.7
Total	100.0	100.0	100.0	100.0	100.0	100.0

Source: Croatia 1998 Household Budget Survey.

CZECH REPUBLIC: Composition of Poverty, 1996

Poverty line	33% of median	67% of median	50% of median	50% of median	50% of median	
Economies of scale	Theta=.75	Theta=.75	Theta=1	Theta=.75	Theta=.50	
	Share of poor	Share of poor	Share of poor	Share of poor	Share of poor	Share of population
Age in years						
0-15	48.6	38.3	48.5	45.2	31.7	20.0
16-64	51.2	51.4	50.7	53.4	50.0	67.1
65+	0.2	10.3	0.8	1.4	18.3	12.9
Total	100.0	100.0	100.0	100.0	100.0	100.0
Education						
Age less than 15	48.3	37.5	47.5	44.2	31.2	19.1
Elementary	24.0	24.7	20.8	24.4	33.7	20.6
Vocational	18.8	26.8	22.5	21.7	24.3	32.9
General secondary	1.3	2.5	1.9	2.1	3.1	4.7
Specialized secondary	5.4	7.1	5.9	5.8	6.3	16.2
University	2.1	1.4	1.3	1.8	1.4	6.5
Total	100.0	100.0	100.0	100.0	100.0	100.0
Location (1)						
Urban	72.2	63.1	62.9	69.6	70.2	66.3
Rural	27.8	36.9	37.1	30.4	29.8	33.7
Total	100.0	100.0	100.0	100.0	100.0	100.0
Location (2)						
Capital	7.4	6.8	4.1	6.0	8.7	11.7
Cities	11.1	10.4	11.3	11.7	13.3	10.3
Towns	53.7	45.9	47.5	51.9	48.2	44.3
Villages	27.8	36.9	37.1	30.4	29.8	33.7
Total	100.0	100.0	100.0	100.0	100.0	100.0
Region						
Middle	13.3	17.2	15.2	16.0	16.9	22.5
South	40.3	23.5	27.8	33.6	31.1	19.8
West	15.4	25.8	25.2	19.9	22.0	26.7
North	31.0	33.6	31.9	30.6	30.1	31.0
Total	100.0	100.0	100.0	100.0	100.0	100.0
Access to land						
No	93.9	85.6	86.0	90.8	92.4	79.0
Yes	6.1	14.4	14.0	9.2	7.6	21.0
Total	100.0	100.0	100.0	100.0	100.0	100.0
Own automobile						
No	77.9	62.6	61.7	69.6	79.6	38.5
Yes	22.1	37.4	38.3	30.4	20.4	61.5
Total	100.0	100.0	100.0	100.0	100.0	100.0
Household typology						
Single parent with child(ren)	35.2	16.0	18.9	29.1	29.6	3.9

(Table continues on next page)

CZECH REPUBLIC (continued)

Poverty line Economies of scale	33% of median Theta=.75 Share of poor	67% of median Theta=.75 Share of poor	50% of median Theta=1 Share of poor	50% of median Theta=.75 Share of poor	50% of median Theta=.50 Share of poor	Share of population
Other households						
with child(ren)	58.6	72.7	80.0	66.4	41.6	87.4
Single elderly man	4.0	2.3	0.7	2.4	7.2	2.8
Single elderly women	2.2	8.7	0.4	2.0	21.4	5.4
Other households						
without child(ren)	0.0	0.2	0.0	0.1	0.1	0.4
Total	100.0	100.0	100.0	100.0	100.0	100.0
No. of children under 15						
Zero	11.4	23.2	6.5	13.9	39.6	51.9
One	23.0	19.3	18.7	23.7	21.4	21.2
Two	32.3	36.3	39.2	34.4	25.1	21.4
Three or more	33.4	21.1	35.6	28.1	13.9	5.5
Total	100.0	100.0	100.0	100.0	100.0	100.0
No. of elderly						
Zero	98.8	73.5	85.1	85.6	67.8	67.5
One	0.4	22.1	12.4	13.0	30.8	19.5
Two	0.8	4.4	2.5	1.4	1.4	12.4
Three or more	0.0	0.0	0.0	0.0	0.0	0.7
Total	100.0	100.0	100.0	100.0	100.0	100.0
Household head, gender						
Male	61.5	71.5	77.8	66.6	46.3	87.3
Female	38.5	28.5	22.2	33.4	53.7	12.7
Total	100.0	100.0	100.0	100.0	100.0	100.0
Household head, labor market status						
Employed	3.5	49.8	44.5	28.0	17.9	64.9
Self-employed or employer	16.1	12.6	15.9	15.7	11.1	11.7
Unemployed, but						
looking for work	50.4	10.2	18.0	26.2	23.1	1.6
Not in workforce	28.8	6.4	11.6	17.7	16.7	0.8
Retired	1.2	20.9	10.0	12.4	31.2	21.0
Total	100.0	100.0	100.0	100.0	100.0	100.0
No. of income earners						
Zero	75.8	32.8	32.5	49.7	67.9	17.9
One	19.2	50.2	52.0	43.3	27.7	27.8
Two	5.0	16.4	14.1	6.3	4.1	40.6
Three or more	0.0	0.7	1.3	0.8	0.3	13.7
Total	100.0	100.0	100.0	100.0	100.0	100.0

Source: Czech Republic Microcensus 1996.

ESTONIA: Composition of Poverty, 1998

Poverty line	33% of median	67% of median	50% of median	50% of median	50% of median	
Economies of scale	Theta=.75	Theta=.75	Theta=1	Theta=.75	Theta=.50	
	Share of poor	Share of poor	Share of poor	Share of poor	Share of poor	Share of population
Location						
City	71.2	67.4	63.5	64.8	68.5	70.0
Town	1.4	2.1	2.6	2.0	1.5	3.3
Settlement	3.8	5.0	4.8	4.5	4.0	6.6
Bigger village	7.1	8.3	9.0	8.7	7.6	7.3
Village	16.4	17.3	20.1	20.1	18.4	12.8
Total	100.0	100.0	100.0	100.0	100.0	100.0
No. of children under 15						
Zero	67.4	67.5	55.4	71.2	82.7	69.2
One	14.1	15.7	17.4	13.5	9.0	17.7
Two	9.4	12.2	17.4	10.9	5.8	9.7
Three or more	9.1	4.6	9.8	4.4	2.5	3.3
Total	100.0	100.0	100.0	100.0	100.0	100.0
Household head, gender						
Male	25.8	39.5	41.7	45.4	40.3	46.6
Female	74.2	60.5	58.3	54.6	59.7	53.4
Total	100.0	100.0	100.0	100.0	100.0	100.0
Household head, labor market status						
Employed	29.8	44.7	49.9	44.1	36.2	59.6
Farmer	0.7	0.3	0.4	0.3	0.1	0.9
Self-employed	0.0	0.5	0.4	0.6	0.7	1.0
Owner	0.0	0.4	0.4	0.2	0.0	2.3
Not in workforce	0.0	2.3	2.1	2.2	1.6	1.5
Unemployed, but looking for work	29.8	9.3	16.7	15.4	12.5	3.4
Retired	36.8	42.1	29.3	36.3	48.4	31.0
Other	2.9	0.4	0.9	0.8	0.5	0.2
Total	100.0	100.0	100.0	100.0	100.0	100.0

Source: Estonia, Household Income and Expenditures Survey 1998 (Q4).

GEORGIA: Composition of Poverty, 1996–97

Poverty line	33% of median	67% of median	50% of median	50% of median	50% of median	
Economies of scale	Theta=.75	Theta=.75	Theta=1	Theta=.75	Theta=.50	
	Share of poor	Share of poor	Share of poor	Share of poor	Share of poor	Share of population
Age in years						
0–15	24.3	26.6	29.3	23.4	20.8	23.1
16–64	61.2	57.7	58.0	60.2	60.5	61.6
65+	14.4	15.7	12.6	16.4	18.7	15.3
Total	100.0	100.0	100.0	100.0	100.0	100.0
Education						
Age less than 15	24.3	26.6	29.3	23.4	20.8	23.1
Elementary	6.4	5.4	5.5	6.5	6.7	4.6
Secondary (incomplete)	10.7	9.4	9.4	10.3	10.9	8.3
Secondary	34.6	32.8	32.9	35.5	36.1	30.7
Postsecondary	14.1	13.2	12.6	13.0	13.6	15.4
University	9.8	12.7	10.2	11.3	11.9	17.8
Total	100.0	100.0	100.0	100.0	100.0	100.0
Location						
Capital	21.0	23.1	20.6	20.7	21.7	26.0
Other urban	34.2	29.2	29.8	30.8	31.8	27.2
Rural	44.8	47.7	49.6	48.5	46.6	46.8
Total	100.0	100.0	100.0	100.0	100.0	100.0
Region						
Western	31.1	35.5	35.3	34.9	34.0	30.9
Eastern	23.0	21.6	22.9	23.1	24.0	21.2
Central	30.8	31.9	29.6	30.0	30.7	35.6
South	15.1	11.1	12.2	11.9	11.3	12.3
Total	100.0	100.0	100.0	100.0	100.0	100.0
Access to land						
No	41.4	41.8	39.3	40.5	42.0	39.5
Yes	58.6	58.2	60.7	59.5	58.0	60.5
Total	100.0	100.0	100.0	100.0	100.0	100.0
Own automobile						
No	92.0	88.0	88.6	89.8	91.5	83.0
Yes	8.0	12.0	11.5	10.2	8.6	17.0
Total	100.0	100.0	100.0	100.0	100.0	100.0
Household typology						
Single parent with child(ren)	2.1	1.6	1.4	1.7	2.2	1.2
Other households with child(ren)	73.8	67.9	74.2	69.0	64.0	62.6

(Table continues on next page)

GEORGIA *(continued)*

Poverty line	33% of median	67% of median	50% of median	50% of median	50% of median	
Economies of scale	Theta=.75	Theta=.75	Theta=1	Theta=.75	Theta=.50	
	Share of poor	Share of poor	Share of poor	Share of poor	Share of poor	Share of population
Single elderly male	0.9	0.6	0.4	0.7	1.2	0.5
Single elderly female	2.3	2.1	1.0	2.2	4.2	2.3
Multiple elderly only	3.2	3.1	2.3	3.3	4.4	4.4
Other households without child(ren)	17.8	24.7	20.8	23.2	24.1	29.0
Total	100.0	100.0	100.0	100.0	100.0	100.0
No. of children under 15						
Zero	37.3	35.7	30.8	36.8	42.2	38.4
One	19.0	20.9	19.3	18.6	18.7	21.5
Two	27.5	29.2	31.6	28.6	25.6	27.6
Three or more	16.2	14.3	18.4	16.1	13.6	12.5
Total	100.0	100.0	100.0	100.0	100.0	100.0
No. of elderly						
Zero	45.9	41.6	41.6	43.2	44.4	45.0
One	28.9	31.8	30.4	30.3	31.2	29.9
Two	24.7	25.7	27.0	25.7	23.7	24.1
Three or more	0.5	1.0	1.0	0.8	0.7	1.1
Total	100.0	100.0	100.0	100.0	100.0	100.0
Household head, gender						
Male	62.9	66.7	66.2	61.6	60.1	70.9
Female	37.1	33.3	33.8	38.4	39.9	29.1
Total	100.0	100.0	100.0	100.0	100.0	100.0
Household head, labor market status						
Retired (old age)	6.9	4.8	3.8	5.7	8.3	3.2
Inactive, disabled, otherwise not in workforce	14.2	8.3	9.3	10.7	11.3	4.6
Unemployed but actively looking for work	7.1	4.0	4.5	5.0	5.2	2.8
Self-employed (or employer)	39.8	44.8	45.8	44.2	41.9	47.8
Employed (wage)	32.0	38.1	36.7	34.4	33.3	41.7
Total	100.0	100.0	100.0	100.0	100.0	100.0
No. of income earners						
Zero	26.6	17.5	17.6	21.7	25.1	11.2
One	25.9	25.1	23.6	24.3	25.7	25.1
Two	23.2	29.5	27.7	26.6	26.4	33.0
Three or more	24.3	27.9	31.1	27.4	22.8	30.8
Total	100.0	100.0	100.0	100.0	100.0	100.0

Source: Survey of Georgian Households, 1996–97.

HUNGARY: Composition of Poverty, 1997

Poverty line	33% of median	67% of median	50% of median	50% of median	50% of median	
Economies of scale	Theta=.75	Theta=.75	Theta=1	Theta=.75	Theta=.50	
	Share of poor	Share of poor	Share of poor	Share of poor	Share of poor	Share of population
Age in years						
0-15	30.4	27.3	33.8	29.9	23.5	18.0
16-64	66.7	62.1	62.7	62.0	58.9	67.9
65+	2.9	10.6	3.5	8.1	17.6	14.1
Total	100.0	100.0	100.0	100.0	100.0	100.0
Education						
Age less than 15	30.4	27.3	33.8	29.9	23.5	18.0
Primary or less	60.7	44.7	46.4	52.7	59.1	34.2
General secondary	0.6	3.1	2.0	2.0	2.4	8.0
Vocational	8.2	23.6	17.6	15.1	14.7	32.0
Higher	0.0	1.4	0.2	0.2	0.2	7.8
Total	100.0	100.0	100.0	100.0	100.0	100.0
Location						
Budapest	15.4	8.7	7.6	9.0	6.8	18.6
Other urban	34.4	40.9	37.2	34.0	36.9	43.4
Rural	50.2	50.4	55.2	57.0	56.3	38.0
Total	100.0	100.0	100.0	100.0	100.0	100.0
Region						
Central region	23.5	19.1	19.7	19.9	16.8	28.3
West Trans-Danubia	0.3	7.7	4.2	3.5	5.6	9.8
Central Trans-Danubia	5.6	9.6	9.2	7.9	8.3	11.0
South Trans-Danubia	14.9	11.2	12.3	11.7	12.0	9.8
Northern Hungary	28.4	18.5	22.1	24.5	25.5	12.7
North Great-Plain	16.2	20.7	23.9	23.4	19.7	15.1
South Great-Plain	11.2	13.2	8.6	9.1	12.1	13.4
Total	100.0	100.0	100.0	100.0	100.0	100.0
Access to land						
No	70.2	51.0	54.7	58.3	56.7	52.4
Yes	29.8	49.0	45.3	41.7	43.3	47.6
Total	100.0	100.0	100.0	100.0	100.0	100.0
Own automobile						
No	99.8	84.7	85.1	88.5	93.7	60.3
Yes	0.2	15.3	14.9	11.5	6.3	39.7
Total	100.0	100.0	100.0	100.0	100.0	100.0
Household typology						
Single parent with child(ren)	1.1	2.6	1.5	2.8	3.7	1.6
Other households with child(ren)	69.9	61.5	77.3	65.3	49.8	43.2
Single elderly male	0.3	0.6	0.0	0.6	1.7	1.0

(Table continues on next page)

HUNGARY (continued)

Poverty line	33% of median	67% of median	50% of median	50% of median	50% of median	
Economies of scale	Theta=.75	Theta=.75	Theta=1	Theta=.75	Theta=.50	
	Share of poor	Share of poor	Share of poor	Share of poor	Share of poor	Share of population
Single elderly female	1.9	3.4	0.5	3.1	10.2	4.0
Multiple elderly only	0.7	3.4	1.1	2.2	3.5	4.8
Other households						
without child(ren)	26.1	28.6	19.6	26.0	31.0	45.3
Total	100.0	100.0	100.0	100.0	100.0	100.0
No. of children under 15						
Zero	29.0	36.0	21.3	31.9	46.5	55.1
One	16.0	23.4	23.4	22.0	19.1	21.1
Two	47.3	27.1	34.1	27.6	23.3	17.9
Three or more	7.7	13.5	21.3	18.5	11.1	5.9
Total	100.0	100.0	100.0	100.0	100.0	100.0
No. of elderly						
Zero	97.1	83.5	91.8	87.6	79.8	79.1
One	2.2	11.6	6.1	9.5	16.2	14.8
Two	0.7	4.8	2.2	2.9	4.0	6.0
Three or more	0.0	0.1	0.0	0.0	0.0	0.1
Total	100.0	100.0	100.0	100.0	100.0	100.0
Household head, gender						
Male	94.9	88.4	93.4	88.0	77.0	87.8
Female	5.1	11.6	6.6	12.0	23.0	12.2
Total	100.0	100.0	100.0	100.0	100.0	100.0
Household head, labor market status						
Employed	30.3	53.9	52.1	43.7	33.4	63.8
Self-employed or employer	0.0	0.4	0.5	0.2	0.2	0.3
Unemployed, but						
looking for work	54.0	20.4	29.2	30.4	28.2	7.0
Not in workforce	12.0	15.4	15.8	17.4	18.0	12.9
Retired	3.7	9.9	2.4	8.3	20.2	15.9
Total	100.0	100.0	100.0	100.0	100.0	100.0
No. of income earners						
Zero	42.3	26.4	25.2	35.1	46.7	23.8
One	40.1	41.3	46.9	45.6	38.9	29.5
Two	12.7	26.6	21.8	14.7	12.3	37.8
Three or more	4.9	5.7	6.0	4.6	2.2	8.8
Total	100.0	100.0	100.0	100.0	100.0	100.0

Source: Hungary Household Budget Survey, 1997.

KAZAKHSTAN: Composition of Poverty, 1996

Poverty line	33% of median	67% of median	50% of median	50% of median	50% of median	
Economies of scale	Theta=.75	Theta=.75	Theta=1	Theta=.75	Theta=.50	
	Share of poor	Share of poor	Share of poor	Share of poor	Share of poor	Share of population
Age in years						
0-15	42.5	34.6	38.9	37.4	34.5	31.3
16-64	50.4	56.9	55.0	54.9	54.5	61.9
65+	7.0	8.5	6.1	7.7	11.0	6.8
Total	100.0	100.0	100.0	100.0	100.0	100.0
Education						
Age less than 15	42.5	34.4	38.6	37.1	34.2	31.1
Unknown	7.9	6.0	6.2	5.7	6.2	5.7
Forms 1–7	4.7	6.2	5.0	6.7	8.2	4.9
Forms 8–12	20.8	20.0	21.7	20.4	20.1	14.8
Additional technical education	22.3	27.4	23.7	25.4	26.3	34.5
Some Higher	1.8	6.1	4.8	4.8	5.0	9.0
Total	100.0	100.0	100.0	100.0	100.0	100.0
Location						
Urban	32.0	45.0	38.5	43.1	44.9	49.2
Rural	68.0	55.0	61.5	56.9	55.1	50.8
Total	100.0	100.0	100.0	100.0	100.0	100.0
Region						
Central	19.9	15.1	14.7	17.8	18.1	19.0
Southern	58.4	43.6	48.3	49.5	49.1	20.5
Western	7.3	12.6	13.5	8.1	8.6	13.7
Northern	2.6	4.7	2.9	2.7	3.5	20.0
Eastern	11.7	24.1	20.6	21.9	20.8	26.9
Total	100.0	100.0	100.0	100.0	100.0	100.0
Access to land						
No	61.0	45.9	48.6	52.2	55.8	35.4
Yes	39.0	54.1	51.4	47.8	44.2	64.6
Total	100.0	100.0	100.0	100.0	100.0	100.0
Own automobile						
No	96.2	89.8	89.0	91.2	94.2	77.4
Yes	3.8	10.2	11.0	8.8	5.8	22.6
Total	100.0	100.0	100.0	100.0	100.0	100.0
Household typology						
Single parent with child(ren)	6.2	4.3	3.8	4.8	5.6	3.9

(Table continues on next page)

KAZAKHSTAN *(continued)*

Poverty line	33% of median	67% of median	50% of median	50% of median	50% of median	
Economies of scale	*Theta=.75*	*Theta=.75*	*Theta=1*	*Theta=.75*	*Theta=.50*	
	Share of poor	*Share of poor*	*Share of poor*	*Share of poor*	*Share of poor*	*Share of population*
Other household						
with child(ren)	74.5	68.2	75.6	71.7	63.9	67.0
Single elderly male	0.0	0.2	0.0	0.2	0.4	0.1
Single elderly female	1.5	1.4	0.5	1.2	3.0	1.0
Multiple elderly only	6.2	5.9	5.1	4.6	5.8	3.8
Other households						
without child(ren)	11.7	20.1	14.9	17.5	21.2	24.2
Total	100.0	100.0	100.0	100.0	100.0	100.0
No. of children under 15						
Zero	17.3	25.2	17.9	22.2	29.0	27.6
One	19.4	22.5	21.7	22.6	21.9	30.0
Two	27.3	23.7	24.4	23.8	22.4	26.0
Three or more	36.1	28.6	36.1	31.5	26.7	16.4
Total	100.0	100.0	100.0	100.0	100.0	100.0
No. of elderly						
Zero	87.1	80.0	81.1	84.7	81.9	82.3
One	6.7	13.9	13.5	10.3	12.2	13.7
Two	4.1	5.6	4.7	4.0	4.8	3.8
Three or more	2.1	0.5	0.8	1.0	1.1	0.1
Total	100.0	100.0	100.0	100.0	100.0	100.0
Household head, gender						
Male	75.9	71.9	77.3	72.0	68.6	69.7
Female	24.1	28.1	22.7	28.0	31.4	30.3
Total	100.0	100.0	100.0	100.0	100.0	100.0
Household head, labor market status						
Employed	37.2	46.2	48.1	43.3	41.8	57.8
Owner	20.5	9.0	9.6	12.0	11.4	7.3
Unemployed, but looking for work	2.4	1.5	1.8	1.2	1.4	1.4
Not in workforce	19.4	20.9	22.2	24.4	23.6	16.8
Retired	20.5	22.4	18.4	19.1	21.9	16.7
Total	100.0	100.0	100.0	100.0	100.0	100.0
No. of income earners						
Zero	36.7	30.1	27.0	33.7	38.2	23.4
One	35.2	38.3	38.4	36.4	34.4	35.9
Two	26.7	26.2	30.0	26.4	24.7	33.6
Three or more	1.5	5.3	4.7	3.5	2.7	7.1
Total	100.0	100.0	100.0	100.0	100.0	100.0

Source: Kazakhstan 1996 Living Standards Measurement Survey.

KYRGYZ REPUBLIC: Composition of Poverty, 1997

Poverty line	33% of median	67% of median	50% of median	50% of median	50% of median	
Economies of scale	Theta=.75	Theta=.75	Theta=1	Theta=.75	Theta=.50	
	Share of poor	Share of poor	Share of poor	Share of poor	Share of poor	Share of population
Age in years						
0-15	42.6	42.9	43.0	42.3	41.3	38.4
16-64	51.6	51.2	51.2	51.2	51.1	55.5
65+	5.8	5.9	5.8	6.4	7.6	6.2
Total	100.0	100.0	100.0	100.0	100.0	100.0
Education						
Age less than 15	43.4	43.3	43.5	42.8	41.8	38.6
Unknown	1.9	1.8	1.7	2.1	2.2	1.5
Primary (less than 7 years)	6.1	6.2	6.1	6.6	7.1	7.2
General secondary (8–12 years)	44.3	41.0	42.2	42.5	42.9	36.4
Professional, technical, or technikum	2.9	5.4	4.6	4.4	4.2	9.0
Some higher	1.4	2.3	1.8	1.6	1.8	7.2
Total	100.0	100.0	100.0	100.0	100.0	100.0
Location						
Urban	9.0	13.3	13.8	9.8	11.5	30.0
Rural	91.0	86.7	86.3	90.2	88.5	70.0
Total	100.0	100.0	100.0	100.0	100.0	100.0
Region						
Bishkek	0.0	0.4	0.4	0.0	0.0	10.6
Issuk-Kulskaya	23.3	14.6	15.8	16.6	19.5	12.2
Djala-Abadckaya	21.6	20.0	20.5	22.6	20.1	14.1
Narunskaya	29.5	29.3	36.2	37.9	39.7	13.0
Oshckaya	4.7	21.3	11.6	10.1	8.1	26.1
Talasskaya	20.8	12.2	13.8	11.3	10.3	13.1
Chyiskaya	0.2	2.5	1.6	1.6	2.4	10.9
Total	100.0	100.0	100.0	100.0	100.0	100.0
Access to land						
No	7.3	8.5	9.5	8.3	10.0	11.0
Yes	92.7	91.5	90.6	91.3	90.0	89.0
Total	100.0	100.0	100.0	100.0	100.0	100.0
Own automobile						
No	100.0	97.4	97.7	98.5	99.3	85.0
Yes	0.0	2.6	2.3	1.5	0.7	15.0
Total	100.0	100.0	100.0	100.0	100.0	100.0
Household typology						
Single parent with child(ren)	2.0	1.7	1.0	1.4	2.1	2.1

(Table continues on next page)

KYRGYZ REPUBLIC (continued)

Poverty line	33% of median	67% of median	50% of median	50% of median	50% of median	
Economies of scale	Theta=.75	Theta=.75	Theta=1	Theta=.75	Theta=.50	
	Share of poor	Share of poor	Share of poor	Share of poor	Share of poor	Share of population
Other household						
with child(ren)	88.6	87.2	88.8	87.8	85.1	82.0
Single elderly male	0.2	0.0	0.0	0.0	0.1	0.1
Single elderly female	0.9	0.3	0.2	0.4	0.8	0.5
Multiple elderly only	4.1	6.5	6.8	6.3	6.2	4.2
Other households						
without child(ren)	4.3	4.2	3.1	4.0	5.8	11.1
Total	100.0	100.0	100.0	100.0	100.0	100.0
No. of children under 15						
Zero	5.9	5.2	4.0	5.3	7.7	11.2
One	7.3	12.0	10.2	12.3	15.4	16.1
Two	21.3	18.6	18.1	18.7	20.4	22.0
Three or more	65.5	64.2	67.8	63.6	56.4	50.7
Total	100.0	100.0	100.0	100.0	100.0	100.0
No. of elderly						
Zero	67.9	71.5	68.0	67.6	68.1	75.0
One	28.0	21.8	25.1	25.9	25.3	18.8
Two	4.1	6.5	7.0	6.4	6.7	6.1
Three or more	0.0	0.1	0.0	0.0	0.0	0.2
Total	100.0	100.0	100.0	100.0	100.0	100.0
Household head, gender						
Unknown	1.2	0.8	0.7	0.4	0.4	0.6
Male	77.2	80.1	78.3	77.5	77.4	79.3
Female	21.6	19.2	21.0	22.2	22.2	20.2
Total	100.0	100.0	100.0	100.0	100.0	100.0
Household head, labor market status						
Unknown	6.5	4.5	3.9	4.1	3.8	4.4
Employed	40.9	51.7	46.4	46.2	44.7	53.6
Employer	0.0	0.6	0.3	0.3	0.4	0.6
Unemployed, but						
looking for work	0.9	1.1	1.2	1.0	1.2	2.3
Not in workforce	17.0	12.7	15.7	14.6	17.0	14.1
Retired	34.7	29.3	32.5	33.8	32.9	25.1
Total	100.0	100.0	100.0	100.0	100.0	100.0
No. of income earners						
Zero	28.0	19.7	21.7	22.7	26.1	18.7
One	26.8	19.8	21.9	22.3	23.1	21.1
Two	22.8	24.5	23.8	24.0	25.7	24.6
Three or more	22.5	36.1	32.5	31.1	25.2	35.6
Total	100.0	100.0	100.0	100.0	100.0	100.0

Source: Kyrgyz Republic 1997 Living Standards Measurement Survey.

LATVIA: Composition of Poverty, 1997–98

Poverty line	33% of median	67% of median	50% of median	50% of median	50% of median	
Economies of scale	Theta=.75	Theta=.75	Theta=1	Theta=.75	Theta=.50	
	Share of poor	Share of poor	Share of poor	Share of poor	Share of poor	Share of population
Age in years						
0–15	26.9	23.8	29.2	24.6	19.0	19.3
16–64	63.3	61.3	61.6	61.8	61.1	63.8
65+	9.8	14.9	9.3	13.7	19.9	16.8
Total	100.0	100.0	100.0	100.0	100.0	100.0
Education						
Age less than 15	26.9	23.8	29.2	24.6	19.0	19.3
Primary or less	36.0	33.0	29.6	33.9	39.4	24.6
Secondary (including specialized)	32.2	36.3	35.1	35.4	35.0	42.1
Vocational	3.7	4.0	4.0	4.2	4.4	3.0
Higher	1.2	2.9	2.2	1.9	2.1	10.9
Total	100.0	100.0	100.0	100.0	100.0	100.0
Location						
Riga	18.1	19.4	18.5	19.1	19.4	32.6
Other urban	34.3	36.6	35.3	36.2	38.6	36.6
Rural	47.6	44.0	46.2	44.6	41.9	30.8
Total	100.0	100.0	100.0	100.0	100.0	100.0
Region						
Riga region	26.3	30.8	28.9	29.8	29.7	45.5
Kurzene	21.4	17.6	18.6	19.9	20.3	13.8
Vidzeme	16.0	14.3	15.3	15.3	15.7	11.8
Zemgale	10.0	13.8	12.3	11.9	12.2	13.0
Latgale	26.3	23.4	24.9	23.1	22.1	16.0
Total	100.0	100.0	100.0	100.0	100.0	100.0
Access to land						
No	81.5	79.5	81.0	82.5	83.4	74.6
Yes	18.5	20.5	19.0	17.5	16.6	25.4
Total	100.0	100.0	100.0	100.0	100.0	100.0
Own automobile						
No	91.2	83.6	83.7	88.4	91.4	67.7
Yes	8.8	16.4	16.3	11.6	8.6	32.3
Total	100.0	100.0	100.0	100.0	100.0	100.0
Household typology						
Single parent with child(ren)	3.8	5.3	5.7	5.8	5.7	4.9
Other households with child(ren)	64.7	52.2	64.8	53.2	39.8	43.2
Single elderly male	0.9	1.1	0.4	0.9	2.1	1.1
Single elderly female	1.7	5.1	1.4	4.4	9.2	5.4

(Table continues on next page)

LATVIA *(continued)*

Poverty line	33% of median	67% of median	50% of median	50% of median	50% of median	
Economies of scale	Theta=.75	Theta=.75	Theta=1	Theta=.75	Theta=.50	
	Share of poor	Share of poor	Share of poor	Share of poor	Share of poor	Share of population
Multiple elderly only	1.6	2.6	1.7	2.4	2.9	4.5
Other households						
without child(ren)	27.3	33.6	26.1	33.2	40.3	41.0
Total	100.0	100.0	100.0	100.0	100.0	100.0
No. of children under 15						
Zero	31.5	42.5	29.5	41.0	54.4	51.9
One	31.0	25.7	28.9	26.4	22.1	24.7
Two	23.2	20.3	24.9	19.6	14.8	17.1
Three or more	14.3	11.5	16.6	13.0	8.7	6.3
Total	100.0	100.0	100.0	100.0	100.0	100.0
No. of elderly						
Zero	77.3	73.6	77.4	75.1	70.6	72.9
One	18.5	21.3	18.1	20.5	24.8	19.9
Two	4.2	5.0	4.5	4.4	4.6	7.1
Three or more	0.0	0.1	0.0	0.0	0.0	0.2
Total	100.0	100.0	100.0	100.0	100.0	100.0
Household head, gender						
Male	40.7	41.7	41.8	39.1	36.7	43.8
Female	59.3	58.3	58.2	60.9	63.3	56.2
Total	100.0	100.0	100.0	100.0	100.0	100.0
Household head, labor market status						
Employed	40.6	43.9	47.4	40.8	35.4	52.3
Self-employed or employer	0.0	3.4	3.6	3.0	2.4	4.2
Unemployed, but						
looking for work	20.1	12.0	15.0	16.1	15.3	6.1
Not in workforce	18.3	12.2	13.1	14.0	12.8	8.9
Retired	21.1	28.5	20.9	26.0	34.0	28.5
Total	100.0	100.0	100.0	100.0	100.0	100.0
No. of income earners						
Zero	43.5	40.1	36.2	42.7	52.0	30.0
One	26.7	22.3	23.5	24.3	22.8	20.2
Two	18.7	26.4	27.1	23.3	18.2	33.0
Three or more	11.2	11.2	13.1	9.8	7.0	16.8
Total	100.0	100.0	100.0	100.0	100.0	100.0

Source: Latvia Household Budget Survey, 1997–98.

LITHUANIA: Composition of Poverty, 1999

Poverty line	33% of median	67% of median	50% of median	50% of median	50% of median	
Economies of scale	Theta=.75	Theta=.75	Theta=1	Theta=.75	Theta=.50	
	Share of poor	Share of poor	Share of poor	Share of poor	Share of poor	Share of population
Age in years						
0–15	34.5	28.4	34.3	30.8	24.2	22.2
16–64	53.1	55.6	56.2	55.3	53.6	63.8
65+	12.4	16.0	9.5	13.8	22.2	14.0
Total	100.0	100.0	100.0	100.0	100.0	100.0
Education						
Age less than 15	34.5	28.4	34.3	30.8	24.2	22.2
Less than primary	4.2	4.4	3.1	4.8	7.4	2.6
Primary	11.9	13.9	9.7	12.5	18.1	10.2
Basic vocational	17.9	16.7	17.4	18.9	17.6	13.9
General secondary	21.2	21.8	22.7	21.9	20.5	21.9
Higher	9.1	12.7	11.4	9.9	10.1	19.2
University	1.3	2.1	1.5	1.2	2.1	9.9
Total	100.0	100.0	100.0	100.0	100.0	100.0
Location						
Largest towns	12.5	21.3	18.0	16.7	17.2	39.1
Other towns	31.3	26.6	25.4	28.0	26.4	28.8
Rural	56.2	52.0	56.7	55.3	56.4	32.1
Total	100.0	100.0	100.0	100.0	100.0	100.0
Access to land						
No	33.8	34.6	32.8	35.4	35.3	39.9
Yes	66.3	65.4	67.2	64.7	64.7	60.1
Total	100.0	100.0	100.0	100.0	100.0	100.0
Own automobile						
No	86.4	74.3	72.8	79.8	84.6	51.7
Yes	13.6	25.7	27.2	20.2	15.4	48.3
Total	100.0	100.0	100.0	100.0	100.0	100.0
Household typology						
Single parent with child(ren)	9.8	8.7	8.9	9.0	8.3	4.3
Other households with child(ren)	68.6	55.6	68.1	59.4	45.6	49.9
Single elderly male	0.0	0.6	0.3	0.6	1.4	0.7
Single elderly female	3.7	4.4	1.6	4.5	10.2	3.1
Multiple elderly only	2.8	4.4	1.5	2.6	4.1	4.6
Other households without child(ren)	15.1	26.2	19.6	24.0	30.5	37.5
Total	100.0	100.0	100.0	100.0	100.0	100.0
No. of children under 15						
Zero	21.6	35.6	23.0	31.6	46.2	45.9
One	30.0	23.5	24.6	22.5	20.3	25.5

(Table continues on next page)

LITHUANIA *(continued)*

Poverty line	33% of median	67% of median	50% of median	50% of median	50% of median	
Economies of scale	*Theta=.75*	*Theta=.75*	*Theta=1*	*Theta=.75*	*Theta=.50*	
	Share of poor	*Share of poor*	*Share of poor*	*Share of poor*	*Share of poor*	*Share of population*
Two	23.9	27.5	33.1	28.0	20.9	22.1
Three or more	24.5	13.4	19.3	17.8	12.6	6.5
Total	100.0	100.0	100.0	100.0	100.0	100.0
No. of elderly						
Zero	74.5	71.6	76.2	73.6	66.0	76.3
One	20.0	20.7	18.8	21.2	28.5	16.7
Two	5.5	7.7	5.1	5.2	5.5	6.9
Three or more	0.0	0.0	0.0	0.0	0.0	0.1
Total	100.0	100.0	100.0	100.0	100.0	100.0
Household head, gender						
Female	50.5	47.0	45.2	51.1	54.1	38.9
Male	49.5	53.0	54.9	48.9	45.9	61.2
Total	100.0	100.0	100.0	100.0	100.0	100.0
Household head, labor market status						
Employed	73.7	75.7	79.9	73.9	67.7	81.7
Looking for a job	3.2	3.2	3.4	4.0	3.3	2.9
Retired	14.6	18.1	13.2	17.3	24.5	13.9
Other	8.5	3.0	3.5	4.8	4.5	1.5
Total	100.0	100.0	100.0	100.0	100.0	100.0
No. of income earners						
Zero	2.7	1.5	1.3	1.9	1.9	0.6
One	24.1	26.5	22.9	28.2	36.8	20.9
Two	39.9	46.6	44.7	42.5	40.7	55.7
Three or more	33.3	25.5	31.0	27.4	20.6	22.8
Total	100.0	100.0	100.0	100.0	100.0	100.0
Alternative household typology						
Single	4.3	7.9	2.4	7.5	18.0	8.6
Single parent	9.8	9.2	9.3	9.5	9.1	4.6
Couple no child(ren)	2.6	8.4	3.4	5.1	8.4	14.5
Couple with child(ren)	30.3	34.2	38.5	32.7	25.7	35.2
Other households without child(ren)	40.2	23.7	31.8	28.5	22.1	18.6
Other households with child(ren)	12.7	16.6	14.7	16.7	16.7	18.6
Total	100.0	100.0	100.0	100.0	100.0	100.0

Source: Lithuania Household Budget Survey 1999.

FORMER YUGOSLAV REPUBLIC OF MACEDONIA: Composition of Poverty, 1996

Poverty line	33% of median	67% of median	50% of median	50% of median	50% of median	
Economies of scale	Theta=.75	Theta=.75	Theta=1	Theta=.75	Theta=.50	
	Share of poor	Share of poor	Share of poor	Share of poor	Share of poor	Share of population
Age in years						
0–15	33.6	29.3	32.2	31.3	28.0	24.6
16–64	57.0	61.6	60.7	60.4	60.2	66.4
65+	9.5	9.1	7.1	8.4	11.8	9.0
Total	100.0	100.0	100.0	100.0	100.0	100.0
Education						
Age less than 15	32.2	28.7	31.3	30.5	27.5	24.3
Unknown	4.2	2.2	3.2	2.6	2.0	1.4
None	9.0	7.4	6.2	7.2	9.8	5.5
Incomplete primary (less than 4 years)	8.9	13.2	13.8	13.1	14.1	11.1
Primary (5–8 years)	30.9	27.5	28.3	28.1	27.2	25.5
Secondary	11.3	19.0	15.6	16.4	17.0	25.9
Some Higher	3.6	2.1	1.7	2.0	2.4	6.1
University	0.0	0.0	0.1	0.0	0.0	0.2
Total	100.0	100.0	100.0	100.0	100.0	100.0
Location						
Urban	37.2	43.8	38.4	40.7	42.2	54.4
Rural	62.8	56.2	61.6	59.3	57.8	45.6
Total	100.0	100.0	100.0	100.0	100.0	100.0
Region						
Capital	20.9	17.9	17.1	16.3	18.6	24.7
Rest of republic	79.1	82.1	82.9	83.7	81.4	75.3
Total	100.0	100.0	100.0	100.0	100.0	100.0
Access to land						
No	78.9	67.3	65.3	69.7	76.0	63.3
Yes	21.1	32.7	34.7	30.3	24.0	36.7
Total	100.0	100.0	100.0	100.0	100.0	100.0
Own automobile						
No	89.0	69.4	73.6	74.5	80.3	51.2
Yes	11.0	30.6	26.4	25.5	19.7	48.8
Total	100.0	100.0	100.0	100.0	100.0	100.0
Household typology						
Single parent with child(ren)	0.0	0.2	0.3	0.4	0.5	0.4
Other households with child(ren)	67.2	69.6	74.8	69.7	60.8	60.3
Single elderly male	0.0	0.2	0.1	0.3	0.5	0.3
Single elderly female	0.0	0.5	0.0	0.1	1.0	0.5

(Table continues on next page)

FORMER YUGOSLAV REPUBLIC OF MACEDONIA *(continued)*

Poverty line	33% of median	67% of median	50% of median	50% of median	50% of median	
Economies of scale	Theta=.75	Theta=.75	Theta=1	Theta=.75	Theta=.50	
	Share of poor	Share of poor	Share of poor	Share of poor	Share of poor	Share of population
Multiple elderly only	16.4	9.2	9.1	11.0	12.8	10.5
Other households without child(ren)	16.5	20.2	15.6	18.6	24.5	28.0
Total	100.0	100.0	100.0	100.0	100.0	100.0
No. of children under 15						
Zero	19.1	24.7	18.0	22.6	31.7	32.3
One	17.3	15.9	14.6	15.6	17.2	21.4
Two	22.0	30.9	31.4	27.3	23.5	29.3
Three or more	41.7	28.5	36.0	34.5	27.6	17.0
Total	100.0	100.0	100.0	100.0	100.0	100.0
No. of elderly						
Zero	64.6	73.3	73.5	74.5	71.9	73.4
One	19.1	17.5	17.4	14.5	15.3	16.0
Two or more	16.4	9.2	9.1	11.0	12.8	10.6
Total	100.0	100.0	100.0	100.0	100.0	100.0
Household head, gender						
Male	92.2	92.5	94.0	94.3	91.2	89.9
Female	7.9	7.5	6.1	5.7	8.8	10.1
Total	100.0	100.0	100.0	100.0	100.0	100.0
Household head, labor market status						
Employed (nonfarm)	28.1	37.9	35.8	36.6	33.9	37.9
Farmer	15.6	11.9	13.0	10.9	10.8	9.7
Unemployed	13.8	11.1	11.0	10.7	10.9	7.2
Pensioner	19.9	20.3	20.2	20.0	23.8	22.4
Employed (farmer)	6.5	3.7	3.4	4.4	5.4	2.8
Pensioner (farmer)	3.0	6.7	6.9	7.4	6.3	9.9
Seasonal worker	4.3	4.9	5.8	5.5	3.2	7.7
Other (includes students, homemakers, social assistance recipients)	8.8	3.6	3.9	4.6	5.7	2.3
Total	100.0	100.0	100.0	100.0	100.0	100.0
No. of income earners						
Zero	53.0	37.8	38.6	40.9	46.4	27.7
One	45.5	42.3	43.8	43.9	41.3	40.3
Two	1.5	16.3	14.1	12.0	10.6	25.5
Three or more	0.0	3.7	3.5	3.1	1.7	6.5
Total	100.0	100.0	100.0	100.0	100.0	100.0

Source: FYR Macedonia 1996 Household Budget Survey.

MOLDOVA: Composition of Poverty, 1997

Poverty line Economies of scale	33% of median Theta=.75 Share of poor	67% of median Theta=.75 Share of poor	50% of median Theta=1 Share of poor	50% of median Theta=.75 Share of poor	50% of median Theta=.50 Share of poor	Share of population
Age in years						
0–15	25.1	25.7	28.6	25.5	22.4	23.7
16–64	64.7	63.2	63.7	63.7	62.6	65.9
65+	10.2	11.0	7.7	10.8	15.0	10.4
Total	100.0	100.0	100.0	100.0	100.0	100.0
Education						
Age less than 15	25.1	25.7	28.6	25.5	22.4	23.6
Primary or less	11.8	13.7	11.2	13.4	16.9	12.3
General secondary	36.4	39.0	39.0	38.6	37.4	35.8
Vocational or technical	22.3	17.1	17.5	17.8	18.6	18.8
Higher	4.5	4.5	3.7	4.6	4.7	9.4
Total	100.0	100.0	100.0	100.0	100.0	100.0
Location						
Chisinau or Tiraspol	6.0	9.7	8.4	9.3	11.3	17.4
Other urban	20.4	24.6	22.9	23.2	24.7	24.2
Rural	73.6	65.6	68.7	67.5	64.0	58.4
Total	100.0	100.0	100.0	100.0	100.0	100.0
Region						
Right bank	88.8	83.5	85.9	85.3	83.8	82.9
Transnistria	11.2	16.5	14.1	14.7	16.2	17.1
Total	100.0	100.0	100.0	100.0	100.0	100.0
Access to land						
No	95.7	87.4	89.9	89.8	90.8	86.2
Yes	4.3	12.6	10.1	10.2	9.2	13.8
Total	100.0	100.0	100.0	100.0	100.0	100.0
Own automobile						
No	97.6	91.0	94.7	94.4	94.2	83.4
Yes	2.4	9.0	5.3	5.6	5.8	16.6
Total	100.0	100.0	100.0	100.0	100.0	100.0
Household typology						
Single parent with child(ren)	2.2	2.2	2.0	2.3	2.7	2.5
Other households with child(ren)	62.0	63.6	70.6	63.1	53.6	59.1
Single elderly male	0.3	0.2	0.1	0.2	0.4	0.5
Single elderly female	1.7	2.9	0.9	3.1	5.7	2.3
Multiple elderly only	4.0	3.2	2.9	3.4	4.9	2.9
Other households without child(ren)	29.8	27.9	23.4	27.7	32.7	32.7
Total	100.0	100.0	100.0	100.0	100.0	100.0

(Table continues on next page)

MOLDOVA *(continued)*

Poverty line	33% of median	67% of median	50% of median	50% of median	50% of median	
Economies of scale	Theta=.75	Theta=.75	Theta=1	Theta=.75	Theta=.50	
	Share of poor	Share of poor	Share of poor	Share of poor	Share of poor	Share of population
No. of children under 15						
Zero	35.8	34.2	27.4	34.5	43.6	38.4
One	24.5	26.3	24.2	24.3	23.7	28.4
Two	23.3	28.7	33.8	30.3	23.8	24.7
Three or more	16.4	10.7	14.5	10.8	8.8	8.5
Total	100.0	100.0	100.0	100.0	100.0	100.0
No. of elderly						
Zero	81.2	78.8	83.1	81.5	78.6	79.2
One	10.2	16.2	11.6	12.6	14.7	15.7
Two	8.5	4.8	5.3	5.9	6.6	5.0
Three or more	0.0	0.2	0.0	0.0	0.0	0.1
Total	100.0	100.0	100.0	100.0	100.0	100.0
Household head, gender						
Male	77.5	70.6	73.3	72.3	69.4	72.8
Female	22.5	29.4	26.7	27.7	30.6	27.2
Total	100.0	100.0	100.0	100.0	100.0	100.0
Household head, labor market status						
Employed	75.8	67.0	70.5	68.3	66.6	69.4
Self-employed or employer	0.0	0.8	0.7	0.7	0.0	1.8
Unemployed	0.0	0.4	0.4	0.4	0.0	0.4
Not in workforce	4.7	7.8	8.2	7.1	6.5	6.9
Retired	19.5	24.0	20.3	23.5	26.8	21.6
Total	100.0	100.0	100.0	100.0	100.0	100.0
No. of income earners						
Zero	14.9	16.4	11.3	16.4	23.5	15.2
One	27.3	24.3	23.6	23.1	26.1	27.6
Two	36.5	44.7	48.3	44.8	37.5	44.7
Three or more	21.3	14.6	16.8	15.6	12.9	12.4
Total	100.0	100.0	100.0	100.0	100.0	100.0

Source: Moldova Household Budget Survey, Q3 1997.

POLAND: Composition of Poverty, 1998

Poverty line	33% of median	67% of median	50% of median	50% of median	50% of median	
Economies of scale	Theta=.75	Theta=.75	Theta=1	Theta=.75	Theta=.50	
	Share of poor	Share of poor	Share of poor	Share of poor	Share of poor	Share of population
Age in years						
0–15	40.6	31.7	36.9	35.5	30.3	22.0
16–64	54.5	60.9	58.1	58.2	58.6	66.9
65⁺	4.9	7.4	5.0	6.3	11.0	11.1
Total	100.0	100.0	100.0	100.0	100.0	100.0
Education						
Age less than 15	40.6	31.8	37.0	35.6	30.4	22.1
Primary	32.6	32.9	30.7	33.2	39.1	27.8
Basic vocational	20.9	24.4	23.6	23.3	22.6	22.0
General secondary	5.5	9.9	8.0	7.4	7.3	21.1
Higher	0.4	1.0	0.7	0.5	0.6	7.2
Total	100.0	100.0	100.0	100.0	100.0	100.0
Location						
Warsaw	0.0	1.0	0.6	0.7	0.5	4.4
Urban	40.2	41.8	36.7	37.3	40.1	56.8
Rural	59.8	57.2	62.7	62.0	59.4	38.9
Total	100.0	100.0	100.0	100.0	100.0	100.0
Region						
North	18.6	16.8	17.6	17.4	16.4	15.7
Center	17.9	20.6	19.0	19.3	20.9	23.5
East	25.6	23.4	25.1	25.0	23.9	17.8
West	17.7	14.3	14.4	14.6	14.9	15.7
South	20.2	24.9	23.9	23.7	23.9	27.4
Total	100.0	100.0	100.0	100.0	100.0	100.0
Access to land						
No	42.3	39.4	34.7	37.2	40.7	49.9
Yes	57.7	60.6	65.3	62.8	59.3	50.1
Total	100.0	100.0	100.0	100.0	100.0	100.0
Own automobile						
No	80.0	64.5	64.0	70.7	77.4	49.3
Yes	20.0	35.5	36.0	29.4	22.6	50.7
Total	100.0	100.0	100.0	100.0	100.0	100.0
Household typology						
Single parent with child(ren)	4.7	2.9	2.9	3.8	4.7	1.9
Other households with child(ren)	83.1	77.7	86.7	80.6	67.5	62.5
Single elderly male	0.0	0.2	0.0	0.1	0.6	0.4
Single elderly female	0.5	1.2	0.2	0.8	3.6	2.4
Multiple elderly only	0.7	1.6	0.6	1.2	2.2	3.1

(Table continues on next page)

POLAND *(continued)*

Poverty line	33% of median	67% of median	50% of median	50% of median	50% of median	
Economies of scale	Theta=.75	Theta=.75	Theta=1	Theta=.75	Theta=.50	
	Share of poor	Share of poor	Share of poor	Share of poor	Share of poor	Share of population
Other households						
without child(ren)	11.0	16.5	9.7	13.6	21.4	29.7
Total	100.0	100.0	100.0	100.0	100.0	100.0
No. of children under 15						
Zero	16.7	26.2	15.8	20.8	33.4	44.2
One	14.0	22.0	20.3	20.3	18.9	23.9
Two	26.3	25.9	28.5	26.3	23.0	20.0
Three or more	43.0	25.8	35.4	32.5	24.8	11.9
Total	100.0	100.0	100.0	100.0	100.0	100.0
No. of elderly						
Zero	85.6	81.1	82.0	82.4	79.7	78.5
One	11.5	14.0	13.3	13.3	15.7	15.3
Two	2.9	4.9	4.6	4.3	4.5	6.1
Three or more	0.0	0.1	0.1	0.1	0.1	0.1
Total	100.0	100.0	100.0	100.0	100.0	100.0
Household head, gender						
Female	29.8	28.2	26.2	29.0	34.7	28.4
Male	70.2	71.8	73.8	71.0	65.3	71.6
Total	100.0	100.0	100.0	100.0	100.0	100.0
Household head, labor market status						
Employed	64.9	78.6	81.1	75.6	66.5	78.0
Unemployed	12.5	3.6	4.6	6.1	7.4	1.3
Retired	9.7	8.9	6.0	8.0	13.7	14.5
Other	13.0	9.0	8.3	10.3	12.4	6.2
Total	100.0	100.0	100.0	100.0	100.0	100.0
No. of income earners						
Zero	46.5	32.4	30.9	36.9	46.2	27.2
One	43.8	44.1	46.4	46.0	41.9	35.9
Two	8.2	20.1	19.4	15.0	10.4	31.4
Three or more	1.6	3.4	3.4	2.1	1.5	5.4
Total	100.0	100.0	100.0	100.0	100.0	100.0
Alternative household typology						
Single	1.7	2.6	0.5	2.2	8.2	5.7
Single parent	5.2	3.2	3.0	4.0	5.1	2.3
Couple no child(ren)	2.3	4.4	1.7	3.2	6.3	12.3
Couple with child(ren)	34.1	38.3	35.9	38.2	36.0	39.0

(Table continues on next page)

POLAND *(continued)*

Poverty line Economies of scale	*33% of* *median* *Theta=.75* Share of poor	*67% of* *median* *Theta=.75* Share of poor	*50% of* *median* *Theta=1* Share of poor	*50% of* *median* *Theta=.75* Share of poor	*50% of* *median* *Theta=.50* Share of poor	Share of population
Other households without child(ren)	35.2	27.0	29.7	29.0	27.4	22.3
Other households with child(ren)	21.6	24.5	29.3	23.5	16.9	18.5
Total	100.0	100.0	100.0	100.0	100.0	100.0
Own labor market status						
Employed	23.2	34.3	32.1	30.7	29.8	40.9
Unemployed	11.5	6.2	6.6	7.7	8.7	3.4
Retired	5.7	7.8	5.1	6.5	11.5	14.1
Other	19.0	20.0	19.2	19.5	19.7	19.5
Age less than 15	40.6	31.7	36.9	35.5	30.3	22.0
Total	100.0	100.0	100.0	100.0	100.0	100.0

Source: Poland Household Budget Survey 1998.

ROMANIA: Composition of Poverty, 1998

Poverty line	33% of median	67% of median	50% of median	50% of median	50% of median	
Economies of scale	Theta=.75	Theta=.75	Theta=1	Theta=.75	Theta=.50	
	Share of poor	Share of poor	Share of poor	Share of poor	Share of poor	Share of population
Age in years						
0–15	36.4	28.0	34.9	31.2	23.0	20.5
16–64	55.3	59.8	59.9	58.9	53.6	66.7
65+	8.3	12.2	5.2	9.9	23.4	12.8
Total	100.0	100.0	100.0	100.0	100.0	100.0
Education						
Age less than 15	36.4	28.0	34.9	31.2	23.0	20.5
None	10.9	4.5	4.4	6.4	8.7	2.3
Primary (less than 8 years)	35.4	37.5	33.3	37.1	46.1	30.4
Vocational	6.8	11.5	10.9	9.8	8.4	13.8
High school (9-12) or post-high school	10.2	17.8	16.1	15.1	13.3	28.1
Higher (college or university)	0.4	0.6	0.4	0.4	0.4	5.0
Total	100.0	100.0	100.0	100.0	100.0	100.0
Location						
Urban	34.8	39.4	35.3	33.5	33.2	54.5
Rural	65.2	60.6	64.7	66.5	66.8	45.5
Total	100.0	100.0	100.0	100.0	100.0	100.0
Region						
Northeast	32.6	23.7	26.5	25.4	24.8	17.0
Southeast	10.8	13.6	13.6	14.0	13.9	13.1
South	7.0	15.9	15.4	13.7	13.1	15.6
Southwest	8.9	9.4	8.9	9.9	10.2	10.8
West	11.2	8.3	8.0	8.3	9.0	9.1
Northwest	10.5	11.2	10.7	11.3	11.7	12.7
Center	16.4	12.0	12.0	12.8	13.5	11.8
Bucharest	2.5	5.9	4.9	4.6	3.7	10.1
Total	100.0	100.0	100.0	100.0	100.0	100.0
Access to land						
No	54.6	45.1	43.8	45.8	44.8	52.9
Yes	45.4	54.9	56.2	54.2	55.2	47.1
Total	100.0	100.0	100.0	100.0	100.0	100.0
Own automobile						
No	98.5	93.8	94.2	96.2	97.3	76.3
Yes	1.5	6.2	5.8	3.8	2.7	23.7
Total	100.0	100.0	100.0	100.0	100.0	100.0
Household typology						
Single parent with child(ren)	2.7	1.9	1.6	2.5	3.0	1.2

(Table continues on next page)

ROMANIA *(continued)*

Poverty line	33% of median	67% of median	50% of median	50% of median	50% of median	
Economies of scale	Theta=.75	Theta=.75	Theta=1	Theta=.75	Theta=.50	
	Share of poor	Share of poor	Share of poor	Share of poor	Share of poor	Share of population
Other households						
with child(ren)	76.6	65.1	79.4	69.6	50.2	52.4
Single elderly male	1.1	0.7	0.2	0.8	2.4	0.9
Single elderly female	3.9	3.9	0.9	3.5	12.7	3.0
Number of elderly	0.8	3.7	1.0	2.3	4.6	4.3
Other households						
without child(ren)	14.9	24.7	16.9	21.3	27.0	38.1
Total	100.0	100.0	100.0	100.0	100.0	100.0
No. of children under 15						
Zero	20.7	33.0	19.0	27.9	46.8	46.3
One	19.9	23.1	22.2	21.9	18.5	26.1
Two	20.3	22.7	25.5	22.8	17.4	18.5
Three or more	39.1	21.2	33.3	27.4	17.4	9.1
Total	100.0	100.0	100.0	100.0	100.0	100.0
No. of elderly						
Zero	84.7	79.2	85.3	82.2	70.3	78.2
One	13.6	14.9	11.3	13.8	24.1	15.0
Two	1.7	5.8	3.3	4.0	5.6	6.7
Three or more	0.0	0.1	0.1	0.0	0.0	0.1
Total	100.0	100.0	100.0	100.0	100.0	100.0
Household head, gender						
Male	74.4	80.4	83.7	78.1	66.2	84.5
Female	25.6	19.6	16.3	21.9	33.8	15.5
Total	100.0	100.0	100.0	100.0	100.0	100.0
Household head, labor market status						
Employee	8.3	29.6	29.4	21.7	13.6	44.5
Employer	0.0	0.1	0.1	0.1	0.1	0.8
Self-employed						
(nonagricultural activity)	18.8	6.7	8.6	10.0	9.3	3.6
Farmer	25.0	18.8	22.5	23.7	20.8	9.6
Unemployed, but						
looking for work	16.4	9.3	11.1	11.9	11.9	4.8
Pensioner	16.9	30.3	21.8	25.2	36.6	34.2
Not in workforce	14.6	5.2	6.6	7.4	7.8	2.6
Total	100.0	100.0	100.0	100.0	100.0	100.0
No. of income earners						
Zero	22.3	7.3	9.2	11.4	12.9	3.0
One	35.7	35.9	31.1	34.9	46.6	26.2
Two	25.9	34.4	31.5	32.1	27.3	47.3
Three or more	16.1	22.4	28.1	21.5	13.2	23.5
Total	100.0	100.0	100.0	100.0	100.0	100.0

Source: Romania 1998 Living Standards Measurement Survey.

RUSSIAN FEDERATION: Composition of Poverty, 1998

Poverty line	33% of median	67% of median	50% of median	50% of median	50% of median	
Economies of scale	Theta=.75	Theta=.75	Theta=1	Theta=.75	Theta=.50	
	Share of poor	Share of poor	Share of poor	Share of poor	Share of poor	Share of population
Age in years						
0–15	36.7	36.4	39.8	36.7	32.4	34.0
16–64	50.2	51.1	49.5	50.0	51.5	54.9
65+	13.1	12.5	10.7	13.3	16.1	11.1
Total	100.0	100.0	100.0	100.0	100.0	100.0
Education						
Age less than 15	34.8	34.9	37.7	34.8	31.2	32.0
High school	40.4	39.4	37.9	39.8	42.2	36.8
Technical or vocational	20.7	19.9	19.7	21.1	21.9	21.2
University	4.1	5.8	4.7	4.4	4.8	10.0
Total	100.0	100.0	100.0	100.0	100.0	100.0
Location						
Urban	60.5	60.3	59.8	59.6	59.2	63.4
Semi-urban	7.7	7.4	8.6	7.0	6.9	5.9
Rural	31.8	32.3	31.6	33.4	33.9	30.8
Total	100.0	100.0	100.0	100.0	100.0	100.0
Region						
Metropolitan areas: Moscow and St. Petersburg	1.0	2.9	2.4	1.6	1.9	6.5
Northern and Northwestern	6.3	8.1	8.6	6.5	6.2	7.1
Central and Central Black Earth	20.1	19.5	19.2	21.3	22.3	18.2
Volga-Vaytski and Volga Basin	25.1	22.8	24.1	25.1	26.1	18.4
Caucasian	12.5	12.2	11.4	10.6	9.6	15.1
Ural	19.7	18.7	18.4	19.4	19.3	15.4
Western Siberian	9.9	10.3	10.5	10.2	9.9	10.3
Eastern Siberian and Far Eastern	5.5	5.5	5.4	5.3	4.8	9.0
Total	100.0	100.0	100.0	100.0	100.0	100.0
Own automobile						
Yes	5.9	15.2	13.5	11.6	8.9	29.4
No	94.1	84.8	86.5	88.4	91.1	70.6
Total	100.0	100.0	100.0	100.0	100.0	100.0
Household typology						
Single parent with child(ren)	15.3	9.9	10.3	11.6	13.3	7.6
Other households with child(ren)	56.4	62.7	67.3	61.2	52.9	64.5
Single elderly male	0.4	0.5	0.3	0.4	0.8	0.6

(Table continues on next page)

RUSSIAN FEDERATION *(continued)*

Poverty line	33% of median	67% of median	50% of median	50% of median	50% of median	
Economies of scale	Theta=.75	Theta=.75	Theta=1	Theta=.75	Theta=.50	
	Share of poor	Share of poor	Share of poor	Share of poor	Share of poor	Share of population
Single elderly female	7.0	4.8	3.6	5.8	8.4	3.5
Multiple elderly only	5.5	6.3	5.3	6.1	7.1	6.5
Other households						
without child(ren)	15.3	15.8	13.3	15.0	17.4	17.3
Total	100.0	100.0	100.0	100.0	100.0	100.0
No. of children under 15						
Zero	31.0	29.5	23.9	29.7	37.0	30.0
One	28.5	29.2	29.8	29.2	29.1	34.1
Two	27.0	30.5	32.4	29.3	24.4	30.0
Three or more	13.5	10.9	13.9	11.7	9.6	9.0
Total	100.0	100.0	100.0	100.0	100.0	100.0
No. of elderly						
Zero	67.9	62.8	65.1	63.3	61.1	63.3
One	23.0	25.1	24.7	25.8	27.5	23.2
Two	8.1	11.2	9.6	10.3	11.0	12.3
Three or more	1.0	1.0	0.7	0.6	0.5	1.1
Total	100.0	100.0	100.0	100.0	100.0	100.0
Household head, gender						
Male	73.8	81.1	81.7	78.0	74.1	85.1
Female	26.2	18.8	18.3	21.9	25.8	14.8
Unknown		0.1	0.1	0.1	0.1	0.0
Total	100.0	100.0	100.0	100.0	100.0	100.0
Household head, labor market status						
Unknown	9.9	6.6	7.0	7.2	7.7	6.1
Employed	48.8	53.6	53.8	52.4	51.0	61.7
Self-employed or employer	1.1	1.3	1.3	1.4	1.2	3.8
Unemployed, but looking for work	22.9	22.2	24.4	23.3	20.2	14.9
Not in workforce	2.2	2.0	1.6	1.6	1.8	1.0
Retired	15.2	14.2	11.8	14.0	18.2	12.6
Total	100.0	100.0	100.0	100.0	100.0	100.0
No. of income earners						
Zero	29.3	22.2	20.6	23.8	27.8	16.7
One	34.5	33.8	34.2	35.2	35.9	29.8
Two	29.1	35.5	35.5	32.6	29.2	41.7
Three or more	7.2	8.5	9.8	8.4	7.1	11.8
Total	100.0	100.0	100.0	100.0	100.0	100.0

Source: Russian Longitudinal Monitoring Survey 1998.

SLOVENIA: Composition of Poverty, 1997–98

Poverty line	33% of median	67% of median	50% of median	50% of median	50% of median	
Economies of scale	Theta=.75	Theta=.75	Theta=1	Theta=.75	Theta=.50	
	Share of poor	Share of poor	Share of poor	Share of poor	Share of poor	Share of population
Age in years						
0–15	17.2	21.1	23.2	18.4	13.4	18.7
16–64	61.2	61.3	60.5	60.1	55.7	68.3
65+	21.5	17.6	16.3	21.5	31.0	13.0
Total	100.0	100.0	100.0	100.0	100.0	100.0
Education						
Age less than 15	17.2	21.1	23.2	18.4	13.4	18.7
None	1.1	0.5	0.4	0.4	0.6	0.4
Primary or middle	57.8	41.3	44.3	50.8	56.1	29.2
Secondary	23.5	35.1	30.8	29.5	28.7	42.5
Higher	0.4	2.0	1.2	1.0	1.3	9.2
Total	100.0	100.0	100.0	100.0	100.0	100.0
Access to land						
No	52.2	37.6	37.4	49.2	48.9	41.0
Yes	47.8	62.4	62.6	50.8	51.1	59.1
Total	100.0	100.0	100.0	100.0	100.0	100.0
Own automobile						
No	72.0	31.3	36.1	50.3	59.7	14.3
Yes	28.0	68.7	63.9	49.7	40.3	85.7
Total	100.0	100.0	100.0	100.0	100.0	100.0
Household typology						
Single parent with child(ren)	2.7	2.1	1.3	1.7	2.3	1.5
Other households with child(ren)	43.1	53.4	59.7	46.7	31.8	48.9
Single elderly male	0.0	0.6	0.3	0.4	1.8	0.3
Single elderly female	2.3	3.1	1.1	2.9	8.5	2.7
Multiple elderly only	12.8	5.9	5.7	9.4	12.0	3.9
Other households without child(ren)	39.1	34.9	32.0	38.9	43.6	42.8
Total	100.0	100.0	100.0	100.0	100.0	100.0
No. of children under 15						
Zero	54.2	44.6	39.0	51.6	65.9	49.6
One	19.2	23.4	21.3	19.4	14.9	24.9
Two	13.8	22.6	24.7	20.9	14.0	19.9
Three or more	12.8	9.5	15.0	8.1	5.2	5.6
Total	100.0	100.0	100.0	100.0	100.0	100.0

(Table continues on next page)

SLOVENIA *(continued)*

Poverty line	33% of median	67% of median	50% of median	50% of median	50% of median	
Economies of scale	Theta=.75	Theta=.75	Theta=1	Theta=.75	Theta=.50	
	Share of poor	Share of poor	Share of poor	Share of poor	Share of poor	Share of population
No. of elderly						
Zero	65.7	62.9	57.5	61.8	55.7	73.4
One	21.5	26.3	29.8	26.8	30.3	18.8
Two	12.8	10.9	12.7	11.4	13.9	7.7
Three or more	0.0	0.0	0.0	0.0	0.0	0.1
Total	100.0	100.0	100.0	100.0	100.0	100.0
Household head, gender						
Male	42.9	58.8	61.0	54.5	50.7	57.6
Female	57.1	41.2	39.0	45.5	49.3	42.4
Total	100.0	100.0	100.0	100.0	100.0	100.0
Household head, labor market status						
Employed	43.3	57.1	55.9	42.5	35.6	67.8
Unemployed	7.1	6.6	7.4	9.6	7.3	2.7
Not in workforce	49.6	36.4	36.7	47.8	57.1	29.5
Total	100.0	100.0	100.0	100.0	100.0	100.0
No. of income earners						
Zero	35.5	24.9	22.8	38.3	48.9	16.8
One	23.9	26.2	25.5	26.9	26.8	23.1
Two	26.5	36.5	34.1	25.4	17.2	45.7
Three or more	14.1	12.4	17.6	9.5	7.1	14.3
Total	100.0	100.0	100.0	100.0	100.0	100.0

Source: Slovenia 1997–98 Household Income and Expenditures Survey.

TAJIKISTAN: Composition of Poverty, 1999

Poverty line	33% of median	67% of median	50% of median	50% of median	50% of median	
Economies of scale	Theta=.75	Theta=.75	Theta=1	Theta=.75	Theta=.50	
	Share of poor	Share of poor	Share of poor	Share of poor	Share of poor	Share of population
Age in years						
0–15	50.9	48.2	48.4	48.0	48.6	44.9
16–64	44.3	47.0	47.6	48.0	46.5	50.7
65⁺	4.8	4.8	4.0	4.0	4.9	4.3
Total	100.0	100.0	100.0	100.0	100.0	100.0
Education						
Age less than 15	50.9	48.2	48.4	48.0	48.6	44.9
Unknown	2.0	1.8	1.6	1.7	1.7	2.0
None	2.5	2.0	2.2	2.2	2.3	1.6
Primary (less than 7 years)	6.6	5.7	5.2	5.3	5.9	5.6
General secondary (8–12 years)	30.6	33.2	34.4	34.2	33.3	32.7
Vocational or specialized secondary	6.3	7.3	6.5	6.7	6.6	9.2
Some higher	1.0	1.9	1.7	1.9	1.7	4.0
Total	100.0	100.0	100.0	100.0	100.0	100.0
Location						
Urban	26.3	20.4	19.9	22.4	21.9	21.9
Rural	73.7	79.6	80.1	77.6	78.1	78.1
Total	100.0	100.0	100.0	100.0	100.0	100.0
Region						
Dushanbe (capital)	3.3	2.3	1.8	2.0	2.9	6.4
GBAO	10.1	7.0	8.2	8.3	7.5	3.9
RRS	15.9	16.9	19.7	16.5	14.8	25.3
Leninabad	25.8	27.6	25.8	30.2	30.0	26.1
Khatlon	44.8	46.1	44.5	43.0	44.7	38.1
Total	100.0	100.0	100.0	100.0	100.0	100.0
Access to individual garden plot						
No	21.2	15.8	16.6	18.7	21.1	16.0
Yes	78.8	84.2	83.4	81.3	78.9	84.0
Total	100.0	100.0	100.0	100.0	100.0	100.0
Own automobile						
No	100.0	97.1	98.5	98.8	98.6	86.5
Yes	0.0	2.9	1.5	1.2	1.4	13.5
Total	100.0	100.0	100.0	100.0	100.0	100.0
Household typology						
Single parent with child(ren)	6.3	2.5	2.3	3.0	4.9	1.3

(Table continues on next page)

TAJIKISTAN *(continued)*

Poverty line	*33% of median*	*67% of median*	*50% of median*	*50% of median*	*50% of median*	
Economies of scale	*Theta=.75*	*Theta=.75*	*Theta=1*	*Theta=.75*	*Theta=.50*	
	Share of poor	*Share of poor*	*Share of poor*	*Share of poor*	*Share of poor*	*Share of population*
Other households						
with child(ren)	91.1	95.3	96.5	94.9	91.4	95.0
Single elderly male	0.0	0.0	0.0	0.0	0.1	0.0
Single elderly female	0.0	0.1	0.0	0.0	0.4	0.1
Multiple elderly only	1.0	0.6	0.4	0.6	1.3	0.3
Other households						
without child(ren)	1.5	1.5	0.8	1.4	1.8	3.2
Total	100.0	100.0	100.0	100.0	100.0	100.0
No. of children under 15						
Zero	2.5	2.2	1.2	2.1	3.7	3.7
One	5.6	6.9	5.7	7.0	8.3	8.4
Two	12.9	13.9	11.3	13.8	15.8	13.9
Three or more	79.0	77.0	81.8	77.1	72.2	74.0
Total	100.0	100.0	100.0	100.0	100.0	100.0
No. of elderly						
Zero	67.6	61.0	59.3	63.9	67.9	61.0
One	23.5	23.3	24.2	21.4	19.2	22.2
Two	8.9	15.7	16.5	14.6	12.8	16.6
Three or more	0.0	0.0	0.0	0.0	0.0	0.2
Total	100.0	100.0	100.0	100.0	100.0	100.0
Household head, gender						
Male	72.7	79.4	77.0	77.4	76.3	84.4
Female	27.3	20.6	23.0	22.6	23.7	15.6
Total	100.0	100.0	100.0	100.0	100.0	100.0
Household head, labor market status						
Employed	67.8	61.3	61.3	62.9	64.4	63.4
Unemployed, but						
looking for work	3.3	5.9	4.5	5.2	4.0	6.3
Not in workforce	15.4	10.2	13.2	14.2	14.5	7.3
Retired	13.4	20.9	19.6	15.9	14.4	21.2
Unknown	0.0	1.8	1.5	1.8	2.8	1.7
Total	100.0	100.0	100.0	100.0	100.0	100.0
No. of adults employed						
Zero	14.2	11.6	10.5	11.0	14.8	10.8
One	39.2	34.9	35.7	40.0	41.2	30.6
Two	27.1	30.5	28.5	26.1	24.6	28.9
Three or more	19.5	23.0	25.3	22.9	19.4	29.7
Total	100.0	100.0	100.0	100.0	100.0	100.0

Source: Tajikistan 1999 Living Standards Measurement Survey.

TURKMENISTAN: Composition of Poverty, 1998

Poverty line	33% of median	67% of median	50% of median	50% of median	50% of median	
Economies of scale	Theta=.75	Theta=.75	Theta=1	Theta=.75	Theta=.50	
	Share of poor	Share of poor	Share of poor	Share of poor	Share of poor	Share of population
Age in years						
0–15	49.3	45.2	45.5	45.8	46.4	39.8
16–64	47.3	51.5	51.8	51.3	49.8	55.8
65+	3.4	3.3	2.7	3.0	3.9	4.4
Total	100.0	100.0	100.0	100.0	100.0	100.0
Education						
Age less than 15	49.3	45.2	45.5	45.8	46.4	39.8
Unknown	5.8	4.6	5.2	5.2	5.5	3.5
None	0.5	0.4	0.4	0.4	0.4	0.3
Primary (less than 7 years)	4.9	4.8	4.3	4.2	4.5	5.9
General secondary (8–9 years)	32.2	35.5	36.0	35.5	34.1	33.7
Higher education	7.3	9.5	8.7	8.8	9.2	16.8
Total	100.0	100.0	100.0	100.0	100.0	100.0
Location						
Urban	10.3	24.5	20.6	18.7	19.7	43.0
Rural	89.7	75.5	79.4	81.3	80.3	57.0
Total	100.0	100.0	100.0	100.0	100.0	100.0
Access to land						
No	24.4	28.1	26.4	25.8	28.3	37.5
Yes	75.6	71.9	73.6	74.2	71.7	62.5
Total	100.0	100.0	100.0	100.0	100.0	100.0
Own automobile						
No	73.6	68.0	69.4	71.7	75.6	58.8
Yes	26.4	32.0	30.6	28.3	24.4	41.2
Total	100.0	100.0	100.0	100.0	100.0	100.0
Household typology						
Single parent with child(ren)	0.5	0.4	0.2	0.3	0.7	1.1
Other households with child(ren)	95.4	95.2	96.6	95.3	93.4	89.3
Single elderly male		0.0			0.1	0.1
Single elderly female		0.1		0.0	0.2	0.3
Multiple elderly only	0.3	0.2	0.1	0.1	0.4	0.3
Other households without child(ren)	3.7	4.0	3.1	4.2	5.2	8.9
Total	100.0	100.0	100.0	100.0	100.0	100.0

(Table continues on next page)

TURKMENISTAN *(continued)*

Poverty line	33% of median	67% of median	50% of median	50% of median	50% of median	
Economies of scale	*Theta=.75*	*Theta=.75*	*Theta=1*	*Theta=.75*	*Theta=.50*	
	Share of poor	*Share of poor*	*Share of poor*	*Share of poor*	*Share of poor*	*Share of population*
No. of children under 15						
Zero	4.1	5.4	4.1	5.7	7.1	10.8
One	5.6	9.4	7.5	7.8	9.4	13.4
Two	15.8	16.5	14.1	15.2	15.7	21.2
Three or more	74.6	68.8	74.3	71.3	67.9	54.5
Total	100.0	100.0	100.0	100.0	100.0	100.0
No. of elderly						
Zero	81.0	82.2	81.6	81.9	82.0	79.7
One	14.4	14.5	15.5	15.2	14.6	15.5
Two or more	4.6	3.3	2.9	2.9	3.4	4.8
Total	100.0	100.0	100.0	100.0	100.0	100.0
Household head, gender						
Unknown	0.0	0.0	0.0	0.0	0.0	0.0
Male	85.3	84.5	85.4	86.0	84.3	82.3
Female	14.7	15.5	14.6	14.0	15.7	17.7
Total	100.0	100.0	100.0	100.0	100.0	100.0
Household head, labor market status						
Unknown	3.2	2.2	2.3	2.3	2.3	2.0
Employed	44.9	53.3	49.6	50.8	53.3	54.9
Self-employed or employer	8.5	5.0	6.2	6.6	7.1	7.3
Unemployed, but looking for work	19.5	9.7	11.2	12.8	13.9	6.4
Not in workforce	8.1	8.2	6.6	6.1	6.2	7.7
Retired	15.8	21.6	24.0	21.4	17.3	21.8
Total	100.0	100.0	100.0	100.0	100.0	100.0
No. of income earners						
Zero	27.3	18.2	17.8	17.8	21.2	13.1
One	22.7	26.5	24.2	27.1	28.8	28.9
Two	27.8	25.9	24.6	23.3	25.2	28.1
Three or more	22.2	29.4	33.2	31.8	24.9	29.8
Total	100.0	100.0	100.0	100.0	100.0	100.0

Source: Turkmenistan 1998 Living Standards Measurement Survey.

UKRAINE: Composition of Poverty, 1996

Poverty line	33% of median	67% of median	50% of median	50% of median	50% of median	
Economies of scale	Theta=.75	Theta=.75	Theta=1	Theta=.75	Theta=.50	
	Share of poor	Share of poor	Share of poor	Share of poor	Share of poor	Share of population
Age in years						
0–15	22.2	21.7	24.7	20.7	15.7	21.7
16–64	53.7	54.9	57.7	54.0	50.3	61.0
65+	24.1	23.4	17.6	25.3	34.0	17.3
Total	100.0	100.0	100.0	100.0	100.0	100.0
Education						
Age less than 15	22.2	21.7	24.7	20.7	15.7	21.7
Unknown	0.0	0.2	0.2	0.3	0.6	0.2
None	2.7	2.9	2.8	4.1	4.5	1.7
Primary (less than 7 years)	14.4	11.4	9.3	12.7	16.0	10.0
General secondary	30.4	30.2	28.4	28.7	30.3	28.7
Vocational or specialized secondary	12.5	10.3	11.8	10.4	10.2	9.4
Some higher	17.9	23.1	22.8	23.2	22.8	28.5
Total	100.0	100.0	100.0	100.0	100.0	100.0
Location						
Urban	69.2	56.9	60.4	59.8	61.9	44.9
Semi-urban	4.0	6.4	6.7	5.4	6.7	7.2
Rural	26.8	36.7	32.9	34.9	31.4	47.9
Total	100.0	100.0	100.0	100.0	100.0	100.0
Region						
South	14.1	21.6	20.3	19.5	18.4	24.0
West	12.0	18.2	17.8	13.2	13.4	27.9
Central	20.7	28.2	25.7	25.3	23.3	29.2
East	53.3	32.0	36.2	42.1	44.9	19.0
Total	100.0	100.0	100.0	100.0	100.0	100.0
Access to land						
No	68.5	41.4	44.9	47.7	54.1	23.8
Yes	31.5	58.6	55.1	52.3	45.9	76.2
Total	100.0	100.0	100.0	100.0	100.0	100.0
Own automobile						
No	93.8	86.4	86.6	88.7	89.6	78.5
Yes	6.2	13.6	13.4	11.3	10.4	21.5
Total	100.0	100.0	100.0	100.0	100.0	100.0
Household typology						
Single parent with child(ren)	5.4	5.4	3.5	3.6	2.9	4.8
Other households with child(ren)	46.4	49.7	60.4	48.5	36.7	51.7

(Table continues on next page)

UKRAINE (continued)

Poverty line	33% of median	67% of median	50% of median	50% of median	50% of median	
Economies of scale	Theta=.75	Theta=.75	Theta=1	Theta=.75	Theta=.50	
	Share of poor	Share of poor	Share of poor	Share of poor	Share of poor	Share of population
Single elderly male	0.4	0.9	0.5	0.9	1.7	0.5
Single elderly female	10.5	6.3	4.3	8.3	13.3	3.8
Multiple elderly only	10.5	11.5	8.8	11.4	14.9	9.3
Other households without child(ren)	26.8	26.2	22.6	27.3	30.6	29.9
Total	100.0	100.0	100.0	100.0	100.0	100.0
No. of children under 15						
Zero	43.1	42.6	33.5	45.7	58.0	41.2
One	37.3	27.4	30.1	28.2	26.7	31.4
Two	11.2	24.2	29.7	20.5	11.7	22.2
Three or more	8.3	5.8	6.7	5.6	3.7	5.2
Total	100.0	100.0	100.0	100.0	100.0	100.0
No. of elderly						
Zero	58.3	58.7	61.1	56.5	52.2	65.7
One	31.2	29.1	29.7	32.1	33.0	24.5
Two	10.5	12.2	9.3	11.4	14.9	9.5
Three or more	0.0	0.0	0.0	0.0	0.0	0.3
Total	100.0	100.0	100.0	100.0	100.0	100.0
Household head, gender						
Unknown	4.7	5.5	6.4	5.9	4.3	5.6
Male	30.1	42.3	41.7	37.8	37.2	49.0
Female	65.2	52.3	51.9	56.3	58.5	45.4
Total	100.0	100.0	100.0	100.0	100.0	100.0
Household head, labor market status						
Unknown	14.9	11.9	15.3	14.2	12.4	10.9
Employed	15.2	25.1	23.5	20.5	19.6	34.3
Employer	0.0	0.0	0.0	0.0	0.0	0.6
Self-employed	0.0	2.1	1.9	1.9	1.1	2.7
Unemployed, but looking for work	0.0	0.2	0.4	0.5	0.0	0.4
Not in workforce	9.8	3.9	4.0	4.2	5.0	3.9
Retired	60.1	56.9	55.0	58.7	62.0	47.3
Total	100.0	100.0	100.0	100.0	100.0	100.0
No. of income earners						
Zero	50.7	41.2	37.2	45.7	53.9	29.9
One	35.5	32.7	32.2	32.1	28.5	34.5
Two	5.4	19.5	21.1	16.3	12.5	26.7
Three or more	8.3	6.6	9.4	5.9	5.1	9.0
Total	100.0	100.0	100.0	100.0	100.0	100.0

Source: Ukraine 1996 Household Income and Expenditures Survey.

Poverty Risk

ALBANIA: Poverty Risk, 1996

Poverty line	33% of median	67% of median	50% of median	50% of median	50% of median
Economies of scale	Theta=.75	Theta=.75	Theta=1	Theta=.75	Theta=.50
	Poverty risk	Poverty risk	Poverty risk	Poverty risk	Poverty risk
Age in years					
0–15	0.7	20.7	11.0	7.0	5.2
16–64	0.2	11.9	4.6	3.0	2.7
65+	0.3	9.7	3.1	2.0	3.3
Total	0.4	15.3	6.9	4.5	3.7
Education					
Age less than 15	0.7	20.7	11.0	7.0	5.2
None	0.6	17.2	6.1	4.8	6.5
Primary (less than 7 years)	0.3	15.2	6.3	4.0	3.6
General secondary (8–12 years)	0.0	3.3	1.2	1.2	0.9
Vocational or specialized secondary	0.0	7.9	1.9	1.1	1.2
Some higher	0.0	1.8	0.5	0.6	0.6
Total	0.4	15.3	6.9	4.5	3.7
Location					
Rural	0.6	21.4	9.8	6.1	4.9
Urban	0.0	3.8	1.5	1.5	1.5
Total	0.4	15.3	6.9	4.5	3.7
Access to land					
No	0.0	5.1	2.3	2.4	2.5
Yes	0.7	21.4	9.7	5.7	4.5
Total	0.4	15.3	6.9	4.5	3.7
Own automobile					
No	0.4	15.6	7.1	4.6	3.8
Yes	0.0	0.0	0.0	0.0	0.0
Total	0.4	15.3	6.9	4.5	3.7
Household typology					
Single parent with child(ren)	0.0	16.2	13.0	13.0	13.0
Other households with child(ren)	0.5	17.5	8.4	5.3	3.9
Single elderly male	0.0	0.0	0.0	0.0	22.4
Single elderly female	0.0	18.6	0.0	7.6	18.6
Multiple elderly only	0.0	8.3	0.0	0.0	8.3
Other households without child(ren)	0.1	5.5	0.7	0.9	2.1
Total	0.4	15.3	6.9	4.5	3.7

(Table continues on next page)

ALBANIA *(continued)*

Poverty line	33% of median	67% of median	50% of median	50% of median	50% of median
Economies of scale	Theta=.75	Theta=.75	Theta=1	Theta=.75	Theta=.50
	Poverty risk	Poverty risk	Poverty risk	Poverty risk	Poverty risk
No. of children under 15					
Zero	0.1	5.8	0.7	1.0	2.5
One	0.0	10.0	2.2	1.4	1.3
Two	0.1	8.7	2.8	2.3	2.0
Three or more	1.2	31.6	18.4	10.9	7.9
Total	0.4	15.3	6.9	4.5	3.7
No. of elderly					
Zero	0.4	16.4	7.7	5.1	4.1
One	0.3	12.9	4.4	3.1	2.7
Two or more	1.0	9.5	5.4	1.3	1.9
Total	0.4	15.3	6.9	4.5	3.7
Household head, gender					
Male	0.3	15.3	6.8	4.1	3.3
Female	1.4	14.5	8.7	7.9	8.1
Total	0.4	15.3	6.9	4.5	3.7
Household head, labor market status					
Unknown	0.0	13.6	6.5	6.4	5.8
Employed	0.0	6.8	1.6	1.4	1.1
Self-employed or employer	0.5	22.2	10.8	5.8	4.1
Not in workforce	0.0	19.3	8.5	6.4	7.6
Retired	0.8	6.7	2.9	2.2	2.1
Total	0.4	15.3	6.9	4.5	3.7
No. of income earners					
Zero	0.4	12.8	5.8	5.6	6.2
One	0.7	12.8	7.2	6.0	4.4
Two	0.4	18.3	7.5	3.7	3.4
Three or more	0.0	15.9	6.6	2.6	1.0
Total	0.4	15.3	6.9	4.5	3.7

Source: Albania 1996 Employment and Welfare Survey.

ARMENIA: Poverty Risk, 1998/99

Poverty line	33% of median	67% of median	50% of median	50% of median	50% of median
Economies of scale	Theta=.75	Theta=.75	Theta=1	Theta=.75	Theta=.50
	Poverty risk	Poverty risk	Poverty risk	Poverty risk	Poverty risk
Age in years					
0–15	2.4	25.5	15.8	11.1	8.5
16–64	2.1	22.3	12.5	9.1	7.6
65+	2.6	25.5	12.1	11.1	12.2
Total	2.2	23.6	13.4	9.9	8.3
Education					
Age less than 15	2.4	25.5	15.8	11.1	8.5
None	2.4	22.5	15.8	9.5	7.9
Primary	2.8	27.7	16.1	13.0	11.4
Secondary or special secondary	2.4	24.1	13.5	10.1	8.6
Higher	1.0	15.7	6.6	5.4	5.6
Total	2.2	23.6	13.4	9.9	8.3
Location					
Urban	1.9	24.1	13.2	10.1	9.0
Rural	2.6	22.9	13.6	9.7	7.3
Total	2.2	23.6	13.4	9.9	8.3
Region					
Aragotsotn	7.2	30.4	21.2	15.6	11.0
Ararat	0.1	23.3	10.7	9.0	6.6
Armavir	0.6	12.1	7.4	4.3	4.4
Gegarkunik	2.7	25.1	16.2	13.0	8.7
Lori	4.9	35.7	22.3	18.1	16.5
Kotaik	2.4	25.4	16.3	8.9	7.9
Shirak	3.0	33.1	15.2	14.1	13.2
Sunik	1.2	19.1	11.3	10.2	7.3
Vaits Dzor	2.7	21.1	11.6	9.5	5.4
Tavush	0.0	4.2	1.3	0.4	0.7
Capital	1.6	22.0	11.7	7.8	6.8
Total	2.2	23.6	13.4	9.9	8.3
Access to land					
No	2.0	26.6	14.3	10.6	9.9
Yes	2.4	20.8	12.6	9.2	6.7
Total	2.2	23.6	13.4	9.9	8.3
Own automobile					
No	2.7	27.5	15.7	11.8	10.1
Yes	0.7	10.5	5.7	3.3	2.2
Total	2.2	23.6	13.4	9.9	8.3

(Table continues on next page)

ARMENIA *(continued)*

Poverty line	33% of median	67% of median	50% of median	50% of median	50% of median
Economies of scale	Theta=.75	Theta=.75	Theta=1	Theta=.75	Theta=.50
	Poverty risk	Poverty risk	Poverty risk	Poverty risk	Poverty risk
Household typology					
Single parent with child(ren)	2.4	36.7	19.4	18.8	20.9
Other households with child(ren)	2.4	24.7	15.5	10.6	7.7
Single elderly male	0.0	8.8	0.0	5.9	8.8
Single elderly female	4.1	30.6	5.0	14.9	34.7
Multiple elderly only	0.9	21.7	1.9	5.7	11.3
Other households without child(ren)	1.6	18.4	6.8	6.7	7.9
Total	2.2	23.6	13.4	9.9	8.3
No. of children under 15					
Zero	1.7	18.9	6.4	6.9	9.0
One	1.8	19.5	10.2	8.3	7.5
Two	2.8	24.5	14.3	10.6	8.2
Three or more	2.2	29.8	21.1	13.0	8.2
Total	2.2	23.6	13.4	9.9	8.3
No. of elderly					
Zero	2.0	21.9	11.9	8.8	7.6
One	2.5	26.9	16.2	12.3	10.2
Two	3.3	28.7	17.9	12.3	8.8
Three or more	0.0	0.0	0.0	0.0	0.0
Total	2.2	23.6	13.4	9.9	8.3
Household head, gender					
Male	2.1	22.7	13.0	9.2	7.1
Female	2.7	26.9	14.8	12.5	12.7
Total	2.2	23.6	13.4	9.9	8.3
Household head, labor market status					
Inactive	3.5	28.5	16.8	12.9	11.5
Unemployed	2.1	31.5	16.4	11.7	10.0
Employed	1.6	18.7	10.7	7.8	6.0
Total	2.2	23.6	13.4	9.9	8.3
No. of income earners					
Zero	3.2	34.7	17.9	14.5	14.7
One	1.8	21.8	11.8	9.2	8.2
Two	1.9	20.2	11.1	9.0	6.3
Three or more	2.2	19.2	14.0	7.2	4.3
Total	2.2	23.6	13.4	9.9	8.3

Source: Armenia 1998/99 Integrated Survey of Living Standards.

AZERBAIJAN: Poverty Risk, 1999

Poverty line	33% of median	67% of median	50% of median	50% of median	50% of median
Economies of scale	Theta=.75	Theta=.75	Theta=1	Theta=.75	Theta=.50
	Poverty risk	Poverty risk	Poverty risk	Poverty risk	Poverty risk
Age in years					
0–15	4.9	30.5	16.6	13.8	13.1
16–64	5.2	26.8	14.2	12.7	12.2
65+	3.0	31.2	15.2	13.6	13.3
Total	5.0	28.1	14.9	13.1	12.5
Education					
Age less than 15	4.9	30.5	16.6	13.8	13.1
Unknown	0.0	24.9	0.0	12.4	12.4
None	5.5	37.6	22.7	20.4	19.6
Primary	14.6	50.9	37.2	34.2	35.2
Incomplete secondary	5.3	34.3	14.7	12.6	11.1
General secondary	6.6	31.1	16.7	14.4	14.1
Technical secondary	4.5	18.5	9.0	8.2	8.2
Professional	3.7	25.7	14.7	15.2	13.9
Higher	1.3	12.3	5.2	4.4	4.4
Total	5.0	28.1	14.9	13.1	12.5
Location					
Baku	1.2	17.3	7.4	8.0	6.9
Non-Baku	6.3	32.0	17.6	14.9	14.5
Total	5.0	28.1	14.9	13.1	12.5
Household typology					
Single parent with child(ren)	4.0	30.9	14.9	14.9	21.0
Other households with child(ren)	5.2	29.2	16.0	13.5	12.7
Single elderly female	0.0	0.0	0.0	0.0	0.0
Multiple elderly only	1.9	40.9	81.9	14.9	12.0
Other households without child(ren)	5.3	21.4	9.9	11.1	11.4
Total	5.0	28.1	14.9	13.1	12.5
No. of children under 15					
Zero	5.0	21.7	9.6	11.2	11.4
One	4.6	23.0	11.7	11.9	12.6
Two	5.7	34.0	17.9	14.3	13.2
Three or more	4.4	31.1	18.9	14.4	12.7
Total	5.0	28.1	14.9	13.1	12.5
No. of elderly					
Zero	5.7	26.7	14.4	13.1	12.5
One	3.2	29.5	14.6	12.4	12.5
Two or more	1.9	40.9	21.9	14.9	12.0
Total	5.0	28.1	14.9	13.1	12.5

(Table continues on next page)

AZERBAIJAN *(continued)*

Poverty line	33% of median	67% of median	50% of median	50% of median	50% of median
Economies of scale	Theta=.75	Theta=.75	Theta=1	Theta=.75	Theta=.50
	Poverty risk	Poverty risk	Poverty risk	Poverty risk	Poverty risk
Household head, gender					
Male	4.8	26.0	13.6	11.7	11.0
Female	5.7	36.8	20.5	18.7	18.9
Total	5.0	28.1	14.9	13.1	12.5
Household head, labor market status					
Unknown	0.0	69.8	40.7	0.0	0.0
Government	3.6	18.8	8.6	8.0	7.6
Education	10.4	21.1	10.4	10.4	10.4
Health	0.0	7.2	7.2	7.2	7.2
Agriculture	3.1	34.3	11.5	9.6	10.4
Private industry	6.6	14.0	6.6	6.6	6.6
Trade	8.9	23.1	15.8	13.4	10.5
Housekeeping	4.8	33.8	17.8	15.6	15.7
Unemployed	5.7	35.7	20.3	17.3	15.4
Other	2.0	16.5	12.3	12.3	12.3
Total	5.0	28.1	14.9	13.1	12.5
No. of income earners					
Zero	11.8	51.3	22.5	22.5	22.5
One	4.3	41.0	21.2	20.6	20.7
Two	7.0	19.6	12.2	12.3	11.1
Three	4.7	23.2	13.4	12.8	13.9
Four	4.6	21.7	10.3	9.0	9.0
Five or more	4.2	30.4	18.3	14.3	12.7
Total	5.0	28.1	14.9	13.1	12.5

Source: Azerbaijan 1995 Living Standards Measurement Survey.

BELARUS: Poverty Risk, 1999

Poverty line	33% of median	67% of median	50% of median	50% of median	50% of median
Economies of scale	Theta=.75	Theta=.75	Theta=1	Theta=.75	Theta=.50
	Poverty risk	Poverty risk	Poverty risk	Poverty risk	Poverty risk
Age in years					
0–15	0.9	22.6	13.3	7.5	4.7
16–64	0.7	15.9	8.1	5.4	4.1
65+	1.0	22.8	6.5	8.1	11.8
Total	0.8	18.2	9.0	6.2	5.2
Education					
Age less than 15	0.9	22.4	13.3	7.6	4.8
Unknown	0.6	19.1	9.1	7.2	3.4
None	1.9	32.3	10.2	12.4	18.9
Primary (less than 7 years)	1.3	25.0	10.0	8.4	10.1
General secondary (8–12 years)	0.7	19.0	10.3	7.3	5.3
Vocational or specialized secondary	0.6	14.5	6.8	4.5	3.4
Some higher	0.0	5.2	1.9	1.2	0.9
Total	0.8	18.2	9.0	6.2	5.2
Location					
Urban	0.6	12.3	5.6	4.3	3.7
Semi-urban	1.3	17.2	9.5	7.5	5.8
Rural	0.6	26.3	12.9	7.8	6.8
Total	0.8	18.0	8.9	6.2	5.2
Region					
South (Brest and Gomel oblasts)	1.0	20.3	10.7	7.3	5.9
Central (Minsk and Minsk oblasts)	0.8	13.2	6.4	4.6	3.8
West (Grodno oblast)	0.7	16.0	6.5	3.0	3.2
East (Mogilev, Vitebsk)	0.6	22.0	10.9	8.3	7.1
Total	0.8	18.0	8.9	6.2	5.2
Access to land					
No	1.1	16.1	7.8	5.8	5.2
Yes	0.6	19.0	9.5	6.4	5.2
Total	0.8	18.0	8.9	6.2	5.2
Own automobile					
No	1.0	22.1	10.8	7.7	6.6
Yes	0.3	5.8	3.2	1.7	1.1
Total	0.8	18.0	8.9	6.2	5.2

(Table continues on next page)

BELARUS *(continued)*

Poverty line	33% of median	67% of median	50% of median	50% of median	50% of median
Economies of scale	Theta=.75	Theta=.75	Theta=1	Theta=.75	Theta=.50
	Poverty risk	Poverty risk	Poverty risk	Poverty risk	Poverty risk
Household typology					
Single parent with child(ren)	1.5	27.9	12.6	11.7	12.9
Other households with child(ren)	0.8	19.8	11.8	6.7	3.8
Single elderly male	0.0	13.2	0.0	6.9	11.6
Single elderly female	2.1	29.7	4.8	12.5	24.8
Multiple elderly only	0.3	20.1	5.5	6.1	7.7
Other households without child(ren)	0.6	12.9	5.0	4.2	4.6
Total	0.8	18.0	8.9	6.2	5.2
No. of children under 15					
Zero	0.7	15.0	5.0	5.1	6.6
One	0.5	15.7	8.1	5.6	3.6
Two	1.6	21.4	11.8	7.6	4.8
Three or more	0.0	43.6	34.9	12.5	5.1
Total	0.8	18.0	8.9	6.2	5.2
No. of elderly					
Zero	0.7	17.2	9.3	5.8	4.2
One	1.5	20.2	6.8	8.1	10.4
Two	0.2	22.7	9.5	7.0	6.2
Three or more	0.0	20.3	0.0	0.0	0.0
Total	0.8	18.0	8.9	6.2	5.2
Household head, gender					
Male	0.5	17.5	9.2	5.3	3.4
Female	1.1	18.5	8.6	7.0	7.0
Total	0.8	18.0	8.9	6.2	5.2
Household head, labor market status					
Unknown	8.9	15.0	12.0	12.0	15.0
Employed	0.8	15.8	8.6	5.1	3.3
Self-employed or employer	0.0	10.2	5.0	3.7	0.0
Unemployed, but looking for work	1.0	30.4	17.1	13.0	10.5
Not in workforce	1.1	21.4	15.2	12.0	9.5
Retired	0.8	23.1	8.1	8.0	10.0
Total	0.8	18.0	8.9	6.2	5.2
No. of income earners					
Zero	1.4	25.0	7.0	9.6	14.3
One	1.4	22.5	10.7	8.3	7.4
Two	0.5	15.1	8.6	4.6	2.5
Three or more	0.0	12.6	8.9	4.3	1.1
Total	0.8	18.0	8.9	6.2	5.2

Source: Belarus 1999 Household Income and Expenditures Data.

BULGARIA: Poverty Risk, 1997

Poverty line	33% of median	67% of median	50% of median	50% of median	50% of median
Economies of scale	Theta=.75	Theta=.75	Theta=1	Theta=.75	Theta=.50
	Poverty risk	Poverty risk	Poverty risk	Poverty risk	Poverty risk
Age in years					
0–15	5.3	25.3	17.9	13.1	9.2
16–64	2.8	20.1	12.4	10.1	7.9
65+	3.3	29.0	12.1	14.7	16.6
Total	3.3	22.5	13.3	11.4	9.7
Education					
Age less than 15	5.3	25.3	17.9	13.1	9.2
Unknown	12.5	47.9	38.5	37.5	28.1
None	5.7	34.1	18.7	18.6	17.6
Primary (less than 7 years)	2.7	22.0	13.2	11.8	9.7
General secondary (8–12 years)	1.4	14.2	7.4	5.6	4.7
Vocational or specialized secondary	0.6	14.2	6.4	4.4	4.1
Some higher	4.0	20.0	17.1	14.9	11.4
Total	3.3	22.5	13.3	11.4	9.7
Location					
Urban	2.3	19.9	11.2	9.6	8.5
Rural	4.8	27.4	17.2	14.6	11.6
Total	3.3	22.5	13.3	11.4	9.7
Region					
Sofia	3.5	22.5	12.3	10.4	9.5
Other urban	2.0	19.3	10.9	9.4	8.2
Other rural	4.8	27.4	17.2	14.6	11.6
Total	3.3	22.5	13.3	11.4	9.7
Access to land					
No	4.9	26.5	15.9	14.0	12.0
Yes	0.9	16.9	9.5	7.9	6.3
Total	3.3	22.5	13.3	11.4	9.7
Own automobile					
No	5.4	31.6	18.8	17.2	15.1
Yes	0.4	10.4	5.8	4.0	2.6
Total	3.3	22.5	13.3	11.4	9.7

(Table continues on next page)

BULGARIA *(continued)*

Poverty line	33% of median	67% of median	50% of median	50% of median	50% of median
Economies of scale	*Theta=.75*	*Theta=.75*	*Theta=1*	*Theta=.75*	*Theta=.50*
	Poverty risk	Poverty risk	Poverty risk	Poverty risk	Poverty risk
Household typology					
Single parent with child(ren)	0.0	27.9	4.9	11.5	11.5
Other households with child(ren)	4.6	22.9	16.9	12.1	8.4
Single elderly male	2.8	29.2	4.2	15.3	23.6
Single elderly female	5.4	37.4	11.3	21.2	32.0
Multiple elderly only	3.9	31.7	16.5	16.0	14.3
Other households without child(ren)	1.8	18.2	9.4	9.0	7.7
Total	3.3	22.5	13.3	11.4	9.7
No. of children under 15					
Zero	2.0	21.1	9.8	10.3	10.3
One	2.3	18.1	11.7	8.7	5.3
Two	4.3	23.7	16.4	11.2	7.7
Three or more	24.2	64.7	60.6	46.1	36.4
Total	3.3	22.5	13.3	11.4	9.7
No. of elderly					
Zero	3.0	20.4	12.5	9.8	7.8
One	3.9	24.0	14.0	14.5	13.0
Two	3.9	31.0	16.2	15.2	14.0
Three or more	0.0	100.0	42.9	42.9	42.9
Total	3.3	22.5	13.3	11.4	9.7
Household head, gender					
Male	3.0	21.0	12.9	10.7	8.4
Female	5.2	31.8	15.8	15.9	17.2
Total	3.3	22.5	13.3	11.4	9.7
Household head, labor market status					
Unknown	12.4	30.0	22.6	21.7	18.3
Employed	1.7	15.7	9.6	6.7	4.3
Self-employed or employer	1.2	8.7	1.2	2.4	2.4
Unemployed, but looking for work	9.8	38.1	30.8	25.5	23.5
Not in workforce	0.0	25.3	15.4	9.9	3.9
Retired	2.6	26.5	12.9	12.9	12.2
Total	3.3	22.5	13.3	11.4	9.7
No. of income earners					
Zero	7.4	35.1	20.7	21.5	20.9
One	2.1	22.0	12.7	10.1	7.6
Two	0.9	15.2	8.5	5.2	3.0
Three or more	2.3	9.4	8.5	5.6	3.9
Total	3.3	22.5	13.3	11.4	9.7

Source: Bulgaria 1997 Integrated Household Survey.

CROATIA: Poverty Risk, 1998

Poverty line	33% of median	67% of median	50% of median	50% of median	50% of median
Economies of scale	Theta=.75	Theta=.75	Theta=1	Theta=.75	Theta=.50
	Poverty risk	Poverty risk	Poverty risk	Poverty risk	Poverty risk

Age in years					
0–15	1.0	18.0	11.8	5.4	3.6
16–64	1.5	15.1	8.0	5.4	5.3
65+	4.1	38.1	13.3	15.4	23.1
Total	1.8	19.4	9.6	7.1	7.9
Education					
Age 15 and below	1.0	18.0	11.8	5.4	3.6
Primary	4.1	33.0	14.9	13.6	17.0
Basic vocational	1.0	17.6	8.9	5.8	5.9
Secondary	0.5	9.1	4.6	2.7	2.6
Higher	0.1	3.9	1.0	0.9	1.4
Total	1.8	19.4	9.6	7.1	7.9
Location					
Zagreb	1.1	15.6	8.3	5.3	7.1
City	1.6	18.0	8.6	6.5	7.5
Rural	2.6	24.2	12.2	9.1	9.1
Total	1.8	19.4	9.6	7.1	7.9
Region					
Zagreb	1.1	16.9	8.6	5.5	6.7
Central	2.7	23.4	13.5	10.7	10.4
Istra (N. Coast)	0.3	17.5	7.6	5.9	7.8
Dalmacija (S. Coast)	1.6	13.2	5.3	4.1	5.1
Slavonia	3.1	25.2	11.8	8.5	9.3
Total	1.8	19.4	9.6	7.1	7.9
Access to land					
No	2.0	18.0	8.1	7.0	8.6
Yes	1.7	20.6	11.0	7.1	7.2
Total	1.8	19.4	9.6	7.1	7.9
Own automobile					
No	4.6	38.1	17.9	15.9	19.2
Yes	0.2	8.4	4.7	1.9	1.3
Total	1.8	19.4	9.6	7.1	7.9
Household typology					
Single parent with child(ren)	0.7	23.4	6.4	4.4	6.4
Other households with child(ren)	1.0	17.0	11.6	5.2	3.1
Single elderly male	7.5	28.8	10.1	10.8	28.8

(Table continues on next page)

CROATIA *(continued)*

Poverty line	33% of median	67% of median	50% of median	50% of median	50% of median
Economies of scale	Theta=.75	Theta=.75	Theta=1	Theta=.75	Theta=.50
	Poverty risk	Poverty risk	Poverty risk	Poverty risk	Poverty risk
Single elderly female	5.1	50.5	8.7	21.0	46.3
Multiple elderly only	5.0	45.9	13.8	19.0	24.7
Other households without child(ren)	2.0	15.9	7.0	6.6	7.7
Total	1.8	19.4	9.6	7.1	7.9
No. of children under 15					
Zero	2.6	21.4	7.9	8.9	12.3
One	1.0	13.8	7.6	4.2	2.9
Two	0.7	18.7	11.6	5.7	3.6
Three or more	1.8	23.1	21.2	6.5	3.5
Total	1.8	19.4	9.6	7.1	7.9
No. of elderly					
Zero	1.4	14.1	7.5	4.9	4.8
One	2.0	26.8	11.1	10.1	14.2
Two	4.5	38.6	19.7	15.2	15.9
Three or more	0.0	44.3	31.3	7.0	7.0
Total	1.8	19.4	9.6	7.1	7.9
Household head, gender					
Female	2.5	24.5	8.8	9.6	14.2
Male	1.6	17.9	9.8	6.3	6.1
Total	1.8	19.4	9.6	7.1	7.9
Household head, labor market status					
Employed	0.6	12.7	6.7	3.5	3.0
Unemployed	7.9	45.4	30.9	20.5	17.4
Retired	2.3	26.2	10.9	9.8	14.1
Other	8.7	38.7	21.9	22.4	20.6
Total	1.8	19.4	9.6	7.1	7.9
No. of income earners					
Zero	6.0	37.9	15.3	19.6	25.7
One	2.6	26.5	12.8	9.9	11.0
Two	0.1	9.6	4.9	1.8	1.3
Three or more	0.5	9.5	8.0	2.2	1.1
Total	1.8	19.4	9.6	7.1	7.9

Source: Croatia 1998 Household Budget Survey 1998.

CZECH REPUBLIC: Poverty Risk, 1996

Poverty line	33% of median	67% of median	50% of median	50% of median	50% of median
Economies of scale	Theta=.75	Theta=.75	Theta=1	Theta=.75	Theta=.50
	Poverty risk	Poverty risk	Poverty risk	Poverty risk	Poverty risk
Age in years					
0–15	1.3	20.8	12.1	6.4	4.2
16–64	0.4	8.3	3.8	2.2	2.0
65⁺	0.0	8.7	0.3	0.3	3.7
Total	0.6	10.8	5.0	2.8	2.6
Education					
Age less than 15	1.4	21.3	12.4	6.5	4.3
Elementary	0.6	13.0	5.1	3.3	4.3
Vocational	0.3	8.8	3.4	1.9	1.9
General secondary	0.2	5.8	2.0	1.3	1.7
Specialized secondary	0.2	4.8	1.8	1.0	1.0
University	0.2	2.3	1.0	0.8	0.6
Total	0.6	10.8	5.0	2.8	2.6
Location (1)					
Urban	0.6	10.3	4.8	3.0	2.8
Rural	0.5	11.9	5.5	2.5	2.3
Total	0.6	10.8	5.0	2.8	2.6
Location (2)					
Capital	0.3	6.3	1.7	1.4	1.9
Cities	0.6	11.0	5.5	3.2	3.4
Towns	0.7	11.2	5.4	3.3	2.9
Villages	0.5	11.9	5.5	2.5	2.3
Total	0.6	10.8	5.0	2.8	2.6
Region					
Middle	0.3	8.3	3.4	2.0	2.0
South	1.1	12.9	7.0	4.8	4.1
West	0.3	10.5	4.7	2.1	2.2
North	0.5	11.7	5.1	2.8	2.5
Total	0.6	10.8	5.0	2.8	2.6
Access to land					
No	0.7	11.7	5.5	3.2	3.1
Yes	0.2	7.5	3.3	1.2	0.9
Total	0.6	10.8	5.0	2.8	2.6
Own automobile					
No	1.1	17.6	8.0	5.1	5.4
Yes	0.2	6.6	3.1	1.4	0.9
Total	0.6	10.8	5.0	2.8	2.6

(Table continues on next page)

CZECH REPUBLIC *(continued)*

Poverty line	33% of median	67% of median	50% of median	50% of median	50% of median
Economies of scale	Theta=.75	Theta=.75	Theta=1	Theta=.75	Theta=.50
	Poverty risk	Poverty risk	Poverty risk	Poverty risk	Poverty risk
Household typology					
Single parent with child(ren)	5.0	44.6	24.3	21.1	19.9
Other households with child(ren)	0.4	9.0	4.6	2.1	1.2
Single elderly male	0.8	9.0	1.2	2.4	6.8
Single elderly female	0.2	17.3	0.4	1.0	10.3
Other households without child(ren)	0.0	6.2	0.4	0.4	0.8
Total	0.6	10.8	5.0	2.8	2.6
No. of children under 15					
Zero	0.1	4.8	0.6	0.8	2.0
One	0.6	9.9	4.4	3.2	2.6
Two	0.8	18.4	9.2	4.5	3.1
Three or more	3.4	41.9	32.7	14.5	6.7
Total	0.6	10.8	5.0	2.8	2.6
No. of elderly					
Zero	0.8	11.8	6.3	3.6	2.6
One	0.0	12.3	3.2	1.9	4.2
Two	0.0	3.9	1.0	0.3	0.3
Three or more	0.0	0.0	0.0	0.0	0.0
Total	0.6	10.8	5.0	2.8	2.6
Household head, gender					
Male	0.4	8.9	4.5	2.2	1.4
Female	1.7	24.4	8.7	7.4	11.1
Total	0.6	10.8	5.0	2.8	2.6
Household head (labor market status)					
Employed	0.0	8.3	3.4	1.2	0.7
Self-employed or employer	0.8	11.7	6.8	3.8	2.5
Unemployed, but looking for work	17.1	68.3	55.5	45.6	37.3
Not in workforce	18.9	82.9	68.9	59.4	52.2
Retired	0.0	10.8	2.4	1.7	3.9
Total	0.6	10.8	5.0	2.8	2.6
No. of income earners					
Zero	2.3	19.9	9.1	7.8	10.0
One	0.4	19.5	9.4	4.4	2.6
Two	0.1	4.4	1.7	0.4	0.3
Three or more	0.0	0.5	0.5	0.2	0.1
Total	0.6	10.8	5.0	2.8	2.6

Source: Czech Republic Microcensus 1996.

ESTONIA: Poverty Risk, 1998

Poverty line	33% of median	67% of median	50% of median	50% of median	50% of median
Economies of scale	Theta=.75	Theta=.75	Theta=1	Theta=.75	Theta=.50
	Poverty risk	Poverty risk	Poverty risk	Poverty risk	Poverty risk
Location					
City	2.2	21.1	7.9	8.9	12.1
Town	0.9	13.9	6.8	5.9	5.5
Settlement	1.2	16.4	6.3	6.5	7.5
Bigger village	2.1	25.1	10.8	11.6	13.0
Village	2.7	29.6	13.6	15.1	17.8
Total	2.1	21.9	8.7	9.7	12.4
No. of children under 15					
Zero	2.1	21.4	7.0	9.9	14.8
One	1.7	19.5	8.5	7.4	6.3
Two	2.0	27.5	15.5	10.8	7.4
Three or more	5.8	30.2	25.6	12.7	9.4
Total	2.1	21.9	8.7	9.7	12.4
Household head, gender					
Male	1.2	18.6	7.8	9.4	10.7
Female	2.9	24.8	9.5	9.9	13.8
Total	2.1	21.9	8.7	9.7	12.4
Household head, labor market status					
Employed	1.1	16.5	7.3	7.1	7.5
Farmer	1.7	6.9	3.5	3.5	1.7
Self-employed	0.0	10.2	2.9	5.9	8.7
Owner	0.0	3.9	1.3	0.9	0.0
Not in workforce	0.0	32.3	11.9	13.8	12.8
Unemployed, but looking for work	18.6	60.1	42.7	43.7	45.4
Retired	2.5	29.8	8.2	11.3	19.3
Other	35.5	47.4	47.4	47.4	35.5
Total	2.1	21.9	8.7	9.7	12.4

Source: Estonia 1998 Household Income and Expenditures Survey.

GEORGIA: Poverty Risk, 1996/97

Poverty line	33% of median	67% of median	50% of median	50% of median	50% of median
Economies of scale	Theta=.75	Theta=.75	Theta=1	Theta=.75	Theta=.50
	Poverty risk	Poverty risk	Poverty risk	Poverty risk	Poverty risk
Age in years					
0–15	7.3	33.7	25.3	17.2	13.4
16–64	7.0	27.5	18.8	16.7	14.7
65+	6.6	30.1	16.5	18.3	18.3
Total	7.0	29.3	19.9	17.0	15.0
Education					
Age less than 15	7.3	33.7	25.3	17.2	13.4
Elementary	9.6	34.2	23.6	23.8	21.7
Secondary (incomplete)	9.1	33.2	22.7	21.2	19.7
Secondary	7.9	31.3	21.4	19.7	17.6
Postsecondary	6.4	25.1	16.4	14.4	13.3
University	3.9	20.8	11.4	10.8	10.0
Total	7.0	29.3	19.9	17.0	15.0
Location					
Capital	5.6	26.1	15.8	13.5	12.4
Other urban	8.8	31.5	21.8	19.3	17.5
Rural	6.7	29.9	21.2	17.7	14.9
Total	7.0	29.3	19.9	17.0	15.0
Region					
Western	7.0	33.7	22.8	19.3	16.5
Eastern	7.6	29.8	21.6	18.6	16.9
Central	6.1	26.3	16.6	14.4	12.9
South	8.5	26.3	19.7	16.5	13.7
Total	7.0	29.3	19.9	17.0	15.0
Access to land					
No	7.5	31.4	20.2	17.7	16.1
Yes	6.9	28.6	20.4	17.0	14.5
Total	7.0	29.3	19.9	17.0	15.0
Own automobile					
No	7.7	31.1	21.3	18.5	16.5
Yes	3.3	20.7	13.4	10.2	7.5
Total	7.0	29.3	19.9	17.0	15.0
Household typology					
Single parent with child(ren)	11.5	36.9	22.2	23.4	26.7
Other households with child(ren)	8.2	31.8	23.6	18.8	15.3
Single elderly male	13.1	36.6	14.8	24.6	36.6
Single elderly female	7.3	27.5	9.2	16.8	28.0

(Table continues on next page)

GEORGIA *(continued)*

Poverty line	*33% of median*	*67% of median*	*50% of median*	*50% of median*	*50% of median*
Economies of scale	*Theta=.75*	*Theta=.75*	*Theta=1*	*Theta=.75*	*Theta=.50*
	Poverty risk	*Poverty risk*	*Poverty risk*	*Poverty risk*	*Poverty risk*
No. of children under 15					
Zero	6.8	27.2	16.0	16.3	16.4
One	6.2	28.6	17.9	14.7	13.0
Two	7.0	31.0	22.8	17.6	13.9
Three or more	9.0	33.4	29.3	21.9	16.2
Total	7.0	29.3	19.9	17.0	15.0
No. of elderly					
Zero	7.1	27.1	18.4	16.4	14.8
One	6.8	31.2	20.3	17.3	15.6
Two	7.2	31.2	22.4	18.2	14.7
Three or more	3.2	27.6	19.3	13.0	9.9
Total	7.0	29.3	19.9	17.0	15.0
Household head, gender					
Male	6.2	27.6	18.6	14.8	12.7
Female	8.9	33.6	23.2	22.5	20.6
Total	7.0	29.3	19.9	17.0	15.0
Household head, labor market status					
Retired (old age)	15.2	44.4	23.9	30.8	39.4
Inactive, disabled, otherwise not in workforce	21.5	53.1	40.2	39.6	36.9
Unemployed, but actively looking for work	17.6	41.6	31.5	30.1	27.7
Self-employed (or employer)	5.8	27.4	19.1	15.8	13.1
Employed (wage)	5.4	26.8	17.6	14.1	11.9
Total	7.0	29.3	19.9	17.0	15.0
No. of income earners					
Zero	16.6	45.9	31.4	33.1	33.5
One	7.2	29.3	18.8	16.5	15.3
Two	4.9	26.3	16.7	13.8	12.0
Three or more	5.5	26.6	20.2	15.2	11.1
Total	7.0	29.3	19.9	17.0	15.0

Source: Survey of Georgian Households 1996–97.

HUNGARY: Poverty Risk, 1997

Poverty line	33% of median	67% of median	50% of median	50% of median	50% of median
Economies of scale	Theta=.75	Theta=.75	Theta=1	Theta=.75	Theta=.50
	Poverty risk	Poverty risk	Poverty risk	Poverty risk	Poverty risk
Age in years					
0–15	1.9	27.2	14.8	10.1	7.3
16–64	1.1	16.4	7.3	5.6	4.8
65+	0.2	13.5	2.0	3.5	7.0
Total	1.1	18.0	7.9	6.1	5.6
Education					
Age less than 15	1.9	27.2	14.8	10.1	7.3
Primary or less	2.0	23.5	10.7	9.4	9.6
General secondary	0.1	6.9	2.0	1.6	1.7
Vocational	0.3	13.3	4.3	2.9	2.6
Higher	0.0	3.1	0.2	0.2	0.2
Total	1.1	18.0	7.9	6.1	5.6
Location					
Budapest	0.9	8.5	3.2	3.0	2.0
Other urban	0.9	16.9	6.7	4.8	4.8
Rural	1.5	23.8	11.4	9.1	8.3
Total	1.1	18.0	7.9	6.1	5.6
Region					
Central region	0.9	12.1	5.5	4.3	3.3
West Trans-Danubia	0.0	14.2	3.4	2.2	3.2
Central Trans-Danubia	0.6	15.7	6.6	4.4	4.2
South Trans-Danubia	1.7	20.7	10.0	7.3	6.9
Northern Hungary	2.5	26.1	13.7	11.7	11.2
North Great Plain	1.2	24.6	12.4	9.4	7.3
South Great Plain	0.9	17.7	5.1	4.2	5.1
Total	1.1	18.0	7.9	6.1	5.6
Access to land					
No	1.5	17.5	8.2	6.8	6.0
Yes	0.7	18.5	7.5	5.3	5.1
Total	1.1	18.0	7.9	6.1	5.6
Own automobile					
No	1.8	25.2	11.1	8.9	8.7
Yes	0.0	6.9	3.0	1.8	0.9
Total	1.1	18.0	7.9	6.1	5.6
Household typology					
Single parent with child(ren)	0.8	28.5	7.2	10.5	12.8
Other households with child(ren)	1.8	25.6	14.1	9.2	6.4

(Table continues on next page)

HUNGARY *(continued)*

Poverty line	33% of median	67% of median	50% of median	50% of median	50% of median
Economies of scale	Theta=.75	Theta=.75	Theta=1	Theta=.75	Theta=.50
	Poverty risk	Poverty risk	Poverty risk	Poverty risk	Poverty risk
Single elderly male	0.3	11.2	0.3	4.0	9.9
Single elderly female	0.5	15.0	1.0	4.7	14.1
Multiple elderly only	0.2	12.7	1.8	2.8	4.1
Other households without child(ren)	0.6	11.3	3.4	3.5	3.8
Total	1.1	18.0	7.9	6.1	5.6
No. of children under 15					
Zero	0.6	11.7	3.0	3.5	4.7
One	0.8	20.0	8.8	6.4	5.1
Two	2.9	27.3	15.0	9.4	7.3
Three or more	1.4	41.0	28.3	19.1	10.5
Total	1.1	18.0	7.9	6.1	5.6
No. of elderly					
Zero	1.4	19.0	9.1	6.8	5.6
One	0.2	14.1	3.2	3.9	6.1
Two	0.1	14.3	2.8	2.9	3.7
Three or more	0.0	17.0	0.0	0.0	0.0
Total	1.1	18.0	7.9	6.1	5.6
Household head, gender					
Male	1.2	18.1	8.4	6.1	4.9
Female	0.5	17.2	4.3	6.0	10.6
Total	1.1	18.0	7.9	6.1	5.6
Household head, labor market status					
Employed	0.5	15.2	6.4	4.2	2.9
Self-employed or employer	0.0	20.6	13.3	3.4	3.4
Unemployed, but looking for work	8.5	52.1	32.7	26.4	22.4
Not in workforce	1.0	21.5	9.6	8.2	7.8
Retired	0.3	11.2	1.2	3.2	7.1
Total	1.1	18.0	7.9	6.1	5.6
No. of income earners					
Zero	2.0	19.9	8.3	9.0	10.9
One	1.5	25.2	12.5	9.4	7.4
Two	0.4	12.6	4.5	2.4	1.8
Three or more	0.6	11.6	5.4	3.2	1.4
Total	1.1	18.0	7.9	6.1	5.6

Source: Hungary Household Budget Survey, 1997.

KAZAKHSTAN: Poverty Risk, 1996

Poverty line Economies of scale	33% of median Theta=.75 Poverty risk	67% of median Theta=.75 Poverty risk	50% of median Theta=1 Poverty risk	50% of median Theta=.75 Poverty risk	50% of median Theta=.50 Poverty risk
Age in years					
0–15	6.5	30.2	22.6	17.3	14.1
16–64	3.9	25.1	16.1	12.9	11.3
65+	4.9	34.4	16.3	16.5	20.8
Total	4.8	27.4	18.2	14.5	12.8
Education					
Age less than 15	6.5	30.2	22.6	17.3	14.1
Unknown	6.6	28.6	19.7	14.6	13.8
Forms 1–7	4.6	35.0	18.8	19.9	21.7
Forms 8–12	6.6	36.8	26.6	20.0	17.4
Additional technical education	3.1	21.7	12.5	10.7	9.8
Some higher	0.9	18.4	9.7	7.7	7.0
Total	4.8	27.4	18.2	14.5	12.8
Location					
Urban	3.1	25.0	14.2	12.7	11.7
Rural	6.3	29.6	22.0	16.2	13.9
Total	4.8	27.4	18.2	14.5	12.8
Region					
Central	5.0	21.8	14.1	13.6	12.2
Southern	13.5	58.2	42.9	35.1	30.8
Western	2.5	25.1	17.8	8.6	8.0
Northern	0.6	6.4	2.6	1.9	2.2
Eastern	2.1	24.5	14.0	11.8	9.9
Total	4.8	27.4	18.2	14.5	12.8
Access to land					
No	8.2	35.5	24.9	21.4	20.2
Yes	2.9	22.9	14.5	10.7	8.8
Total	4.8	27.4	18.2	14.5	12.8
Own automobile					
No	5.9	31.7	20.9	17.1	15.6
Yes	0.8	12.4	8.9	5.7	3.3
Total	4.8	27.4	18.2	14.5	12.8
Household typology					
Single parent with child(ren)	7.4	29.9	17.6	17.6	18.3
Other households with child(ren)	5.3	27.8	20.5	15.5	12.2
Single elderly male	0.0	66.7	0.0	33.3	66.7

(Table continues on next page)

KAZAKHSTAN *(continued)*

Poverty line	*33% of median*	*67% of median*	*50% of median*	*50% of median*	*50% of median*
Economies of scale	*Theta=.75*	*Theta=.75*	*Theta=1*	*Theta=.75*	*Theta=.50*
	Poverty risk	*Poverty risk*	*Poverty risk*	*Poverty risk*	*Poverty risk*
Single elderly female	7.0	38.0	9.9	18.3	39.4
Multiple elderly only	7.7	42.3	24.5	17.5	19.7
Other households without child(ren)	2.3	22.6	11.2	10.5	11.2
Total	4.8	27.4	18.2	14.5	12.8
No. of children under 15					
Zero	3.0	25.0	11.8	11.7	13.5
One	3.1	20.6	13.2	10.9	9.4
Two	5.0	24.6	17.0	13.3	11.0
Three or more	10.4	47.7	40.0	27.9	20.9
Total	4.8	27.4	18.2	14.5	12.8
No. of elderly					
Zero	5.0	26.6	17.9	14.9	12.8
One	2.3	27.7	17.8	10.9	11.4
Two	5.1	39.9	22.1	15.2	15.9
Three or more	70.0	100.0	100.0	100.0	100.0
Total	4.8	27.4	18.2	14.5	12.8
Household head, gender					
Male	5.1	28.2	20.2	15.0	12.6
Female	3.8	25.4	13.6	13.4	13.3
Total	4.8	27.4	18.2	14.5	12.8
Household head, labor market status					
Employed	3.1	21.9	15.1	10.9	9.3
Owner	13.2	33.5	23.6	23.6	19.9
Unemployed, but looking for work	8.2	29.6	23.5	13.3	13.3
Not in workforce	5.5	34.1	24.1	21.1	18.1
Retired	5.8	36.6	20.0	16.6	16.8
Total	4.8	27.4	18.2	14.5	12.8
No. of income earners					
Zero	7.4	35.3	21.0	20.9	21.0
One	4.6	29.2	19.4	14.7	12.3
Two	3.8	21.3	16.2	11.4	9.4
Three or more	1.0	20.6	12.1	7.2	4.9
Total	4.8	27.4	18.2	14.5	12.8

Source: Kazakhstan 1996 Living Standards Measurement Survey.

KYRGYZ REPUBLIC: Poverty Risk, 1997

Poverty line	33% of median	67% of median	50% of median	50% of median	50% of median
Economies of scale	Theta=.75	Theta=.75	Theta=1	Theta=.75	Theta=.50
	Poverty risk	Poverty risk	Poverty risk	Poverty risk	Poverty risk
Age in years					
0–15	5.3	37.1	22.3	18.6	14.6
16–64	4.4	30.6	18.4	15.6	12.5
65+	4.5	31.8	18.8	17.6	16.8
Total	4.8	33.3	20.0	17.0	13.6
Education					
Age less than 15	5.3	37.1	22.3	18.6	14.6
Unknown	5.9	38.1	22.8	22.8	19.3
Primary (less than 7 years)	4.0	28.3	16.8	15.3	13.3
General secondary (8–12 years)	5.7	37.3	23.0	19.5	15.9
Professional, technical or technikum	1.5	19.9	10.2	8.2	6.3
Some higher	0.9	10.7	5.0	3.7	3.3
Total	4.8	33.3	20.0	17.0	13.6
Location					
Urban	1.4	14.8	9.2	5.6	5.2
Rural	6.2	41.2	24.6	21.9	17.2
Total	4.8	33.3	20.0	17.0	13.6
Region					
Bishkek	0.0	1.1	0.8	0.0	0.0
Issuk-Kulskaya	9.1	39.7	25.9	23.1	21.6
Djala-Abadckaya	7.4	47.1	29.1	27.2	19.3
Narunskaya	10.9	74.8	55.6	49.4	41.3
Oshckaya	0.9	27.1	8.9	6.6	4.2
Talasskaya	7.6	30.8	21.0	14.6	10.7
Chyiskaya	0.1	7.5	3.0	2.5	3.0
Total	4.8	33.3	20.0	17.0	13.6
Access to land					
No	3.2	25.9	17.3	12.8	12.3
Yes	5.0	34.3	20.4	17.5	13.7
Total	4.8	33.3	20.0	17.0	13.6
Own automobile					
No	5.6	36.4	21.6	18.3	14.4
Yes	0.0	5.6	2.8	1.6	0.6
Total	4.8	33.3	20.0	17.0	13.6
Household typology					
Single parent with child(ren)	4.7	28.5	9.9	11.7	14.2
Other households with child(ren)	5.2	35.4	21.7	18.2	14.1

(Table continues on next page)

KYRGYZ REPUBLIC *(continued)*

Poverty line	*33% of median*	*67% of median*	*50% of median*	*50% of median*	*50% of median*
Economies of scale	*Theta=.75*	*Theta=.75*	*Theta=1*	*Theta=.75*	*Theta=.50*
	Poverty risk	*Poverty risk*	*Poverty risk*	*Poverty risk*	*Poverty risk*
Single elderly male	7.1	14.3	7.1	7.1	14.3
Single elderly female	8.7	20.3	8.7	14.5	20.3
Multiple elderly only	3.2	35.5	22.5	17.7	13.9
Other households without child(ren)	2.2	14.9	6.6	7.3	8.3
Total	4.8	33.3	20.0	17.0	13.6
No. of children under 15					
Zero	2.5	15.5	7.1	8.1	9.4
One	2.2	24.7	12.6	13.0	13.0
Two	4.7	28.2	16.4	14.4	12.6
Three or more	6.2	42.2	26.7	21.3	15.1
Total	4.8	33.3	20.0	17.0	13.6
No. of elderly					
Zero	4.4	31.7	18.1	15.3	12.3
One	7.2	38.7	26.7	23.4	18.3
Two	3.2	35.6	22.8	18.0	14.8
Three or more	0.0	26.1	0.0	0.0	0.0
Total	4.8	33.3	20.0	17.0	13.6
Household head, gender					
Unknown	9.9	42.0	24.7	9.9	9.9
Male	4.7	33.6	19.8	16.6	13.2
Female	5.2	31.7	20.8	18.7	14.9
Total	4.8	33.3	20.0	17.0	13.6
Household head, labor market status					
Unknown	7.2	34.6	17.9	16.0	11.9
Employed	3.7	32.1	17.3	14.6	11.3
Employer	0.0	31.4	9.3	9.3	9.3
Unemployed, but looking for work	1.9	16.6	10.8	7.0	7.0
Not in workforce	5.8	30.0	22.3	17.6	16.4
Retired	6.6	38.9	25.9	22.9	17.8
Total	4.8	33.3	20.0	17.0	13.6
No. of income earners					
Zero	7.2	35.1	23.2	20.6	18.9
One	6.1	31.1	20.7	17.9	14.8
Two	4.5	33.1	19.4	16.5	14.2
Three or more	3.0	33.7	18.3	14.9	9.6
Total	4.8	33.3	20.0	17.0	13.6

Source: Kyrgyz Republic 1997 Living Standards Measurement Survey.

LATVIA: Poverty Risk, 1997/98

Poverty line	33% of median	67% of median	50% of median	50% of median	50% of median
Economies of scale	Theta=.75	Theta=.75	Theta=1	Theta=.75	Theta=.50
	Poverty risk	Poverty risk	Poverty risk	Poverty risk	Poverty risk
Age in years					
0–15	4.7	27.8	18.9	14.2	10.7
16–64	3.4	21.7	12.1	10.8	10.5
65+	2.0	20.0	6.9	9.1	12.9
Total	3.4	22.6	12.5	11.1	10.9
Education					
Age less than 15	4.7	27.8	18.9	14.2	10.7
Primary or less	4.9	30.3	15.0	15.3	17.5
Secondary (including specialized)	2.6	19.4	10.4	9.4	9.1
Vocational	4.1	29.6	16.3	15.5	15.9
Higher	0.4	6.1	2.5	2.0	2.1
Total	3.4	22.6	12.5	11.1	10.9
Location					
Riga	1.9	13.4	7.1	6.5	6.5
Other urban	3.2	22.6	12.1	11.0	11.5
Rural	5.2	32.3	18.7	16.2	14.9
Total	3.4	22.6	12.5	11.1	10.9
Region					
Riga region	2.0	15.3	7.9	7.3	7.1
Kurzene	5.3	28.9	16.9	16.1	16.1
Vidzeme	4.6	27.3	16.1	14.4	14.5
Zemgale	2.6	24.1	11.8	10.2	10.3
Latgale	5.6	33.1	19.5	16.1	15.1
Total	3.4	22.6	12.5	11.1	10.9
Access to land					
No	3.7	24.1	13.6	12.3	12.2
Yes	2.5	18.2	9.3	7.7	7.1
Total	3.4	22.6	12.5	11.1	10.9
Own automobile					
No	4.6	27.9	15.4	14.5	14.7
Yes	0.9	11.5	6.3	4.0	2.9
Total	3.4	22.6	12.5	11.1	10.9
Household typology					
Single parent with child(ren)	2.7	24.4	14.5	13.2	12.8
Other households with child(ren)	5.1	27.3	18.7	13.7	10.1
Single elderly male	2.7	23.4	4.1	9.5	20.5

(Table continues on next page)

LATVIA *(continued)*

Poverty line	*33% of median*	*67% of median*	*50% of median*	*50% of median*	*50% of median*
Economies of scale	*Theta=.75*	*Theta=.75*	*Theta=1*	*Theta=.75*	*Theta=.50*
	Poverty risk	Poverty risk	Poverty risk	Poverty risk	Poverty risk
Single elderly female	1.1	21.6	3.3	9.3	18.8
Multiple elderly only	1.2	13.3	4.7	6.0	7.0
Other households without child(ren)	2.3	18.5	8.0	9.0	10.7
Total	3.4	22.6	12.5	11.1	10.9
No. of children under 15					
Zero	2.1	18.5	7.1	8.8	11.5
One	4.2	23.5	14.6	11.9	9.7
Two	4.6	26.8	18.2	12.8	9.5
Three or more	7.7	41.4	33.1	23.0	15.0
Total	3.4	22.6	12.5	11.1	10.9
No. of elderly					
Zero	3.6	22.8	13.3	11.5	10.6
One	3.2	24.3	11.4	11.5	13.6
Two	2.0	15.9	7.9	6.9	7.1
Three or more	0.0	10.7	0.0	0.0	0.0
Total	3.4	22.6	12.5	11.1	10.9
Household head, gender					
Male	3.1	21.5	11.9	10.0	9.1
Female	3.6	23.4	12.9	12.1	12.3
Total	3.4	22.6	12.5	11.1	10.9
Household head, labor market status					
Employed	2.6	19.0	11.3	8.7	7.4
Self-employed or employer	0.0	18.4	10.8	8.1	6.3
Unemployed, but looking for work	11.1	44.4	30.7	29.4	27.5
Not in workforce	7.0	31.0	18.5	17.6	15.7
Retired	2.5	22.6	9.2	10.2	13.0
Total	3.4	22.6	12.5	11.1	10.9
No. of income earners					
Zero	4.9	30.2	15.1	15.8	18.9
One	4.5	24.9	14.5	13.4	12.3
Two	1.9	18.1	10.3	7.9	6.0
Three or more	2.2	15.0	·9.8	6.5	4.5
Total	3.4	22.6	12.5	11.1	10.9

Source: Latvia Household Budget Survey, 1997–98.

LITHUANIA: Poverty Risk, 1999

Poverty line	33% of median	67% of median	50% of median	50% of median	50% of median
Economies of scale	Theta=.75	Theta=.75	Theta=1	Theta=.75	Theta=.50
	Poverty risk	Poverty risk	Poverty risk	Poverty risk	Poverty risk
Age in years					
0–15	3.6	28.1	20.7	13.8	8.8
16–64	2.0	19.2	11.8	8.6	6.8
65⁺	2.1	25.2	9.1	9.9	12.9
Total	2.4	22.0	13.4	10.0	8.1
Education					
Age less than 15	3.6	28.1	20.7	13.8	8.8
Less than primary	3.8	37.6	15.8	18.3	23.1
Primary	2.7	30.0	12.7	12.2	14.3
Basic vocational	3.0	26.4	16.8	13.5	10.2
General secondary	2.3	21.9	13.9	10.0	7.5
Higher	1.1	14.5	8.0	5.1	4.3
University	0.3	4.6	2.0	1.2	1.7
Total	2.4	22.0	13.4	10.0	8.1
Location					
Largest towns	0.8	12.0	6.2	4.3	3.5
Other towns	2.6	20.3	11.8	9.7	7.4
Rural	4.1	35.7	23.7	17.2	14.2
Total	2.4	22.0	13.4	10.0	8.1
Access to land					
No	2.0	19.0	11.0	8.8	7.2
Yes	2.6	24.0	15.0	10.7	8.7
Total	2.4	22.0	13.4	10.0	8.1
Own automobile					
No	3.9	31.6	18.9	15.4	13.2
Yes	0.7	11.7	7.6	4.2	2.6
Total	2.4	22.0	13.4	10.0	8.1
Household typology					
Single parent with child(ren)	5.4	45.2	28.0	21.0	15.7
Other households with child(ren)	3.2	24.6	18.3	11.9	7.4
Single elderly male	0.0	18.6	5.1	8.0	15.6
Single elderly female	2.8	31.1	6.9	14.3	26.5
Multiple elderly only	1.5	21.1	4.5	5.6	7.2
Other households without child(ren)	0.9	15.4	7.0	6.4	6.6
Total	2.4	22.0	13.4	10.0	8.1

(Table continues on next page)

LITHUANIA *(continued)*

Poverty line	33% of median	67% of median	50% of median	50% of median	50% of median
Economies of scale	Theta=.75	Theta=.75	Theta=1	Theta=.75	Theta=.50
	Poverty risk	Poverty risk	Poverty risk	Poverty risk	Poverty risk

No. of children under 15

Zero	1.1	17.1	6.7	6.9	8.1
One	2.8	20.2	12.9	8.8	6.4
Two	2.5	27.4	20.1	12.6	7.7
Three or more	8.9	45.5	39.8	27.3	15.7
Total	2.4	22.0	13.4	10.0	8.1

No. of elderly

Zero	2.3	20.6	13.4	9.6	7.0
One	2.8	27.2	15.0	12.6	13.8
Two	1.9	24.8	9.9	7.6	6.5
Three or more	0.0	0.0	0.0	0.0	0.0
Total	2.4	22.0	13.4	10.0	8.1

Household head, gender

Female	3.1	26.6	15.6	13.1	11.3
Male	1.9	19.1	12.0	8.0	6.1
Total	2.4	22.0	13.4	10.0	8.1

Household head, labor market status

Employed	2.1	20.4	13.1	9.0	6.7
Looking for a job	2.6	24.5	15.9	13.8	9.3
Retired	2.5	28.6	12.7	12.4	14.2
Other	13.4	44.3	31.7	32.4	24.6
Total	2.4	22.0	13.4	10.0	8.1

No. of income earners

Zero	10.5	54.6	29.4	31.2	25.5
One	2.7	27.8	14.7	13.4	14.2
Two	1.7	18.4	10.8	7.6	5.9
Three or more	3.4	24.6	18.3	12.0	7.3
Total	2.4	22.0	13.4	10.0	8.1

Alternative household typology

Single	1.2	20.4	3.8	8.7	17.0
Single parent	5.0	43.7	27.0	20.5	15.9
Couple no child(ren)	0.4	12.7	3.2	3.5	4.7
Couple with child(ren)	2.0	21.4	14.7	9.3	5.9
Other households with child(ren)	5.1	28.0	22.9	15.3	9.6
Other households without child(ren)	1.6	19.7	10.6	9.0	7.3
Total	2.4	22.0	13.4	10.0	8.1

Source: Lithuania 1999 Household Budget Survey.

FORMER YUGOSLAV REPUBLIC OF MACEDONIA: Poverty Risk, 1996

Poverty line	33% of median	67% of median	50% of median	50% of median	50% of median
Economies of scale	Theta=.75	Theta=.75	Theta=1	Theta=.75	Theta=.50
	Poverty risk	Poverty risk	Poverty risk	Poverty risk	Poverty risk
Age in years					
0–15	5.9	34.0	25.6	21.1	15.3
16–64	3.7	26.5	17.8	15.1	12.1
65+	4.5	28.9	15.3	15.4	17.6
Total	4.4	28.8	19.9	16.8	13.5
Education					
Age less than 15	5.9	34.0	25.6	21.1	15.3
Unknown	13.8	47.7	46.5	33.0	20.0
None	7.1	38.5	22.3	21.8	23.9
Incomplete primary (less than 4 years)	3.6	34.2	24.7	20.0	17.1
Primary (5–8 years)	5.4	31.1	22.1	18.6	14.4
Secondary	1.9	21.1	11.9	10.7	8.8
Some higher	2.6	9.8	5.5	5.5	5.2
University	0.0	4.5	4.5	0.0	0.0
Total	4.4	28.8	19.9	16.8	13.5
Location					
Urban	3.0	23.2	14.0	12.6	10.5
Rural	6.1	35.6	26.9	21.9	17.1
Total	4.4	28.8	19.9	16.8	13.5
Region					
Capital	3.7	20.9	13.7	11.1	10.2
Rest of republic	4.6	31.5	21.9	18.7	14.6
Total	4.4	28.8	19.9	16.8	13.5
Access to land					
No	5.5	30.7	20.5	18.5	16.2
Yes	2.5	25.7	18.8	13.9	8.8
Total	4.4	28.8	19.9	16.8	13.5
Own automobile					
No	7.7	39.1	28.6	24.5	21.2
Yes	1.0	18.1	10.8	8.8	5.4
Total	4.4	28.8	19.9	16.8	13.5
Household typology					
Single parent with child(ren)	0.0	15.3	15.3	15.3	15.3
Other households with child(ren)	4.9	33.3	24.7	19.5	13.6
Single elderly male	0.0	25.9	10.0	16.2	25.9

(Table continues on next page)

FORMER YUGOSLAV REPUBLIC OF MACEDONIA *(continued)*

Poverty line	33% of median	67% of median	50% of median	50% of median	50% of median
Economies of scale	Theta=.75	Theta=.75	Theta=1	Theta=.75	Theta=.50
	Poverty risk	Poverty risk	Poverty risk	Poverty risk	Poverty risk
Single elderly female	0.0	26.0	0.0	1.9	26.0
Multiple elderly only	6.9	25.5	17.3	17.6	16.5
Other households without child(ren)	2.6	20.8	11.1	11.2	11.8
Total	4.4	28.8	19.9	16.8	13.5
No. of children under 15					
Zero	2.6	22.1	11.1	11.8	13.3
One	3.6	21.5	13.6	12.3	10.8
Two	3.3	30.4	21.3	15.7	10.8
Three or more	10.8	48.2	41.9	34.0	21.9
Total	4.4	28.8	19.9	16.8	13.5
No. of elderly					
Zero	3.9	28.8	19.9	17.1	13.2
One	5.3	31.5	21.6	15.3	12.9
Two or more	6.8	25.1	17.1	17.4	16.3
Total	4.4	28.8	19.9	16.8	13.5
Household head, gender					
Male	4.5	29.7	20.8	17.6	13.7
Female	3.4	21.4	11.9	9.5	11.8
Total	4.4	28.8	19.9	16.8	13.5
Household head, labor market status					
Employed (nonfarm)	3.3	28.8	18.7	16.2	12.1
Farmer	7.1	35.1	26.6	18.7	15.0
Unemployed	8.5	44.5	30.3	24.9	20.5
Pensioner	3.9	26.1	17.9	15.0	14.3
Employed (farmer)	10.3	37.8	24.4	26.5	25.9
Pensioner (farmer)	1.3	19.5	13.9	12.6	8.6
Seasonal worker	2.5	18.4	14.8	11.9	5.5
Other (includes students, homemakers, social assistance recipients)	17.0	44.8	33.6	33.6	33.6
Total	4.4	28.8	19.9	16.8	13.5
No. of income earners					
Zero	8.5	39.3	27.7	24.9	22.6
One	5.0	30.3	21.6	18.3	13.8
Two	0.3	18.4	11.0	8.0	5.6
Three or more	0.0	16.4	10.7	8.0	3.4
Total	4.4	28.8	19.9	16.8	13.5

Source: FYR Macedonia 1996 Household Budget Survey.

MOLDOVA: Poverty Risk, 1997

Poverty line	33% of median	67% of median	50% of median	50% of median	50% of median
Economies of scale	Theta=.75	Theta=.75	Theta=1	Theta=.75	Theta=.50
	Poverty risk	Poverty risk	Poverty risk	Poverty risk	Poverty risk
Age in years					
0–15	5.5	28.8	17.7	15.3	12.5
16–64	5.1	25.4	14.2	13.7	12.5
65+	5.1	28.1	10.8	14.7	19.0
Total	5.2	26.5	14.7	14.1	13.2
Education					
Age less than 15	5.5	28.8	17.7	15.3	12.5
Primary or less	4.9	29.4	13.3	15.4	18.1
General secondary	5.3	28.8	16.0	15.3	13.8
Vocational or technical	6.1	24.0	13.6	13.3	13.0
Higher	2.5	12.9	5.8	7.0	6.6
Total	5.2	26.5	14.7	14.1	13.2
Location					
Chisinau or Tiraspol	1.8	14.8	7.1	7.6	8.6
Other urban	4.4	27.0	13.9	13.5	13.5
Rural	6.5	29.7	17.3	16.3	14.5
Total	5.2	26.5	14.7	14.1	13.2
Region					
Right Bank	5.6	26.7	15.2	14.6	13.4
Transnistria	3.4	25.5	12.0	12.1	12.5
Total	5.2	26.5	14.7	14.1	13.2
Access to land					
No	5.8	26.9	15.3	14.7	13.9
Yes	1.6	24.1	10.8	10.5	8.8
Total	5.2	26.5	14.7	14.1	13.2
Own automobile					
No	6.1	28.9	16.6	16.0	14.9
Yes	0.8	14.3	4.7	4.8	4.6
Total	5.2	26.5	14.7	14.1	13.2
Household typology					
Single parent with child(ren)	4.5	22.8	11.5	13.1	14.5
Other households with child(ren)	5.4	28.5	17.5	15.1	12.0
Single elderly male	3.7	9.8	3.7	6.8	9.8

(Table continues on next page)

MOLDOVA *(continued)*

Poverty line	*33% of median*	*67% of median*	*50% of median*	*50% of median*	*50% of median*
Economies of scale	*Theta=.75*	*Theta=.75*	*Theta=1*	*Theta=.75*	*Theta=.50*
	Poverty risk	*Poverty risk*	*Poverty risk*	*Poverty risk*	*Poverty risk*
Single elderly female	3.9	32.8	6.0	19.2	32.8
Multiple elderly only	7.1	29.6	14.9	16.8	22.1
Other households without child(ren)	4.7	22.6	10.5	12.0	13.2
Total	5.2	26.5	14.7	14.1	13.2
No. of children under 15					
Zero	4.8	23.6	10.5	12.7	15.0
One	4.5	24.5	12.5	12.2	11.0
Two	4.9	30.8	20.1	17.4	12.7
Three or more	9.9	33.3	25.0	17.9	13.7
Total	5.2	26.5	14.7	14.1	13.2
No. of elderly					
Zero	5.3	26.3	15.4	14.6	13.1
One	3.4	27.3	10.9	11.4	12.4
Two	8.9	25.5	15.5	16.6	17.6
Three or more	0.0	49.7	0.0	0.0	0.0
Total	5.2	26.5	14.7	14.1	13.2
Household head, gender					
Male	5.5	25.7	14.8	14.0	12.6
Female	4.3	28.6	14.4	14.4	14.9
Total	5.2	26.5	14.7	14.1	13.2
Household head, labor market status					
Employed	5.7	25.5	14.9	13.9	12.7
Self-employed or employer	0.0	12.4	5.7	5.7	0.0
Unemployed	0.0	28.7	17.0	17.0	0.0
Not in workforce	3.6	29.9	17.4	14.6	12.5
Retired	4.7	29.5	13.8	15.4	16.4
Total	5.2	26.5	14.7	14.1	13.2
No. of income earners					
Zero	5.1	28.5	10.8	15.2	20.3
One	5.1	23.3	12.5	11.8	12.5
Two	4.2	26.5	15.8	14.2	11.1
Three or more	8.9	31.2	19.9	17.8	13.7
Total	5.2	26.5	14.7	14.1	13.2

Source: Moldova Household Budget Survey, Q3 1997.

POLAND: Poverty Risk, 1998

Poverty line	33% of median	67% of median	50% of median	50% of median	50% of median
Economies of scale	Theta=.75	Theta=.75	Theta=1	Theta=.75	Theta=.50
	Poverty risk	Poverty risk	Poverty risk	Poverty risk	Poverty risk
Age in years					
0–15	3.1	37.8	28.3	17.5	10.0
16–64	1.4	23.9	14.7	9.4	6.3
65+	0.7	17.7	7.6	6.2	7.2
Total	1.7	26.3	16.9	10.8	7.2
Education					
Age less than 15	3.1	37.8	28.3	17.5	10.0
Primary	2.0	31.1	18.7	13.0	10.2
Basic vocational	1.6	29.2	18.2	11.5	7.5
General secondary	0.4	12.4	6.4	3.8	2.5
Higher	0.1	3.8	1.6	0.8	0.6
Total	1.7	26.3	16.9	10.8	7.2
Location					
Warsaw	0.0	6.0	2.4	1.7	0.8
Urban	1.2	19.3	10.9	7.1	5.1
Rural	2.6	38.6	27.2	17.3	11.1
Total	1.7	26.3	16.9	10.8	7.2
Region					
North	2.0	28.2	19.0	12.1	7.6
Center	1.3	23.0	13.7	8.9	6.4
East	2.4	34.6	23.9	15.3	9.7
West	1.9	23.9	15.4	10.1	6.9
South	1.2	23.9	14.8	9.4	6.3
Total	1.7	26.3	16.9	10.8	7.2
Access to land					
No	1.4	20.7	11.7	8.1	5.9
Yes	1.9	31.7	22.0	13.6	8.6
Total	1.7	26.3	16.9	10.8	7.2
Own automobile					
No	2.7	34.4	22.0	15.5	11.4
Yes	0.7	18.4	12.0	6.3	3.2
Total	1.7	26.3	16.9	10.8	7.2
Household typology					
Single parent with child(ren)	4.1	40.1	25.2	21.3	17.6
Other households with child(ren)	2.2	32.7	23.5	14.0	7.8
Single elderly male	0.0	11.5	0.5	2.9	9.0
Single elderly female	0.4	13.1	1.2	3.6	11.1
Multiple elderly only	0.4	13.1	3.5	4.2	5.2
Other households without child(ren)	0.6	14.5	5.5	4.9	5.2
Total	1.7	26.3	16.9	10.8	7.2

(Table continues on next page)

POLAND *(continued)*

Poverty line	*33% of median*	*67% of median*	*50% of median*	*50% of median*	*50% of median*
Economies of scale	*Theta=.75*	*Theta=.75*	*Theta=1*	*Theta=.75*	*Theta=.50*
	Poverty risk	*Poverty risk*	*Poverty risk*	*Poverty risk*	*Poverty risk*
No. of children under 15					
Zero	0.6	15.6	6.1	5.1	5.5
One	1.0	24.2	14.3	9.2	5.7
Two	2.2	34.0	24.0	14.2	8.3
Three or more	6.0	57.2	50.5	29.8	15.1
Total	1.7	26.3	16.9	10.8	7.2
No. of elderly					
Zero	1.8	27.1	17.7	11.4	7.3
One	1.3	24.0	14.7	9.4	7.4
Two	0.8	21.0	12.8	7.6	5.3
Three or more	0.0	16.1	13.6	4.9	4.9
Total	1.7	26.3	16.9	10.8	7.2
Household head, gender					
Female	1.7	26.1	15.6	11.1	8.9
Male	1.6	26.3	17.4	10.7	6.6
Total	1.7	26.3	16.9	10.8	7.2
Household head, labor market status					
Employed	1.4	26.4	17.6	10.5	6.2
Unemployed	15.5	69.6	58.0	49.2	40.1
Retired	1.1	16.1	7.0	6.0	6.8
Other	3.5	38.5	22.7	18.2	14.5
Total	1.7	26.3	16.9	10.8	7.2
No. of income earners					
Zero	2.8	31.3	19.2	14.7	12.3
One	2.0	32.2	21.8	13.9	8.4
Two	0.4	16.8	10.4	5.2	2.4
Three or more	0.5	16.6	10.6	4.3	2.0
Total	1.7	26.3	16.9	10.8	7.2
Alternative household typology					
Single person	0.5	12.2	1.4	4.2	10.5
Single parent	3.7	36.4	21.5	18.4	16.0
Couple with no child(ren)	0.3	9.5	2.4	2.8	3.7
Couple with child(ren)	1.5	25.8	15.5	10.6	6.7
Other households without child(ren)	2.6	31.8	22.5	14.1	8.9
Other households with child(ren)	1.9	34.6	26.7	13.7	6.6
Total	1.7	26.3	16.9	10.8	7.2
Own labor market status					
Employed	0.9	22.0	13.2	8.1	5.3
Unemployed	5.6	47.7	32.7	24.4	18.4
Retired	0.7	14.5	6.2	5.0	5.9
Other	1.6	26.9	16.7	10.8	7.3
Age less than 15	3.1	37.8	28.3	17.5	10.0
Total	1.7	26.3	16.9	10.8	7.2

Source: Poland 1998 Household Budget Survey 1998.

ROMANIA: Poverty Risk, 1998

Poverty line	33% of median	67% of median	50% of median	50% of median	50% of median
Economies of scale	Theta=.75	Theta=.75	Theta=1	Theta=.75	Theta=.50
	Poverty risk	Poverty risk	Poverty risk	Poverty risk	Poverty risk
Age in years					
0–15	2.3	28.8	21.4	11.6	6.1
16–64	1.1	19.0	11.3	6.8	4.3
65⁺	0.9	20.0	5.1	5.9	9.9
Total	1.3	21.1	12.6	7.6	5.4
Education					
Age less than 15	2.3	28.8	21.4	11.6	6.1
None	6.4	42.5	24.7	21.8	20.9
Primary (less than 8 years)	1.5	26.0	13.8	9.3	8.2
Vocational	0.6	17.7	9.9	5.4	3.3
High school (9–12 years) or post–high school	0.5	13.4	7.2	4.1	2.6
Higher (college or university)	0.1	2.5	0.9	0.6	0.4
Total	1.3	21.1	12.6	7.6	5.4
Location					
Urban	0.8	15.3	8.1	4.7	3.3
Rural	1.9	28.1	17.9	11.2	7.9
Total	1.3	21.1	12.6	7.6	5.4
Region					
Northeast	2.5	29.5	19.6	11.4	7.9
Southeast	1.1	22.0	13.1	8.2	5.7
South	0.6	21.6	12.4	6.7	4.6
Southwest	1.1	18.4	10.4	7.0	5.1
West	1.6	19.4	11.1	7.0	5.4
Northwest	1.1	18.6	10.6	6.8	5.0
Center	1.8	21.5	12.8	8.3	6.2
Bucharest	0.3	12.4	6.1	3.5	2.0
Total	1.3	21.1	12.6	7.6	5.4
Access to land					
No	1.4	18.0	10.4	6.6	4.6
Yes	1.3	24.6	15.0	8.8	6.3
Total	1.3	21.1	12.6	7.6	5.4
Own automobile					
No	1.7	26.0	15.5	9.6	6.9
Yes	0.1	5.5	3.1	1.2	0.6
Total	1.3	21.1	12.6	7.6	5.4

(Table continues on next page)

ROMANIA *(continued)*

Poverty line	33% of median	67% of median	50% of median	50% of median	50% of median
Economies of scale	Theta=.75	Theta=.75	Theta=1	Theta=.75	Theta=.50
	Poverty risk	Poverty risk	Poverty risk	Poverty risk	Poverty risk
Household typology					
Single parent with child(ren)	2.9	31.9	16.3	15.3	13.3
Other households with child(ren)	1.9	26.2	19.0	10.1	5.2
Single elderly male	1.6	18.1	2.9	6.9	14.9
Single elderly female	1.7	27.2	3.8	8.9	22.9
Multiple elderly only	0.2	18.1	2.8	4.1	5.8
Other households without child(ren)	0.5	13.7	5.6	4.3	3.8
Total	1.3	21.1	12.6	7.6	5.4
No. of children under 15					
Zero	0.6	15.1	5.1	4.6	5.5
One	1.0	18.7	10.7	6.4	3.8
Two	1.4	25.9	17.3	9.4	5.1
Three or more	5.7	49.3	46.1	23.1	10.3
Total	1.3	21.1	12.6	7.6	5.4
No. of elderly					
Zero	1.4	21.4	13.7	8.0	4.9
One	1.2	21.0	9.4	7.0	8.7
Two	0.3	18.1	6.1	4.5	4.5
Three or more	0.0	21.1	18.0	0.0	0.0
Total	1.3	21.1	12.6	7.6	5.4
Household head, gender					
Male	1.2	20.1	12.5	7.1	4.2
Female	2.2	26.7	13.2	10.8	11.8
Total	1.3	21.1	12.6	7.6	5.4
Household head, labor market status					
Employee	0.2	14.0	8.3	3.7	1.6
Employer	0.0	3.8	1.0	0.6	0.6
Self-employed (nonagricultural activity)	7.0	39.8	30.2	21.4	14.1
Farmer	3.4	41.5	29.6	18.9	11.7
Unemployed, but looking for work	4.5	41.1	29.2	19.1	13.4
Pensioner	0.7	18.7	8.0	5.6	5.8
Not in workforce	7.3	41.8	31.6	21.4	16.0
Total	1.3	21.1	12.6	7.6	5.4
No. of income earners					
Zero	9.9	52.0	39.1	29.4	23.4
One	1.8	29.0	14.9	10.2	9.6
Two	0.7	15.4	8.4	5.2	3.1
Three or more	0.9	20.1	15.0	7.0	3.0
Total	1.3	21.1	12.6	7.6	5.4

Source: Romania 1998 Living Standards Measurement Survey.

RUSSIAN FEDERATION: Poverty Risk, 1998

Poverty line	33% of median	67% of median	50% of median	50% of median	50% of median
Economies of scale	Theta=.75	Theta=.75	Theta=1	Theta=.75	Theta=.50
	Poverty risk	Poverty risk	Poverty risk	Poverty risk	Poverty risk
Age in years					
0–15	9.4	33.4	25.6	20.0	16.1
16–64	8.0	29.0	19.7	16.9	15.8
65+	10.3	35.1	21.1	22.3	24.5
Total	8.7	31.2	21.9	18.6	16.9
Education					
Age less than 15	9.5	34.0	25.8	20.2	16.4
High school	9.6	33.4	22.6	20.1	19.4
Technical or vocational	8.5	29.3	20.3	18.5	17.5
University	3.5	18.0	10.2	8.1	8.0
Total	8.7	31.2	21.9	18.6	16.9
Location					
Urban	8.3	29.7	20.6	17.5	15.8
Semi-urban	11.3	39.1	31.9	22.1	19.8
Rural	9.0	32.7	22.5	20.2	18.6
Total	8.7	31.2	21.9	18.6	16.9
Region					
Metropolitan areas: Moscow and St. Petersburg	1.3	14.0	8.1	4.6	4.8
Northern and Northwestern	7.8	35.7	26.5	17.0	14.7
Central and Central Black Earth	9.6	33.3	23.1	21.8	20.7
Volga-Vaytski and Volga Basin	11.9	38.6	28.7	25.3	23.9
North Caucasian	7.2	25.2	16.6	13.1	10.8
Ural	11.2	37.9	26.1	23.4	21.2
Western Siberian	8.3	31.1	22.3	18.4	16.2
Eastern Siberian and Far Eastern	5.3	19.2	13.0	11.0	8.9
Total	8.7	31.2	21.9	18.6	16.9
Own automobile					
Yes	1.7	16.1	10.1	7.3	5.1
No	11.6	37.5	26.8	23.3	21.8
Total	8.7	31.2	21.9	18.6	16.9
Household typology					
Single parent with child(ren)	17.5	40.5	29.6	28.1	29.4
Other households with child(ren)	7.6	30.3	22.8	17.6	13.8
Single elderly male	6.0	29.9	10.5	13.4	25.4

(Table continues on next page)

RUSSIAN FEDERATION *(continued)*

Poverty line	33% of median	67% of median	50% of median	50% of median	50% of median
Economies of scale	Theta=.75	Theta=.75	Theta=1	Theta=.75	Theta=.50
	Poverty risk	Poverty risk	Poverty risk	Poverty risk	Poverty risk
Single elderly female	17.3	42.5	22.4	30.6	40.2
Multiple elderly only	7.4	30.4	17.8	17.5	18.7
Other households without child(ren)	7.8	28.5	16.8	16.1	17.0
Total	8.7	31.2	21.9	18.6	16.9
No. of children under 15					
Zero	9.0	30.7	17.4	18.5	20.9
One	7.3	26.7	19.1	16.0	14.4
Two	8.7	35.3	26.3	20.2	15.3
Three or more	13.1	37.7	33.9	24.2	18.0
Total	8.7	31.2	21.9	18.6	16.9
No. of elderly					
Zero	9.4	30.9	22.5	18.6	16.3
One	8.6	33.6	23.2	20.7	20.0
Two	5.8	28.3	17.0	15.5	15.0
Three or more	7.6	28.2	14.5	9.9	7.6
Total	8.7	31.2	21.9	18.6	16.9
Household head, gender					
Male	7.6	29.7	21.0	17.0	14.7
Female	15.5	39.6	27.0	27.4	29.5
Unknown	n.a.	40.0	40.0	40.0	40.0
Total	8.7	31.2	21.9	18.6	16.9
Household head, labor market status					
Unknown	14.2	34.2	25.4	22.1	21.5
Employed	6.9	27.1	19.1	15.8	14.0
Self-employed or employer	2.6	10.8	7.7	7.1	5.5
Unemployed, but looking for work	13.4	46.4	35.8	29.0	22.8
Not in workforce	18.6	61.3	34.7	29.8	29.0
Retired	10.5	35.3	20.5	20.7	24.4
Total	8.7	31.2	21.9	18.6	16.9
No. of income earners					
Zero	15.3	41.6	27.0	26.6	28.2
One	10.1	35.3	25.1	22.0	20.3
Two	6.1	26.5	18.6	14.5	11.8
Three or more	5.3	22.5	18.1	13.2	10.2
Total	8.7	31.2	21.9	18.6	16.9

Source: Russian Longitudinal Monitoring Survey, 1998.

SLOVENIA: Poverty Risk, 1997/98

Poverty line	33% of median	67% of median	50% of median	50% of median	50% of median
Economies of scale	Theta=.75	Theta=.75	Theta=1	Theta=.75	Theta=.50
	Poverty risk	Poverty risk	Poverty risk	Poverty risk	Poverty risk
Age in years					
0–15	1.3	20.8	10.3	6.4	4.8
16–64	1.3	16.5	7.4	5.7	5.5
65+	2.4	25.0	10.4	10.8	16.0
Total	1.4	18.4	8.3	6.5	6.7
Education					
Age less than 15	1.3	20.8	10.3	6.4	4.8
None	4.1	25.2	9.6	7.0	9.8
Primary or middle	2.8	26.1	12.6	11.3	12.9
Secondary	0.8	15.2	6.0	4.5	4.5
Higher	0.1	3.9	1.1	0.7	0.9
Total	1.4	18.4	8.3	6.5	6.7
Access to land					
No	1.8	16.9	7.6	7.8	8.0
Yes	1.2	19.5	8.8	5.6	5.8
Total	1.4	18.4	8.3	6.5	6.7
Own automobile					
No	7.2	40.2	20.9	22.8	27.8
Yes	0.5	14.8	6.2	3.8	3.2
Total	1.4	18.4	8.3	6.5	6.7
Household typology					
Single parent with child(ren)	2.6	26.0	7.4	7.4	10.5
Other households with child(ren)	1.3	20.1	10.2	6.2	4.4
Single elderly male	0.0	38.0	7.4	7.4	38.0
Single elderly female	1.2	21.4	3.3	7.1	21.4
Multiple elderly only	4.8	28.3	12.2	15.9	20.8
Other households without child(ren)	1.3	15.0	6.2	5.9	6.8
Total	1.4	18.4	8.3	6.5	6.7
No. of children under 15					
Zero	1.6	16.5	6.5	6.8	8.9
One	1.1	17.3	7.1	5.1	4.0
Two	1.0	20.9	10.3	6.8	4.7
Three or more	3.3	31.3	22.4	9.4	6.3
Total	1.4	18.4	8.3	6.5	6.7

(Table continues on next page)

SLOVENIA *(continued)*

Poverty line	*33% of median*	*67% of median*	*50% of median*	*50% of median*	*50% of median*
Economies of scale	*Theta=.75*	*Theta=.75*	*Theta=1*	*Theta=.75*	*Theta=.50*
	Poverty risk	*Poverty risk*	*Poverty risk*	*Poverty risk*	*Poverty risk*
No. of elderly					
Zero	1.3	15.8	6.5	5.5	5.1
One	1.7	25.7	13.2	9.3	10.8
Two	2.4	26.0	13.7	9.6	12.1
Three or more	0.0	0.0	0.0	0.0	0.0
Total	1.4	18.4	8.3	6.5	6.7
Household head, gender					
Male	1.1	18.8	8.8	6.2	5.9
Female	1.9	17.9	7.7	7.0	7.8
Total	1.4	18.4	8.3	6.5	6.7
Household head, labor market status					
Employed	0.9	15.5	6.9	4.1	3.5
Unemployed	3.8	44.4	22.6	23.1	17.9
Not in workforce	2.4	22.7	10.4	10.5	13.0
Total	1.4	18.4	8.3	6.5	6.7
No. of income earners					
Zero	3.0	27.3	11.3	14.8	19.4
One	1.5	20.9	9.2	7.6	7.8
Two	0.8	14.7	6.2	3.6	2.5
Three or more	1.4	15.9	10.2	4.3	3.3
Total	1.4	18.4	8.3	6.5	6.7

Source: Slovenia 1997–98 Household Income and Expenditures Survey.

TAJIKISTAN: Poverty Risk, 1999

Poverty line	33% of median	67% of median	50% of median	50% of median	50% of median
Economies of scale	Theta=.75	Theta=.75	Theta=1	Theta=.75	Theta=.50
	Poverty risk	Poverty risk	Poverty risk	Poverty risk	Poverty risk
Age in years					
0–15	3.2	23.7	13.0	11.6	10.4
16–64	2.4	20.5	11.4	10.3	8.8
65⁺	3.2	24.5	11.1	10.0	10.9
Total	2.8	22.1	12.1	10.9	9.6
Education					
Age less than 15	3.2	23.7	13.0	11.6	10.4
Unknown	2.9	19.9	10.1	9.4	8.3
None	4.4	27.6	16.2	14.9	13.6
Primary (less than 7 years)	3.3	22.4	11.1	10.1	10.0
General secondary (8–12 years)	2.6	22.5	12.7	11.4	9.8
Vocational or specialized secondary	1.9	17.5	8.6	7.9	6.8
Some higher	0.7	10.4	5.2	5.4	4.1
Total	2.8	22.1	12.1	10.9	9.6
Location					
Urban	3.4	20.6	11.0	11.1	9.6
Rural	2.6	22.5	12.4	10.8	9.6
Total	2.8	22.1	12.1	10.9	9.6
Region					
Dushanbe (capital)	1.4	7.9	3.4	3.4	4.4
GBAO	7.2	39.2	25.3	22.8	18.3
RRS	1.8	14.8	9.4	7.1	5.6
Leninabad	2.8	23.4	11.9	12.6	11.0
Khatlon	3.3	26.7	14.1	12.3	11.2
Total	2.8	22.1	12.1	10.9	9.6
Access to individual garden plot					
No	3.5	21.8	12.5	12.6	12.4
Yes	2.5	22.1	12.0	10.4	8.9
Total	2.7	22.1	12.1	10.9	9.6
Own automobile					
No	3.2	24.8	13.8	12.4	10.9
Yes	0.0	4.7	1.3	1.0	1.0
Total	2.8	22.1	12.1	10.9	9.6
Household typology					
Single parent with child(ren)	13.3	41.0	21.3	24.5	35.6
Other households with child(ren)	2.7	22.2	12.3	10.9	9.2

(Table continues on next page)

TAJIKISTAN *(continued)*

Poverty line	33% of median	67% of median	50% of median	50% of median	50% of median
Economies of scale	Theta=.75	Theta=.75	Theta=1	Theta=.75	Theta=.50
	Poverty risk	Poverty risk	Poverty risk	Poverty risk	Poverty risk
Single elderly male	0.0	20.0	0.0	0.0	40.0
Single elderly female	0.0	23.1	0.0	0.0	38.5
Multiple elderly only	8.7	39.1	13.0	21.7	39.1
Other households without child(ren)	1.3	10.4	3.1	4.9	5.5
Total	2.8	22.1	12.1	10.9	9.6
No. of children under 15					
Zero	1.9	13.3	3.9	6.2	9.7
One	1.9	18.4	8.2	9.1	9.5
Two	2.6	22.1	9.8	10.8	10.9
Three or more	3.0	23.0	13.4	11.3	9.4
Total	2.8	22.1	12.1	10.9	9.6
No. of elderly					
Zero	3.1	22.1	11.8	11.4	10.7
One	3.0	23.1	13.2	10.5	8.3
Two	1.5	20.9	12.0	9.6	7.4
Three or more	0.0	0.0	0.0	0.0	0.0
Total	2.8	22.1	12.1	10.9	9.6
Household head, gender					
Male	2.4	20.8	10.0	10.0	8.7
Female	4.9	29.1	17.8	15.8	14.6
Total	2.8	22.1	12.1	10.9	9.6
Household head, labor market status					
Employed	3.0	21.4	11.7	10.8	9.7
Unemployed, but looking for work	1.4	20.5	8.6	8.9	6.0
Not in workforce	5.9	30.7	21.7	21.2	18.9
Retired	1.8	21.7	11.2	8.1	6.5
Unknown	0.0	22.7	10.3	11.6	15.7
Total	2.8	22.1	12.1	10.9	9.6
No. of adults employed					
Zero	3.7	23.8	11.0	11.1	13.2
One	3.6	25.2	14.1	14.2	12.9
Two	2.6	23.3	11.9	9.8	8.2
Three or more	1.8	17.2	10.3	8.4	6.2
Total	2.8	22.1	12.1	10.9	9.6

Source: Tajikistan 1999 Living Standards Measurement Survey.

TURKMENISTAN: Poverty Risk, 1998

Poverty line	33% of median	67% of median	50% of median	50% of median	50% of median
Economies of scale	Theta=.75	Theta=.75	Theta=1	Theta=.75	Theta=.50
	Poverty risk	Poverty risk	Poverty risk	Poverty risk	Poverty risk
Age in years					
0–15	6.0	35.0	22.7	20.0	17.4
16–64	4.1	28.4	18.5	16.0	13.3
65⁺	3.8	22.9	12.4	11.8	13.1
Total	4.9	30.8	19.9	17.4	14.9
Education					
Age less than 15	6.0	35.0	22.7	20.0	17.4
Unknown	8.1	41.0	29.6	26.1	23.5
None	7.9	36.8	23.7	23.7	18.4
Primary (less than 7 years)	4.0	25.0	14.5	12.4	11.4
General secondary (8–9 years)	4.6	32.4	21.3	18.3	15.1
Higher education	2.1	17.3	10.3	9.1	8.2
Total	4.9	30.8	19.9	17.4	14.9
Location					
Urban	1.2	17.6	9.5	7.6	6.8
Rural	7.6	40.7	27.7	24.7	21.0
Total	4.9	30.8	19.9	17.4	14.9
Access to land					
No	3.2	23.0	14.0	11.9	11.3
Yes	5.9	35.4	23.4	20.6	17.2
Total	4.9	30.8	19.9	17.4	14.9
Own automobile					
No	6.1	35.6	23.5	21.2	19.2
Yes	3.1	23.9	14.8	11.9	8.8
Total	4.9	30.8	19.9	17.4	14.9
Household typology					
Single parent with child(ren)	2.3	12.4	4.7	4.7	10.1
Other household with child(ren)	5.2	32.8	21.5	18.5	15.6
Single elderly male	0.0	10.0	0.0	0.0	10.0
Single elderly female	0.0	9.4	0.0	3.1	9.4
Multiple elderly only	5.0	20.0	5.0	4.7	20.0
Other households without child(ren)	2.0	14.0	6.8	8.2	8.8
Total	4.9	30.8	19.9	17.4	14.9

(Table continues on next page)

TURKMENISTAN *(continued)*

Poverty line	33% of median	67% of median	50% of median	50% of median	50% of median
Economies of scale	Theta=.75	Theta=.75	Theta=1	Theta=.75	Theta=.50
	Poverty risk	Poverty risk	Poverty risk	Poverty risk	Poverty risk
No. of children under 15					
Zero	1.8	15.2	7.5	9.1	9.7
One	2.0	21.5	11.2	10.1	10.4
Two	3.6	23.9	13.2	12.4	11.0
Three or more	6.7	38.8	27.1	22.7	18.6
Total	4.9	30.8	19.9	17.4	14.9
No. of elderly					
Zero	4.9	31.7	20.4	17.8	15.4
One	4.5	28.8	19.9	17.1	14.0
Two or more	4.6	21.2	12.0	10.5	10.7
Total	4.9	30.8	19.9	17.4	14.9
Household head, gender					
Male	5.0	31.6	20.7	18.2	15.3
Female	4.0	26.8	16.4	13.7	13.2
Total	4.9	30.8	19.9	17.4	14.9
Household head, labor market status					
Unknown	7.9	34.4	23.2	19.9	17.4
Employed	4.0	29.9	18.0	16.1	14.5
Self-employed or employer	5.7	21.3	16.9	15.8	14.7
Unemployed, but looking for work	14.9	46.8	35.1	34.8	32.5
Not in workforce	5.1	32.7	17.1	13.8	12.0
Retired	3.5	30.4	21.9	17.1	11.8
Total	4.9	30.8	19.9	17.4	14.9
No. of income earners					
Zero	10.1	42.7	26.9	23.5	24.1
One	3.8	28.2	16.8	16.3	14.9
Two	4.8	28.4	17.4	14.4	13.4
Three or more	3.6	30.3	22.1	18.5	12.5
Total	4.9	30.8	19.9	17.4	14.9

Source: Turkmenistan 1998 Living Standards Measurement Survey.

UKRAINE: Poverty Risk, 1996

Poverty line	33% of median	67% of median	50% of median	50% of median	50% of median
Economies of scale	Theta=.75	Theta=.75	Theta=1	Theta=.75	Theta=.50
	Poverty risk	Poverty risk	Poverty risk	Poverty risk	Poverty risk
Age in years					
0–15	3.9	24.1	16.0	11.2	7.6
16–64	3.3	21.7	13.3	10.3	8.6
65+	5.3	32.5	14.2	17.1	20.6
Total	3.8	24.2	14.0	11.8	10.5
Education					
Age less than 15	3.9	24.1	16.0	11.2	7.6
Unknown	0.0	40.0	20.0	20.0	40.0
None	6.0	41.4	23.3	28.5	27.6
Primary (less than 7 years)	5.4	27.6	13.1	14.8	16.7
General secondary (8–12 years)	4.0	25.4	13.9	11.7	11.0
Vocational or specialized secondary	5.0	26.5	17.6	12.9	11.4
Some higher	2.4	19.6	11.2	9.5	8.4
Total	3.8	24.2	14.1	11.8	10.5
Location					
Urban	5.9	30.8	19.2	15.9	14.6
Semi-urban	2.1	21.5	13.2	8.8	9.8
Rural	2.2	18.7	9.8	8.7	6.9
Total	3.8	24.2	14.1	11.8	10.5
Region					
South	2.3	21.9	12.1	9.7	8.1
West	1.7	15.9	9.1	5.6	5.1
Central	2.7	23.4	12.6	10.3	8.4
East	10.8	41.1	27.3	26.5	25.1
Total	3.8	24.2	14.1	11.8	10.5
Access to land					
No	11.1	42.4	26.9	23.9	24.1
Yes	1.6	18.7	10.3	8.2	6.4
Total	3.8	24.2	14.1	11.8	10.5
Own automobile					
No	4.6	26.8	15.7	13.5	12.1
Yes	1.1	15.4	8.9	6.3	5.1
Total	3.8	24.2	14.1	11.8	10.5
Household typology					
Single parent with child(ren)	4.4	27.5	10.5	9.1	6.4
Other households with child(ren)	3.4	23.4	16.7	11.2	7.5

(Table continues on next page)

UKRAINE (continued)

Poverty line	33% of median	67% of median	50% of median	50% of median	50% of median
Economies of scale	Theta=.75	Theta=.75	Theta=1	Theta=.75	Theta=.50
	Poverty risk	Poverty risk	Poverty risk	Poverty risk	Poverty risk
Single elderly male	2.6	42.1	13.2	21.1	34.2
Single elderly female	10.6	40.4	16.0	25.8	36.7
Multiple elderly only	4.3	29.9	13.4	14.6	16.8
Other households without child(ren)	3.4	21.3	10.8	10.9	10.8
Total	3.8	24.2	14.1	11.8	10.5
No. of children under 15					
Zero	4.0	25.2	11.6	13.2	14.9
One	4.6	21.3	13.7	10.7	9.0
Two	1.9	26.5	19.1	11.0	5.6
Three or more	6.1	26.8	18.3	12.7	7.4
Total	3.8	24.2	14.1	11.8	10.5
No. of elderly					
Zero	3.4	21.7	13.3	10.3	8.4
One	4.9	29.0	17.3	15.6	14.3
Two	4.2	31.1	13.9	14.3	16.5
Three or more	0.0	0.0	0.0	0.0	0.0
Total	3.8	24.2	14.1	11.8	10.5
Household head, gender					
Unknown	3.2	23.7	16.3	12.6	8.1
Male	2.4	21.0	12.1	9.2	8.0
Female	5.5	28.0	16.3	14.8	13.6
Total	3.8	24.2	14.1	11.8	10.5
Household head, labor market status					
Unknown	5.2	26.6	20.1	15.6	12.0
Employed	1.7	17.8	9.8	7.1	6.0
Employer	0.0	0.0	0.0	0.0	0.0
Self-employed	0.0	18.8	9.9	8.3	4.2
Unemployed, but looking for work	0.0	14.3	14.3	14.3	0.0
Not in workforce	9.7	24.5	14.8	13.0	13.7
Retired	4.9	29.3	16.6	14.8	13.9
Total	3.8	24.2	14.1	11.8	10.5
No. of income earners					
Zero	6.5	33.5	17.7	18.2	19.0
One	4.0	23.1	13.4	11.1	8.8
Two	0.8	17.8	11.3	7.3	5.0
Three or more	3.6	17.8	15.0	7.9	6.1
Total	3.8	24.2	14.1	11.8	10.5

Source: Ukraine 1996 Household Income and Expenditures Survey.